Critical Issues in Criminal Justice

Critical Issues in Criminal Justice

Edited by

R. G. Iacovetta and Dae H. Chang

1979
Carolina Academic Press
Durham, North Carolina

Carolina Academic Press
P.O. Box 8971, Forest Hills Station
Durham, North Carolina 27707

Contents

Part III
Law, Legitimacy and the Court

Part IV
Issues in Corrections

Part V
Issues in Juvenile Crime/Juvenile Justice

Part VI
Why Not Capital Punishment?

Preface

THIS TEXT ADDRESSES a select set of "critical issues" pertinent to today's criminal justice system and its operation. While there are differences of opinion as to what constitutes a "critical issue" in criminal justice, as evidenced by the plethora of debatable and controversial issues in the field, the editors have selected those issues which keenly discern areas of contemporary interest, debate, and concern. Each chapter represents a departure point from which students can enter into serious discussion, analysis, and reflection. Some chapters present both "pros and cons" with respect to a particular issue under consideration. Some take a definite "pro" or "con" position on a particular issue. The papers' object is to develop a point of view on a given topic. The editors' goal is to place the reader in an arena in which ideas are presented. It is the readers' responsibility to weigh and to evaluate the persuasiveness of the conflicting arguments.

The text is designed to provide students of criminology and criminal justice a perspective from which to begin the search for solutions to the problems of crime and criminal justice in our society. The first step in arriving at viable solutions to these problems is the asking of pertinent questions based up a careful study of all relevant factual information and scientific data. By definition, therefore, the text focuses upon "issues" or "concerns" that are in need of concerted analyses and/or resolution. The primary purpose of the text is to provoke maximum reflection and debate as it relates to a particular issue.

Notwithstanding the enormous amount of controversy and debate which exists within the criminal justice system today, most of the nation's colleges and univesities have only recently begun offering courses in "Critical Issues in Criminal Justice" or "Contemporary Issues in Criminal Justice." Moreover, there is no single book which is adequately devoted to a critical analysis of a broad range of such issues.

The book contains, altogether, 41 chapters. The chapters are grouped under the following topics: 1.) General Issues in Criminal Justice; 2.) Issues in Law Enforcement; 3.) Law, Legitimacy, and the Court; 4.) Issues in Corrections; 5.) Issues in Juvenile Crime/Juvenile Justice; and 6.) The Issue of Capital Punishment.

The editors have arranged the sequence of materials in the book in such a fashion as to maximize the student's familiarity and understanding of the respective issues. The text is designed to be used in a wide variety of criminal justice courses at both the undergraduate and graduate levels. The diversity of "issues" and the manner of treatment should provide adequate fuel for thought by both groups. The material reflects current concerns and issues germane to the criminal justice system and its operation and does not dwell upon historical trends or events. Many chapters contain provocative materials that could generate theses, dissertations, or book projects. Indeed, the text has the potential of great versatility in a variety of courses as either a main text or a supplemental text to augment other course material. More important, perhaps, is the good possibility that the text may have broad appeal within the criminal justice system itself.

The text contains original contributions from a diverse group of accomplished criminal justice academicians and criminal justice practitioners. The chapters were solicited to represent the vast range of knowledge and opinion present in contemporary criminal justice. All chapters are presented from the particular perspective of the contributing author(s) and do not, necessarily, represent the views of the editors.

The editors do not pretend that the text is exhaustive. Rather, the editors consider this book to be a first step toward a more comprehensive evaluation of critical issues. Nor do we feel that debate, reflection, and concerted study of an issue will naturally lead to eventual solutions. Rather, we hope the text will stimulate the kind of evaluation and focus necessary for students (and others) to begin the search for viable solutions. The text represents a beginning of that search.

Acknowledgements

THE EDITORS would like to acknowledge the debts which have accumulated in the preparation of this book. The contributing authors, first and foremost, deserve commendation for their originality, imagination and critical evaluation of their respective topic. Without their vision, foresight and dedication this book would not have been possible. We would also like to acknowledge the invaluable help of our Graduate Assistant, Mr. Tim Eley and our secretariat staff, particularly Mary Ann Gertsen and Marjorie Jack for their continued support and assistance.

Above all, we would like to thank our wives, Sherry and Sueng Hi, for their support and encouragement during the duration of this project. We dedicate this book to our children, Danielle and Lara Iacovetta and Morris and Ricky Chang for forgiving us for our absences, and in the hope that many of the "Critical Issues in Criminal Justice" that are addressed in the book will be resolved by their generation.

Introduction

THE STUDY OF CRIME and criminal justice is a fascinating subject. However, despite all the rhetoric, there is more focus upon the nature, scope, and causes of crime than upon concerted attempts at resolution. Due to publicity, crime has produced fear and caution. On the other hand, popular magazines, television shows, movies and the daily news create in the mind of the general public an obsessed interest in crime, even an envy for "successful crime." Moreover, the media feed us a steady diet of sensationalized crime related information.

The problem of crime is often a political commodity. Witness, for example, election campaign speeches. Many candidates for municipal, state, or federal offices insist that crime is our nation's number one problem and that an all out war is absolutely necessary to maintain civil order. However, local, state, and federal officials, once elected, tend to offer only lip service to the problem of crime. In fact, in order to save money, the most popular area for budget cutting is often law enforcement. The bulk of tax revenues are spent on public works, military appropriations, highways, and a multitude of social programs at the state and federal level, rather than on crime related appropriations; only a fraction of the total budget is earmarked for crime control strategies.

"Critical Issues" are herein defined as those social discussions, arguments, or interests that require urgent attention by any segment of society, in an effort to maintain public order, safety and peace. Critical often implies peril, danger or even crisis. Critical issues are not always viewed in the same magnitude, nor do all strata in a given society always agree on the same issue. For instance, in recent years, "gun control" has become an issue because of the number of killings done with handguns, particularly the so-called "Saturday Night Special." The American Rifle Association affiliates and its members undoubtedly view possession of handguns as a "critical issue," although in a different context than do other segments of the public. Moreover, welfare recipients may view the welfare system which exists in the United States as "a critical issue," but not in the same context as middle-class Americans. Nevertheless, successive presidents have indicated that "welfare reform" is critical to all citizens of the United States.

This book, "Critical Issues in Criminal Justice," is timely and the compilation of various issues presented are only in response to the long term demand for such a book. Authors of textbooks and journal articles, and the mass media—radio, television and newspapers—have agonized over the problem of crime, particularly of violent crimes. Yet, to this date, even though various policy formulas have been advocated by various groups, there are no effective and viable solutions to crime problems. "What to do," "Where do we go from here," "There must be a solution," "We haven't done enough," and a host of similar comments are made daily among those in criminal justice circles. The clear indication is that "something needs to be done."

When a large majority of people agree, or a large majority of legislators, or public policy-makers agree on a given issue, the issue usually is translated into "public policy," thereby becoming a law, enactment, ordinance, or executive order, and the populace is expected to abide by it under the threat of Criminal or Civil penalty. Social policy formulation is often based upon the moral, ethical, and value judgments of the people (or special interest groups within the society), rather than upon rational, objective evaluation of the available scientific data. Unfortunately, social policy often only addresses the effects of a problem and not the problem itself. Issue resolution and policy formulation are, therefore, often distinct and disparate objectives.

In a democratic society where citizens are allowed to express their views through legitimate channels, discussions, conferences, meetings and debate usually lead to information and the formulation of issues that can be understood by the population. In a dictatorial society, we may not find many critical issues because information flow is severely restricted. However, the absence of public debate, controversy or demonstration does not necessarily mean the absence of "critical issues." In fact, throughout history, when dictators tried to control the masses by means of "information control," or in some instances by means of "brainwashing" techniques, riots, strikes, and even revolutions were often the result. However, in a heterogeneous, democratic society like ours, there are a great many issues that confront us. Confrontation of issues, critical or otherwise, represents an essential ingredient for issue resolution and public policy formulation. Therefore, assessment and demonstration with respect to a particular issue is functional and necessary if viable solutions are to be found.

In a heterogeneous society, where various racial, ethnic, religious, and sub-cultural groups come in contact with each other, a certain amount of friction or conflict might be anticipated. Such a society also contains numerous sub-groups and groups that possess differential value orientation, differential degrees of tolerance, differential levels of prejudice toward other groups and the like. Each group conceives issues, problems, and public policies with different intensity and importance. Consequently, such terms as "pro," "con," and "neutral" are common terms to which we are all exposed. When we are confronted with problems or issues, we react, or respond, according to our frame of reference. The socialization process dictates that we respond appropriately to a given situation according to cultural or sub-cultural norms. For example, in homogeneous and agrarian societies, one usually solicits the advice of family members and relatives in solving problems. In a complex heterogeneous, urbanized, industrialized, and secular society, however, problem solution often takes place outside the family milieu. Thus, critical issues must be differentiated according to the type of society in which they appear.

There are literally hundreds of critical issues awaiting our eventual collective solutions. Is the death penalty an effective method of handling capital offenders? Should the juvenile court be abolished? How about rising female criminality and female juvenile offenders and what to do with them? Has it been demonstrated that prisons are outmoded and ineffective and that they should give way to "community correctional facilities?" For years police fraternal organizations insisted that police be unionized. Should unions be viable solutions for that profession? Should victims of crime be compensated by the State? What is the role of the private insurance company? Why are those who are processed through the criminal justice system over-represented by those in the lower social class and, particularly, of minority groups? Can law be more equitable? Would the old dictum: "criminals should be locked up and the keys thrown away" work in an enlightened "human rights" conscious country like the United States? Is victim compensation viable? Why can't the police stop crime? Should the police be reorganized? Should we abolish indeterminate sentencing? What about plea bargaining? Can Corrections really correct? Should we make the offender pay? Should prostitution be legalized? Should abortion be condoned throughout the United States? Should pornography be altogether banned? What about gambling? The list is endless.

The failure of local, state, and federal government to resolve the omnipresent concerns of the people is often blamed upon "the bureaucracy" of the system. As a result, many have concluded that "nothing can be done" and have found comfort in the notion that "no matter what I do, nothing will happen anyway—so why should I bother?"

Finally, it must be stated that the operation of the criminal justice system in the future will be in the hands of a new generation. Young people with keen interest and vision will eventually chart the future. In its 1967 report on the American Criminal Justice System, the *President's Commission on Law Enforcement and Administration of Justice* stated: "Probably the single greatest limitation on the system's ability to make decisions wisely and fairly, is that people in the system often are required to decide issues without enough information . . . only by combining research with action can future programs be founded on knowledge rather than informed or perceptive guesswork. Moreover, once knowledge is acquired, it is wasted if it is not shared." If this book instills in students some sense of urgency in dealing with the multitude of critical issues which confront us on the battleground of crime and criminal justice, then the editors' goal is partially fulfilled.

R. G. IACOVETTA
DAE H. CHANG

Wichita, Kansas
July 20, 1979

Contributors

LAWRENCE A. BENNETT is the Director of the Center for the Study of Crime, Delinquency and Corrections at Southern Illinois University having recently assumed that position after nine years as Chief of Research, California Department of Corrections. His research and writing interests have ranged from psychological studies to the application of research to administrative problems. Recently, his efforts have been directed toward term-setting policies and the effects of long-term confinement. He received his Master's and Doctorate in Psychology from Claremont Graduate School in California.

GEORGETTE BENNETT-SANDLER is a network correspondent specializing in sociological, economic, and financial issues for NBC-TV News. Dr. Bennett-Sandler has held various positions in the New York City government and holds the title of Visiting Associate Professor of Sociology at the Graduate Center, City University of New York. She is author of the forthcoming text *Law Enforcement: An Introduction* (1979). She received her Ph.D. from New York University.

DON BRADEL is the Director of the Criminal Justice Program at Bemidji State University (Minnesota). He held various academic posts at the University of Minnesota and Southern Illinois University prior to assuming the directorship in 1975. Dr. Bradel received his Ph.D. from the University of Minnesota.

WILLIAM R. BROWN is an Associate Professor of Sociology at Florida Technological University in Orlando. His research interests have led to numerous publications in the areas of juvenile delinquency and the sociology of education. Dr. Brown is currently involved in formulating a general social psychological model of decision-making processes. He is a graduate of Purdue University.

ORDWAY P. BURDEN is the President and Treasurer of the Law Enforcement Assistance Foundation. He has served in a wide range of national and local law enforcement positions and his articles have appeared in a number of professional publications.

STEPHEN A. CERNKOVICH is presently an Assistant Professor of Sociology at Bowling Green State University. His current research concerns include the extent and nature of changing patterns of female delinquency involvement. He earned his Ph.D. from Southern Illinois University.

ARTHUR J. CROWNS, JR. is a Professor in the Department of Administration of Justice at Wichita State University. He has experience as a State Legislator and has over 10 years experience as a practicing attorney. He earned his J.D. from the University of Wisconsin and his Ph.D. from Florida State University.

MICHAEL E. ENDRES is a professor of corrections and sociology at Xavier University in Cincinnati, Ohio. His areas of research are in the sociology of crime and delinquency, evaluation research and social stratification. Dr. Endres authored the text *On Defusing the Population Bomb* and his articles have appeared in professional journals. He has participated in numerous funded institutes, workshops and program evaluation in correction.

DON EVANS is an instructor in the Department of Sociology at Mercer University, Macon, Georgia. He served for 13 months as the head chaplain at the Louisiana Correction Institute for Women. Mr. Evans has conducted field research in Mexican prisons and most recently spent nine weeks in the jungles of Guatemala gathering data about Mayan Indians.

JAMES A. FAGIN is an assistant professor of the Department of Administration of Justice at Wichita State University. He received his Ph.D. from Southern Illinois University at Carbondale. He served as Security Consultant and Crowd Control Instructor for the 1976 Republican National Convention. He has directed reorganizational studies for several municipal police departments, municipal courts, and county jails including proposals for the unification of police services. He has published articles on police unionism and police-community relations. Dr. Fagin is a reserve police officer and continues to regularly participate in the criminal justice system not only as an instructor but also as a uniformed police patrol officer in the field.

RAYMON C. FORSTON is Professor of Sociology at Houston Baptist University. His primary research and teaching interests are in criminology, corrections, criminal victimization, and deviant behavior. His 1973 victimization study of an inner city area of Houston has been widely used by criminal justice planners throughout the United States and Canada. He obtained his Ph.D. in Sociology from Indiana University.

DAVID O. FRIEDRICHS is Assistant Professor of Sociology/Law Enforcement at the University of Scranton (Pennsylvania). His research has been primarily concerned with various aspects of the legitimacy problem, historical dimensions of criminal justice, and questions pertaining to police education and jury trials. He has edited a classroom reader, *Crime & Justice: Perspectives from the Past* and has published in several academic journals. He has an M.A. from New York University and is currently pursuing his doctorate from the same institution.

BURT GALAWAY is on the faculty, School of Social Development at the University of Minnesota. Mr. Galaway is, most recently, co-editor of *Offender Restitution in Theory in Action* and *Restitution in Criminal Justice.* He has published numerous professional articles in relation to criminal justice restitution, victim compensation and child welfare. Mr. Galaway is a candidate for a Ph.D. at the University of Minnesota.

PEGGY C. GIORDANO is an Assistant Professor of Sociology at Bowling Green State University. Her current research interests include the impact of changes in sex-role related attitudes and behavior on females involvement in crime. She received her Ph.D. from the University of Minnesota.

FRANKLIN GOULD is an Associate Professor of Psychology at the State University College of Oneota, New York. He has devoted much time and effort to interviewing ex-convicts who have been successfully reintegrated into society.

MARTIN GREENBERG is an instructor and Coordinator of the Police Science Program at Hawaii Community College in Hilo, Hawaii. His lengthy involvement as an auxilary police officer in New York City, coupled with his legal training, makes him well-qualified to write on the subject of police volunteers. Dr. Greenberg obtained his J.D. in 1969 from New York Law School.

LEONARD J. HIPPCHEN is a member of the faculty at Virginia Commonwealth University and has worked in the field of crime and delinquency for the past 20 years. He has served as a research director for the U.S. Air Force, DHEW and as a consultant for numerous research projects. He is the author of numerous correctional publications and serves as chairman of the committee on classification and treatment of the American Correctional Association. Dr. Hippchen is the editor of the recently published text *Ecologic-Biochemical Approaches to Treatment of Delinquents and Criminals* and *Handbook on Correctional Classification: Programming for Treatment and Reintegration.*

FREDERIC HOMER is the head of Political Science Department and the Department of Administration of Justice at the University of Wyoming. He is the author of *Guns and Garlic: Myths and Realities of Organized Crime* and has written journal articles on organized crime, violence and terrorism.

GALAN M. JANEKSELA is an Assistant Professor of Administration of Justice at Wichita State University. His specialty areas include corrections, juvenile justice, conflict management and research methods. Dr. Janeksela has published widely in the field of criminal justice and has served as a criminal justice consultant, planner, and evaluator. Dr. Janeksela received his Ph.D. from Iowa State University.

CLINTON B. JONES is the Associate Dean of the College of Urban Life at Georgia State University. He has served as a correctional officer and youth counselor and has held faculty positions at the University of Nebraska and Howard University. Dr. Jones' research interests are in the areas of national criminal justice policy, minority work force issues in criminal justice and correctional education programs. He received his Ph.D. from Claremont Graduate School.

RICHARD KANIA is the Criminal Justice Planner for the Thomas Jefferson Planning District, a regional, Virginia governmental administrative agency. Previously he had served three years as a police officer with the Charlottesville, Virginia Police Department. Mr. Kania earned his M.A. at the University of Virginia in 1974, and has continued graduate studies in public administration, sociology, anthropology and criminal justice. His interests are in the area of human social organization, deviancy and social control.

JACK M. KRESS is an Assistant Professor at the State University of New York at Albany. Prior to that, Mr. Kress was an Assistant District Attorney in New York County and has served as a criminal justice consultant for various state, national, and international organizations. His published works are in the area of evidence, sentencing and related topics. He received his J.D. from Columbia Law School.

ROBERT F. KRONICK is the director of the Program in Human Services at the University of Tennessee. He has served as director and consultant on various state and local programs dealing with human services. His areas of interest include deviant behavior, criminology and sociology of mental health. Dr. Kronick has presented numerous papers and his publications have appeared in various professional journals. Dr. Kronick's doctoral degree was earned at the University of Tennessee.

G.L. KUCHEL is a Professor in the Department of Criminal Justice at the University of Nebraska at Omaha. He is currently a member of the Nebraska Commission on Law Enforcement and Criminal Justice. His experience in corrections ranges from corrections officer to being a member of the State Parole Board.

RICHARD J. LUNDMAN is an Associate Professor of Sociology at Ohio State University. His research and numerous publications have centered on deviance, criminology and social control. Dr. Lundman has forthcoming books, *Police and Policing: A Sociological Introduction* and *Organizational Deviance: Towards a Sociology of Crime and Social*

Problems (1979). In 1972, Dr. Lundman was awarded a Ph.D. from the University of Minnesota.

DONALD MCLEOD is the present director of the Rockland County Police Training Center in Pomona, New York. He was a New York City Detective and has served as a management consultant and as an Adjunct Assistant Professor to Manhattan College. Mr. McLeod is the author of *The Function of the Police in Crisis Intervention and Conflict Management* and "Murder One" *Handbook of Structured Experiences.* Mr. McLeod earned his M.A. from the John Jay College of Criminal Justice.

CLAUDE T. MANGRUM is the Director of the Adult Services Division, San Bernardino County (CA) Probation Department. He has been involved in adult and juvenile probation since 1957 and has taught at both Chapman College and Riverside City College. Mr. Mangrum authored *The Professional Practitioner in Probation* and has had numerous articles published in professional journals. His areas of interest are in adult probation and correctional administration.

GUYON MERSEREAU is an Assistant Professor at McMaster University (Hamilton, Ontario) as well as a medical staff consultant to several area psychiatric facilities. Dr. Mersereau has taught criminology and penology at various universities in both the United States and Canada. His expertise is in the areas of criminal psychiatry and psychotherapy. He earned his medical degree at McGill University (Montreal).

RAYMOND MICHALOWSKI is an Associate Professor of Sociology at the University of North Carolina at Charlotte. He has published articles dealing with vehicular homicide, criminological theory, violent death, shock probation and political repression. He co-authored the text *Thinking the Thinkable: Investment in Human Survival.* Dr. Michalowski received his Ph.D. from Ohio State University.

GARY R. PERLSTEIN is an Associate Professor of Administration of Justice at Portland State University. He is a co-editor of *Alternatives to Prison.* His expertise is in the area of correctional theory and correctional problems.

JERALD K.M. PHILLIPS is a candidate for the Ph.D. in Urban Affairs at Portland State University. Previously, he was Administrative Assistant to the Director of Justice Services, Multnomah County, Oregon. His special areas of expertise are in the field of Administration and planning.

R.V. PHILLIPSON is a psychiatrist with the National Institute on Drug Abuse and a former senior medical officer with the Mental Health Division, Ministry of Health of England and Wales, where he was involved with drug dependence issues and assisted in the establishment of the British System of Heroin Maintenance. His research efforts have centered around drug dependency, child psychiatry and mental subnormality. He has published numerous articles in both British and American professional journals. Dr. Phillipson is a graduate of the Royal College of Physicians and Surgeons in Dublin, Ireland.

TONY G. POVEDA is presently an Associate Professor of Sociology at the State University of New York at Plattsburgh. His research has centered around delinquency, sociology of youth and white-collar crime. Currently, his research centers on domestic intelligence activities. Dr. Poveda earned his Ph.D. from the University of California at Berkeley.

NICHOLAS A. REUTERMAN is an Associate Professor and Acting Director of Delinquency Study and Youth Development Center at Southern Illinois University at Edwardsville. His research has dealt with delinquent causation, juvenile justice and program evaluation. Dr. Reuterman earned both his Master's degree and his Ph.D. from the University of Colorado.

JOSEPH W. ROGERS is Professor of Sociology at New Mexico State University. He served six years as an Assistant Probation Officer with the San Diego County Probation Department, Juvenile Division and has taught on the campuses of Washington State University and Kansas State University. In addition to numerous articles and book reviews, he is the author of *Why Are You Not a Criminal?* His major areas of teaching and research include criminology, juvenile delinquency, justice systems, deviance and social problems. He received his Ph.D. in 1965 from the University of Washington.

STEPHEN ROWE is a graduate student at San Jose State University, pursuing a degree in criminal justice administration. His areas of research interest included prostitution, white-collar crime, crime etiology, and criminal justice planning.

HARRY RUBENSTEIN operates a short term client Intensive Treatment Unit at the Buffalo Psychiatric Center. Previously, he piloted and directed a special psychiatric unit at Attica Correctional facility from late 1973 to 1977. Dr. Rubenstein also instructs at the State University of New York at Buffalo. His medical training was obtained from the Philadelphia College of Osteopathic Medicine and Surgery.

LYNDA J. STRIEGEL is an attorney in Washington, D.C.

GERALD F. UELMAN is a Professor of Law at Loyola Law School. Mr. Uelman has served as both a defense counsel and as an Assistant U.S.

Attorney. He has acted as a consultant on numerous committees and projects on matters related to criminal justice and criminal law. Mr. Uelman's research efforts have centered on drug law, drug abuse and drug addiction.

CHARLES M. UNKOVIC is Chairman and Professor of the Department of Sociology at Florida Technological University, Orlando, Florida. Dr. Unkovic has had extensive research experience and has published numerous articles in the areas of penal reform, criminology, alcoholism, juvenile delinquency, and suicide. He has contributed much of his time to various national level organizations that deal with social problems. Dr. Unkovic received his Ph.D. from the University of Pittsburgh.

S. GEORGE VINCENTNATHAN is an Associate Professor in the Department of Criminal Justice at the University of Wisconsin-Plattesville. His areas of research and teaching interests are criminological theory, juvenile justice, juvenile delinquency and criminal justice planning. He earned his doctorate from the University of California, Berkeley.

SAMUEL WALKER is an Associate Professor of Criminal Justice at the University of Nebraska. He is the author of *A Critical History of Police Reform: The Emergence of Professionalism* and the forthcoming text *Popular Justice: A History of American Criminal Justice* (1979). His principal interests center on the history of American criminal justice and the police. Dr. Walker earned his Ph.D. from Ohio State University in American History.

JOHN C. WATKINS is a Professor of Criminal Justice at the University of Alabama. He has held a variety of legal positions at both the federal and state level and has taught at several universities around the country. His research interests have centered around criminal law and procedure, juvenile justice and theoretical criminology. Dr. Watkins earned his J.D. from the University of Alabama and his L.L.M. from Northwestern University.

RAY H. WILLIAMS is presently an Associate Attorney, Criminal Division, Legal Aid Society, of the City of New York, Former Director of the Administration of Justice Program, Institute for Urban Affairs and Research, Howard University, Washington, D.C. He holds a B.A. Degree from the City University of New York and received his J.D. Degree from the Brooklyn Law School in New York.

1

Criminal Justice for Whom?
A Critical Appraisal

RAYMOND J. MICHALOWSKI

Introduction

OUR POPULAR IMAGE OF CRIMINAL JUSTICE IS THAT OF A MORALITY PLAY. Through official statements, the news media and our popular entertainments we are presented with the view that the administration of justice is a simple struggle between the forces of good and evil. On one side exists the "criminal element;" violent, cruel and self-seeking individuals who will stop at nothing to satisfy their illegitimate, personal desires. On the other side exists the forces of order; dedicated, selfless and law-abiding individuals who are ready to give their all in the "never ending battle for truth, justice and the American way."

This simple image, so common in our everyday world, reflects the generally held belief that the *primary* purpose of criminal justice is to protect citizens from threats to their person or property by capturing criminals and preventing crime. It also reflects the belief that the criminal justice system operates in the best interests of *all* law-abiding citizens.

This chapter presents an alternative view of criminal justice in modern, capitalist America. This alternative view consists of four major assertions:

1. The *primary* purpose of the justice system is to preserve the system of power and privilege characteristic of American capitalism. Protecting individual citizens from harm to either their person or property is of secondary importance.

2. Contemporary criminal justice is focused on an inadequate and outdated conception of what constitutes harm to persons and property.

3. Maintenance of this outdated conception of harm to persons and property is in the advantage of those who must benefit from the current system of privilege and power.

4. If criminal justice were to adequately fulfill its task of protecting individuals from harm to their person or property, it would have to radically revise its targets for control. Specifically, it would have to

3

de-emphasize the individual common-law offender, and devote considerably more attention than it does to the crimes committed by corporations and businesses in their pursuit of profit.

Some may find these assertions a bit unfair, as well as finding the
suggested reorientation of criminal justice unrealistic. This is not a disclaimer. It is an invitation—an invitation to read carefully and think
seriously about the most critical issue facing criminal justice. That issue is:
"What is the purpose of a justice system?" It is my hope that serious
consideration of this question will stimulate an understanding of criminal
justice, not as a collection of individual crime fighters valiantly struggling
to protect society from that group of individual miscreants known as the
"criminal element," but as a systematic arrangement arising from the very
nature of our social order.

Before examining these contentions further, it should be noted that our
concern is *not* with the individual motivations of those who work in the
justice system. Nor is it with the more immediate personal motivations of
those who enjoy substantial control over political and economic establishments. These are actors in a social system, selected for their parts because
they are well trained according to the cultural rules of that system. Our
concern is not with individual motivations, but with the particular social
system of which our criminal justice system is but one component.

Any social system is greater than the sum of its parts, and it cannot be
adequately understood by simply examining its parts separately. The relationship between a particular organizational unit within a social system
(e.g. the criminal justice system) and the other components of that system
must always be part of examination if we are to truly understand the
organizational unit we are studying. Focusing on the personal motivations
of individuals within a particular organizational unit is probably the least
adequate way of understanding that unit. If all the reasons why individuals
work in the criminal justice system were laid end to end, they would not
explain the existence or the nature of that system. What we must seek to
understand is the way in which criminal justice fits within the larger social
order which it is designed to protect.

The Primary Purpose

The primary purpose of criminal justice is to preserve the particular
distribution of power and privilege characteristic of American society. As an
advanced capitalist nation, America is characterized by great, systematic
inequities in the distribution of wealth and power, as well as the fact that the

means of production are owned and controlled by a few. These are not ideological statements; they are demonstrable consequences of our economic system.

The top 20% of the American population, in terms of wealth, owns approximately 76% of all wealth.[1] This means that the remaining 80% of the American population have only 24% of the nation's wealth to divide among themselves. The division of this remaining 24% results in even further inequities. The bottom 40% of the population in terms of wealth, for example, owns only 2.3% of the total wealth.[2] This bottom group is essentially excluded from sharing in the nation's wealth in any meaningful way, and constitutes an almost propertyless underclass. On the average, each individual in the top 20% has a share of the nation's wealth, that is, 7,600% greater than the average share held by individuals in the bottom 40%.

More important than these figures, however, is the fact that the industries and other property of the United States are owned by a very few. Approximately 6.4% of the American poulation own 89% of all publicly traded stocks, 63% of all real estate, 72% of all mortgage assets and 80% of all other investments.[3] The notion that American industry and investments are owned and controlled by a large group of small, middle-class investors and stockholders is a myth. It is rather a small group of economic elites who constitute America's ruling class. It is they who own America; the rest of the population lives here as their tenants.

This distribution of wealth is not a new phenomenon. Since colonial days America has had substantial inequities in the distribution of wealth and power. As Turner and Starnes note:

> To some extent, a New World landed upper class was inevitable because of the manner in which the colonies were established. Nearly all of the original colonial grants were made to already wealthy and powerful Engishmen.[4]

This landed upper class, in turn, imported large numbers of poor and dissatisfied Englishmen to serve as a pool of cheap agricultural labor. After the revolutionary war, this class system did not change noticeably. A large portion of the landholdings of wealthy colonists who had remained loyal to the crown were simply transferred to wealthy Patriots.[5] During the first half of the 19th Century with its expanding industrial development, this concentration of wealth became even greater. In Boston, for example, the wealthiest 4% of the population increased its share of the total wealth from 59% in 1833 to 64% by 1848.[6] From 1810 until 1929 the wealthiest 1% of the American population increased its share of the wealth from 21% to

36%. While they never regained their predepression level, by 1969, the wealthiest *1%* of the population controlled 24% of the total wealth.[7] This equalled their level of wealth in 1860, despite the various supposed "levelers" such as income tax and social welfare programs characteristic of post-industrial America.

Through their control of the productive wealth of the nation, a small number of economic elites has always had disproportionate access to political power. After the revolution, mass participation in government through voting was limited to free, white males—and some felt that even this was too extensive. Alexander Hamilton, in expressing this elitist position, wrote:

> All communities divide themselves into the few and the many. The first are the rich and well-born, the other the masses of people. The voice of the people has been said to be the voice of God; and however generally this maxim has been quoted and believed, it is not true in fact. The people are turbulent and changing, they seldom judge or determine right.[8]

While Hamilton's view did not prevail with respect to voting (at least where free white males were concerned), it did characterize actual participation in the daily affairs of government. The majority of those who served, and do serve, in the higher levels of government, as well as those in the private sector consulted by government officials, are drawn from a relatively small group of economic elites.[9] Since 1953, five out of seven Secretaries of Defense, three out of four Secretaries of State and six out of seven Secretaries of the Treasury have been officers of major American corporations. In most cases they have been presidents, chairmen of the board, or members of the boards of directors of these corporations. The few who have not held such positions have been either senior partners or officers in elite law firms, investment firms or foundations.[10]

This pattern is characteristic not only of the executive branch of government. In his analysis of institutional leadership in America, Thomas Dye found that:

> . . . congressional committees are an important communication link between governmental and non-governmental elites; they serve as a bridge between the executive and military bureaucracies and the major non-governmental elites in American society.[11]

Dye's research also demonstrates that the initial development of public policy is likely to reflect the perspectives and interests of economic elites. "The initial resources for research, study, planning and formulation of policy come from corporate and personal wealth."[12] Studies of state and local power structures have shown, for the most part, that economic elites also have similar disproportionate power at these levels of government.

Middle and lower class Americans have not been totally without political power, but what power they have had has been small in proportion to their numbers. Only by pooling their individually miniscule amounts of political power can thousands of auto workers, for example, hope to counteract the political leverage held by a *few* key stockholders and corporate managers in the auto industry.

Our system of government allows both a professional lobbyist working for the Dow Chemical Corporation and an ecology-minded school teacher to prowl the halls and offices of Congress seeking to influence legislation concerning the use of pesticides. For the former, this is a well-paid full-time occupation. For the latter, who must work at some other full-time occupation in order to survive, such lobbying activity must be supported out of whatever time and money is left over from the everyday demands of life. The idea that all Americans, whether as private citizens or as corporate representatives, have an equal opportunity to influence the actions of government is a theoretical possiblity, not a practical reality.

Economic elites have always had greater opportunities to influence legislation and other types of governmental decision-making. As a result, America has developed a justice system which reflects, first of all, the interests of this privileged class, and only secondly the interests of the mass of citizens to be free from threats to their person or property.

The criminal justice system in America devotes the majority of its efforts to controlling harms which DO NOT support the system of privilege and power beneficial to the capitalist ruling class. Harms which DO support the economic and political privileges of the capitalist ruling class are given much less attention — regardless of the degree to which they represent actual threats to individual lives or property.

The criminal justice system helps legalize the inequities which result from a capitalistic economic system. When members of the propertyless underclass react in frustration by committing property crimes or engaging in violent outbursts, the justice system devotes considerable energy to their capture and punishment. Little attention is paid to the system of social inequities which increase the likelihood of such behavior. When corporate or political elites engage in acts which threaten the well being of the average citizen, these acts are either defined as not the law's concern, or if they are considered crimes, the justice system's response is usually less vigorous than in the case of common law offenses.

The average citizen may feel that he or she is being protected by the efforts of the criminal justice system. However, it must be remembered that the context in which this "protection" occurs increases the likelihood of the need for this protection. Furthermore, this "protection" does not provide freedom from being victimized by corporate and political crimes. The primary beneficiaries of our criminal justice system are the economic and political elites who can enjoy their considerable privilege and power with little interference from the justice system.

Protecting Elite Interests

The desires of human individuals to be free from unwarranted threats to their physical well being as well as from the theft of their "property" antedate both the political state and the era of industrial development. Most primitive, non-state societies have had some mechanism for controlling such behaviors. In many instances, these mechanisms consisted of highly complex and well-established routines for providing the victim of a "crime" or his or her relatives with compensation for the harm done. Among the Ifugao, for example, an intermediary relays offers and counter-offers between the victim and the offender until an acceptable compensation for the harm done is determined.[13]

With the emergence of a political state several significant transformations generally take place in the manner in which individuals are "protected" from unwarranted harms. First, all violence, except that authorized by the state, is generally outlawed. The mechanisms for controlling unwarranted harms in *non-state* societies are usually underscored by the potentiality of violent retribution by the victim or his kin should the offender or his kin not cooperate in the process of arriving at satisfactory compensation. In a sense the various clans and tribes of a non-state society comprise mini-armies. The existence of these armed groups with the potentiality, however remote, for independent warfare is inimical to the development of a centralized political authority. The process of subduing the various independent armed groups in the attempt to forge a unified political state is often a long and arduous one. Where successful, however, not only does the state succeed in defining all violence *except* its own as illegitimate, but it also succeeds in destroying the traditional basis upon which individuals were protected from unwarranted harms. Thus, the creation of the political state makes individuals dependent upon that state for protection.

Second, the individual disputants in a conflict are generally no longer permitted to settle the matter between themselves or their representatives. With the emergence of the English monarchy, for example, individuals were required to submit their disputes to one of the King's chancellors for resolution.[14]

Third, over time, crimes cease to be treated as harms against individuals. As a means of emphasizing the *order* of the political state, crimes are generally redefined as harms against the ruler's order, and later simply as harms against the state.[15] Our modern criminal prosecutions, for example, specify the State v. Offender and not Offender v. Victim. The emphasis is upon reaffirming the order of the state, not on meeting the needs of victims to be reinstated to their condition before the crime.

Along with the decline of feudalism and the emergence of capitalism in Europe and England came several other significant changes in "protecting" individuals from harm. The laws governing property relations had to be modified to accommodate the needs of the growing capitalist class. Criminal law became a significant tool with which to protect the interests of this emerging economic elite. The development of the laws of theft in England, for example, proceeded not with the interest of the average individual in mind, but specifically to protect the interests of a developing mercantile class.[16] The laws of vagrancy were rewritten and reactivated to insure the economic elites a supply of cheap labor.[17] Other laws were established to insure the dominance of the emerging capitalist class.

> Criminal laws strangled the ability of the lower classes (those alienated from landed feudal ties who had migrated to the cities as 'free labor') to possess tools or capital goods, raw materials, and also under pain of heavy penal sanction, forbade association with guild masters.[18]

It was during this period of early capitalist development that the concept of *crime* was narrowly defined to incorporate primarily those harms committed by lower class members and which threatened the economic and political order advantageous to the developing capitalist ruling class. The "harms" committed *against* the lower classes by economic elites in their pursuit of profit were totally excluded from the criminal law. Pitiful wages, unsafe and unsanitary working conditions, child labor, woefully inadequate housing and all of the other oppression of the early industrial era were barely noticed by the legal system of the emerging capitalist state. Calling upon the concept of "individualism" these harms were absolved as the just condition of those who were less fit to compete in the capitalist market place.

Harms committed by members of the capitalist ruling class against other ruling class members—that is, harms which threatened to disrupt the developing economic order—were handled within the legal system. However, these acts were not treated as crimes. Instead they were managed by the system of civil law which absolved the disputants both from penal sanctions and the stigma of being viewed as threats to the social order. As Mark Kennedy notes, under English law the state:

> . . . created two classes of citizens—one bound by criminal laws and penal sanctions, and another bound only by non-punitive civil laws . . .

> Under the formally rational State, second-class citizens are never in a
> position to be governed only by civil law—they are never, therefore,
> beyond incrimination."[19]

English law, the direct parent of our American legal system, developed in a
manner suited primarily to protecting the economic and political order
advantageous to capitalist elites. It did not develop with its primary concern
being the protection of *average* citizens from the various harms possible in
that society.

Outdated Concepts

Developed from English common law, our modern day concept of crime
emphasizes anti-social acts committed by *specific individuals* with the *specific
intent* to either directly (as in the case of violent crime), or indirectly (as in
the case of property crime) cause harm to some other *specific individual(s)*. For
anti-social behavior to be considered truly serious crime in modern America
it normally must involve these three factors. As a result, our everyday image
of crime centers around behaviors such as murder, rape, robbery, assault,
burglary and larceny. While we have in modern times added a number of
public order offenses such as drunkenness, traffic violations and gambling,
these are considered to be of a relatively minor nature. The one variant is
drug-related offenses. While lacking both specific victims and specific
intent to cause harm, they are considered relatively serious offenses.

The overall effect of this emphasis upon specific offenders, specific victims
and specific intent is to limit the focus of criminal justice. Common law
offenses against persons and property meet the specific requirements of our
historical definition of "crime." The harms committed by economic and
political elites in their search for power and profit, as well as harms which are
unique to the modern, industrialized world fit this older concept of crime
much less easily. As a result the criminal justice system "protects" the
average citizen from only one class of harms—those most easily committed
by common citizens who are not members of economic and political elite.
Another entire class of harms—those more easily committed by elites or
whose non-control benefits elite interests—are either not prohibited by the
law, or when they are, they are not considered to be "real" crimes. The
criminal justice system offers little or no protection from this second class of
harms despite the fact that the harm caused often equals or exceeds the harm
from analogous common law crimes.

While it is not possible to enumerate the entire range of these second class
harms in the space of this paper, it is worthwhile to examine several
examples from which the criminal justice system offers very little protection.

Corporate Harms

The world of corporate harms encompasses a broad range of negative consequences resulting from the search for corporate profit. These include harms to the environment, harms to workers, harms to consumers through false or misleading advertising, harms to consumers through unsafe products, and harms to consumers through price fixing, corporate collusion and other types of illegal marketing practices. While some of these harms are considered to be violations of law, many are not. However, even those which are *crimes* enjoy a special status because they do not meet the tests of specific offenders, victims and intent.

In one sense, all corporate crimes can be considered "white collar crime" because they occur during the conduct of business relations. However, they differ from the more personally motivated white collar crimes such as embezzlement, graft and employee theft. These offenses are committed by specific offenders, with clear intent to achieve a *direct* personal gain, and they generally have specific victims such as banks, stockholders or investors. Corporate crimes often lack these components of "crime." They are frequently committed not by a specific individual, but result from the interaction of a number of persons. While Sutherland found that the Federal Trade Commission identified approximately 50,000 questionable and 1,500 patently false advertisements per year, the *specific* offenders in such cases are not readily apparent.[20] Is the advertising agency which devised the advertising campaign the criminal? Or, is it the particular executive who authorized the particular advertising campaign the "criminal?" Or, is the "criminal" the corporation's president who knew that a particular executive authorized a particular advertising agency to develop a particular advertising campaign? The diffuse nature of responsibility for corporate crimes makes it quite difficult to think in terms of an "offender", yet our historical definition of crime requires that we be able to identify a specific offender.

This problem becomes even more acute in the case of harms which result form general corporate policy rather than specific decisions. A given company may be generally lax in implementing required safety standards for its workers, and as a result the amount of injury and death to workers may be unnecessarily high. Yet, there is no specific individual clearly apparent to our observation who is responsible for these safety lacks. It may be possible to legally *assign* responsibility, but this assignment does not have the clarity of the relationship, for example, between an armed robber and his victim. As a result, corporate personnel who may be "assigned" responsibility do not appear to us as "real" criminals. Rather they seem to be the *victims* of some legal ruling.

A second problem in accepting corporate crime as real crime is the issue of intent. Normal crimes require that the offender have some intent to cause harm, and this intent is usually made comprehensible by some direct gain which will be enjoyed by the offender as a result of causing harm — the motive. There is evidence that "more profitable firms do not violate the law as easily and quickly as the less profitable ones."[21] That is, the intent of corporate crime is related to improving the economic position of the company. However, analysis of the "Great Electrical Conspiracy" found that many of the actual participants in the price fixing activities did so for the sake of indirect rather than direct personal gain. Participation in illegal activities appeared to have been significantly related to advancement within the organization.[22] While not receiving direct gain for their activity, corporate executives who advanced the company's economic position through price fixing were rewarded indirectly through swift promotion. Furthermore, failure to participate might lead, not only to lack of advancement, but to other types of censure. As Geis reported:

> . . . the General Electric witnesses specified clearly that it was not their job with the company that would be in jeopardy if they failed to price-fix, but rather the particular assignment they had. 'If I didn't do it, I felt that somebody else would,' said one, with an obvious note of self-justificatoin. 'I would be removed, and somebody else would do it.'[23]

Because the intent to violate the law is related to indirect reward from the organization, rather than direct reward through harming some victim, we find it more difficult to understand corporate crime as "real" crime. In one sense, the individual appears not to have the intent of harming others, but rather the intent to do his job well. It is hard to view such a person as a "criminal," and it is even harder to view the diffuse organizational structure within which doing one's job well involves violating the law as the "criminal." The result of this lack of clear "intent" to cause harm results in corporate crimes being given special treatment under the law.

> . . . the question of intent, so prominent in the criminal code is irrelevant to conviction under many regulatory laws . . . In this' respect, white-collar violations are legally much more like traffic laws and municipal ordinances than statutes of the criminal code.[23]

In essence, corporate crimes — whose cost to consumers and whose harm to the physical well being of both individuals and environment may well exceed that of common law crimes — are assigned a legal status which makes them appear similar to other "minor" offenses.

The third difficulty presented by corporate crimes is the lack of specific victims. The actual victims of corporate crime may be many times removed from the actual violation of law. The excessively high prices paid by the purchasers of electrical generating equipment as a result of the Great Electrical Conspiracy would have ultimately been passed on to the individuals who bought electric power from the various municipalities and utilities that had originally purchased the generating equipment. Similarly, the recent charges by the government that various oil companies illegally manipulated their supplies during the 1974 Arab oil embargo thereby obtaining an additional 33 million dollars in revenue, brings to mind no "victim" other than the faceless mass of "consumers."[25]

The diffuse nature of victimization by corporate crimes makes it difficult to view such acts as real crimes. At the same time, this diffuse victimization is the basis for the enormous total economic and physical costs of corporate crime. As Sutherland noted:

> If you consider the life of a person, you find that from the cradle to the grave he has been using articles which were sold or distributed in violation of the law.[26]

While the individual loss may be small for each specific victimization, the total cost over a lifetime may be substantial, and the total cost to the nation on an annual basis has been estimated to far exceed the cost of common law crime. Unfortunately, because of the limited attention given to such offenses by the justice system, we do not have the same extensive data on corporate crimes that we have for common law offenses. The lack of such data obscures such crimes from the public's view and makes it difficult to assess the true cost of corporate crime.

Each purchase of a service or commodity whose price is higher than it would have been if the corporation or business involved had not violated the law is a theft. Every death or illness resulting from a violation of pollution or safety standards is a crime of violence. Yet, because of our adherence to the concepts of specific offenders, specific victims and specific intent to cause harm, the criminal justice system does not recognize such acts as significant threats to the persons and property it is designed to "protect."

Corporate crimes are but one example of diffuse harms which do not receive the full attention of the justice system. Systematic forms of discrimination and oppression which rob individuals of their freedom, the opportunity to develop their human potential and, in many cases, of their health and life are so diffuse in character that they are seldom defined as criminal acts. The Supreme Court, for example, recently affirmed the need for specificity of intent in cases of discrimination by ruling that where no *specific intent* to discriminate can be shown, no illegal discrimination can be charged.[27] Decisions such as these exemplify the degree to which our concept of "crime" is dependent upon a specificity which cannot incorporate many of the harms possible in a complex society.

Our definition of crime is tied to concepts which are historically outdated, and which in many ways were fostered, not by the need of individuals to be free from threats to their person and property, but by the needs of capitalist elites to be free from legal controls on their search for profit. While there have been many modifications and additions to our concept of law and justice since the era of early capitalist development, the basic element remains. The criminal justice system will strive to protect individuals from harms which are not beneficial to the economic elite. It will, however, offer very little protection to individuals from harms whose existence benefits the ruling class.

Criminal Justice and the Preservation of Inequality

Criminal justice operates according to a definition of crime which requires specific offenders, specific victims and specific intent to cause harm. Adherence to this concept of "crime" helps preserve the system of political and economic inequality advantageous to the capitalist ruling class by (1) contributing to the maintenance of ruling class hegemony and (2) focusing attention on the disruptive behaviors of the economic underclass.

Hegemony refers to a condition in society where the rules for defining acceptable and unacceptable behavior characteristic of a particular world view becomes "so ingrained in mass thinking that they are taken for granted."[28] The attainment of hegemony occurs, not through the direct application of force, but through the more indirect processes of controlling the essential social arrangements within which the masses lead their lives. Human individuals learn the meaning of various behaviors by observing or directly experiencing the consequences of these behaviors. Behaviors we observe being punished we come to think of as "bad." Behaviors we observe being rewarded we come to think of as "good." The more severely a behavior is punished the "worse" we think it is. By controlling the selection of behaviors for punishment or reward, over a long period of time, a dominant social group can establish within a culture an understanding of right and wrong which serves primarily the interests of that dominant group and not the interests of the society as a whole.

Our criminal justice system devotes its manpower and money to "protecting" citizens from common law crimes. By comparison it provides very little protection from harms whose annual cost and whose certainty of victimization exceeds that of common law offenses. Corporate harms and other quasi-crimes, when they are controlled at all, are done so primarily through civil mechanisms which lack the stigma of criminal prosecutions and serve to deemphasize the seriousness of the harms being adjudicated. Sutherland, in his seminal study of white collar crime found that:

> The crimes of the lower class are handled by policemen, prosecutors and judges with penal sanctions in the forms of fines, imprisonment and death. The crimes of the upper class either result in no official action at all, or result in suits for damages in civil courts, or are handled by inspectors and by administrative boards or commissions with penal sanctions in the form of warnings, orders to cease and desist, occasionally the loss of a license, and only in extreme cases by fines and prison sentences. Thus, the white-collar criminals are segregated administratively from other criminals, and, largely *as a consequence of* this, are not regarded as real criminals by themselves, the general public, or the criminologists."[29] (my emphasis)

This is but one example of the important educational function performed by the justice system. By the stringency of its response to common law crimes and the laxity of its response to corporate crimes, the justice system helps the public understand that common law offenders are the "dangerous" criminals of our society, while corporate criminals are little more than the victims of "technical" regulations. This definition of "serious" and "not so serious", however, is more beneficial to ruling class interests than the interests of the society as a whole. It guarantees that the majority of harms most easily committed by ruling class members will go relatively uncontrolled, and furthermore that the public will be slow to demand greater control of ruling class harms because, by observation, the mass of citizens have learned that ruling class harms are not really "serious" crimes. However, it also guarantees that the mass of citizens will remain relatively unprotected from these crimes.

In addition to deemphasizing the harms committed by ruling class members, the criminal justice system serves to legalize inequality and foster the image that the lower class is the "dangerous" class. Criminal justice legalizes inequality by focusing the blame for the consequences of inequality on the victims rather than the perpetrators of inequality. In essence, criminal justice serves to maintain a capitalist definition of material relations. Basic to this capitalist definition of appropriate material relations is the concept that individuals have a right not only to the *personal* property needed for daily life, but also a right to own and control productive property. The ownership of productive property makes possible the exploitation of labor. Those who own productive property (mines, factories, stores, oil wells, etc.) can command the labor of those who, not owning such property themselves, must enter into wage labor for their survival. Because of their advantaged position, the owners of productive property can always pay workers less than the real value of their labor. According to Marx's theory of the surplus value of labor, this difference between the *real* value of labor and what is actually paid for it constitutes *profit*. Profit is the value created by workers which is not returned to them in the form of wages.

Profit accrues, not to the worker, but to the owner of the productive property. This profit facilitates the purchase of additional productive property, which in turn can be used to produce more profit. The worker receives only enough return for his or her labor to meet the average daily needs as defined by the material level of the society. Few receive salaries which are sufficiently large as to allow the purchase of their own productive property. Thus workers' existences are characterized by a fragile dependency upon the owners of productive property. This insures the continuation of a class system whose essential characteristic is a division between those who own productive property and those who do not.

In the advanced capitalist state a portion of the workers receive substantial salaries and their material condition is vastly improved over that of workers during the early industrial era. However, the essential division between those who control productive property and those who are dependent upon them remains. By providing relatively comfortable material existences for a *portion* of the society, the advanced capitalist nation obtains a degree of increased productive efficiency and relative freedom from unrest. However, it is also advantageous to maintain a parallel pool of relatively cheap and manipulatable labor. These individuals who are either unemployed or chronically underemployed can be shifted in and out of the job market as the requirements of industrial efficiency dictate. It is for this reason, for example, that welfare and other income subsidies given to the poor are always lower than the lowest wages paid in a given region.[30] This insures a pool of persons who will be willing to accept low paying jobs should the productive system have a need for them.

The desires of those who own and control productive property for efficient utilization of this property—that is, the maintenance or expansion of margins of profit—is the essential guiding force of the advanced capitalist state. Human needs are secondary. If it is efficient to reduce the payroll— i.e. close off some wage laborers from their source of economic survival— there is little question but that it is, while perhaps regrettable, certainly legitimate to do so.

There are also other processes which contribute to the maintenance of an economic underclass with little access to the economic and social rewards of American society. Racism and other forms of discrimination serve as handy levers for holding some individuals out of more lucrative job markets, and in the pool of manipulatable, cheap labor. In a society where productive efficiency, rather than creating meaningful spaces for all individuals is the primary goal, individuals must compete to obtain some survival niche. Individuals become alienated from one another insofar as each other individual may be a potential competitor for one's own survival niche. Thus, discrimination not only serves to keep the labor force down to the minimum needed by the productive system, but it also receives general support from a substantial proportion of those who have managed to enter the work force. Each uneducated and unemployed minority individual is just one more person who cannot compete effectively for the job held by someone employed.

The common law crimes emphasized by the justice system are not generally committed by individuals with access to the average material and social rewards of the society. Executives earning $25,000 a year do not normally burglarize houses, and fully employed factory workers earning a $9.00 hourly wage do not normally commit armed robberies. The types of crimes given the greatest attention are committed most frequently by members of the economic underlcass, that body of individuals who have been historically, economically, socially and culturally excluded from legitimate access to the benefits of society.

A society cannot maintain a substantial concentration of wealth in the hands of a few without also maintaining a substantial number of poor. The relationship between inequality, poverty and common law crime is a complex one, however, the simple fact remains that the majority of offenses handled by the justice system (excluding public order crimes) are crimes for relatively petty economic gain committed by the poor. In 1975 approximately 95% of all felony offenses known to the police were for economic gain. Violent crimes, although given substantial public attention constituted only 5% of the felony offenses known that year.[31] The average gain from these crimes was relatively small. In 1975, for robbery the average value taken was $331, for burglarly $422 and for larcency $166, and there is a real possibility that these "average" figures are inflated by a few offenses involving very large sums as well as overestimation of loss by victims for the purposes of insurance compensation.

The majority of those who commit the common law offenses emphasized by the justice system live in a world where such crimes can appear as viable alternatives for meeting one's economic and psychological survival needs. That is, the rewards from crime can appear nearly as attractive as the rewards from legitimate activity. This is not because the rewards from crime are so high, but because the potential rewards from legitimate activity are so low. The majority of the poor are law abiding but this is because they have in some way come to terms with the low rewards they will receive for whatever work or public assistance they can find. For those who cannot come to terms with these inequities, casual or career crime appears as a viable alternative. While this may be oversimplifying very complex social psychological processes, the fact is the poor must try to cope with a world of inequities which was not of their making. Inevitably, some will fail to come to terms with it in the way in which we would like.

The wealthy and the affluent of our society benefit by the existence of the poor. It is through the maintenance of some at low economic levels that others can enjoy substantially large shares of the overall wealth. When the poor fail to adequately cope with the pressures of their economic and social poverty, the justice system attempts to apprehend and punish their misdeeds. The very act of punishing, or attempting to punish, such individuals emphasizes that *the failure was theirs.* The system of inequality is preserved by blaming its victims. Furthermore, because it is the poor who receive the bulk of the justice system's attention, they appear to be the "dangerous class" within society. It is the poor that we observe being apprehended, adjudicated and imprisoned for committing harms to society. Since the criminals we have available for observation are from the underclass, we tend to associate the underclass with "crime." In this way the entire society is focused upon the poor as the social group most needing control and away from economic elites whose harms may be equally or more dangerous, but whom we do not see paraded through the spectacle of criminal prosecution.

Conclusion

Presently the criminal justice system is oriented toward protecting individuals from common law crimes which threaten their person or property. By contrast, the justice system can offer only very limited protection from corporate crimes and harms resulting from racial discrimination and class oppression. The immediate reason for this is the fact that the justice system is guided by a legal concept which emphasizes specific offenders, specific victims and specific intent to cause harm as the basic components of crime. This definition of crime, however, reflects the needs of the capitalist ruling class to be relatively free from controls, and was forged during the early period of capitalist development. Through a historic process covering almost 500 years, this concept of criminal harm has become entrenched in Western culture as a result of ruling class hegemony. While accepted by the mass of Americans, the primary beneficiaries of this concept of crime remain those who own and control the means of production.

The predatory common law crimes from which the criminal justice system attempts to offer some degree of protection are real, as is the need for this protection under the present circumstances. However, the very prevalence of these crimes results from one of the major cultural contradictions of the advanced capitalist state — the persistence of poverty amidst both great wealth and general affluence. Thus, the criminal justice system functions primarily to control one of the negative consequences of a capitalist society, the existence of an underclass, some members of which will occasionally resort to predatory crimes to meet what they define as their survival needs.

The criminal justice system is designed to provide only the narrowest form of justice; justice as defined within a social system based on inequality. This concept of justice serves not the mass of the people, but those who most benefit from the system of economic and social inequality. The justice system of itself can do little to change this. It exists essentially as a tool of the larger political state which is organized primarily to promote the interests of the capitalist economic system. Only in a society organized to aggressively promote the concepts of equality and social justice can the justice system begin to protect the general population from the true range of harms possible in the modern state.

Discussion Questions

1. Identify three examples of news reporting and three examples of popular drama (T.V., movies or books) which reinforce the image of crime as a "morality play". How do they reinforce this image?

2. Imagine you have recently bought a used car. After several days it begins to run very badly and you discover through a chance meeting with the car's former owner that the odometer has been turned back 50,000 miles and the engine is in need of major repair, despite the car dealers statement that it was "almost new and in perfect shape.
   A. What are your options for obtaining legal redress?
   B. How do these options differ from those which would be available to you if you were the victim of a common theft and knew who was the offender?

3. Recent estimates place the cost of white collar crime at 40 times greater than the cost of all common crime (40 billion vs. 1 billion). Why does such a costly form of law-breaking result in very few prosecutions and relatively light sentences?

Notes

1. Executive Office of the President: Office of Management and Budget, *Social Indicators 1973* (Washington, D.C.: U.S. Government Printing Office, 1973) p. 164.

2. ibid. p. 164.

3. Dorothy S. Projector and Gertrude S. Weiss, *Survey of Financial Characteristics of Consumers* (Washington, D.C.: Board of Governors of the Federal Reserve System, 1966) p. 136.

4. Jonathan H. Turner and Charles E. Starnes, *Inequality: Privilege and Poverty in America* (Pacific Palisade, California: Goodyear Publishing Co., 1976) p. 12.

5. ibid., p. 13.

6. Edward Pessen, "The Egalitarian Myth and the American Social Reality: Wealth, Mobility and Equality in the 'Era of the Common Man';" American Historical Review 76, 4 (October, 1971): 989–1034.

7. Turner and Starnes, p. 19.

8. Alexander Hamilton, Records of the Federal Convention of 1797, quoted in Thomas R. Dye, *Who's Running America,* (Englewood Cliffs, N.J.: Prentice Hall, 1976) p. 4.

9. Turner and Starnes, pp. 77–78.

10. Dye, pp. 56–58.

11. ibid, p. 90.

12. ibid, p. 204.

13. E. Adamson Hoebel, *The Law of Primitive Man* (Chicago: University of Chicago Press, 1954) pp. 114–117.

14. Richard Quinney, *Criminology: Analysis and Critique of Crime in America* (Boston: Little, Brown and Co., 1975) p. 47.

15. ibid, p. 47.

16. Jerome Hall, *Theft, Law and Society,* 2nd ed. (Indianapolis, Ind.: Bobbs-Merrill, 1952).

17. William J. Chambliss, "A Sociological Analysis of the Law of Vagrancy", *Social Problems* 12 (Summer, 1964) pp. 67–77.

18. Mark C. Kennedy, "Beyond Incrimination: Some Neglected Facets of the Theory of Punishment", *Catalyst* No. 5 (Summer, 1970) p. 15.

19. ibid, p. 15.

20. Edwin Sutherland, "Crime of Corporations", in Gilbert Geis and Robert F. Meier (eds.) *White Collar Crime* (New York: The Free Press, 1977) p. 74.

21. Robert E. Lane, "Why Businessmen Violate the Law" in Geis and Meier (eds.) p. 105.

22. Gilbert Geis, "The Heavy Electrical Equipment Conspiracy Case of 1961" in Geis and Meier (eds.) p. 124.

23. ibid, p. 124.

24. Donald J. Newman, "White Collar Crime: An Overview and Analysis" in Geis and Meier (eds.) p. 53.

25. New York Times, April 29, 1977, p. 1.

26. Sutherland, p. 73.

27. New York Times, January 12, 1972, pp. 1 & 6B.

28. Barry Krisberg, *Crime and Privilege* (Englewood Cliffs, N.J.: Prentice Hall, 1975) p. 55.

29. Edwin Sutherland, "White Collar Criminality" in Geis and Meier (eds.) p. 45.

30. Joe R. Feagin, *Subordinating the Poor* (Englewood Cliffs, N.J.: Prentice Hall, 1975) p. 71.

31. U.S. Dept of Justice, *Uniform Crime Reports, 1975* (Washington D.C.: U.S. Government Printing Office, 1976).

2

The Criminal Justice/Racial Justice Nexus

CLINTON B. JONES

Introduction

SINCE THE EARLY 17TH CENTURY, RACE[1] AND CRIME have been America's two most persistent, complex and politically divisive domestic issues. Of course, crime problems are not unique to America, but are common to most organized societies. When blacks entered Jamestown, Virginia in 1619 as indentured servants, racial issues joined with issues of crime to become colonial America's two most challenging domestic issues.

Within colonial America's hierarchically arranged social structure, wealthy whites were situated at the top echelon and blacks, both slave and free, were at the very bottom. The comparative social statuses of colonial whites and blacks were supported at the time by a widely accepted ideology of white supremacy and, correspondingly, of black inferiority; this ideology pervaded all aspects of American life during slavery, including its criminal justice institutions.[2] Out of this beginning, evolved the merger of the two issues. They merged primarily because of (1) the criminal justice system's responsibility for enforcing laws of white supremacy; (2) active black resistance to laws and customs of white supremacy; and (3) the criminal justice system's responsibility for repressing such resistance. Although conflicting, racial and criminal justice issues came together early in American history.

Too often analysts have sought to study the two issues separately. However, they are so inextricably interwoven into the American experience that extrapolation of one for analysis to the exclusion of the other is virtually impossible. More explicitly, it is self defeating for one to conduct problem solving oriented analyses of crime in the United States without considering race as a factor in the administration of justice process; nor may one seriously contemplate eradicating racism in the United States without considering the role of criminal justice institutions in either fostering or hindering racial justice. Both of the foregoing assertions will become more evident during the progress of this presentation.

Why are racial and criminal justice issues so interrelated? What is the nature of the kinship? How have they impacted on each other? What policies and programs are most likely to foster harmonious rather than conflictual relations between the issues? It is the purpose of this chapter to provide answers to these questions. Therefore, for convenience of presentation, the discussion will proceed under the following headings: (1) Historical Antecedents; (2) The Current Racial/Criminal Justice Nexus; (3) Current Programs and Policies; and (4) Conclusions.

Historical Antecedents

While the primary concern here is with analysis of current relationships between the issues, a brief review of their historical nexus is a prerequisite for such analysis. Since entering North America as involuntary servants, blacks have experienced forms of racism that have ranged from abject slavery to current forms of institutional racism. Regardless of racism's form, racial and criminal justice issues have significantly impacted on each other in the United States.

Slavery

From around 1639 to 1865, most North American blacks were slaves and those not slaves were also victims of discrimination. During this lengthy period of blatant racial oppression, criminal justice institutions, while, underdeveloped, functioned predictably to protect the absolute white domination of blacks. Illustrations of the criminal justice systems role in the oppression of blacks at this time were found in the history and content of two documents that guided the activities of criminal justice institutions and continue to serve as America's two most valued written symbols of liberty, egalitarianism, and justice, i.e., The Declaration of Independence and the United States Constitution.

Notwithstanding international acknowledgement of the Declaration of Independence's status as one of the most uncompromising and eloquent statements of man's natural right to freedom (i.e., freedom is granted by a source higher than man and, therefore, cannot be denied by man), it failed to condemn slavery and, even more contradictory, over one half of the document's signatories were themselves slaveholders.[3] Frederick Douglass, the leading 19th century black opponent of slavery, offers the following black response to white America's professed commitments to human equality and freedom:

> What to the American Slave is your 4th of July? . . . To him, your celebration is a sham; your boasted liberty an unholy license; your national greatness, swelling vanity . . . Your prayers and hymns, your

> sermons and thanksgiving, with all your religious parade and solemnity
> are, to him, mere bombast, fraud, deception, impiety, and hypocrisy . . .
> a thin veil to cover up crimes which would disgrace a nation of savages.[4]

By not condemning slavery, The Declaration of Independence symbolizes
the tendency of whites at this time to exclude nonwhites from their
preachments of human equality.[5] Unlike The Declaration of Independence,
however, the United States Constitution explicitly endorsed slavery. Its
endorsement of slavery resulted from the political compromise agreed to by
the slavery and anti-slavery forces at the Constitutional Convention, and
includes: (1) the "Three-Fifth's Compromise" (i.e., one black slave represented three-fifths of a person in the numerical allocation of Congressional
seats and the apportionment of tax obligations);[6] (2) the "Fugitive Slave
Clause" (i.e., run-away slaves had to be returned to slaveholders);[7] and (3)
the legal continuation of the slave trade until 1801.[8] Thus, both the
Constitution, and the Declaration of Independence, either ignored or
endorsed the existence of slavery. Since American criminal justice institutions were required to enforce the Constitution's anti-black provisions,
conflict between blacks and criminal justice was inevitable.

During the slavery phase of American interracial relations, law enforcement and corrections were severely underdeveloped in comparison with the
courts. They all functioned cooperatively, however, to repress black liberation efforts. Even the U.S. Supreme Court, the most developed component
of the system, at that time, supported slavery through its infamous "Dred
Scott Decision."[9] In summary, until 1865, most black Americans resided in
a system of racist totalitarianism (i.e., racism permeated the entire social
system, including criminal justice).

Reconstruction and Jim Crow, 1865 – 1954

The Civil War ended chattel slavery. Obviously it did not end racial
discrimination. However, immediately following the Civil War, blacks did
experience over a decade during (1865 – 1877) of what has been referred to as
a "golden-age" of black participation.[10] This increased black participation
was due to the defeat of the South, expanded black influence in Southern
politics and, most importantly, to the protective presence of federal troops
in the South. However, after over two decades of bitter regional conflict over
racial issues, Northern whites tired of the financial costs and threats to
national unity that stemmed from protecting black civil rights in the South;
and, in 1877, President Rutherford Hayes withdrew federal troops from
the South and consequently left black Southerners powerless to defend
themselves against the better organized and armed Southern white supre-

macists.[11] Reconstruction's failure to create durable institutions viable enough to ensure racial justice, and the subsequent return of ante-bellum white supremacists to power ushered in the "Jim Crow" phase of interracial relations. Early in this phase, once the federal troops had been withdrawn, white supremacists wrested political influence from Southern blacks and anti-slavery whites and blacks onces again became subjects of the system rather than active participants.[12]

Although many blacks migrated from the South during this time, especially during the two World Wars, most blacks remained in the South throughout the period. The minority of blacks that resided outside of the South, however, was not treated much better than those in the South.[13]

During this time blacks had little influence over criminal justice decision-making and few were employed as criminal justice professionals. Those that were so employed were usually restricted to exercising their authority over blacks and not whites.[14]

The courts, at the beginning of this phase, acquiesced in the disfranchisement of blacks by rendering decisions that served to nullify the effectiveness of civil rights laws passed during Reconstruction, and later on (1896), the Supreme Court openly endorsed Jim Crow institutions with its Plessy v. Ferguson decision.[15]

While not quite as brutally repressive as during slavery, Jim Crow criminal justice institutions exacted a heavy toll from black Americans in the form of disproportionate black arrests, death sentences and quasi-legal lynchings, resulting in pervasive black fear of and alienation from American criminal justice institutions.[16]

Institutional Racism, 1954 to Present

Intentional, overt acts of racial discrimination are no longer permissible in American society. Significantly, it was the act of a criminal justice institution, the United States Supreme Court's Brown v. School Board decision, that initiated the demise of Jim Crow, launched the modern phase of interracial relations commonly referred to as "institutional racism," and signalled the beginning of an alliance between racial justice proponents and the courts that would continue into the 1970's. The landmark *Brown* decision declared racially segregated public schools to be illegal and gave added momentum to the fledging black movement for racial equality. Subsequent civil rights' court decisions, legislation and Executive Orders augmented the impact of *Brown* and combined to prohibit easily proven acts of racial discrimination, leaving unresolved the more subtle and complex discriminatory acts.

One representative definition of institutional racism is:

> Racism attributable to the fundamental operating rules of an institution, and which on the basis of race preempts blacks from effective access to the decision-making process.[17]

A practical illustration of institutional racism may be found in the disproportionate number of blacks eliminated from the competition for law enforcement occupations because of their low scores on ostensibly objective written examinations. However, since these examinations are prepared by whites, they often include items that are culturally biased in favor of whites and they are not valid predictors of on-the-job success. Thus, even though unintentional, blacks are discriminated against in the utilization of such tests as employee selection instruments.[18]

The Current Criminal/Racial Justice Nexus

The Civil Rights Movement's success in destroying Jim Crow discrimination left institutional racism as America's predominate form of discrimination and brought about changes in the nature of relationships between racial and criminal justice issues. As described earlier, criminal justice institutions in the United States functioned, to cooperatively and conspicuously perpetuate black subordination to whites prior to the mid-fifties. Since that time, however, criminal justice agencies rarely practice overt, easily proven racial discrimination.

Criminal justice agencies began to display in the 1960's for the first time, an interest in cultivating the allegiance of black Americans and several even made attempts to become more responsive to black community needs and interests. Unfortunately, this awakening was not self imposed; but stemmed from the pressures of: the Civil Rights Movement; pro-civil rights court decisions; civil rights Executive Orders; the 1964–65 Civil Rights Act; and even more specifically, from the call of several prestigious study groups commissioned by the President of the United States to study causes of urban violence and crime in the United States, and based on their findings to make policy recommendations for alleviating the problems.[19]

Programmatic manifestations of this new interest in blacks are found in the proliferation of: (1) community relations programs, specifically designed to promote among black Americans positive images of the criminal justice system; and (2) minority recruitment programs that emphasize increasing the number of blacks employed in criminal justice careers. More will be said later about both types of programs.

One must be cautioned, however, against an overly optimistic interpretation of current racial and criminal justice interrelations. Long standing attitudes, beliefs and values are not easily purged from a nation's social consciousness, especially when they are deeply ingrained in that nation's way of life, as is racism in the United States. For over three centuries (1619–1954), overt racism was irrefutably an integral part of life in the United States and during this time criminal justice institutions acted as America's most visible protector of the racist status quo. Understandably, then residuals of racism remain in the system, even though the system is much less overtly anti-black than in the past.

Listed below are findings of several studies which reveal the system's continued racially discriminatory features:

> Many white police officers continue to hold prejudiced, anti-black views.[20]
>
> For similar offenses, blacks are more likely than whites to receive prison sentences and serve longer terms.[21]
>
> Blacks are less likely than whites to receive pretrial release on bail.[22]
>
> Blacks are less likely than whites to be selected to serve on juries.[23]
>
> Blacks are more likely than whites to be sentenced to death.[24]

In addition to the above findings, blacks are also disproportionately victims of crime, which indicates a high incidence of black intra-racial crime and/or lax enforcement of laws in black communities.[25] As a matter of fact, crime and the fear of crime have become so pervasive among urban blacks that grassroots crime fighting organizations have proliferated throughout urban America.[26]

Of course some would argue that high black arrest and victimization rates are not due to racism, but that they more probably reflect black racial and/or socio-cultural inferiority. The racial inferiority position has few adherents, even though it attracted enormous media attention following publication of Arthur Jensen's claim of black inferiority.[27] This position asserts that blacks are intellectually inferior to whites and are, therefore, more likely to commit crimes than are whites because of the demonstrated association between low "intelligence" and criminal behavior. This position is attacked for basing the extreme conclusion of black intellectual inferiority on intelligence tests that may be culturally biased to favor whites and for ignoring the representation of blacks among the top scorers on all "intelligence" tests.[28] The policy implications of this position suggest that emphasis should be placed on stringent crime control measures to reduce black crime because of the posited biologically determined black predisposition to commit crimes.

The socio-cultural inferiority position has greater support among reputable behavioral scientists than the racial inferiority one. It argues that there are "pathological" attitudinal and behavioral patterns operating in low-income black communities that encourage criminal behavior; such as broken homes, single parent homes, tendencies toward violent resolutions of conflict, low levels of educational achievement, and lowered socioeconomic aspirations. This position relates the above posited black cultural "pathologies" to black life experiences that have included efforts to adapt to and survive in oppressive anti-black environments in the United States, but it rejects arguments of innate black inferiority.[29] The policy implications of this position support programs designed to lower black crime rates by bringing about ameliorative social change in black environments.

Notwithstanding the racial and socio-cultural explanations for crime, the preponderance of criminal justice literature agrees that high black arrest and victimization rates indicate the continued existence of racial discrimination in the American system of justice.

While blacks are statistically over-represented as perpetrators and victims of crimes, they are under-represented as professionals in the system. The under-employment of blacks in criminal justice professions has been identified as contributing to high black crime rates. The argument usually proceeds as follows: (1) black criminal justice professionals share common physical and cultural traits with other blacks; (2) they understand the nuances of black life; and (3) are therefore better able than whites to inconspicuously work in black surroundings to establish contacts in order to gather information needed to prevent and solve crimes.[30]

Another highly visible consequence of black under-employment in criminal justice is the common situation wherein white police officers patrol predominantly black neighborhoods; thereby lending credence to the proposal, popular during the late 1960's, that black communities were analogous to the colonial model of European domination of non-whites and that, consistent with this model, white police officers performed the role of alien occupation troops whose only raison d'etre was to protect white (i.e., the colonial rulers) property in black communities and maintain white domination of blacks.[31] Therefore, many believe that increased black employment in law enforcement will increase black identification with the system and a resultant lowering of black alienation from the system.

In summary, the nature of the current merger of the two issues is mixed; while the system continues to function in a manner that has negative consequences for black Americans, it has made strides toward becoming more responsive to black needs. In addition, the current-phase, "institutional racism" provides an excellent opportunity for further improvement in the relationship between the issues; however, if criminal justice theorists and practitioners do not expeditiously act to exploit these opportunities, continued conflict between blacks and criminal justice agencies seem inevitable. The following section will analyze several programmatic attempts to fight crime and simultaneously promote equality of opportunity and treatment.

Current Programs and Policies

Consistent with the relatively improved interracial atmosphere of the late 1960's, criminal justice agencies began at this time to implement a variety of programs which were expressly designed to increase black support of the system, as well as improve the quality of criminal justice service provided black communities. Of these programs, the following three are analyzed: (1) Community Relations Programs; (2) Minority Recruitment Programs; and (3) Federal Legislation.

Community Relations Programs

In reaction to overt black expressions of hostility, and in conformity with what was fashionable at the time, community relations programs began cropping up all over the United States in the late sixties. While these programs differed in terms of goals and objectives, most shared the following objectives: (1) to replace negative black perception of criminal justice with positive ones; (2) to create positive attitudes where apathy exist; and (3) to reinforce existing positive attitudes.

The effectiveness of these programs have varied from absolute failure to moderate success, with failure being the most frequent result. An experienced director of community relations offers the following examples of poorly conceived programs:

> Many (community relations programs) were hastily established because it was "fashionable" to have one. Some were created to "prevent riots." . . . A major community relations endeavor of one city consisted of an expensive public campaign involving radio, television and billboards encouraging the public to "Wave at a Cop . . . He's Human Too." Another city's sole community relations program consisted of sewing the American flag on the officers' uniform.[32]

Major determinants of program effectiveness include: the financial and human resources committed to the programs; the over-all racial climate of the community, which heavily influences the criminal justice system's racial policies; credibility of the message (the degree to which police behavior corresponds with the messages of interracial harmony); and the visibility of blacks in the agency.

In terms of specific strategies the more comprehensive programs sought to combine the persuasive and the experiential by: holding informal discussion groups comprised of community residents and criminal justice personnel; assigning officers to foot patrols and motor scooters in black communities to increase face-to-face contact between officers and community residents; in-service training programs in cultural awareness and interracial relations; assigning very personable officers (e.g., "Officer Friendly") to public schools and community centers; sending interracial messages through the mass media; and sponsoring youth recreational activities.[33]

Although community relations programs are no longer fashionable, they are still potentially effective as strategies for improving relations between blacks and criminal justice personnel, particularly if criminal justice decision-makers have learned from the programmatic failures of the late sixties, and are willing to take the necessary corrective measures to insure the future viability of such programs.

Minority Recruitment Programs

The statistical under-employment of minorities in criminal justice is recognized as a problem by civil rights and criminal justice spokespersons alike. Minority under-employment is usually atrributed to: (1) negative minority perceptions of criminal justice professions; (2) minority reluctance to apply for criminal justice positions because of high minority rates of failure in the job competition process; and (3) racially discriminatory hiring practices. Thus, any sincere effort to recruit minorities must address all three of the above phenomena.[34]

Minority recruitment program emphasis on fostering positive minority perceptions of the system in order to attract larger numbers of minority job applications is firmly based in empirical research which has demonstrated a strong correlation between an individual's image of a particular profession and the same individual's willingness to seek employment in that profession. Thus, improved minority perceptions of the system should be accompanied by concurrent increases in minority applications for criminal justice jobs.[35]

These programs utilized a variety of tactics, including:

Assigning minorities to highly visible and responsible positions in the recruitment program.

Presenting interracial themes and pictures in all recruiting literature.

Exploitation of themes of racial and ethnic consciousness (e.g., accept a criminal justice position in order to better serve and protect the black community).

Exploitation of minority interests in bringing about ameliorative social change (e.g., help the criminal justice system become more responsive to minority needs by becoming a part of it).

Exploitation of minority drives toward socioeconomic advancement (e.g., criminal justice careers often pay salaries that exceed those of many professions that require more education and/or experience).

Utilization of minority oriented media and organizations for the dissemination of employment opportunities.

Providing minority applicants with tutorial and remedial assistance in preparing for entrance and promotional examinations.

These programs have achieved mixed results. They are most successful in attracting minority applicants for criminal justice jobs and least successful in actually making placements. Reasons for this may be ascribed to: (1) non-enforcement of equal employment opportunity (EEO) requirements; (2) the economic recession of the 1970's and (3) the adverse impact of employee screening instruments on minority employment opportunities.

Weak EEO enforcement during the 70's is thoroughly documented and such enforcement undoubtedly served to perpetuate racially discriminatory hiring practices in criminal justice.[36]

The simplistic cliché "blacks are last hired but first fired" accurately describes the employment history of black Americans. The cliché refers to the tendency of the American economy to function in such a manner that black employment chances are enhanced considerably during periods of economic prosperity when white employment needs are readily met; and, contrariwise, blacks are more likely to lose their jobs or be denied employment than are whites during periods of economic decline when jobs are scarce.[37] Consistent with the above, many minority recruitment programs were unable to place their minority recruits in the 70's because of the economic recession at the time.

Perhaps the most formidable barriers to the actual hiring and promotion of minorities in criminal justice are the institutionalized employee screening instruments, especially written examinations and background investigations. In addition to disproportionately failing written examinations blacks are more likely than whites to fail background investigations because they are arrested more frequently than whites and are therefore more likely to possess criminal records.

The failure of minority recruitment programs to place large numbers of minority persons graphically reveal the ineffectiveness of piecemeal solutions to very complex social problems and the necessity for the consideration of political (i.e., EEO enforcement) as well as economic issues in planning criminal justice policy. Future minority recruitment policies must more forcefully address the negative impact of institutional factors (i.e., tests and background investigations) and economic conditions on black employment opportunities.

Federal Legislation

Because criminal justice is primarily a state and local concern, the federal government's functions in the area are restricted to enforcing federal criminal codes, administering federal correctional facilities and providing financial and technical assistance to state and local criminal justice agencies. However, in carrying out its legislative functions, the federal government has enormous potential for encouraging racial justice within an effectively administered criminal justice system.

The Omnibus Crime Control and Safe Streets Act of 1968 and its subsequent amendments in 1973 and 1976 (hereinafter referred to as the Act) represents America's most comprehensive piece of crime control legislation ever, and provides an excellent illustration of current contradictions in the relationships between racial and criminal justice issues. The Act created The Law Enforcement Assistance Administration (LEAA) to distribute federal funds to state, local and private citizens' organizations and to monitor the expenditure of such funds.

The Act is unquestionably a product of conservative "law and order" and "new federalism" movements of the 1960's and its easy passage through both houses of Congress was made possible by pervasive moods of white hostility towards the urban violence occurring at that time, which they often associated with blacks. Thus, the Act's major provisions stressed crime control activities; however its Section 518(c) explicitly forbids discrimination on the basis of race, color, national origins, or sex in all of its funded programs; furthermore, it authorizes LEAA to apply severe administrative sanctions (i.e., withholding or withdrawing funds) to discriminating recipient agencies and to, concurrently seek legal redress through the federal courts.

Although LEAA's enforcement of Section 518(c)'s provision has been lukewarm at best, the Acts civil rights provisions significantly illustrate how racial and criminal justice issues may harmoniously merge in legislation and that stringent crime control legislation need not be anti-black.

Summary

The blending together of racial and criminal justice issues have undergone several evolutionary changes since blacks first entered North America as indentured servants, with each evolutionary stage representing an expansion of black political and socioeconomic opportunities but stopping short of full equality. Essentially, these changes have involved a progression in the interrelatedness between the issues from blatant conflict to the current relationships which are characterized by a mixture of harmony and conflict.

In many ways, the older, more manifest forms of racial discrimination were easier to combat than the current more subtle forms. The older forms could be effectively addressed by simply enforcing legal prohibitions against racial discrimination. Today's institutionalized forms, however, are much more formidable and as a consequence require approaches and programs that take "affirmative actions" to alleviate the disadvantaged status of blacks and certain other minorities in competing for society's benefits. Below are several examples of affirmative action efforts:

> (1) Establishment of minority employment goals and timeframes within which the goals are to be met.

> (2) Special funds to assist minorities in acquiring educational and vocational skills.

> (3) Granting priority to improving quality of goods and services provided black neighborhoods in such areas as health, educational and social services.

> (4) Actively seeking minorities to integrate certain professions, schools and neighborhoods.

Because these "affirmative action" programs stress granting special considerations to minorities, they are controversial and often evoke charges of "preferential treatment" and "reverse discrimination" from many whites. Notwithstanding the controversy and charges, it seems clear that the old remedies designed to prevent discrimination are woefully inadequate in combating current forms of institutional racism.

Furthermore, in formulating policies, criminal justice planners need to consider more seriously the system's economic class biases and how these biases negatively impact on minorities. As a matter of fact, economic factors have become so significant in the administration of justice process that it is extremely difficult to determine whether blacks are victimized by the criminal justice system more because of race or economic status.

Finally, because the criminal justice system is responsive to the political system's demands, those committed to both racial justice and effective criminal justice administration must organize coalitions and devote more attntion to political strategies in order to bring about a more effectively administered system of justice in which race ceases to serve as a basis for discriminatory decision making.

Discussion Questions

1. Based on the historical relationship between racial and criminal justice issues, what do you predict will be future relationship between the issues? Present a detailed justification for your prediction.

2. List and critique several proposals for making the American criminal justice system more responsive to the needs and interests of minorities and women.

3. Why is it so difficult to separate race from economic class in explaining black American experiences within the American criminal justice system?

Notes

1. Because of inconsistencies and contradictions in racial designations in the United States; race, as used in this chapter, refers to socially determined rather than physiological or biological definitions of race.

2. For a widely read description of black life in colonial America see: John Hope Franklin, *From Slavery to Freedom* (New York: Vintage books, 1969) pp. 71–165; and for a special emphasis on black relationships with law enforcement see: Robert F. Wintersmith, *The Police and the Black Community* (Lexington, Mass.: Lexington Books, 1974)

3. Analyses of racism in both documents are found in: Mary Berry, *Black Law/White Resistance* (New York: Appleton-Croft Century, 1971), 7–32.

4. Douglass 4th of July is quoted in Lerone Bennett, Jr. *Before The Mayflower* (Baltimore: Penguin Books, 1966), 156–157.

5. Two representative statements of black exclusion for American pronouncements of political and social egalitarianism are: Gunnar Myrdal, *An American Dilemma* (New York: Harper and Row, 1944); and Lerone Bennett, "The Politics of the Outsider," *Negro Digest.* 17 (July, 1968), 4–9, 30–35.

6. U.S. Constitution; Article I, Section 2.

7. U.S. Constitution; Article IV, Section 2.

8. U.S. Constitution; Article I, Section 9.

9. The Dred Scott decision rendered in 1857 by the United States Supreme Court, endorsed slavery by: upholding laws requiring the return of fugitive slaves to slavery; permitting slavery in the new territories; and by denying citizenship rights to blacks.

10. For review of black political power during Reconstruction see: Chuck Stone, *Black Political Power in America* (New York: Delta Books, 1968) 11–25.

11. A summary of events leading to the demise of Reconstruction may be found in: Lerone Bennett, Jr., *Ibid,* 183–219.

12. *Ibid.*

13. For a review of black oppression outside the South during the Jim Crow period see: Rayford Logan, *The Betrayal of the Negro* (New York: Collier Books, 1967).

14. Wintersmith, *Ibid.*

15. Role of Court in disfranchisement of blacks is described in: Henry J. Abraham, *Freedom and the Court* (New York: Oxford University Press, 1972), 292–313

16. For a detailed chronicling of brutalization of blacks during Jim Crow are: Logan, *Ibid.*

17. Edward Greenberg, Neal Milner and David Olson, *Black Politics* (New York: Holt, Rinehart and Winston, 1971).

18. For criticisms of reliance on aptitude test scores for predicting student and employee performance see: *Journal of Afro-American Issues.* 3 (Winter, 1975); and Robert Sadacca, "The Validity and Discriminatory Impact of the Federal Service Entrance Examination," *An Urban Institute Paper* (Washington, D.C.: The Urban Institute, 1971).

19. "The Challenge of Crime in a Free Society," *The President's Commission on Law Enforcement and Administration of Justice* (Washington, D.C.: Government Printing Office, 1967; and *Report of The National Advisory Commission on Civil Disorders* (New York: Bontom Books, 1968), 283–315.

20. *Supplemental Studies for the National Advisory Commission on Civil Disorders* (Washington, D.C.: Government Printing Office, 1969), 103–119.

21. Haywood Burns, "Can A Black Man Get A Fair Trial In This Country," *Readings in Africana Studies* (Rutgers: The Department of Africana Studies).

22. Andrew Overby, "Discrimination in the Administration of Justice" in Norman Johnson, Leonard Savity, and Marvin Wolfgang (eds.), *The Sociology of Punishment and Correction* (New York: John Wiley and Sons, 1970), 261–270.

23. Burns, *Ibid.*

24. *The Case Against Capital Punishment* (Washington, D.C.: The Washington Research Project, 1971).

25. *Criminal Victimization in the United States* (Washington, D.C.: The Law Enforcement Assistance Administration).

26. Ethel L. Payne, "Citizen Action As A Deterrent to Crime," in Lawrence E. Gary and Lee P. Brown (eds.), *Crime and Its Impact on the Black Community* (Washington, D.C.: Institute For Urban Affairs and Research, 1975), 121–125; and Elsie L. Scott, "Black Attitudes Toward Crime and Crime Prevention," in Gary and Brown (eds.), *Ibid,* 13–30.

27. Arthur Jensen, "How Much Can We Boost I.Q. and Scholastic Achievement," *Harvard Educational Review.* 39. (Winter, 1969) 1–123.

28. For a cogent critique of Jensen and summary of other criticisms see: Howard F. Taylor, "Quantitative Racism: A Partial Documentation," *Journal of Afro-American Issues.* (Winter, 1975) 19–42; for an excellent explication of race and

criminal behavior relationships see: Marvin E. Wolfgang and Bernard Cohen, *Crime and Race: Conceptions and Misconceptions* (Washington, D.C.: Institute for Human Relations Press, 1970).

29. A representative presentation of this view may be found in Edward Green, "Inter- and Intra-Racial Crime Relative to Sentencing," *Journal of Criminal Law, Criminology and Police Science*. 55 (September, 1964), 348–358.

30. President's Commission on Law Enforcement and Administration of Justice, *Ibid,;* and *National Advisory Commission on Civil Disorders, Ibid.*

31. For a thorough and succinct analysis of internal black colony position see: Robert Blauner, "Internal Colonialism and Ghetto Revolt," *Social Problems*. 4 (Spring, 1969), 383–408.

32. Lee P. Brown, "The Death of Police Community Relations," *Occasional Paper* (Washington, D.C.: Institute for Urban Affairs and Research, 1973).

33. *Ibid;* and Ben Holman, "Community Relations Units in Police Departments," in Harrington J. Bryce, *Black Crime* (Washington, D.C.: Joint Center for Political Studies, 1977), 91–107.

34. Information concerning minority recruitment programs is based on author's survey of staff employed by the National Urban League to conduct The Law Enforcement Assistance Administration.

35. See: Frank K. Gibson and George A. James, "Student Attitudes Toward Government Employees and Employment," *Public Administration Review*. 27 (December, 1967), 429–435; and Morris Janowitz and Deil Wright, "The Prestige of Public Employment: 1929 and 1954," *Public Administration Review*. 16 (Winter, 1956), 15–21.

36. *The Federal Civil Rights Enforcement Effort—1974* (Washington, D.C.: United States Commission on Civil Rights, 1977).

37. See: Gunmar Myrdal, *Ibid,* p. 207.

The Criminal Justice System:
A Trip with Alice (Alex) in Wonderland*

ROBERT F. KRONICK

This chapter deals with the criminal justice system. It is a look at the interaction which go on within it and how these interactions work to the benefit or detriment of the offender, the victim and the social system. The criminal justice system encompasses police, courts, incarceration, either training school or prison, and after-care. It is not very often that criminal justice is looked upon as an integrated whole and this chapter will focus on the parts of the system as well as the system as a functioning unit, while showing the linkages which exist within the entire system.

> The criminal justice system is the institutional representation of the "American Creed" of equality for all—Gunnar Myrdal

Police

Police get involved in a criminal case in one of two ways. They see the criminal act occurring and act accordingly, or they are called and informed of its occurrence either while ongoing or after the fact. The visibility of the offender and the act has a great deal to do with the act being detected and the accused being caught. The two main factors influencing apprehension of the offender are his/her status characteristics and situational factors. A study of shoplifiting[1] showed the shoplifters were poorly dressed, had long hair (if males) and were generally unruly looking, were significantly more likely to be reported to police and apprehended than those who just as visibly shoplifted but who were neatly dressed, had acceptable hair length and were generally well groomed. Once the deviating act occurs and is discovered the police are the first on the scene and first to react to the behavior in question.

The reaction of the policeman may vary due to his personal background[2], values[3] or training experience[4]. Wambaugh's *The New Centurions, The Blue Knight,* and television's adaptation of "Police Story" give vivid accounts of

---

*I am indebted to James Bell, Larry Gibney, Larry Lively, Mike Harkleroad, Jim Ball, Richard Ray Ford, and Dorman Fracisco for their aid in preparing this chapter. All faults are those of the author.

the role that personal factors such as background and values play in the life of the policeman and the execution of his duties. Events which the policeman experiences in his daily routine turn around and also influence his present value structure so that past and present play an especially strong role in the total life of the policeman.

Jerome Skolnick's[5] "Why Cops Behave as They Do," states that the policeman's personality or role contains two principal variables, *danger* and *authority*, which should be interpreted in the light of a constant pressure to appear *efficient*. The element of danger seems to make the policeman especially attentive to signs indicating a potential for violence and lawbreaking. As a result, the policeman is generally a *suspicious* person. Furthermore, the nature of a policeman's work makes him less desirable as a friend, since norms of friendship implicate others in his work. Accordingly the element of danger isolates the policeman socially from that segment of the citizenry that he regards as symbolically dangerous and also from the conventional citizenry with whom he identifies.

Closely related to the policeman's authority based problems are difficulties associated with his injunction to regulate public morality. Often he is likely to cause resentment because of the suspicion that the policeman himself does not strictly conform to the moral norms he is enforcing. Thus the policeman faced with enforcing a law against fornication, drunkeness or gambling is easily liable to a charge of hypocrisy.[6] It is this picture of the ghetto policeman which James Baldwin presents in the following passage: their very presence is an insult and it would be, even if they spent their entire day feeding gumdrops to children. They represent the force of the white world and that world's criminal profit and ease, to keep the black man/woman corraled up here in his/her place. The badge, the gun in the holster and the swinging club make vivid what will happen should his/her rebellion become overt.[7]

All occupational groups share a measure of inclusiveness and identification and policemen are a prime example of how organizational effects[8] exert influence over those who work within their confines. People are brought together simply by doing the same work and having similar career problems. The organization within which the policeman works plays a tremendous role in how he acts and reacts as a policeman and as a citizen. This probably is true for policemen more than for most other occupational groups.

Thus it may be *generalized* that policeman are conservative both politically and emotionally, but that there are some variations to this pattern especially among younger and newer recruits. As the novices become older and more experienced, however, they become organizationally co-opted and adhere assiduously to the goals of the police organization. Because of the type of people he deals with, the policeman quite often builds in a mind set to status characteristics, and situational factors and responds in a generally set way to the deviating acts ranging from crimes without victims such as homosexual behavior to street violence including rape, murder and riots.

COURTS: Adult

Generally, an individual is ordinarily arrested on a warrant or without a warrant, charged with a felony or misdemeanor. In numerous jurisdications, if arrested upon a misdemeanor, he/she may, with the concurrence of the magistrate, have a trial on the merits in what has traditionally been called the Sessions Court or Trial Justice Court. In the event the individual is charged with a felony, the case is set for a preliminary hearing, where the only issues before the court are whether or not there is probable cause to believe that a crime has been committed in the county of the court's jurisdiction and whether or not there is probable cause to believe that the act was committed by the individual before the court.

Oftentimes, an individual initially arrested on a felony warrant will have it reduced to a misdemeanor as a result of plea bargaining or when the court at the preliminary hearing ascertains that no felony has been committed.

After the preliminary hearing, the matter is now in "hiatus status" wherein no court has jurisdiction, although the individual remains under bond. At this stage, the Grand Jury convenes to ascertain the same issues that were determined at the Trial Justice Court or Sessions Court. In the event that these issues are answered affirmatively, the Grand Jury returns what has traditionally been termed an indictment. If the Grand Jury answers the issues negatively, they will return a "no true bill" which may or may not end the case at that point. If the individual is indicted, his/her case history is handed to the Criminal Court, where a day is set for arraignment.

Note, however, that a return of a "no true bill" inquiry does not necessarily mean there is a successful completion of the charges. For example, a Grand Jury may not indict X as the assailant of V, who claims to have been raped by X. V's credibility is shown to be impeachable and likewise her reputation for morality. However, the Attorney General, may at some later point, have corroborating evidence, i.e., showing semen in the vaginal area, bruises, abrasions and the like. Then, the male is resubmitted to Grand Jury for redetermination of probable cause on the crime and identity of the assailant. If a true bill is returned in this instance, a "capias" is issued to bring the individual back into court.

A special case that will circumvent the Sessions Court area is a presentment. A presentment is used in such areas as drug abuse cases where undercover agents were employed. The agent may come right to the grand jury and tell them that he/she made so-many buys from such-and-such a person on such-and-such a date and thus will not have to jeopardize his cover as an undercover agent, and the case will go right to the grand jury.

Once the individual has been bound over to criminal court, the chief judge will assign the case to one of three courts. Then the individual will go on to court for arraignment and will enter a plea. At this point he/she will have a trial with the state in which the state must show beyond a reasonable doubt that the event was committed and that it was committed by the person who stands before them. If the individual is convicted he/she may file a motion for a new trial and if his/her sentence is ten years or less he/she may apply for probation. During the probation hearing which is held in Criminal Court, the individual may bring in witnesses in order to prove to the judge that he/she should be entitled to probation. If the individual is convicted, an appeal to the Court of Criminal Appeals can be made to show where points of law have been violated. The individual then applies for a new trial.

A final note on a recent case should be added at this point and that is that the Attorney General is under the aegis of moral ethics to recommend probation if it is his/her contention that the individual has absolutely no factors in his/her life that would make him/her unsuitable for probation. Thus, not only may the Attorney General prove or try to prove that this individual needs to be incarcerated he/she is now bound by statute to recommend probation when it is his/her opinion that probation is the best alternative for this particular individual.

As can be readily seen, there are many informal factors that are at work as the defendant progresses up to this point in the court system. Among these is the influence of the individual's lawyer. The lawyer's influence with the judge and Attorney General's office may play a major role in the offer of a plea bargain. If the defendant is represented by a court-appointed attorney or a Public Defender he/she is more likely to be advised to accept the plea bargain than if he/she secures his/her own attorney. Thus there are factors that tend to operate within the court system that will affect the outcome of a court decision that ostensibly are unrelated to justice within the courts but which are truly at the core of judicial decision-making. At the level of sentencing, the judge may recommend several diversionary programs such as a voluntary probation counselor (Project First Offender in Tennessee) or grant probation under the supervision of the State Department of Probation and Parole. Many of these decisions follow no set pattern, but rather, emerge for each individual case. Ideally the system appears as follows;

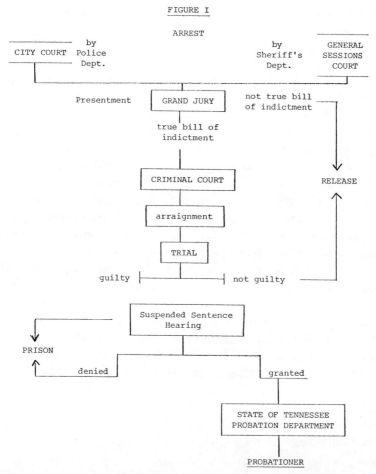

FIGURE I

ARREST

CITY COURT — by Police Dept. — by Sheriff's Dept. — GENERAL SESSIONS COURT

Presentment — GRAND JURY — not true bill of indictment

true bill of indictment

CRIMINAL COURT — RELEASE

arraignment

TRIAL

guilty — not guilty

Suspended Sentence Hearing

PRISON — denied — granted

STATE OF TENNESSEE PROBATION DEPARTMENT

PROBATIONER

(Source: Daniel Glaser's THE EFFECTIVENESS OF A PRISON AND PAROLE SYSTEM)

COURTS: *Juvenile: Non-Status Offenders*

The juvenile justice system is run somewhat differently than the adult system and so a process model of juvenile justice is now presented.

Juvenile courts were originally set up to remove the child from the harsh realities of adult court. It was assumed that the child needed protection in legal matters and the juvenile court was set up to protect the child in just such matters. However in 1967 the Gault[9] decision was rendered which stated that juveniles were entitled to legal rights and protections that are accorded adults. What had happened was the child in juvenile court was being denied his/her constitutional rights. A court that had originally been set up to protect the child was now systematically denying his/her rights and protection.

As was done in the case of adults let us now look at an idealized version of how the juvenile becomes involved with the juvenile justice system. It should be remembered that this is an idealized representation with a great many variations existing. As with the adult model let us start with initial arrest or referral.

Within the juvenile justice system there is a dichotomy of status and non-status offender. The status offender is one who commits an act that if he/she were an adult would not be a crime. Status offenses include truancy, unruly behavior and curfew violations. Non-status offenses are regarded as crimes whether they are committed by juveniles or adults. The status offenders may be referred to the juvenile court by the school or by the parents by the swearing out of a petition. The non-status offender is generally caught by the police and they are the first to deal with him/her.

Let us now follow both the status and the non-status offender in his/her progression through the criminal justice system stopping, in this section, with court adjudication; first, the non-status offender.

Once arrested the non-status offender has several options depending on the offense. The police department through its juvenile bureau has the prerogative of handling the offender by dealing with him/her and his/her parents. Generally there is a bargain struck among the child and his/her parents and the victim, where restitution is to be worked out between the victim and the offender. This situation is left to the discretion of the juvenile bureau within the police department. If the contract is met and satisfied with compensation to the victim, generally the juvenile's record is wiped clean.

If the juvenile bureau does not want to handle the case itself, the case is referred to the Juvenile Court. The Juvenile Court may now choose to handle the case formally or informally. If the case in handled informally by the Juvenile Court, much the same procedure as described above for the juvenile bureau of the police department is followed with parents and victim being called in. If the case is handled formally then the juvenile is brought to court before the Juvenile Judge. The judge has total power to decide the outcome of the case and only in rare instances are juveniles represented by attorneys. When they are, however, they generally fare much better than when not so represented. It goes without saying that those juveniles represented by attorneys generally come from more well-to-do families than those not represented.

The non-status offender is one who has committed a criminal act and while he/she should be handled in a special way, he/she should not necessarily be regarded as an adult. It is a moot point if the juvenile justice system has the resources to handle this ticklish situation. A prime example of ticklish situations facing the juvenile justice system is the *transfer* hearing. The transfer hearing involves transferring a child from juvenile to adult court. This is most often done when the juvenile judge does not want to hear the case based on the nature of the offense, i.e., murder, rape, aggravated assault. What must be proved in a transfer hearing is that the juvenile is not amenable to treatment under existing programs for children and youth. A peculiar dilemma evolves in the incarceration of such offenders and is covered in the following section dealing with incarceration.

Another interesting event with certain parallels in the adult system is the Juvenile Court Committal Order (JCCO)*. The JCCO is issued when the juvenile judge decides a mental health commitment is more appropriate than a correctional commitment. This commitment order is made in the light of many factors but generally in regards to non-status offenders. The judge may arbitrarily decide that a JCCO is more appropriate than a training school commitment. The factors underlying such decisions are as mysterious as those mentioned in the adult court section on page 4 of this chapter. These questions, like many others raised in this chapter, are excellent topics for further in-depth research, but are too complex to be discussed in detail here.

COURTS: *Juvenile: Status Offenders*

The status offender as mentioned earlier is a juvenile who commits an act that if he/she were an adult would not be a crime, i.e., truancy, beyond control of parents. The sentencing procedure for the status offender is much the same as that for the non-status offender, except that parents or school officials are the ones who take out and file the petition rather than the police. Staffings involving school psychologists, parents and other interested parties are more likely to be carried out in the disposition of status as opposed to non-status offenders. Special difficulties with status offenders are presented in the next section dealing with incarceration. The role of the juvenile counselor is especially important in the sentencing or disposition process because in many cases the judge will follow the recommendations of the juvenile counselor to the letter in making his/her judicial decision. The power and influence of the juvenile counselor with regard to the social history that he/she submits on each offender is another topic in need of more in-depth study. This power and influence is also true of pre-sentence

---

*The JCOO is for observation not treatment from the court's perspective.

investigation done by the pre-sentence investigator under the adult court set-up.

A final comment should be made regarding the juvenile court judge. There is a vast move today to require all juvenile judges to be lawyers. In Tennessee only in the major metropolitan counties are juvenile judges lawyers—or it is possible that the county judge will assume the juvenile judgeship as one of his/her duties. Whether or not juvenile judges should be attorneys is a complicated issue. Perhaps the simplest way of handling this situation is to bring in referees who are lawyers when points of law are involved in the case, or to transfer the case to a judge who is an attorney. Regardless of how this issue is resolved hopefully it will bring more light to the juvenile justice system instead of more heat.

INCARCERATION: Adults

Once sentence has been set by the judge and probation is not granted, the offender is sent from the county or city jail where he/she was arrested, though generally the individual is transferred to the county jail awaiting transfer, to the state's main prison for classification. Classification generally lasts three weeks. During this time the offender's personality and needs, as well as age, number of prior offenses and type of offense are taken into consideration in deciding which one of the state's institutions the offender will be sent to.

The types of institutions within the state generally include one for youthful offenders, those between 18–25 years of age, and those who are generally first offenders. A maximum security institution for those deemed as too dangerous to be in open population or who have been in trouble with guards or with other inmates in a different institution is also available. Then, of course, there is the state's main prison to which the individual may be sent from the classification unit and there is generally also at least one institution that is geared to farming to which the offender may be sent. Once the offender is housed in one of these institutions, he/she becomes a convict, inmate or resident depending on the role he/she chooses to assume.

Each institution has its differences but there are certain similarities which tend to hold for all. It is these all-encompassing characteristics which Goffman[10] had in mind in *Asylums*. Regardless of the orientation of the institution as "custodially" oriented or "treatment" oriented, there are certain commonalities that exist within the institution according to Goffman. These organizational effects will influence the inmate as much as the police organization influences the policeman as noted earlier in this chapter.

The characteristics which Goffman noted as being common to total institutions or asylums such as prisons are: 1) the bureaucratic handling of human needs; 2) the difficulty of social intercourse with the outside world; 3) narrow stereotypical views that staff have of inmates and that inmates have of staff; 4) the breaking down of barriers that separate sleep, work, and play. These along with argot-roles which Sykes[11] describes as modes of adaptations within the prison illustrate that those who adapt well within the prison may be those who are least able to adapt successfully in the outside world. It is this idea of institutional counseling which is a most important point at this juncture rather than true treatment that may reflect why recidivism is so high in prisons today. In other words, we are teaching people how to adapt to the institution rather than how to live outside of the institution.

The idea of adaption to prison conditions being counter-productive to rehabilitation is certainly radical and bears further investigation. The most that has been said to this point is that certain inmates become prisonized[12] during their incarceration.

When the court has sentenced a man/woman to prison for armed robbery for ten (10) years the public assumes that he/she will be there for ten (10) years. However this is not always the case. Through good, honor and incentive time, the convict may serve his/her ten (10) year sentence in a considerably shorter period of time. These devices are probably essential to the smooth running of the institution and gaining the acquiescence of the inmate, but it is confusing and maddening to the public when they see the man/woman they know went to prison for ten (10) years out on the street in what seems to them a very short time.

It is the policy of the (Tennessee) Department of Correction that all available resources be directed toward the correction of the offender. In this connection the Good and Honor time program will be used as a positive factor in encouraging inmates to establish good behavior patterns, attitudes, and habits. Each inmate entering the system will have a thorough orientation on the program in order that he/she may more fully understand what will be expected of him/her and as a result be motivated toward better behavior patterns.

Each inmate entering the (Tennessee) penal system will be placed in an honor grade and honor time accrued starts as of the date of sentence. This will permit him/her to secure two (2) months of honor time for each year of his/her sentence served so long as his/her behavior and attitude remain good and he/she does not violate prison rules and regulations. Such violations will result in loss of honor time.

Residents will be eligible for incentive time at the beginning of the first grading period after they complete classification. Those who attend school will receive incentive time provided they attend regularly, make an effort in participation and have no disciplinary convictions. Those facilities that have privileged visiting areas will award these privileges to those men/women who qualify for incentive time provided their security requirements are suitable. Privileged housing will be governed in the same manner.[13] However as can be seen in the following memorandum the availability of housing facilities present a desperate situation.

> RE: Emergency Restoration of Good and/or Honor Time
>
> The Department of Correction is in a desperate situation regarding overcrowding of institutions. The population is at an all time high and climbing each day. Currently, the Tennessee State Penitentiary has 2601 residents. Every effort must be made to reduce this population.
>
> Beginning immediately each institution will prepare a list of all residents who have lost Good and/or Honor time more than 90 days ago. Those who have not had discipline *convictions* during this time will be considered for restoration of lost Good and/or Honor time.
>
> The Behavioral Review Committee at each facility will work full-time on reviewing the residents on the list. Please give this effort priority attention.
>
> Residents who would qualify for immediate release if time restoration is made should be considered first.
>
> Please make every effort to have this work completed and your committee recommendations signed and in this office as soon as possible.
>
> Your usual cooperation is appreciated.

Coupled with this problem is the reality that today every inmate (in Tennessee) comes out on 90 day mandatory release. This too is because of overcrowded conditions existing within the state institutions. Generally the convicts do not favor this release plan because if they violate during this 90 day release period all good and honor time is lost. The concept of sentencing, release, and good and honor time play a major role in the criminal justice system and touch it at several levels.

Figure II shows how good, honor and incentive time is computed.

FIGURE II

Sentence	Honor Time	Good Time	Sentence Built In	
1 year	2 months	1 month	0 years	9 months
2 years	4 months	3 months	1 year	9 months
3 years	6 months	6 months	2 years	0 months
4 years	8 months	9 months	2 years	2 months
5 years	10 months	12 months	3 years	2 months
6 years	12 months	15 months	3 years	9 months
7 years	14 months	18 months	4 years	4 months
8 years	16 months	21 months	4 years	11 months

9 years	18 months	24 months	5 years	6 months
10 years	20 months	27 months	6 years	1 month

99 years is built in 50 years and 7 months. This applies to the Tennessee State Prisons only.

Honor Time — 2 months of each year of the term of sentence

Good Time — 1 month first year
                    3 months each year to 10 years
                    4 months each year thereafter

(Source: Tennessee State Department of Correction)

This concept of the indeterminate sentence, as it is illustrated above, is yet another topic worthy of further in-depth discussion.

Adult prisons for women are not as numerous, and there tends to be one central institution for all adult female offenders. This is certainly due to the much smaller numbers of female offenders as compared with male offenders. However, recent statistics show female crime to be catching up to that of male crime. This may be a dubious product of women's liberation as well as other social factors.

Women in prison tend to adapt much the same as men do except that their homosexual behavior is much more family oriented with "extended" families being formed. Homosexual behavior in men's prisons tends to be much more episodic and does not have the family orientation of that of the female inmates. Not much is known about the prison life of women but Rose Gialombardo's[14] *Society of Women* is an excellent starting point for the reader interested in women's prisons.

Adult prisons for both men and women are the subject of much controversy regarding their success as rehabilitation agents. Perhaps the strongest attacks on the abysmal failure of prisons and correctional schools as rehabilitative agents have been leveled by Robert Martinson.[15] A summary of his contentions is presented at the end of this section on incarceration.

INCARCERATION: *Juveniles*

Incarceration of juveniles takes an even more erratic stance than that for adults. The first problem that arises is whether to incarcerate status offenders with non-status offenders. That is, putting a truant child within the same confines as a youth "being treated" for such various offenses as armed robbery, assault and battery or breaking and entering. We know that a child who goes to a training school under such conditions emerges a very different person than when he/she went in. This is, of course, true for adult offenders also.

In 1976 the federal government decreed that no federal money would be made available to those programs which housed both status and non-status offenders together. Most states, including Tennessee, were not able to meet these requirements. Thus in most if not every state the process of incarcerating status with non-status offenders continues.

A lucid example of how juveniles are handled is presented in a recent film entitled "Children in Trouble".[16] This film depicts the varied conditions under which juveniles are incarcerated ranging from county jails where the juvenile is housed with adult offenders to community-oriented programs. The training school is still the heart of the incarceration process for juveniles, but other options are beginning to appear. They include group homes, halfway houses and other general forms of community based treatment.

COMMUNITY BASED TREATMENT

There is a move afoot today based on research that shows that to reduce recidivism appreciably treatment must be carried on within the community where the individual lives. This is sometimes referred to as an environmental design. The aegis here is that it is environmental and community factors which shape the individual's behavior and that it is these factors which should be considered in the rehabilitation of the young offender.

Group homes are generally used as an alternative to incarceration. The child is remanded to the group home directly by the juvenile judge, and his/her custody remains with his/her parents. Halfway houses generally follow the same model as group homes with the exception that they will take young people half way out as well as half way in. That is, juveniles who have been sent to a training school may, as part of their treatment plan be sent to the halfway house before their final release into the community. The average length of stay in these community based programs is six months, but due to the lack of appropriate or suitable referrals this stay may be extended.

The progenitor of community based programs for juveniles and the one that is probably best known is Achievement Place initiated by Montrose Wolf and others at Lawrence, Kansas, and run in conjunction with the behavioral branch of the Department of Psychology at The University of Kansas. Other notable group home and halfway house programs are Cooper House in Knoxville, Tennessee, an adjunct of Lakeshore Mental Health Institute, and The Center for Youth Development and Achievement in Tucson, Arizona, under the direction of Dr. V.R. Harris. The success rate of these types of programs vary, but it is argued both from a cost efficiency basis as well as a humanitarian point of view that the community-environmentally oriented program is the most effective manner in which to work with juvenile offenders. There is a great deal of variety in the way in which juvenile incarceration may work but the main emphasis should always be that the person got no worse from being in the program.

Juvenile institutions may well be the breeding ground of adult crime but this is mere hypothesis at this point in time. The point is that a great deal of work needs to be done in the area of incarceration for juveniles as well as adults. Hopefully this chapter may spur others to initiate action research in these areas and that social scientists will begin to initiate policy-oriented studies and follow them to their conclusion of policy making in the areas of incarceration for juveniles and adults.

As mentioned, Robert Martinson has been most critical of almost any treatment program in the area of corrections, both juvenile and adult, and of studies done on these programs. Martinson contends that there has been no treatment (plan) which has been shown to work systematically in the correctional field. Martinson includes here studies of institutional programs, community programs, as well as various forms of treatment modalities. Martinson's work has prompted a great deal of response within the corrections community and his criticisms cannot be taken lightly. What this author suggests is that the challenge presented by Martinson be responded to by establishing top-flight programs with built-in evaluations that are solid methodologically.

A first step in this most pressing process is to secure competent, humanistic workers in the field and then to consider locating the facilities of detention in central cities where they are not out-of-sight/out-of-mind. Today many institutions for juveniles as well as adults are placed in locales known only to the Sierra Club. The feeling here being that if the facilities are off in some far away place then I am exonerated of having any part in the juvenile problem. The juvenile's problems are of his/her own making as sure as if they were organically caused. This of course adds to the medical model of deviance and denies the social learning approach. This is, of course, a difficult idea to overthrow, and why not? Why should I want to be considered part of the problem simply because I am part of the child's environment.

AFTER-CARE: *Adults and Juveniles*

After-care is a central part of correction both for juveniles and adults. For adults no euphemism is used; after-care is called parole. In most states every person comes out on some type of parole plan, usually referred to as an

FIGURE III

A. New Intake for Year 1976 (By Sex):

Month	Male	Female
January	25	5
February	37	11
March	32	14
April	34	14
May	41	7
June	38	3
July	25	14
August	26	9
September	20	11
October	34	8
November	38	7
December	40	8
Total	390	111

B. Total Number of Probation and After-Care Caseload by Month:

Month	Probation	After-Care	(Inst.	—Comm.)
January	257	468	240	228
February	265	460	247	213
March	270	468	272	196
April	282	473	274	199
May	290	490	199	291
June	283	487	201	286
July	274	480	199	281
August	270	468	199	269
September	266	475	233	252
October	270	493	212	281
November	279	489	227	262
December	289	504	274	257
Average	274.6	479.6	228.3	251.3

C. Recidivism (By Numbers):

Month	Probation	After-Care
January	0	8
February	5	11
March	4	21
April	2	12
May	9	9
June	4	16
July	3	15
August	2	10
September	4	19
October	5	17
November	3	22
December	7	16
	48	176

D. Recidivism Rate By Month:

Month	Probation	After-Care
January	0.00%	3.41%
February	1.81%	5.16%
March	1.40%	10.70%
April	0.71%	6.03%
May	3.10%	3.10%
June	1.06%	5.50%
July	1.10%	5.30%
August	0.74%	3.72%
September	1.50%	4.00%
October	1.85%	6.04%
November	1.08%	7.61%
December	2.42%	6.22%
	16.77%	66.79%
Average	1.40%	5.57%

Note: C and D include new offenses and departmental violations
(Source: Tennessee State Department of Corrections)

accelerated discharge program. Because of over-crowded conditions no one tends to come out on flat time but rather with a minimum of 90 days parole time.

The type of supervision that is given on parole varies by institutions and probation and parole departments. While on parole the man or woman is subject to a great many pressures, and he/she may violate in one of two ways: 1) by committing a new crime whereby the procedure described herein begins anew or 2) by violating rules of parole. Each after-care program has a Parole Hearings officer. If he/she decides that there is probable cause that a violation was committed, then the offender is referred to the Parole Board where he/she is either returned to prison where he/she looses good and honor time already built or if found innocent returned to parole. The vast majority at this stage are returned to prison for the commission of new offenses. That is, parole boards generally try to work with the person and his/her environment in trying to help him/her work out problems rather than to send him/her back to the penitentiary for a technical violation. It is in this fashion that recidivism rates are determined. The breakdown of new crimes as opposed to parole violation is approximately 80% new crimes and 20% violation for adults and the reverse, 20% new crimes and 80% violations for juveniles. (See Figure III-D, page 51.) Thus evaluation of the success of the criminal justice system, realizing that the individual has come through the system in its entirety at this point is right before the public's eye. When a person fails on aftercare or parole it may be due to a myriad of social, psychological or political factors. The failures show in parole but they may be due to problems that arose at any of the four levels of organizational processing within the criminal justice system.

After-care and parole case loads are gigantic, averaging 65 cases per counselor, so that it is no wonder that so little counseling or treatment is possible, but merely crisis intervention.

Nonetheless, Martinson has stated that caseload size is meaningless and that violations even increase with smaller caseloads. Of course, what this means is that closer supervision is possible with these smaller caseloads and the detection of violation becomes much easier.

A look at the following caseload sizes and repeated violations both technical and new offenses for juveniles and adults should give some insight into what after-care and parole caseload sizes look like and how violations occur, at least in 16 counties in East Tennessee. No generalizations to other areas of the country are necessarily implied.

When looking at national data of this nature, there are many variations present, ranging from type of reporting to rules and regulations of parole officers and after-care counselors.

FIGURE IV

After-Care Violations Filed by Counselor (By Offense):

Offense	Males	Females
Failure to adjust to Foster Care	3	2
Run away from home (including foster home)	26	46
Curfew and late hours	1	7
Failure to obey rules of after-care	1	1
Traffic violations	1	0
Truancy	12	1
Paint sniffing	1	0
Leaving Freedom House	3	1
Drugs	1	1
Alcohol	2	0
Abscond from Riverbend	1	0
Abscond from Barret Hall	0	3
Auto Larceny	3	0
Breaking and entering	1	0
TOTAL	56	62

Probation: 275 cases
48 violations
48/275 = 17%
    48 + 176 = 224 violations

After-care: 479 cases
176 violations
176/479 = 36%

New offenses 58/176 = 32%
Violations 118/176 = 68%
176 re-committed
118 violations
58 new offenses

(Source: Tennessee State Department of Corrections)

These figures reveal two interesting facts: 1) females were "violated" more often than males; 2) those violated were most often violated for running away from home, a status offense!

It is this author's contention that community alternatives to incarceration such as parole, or some forms of pre-trial diversion which utilize the community in some fashion will increase. This will be true if for no other reason than the fact that courts and institutions are too crowded to handle these cases effectively.

SUMMARY

It has been the purpose of this chapter to take the reader on a journey through the criminal justice system beginning with arrest and ending with some type of after-care arrangement. The labelling process as presented illustrates how in a social-psychological sense one traverses the criminal justice system and is either deterred or labelled (and becomes a deviant) by the organizational processing of the criminal justice system.

FIGURE V

Labeling Processes

Predictor

Variables

Status
Characteristics

| Situational factors | Deviating acts | Interpersonal relations | Organizational processing | "Deviants" |

Social-
psychological
factors

(Source: Edwin M. Schur's *Labeling Deviant Behavior*

In terms of improving the system the following suggestions should prove helpful:

1. Increase the social treatment skills of policemen. Policemen should be better trained and better paid. A return to respect for the law must begin with respect for and trust in the police. A good example of the success of a program where policemen are seen as social treatment specialists is in the Police Department of Portland, Maine[17]. Though it is too early to evaluate the success of this new program, the initial results are quite favorable. Secondly the tying of police officer's promotions and raises to politics should somehow be eliminated. Their promotions should not be linked to the comings and goings of a new mayor or city council. Morale among police departments can be improved if this straightforward but complex step of removing politics from the role and scope of the policeman is taken.

Finally the aspect of better pay for policemen must be addressed. Too often the policeman comes to court too tired to do a good job of presenting evidence. This may be because he is working a second job to earn a liveable income. Better pay for policemen along with working conditions where he is not coming off a shift and then going to court will make for greater efficiency in the criminal justice system and will guarantee greater possibilities for justice in the courts and a boost to morale for the policeman. Given all the gains, a suitable wage for the policeman is a must!

2. From the court's perspective two changes should bring about some immediate relief:

a. Eliminate the variety of ways in which delays may be granted either before or during the trial. From a behavioral point of view there must be some linkage between the offense and the punishment. If time delays are permitted here, correlation between behavior and response is lost. Hence the behavior is bound to continue. A collateral aspect of this problem is the fact that so little education-information is provided to the individual while he/she is being processed through the system and he/she quite often never understands what is happening to him/her.

b. The second area of concern that is in need of change is sentencing. Uniformity of sentencing would do away with a great deal of the confusion which exists in the court system today. Fines, sentences and suspended sentences for the same offense only serve to muddle the efficient running of the court and the criminal justice system.

3. It must be realized that settings have a strong impact on human behavior and that the very nature of prison settings has a strong deleterious effect on both inmates and guards. A study by Zimbardo[18] showed the oppressive roles taken by student-guards and the passive roles taken by student-inmates. Zimbardo was forced to stop the experiment after six days because of the horrible effect which he saw taking place. Thus the very nature of the prison setting itself is deleterious to treatment and rehabilitation. Only a small percentage of men/women need to be incarcerated and putting others in with them only serves to make this latter group come out worse than when they went in.

4. For true correctional reform to take place it should not be tied into the existing power structure. Real change probably will come from those who are not part of the system and they should be allowed to grow and prosper rather than to be co-opted or beaten down. The key concept here is de-centralization; the creation of smaller units to treat clients and an emphasis on community-based treatment programs.

What must be answered in the final analysis is whether or not this criminal justice processing reduces the crime rate in any significant sense, or is it that nothing really works!!

Discussion Questions

1. What are the four component parts of the Criminal Justice system as it now exists? How do they fit together as an integrated whole?

2. What suggestions do you have to increase the efficiency and human-

ness of the Criminal Justice system? What are some limitations to
your suggestions?

3. Distinguish between delinquent (non-status) and status offenders.
How are these two groups presently handled?

4. What are some problems peculiar to after-care? Describe after-care as
it is utilized in "treating" both juveniles and adults.

Notes

1. Steffensmeier, Darrel J. and Robert M. Terry. "Deviance and Respectability: An Observational Study of Reaction to Shoplifting". *Social Forces*, Vol. 51, No. 4, June 1973.

2. Wambaugh, Joseph. *The New Centurions*. Boston, Little Brown, 1970.

3. Skolnick, Jerome. "Why Cops Behave as They Do" in *Deviance:* Studies in the Process Stigmatization and Societal Reaction; Simon Dinitz, Russel Dynes, and Alfred C. Clarke (editors). Oxford University Press, New York, 1969, pp. 40–47.

4. Niederhoffer, Arthur. *Behind the Shield*. Doubleday and Co., Inc.

5. op. cit. Skolnick, p. 44.

6. op. cit. Skolnick, p. 45.

7. op. cit. Skolnick, p. 43.

8. Kronick, Robert F. "The Impact of Perceived Organizational Climate Upon Academic Performance and Attitude Toward Learning". Unpublished Doctoral Dissertation, The University of Tennessee, March 1971.

9. In Re Gault 397 United States 1 (1967).

10. Goffman, Erving. *Asylums*. Doubleday and Co., Inc., Garden City, New York, 1961.

11. Sykes, Gresham. *The Society of Captives*. Atheneum Publishers, New York, 1966.

12. Clemmer, Donald. *The Prison Community*. Rinehart, New York, 1958.

13. Policy Memo #41, State of Tennessee, Department of Corrections, March 19, 1976.

14. Gialombardo, Rose. *Society of Women*. John Wiley & Sons, Inc., New York, 1966.

15. Martinson, Robert. "What Works? Questions and Answers about Prison Reform". *The Public Interest*. Spring 1974, pp. 22–54.

16. "Children in Trouble". (film)

17. Adams, Stuart. "Evaulation: A Way Out of Rhetoric" in *Rehabilitation, Recidivism and Research*. Robert Martinson, Ted Palmer and Stuart Adams (editors). National Council on Crime and Delinquency, 1976, p. 83.

18. Zimbardo, P. "Psychological Power and Pathology of Imprisonment" in *Behavior Disorders*. Robert G. Walker and Ohmer Milter (editors). J.B. Lippincott, 1973, pp. 151–161.

The Psychiatrist as Servant of the System: A Hippocratic Dilemma

GUYNON MERSEREAU

When is a patient not a patient?

Answer: When he is the subject (i.e. object) of a psychiatrist's examination for a court of law.

A PSYCHIATRIST, like any medical specialist, is a physician first. His training and his job are to treat his patients. He is often consulted by persons who are not his patients, usually other physicians concerned about psychiatric problems in their patients. The patients usually understand this, at least after it's explained to them, but when the person asking for help is neither doctor nor patient, the relationship becomes a bit strange.

Of course when doing examinations for the court the psychiatrist follows, as a rule, the rule of telling the person about to be examined that this is a forensic interrogation. The actual examination differs from a general initial psychiatric assessment mainly in the extra attention it gives to illegal behaviour and the subject's comprehension of his situation *vis à vis* the courts. In this process it is quite clear that the examiner is a doctor. It is usually not so clear that the subject is *not* a patient. He is treated like a patient and he acts like one, and is frequently called a patient. He is thus, in spite of the initial warning, seduced into behaving like someone undergoing treatment rather than someone being questioned for a court before which he stands accused of committing some crime.

Thomas Szasz has written extensively on the role of the psychiatrist as an agent of social control, describes the profession as fraudulent in its exercise of this power, and proposes for this reason that it get out of the labelling business altogether[1]. His arguments are attractive and quite compelling. His humanistic reasoning can also find support in the pantheistic Hippocratic oath. Still further support may be found in the simple practicalities of the different work done by different systems: legal and health. Work in the health system is often categorized into diagnosis and treatment. Health practitioners take it for granted that the one requires the other: treatment following diagnosis (though sometimes it goes that other way). The courts, however, are not primarily concerned with these functions. When they consult a psychiatrist they are looking for help in things like fitness to stand trial, criminal responsiblity and future danger. Somehow they seem to feel that his diagnostic, but not his treatment, skills will have some bearing on their legal issues in the odd-looking case before them. Thus the diagnostic arts, developed for the purpose of rational treatment, are applied to purposes quite alien to those for which they were designed.

Well, the system at this point gets to look crazier than some of its more insane subjects.[2] Let's see if we can look at *it,* the legal system, as a patient for a while and try to make some sense of it. A patient is often best understood in terms of his value system, which is based on where his emotional investments are. The social analog is where the money is. In the criminal justice system, at least in much of the U.S.A. and Canada, the pay for psychiatrists is usually better for court work than it is for treatment of patients, usually in prison. In the Province of Ontario, Canada, now this differential is 7:4.

Another measure of where the values are is who uses the hospitals and for what. In one Canadian city (pop. 300,000) 78 inmates were psychiatrically hospitalized from the county jail over a two-year period. Of these, 65 were sent on court orders for assessment (the vast majority pre-trial); the remaining 13 were referred by the jail psychiatrist for treatment.

Norval Morris[3] has cogently criticised this imbalance in the relative use of psychiatric resources by court and correctional agencies. Police, whose need is probably greater than that of either of the other two agencies, often have the least access to these same resources. Where are our priorities?

The legally innocent jail inmate, caught and held, often for months, in that pre-trial limbo, and usually pretty upset even before his arrest, is frequently in critical need of some psychiatric-type help soon after his arrival. He may ask for a psychiatrist himself or somebody may make the request for him. Looking for help, he gets an examination. He may reasonably expect this to be the first step in getting the help he needs. He may well hear the result of his examination in court: usually centering around a label like "personality disorder". The diagnostic exercise seems to make little difference to the sentence he gets, let alone any help or treatment, and afterwards the whole thing is pretty well forgotten: an empty ritual.

So what does it mean and why is it done? Szasz in his Manufacture of Madness[4] describes the striking similarity between the modern madman and the medieval witch. Michel Foucault[5] traces the growth of the undifferentiated *hôpital* or workhouse from the declining leprosaria. His description of the transitional "Ship of Fools" is very reminiscent of the British hulks when transportation of criminals stopped. Something must be done with the misfits and what is done must demonstrate, as dramatically as possible, how bad and/or how ill it is to be a misfit, i.e. not fit well.

Unfitness in the criminal legal process, variously defined in statutes setting forth criteria for fitness to plead, to stand trial or simply "to proceed" (N.Y., CPL #730), is drawing more psychiatrists into court as the use of the insanity plea declines* and the criteria for civil commitment become tighter. Increasingly, it is the procedure for diversion from criminal justice to "mental health" streams. The role of the psychiatrist here is essentially that of any physician saying a person is too sick to do what is expected of him, e.g. work. It's something that any doctor may expect to do occasionally when the issue arises with a patient he has under treatment at the time. Under these circumstances making such an excuse comes naturally enough, provided it is valid and not abused, even though it is not directly necessary for treatment. It comes not so naturally when the person seeking the excuse is not a patient undergoing treatment by that particular doctor, and maybe not being treated by *any* doctor. It gets even more unnatural, more unmedical, when the examining doctor is engaged not by the complainant but by another interested party, e.g. the employer. This is the situation in much, and probably most, forensic psychiatry. The psychiatrist is brought in to make a report advising a decision-making body as an expert witness. Scientific objectivity is expected of his report just as impartiality is expected of the court. In this situation the reporting tail is wagging the medical dog. Hippocrates, the cultic father of scientific medicine, dazzled as he would be by our scientific and technical advances, would be aghast at such a distortion—even perversion—of the medical art. Small wonder then that it's hard, even with the extra remuneration involved, to get physicians to testify in court and when they do they're like a fish out of water.

But enough now of the psychiatrist in court, and enough even of forensic psychiatry as such. What about treatment for those whom the courts process, those officially labelled delinquent? We know the treatment needs are there. This group has been well-described as more socially inadequate than anti-social. This should be hardly surprising as the mere fact of their appearance in the legal-penal system is the result of their failure to be

---

*Louis McGarry reports 2,101 pre-trial court commitments in Mass. in 1970 during which time *no* one was committed as not guilty by reason of insanity.[6]

successfully delinquent. All officially labelled criminals are thus *ipso facto* ex-criminals. They are the failures and one should expect to find in this population more than its share of mental or personality disorders. Careful surveys of prison populations have indeed shown this to be so, at least for some disorders.[7]* What can we do about it?

So far, we have been looking at the problem from a traditional medical perspective. We have identified a population in need, the medical (psychiatric) service for which is meeting not so much its needs as the needs of another group, the decision-makers. The unmet needs are for treatment, but what treatment?

Here, traditional medicine has been a disappointment. It has served well in psychiatry for the treatment of the middle-class neurotic who does well on a regular (say, weekly) office visit; somewhat less well, but still fairly well, for the treatment of (usually poorer) psychotics, usually in hospital; but least well in the treatment of personality disorders, such as those which bring people to jail. For this last group, the newer and more intensive group or milieu therapies have shown the most promise.[9], [10], [11], [12] They are sufficiently different from the more traditional methods that special training and aptitudes are required of the treatment personnel, who need not have had much medical training as such. But still, different and difficult though it be, this kind of treatment can be, and is being done.

The question often asked of the providers of this treatment is: Which side are you on, theirs (the penal authority) or ours? We have been looking at this question from both a medical and a legal perspective. There is still another perspective and dimension to this problem. The very question, "which side are you on?", implies a marked polarization. The penal psychotherapist is part of a "cops and robbers" game, which seems to require it, but when he becomes identified with one side or the other, he becomes more a part of the problem than the solution. He is usually engaged by a counter-criminal system to serve the criminal. This may look like an impossible situation— and indeed it does seem to get that way at times—but it has the potential for bridging the gap, reconciling the opposing factions, both internal and external, and thus developing a dialectical synthesis. This is the challenge, and when it is met, it becomes the highest achievement of the therapeutic art in this field.

---

*In view of the elaborate screening and diversion procedures discussed above, it may seem at first surprising that in prison, the major psychoses appear at about the normal rate for the general population. Obviously, if these procedures are operative at all, the entry rate for these disorders must be *higher* than normal. This is supported by more recent studies of jail populations, which include those held pre-trial, which do show higher rates of psychiatric illness in this group.[8]

The Politics of Treatment

To undergo treatment is to enter a relationship dominated by the person doing the treatment. Traditionally, this dominant person is the physician. He, being literally the treatment agent, those under his care are called his "patients", thus etymologically furthering the polarization of an active-passive role complement. This scheme — active doctor, passive patient — is quite useful in the acute phase of treatment, notably where this involves major surgery.* It gets less useful in the later phases as recovery proceeds when more is expected of the "patient", and less of the doctor. In the last two or three decades, there has been a growing recognition of that group of iatrogenic disorders based on the failure of this shift from passivity to activity to occur fast enough. Deaths from pulmonary embolism arising from phlebothrombosis (clotting) in the subacute phase of myocardial infarction (heart attacks), major surgery, multiple fractures and complicated childbirth, are clearly related to patient inactivity. Stasis pneumonia in similar conditions is another, if somewhat less dramatic, cause of death from staying too long (and too still) in bed. Staying too long in hospital increases mortality from antibiotic-resistant infections and morbidity from such things as chronic chest disease, arthritis, and strokes, as well as those conditions already mentioned.

Psychiatrically, Freud in 1912 described the transference neurosis, characterized by a morbid attachment to the therapist, as a necessary phase of a successful psycho-analysis. He added: "Institutions and homes for the treatment of nervous patients . . . provide instances of transference . . . extending even to complete subjection."[13] More recently the "institutional neuroses" of excessive passive dependency on the place has been described as accounting for much of the phenomena which were previously thought to be part of such psychoses as schizophrenia. Spitz made similar observations in the very young in foundling homes, where the outcome was sometimes fatal.[14] Basically, the same problem occurs in prisons. Here, Cormier describes it as the basis for pre-liberation anxiety, or "gate fever."[15] The institution has become home, those in it family, and the inmate the baby. For the prisoner to grow up and mature before he leaves it, the traditional authoritarian structure must be modified. The most successful modification has been the therapeutic community, or some near variant of it. The name was coined, and the technique popularized by Maxwell Jones, though he was not the first to use it. Basically, it is a living-in group therapy situation,

---

*An exception to this is some brain surgery, a crucial phase of which requires the active experiential report of the patient.

structured as democratically as possible, with considerable responsibility expected of each member.[16] It has helped in the few instances where it has been tried, especially in Denmark,[17] and Holland,[18] where good clinical follow-up has been provided. It still remains to be seen whether comparable results are possible in North America. Power, authority, and privilege are hard to relinquish. Doctors and administrators in our culture are expected to hold and wield these perquisites, but frequently do not learn well the art of tailoring such exercise of authority to the current need of their patients.

Thus, we come to the need for professional development. There is a general skill in therapeutic community administration for which there is a general need. There is a more specific skill in its use with prisoners. This latter can be taught only in part. The rest is native aptitude found in people who enjoy working with criminals, often because they are somewhat that way themselves. To find such aptitudes, and teach these skills, the only way is by having people do it. The therapeutic community, therefore, selects and trains staff as well as doing its immediate job of rehabiliation.

It becomes quickly apparent, especially when one sees the actual operation of such treatment and rehabilitation centres, that treatment and training are two sides of the same coin: one concerned with patients (or inmates), the other with the staff. Such is the reciprocity of such milieu that one may well wonder who is treating whom.[19] Certainly, the training function is bilateral, for the patients well along in treatment are quite regularly a major influence in drawing the new arrival into the treatment process. Thus, patients too are trained as therapists. Through this treatment, and training, growth towards self-sufficiency takes place—if the job is being done. For what is the purpose of any job but to work itself out of existence?

This job, however, by its very nature, can be begun, but never finished behind walls. No matter how well the lessons have been learned and applied within the therapeutic community, they still have to be re-learned in, and re-applied to, the outside natural community. It is in this transition from inside to outside in living that most programmes fail. The Dannemora project group returned at the same rate as the control group (though for lesser offences).[20] An outpatient treatment phase with ready availability for crises is at least as important for this group as it is for other patients.

Why, then is proper clinical follow-up so rarely provided? Here, we must turn from the internal politics of treatment to the external politics and economics of establishing and funding such programmes. It is difficult, and often impossible, to provide follow-up care when the treatment centre is far removed from the population centre, yet this is usually the case when treatment is done in prison. It is an old criticism of prisons that they are so out-of-the-way, yet little has been done to change this. Why? One reason seems to be that prisons are not only prisons, but government-owned industries, with fairly substantial budgets. Like universities, hospitals, and other such enterprises, they can be a major economic resource to a small community, even its life-blood. Dannemora ("Little Siberia") was a failing pocket of poverty with an exhausted mine shaft before the prison was built. Springhill, Nova Scotia, was rescued from its coal mine disaster by building a penitentiary there. Besides meeting such real economic needs, projects like these frequently serve less substantial, but real enough to those involved, political needs. Three mental hospitals in the province of Quebec were built by one administration, each in the constituency of a cabinet minister (Health, Labour and Public Works being the respective port-folios). This came at a time when tuberculosis sanitoria had recently closed.[21] A parallel with Foucault's observation of madness increasing as leprosy declined in Europe is rather striking. Hospitals and prisons now take the place of sanitoria and leprosaria.

Outpatient services could employ as many voters, but as monuments to local politicians and/or their constituents, they are neither so dramatic nor concrete. North American society seems to lack the political imagination, if not the managerial expertise, to make the changes it needs. Now, with the decline of religious institutions, there seems to be greater need than ever for objects to symbolize and carry society's scapegoating rituals.

Charles Taylor describes the "sacralization" of politics,[22] which is part of this trend, which can be seen extending through other institutions like those of health and criminal justice. Social scapegoating, whether of individuals (e.g. criminals, lunatics) or institutions (e.g. "police brutality") is commonly seen as a phenomenon of negative valuation. The original ritual scapegoat, however, is a highly valued object, bearing like Jesus Christ the sins of the community for its redemption. Now, as we personify our sins, the jails and asylums becomes our saviors — scapegoats in the original sense. We need our prisons and hospitals as much as we need our criminals and fools.

Luckily for the authors, this book only purports to raise issues, not necessarily solve them. Obviously, the solution of this one is beyond psychiatry. The issues are more existential than morbid, and call — even cry out — for a prophet rather than a physician. As in so much of his work, the doctor watches and waits while God or fate does its (or His) work.

Some needs for action, however, have fairly clearly emerged. We can't ignore Szasz' and others' warnings of the mischief done by psychiatric labelling, and Norville Morris' opinion that the psychiatrist (or his report) in court is usually a relative waste of time (both his and the court's). Society would probably be better off if *both* criminal responsibility ("insanity") and procedural competency (fitness to plead, stand trial, etc.) statutes were simply abolished, and the psychiatrists, like any physicians, were used by the courts only on clearly medical matters like treatment and disability. Then the madman on the streets, with his new-found civil liberty will, when he goes to jail, be seen more pragmatically, more as someone needing treatment and support, than as an unfit defendant.

Obviously, more treatment and rehabilitation programmes geared specifically to the needs of the socially disabled population now in our prisons are needed, and must be implemented. However, let's not do just half a job again. As well as halfway houses, full programmes are needed. The critical phase of reintegration into the community needs far more attention than it has been given. As much as this has been talked about, still little has been seriously done. This brings us again to the larger social and political issues, which are beyond the scope of this article.

Finally, the vast virgin territory of research needs must be mentioned. Even data, which are supposed to be fairly available, like comparable rates of utilization of the different systems, are either unavailable or unreliable. More basic studies, e.g. of homicidal (or even assaultive) interactions, and the phenomenology of shifts in time and space as movement into or out of the system occurs, have yet to be done. New jails and related structures are being built all the time, still without knowing how they affect the watchers, the watched, or their relationships. If the interactional dialectics of relationships between individuals are getting so little attention, still less are they being studied at the level of the larger systems. There is now a fair amount of descriptive material on prison riots and related phenomena, but still penology remains one of our most primitive sciences, not having moved much beyond these descriptions with either good theoretical or practical studies.

In sum, this overview has considered the psychiatrist in the legal-penal system from several different *optiques,* including that of the psychiatrist himself. As well as the more usual medical and legal views, it has been approached from ethical, political, and economic perspectives. In attempting to put it together, there has been added a sprinkling of general systems theory, and just a dash of religion. The problems seen are mainly chronic ones of closed institutions in a "free" society, but some of them are becoming acute as present trends continue. These trends include the growing civil liberties movement, the secularization of society, and economic recession with its concomitant public budgetary constraints. Even technologic advances in apparently unrelated fields, maybe most specifically in the mass media, contribute through "the revolution of rising expectations" to such phenomena as prison riots.

Summary

This brief survey has been an attempt to take a fresh look at the now not-so-popular role of the psychiatrist in the criminal justice system. The critics who say that in the court, this role must be severely limited, and in some areas (e.g. insanity defense), eliminated altogether, are given comfort and support. When it comes to the penal (often still called "correctional") system, however, it becomes readily apparent that psychiatric skills are woefully underutilized. Some of the ways they have been and still can be used to make the existing system work better have been reviewed. It makes sense not to discard something so potentially useful as psychiatric rehabilitative and treatment methods without first really trying them. There remain, however, larger issues that cannot be totally ignored. The watcher and the watched are not basically different. Criminal and counter-criminal systems together serve important socio-cultural needs which are both symbolic and destructive. Black sheep and scapegoats are seen as individual expressions of these larger needs; but could these needs not be met more symbolically and less destructively? It is within the context of such broader and more radical issues that the lesser and more psychiatric issues must be understood.

Time is running out. These are indeed critical issues.

Discussion Questions

1. How effective are forensic (court-related) psychiatric screening and diversion procedures?
   Which of these functions could be performed as well or better non-psychiatrically?

2. How effective is penal psychiatric treatment?
   —for psychoses?
   —for personality disorders?
   How could these be improved?

3. Where in your experience has the psychiatrist figured in the interaction of criminal and counter-criminal systems?
   —in their polarization?
   As agent of change?

4. What *non*-criminal black sheep and scapegoats do we have?
   How do their roles compare with and differ from the criminal ones?
   and how do they affect the balance between movements for social
   control vs. those for civil liberty?

5. Has penal psychiatry been tried and found wanting?
   Has it been tried?
   Is there a valid analogy between "therapeutic" and other experimental
   (e.g. religious) communities?

Notes

1. Szasz, T.S. *Law, Liberty, and Psychiatry,* N.Y. MacMillan, 1963.

2. Mersereau, G.P.M. The Criminal in General Systems: A Mental Health Consultation Service to the Criminal Justice System in One County, in: *Politics, Crime and the International Scene,* Adler, F. and Mueller, G.O.W., eds. San Juan, P.R. North-South Centre Press, 1972.

3. Morris, N. and Hawkins, G. *The Honest Politician's Guide to Crime Control,* pp. 173–201 Chicago, Univ. Chicago Press, 1970.

4. Szasz, T.S. *The Manufacture of Madness: A Comparative Study of the Inquisition and the Mental Health Movement.* N.Y. Dell, 1970.

5. Foucault, M. *Madness and Civilization,* N.Y. Vintage, 1973.

6. McGarry, L. Competency to Stand Trial and Mental Illness, in: *Crime and Delinquency Issues,* NIMH monograph, DHEW Publication No. (HSM) 73-9105 (Rockville, Md., 1972).

7. Guze, S.B., Tuason V.B., Gatfield, P.D. et al. Psychiatric Illness and Crime with particular Reference to Alcoholism: A Study of 223 criminals. *J. Nerv. Ment. Dis.* 134: 512–521, 1962.

8. Petrich, J. Rate of Psychiatric Morbidity in a Metropolitan County Jail Population. *Am. J. Psychiat.* 133:1439–1444, 1976.

9. Barker, E.T. and Mason, M.H. Buber Behind Bars. *Canad. Psychiat. Assoc. J.* 13:61–72, 1968.

10. Cormier, Bruno M. *The Watcher and the Watched,* Montreal, Tundra, 1975.

11. Jones, Maxwell. *Social Psychiatry in Practice: The Idea of the Therapeutic Community.* Harmondsworth, Penguin, 1968.

12. Sturup, George K. *Treating the "Untreatable" Chronic Criminals.* Isaac Ray Lectures, Baltimore, John Hopkins University Press, 1968.

13. Freud, S. Dynamics of the Transference In: *Therapy and Technique.* N.Y. Collier 1963, p. 108.

14. Spitz, R.A. Hospitalism, A Follow-up Report on Investigation described in Vol. 1, 1945. *Psychoanal. Study Child* 2:255, 1946.

15. Cormier, Bruno M op. cit.

16. Jones, Maxwell op. cit.

17. Sturup, George K. op. cit.

18. Cormier, Bruno M. op. cit.

19. Angliker, C.C.J. The Therapeutic Community—Whom Are We Treating? *Laval Medical* 42, 1971.

20. Cormier, Bruno M. op. cit.

21. Lemieux, Marcel. Personal Communication.

22. Taylor, Charles. *The Pattern of Politics,* Montreal, McClelland and Stewart, 1970 p. 110.

5

Radical Changes in Criminal Justice: From Non-System to System

GALAN M. JANEKSELA

Introduction

THE CRIMINAL JUSTICE SYSTEM in America is in danger! The courts face alarmingly overcrowded calendars; corrections suffers from a lack of resources for facilities and services; and the police stand in awe while second and third time offenders are released back to the streets before they have completed the paperwork on the case.

> . . . most practitioners in the field (police officers, correctional workers, judges, prosecutors, public defenders and private attorneys as well as the academicians) often state that the entire criminal justice system is rapidly approaching a crisis—or may now be in a crisis—and is alarmingly close to a breakdown.[1]

This crisis affects every segment of the criminal justice system. The criminal justice system has reached the critical point; it is time for change.

Many theoreticians argue that criminal justice is not a system; it is a fragmented non-system. This chapter addresses the system vs. non-system controversy, and the author forwards structural changes for improving the "system's" operations.

Criminal Justice: The Non-System Viewpoint

A system implies continuity of purpose among component parts. In reality, each component within criminal justice is an entity in itself. The relationship between the components is adversary in nature because the *primary goals* of each component are different. The police are charged with law enforcement, prevention of crime, preservation of peace, and protection of life and property. The courts are concerned with due process and the protection of the individual's rights. The mandate of corrections is to carry out the sentence of the court, and to rehabilitate and return the offender to society at the most opportune time.[2]

The police see the courts as "enemies," judges view the police as violators of individual rights, and both the police and the courts view correctional programs as failures. The public perceives that all three criminal justice sub-systems are ineffective; e.g., the police are the "gestapo" or "goon-squads"; the courts cater to the rich; and corrections is unable to keep the "common criminal" from preying on the citizens of the community.

Each component views the commission of crime and the administration of justice differently. The police see the real agony of the victim; the courts see crime from a more remote and neutral position; and corrections de-emphasizes the crime and focuses on rehabilitating the offender. Consequently, these differing perspectives result in frustration for nearly every official and agency within this process. As a result, each component becomes the subject of criticism by the other components,[3] and each component negatively stereotypes the other components.

> . . . conflicts arising from value differences require that so much of a criminal justice system's resources must be allocated toward internal surveillance measures (in an effort to maintain system equilibrium) that the basic goal of the system is subverted, providing the goal is the elimination of crime.[4]

The System's Structure as a Source of Conflict

Criminal justice conflict is intensified by the fact that the training of manpower focuses solely on its distinct primary function, that being law enforcement, adjudication, or correction. Training programs rarely acknowledge that there is a "system" of criminal justice.

The existing agencies in the criminal justice process operate largely in isolation from each other,[5] therefore, many "experts" believe that a 'system' of criminal justice does not exist in the United States from either a theoretical or a practical point of view. A system implies some unity of purpose and organized interrelationships among component parts. If the criminal justice system fails to meet these criteria, it is not a system, but a well-defined process, a continuum through which each accused offender may pass.[6]

Judges, police administrators, and prison officials, seldom confer on common problems. The common perception is: 'We have enough problems of our own, without concern for the problems of other agencies within the system.' The end result is that each criminal justice agency attempts to achieve its own interests with little regard for other agencies.[7]

The structure of the criminal justice system is a loose federation of offices and agencies whose formal relationship is amorphous because they are structurally independent. Each agency has its own purpose, job tasks and standards for performance evaluation. In other words, there is not a homogeneous continuum for the processes within the criminal justice structure.[8]

In a system, each component views its role and function as part of a whole. However, the process of criminal justice is a series of segments separated by differences in philosophy, purpose, and practice which are best characterized by internal conflict and confusion. With this antagonism towards one another, each component isolates itself from the others, rather than working toward solutions of common probelms.

Each component jealously adopts a narrow view of its role in the administration of justice and refuses to function beyond its narrowly defined parameters. This narrow view of criminal justice is intensified by the many conflicting demands placed on the criminal justice system. In short, the roots of the conflict may be operational in nature, i.e., the functions of the major components are not consistent.

Conflicts within the criminal justice spectrum are compounded by the fact that each component must compete for the budgetary dollar. Cities, states, and the federal government, allocate a part of their total budget to the "fight against crime." This creates a continuing debate between the various components of criminal justice as to the most effective means of controlling crime (e.g., increasing the number of personnel in law enforcement, a more effective judicial process, or more comprehensive treatment centers for treating the offender).

Criminal justice agencies are so independently structured that there are no clear political boundaries within which each of the components can function; police are generally funded at the city level; judges are sometimes elected, sometimes appointed, and are answerable to either state, county or local constituencies; and, correctional agencies are a composite of federal, state, county and local facilities, with probation and parole systems being directed by courts and/or executive agencies. Each agency:

> . . . sees its own special mission being undercut by the cross-purpose, frailties, or malfunctions of others. As they find their places along the spectrum between the intense concern with victims at one end, and total preoccupation with reforming convicted lawbreakers at the other, so do they find their daily perceptions of justice varying or in conflict.[10]

Illustrations of Police-Court Conflict

This section analyzes police-court conflicts to illustrate the nature of intra-system conflicts. The police dilemma is one of law vs. order. The court stresses the technicalities of the law while the police are attempting to maintain order using available methods which may violate the rules of law. Often, the end result is that the courts may dismiss a case on a technicality, and the police are likely to interpret this as an unnecessary blockade which prevents them from performing their duties.[11]

Police officers spend time and resources to attain evidence on a criminal, however, frequently this evidence can only be achieved via methods which violate rules of evidence. The police feel justified in their actions in that the community's safety is at stake, but the court refuses such evidence. The result is a hostile relationship between the police and the judiciary.[12]

Police officers become frustrated because 60% of their tickets for traffic violations are forgiven by the court; i.e. the court finds the "violator" not guilty. In addition, there are inconsistencies within the same jurisdictions regarding the decisions of the traffic court. For example, one judge may find a defendant not guilty while another judge will find another party guilty under similar circumstances.

Police hostility is often overtly expressed in the form of verbal assault upon the court, within police groups or in the presence of the judge. Many incidents of police-judge conflicts can be illustrated. For example, an officer, in response to a judge's refusal to find the defendant guilty, uttered in audible volume, "M-I-C-K-E-Y M-O-U-S-E." In reaction to this, the judge called the officer into his chambers and threatened him with contempt of court. In another incident, a police officer verbally assaulted the judge in the presence of several attorneys. Fortunately for the police officer, this judge responded by taking an empathetic position regarding the police plight.[13]

Criminal Justice: The "System" Viewpoint*

Many theoreticians and practitioners believe that a system of criminal justice does exist. This viewpoint will be discussed in this section. Diverse agencies within the criminal justice system do share an allegiance to the common objectives of crime control and prevention, and the actions of any one of the agencies within the process of criminal justice directly affects the other components. It is not unusual to see a police officer, a prosecutor, a defense attorney, and possibly a parole officer collaborating within a court of law, to determine the appropriate disposition for an offender. Although the interrelationships between the various component parts (law enforcement, courts, and corrections) is not as extensive as it should be, interrelationships do exist.

---

* This section is an expanded version of material contained in my article entitled "Systems Analysis in Juvenile Justice," *Juvenile and Family Court Journal* (August, 1978), pages 9–15.

Many experts believe that the components are separate entitites, each having its own goals, procedures, practices, and functions. Functional analysis of criminal justice helps the researcher to identify problems, issues, and even techniques that are not localized in agencies, but, that occur repeatedly at various points in the process. For example, when this approach is used, it becomes clear that the functions of interrogation, search, and arrest are not issues limited only to law enforcement. Probation officers, wardens, custodial officers, and parole agents also perform these tasks.

Advocates of a criminal justice "system" do not deny that each component is distinct, since a system has to be specifiable (an organization of people, devices, and procedures intended to perform some function). They believe the functional interrelationships between the components creates the cement that binds the system together. The decision of one agency directly affects the other component parts . . . "no single agency or office is in itself a complete criminal justice system; the police serve as the intake agency for correctional populations, and in turn corrections returns to the community ex-inmates who are hoped to be rehabilitated, but who soon again become police problems."[14] The flow of persons through the system, or diverted from it, indicate the system's parameters and provides the most comprehensive way of dealing with the system in its total context.

The fact that an individual can (1) enter the system as an input via the police, (2) be processed from one criminal justice component to another, and (3) be released as an output by corrections, supports the notion that criminal justice is a "system."

The criminal justice system consists of the police, the courts, and corrections. However, these sub-systems are not independent of each other. The President's Commission on Law Enforcement and Administration of Justice recognized the interrelationships between sub-systems as evidenced by the following statement:

> What each one does and how it does it has a direct effect on the work of the others. The courts must deal, and can only deal, with those whom the police arrest; the business of corrections is with those delivered to it by the courts. How successfully corrections reforms convicts determines whether they will once again become police business and influence the sentences the judge pass; police activities are subject to court scrutiny and are often determined by court decisions. And so reforming or reorganizing any part or procedure of the system changes other parts or procedures. Furthermore, the criminal process, the method by which the system deals with individual cases, is not a hodgepodge of random actions. It is rather a continuum—an orderly progression of events— some of which, like arrest and trials, are highly visible and some of which, though of great importance, occur out of public view. A study of the system must begin by examining it as a whole.[15]

In the sixties, the civil rights decisions by the Supreme Court directly affected police enforcement techniques and correctional treatment strategies. All component parts were directly affected by the Supreme Court's decisions regarding the Fourteenth Amendment, and the carry-over amendment guaranteeing individual rights both in federal and state courts. This Constitutional guarantee greatly hampered the effectiveness of all components pursuing a decrease in the rise of crime, and reinforced their divergent differences by this "apparent assault" on criminal justice by the highest court in the land.

The criminal justice system includes a set of systems which relate to and affect each other. Decisions made by one component pervasively affects the decisions of the other components. Responses to decisions made by one component may take the form of formal changes or informal changes in practice:

> . . . any effort radically to interfere with an existing system of criminal justice would be met first by some form of compensation with the system. An effort to intervene at one level would likely be compensated for at another. For example, if efforts were made to discourage the taking of guilty pleas there would, of course, be more trials, likely with a greater proportion of guilty verdicts and harsher sentences in cases where a plea of guilty would previously have been the response considered appropriate. The police are commonly believed to attempt to compensate for the increased protection now being afforded defendants in court by administering their own officially unrecognized criminal justice system entirely independent of the courts. The maximum penalty that can be administered within the police system is the hardship connected with arrest, detention, and perhaps holding to preliminary hearing.[16]

The Community Justice Center

It is evident that as long as the various agencies continue to compete for the same tax dollars, are inefficiently run, are understaffed and underpaid, lack common goals and purposes, and view each other agency as "the enemy," the criminal justice system will breed chaos and stagnation. Part of the problem is operational in nature. Even within an efficiently run criminal justice system, law enforcement will still be charged with the control of crime; the courts will be concerned with due process and individual rights; and, corrections will carry out the sentence of the court while attempting to rehabilitate and return the offender to society at the most opportune time. This approach prevents inter-departmental cooperation. Sub-systems are segregated and they each see only what is relevant to their own responsibilities.

It is not impossible for the system of criminal justice to become: (1) effective in the prevention of crime; and (2) efficient as a complex network of agencies with a multiplicity of goals, purpose, and functions. One method by which criminal justice can be improved is the formation of a "community justice center"; i.e., a centralized criminal justice facility which would allow daily contact between criminal justice components.

A "community justice committee" would establish policy, and the center's director would implement the policies. The committee would include representatives from law enforcement, courts, corrections, and the community. Representatives would be encouraged to offer a professional point of view, without threat of repercussions. This would create an awareness of the problems of the overall system (i.e., procedures, techniques, errors in judgement, or lack of communication) that affect the other agencies within the system. Changes made in each sub-system would be planned by the committee. Rules and procedures for planning and implementation of change would be established by the committee.

The director's primary purpose would be to: (1) oversee the daily operations of the various criminal justice agencies of law enforcement, courts, and corrections; and (2) facilitate a shared goal-orientation throughout the field of criminal justice. This type of centralized organizational structure furnishes a rather intricate mechanism for establishing policies and decisions. Since it is presumed that the decisions are the best possible for the achievement of a common purpose and goal, it is expected that the personnel within each agency will be committed to implementing the policies as directed, and that these policies will have support from the community.

Organizational centralization of the various components within the community justice center would create the consistency and unified goal-orientation that would overcome the adversary relationship that exists today. The budget would be administered by the director of the community justice center in accordance with the committee's recommendations regarding the requests from the various departmental heads.

Criminal justice personnel would be periodically trained in new methods of crime control, innovative treatment techniques, law, recent Supreme Court rulings, and the rights of the individual. This training would enhance the effectiveness of crime prevention, detection of crime, due process of law, and positive corrective techniques in rehabilitating the offender, without increasing the tax base for the community.

The community justice center concept includes feedback mechanisms at each stage of the criminal justice system; e.g., decisions made by the law enforcement agencies would be communicated to the courts, corrections, and sub-systems. Feedback mechanisms would include feedback regarding decisions made at each step of the criminal justice system. This continuous flow of information between the various criminal justice agencies would, in turn, create harmony of purpose, prevent continued dissension between the agencies, and create an open channel of communication between department heads. This would result in communal problem-solving and decision-making, and an awareness of the other components.

The "community justice center" concept is needed, and it is more than a theoretical construct; it has operational significance in that a "system" requires that each agency in the system (and each person in each agency) must view its role and function as part of the whole.[17] Through the total system concept, the nation's criminal justice process could be converted from a diffused group of fragmented agencies (each without any regard for the other) into a unified system which has common goals.

The actuality of an effective community justice center will be realized only if the various criminal justice agencies allow a centralized administrative structure to assume the authority to manage community criminal justice processes. Breakdowns in communication, dissension among the various agencies, biased decision-making, and political favoritism must be minimized.

Implementation of this model could diminish the debate over the use of the concept of "system" in criminal justice. A radical implementation of a systems approach in criminal justice is necessary in order to dissolve a "process" or "continuum" that both theoreticians and practitioners agree, is out-moded, antiquated, decadent, and most of all, dysfunctional.

The advantages and disadvantages of this approach can be determined by a pilot program. The author recommends that a pilot "community justice center" be established in a community which has between 100,000–250,000 people. This size city is more able to assist in the financial support of the "center" than smaller communities. However, it is likely that the "center" concept will work in smaller communities in that this approach focuses on a Gemeinschaft community wherein the community takes responsibility for its deviance. In other words, the "community justice center" will be most effective in communities characterized by an attitude of responsibility for problems which occur within the community.[18]

Discussion Questions

1. Construct a model of criminal justice as it exists in your community
   a. Is there interaction between the various components?
   b. Is there cooperation between the various components?
   c. If there is cooperation, what agencies are cooperating?

2. Identify conflicts between the components of criminal justice.

a. What causes each conflict identified above? (goals, values, ig-norance, etc.)

b. What can be done to prevent, resolve, or eliminate these con-flicts?

3. How can criminal justice become a system? Assume that you had the resources to implement changes (structural changes, goal changes, etc.), what would you do?

a. Identify a common goal which all subsystems can work toward.

b. How can you make this a realistic and an attainable goal?

c. Discuss the pro's and con's of the community justice center.

Notes

1. Alan R. Coffey and Edward Eldefonso, *Process and Impact of Justice* (Beverly Hills: Glencoe Press, 1975), page 32.

2. Vincent O'Leary and Donald Newman, "Conflict Resolution in Criminal Justice," *Journal of Research in Crime and Delinquency,* 7 (1970): pages 99–119.

3. Daniel Freed, "The Non-System of Criminal Justice," Chapter 13 in *Law and Order Reconsidered,* Report of the Task Force on Law and Law Enforcement to the National Commission on the Causes and Prevention of Violence, (1969): pages 265–284.

4. Bruce T. Olson, "Conflicts in Values in Criminal Justice: A Proposed System Analysis," *Police,* November–December (1969): pages 44–48.

5. Robert Scott, "Problems in Communication and Cooperation in the Administration of Justice," in *Police and Community Relations: A Sourcebook* edited by A.F. Brandstatter and L.A. Radelet, (Glencoe Press and MacMillan Publishing Company, Inc., 1967): pages 430–434.

6. Freed, 1969: 266.

7. Ibid., p. 268.

8. O'Leary and Newman, 1970: 100.

9. Scott, 1967.

10. Freed, 1969.

11. Newman, 1975:7.

12. Jerome Skolnick, *Justice Without Trial: Law Enforcement in Democratic Society* (New York: John Wiley and Sons, Inc., 1966).

13. The above two paragraphs are based on my discussions with police officers.

14. Newman, 1975:7.

15. President's Commission on Law Enforcement and the Administration of Justice, *Challenge of Crime in a Free Society* (Washington, D.C.: U.S. Government Printing Office), page 7.

16. Oaks, Dallin, H., and Warren Lehman, *A Criminal Justice System and the Indigent* (Chicago: The University of Chicago Press, 1968) page 7.

17. O'Leary and Newman, 1970:101.

18. I would like to thank Terry Nida and Fred Bieker for their assistance during my preparation of earlier drafts of this chapter. Mr. Nida and Mr. Bieker were employed as graduate assistants in the Department of Administration of Justice while they assisted me.

6

Victim Compensation for the Poor

S. GEORGE VINCENTNATHAN

THE ECONOMIC COMPENSATION OF CRIME VICTIMS has recently become a significant concern for both the citizens and the federal, state, and local governments in America. People often tend to justify victim compensation on the grounds of a sympathy they have developed based on religious or humanitarian grounds. Since this interest in the compensation of victims has emerged only recently, perhaps other grounds for compensation of victims have not been clearly identified. By applying some ideas borrowed from the behavioral and social sciences, it will be shown that compensation should be made to victims of violent offenses who are economically poor and needy, and that victim compensation programs can be integrated with crime prevention efforts.

Should all victims of crimes be eligible for compensation? To do economic justice both to victims and to the citizens whose tax money would fund any compensation program, it is maintained that only needy victims should be compensated. What type of poor victims should be compensated? It is argued that victims of violent offenses should be entitled to victim compensation. To compensate needy victims of property offenses would place an enormous burden on taxpayers since the incidence of victimization through property offenses is much higher than that through violent offenses.

It is contended that victim compensation programs can also activate crime prevention efforts. As systemic components, the society- government structural units, the offender, and the victim are responsible for any instance of crime, and thus the burden of victim compensation is relegated to these systemic agents. If these systemic agents can be made to understand that they are contributing toward crime, and that they are paying for both its control and the compensation of its victims, they would develop the motivation to work toward crime reduction.

This type of endeavor will require integrated federal, state, and local administrative structure. These units can develop uniform standards for the funding and administration of victim compensation programs. The appropriation of money for victim compensation is predominantly a role of the state government. The compensation paid to crime victims should come from the home county of the responsible criminal, regardless of the victim's residence. Taxation based on this compensation framework, coupled with county-wide and community-wide crime prevention efforts can significantly reduce the rates of crimes and victimization and help to lower local tax rates. Finally, a summary of recommendations for victim compensation and crime prevention is presented.

Victim, Class Structure, and Victim Compensation

Because crime strikes without regard for economic class, many victims of violent offenses find that they simply cannot bear the losses. Victims who are poor often do not have the means to deal with economic losses and must have immediate financial assistance. Some in our society may maintain that the inability of some victims to bear the burden of their losses is their own fault. Yet the ultimate responsibility for poverty lies with the institutional structures of society and their failure to help the poor to achieve a better life.

Through its cultural dictates, society has oriented people toward economic achievement, while not providing an equal opportunity for all to reach it. The illiterate, the undereducated, the oppressed, and those vocationally unskilled and semiskilled are examples of people who are disadvantaged in competing with the unimpaired in the attainment of economic goals. Consequently, social classes develop based on levels of economic achievement, each class with a distinctive style of living. In response to the economic hardships and frustrations they bear, those in the lower economic groups develop specific patterns of thought and behavior. These response patterns, aside from simply making up a part of the "subculture of poverty," contain "defense mechanisms without which the poor could hardly carry on."[1] Once a person is caught up in this subculture, a release from it is hard to achieve.

One of the main barriers imposed by this subculture of poverty to its participants is that it does not provide its people the necessary access to obtain education. Because these people develop a desire for the immediate gratification of needs in response to their concern for survival, as opposed to the delayed gratification demonstrated by the upper classes, little concern for education appears. Further, the teachers of lower class children often expect them to perform at a lower academic level. Ryan notes: "In other words, such children who do well — in contradiction to the teachers' expectations — are viewed as difficult and as likely adjustment problems."[2] Minority group youths, especially Black children, experience an additional deprivation due to the prejudice and discrimination they face in the schools. Because of these conditions, education has become an unusually difficult objective for the poor to realize. Most of them become entrapped in the subculture of poverty and remain there throughout their lives.

From the Marxian perspective, the poor in capitalistic societies are viewed as concomitant results of the exploitative endeavors of the rich in the furtherance of their economic aspirations.[3] The drive in capitalistic societies to accumulate private property leads to the concentration of wealth among a few individuals. This wealthy elite wields economic and political power to ensure the permanence of its position. Through political alliances, the rich make possible the creation of laws for the protection of their economic interests. Politically, economically, and educationally, they are in a powerful position to advance their class, while the poor experience few opportunities for betterment of any sort.

Through its institutional structure, then, the society is responsible for both the creation and the underdevelopment of the poor because it failed to make available to the poor the opportunity to develop the abilities that are necessary for economic betterment. A recognition of this key problem makes the importance of compensating those victims of violent crimes who are in the lower income groups even more pressing.

Higher victimization and crime rates are also concentrated in the lower income groups. These crimes result from the frustrations which the poor daily experience. People naturally vent such a rage on those within their reach — in homes and in neighborhoods. Some individuals come to respond to such frustration with violent actions as a matter of course. When many react this way, it develops over a period of time into a subculture of violence. This subculture often overlays the subculture of poverty, and the joint configuration finds frequent expression in the development of a violent orientation among members of the lower class.[4] Often both the offender and victim are oriented toward violence, for victim-precipitated offenses occur with greater frequency in lower income areas.[5] Thus a higher rate of violent crimes has become a real problem in lower income groups. Since the societal neglect of the lower class provides the main reason for its poverty, its victimization, and its tendency toward violence, the government of that society should assume the responsibility for compensating the poor victims of crime.

Higher income areas show lower victimization rates, and those with a larger income stand in a more advantageous economic position to employ crime prevention measures to evade such victimization. When victimization does occur, they have the economic resources to maintain themselves. The expenses related to victimization can be covered by savings, insurance, or the liquidation of assets. Some of their health-related expenses can even be claimed as income tax deductions. Victims from the lower income groups often do not have these advantages available.

In socialist societies, where income levels do not vary as much as in capitalist societies, the compensation of all crime victims is a logically consistent venture. It will serve as a redress mechanism to level the economic imbalance caused by victimization. In capitalistic societies like the United States, with its wide variance in income level, compensating all victims irrespective of economic position would only aid in the perpetuation of economic inequalities. In other words, it would only serve to re-establish the economic position of individuals prior to their victimization. Those wealthy persons with alternate forms of victim compensation (e.g., insurance, tax deductions) may even increase their economic standing. Thus, those who maintain that compensating all crime victims is socialistic are mistaken, for such a program would only perpetuate class differences, not reduce them. Compensating all crime victims may also mean an increase in taxes, which would put a severe burden on the tax-payers, especially the poor.

The poor, then, should be given preferential treatment in economic compensation for victimization, just as they deserve help in other areas of their lives. The poor help to sustain the economy through their labor, so the economically comfortable section of society has an obligation to insure through its government economic justice to needy victims.

Justice for the Victim

Historically, justice has been done to victims of crimes in many different ways. To a large extent, the response of the society to its crime victims relates to the socio-cultural matrix of that society. In a small primitive society like that of the Eskimo, whose population was divided into kinship groups to increase mobility for food gathering and hunting, strong centralized political institutions never developed. Disputes between members of kinship groups were considered private wrongs. The aggrieved or his kin often felt obligated to take revenge on the offender or on one of his kin appointed for that purpose. Murder demanded murder in retaliation.[6] Such settlements created a balance between the parties in the dispute.

As societies grew in complexity, centralized political institutions started evolving. Through their legal organizations, these political institutions began to undermine this private settlement of disputes that led to disturbances to public order. Private wrongs came to be regarded as public wrongs, and private laws were gradually replaced by public laws. An offense committed by one person against another became an offense, a crime, against the public. The prevailing legal conception of an offense as a crime against the state does not conflict with the idea of an offense against the public, because the state is interpreted to embody the public.

In this development of the concept of crime, the victim has been almost forgotten. The offender became the center of attention for legal and social condemnation. As a consequence, the victim often received no assistance within the criminal justice system.[7] Perhaps this neglect stems from the belief that the victim's greatest need is viewing the punishment of his or her assailant.

Apart from the criminal justice system, there has been another way for crime victims to receive economic compensation. After the criminal conviction of the offender, the victim can file a civil suit to claim economic losses incurred because of victimization. Victims rarely use this method, especially victims of violent offenses, because the offenders are usually poor and have little opportunity in prison to earn money for restitution payments.

This victim neglect in the American criminal justice system has lately been increasingly recognized. The pioneering victim compensation programs in England and New Zealand, coupled with the growing sympathy in this country for crime victims, have led to the development of several programs in the United States. Many states have initiated victim compensation programs following the establishment of a California program in 1965.[8] There is now a growing trend to support a state role in compensating crime victims on a regular basis, rather than relying on victim restitution by offenders and economic compensation to "good samaritans."

Many of the victim compensation programs in America are forwarded on the sympathy felt for victims. But such a basis does not use the knowledge available from the fields of criminology, victimology, and other social and behavioral sciences that can help develop victim compensation programs on a sound, rational basis. Justice to victims involves remedying their economic losses. In doing this, the identification of causative agents must precede the assignment of liability. The causative agents can be identified only in an abstract manner: the offender, the victim, and the society-government structures. These three elements share the responsibility for crime and victimization and should therefore divide the responsibility for compensating victims.

Causative Agents and Their Responsibilites

In this section, the degrees of responsibility of the causative agents will be established by articulating the levels of their liability to crime and victimization. Once the degrees of responsibility are determined, these agents can be made to contribute toward the economic compensation of victims in specific terms. In other words, once the causative agents assume varying degrees of responsibility for the crime and victimization, we can distribute fair financial liabilities to them for their contribution to the victim compensation fund.

The poor, then, should be given preferential treatment in economic compensation for victimization, just as they deserve help in other areas of their lives. The poor help to sustain the economy through their labor, so the economically comfortable section of society has an obligation to insure through its government economic justice to needy victims.

Offender Responsibility

The classical theorists assume that all persons have the inherent capacity to distinguish right from wrong and that, if some choose to commit crimes, they do so in a calculated manner.[9] Some hold this view to put the total burden of causative responsibility for the crime on the offender and to justify his restitution to his victim.

Even though this argument makes some sense, it lacks substance in terms of theoretical developments in the behavioral and social sciences. In these fields, the origin of criminal behavior is often explained in terms of social environment. The "anomie" theory of Merton, for instance, views criminal behavior as arising out of the interplay of a major stress on economic attainments and a minor stress on the norms that govern achievement. This should be understood in the context of socially structured barriers that restrict many from developing the skills and abilities necessary to achieve economic success through normal means.[10] The subcultural theorists on crime emphasize that some subcultures contain values, motivations, and incentives for their members to engage in criminal behavior. In his theory of the subculture of violence, Wolfgang sees the origin of violent behavior among individuals as an integration of the subcultural values that support and encourage violence.[11] Such subcultures arise out of the responses of individuals to the frustrating economic conditions of lower class living. Sutherland notes that criminal behavior is learned and that individuals develop this knowledge through their contact with criminal groups that possess values, knowledge, and skills related to criminal behavior. Demands to conform have little effect on such individuals, since their bonds to criminal groups are stronger than those to conventional society. In the conflict perspective on crime, the economic arrangement of society produces crimes and criminals. Because of their political power the rich can create laws to exploit the laborers. Crimes in the lower class serve as symptoms of a potential class war, while crimes among the monied more often reflect simple greed.[12]

The unavoidable implication of these theoretical perspectives is that we are all "norm-free" at birth. We later become either criminals or conformers wholly because of our particular social environment. The criminal, then, is a product of his social circumstances just as much as the conformer.

Therefore, offenders do not bear the full responsibility for their crimes, although they are not guiltless. No offender has a total inclination to commit crimes at all times, since he is a product of a social setting that encourages conformist as well as criminal behavior. The criminal knows the difference between wrong and right, but his knowledge of the right is not enough to keep him from criminal activity. Further, the offender as a citizen is a part of society and shares the responsibility with other members of the society for the crime rate. Of all the causative agents, the offender remains the most visible. Yet the offender is only a secondary causative agent, because his crime is a reaction to the primary cause: the maladies of social structure. For these reasons and for the purpose of identifying the character he must develop to abstain from committing crimes, a partial responsibility for victimizatoin should be assigned to the offender. Hence, the offender should be expected to pay toward the economic compensation of his vicitm.

Economic restitution by offenders works only if the offenders have the necessary economic means. Very few offenders are wealthy, and only these offenders can pay substantial compensation to their victims. Because most offenders are poor and lack adequate skills and opportunities to earn money, offender restitution presents a problem. Because society imprisons those who violate the law, they have no opportunity to work to compensate their victims. Prison industries are archaic and inmate wages cannot support the inmate's family, much less meet the needs of his victim.

Unless the prisons create opportunities for vocational training, offender restitution will remain impossible. Those offenders who are on probation, work-release, or parole can contribute to the compensation of their victims. These offenders have greater economic opportunity than those in prison. Although poor offenders, whether they work in prison industries or participate in other work programs, may not be expected to compensate their victims fully, a nominal amount of money can be fixed for such offenders based on their realistic abilities to work and the actual opportunities available for them to work. Offender restitution in this limited sense can function as a part of the offender rehabilitation program. Offenders who have the desire, the ability, and the oportunity to participate in the offender restitution program can receive such incentives as probation, reduced terms and early parole.

Victim Responsibility

Some may hold that the victim brings about his own victimization and should therefore bear the burden of meeting expenses incurred due to violent offenses. Two arguments bear on this point. First, victims often cannot avoid victimization by their offender. For example, persons walking in the city streets during the late hours of the night may become victims of mugging or rape. A victim may deserve blame because of a negligent attitude toward crime. Second, studies of victim-precipitated offenses reveal that victims could be just as active as their assailants in the encounters preceding the crime itself. In summarizing victim-precipitated homicide studies Sessar notes: Wolfgang reported that 65% of the homicides were victim-precipitated, the Baltimore Criminal Justice Commission reported 45%, Roesner 46%, Bluhn 52%, and Krause 67%.[13] These two contentions, ignorance or negligence and victim-precipitation, should be properly appraised.

Just as offenders cannot be held totally responsible for their crimes, so victims cannot be held totally responsible for their victimization. They often come from the same environment as their assailants, and both usually participate in the subculture of violence. Each has the potential to assume the other's role. Many victims lack the necessary knowledge and discipline to avoid victimization, and they frequently provoke their assailants into the commission of crimes. The social structure which created the subculture of violence assumes most of the blame for this. Yet a partial responsibility can be relegated to those victims who have failed to develop the knowledge necessary to avoid victimization. In a general sense, these victims have directly or indirectly contributed to the crime rate of the society for which they share some responsibility. By failing to avoid potential victimization by not walking on the city streets during the late hours of the night, for example, victims share a partial responsibility. Those victims who have aggravated their assailants can also be held partly responsible for their own victimization. Victims who have brought crimes upon themselves should receive less compensation than ignorant or negligent victims, because they have contributed directly to their victimization. They will then realize that they had a part to play in their own victimization. Such an awareness can reduce both victim recidivism and crime rates.

Other types of victims include good samaritans, innocent bystanders, law enforcement personnel, and those involved in situations where crimes rarely occur. These victims should not be held liable for their victimization, and, if they are needy, they should receive maximum compensation. Similarly, juveniles, the aged, the physically handicapped, the mentally retarded, and the mentally ill who become victims of violent crimes should not be held responsible for their victimization, since they lack the necessary mental or physical abilities to protect themselves. Victims in these categories should also receive the maximum compensation if they prove to be needy victims.

Responsibility of the Government

Beyond the responsibility-controversy centering on the offender and the victim, the federal, state, and local governments can also be blamed for their inability to control crime. The government has contracted with the individual to protect him against aggressors so that he will not have to do so himself. In return, he allows the government to take actions on his behalf. Under the constitutions, the governments must protect and enhance the freedom of the people. In spite of increasing crime control funds allotted to the criminal justice systems, the crime rates have continued to climb. The governmental failure to enhance the personal safety of the citizens by reducing crime is emphasized by holding the governments responsible for compensating crime victims.

Responsibility of Society

Some may relate the responsibility for compensating crime victims to the larger society, since that society is founded on the principles of individual freedom with checks to control the powers of governments. Therefore, governments function only within the limits allowed by the people. The people who do not give full power to governments to regulate their lives for the prevention of crime should assume a responsibility for compensating the victims of crime.

Beyond the fact that society limits the power of government to control crime and victimization, several criminological theories view society as a generator of crime. In the structural and functional explanations of crimes the society which stresses individualism, economic attainments, and pleasure-seeking, without placing limits on their achievement, without providing adequate opportunities for their realization, and without developing among its individuals approved means of realizing these goals, forces some of its members to resort to violence in trying for such goals. This approach views crimes as developing from the social ills which can be solved by governmental leadership with little serious change in the social structure. In the conflict perspective, crimes among the poor are considered as resulting from the economic exploitation of the poor by the monied sections of society. Crimes will continue to exist in this structure unless a revolution brings forth an equal distribution of incomes throughout the society. Nevertheless, in both the structural-functional approach and conflict approach, the society and the government are held responsible as the primary agents of crimes. Since the society and government appear as significant contributors to crime, and victimization, they should likewise be responsible for victim compensation.

Combined Responsibility of the Society-Government Structure

The responsibilities of society and government in the compensation of crime victims are intertwined. The government is an administrative institution of society that exists on financial and social support provided by the society. Even though the agents of government can be blamed for their ignorance of and apathy toward the control of crime, the government can compensate victims only through public funds. Further, government's success or failure in controlling crime, like its success or failure in other aspects of life, depends upon the people. Because of their ignorance, their indifference toward controlling crime, and their part in limiting the powers of government, these people simply cannot control crime. As a result, they have problems in directing the government to the control of crime. Since each has failed in its responsibilities for crime control, both government and society have a responsibility for aiding crime victims.

Degrees of Responsibility and Victim Compensation

So far, the responsibility of victim, offender, and the society-government structure for crime and victimization have each been considered separately. Each of the three agents shares the task of helping the victim of crime.

Related to this shared responsibility is the concept of degrees of responsibility. This concept focuses on the levels of responsibility of victim, offender, and society-government structure in the generation of crime and victimization, and on their particular roles in the economic compensation of victims. It appears that the society-government structure has the crime and victimization rates that it deserves. The offenders and their victims are products and symptoms of the social structure's anomalies. Because crime and victimization rates continue to rise, the failure of the society- government structure to perform its function lies evident. For this, the society through its government should take the primary responsibility and, consequently, aid the victims of crimes. Even though the government, as distinct from society, can be considered a causative agent of crime and victimization, the practical compensation of victims falls on the society, since the government has only the society's money to appropriate.

Next in order of responsibility come the offenders and their victims. Their role is largely a response to the maladies of the society-government structure, and they therefore have reduced liability for crime and victimization, and are consequently less responsible for compensating victims. For becoming involved in the crime because of inadequate knowledge and controls, both offenders and victims must bear partial responsibility for the causation of crime and victimization and should assist in economic help to the victim.

Since, especially in violent offenses, the law allows no victim without a criminal, the criminal as the aggressor bears greater responsibility for the crime than his victim, the aggrieved. Although the offender bears a level of responsibility just beneath that of the society-government structure, he rarely has the ability to compensate his victim because he normally comes from a low economic group. He can nevertheless be encouraged to pay a small amount of money to his victim as part of a rehabilitation program.

The victim bears the least responsibility for the crime. He may have become the victim by virtue of either ignorance or provocation, in which case, a portion of his compensation should be withheld. If his actions directly precipitated the crime, a greater amount of money should be withheld. These measures seem both to create a sense of responsibility for the crime, and to encourage a cautious attitude for the future.

Character Building for Crime Prevention

Victim compensation programs, aside from aiding needy vicitms, can be geared toward crime prevention. Character building involves the development of a collective consciousness among the causative agents for the prevention of crime. Focusing on the concept of distributive justice, divided responsibility and degrees of responsibility, the victim, the offender, the government, and the society can be motivated to develop the character that is essential for reduction of victimization. Building this character can be related to three main concerns. First, the causative agents should realize that they generate crime and victimization. Second, they should understand their responsibilities for compensating the victims of violent offenses. Third, they should engage in crime prevention activities to reduce crime and ultimately to lower the taxes paid to the government for crime control and the compensation of victims.

These ideas can be implemented by developing effective administrative systems. A three-tier administrative system is suggested, including federal, state, and county level administrative units. A federal victim compensation bureau should be instituted to develop uniform standards for compensating victims of crimes throughout the country, to engage in research on victim compensation issues, and to coordinate the state victim compensation bureaus. Further, it should also collect compensation payments from inmates in federal prisons and distribute the money collected to the victims' home state bureaus. This federal bureau should also monitor the transfer of money from the state where the offender is a resident to the state where the victim resides.

The state victim compensation bureau should cooperate with the federal bureau in the development and implementation of uniform standards for the compensation of victims of violent offenses. This state bureau should develop and maintain financial resources for compensating victims and meeting its own administrative costs. There are several ways in which the financial resources can be developed. The state governments can, for example, appropriate tax money for victim compensation and allot this money to the state victim compensation bureau. County taxation would depend on the offender based victim compensation needs. A state should determine the victim compensation tax for each county based on situations where: 1) victim and offender are in county; 2) offender is in county, victim is in another county; and, 3) offender is in county, victim is in another state. The burden of compensating a victim falls on the offender's home county. The state tax for each county in a current year can be determined by pro-rating victim compensation needs experienced in the preceding year.

Apart from this tax-based resource, a state victim compensation bureau can also receive money from bureaus of other states (through the federal victim compensation bureau) in situations where the victims and offenders come from different states. Offenders in federal prisons or in other federal correctional placement can also be encouraged to pay toward compensation of victims. Such money can be collected by the federal victim compensation bureau and distributed to the state offices of the victims. Offenders in state prisons, jails, or other correctional placements can be motivated to contribute toward compensation of their victims. These contributions can be collected by the state office to form a part of the monies distributable to the victims wherever they may reside. It should be recognized that offenders in prison, at either the federal or state level, are usually poor and may not have the opportunity to earn money. It is urged however that offenders be given the chance to work and be motivated to contribute toward the compensation of their victims. Even small contributions from the offenders can have a significant rehabilitative impact.

At the county level, there should be a staff attached to the county court with the responsibility of working with the county judge in all matters involving victim determination and claims issues. Victim compensation claims received should be forwarded to the state victim compensation bureau for review and award determination. In addition, a community organization worker attached to the county welfare department should be responsible for awakening public interest to crime and victimization prevention activities. To achieve this goal, he or she should create cooperation among the public, the agents of county governmental units, the leaders of the communities in developing programs and resources.

By state taxation of counties for victim compensation, offender contributions, withholdings from victim compensation amounts, and community organization efforts, a collective consciousness among people in counties and local communities can be effected for the prevention of crime and victimization. Communities and counties in a state can be encouraged to compete with each other in the crime reduction. People in locales where crime and victimization rates have declined will have the additional incentive of lower taxes. Crime and victimization prevention efforts carried out at the federal and state levels without vigorous involvement of people at the county and local community levels have been failures. Hence the county-centered and community-centered crime and victimization prevention efforts and programs can be successful for they would be at manageable levels for people to increase their involvement in such activities and at the same time see the fruits of their efforts.

Summary of Recommendations

Based upon the preceding discussion, the following recommendations for the development of victim compensation programs are made:

1. Victims of crimes who are poor should receive compensation. The poor are those whose annual incomes are adequate only to cover the basic necessities of life. Based on this consideration a poverty level for individual income and family income can be determined.

2. The compensation of crime victims should be made monetarily.

3. Compensation should be given to victims of violent offenses, but not to victims of property offenses.

4. Since victim compensation programs are quite new, states should often publicize their victim compensation programs.

5. To be eligible for compensation, victims must report their victimization to their local police within 24 hours.

6. The police should inform the victims of violent offenses about the existence of victim compensation programs.

7. If the victim wants to claim victim compensation, a form obtainable from local police departments must be completed. The police will transfer the form to the county victim compensation office, which, in cooperation with state bureau of victim compensation, will make the decision regarding eligibility and the amount of compensation.

8. The amount of compensation should depend on the needs of the victims caused by the crime: medical expenses, psychiatric expenses, and wages lost. If the victim is physically impaired or handicapped and cannot work for one year or more, he should be given the maximum compensation allowed, with a small amount withheld if he precipitated the assault. The amount of compensation should not only include the crime-related expenses of the victim, but also the needs of his immediate family. If the victim needs economic assistance for more than a year because of a prolonged illness due to victimization, such costs can be met by public welfare and health institutions. The immediate family members of dead victims of crimes should receive full compensation if they were dependents of the victim and are needy.

9. The minimum and maximum amount of compensation should be set. The minimum compensation which can be claimed should be $100. The maximum amount of money that should be given for persons who are physically and/or mentally impaired for a year or more should be enough to cover hospitalization expenses and wages lost due to victimization.

10. In determining compensation for any victim, the financial resources of the individual should be determined. The victim who has full insurance coverage can claim economic compensation only if the insurance payments are not adequate. In this situation, the difference between the maximum amount claimable and the money received from insurance sources should be paid. Further precautions should be taken that the victims do not get undue assistance from various public sources.

11. Victims who need immediate economic assistance after their victimization should receive an immediate assurance of commitment for the payment of hospitalization-related expenses from the county judge or district attorney. This assurance can help to obtain immediate medical care in situations where victims have no health insurances. Adjustments from the victim compensation payments can be made later. If such victims are found to be ineligible for victim compensation, they should be required by court order to pay their own medical bills.

12. a) In cooperation with federal and local governments, the state should develop uniform standards for the appropriation of money and for the administration of victim compensation programs. b) The state should tax a county based on the victim compensation needs of victims in that county whose offenders are residents of the same county. c) If an offender is from a county other than that of his victim, the county of the offender within the state should be responsible for bearing the burden of paying toward the compensation of the victims in another county. The state bureau of victim compensation in cooperation with the county victim compensation office of the victim will determine the amount payable to the victim as compensation. d) Similarly, if an offender is from a different state than that of the victim, the state of the offender (in cooperation with its offender's county office) and the state of the victim (in cooperation with its victim's county office) determine the amount of victim compensation to be transferred from the offender's state to that of the victim's state. Such an arrangement can be of great value if people are made to realize that, since they are directly or indirectly responsible for producing the criminal, they will pay toward victim compensation. People can be motivated

through local community organization efforts and shown the tax benefits in reducing local crime.

13. Money should be collected from the offender in correctional placements to be routed to the state bureau of his victim. This money can be used to help pay victim compensation. Offender restitution of this limited nature should be integrated with offender rehabilitation programs.

14. Victims who have directly or indirectly precipitated their own victimization should receive less compensation than if they were guiltless. This will reinforce the idea that victimization under these situations can be avoided through controlled behavior.

15. Juveniles, the elderly, and physically handicapped or mentally impaired victims of crimes should receive full compensation payments if they are economically needy. This same principle holds true for those assaulted while attempting the process of saving others from victimization, or to save another victim, and those victimized in normally safe situations.

Discussion Questions

1. In the context of unequal distribution of wealth and incomes among victims, should all victims of crimes receive equal consideration in economic compensation?

2. Why should the society through its governmental units take the primary burden of compensating the poor victims of violent crimes?

3. Discuss ways by which victim compensation programs can be integrated with crime prevention programs.

4. Devise a procedure for the compensation of the victims of violent crimes whose offenders are not apprehended.

Notes

1. Frank Riessman, *The Culturally Deprived Child* (New York: Harper and Bros., 1962), p. 84.

2. William Ryan, *Blaming the Victim* (New York: Vintage Books, 1972), p. 56.

3. William J. Chambliss, ed., *Sociological Readings in the Conflict Perspective* (Reading, Mass.: Addison-Wesley Publishing Co., 1973), p. 4.

4. Marvin E. Wolfgang and Franco Ferracuti, *The Subculture of Violence* (London: Tavistock Publications, Ltd., 1967), p. 154.

5. Marvin E. Wolfgang, "Victim-Precipitated Criminal Homicide," in *Victimology*, eds. Israel Drapkin and Emilio Viano (Lexington, Mass.: Lexington Books, D.C. Heath and Company, 1974), pp. 83–86.

6. Adamson E. Hoebel, *Anthropology: The Study of Man*, 3rd ed. (New York: McGraw-Hill, 1958), p. 477.

7. William F. McDonald, "Criminal Justice and the Victim: An Introduction," in *Criminal Justice and the Victim*, ed. William F. McDonald (Beverly Hills, California: Sage Publications, 1976), p. 18.

8. Gilbert Geis, "Crime Victims and Victim Compensation Programs," in *Criminal Justice and the Victim*, ed. William F. McDonald (Beverly Hills, California: Sage Publications, 1976), p. 248.

9. Gilbert Geis, "Jeremy Bentham," in *Pioneers in Criminology*, ed. Hermann Mannheim (Montclair, New Jersey: Patterson Smith, 1973), p. 56.

10. Robert Merton, "Social Structure and Anomie," *American Sociological Review* 3 (1938): 672–682.

11. Wolfgang and Ferracuti, *op. cit.*, pp. 158–162.

12. Arnold Birenbaum and Edward Sagarin, *Norms and Human Behavior* (New York: Praeger Publishers, 1976), pp. 89–92.

13. Klaus Sessar, "The Familiar Character of Homicide," in *Victimology*, vol. 4, eds. Israel Drapkin and Emilio Viano (Lexington, Mass.: Lexington Books, D.C. Heath and Company, 1975), pp. 29–42.

7

Social Response to White Collar Crime

MICHAEL E. ENDRES

EDWIN S. SUTHERLAND'S PIONEERING FORMULATION of the concept of White-collar Crime ignited theoretical and practical issues whose embers can still be fanned by events and alerted public interest.[1] Indeed, from the late 1960's on, in the Viet Nam War period and its aftermath, the term White-collar Crime has entered into popular, albeit even less exact use. Events eddying about the war stimulated denunciations of the American "middle class" value system, renewed concern about racial and other social injustices and raised questions about society's service to the interests of what Senator Eugene McCarthy consistently scorned as the Military-Industrial Complex.

During the same era, war protesters rationalized their conflicts with the law as manifestations of conscience acted out against an oppressive state. Thus, they characterized their deviance as political, distinct from crime as traditionally perceived. Astute blacks like Eldridge Cleaver were not long in applying the same rationale to crimes committed by their brothers and ultimately the notion of the traditional criminal as a dispossessed victim of society and the criminal justice system emerged.

Still, the second Nixon Administration—the "Law and Order Administration"—probably did more than anything else to sensitize the general public to White-collar Crime. Initially, there were the many allegations made against Vice President Agnew in the conduct of his office as Governor of Maryland, and his subsequent pleading of no contest to a single income tax charge. There were also his subsequent fine and three years probation and his resignation from office. The Agnew affair was, however, only a prelude to the series of extraordinary revelations that comprised the Watergate scandal. In turn, Watergate was followed by a series of allegations and admissions about the unethical and often illegal conduct of American businessmen and goverment officials with governments and private interests abroad. Meanwhile, the public was outraged by the suspicion of the misuse of public funds in the Hays' case and other alleged sex scandals, and in an unusual departure from policy, on June 2, 1976, the House Ethics Committee voted 11−0 to investigate such charges even though a Justice Department probe was already in progress.[2] These events appear to have rekindled interest in White-collar Crime and it has been increasingly treated in government and business publications and by the daily press and broadcast media.

White-collar Crime is a complex phenomenon, conceived of in a diversity of definitions, typologies, and causal theories. It is also submitted to a variety of value judgments about how society ought to react to it. Some of these issues are of greater theoretic import; some are more pragmatic in nature. They are generally too involved to be considered in common here. Instead, the central problem addressed is that of how the legislature and the criminal justice system ought to respond to White-collar Crime.

The Law, Crime and Justice

The sociologist conceives of the law as developmental and relative to time and place. The sociology of the law is perhaps best keynoted by paraphrasing Holmes' assertion that the life of the law has not been logic but experience.[3] Holmes militates against an absolute interpretation when he writes that the prevailing political philosophy and institutions and even the prejudices of the day have more to do with the law than any syllogism.

In the *Folkways*,[4] William G. Sumner spells out in more detail the organic view of the law's development. Sumner classifies social norms or rules as: (1) folkways; simple, customary practices arising directly out of life's experiences, (2) mores; folkways which acquire an especial significance for society's well-being and (3) laws; which evolve out of folkways and mores through a process of institutionalization and rationalization. The institutionalization of norms refers to a process of making them enduring and of developing specialized structures to effect them (legislatures, law enforcement agencies, courts, etc.). Rationalization refers to a parallel process in which the norm is cognized as a means to some end which has been identified. For example, when moral rules forbidding sexual relations between near relatives are consciously linked to consideration of biological health or to domestic tranquility rather than being justified on traditional grounds alone, the incest taboo emerges as law.

In one sense then, the law is always a matter of morality. That is, the law incorporates the mores which express the prevailing notions of goodness and rightness in a society.[5] In a more general sense, the law expresses the predominant cultural patterns in a society, the complexion of its institutions and its priority of values.[6]

The purported purpose of the criminal law is the protection of the community's well-being. The working distinction between the criminal law with its emphasis on publicly imposed penalties and the civil law and its provision for private redress is consistent with the public interestedness of the criminal law.[7]

The specifics of the criminal law are not only determined by cultural patterns and morality, however. They are also markedly influenced by the distribution of power in society. Quinney[8] and Turk,[9] among others, have strongly assailed the view that the criminal law transcends individuals and group interests and is arrived at as a matter of consensus in an American society characterized by a stable homogeneous value system. Instead, they perceive of American society as pluralistic, characterized by value change and value conflict. They see criminal laws as expressing the values and protecting the interests of those who have power. In their view, the law changes not in automatic response to changing conditions and needs, but in response to the changing interest group structure of society. In other words, the law changes as various groups gain or lose power.

Some traditional crime categories such as homicide, rape, etc. do no doubt transcend particular interests and value differences. Others, such as the movement toward decriminalizing marijuana use, may be representative of a consensus emergent out of inter-group conflict. There is also evidence, however, that the law reflects interests of predominant groups particularly in regard to crimes against property. The preoccupation of the American society with material values, the work ethic and the success drive,[10] leads to a kind of ambivalence with respect to the way in which property rights are perceived. On the one hand, violations of property in a traditionally criminal way, (burglarly, larceny, etc.), are severely condemned and strenuously sanctioned. On the other hand, some questionable commercial processes by which vested interests acquire property and other abuses of power are rationalized as "sharp business practices" or as "politics," etc.[11]

The implications of the foregoing for White-collar Crime and its handling will be elaborated on below. For the present, there is one more dimension of the socio-legal context to be considered; namely, the relationship of justice to the law and the defining of crime. The essential problem here is that while the law is derived from and varies with experience, justice is a transcendent value—an ideal. In other words, the law *is;* justice is concerned with the *fairness* of what is and thus with what *ought to be.* The degree to which the law fails to ensure justice has been recently described by Forer.[12] While this disparity between the law and justice has not apparently been resolved in criminology, it can hardly be ignored in questions of policy and will have to be grappled with here eventually.

It may be noted for the present, that the criminal law has increasingly sought to actuate the due process dimension of justice. The judicial review process has established broadened rights of the accused, and the widespread concern about sentencing and about the rights of the convicted (emphasized, e.g., by the "justice model" in corrections[13]) illustrate the degree to which the law has become absorbed in procedural questions. On the other hand, as implied above, the law has not exhibited an equal concern with the substance of justice.

Definitions of White-collar Crime

There is wide variation in the scope and emphasis of definitions of White-collar Crime. Sutherland's own definition of it as ". . . crime committed by a person of respectability and high status in the course of his occupation,"[14] has frequently been criticized as being unduly restrictive. At the same time, it has often been suggested that Sutherland's definition and the theory and research from which it was derived, imparted a particular class bias to the concept.[15] It limited involvement to those with middle and upper class status and to those with business or professional occupations.

Hartung[16] and Newman[17] take a similar view of the matter, emphasizing the business-connectedness of White-collar Crime. Newman appears to emphasize the role of complex, modern social and economic organization in its incidence. He asserts that it *is* the deviator's occupational role that is after all the critical and only global factor in White-collar Crime. He explains that most of the laws violated are not part of the traditional code because White-collar legislation regulates business, professional activity and administrative procedure.

One of the most recent and more descriptive definitions is contained in *A Handbook on White-collar Crime* prepared under the auspices of the Chamber of Commerce of the United States. Relying heavily on Edelhertz's[18] lengthy restatement of the problem, White-collar Crime is defined as:

> . . . illegal acts characterized by guile, deceit and concealment—and are not dependent upon the application of physical force or violence or the threats thereof. They may be committed by individuals acting independently or by those who are part of a well-planned conspiracy. The objective may be to obtain money, property or services; to avoid the payment or loss of money, property or services; or to secure business or personal advantage.[19]

The *Handbook* argues that the superiority of this definition inheres in that it focuses ". . . on the nature of the violation, rather than on the nature of the violator. . . ."[20] In other words, it removes the class bias or the tendency to isolate White-collar Crime in the executive suite. The *Handbook* also favors the broader definition because ". . . by describing White-collar Crime as 'illegal acts,' this definition avoids the implication that only criminal proceedings and sanctions should be directed at such offenses. As noted later, civil proceedings and remedies can be equally, if not more effective."[21]

In the first case, the universalization of White-collar Crime to include offenders of whatever social status or occupation would appear to be more consistent and logical. Although the *Handbook*'s definition does not mention it explicitly, Sutherland and others noted a quality that hangs about the fringes of the very rationale for singling out and distinguishing the White-collar variety from *crime* in general. That is, the White-collar Crime is not perceived by the violator or the society in the same way as is traditional crime. The distinction may in part originate in and be reinforced by the social statuses and occupations of some White-collar offenders but as shall be discussed at length later, it does not entirely originate or reside there. From this perspective, it is then entirely true as exemplified in the *Handbook,* that blue collar workers may pilfer as well as vice-presidents embezzle. Another advantage of the *Handbook*'s definition is that is is malleable enough to permit the inclusion of such non-business related activities as credit card and income tax fraud or abuses of power. It would then appear to present a substantial improvement over narrow business-related definitions.

On the other hand, the *Handbook*'s endorsement of its own definition of White-collar Crime as "illegal acts" permitting of civil proceedings and remedies is subject to serious qualification. Without quibbling with the wording of the definition itself, the interpretation of its meaning conveys a looseness of logic as well as an ideological conviction that is open to question.

In the first place, to refer to such white collar activities as *criminal* and then to suggest that they are *only illegal* acts and ought not to evoke criminal proceedings and sanctions is to muddle the concept of crime, at least as it has been traditionally understood. Moreover, the *Handbook*'s interpretation of this phrase is issue oriented. It goes to the heart of this article, namely the question of how society ought to respond to such offenses.

Many would disagree with the contention that "civil proceedings and remedies" can be equally if not more effective in controlling White-collar Crime than criminal law deterrrents. It is frequently argued in the criminal justice literature that criminal law sanctions would, if consistently applied, have more deterrent effect on most White-collar criminals than on most traditional criminals. The rationale generally given is that deterrence is workable with individuals who have higher social status and prestigious, economically rewarding occupations and thus, who have much to risk and lose by criminal stigmatization and punishment.[22] The obvious failure of criminal law sanctions to deter many street criminals is, in like manner, explained by their having no "piece of society's action" to lose through apprehension and conviction.

The *Handbook*'s interpretation of this aspect of its definition appears to evidence an ambivalence toward White-collar Crime that is typical of commercial and professional interest groups. The *Handbook* appears to make the value judgment (in the face of its own recognition that the financial and other effects of White-collar crime dwarf those of traditional property crime)[23] that nevertheless, White-collar criminals are different from street criminals and ought to be handled differently. The degree to which this conclusion is arguable is considered below.

Social Response to White-Collar Crime

The preceeding discussion of certain elements of the U.S. Chamber's position on White-collar Crime as specified in its *Handbook,* illustrates the degree to which any response made by society is likely to be controversial. The issue is complex enough when considered in terms of White-collar Crime alone. It has recently been further complicated by the agonizing reassessment of the efficacy of correctional treatment and by all of the shadings among various policy alternatives urged by officials within the cirminal justice establishment as well as by its critics.[24]

Thus, a number of sharply conflicting "solutions" to the correctional dilemma have been offered. On the one hand, there are those who suggest that the institutional system ought to be constricted if not dismantled entirely in favor of a fuller range of community alternatives, as well as, the broader use of fines and restitution. On the other, there are those in the "nothing works" school who variously emphasize "justice," mandatory sentences (on a time-offense or some other basis), or smetimes insist upon incarceration as punishment and not rehabiliation and probation (and parole where retained) as surveillance, rather than assistance.

This ferment in regard to the criminal justice system's handling of its clientele which is heavily biased toward lower socio-economic class traditional criminals is nevertheless relevant to policy questions regarding White-collar criminals. While there are some unique aspects to White-collar Crime, it is still requisite that the treatment of non-traditional criminals have some reference to the general approach taken by the justice system. At the minimum, fundamental conditions of equity, and the avowed purposes of the system would seem to dictate that one should not be considered independent of the other.

Historically, something else has been the case. White-collar Crime has often been handled civilly rather than criminally. "Victims" have declined prosecution. Civil remedies have been applied rather than criminal penalties exacted[25] and even in cases disposed of under criminal sanctions, the penalties assessed White-collar criminals were frequently minimal. So little has the criminal justice system been oriented to this kind of crime, that it has been virtually impossible to aggregate data on White-collar offenses through conventional or official sources. (For example, the FBI's annual Uniform Crime Reports include data on only a very few White-collar offenses, notably embezzlement.)

In its context, (considered below), this mode of response to White-collar Crime is not difficult to understand. At the same time, the increasing concern about its prevalence and growing scruples about unequal justice have led some to conclude that White-collar Crime should be reacted to commensurate to the social damage inflicted. It is suggested, in other words, that such offenses should be vigorously prosecuted, and that criminal sanctions with attendant criminal stigmatization should be imposed. In short, what is suggested is that White-collar Crime be "criminalized" and responded to in parity with the usual response of the system to non-violent property crimes committed by traditional criminals. Before attempting to generalize about the merits of this position, it is necessary to consider the major arguments in favor of this approach, as well as those factors which militate against stronger sanctions.

For A More Vigorous Response

The arguments for criminalizing White-collar Crime may be reduced to these: (1) that it does great financial and moral damage to the Commonweal; (2) that the failure to respond with vigor maintains a dual standard of justice and inequality before the law. A third argument—that such crime is relatively deterable has already been discussed briefly above and will not be reconsidered at this point.

The conviction that punishment ought to be meted out in relation to the gravity of the offense has led some to argue that White-collar Crime ought to be stringently sanctioned.

The virtual absence of official recording of these offenses, and the cross-cutting of categories entailed in more global descriptions such as "crimes against business," which also include traditional offenses, limit the analyses of the cost of White Collar crimes. Whatever the criteria used, however, estimates generally yield the inference that such costs are considerably greater than the aggregate costs of street crime.

The U.S. Chamber of Commerce aggregates the calculable costs of White-collar Crime within business, industry and the professions (i.e., excluding government and organized labor) at no less than $40 billion per year.[26] This figure, which the *Handbook* judges to be enormous, does not include the costs of price fixing illegalities and industrial espionage which are considered to be incalculable.

An inference as to the possible costs of price fixing may be drawn from the celebrated electrical industry case. Here, a conspiracy to fix prices, rig bids and divide markets affected goods approximating $1,750,000,000 in value annually, ". . . on everything from $2 insulators to multi-million dollar turbine generators. . . ." for as long as eight years.[27]

A recent U.S. News and World Report study reveals that White-collar Crime is on the increase. Such offenses have increased by thirty-five percent during the past five years, while business losses have increased by seventy-five percent.[28]

Other related economic costs of crime generally are those of law enforcement, prosecution and adjudication and corrections. If White-collar Crime were responded to with substantially more concern, the costs of running the criminal justice machinery would be greatly increased. This is especially the case, since as will be expanded on below, much of White-collar Crime is complex and requires a heavy in-put of highly specialized law enforcement, prosecutorial and judicial resources.[29]

The moral costs of White-collar Crime though less measurable than the financial are no less significant. There is a strong element of exploitation in such crimes. As Sutherland[30] and Edelhertz,[31] among others, have pointed out, White-collar Crime generally involves a stronger offender and weaker victims. The President's Commission on Law Enforcement and Administration of Justice[32] emphasizes the element of stealth involved in consumer fraud and other White-collar Crimes that make them difficult to detect and prosecute.

The wrong-doing of the community's privileged leaders is bound to have a serious impact on its values and standards. Thus, Sturdivant[33] is quoted as expressing regret that more students in his course in Business and Its Environment are not concerned about ethical issues in business and that a substantial number remain passive about the fraudulent behavior of their simulated corporation in a classroom management game. And in an extraordinary address to the American Chamber of Commerce in October, 1975, Fred T. Allen[34] Chariman and President of Pitney Bowes, expressed his concern about the state of business ethics.

Allen had previously commissioned a survey of businessmen's attitudes about certain aspects of corporate morality. He concluded that some attitudes were startling. Forty-eight percent of his respondents replied that foreign officials should be bribed where bribery was a local practice and sixty-eight percent of those who condoned bribery rationalized that it was a cost of doing business in certain countries. Thirty-eight percent of those condoning bribery considered it to be an established practice, (i.e., that there was not alternative).

Allen is not inclined to minimize the accountability of well-placed executives or to displace wrong-doing on either the impersonal corporation or its underlinings. Noting that business organizations usually reflect the character of their leader, he laments:

> I am sorry to say that nearly all revealed incidents concerning shady practices were authorized by topmost officers—*the kind of men we should have been able to look to not only for corporate leadership but also for national leadership.*[35] (Emphasis added.)

Allen is no advocate of a dual standard of justice, noting that when actual criminality is involved, companies should cooperate with law enforcement officers. "When a company fails to take strong action many employees may assume that unethical acts are accepted standards of corporate behavior."[36]

A final major reason for reassessing the present mode of dealing with White-collar Crime is that there is growing sensitivity to a dual standard of justice. Those events of the Viet Nam War and Watergate eras already alluded to and the "law and order" reaction engendered by social protest and rising crime indicators have pointed up the inconsistencies operating in every phase of criminal justice.

On the one hand, the righteous concern of the middle classes about street crime has stimulated legislatures, courts and parole boards to take an increasingly more punitive approach to offenders. Thus, in spite of the greater availability of community based alternatives, incarcerations have escalated, institutional stays have been prolonged and facilities have become dangerously overcrowded.

On the other hand, apparent increases in White-collar Crime have failed to stimulate any similar concern on the part of the legislature or the criminal justice system. It is not simply the superior financial resources of White-collar criminals — the ability to defend oneself against the apprehension and conviction process — that creates less vulnerability to criminalization. As Sutherland[37] notes, the relatively unorganized resentment of the public against White-collar Crime and the status of businessmen among other things also explains the double standard of justice. Moreover, as Clinard[38] explains, the common social and cultural bonds which legislators and judges share with many White-collar offenders makes them reluctant to make "criminals" of reputable businessmen.

While it may be unrealistic to anticipate the full realization of equality before the law, it is not unreasonable to suggest that the grossest violations of the principle are amenable to adjustment. The dual standard of justice is not only an affront to constitutionalism, it breeds disrespect for the law and provides a ready rationale for the belief that "it's only wrong if you get caught."

Factors Inhibiting Heightened Response

Those factors that in the past militated against a stringent response to White-collar Crime are likely to continue to do so. Prescinding from the social status and power of the bulk of White-collar offenders, vigorous response is inhibited by: (1) the lack of moral indignation toward White-collar Crime in the community; (2) the pragmatic consideration of additional costs of criminal justice attendant on substantially increased involvement of the system; and (3) at the adjudication level by the application of the normal criteria for disposition after conviction.

While there is evidence of aroused public concern about White-collar Criminality, there are a number of reasons why a high-level of adverse public opinion is not sustained. In the first instance, White-collar Crime is often highly complex. It is also victimless in the sense that its impact tends to diffuse over a multiplicity of victims who in general are indirectly or even tenuously connected to the offender. For example, the theft by computer of a fraction of a penny of interest (generally not accredited to the holder anyway) from millions of accounts, works no hardship on any individual whatever the gain to the thief. Consequently, the public is less likely to personalize White-collar offenses and so identify them as criminal as it does, for example, in the case of a car stolen from a city street or a house entered and burglarized in the absence of its owner.

Again, much of traditionally defined criminal behavior presents the possibility of harming the victim's person, even when not inherently violent. The purse snatcher may need to wrestle his victim for the prize, the burglar may be surprised by the return of the householder or the shoplifter may resist apprehension. White-collar offenders rarely pose a physical threat to victims since they are generally remote from one another.

Finally, the distinction in the public's attitude between traditional and White-collar Crime is also moored in American cultural patterns which tend to identify much of the latter with business entities, (e.g., the corporation), rather than with individuals. There is also a related tendency to diminish responsibility for such non-traditional crimes by relying on such rationalizations as "everybody does it," the "press of competition" or "sharp business practices." The open class system and its high social mobility potential also tend to weaken moral censure since such practices are seen as underlying "success" in life.

A second set of considerations militating against a rigorous response is that more legislation, enforcement, prosecution and conviction mean drastically increased costs of criminal justice. It is evident that despite extensive plea bargaining, the justice system is already overwhelmed by its caseload. Moreover, the complexity of much of White-collar Crime creates an especial burden. Detection and prosecution invariably require the services of accountants, engineers, research scientists or other specialists not ordinarily involved in preparing and trying criminal cases traditionally.

A last major impediment to creating an equitable approach to White-collar offenders derives from an unanticipated source, namely, the theory of probation itself. The usual criteria for opting for probation instead of incarceration are highly favorable to White-collar offenders. The nature and circumstances of the present offense and the offender's attitude towards it, previous offense history, employment history, the quality of family and community relationships, potential for employment and amenability to supervision and other similar criteria are those on which White-collar offenders are much more likely than traditional offenders to get high marks.

Summary and Conclusions

In the final analysis, crime is a matter of social perception; crime and the law which defines it are relative to time and place. Cultural patterning and the distribution of power have much to do with what is legislated and with how violations of the law are policed, adjudged and punished.

It is not redundant to observe that the law is the law (and not necessarily just). There is some evidence, however, of a change in public perception. On every side, we hear calls for a repudiation of situation ethics, and for high school, college and professional school courses in ethics. Even businessmen and business organizations are becoming concerned about the state of business affairs.[39]

There is also some evidence of a growing tendency for law enforcement and prosecutorial agencies to focus on White-collar Crime. In 1973, the National District Attorney's Association, under a LEAA grant, began to focus on the area. By the end of 1976, NDAA was partially supporting such programs in 15 jurisdictions.[40] Again, the FBI reported a 7.6% increase in convictions for White-collar Crimes in the first 11 months of 1975, over the same period in 1974.[41]

Independent of how the public feels about White-collar Crime, there are compelling reasons why it must be vigorously confronted. The criminal law purports to protect the well-being of the community, and the principle of proportional punishment is reasonable as well as back in vogue. White-collar Crime is gravely damaging financially to its victims, individually or collectively. It is at least as damaging to the morale of the community. Widespread, unsanctioned deviation among "respectable" members of the community creates distrust and disrespect for the law. The perversion of justice inherent in the dual standard widens the divisions between classes, poisons their relationships and casts the criminal justice system in an apparent one-sided role as the guardian of vested interest.

It might then be logical to insist that society ought to aggressively pursue the White-collar criminal. On the other hand, at the very least, a balanced assessment of the prevalence and gravity of White-collar Crime ought to incline us to respond to *traditional nonviolent property* crime with less vindictiveness. Independent of the efficacy of community based alternatives to the prolonged incarceration of such offenders, justice along would appear to demand their more frequent use.

Discussion Questions

1. Discuss the relationships and distinctions between noneconomic crimes of public officials (e.g., abuses of power such as wiretapping) and the generality of White Collar Crime.

2. Arrive at a functional, realistic definition of crime and discuss behaviors not presently identified as criminal which meet the criteria established by your definition.

3. Discuss alternatives to incarceration for convicted White Collar offenders. In your discussion, consider issues related to both equity and workability.

4. Discuss the technological, sociological and cultural factors related to the prevalance of White Collar Crime in modern American society.

Notes

1. Edwin H. Sutherland, "White-Collar Criminality," *American Sociological Review,* 5 (1940): 1–12; "Crime and Business," *Annals of the American Academy of Political and Social Science,* 118 (1941): 112–118 and *White Collar Crime* (New York: Holt, Rinehart and Winston, 1941).

2. U.S. News and World Report, June 14, 1976, p. 20.

3. Oliver W. Holmes, *The Common Law,* ed. by Mark D. Howe, (Cambridge; Harvard U. Press, 1963).

4. William G. Sumner, *Folkways,* (Boston: Ginn and Company, 1906).

5. The question of priority in the relationship between morality and the law and the issue of legislating private morals could logically arise here. They are, however, somewhat tangential to the present topic and too complex for the present context.

6. For example, in a dynamic society like the American, rational social control (the law) supplants traditional or customary control and thus in one sense criminalizes. Or, a developed division of labor and open class system accentuate materialism, the drive to material success and a hyper-concern about property in the criminal law.

7. As Edwin H. Sutherland and Donald R. Cressey caution, however, the conventional distinction between a crime and a tort is not always clear. For a discussion of the matter see, *Principles of Criminology,* 6th ed. (Chicago: J.B. Lippincott and Company, 1960) pp. 8–9.

8. Richard Quinney, *Crime and Justice in Society,* (Boston: Little, Brown and Company, 1969), and *The Social Reality of Crime,* (Boston: Little, Brown and Company, 1970).

9. Austin T. Turk, "Conflict and Criminality," *American Sociological Review,* 31 (1966): 338–352.

10. See Robert K. Merton, *Social Theory and Social Structure,* rev. ed. (Glencoe, Ill: Free Press, 1957), Chaps. 4–5, and Richard A. Cloward and Lloyd E. Ohlen, *Delinquency and Opportunity,* (New York: The Free Press, 1960).

11. For discrepancies between the practices of sentencing those convicted of White-collar and traditional crimes, see Herbert S. Miller, "Respectability Helps If You're a Crook," The Washington Post, July 7, 1974, pp. B1–B3.

12. Lois G. Forer, *The Death of the Law,* (New York: David McKay Company, Inc., 1975).

13. See David Fogel, *We Are the Living Proof: The Justice Model for Corrections,* (Cincinnati: The W.H. Anderson Company, 1975).

14. Sutherland, *White Collar Crime,* p. 9.

15. Gilbert Geis recounts Sutherland's moralistic outrage towards White-collar criminals despite his own often quoted disclaimer that his only interest in the matter was to reform criminology and not society. See "Associational Crime" in *Handbook of Criminology,* ed. by David Glaser (Chicago: Rand McNally, 1974) pp. 282–283.

16. Frank E. Hartung, "White collar Offenses in the Wholesale Meat Industry in Detroit," *American Journal of Sociology,* 55 (1950): 25–31.

17. Donald J. Newman, "White-collar Crime," *Law and Contemporary Problems,* 23 (1958): 735–573.

18. Herbert Edelhertz, *The Nature, Impact and Prosecution of White Collar Crime,* (Washington, D.C.: National Institute of Law Enforcement and Criminal Justice, Law Enforcement Assistance Administration, U.S. Department of Justice, 1970).

19. Chamber of Commerce of the United States, *A Handbook on White Collar Crime,* (Washington, D.C.: undated) p. 3.

20. *Ibid.* p. 3.

21. *Ibid.* p. 3.

22. For example, see Miller, "Respectability Helps If You're a Crook."

23. *A Handbook on White Collar Crime,* pp. 4–11.

24. The recent literature is full of the debate about the effectiveness of imprisonment, community alternatives and shifting directions in the Criminal Justice System. For example, see Forer, *The Death of the Law,* Norval Morriss, *The Future of Imprisonment,* (Chicago : U. of Chicago Press, 1974). Fogel, *We Are the Living Proof: The Justice Model in Corrections,* James Q. Wilson, *Thinking about Crime,* (New York: Vintage Books, 1977), and Douglas Lipton, Robert Martinson and Judith Wilks, *The Effectiveness of Correctional Treatment* (New York: Praeger Publishers, 1975). The positions of many of these and a number of other widely read writers in the field are capsulized in the March, 1976 issue of *Corrections Magazine.*

25. The conspiracy in the electrical industry tried in 1960 affords a case in point. Although the non-financial penalities in that case were minimal, (7 top executives received 30 days in jail and 24 others received suspended sentences), the case was hailed as precedent-setting because the court imposed personal liability on corporation executives.

26. *Handbook on White-Collar Crime,* p. 5.

27. Richard Austin, "The Incredible Electric Conspiracy," *Delinquency, Crime and Social Process,* edited by Donald R. Cressey and Donald A. Ward (New York: Harper and Row, 1969), pp. 884–912. Some idea of the high costs of some other kinds of White-collar offenses not comprehended by the *Handbook*'s estimate can be gained from Marshall B. Clinard's *The Black Market: A Study of White Collar Crime* (New York: Rinehart and Company, (1952) and Hartung, "White Collar Offenses in the Wholesale Meat Industry in Detroit."

28. The U.S. News and World Report, February 21, 1977, pp. 47–48. This article also provides a number of interesting distributions of White-collar Crime costs to organizations, consumers, etc.

29. For example, computer crimes yield a particularly high pay-off per incident and are extremely difficult to detect and prosecute. See Donn B. Parker, *Computer Abuse* (Washington, D.C.: National Science Foundation, 1973).

30. Edwin H. Sutherland, "White Collar Criminality," in Donald R. Cressey and David A. Ward, *Delinquency and Social Process,* p. 357.

31. Edelhertz, *The Nature, Impact and Prosecution of White Collar Crime,* pp. 5–11.

32. President's Commission on Law Enforcement and Administration of Justice, "White-collar Crimes and the Criminal Process," Task Force Report: *Crime and Its Impact: An Assessment* (Washington: Government Printing Office, 1967) pp. 104–108.

33. The Cincinnati Post, October 1, 1975, p. 46.

34. The Cincinnati Post, October 27, 1975, p. 12.

35. *Ibid.*

36. *Ibid.*

37. Sutherland, *White Collar Crime,* p. 46.

38. Clinard, pp. 231–232.

39. The Cincinnati Post, (March 22, 1976, p. 12), reports that more than five months after his address to the American Chamber of Commerce (cited above), Fred T. Allen said that he had received 200 written responses and 3,000 requests for copies of his speech.

40. *Exemplary Projects: Prosecution of Economic Crime,* LEAA, U.S. Department of Justice (Washington: U.S. Printing Office, 1975).

41. *Crime Control Digest,* January 19, 1976, p. 6. Solid detection and prosecution are still no guarantee of suitable punishment for White-collar offenses. For example, in October, 1975, federal prosecutors gathered in U.S. District Court in Washington to protest a one year sentence of an investment counselor convicted of defrauding his clients of two million. See the *Crime Control Digest,* October 27, 1975, p. 9.

8

Gun Control

WAYNE W. DUNNING

THE CONTROL OF FIREARMS, particularly handguns, in the United States is a matter of considerable public debate. To a certain extent it is unfortunate that one must apply labels such as pro-gun or anti-gun to the subject. To those who see things only in terms of black or white, it might seem that the pro-gun faction suggests, endorses, or condones the idea that anyone should have the complete right to own or carry any sort of weapon at any time in any place. Excluding from any discussion those people who may not be certifiably sane, I seriously doubt that even the staunchest pro-gun person would support any such notion. On the other hand, the anti-gun people are often seen as desiring the complete abolition of all privately owned firearms— handguns in particular. Most regrettably, there are a number of serious, dedicated, outspoken and well financed persons and groups who do indeed have abolition as their goal.

Many people divide the opposing factions into political camps, suggesting that the pro-gun are conservatives, and the anti-gun are liberals. Indeed, the most outspoken anti-gun lawmakers are usually labeled as political liberals. While many of them suggest no penalties for non-victim crimes, they would like to make non-victim criminals out of firearms owners. This I find rather strange in view of some liberal politicians' own definition of liberalism:

Rep. Morris Udall: "One of the central themes is a passion for individual liberty. . . ."

Sen. Adlai Stevenson: "The liberal really . . . tries to protect the freedom of an individual from encroachment by the state and other forces beyond his control, with a minimum of government activity."

Sen. Hubert H. Humphrey: "Liberalism means freedom for the individual from forces of oppression.. . ."

I would suggest therefore, that the conservative/liberal concept has little, if any, applicability to the gun control question.

Lest there be any doubt, I would like to make it clear at this point that I am a member of the pro-gun faction. A number of other points should also be made clear. I have never urged that any citizen possess or carry any firearm, unless they wish to do so and their intentions are lawful. I do urge that anyone possessing or using firearms should know, or learn, how to use them safely, prudently, and lawfully. I do not oppose laws which do, or which would, make it more difficult or dangerous for criminals, drug addicts, alcoholics, mental defectives, etc., to own or use firearms. I do oppose laws whose likely or demonstrated effect is to make it more difficult or dangerous for honest citizens. Having laid that foundation, let us take a very brief look at a little history. Then we will consider some current regulations and their effects, and some proposed laws and their likely benefits or effects, costs, and dangers.

The cornerstone of the entire argument may well be the Second Amendment to the United States Constitution; hopefully, this is familiar to everyone reading this. Basically, the anti-gun argument seems to be that the amendment is out of date — that the National Guard functions for what was the Militia, and that there is therefore no reason nor guarantee for private possession of firearms. I suggest there are at least four flaws in that argument:

1) If this amendment is out of date and is interfering with our "solutions to the crime problem", why not also ignore or dispense with others, such as the fourth, fifth, and sixth. That should aid law enforcement considerably. I, for one, am nowhere near willing to pay the price that would be involved, and I suggest that the Bill of Rights, despite its age, is just as timely and as important as ever — perhaps more so.

2) To the framers of the amendment, the militia was "the whole people, except a few public officials".[1] As late as 1970, the United States Code provides that "The militia of the United States consists of all able-bodied males at least 17 years of age and except as provided in section 313 of title 32, under 45 years of age. . . ."[2] Other definitions by Congress and the Supreme Court over the past two centuries are consistent with the above.

3) The notion that the National Guard is the militia is completely counter to the will and advice of the Nation's Founding Fathers. "What, Sir, is the use of a militia? It is to prevent the establishment of a standing army, the bane of liberty."[3] The makeup and command structure of the National Guard completely neutralizes it as an effective final check against unjust government. Unjust government was one of the great fears of our Founders, and I suggest that history has shown their fears to be well founded.

4) Militia or not, organized or not, the amendment clearly goes on to say, ". . . the right of the people to keep and bear Arms, shall not be infringed."

Not the right of the militia or any other particular group—the right of the people!

There Ought To Be A Law

The substantial lack of public understanding about existing laws is a problem. Since 1934, such weapons as machine guns and sawed-off shotguns (I must admit I rather prefer the English expression: sawn-off) have been regulated and taxed by the National Firearms Act or a recent modification. Many, if not even a majority, of the public appear to believe that Federal law prohibits private ownership of such weapons. This is not the case at all, although some states or municipalities do prohibit them. On the other hand, there are at least a few people who believe that there are essentially no restrictions on them. A recent undercover purchase by a federal agent of an unregistered submachine gun points that out. The seller suggested that its use might be a violation of some game laws. The government did not prosecute in this case, as it was convinced that the seller was merely ignorant of the law.

With such public ignorance after 43 years, it is perhaps not too surprising that the Gun Control Act of 1968 is still widely misunderstood. More than a few television shows which would have us believe that outright violations of that Act are to this day completely legal certainly contribute to the public misunderstanding. It is suggested that mail-order sales of firearms to individuals across state lines, purchases by convicted felons, etc., are still very much a part of unproscribed activities. For readers who may well be unfamiliar with this Act (it is rather long and tedious), a few pertinent and condensed extracts follow:[4]

> It shall be unlawful for any person who is under indictment for, or who has been convicted in any court of, a crime punishable by imprisonment for a term exceeding one year; who is a fugitive from justice; who is an unlawful user of or addicted to marihuana or any depressant or stimulating drug (as defined . . .); or who has been adjudicated as a mental defective or who has been committed to a mental institution; to ship or transport any firearm or ammunition in interstate or foreign commerce, or to receive any firearm or ammunition which has been shipped or transported in interstate or foreign commerce.

> It shall be unlawful for any person to transport, ship, or receive in interstate or foreign commerce any stolen firearm or stolen ammunition, or any firearm which has had the serial number removed, obliterated, or altered.

I would like to suggest that if this law, along with current state and local laws, was understood by the public, properly enforced, prosecuted, and sentences meted and carried out, that there would be considerably less of a problem than we seem to have today. This has not been the situation, and it appears rather unlikely that it will become so. Should there be any significant change, many anti-gun people (especially politicians) would probably be highly displeased.

The average politician's overwhelming goal in life is to be re-elected, either to the same or to a higher office. To do this, he must sufficiently please his electorate. One method is to pass laws that *appear* to attack or resolve a readily recognizable problem, such as crime. Rather than stand up to the problem of doing something about those who commit crimes, they attempt to give us social palliatives like gun control. They attempt to lead us to a benevolent totalitarianism in increments. As anti-gun Rep. John Conyers said, reasoning that the gun legislation being proposed was ineffective, ". . . if it gets passed, and it doesn't do anything, then you come back and say, 'I told you so', which is how we move forward in this incremental political system". There are several great dangers here. One is not in the ineffectiveness of firearms restrictions, but in the belief that they will solve the problem.[5] Another is that we will eventually find ourselves with a government more concerned with security and safety than with the freedom of the people. (The second danger is mentioned on the assumption that we have not already passed that point.)

Their proposals are frequently rather simple-minded: "If handguns are against the law, then police can arrest criminals simply for the possession of a handgun, thus preventing a future crime". Police can already arrest criminals who are in possession of a handgun. Or are we to presuppose that possessors of handguns categorically are future criminals?

Register Here

Registration is one frequently suggested approach. It was very recently proposed by a city official that Wichita enact a gun registration program. The intended benefits included the following: If a gun were stolen and the owner had not kept the proper records, then return could be made upon recovery. Next, if a stolen gun were used in an armed robbery, for example, and the robber was captured and the gun recovered, and the robber had taken less than fifty dollars, then he could be charged with a serious crime—possession of a stolen gun. This official would have us believe that "low-loot" armed robberies are only misdemeanors, and barely worth going to court over. "Let's be able to charge those people with a Serious Crime."

If registration were to be really effective, it would doubtless have to be done on a federal level, and this is frequently proposed. It would, of course, make it much easier to return recovered stolen guns to their rightful owners, and there could be some criminal charges for sale, possession, etc., of stolen property. If there are any other potential benefits (real, not imagined), they are not known to me.

The cost of registration can only be roughly estimated. Based on actual experience in New York City, the cost could exceed $100 per gun. It might be that the federal government, inefficient as it is, could carry out a registration program for half that cost. By the most modest estimates, there are over 200 million privately owned guns in America, of which perhaps 60 million or so are handguns. The reader can estimate the dollar cost of registration programs himself. If the registration were to be effective, it would have to be essentially total (for whatever classes of arms were included). In addition to the cost, the reader should consider the problems inherent in the administrative and police methods to be required for such registration to reach a measureable degree of effectiveness.

How successful have some recent attempts at registration actually been? The City of Cleveland is probably a good example. The April 6, 1977 edition of the *Cleveland Plain Dealer* reports, "City Gun Law Fails Dismally in First Year". Of an estimated 100,000 weapons, only 16,854 were duly registered, and no registered weapons were established as having been used in a crime of violence. Although a majority of Clevelanders declined the dubious honor of having their guns registered, violent crime within the city dropped some 18.3% from the previous year.

The President of the Gun Control Federation of Greater Cleveland reports that he is "dismayed" at the results, and promises further efforts to bind the law-abiding gun owners of Cleveland.[6] It is not clear whether he is dismayed at the drop in crime, or the fact that it dropped despite the costly failure of his pet project.

Cleveland Police Chief Lloyd Garey said, "People who register guns don't commit crimes. . . . I doubt the crime drop has anything to do with gun registrations".

The danger of registration lies not in low benefit at high cost, but in the high potential for the next step—confiscation. Many proponents of registration scoff at their opponents fears of confiscation. They say, "Why would the police want to take your guns? Your car is registered; do you fear its confiscation?"

Thoughtful analysis shows that both questions are stupid. If confiscation legislation is passed, somebody would have to enforce it—or at least try. That would be either the current police, or some new nationwide organization—the beginning of the police state. The tactics that would have to be employed, and the distortion and destruction of our liberties, could be staggering.

I know of no one at the moment who seriously suggests the cars should be confiscated, but attempts have been and are being made to cause and implement firearms confiscation. Nelson Shields, chairman of the National Coalition to Control Handguns, has spelled out their game plan:

> Our ultimate goal—total control of handguns in the U.S.—is going to take time. . . . The first problem is to slow down the increasing number of handguns being produced in this country. The second problem is to get handguns registered. And the final problem is to make the possession of all handguns and handgun ammunition—excpet for the military, policemen, licensed security guards, licensed sporting clubs and licensed gun collectors—totally illegal.

Very simply then: prohibition of handguns. Surely, the alcohol prohibition amendment should have warned this nation of the irreversible damage which absolutely accompanies an unenforceable law. The public simply did not want prohibition, and it therefore could not be enforced. What we did get was a considerable loss of respect for laws, and the establishment of an organized crime colossus, which will be very pleased to supply firearms when, and if, it becomes worth their effort.

Any law affects only the people who obey it. I think it is no less than mindboggling to suggest that the criminal element would obey a confiscation law; there is no conceivable reason why they would start obeying one, and a very good reason why they would most definitely not. If honest citizens did respond to such a law, how much more safe and secure the armed criminal would be. I do not understand how a sane adult can justify disarming himself while knowing that the criminals will remain armed. At the present time, in our country, the only people who would benefit from a handgun ban are the armed criminals.

Massachussetts has some of the most stringent firearms laws in the country, and a very popular U.S. Senator who is very much anti-gun. Attempts to pass a state law banning handguns had failed badly, bringing charges of pro-gun people "buying" the legislature. In November, 1976, an article was finally placed on the ballot that would have required all privately owned handguns to be turned in to state officials, with some financial recompense to be determined by the bureaucracy. Proponents thought that if any state would accept it, Massachussets would. It was billed as the "real showdown on the issue". Antigunners claimed that 85 percent of the voters in the state did not own firearms, and were counting on their support. Public opinion polls predicted that the measure would succeed. One poll predicted passage by 51 to 40: another predicted victory but said the percentage was too close to call. The final result: Less than 738,000 for, over 1,666,000 against—a percentage of over 69 to less than 31. (A very interesting percentage, since a certain television network claims that their polls show 69 percent of the public *opposing* firearms.)

Another reason for confiscation is political overthrow of a free government. Throughout history, no disarmed people have been able to maintain and protect their freedom. Modern dictatorships begin their enslavement of the people by registration of guns (if it has not already been done for them), then by control, and finally by confiscation. In the Philippines a few years ago, the government lifted all criminal sanctions against possessing firearms, *as long as they were registered with the police.* A year later, possession of most firearms was declared a felony. Do I seriously suggest that such a thing could happen here? Do you seriously suggest that it could not? The world's largest democracy, India, gave us some examples of what can happen a few years ago.

Guns As A Cause

If one were to assume that the majority of those persons in this country attempting to disarm us, especially of handguns, are sincere in their efforts to combat crime, we might attempt to trace the course of their thinking.

Some suggest that guns are evil in and among themselves. Depending upon the suggester, that may apply to all guns, or perhaps only to handguns. The difference between handguns and others is that of size and mobility. If guns are evil, or if they have a purpose beyond that of the person using them, then we have a bona-fide case of animism; people who believe in that will probably believe in anything.

It is suggested that "crimes of passion" are made much easier and more convenient by the presence of a firearm, and in some cases again, that the mere presence of the evil gun will cause one person to harm another. I would suggest that this is simply the proponent's own subconscious fears being expressed. For such a person, the gun may well be evil and a dangerous thing for them to have at hand. Since they realize in some fashion that they could not trust themselves with a gun, they cannot trust anyone else either.

Another suggestion is that since a very substantial portion of homicides are committed by people who "know" each other, the absence of guns would automatically put an end to such unpleasant activities. However, while these killers may indeed be acquainted with their victims, they are NOT law abiding citizens. Mostly they are drug users and pushers, pimps, lunatics, felons, drunkards, etc. They usually have criminal records and are already violating laws by possessing or carrying guns. Murderers are not your average, sane, law-abiding citizen.

Help! Police!

In addition to the idea that the handgun threatens our family more than any intruder and has no sporting value, we are told that handguns are useless for self-defense. The evidence apparently consists of television shows, where the defender is always the loser.

There has never been a scholarly study on handguns used in defense to validate such a claim. Even if it should be true, who has the right to say that a citizen may not defend himself? Unfortunately, some jurisdictions are attempting to say this very thing. In any case, these people completely ignore countless cases in which crimes were averted, or injuries prevented, without killing the intruder—sometimes without ever firing a shot. The author has had personal experience of this type.

The notion that the police will give us all the protection we need is quaint, and hopelessly optimistic. The police ordinarily react after the crime is over. They can seldom arrive in time, even assuming that they can be promptly notified, to take over the defense function.

May I See Your License, Please?

Licensing of firearm owners and/or users is a suggestion we sometimes hear. The basic notion is that a license would be required to purchase or possess arms or ammunition, or to use them on public lands. In many respects, there would be similarities between this and the common driver's license. There appears to be considerable merit in this idea, IF it is properly legislated, and reasonably and fairly administered. I would suggest the following points for consideration in such a proposal:

(1) a fair and reasonable written or oral examination on firearms safety and handling; (2) a reasonable charge to help cover administrative costs; (3) denial only on clearly specified grounds (such as inability to pass the examination, or being in one of the groups previously mentioned who are not legally permitted to own firearms); (4) right of appeal if denial appears to be capricious or arbitrary; (5) no provisions, direct or oblique, for registration of any arms now possessed or subsequently purchased.

I do not envision the above as any kind of cure for what ails whomever. However, there could be some benefits that may well be worth the cost and trouble, and it is one of the most reasonable suggestions if more controls are deemed necessary.

Unfortunately, there are suggestions for other proposals that sound very similar to the above, but are in fact extremely and disturbingly different—

primarily because there is no provision for fair and/or reasonable treatment, nor avenues of appeal. Essentially these proposals place in the hands of some nameless, faceless bureaucrat the power to decide who may or may not own or purchase arms and ammunition. "The Secretary may proscribe . . .", is part of the language of these proposals. Basically, the Secretary (of whatever) gets the power to go up or down in his decision elevator, and the citizen gets the shaft. The Secretary will have authority to deny firearms to people who have committed no offense and who bear no evil intent. That is prior constraint—a technique that if allowed to start could become an all-consuming cancer to our basic freedoms. It flies in the face of our cherished presumption of innocence until proven guilty. Based on the political experience of other nations, the class of people allowed to possess firearms will be that class which is "politically safe", or "politically powerful". Once we have reached this stage, it will be too late to point out that a government which cannot trust its people cannot be trusted by its people.

Is Saturday Night Special?

Many efforts are directed toward control or prohibition of the "Saturday Night Special". Allegedly, the term SNS came into use in Detroit some years ago to describe a handgun purchased across the state line in Toledo, Ohio, and used on Saturday night in a crime in the inner city where gun controls were strict. However, if one is going to ban something a much better definition must be found. Various attempts have been made in this area, and factors considered include caliber, barrel length, frame size, price, melting point and/or tensile strength of frame material. Ultimately, the term SNS is used to designate just about any gun to which you wish to apply the term.

Of his bill HR 4692, Rep. Marty Russo of Illinois says:

> I am simply trying to remove from the market those concealable hand-guns that are too poorly constructed or too dangerous for home storage when children are around. . . . (The bill) does not restrict sportsmen or homeowners from purchasing quality handguns for either sporting or defensive purposes.

However, the bill would outlaw the importation or manufacture of approximately three-fourths of all existing models of handguns (based on a frame/barrel length formula) and it would freeze all interstate handgun sales. It would also give the Secretary of the Treasury absolute authority to dictate the type and model of handgun a private citizen would be allowed to buy or sell. It would also give federal authority over intrastate transfers—a power now denied.

Denial of the right to own a firearm on the economic basis that it is cheap is simply a reprehensible rejection of people who are poor. More expensive guns can just as readily be used in crimes but cannot be as readily purchased by many who would wish them for their own defense.

In what manner is "dangerous" defined. All firearms produced by manufacturers with a traceable address in Europe and America today are safe to the user for the purpose for which they were designed, All of them, no matter what their cost or size, are unsafe at the muzzle.

The world "concealable" is increasingly used to describe firearms which are claimed to be socially objectionable. If "concealability" is written into law as a criterion, firearms owners may be in for a terrible surprise. Many people believe that the gun prohibitionists are out to get only handguns, and will not bother owners of rifles and shotguns. "Why not compromise and let them take the handguns? Then they will leave us alone." Unfortunately, the Supreme Court ruled in 1975 that an overall length of 22 inches represented a concealable firearm. Based on experiences with similar legislation, what we could expect would be a ban on those arms which are concealable (that is, under 22 inches overall) or *which may readily be made concealable.* Since a few minutes with a hacksaw can make almost any rifle or shotgun fit that description, the way would be clearly paved for a total gun ban (except, of course, for the economically and politically privileged classes).

If, in some fashion or by some means, all guns could be banned, then the most savage and muscular would rule our streets and pillage our homes (which they often do anyway).

There Will Always Be An England?

Control proponents invariably use England as an example, stating that England has extremely strict controls and little violent crime. Before examining that premise, let us consider a few other foreign countries.

Switzerland, which is virtually armed-to-the-teeth in comparison to the U.S., has very little violent or gun-involved crime. Japan, which bans handguns, has a homicide rate almost six times that of Switzerland. Ceylon has required a police permit to possess any kind of firearm since at least 1917, but has a homicide rate almost twice that of the United States. A few years ago, Jamaica instituted what seem to be the most restrictive firearms and ammunition laws in the world. One could receive an indefinite sentence for mere possession of a live cartridge. Police methods totally foreign to our concepts were utilized in search and seizure procedures. The final result was a short-term decrease in armed crime of about 15%, then a gradual climb back to previous levels. At phenomenal cost, the whale had labored mightily and given birth to a minnow.

The proponents would argue that other countries have different peoples, with different customs and cultures, whereas England is like the U.S. The fact is that England, despite a certain similarity in language, is a very different country and culture than is ours—we separated 200 years ago, and have been drifting apart ever since. In any case, in recent years there have been substantial changes in the control-versus-crime picture in England. In 1964, the incidence of crime involving handguns began to rise at an alarming rate, until in 1969, the number of handgun-related crimes had increased by 700 percent, despite the very severe gun restrictions which have been in effect for some years. Chief Inspector Colin Greenwood, a 19-year police veteran, undertook a study in 1970–71 at the University of Cambridge to ascertain the effectiveness of existing British gun control. He began the study with a firm belief in the effectiveness of the controls. From this study came a book, *Firearms Control,* from which the following quotes seem especially pertinent:

> One of the most glaring defects to be found in most studies of the development of (British gun control) legislation is the almost complete absence of proper research. The statistics produced to support bills were invariably inadequate and lacking in points of comparison.

> The Blackwell Committee had little statistical information before it, and such as it had pointed to a downward trend in the criminal use of firearms. They did not, as far as one can see, research the type of firearms involved in crime, nor the sources, before concluding that controls on pistols and rifles were required. This lack of research lead them to pin all their hopes on the firearms certificate system as a means of preventing criminal use of firearms; so much so, that they did not recommend legislation concerning the actual use of firearms.

> One thing is certain, the statistics produced in Parliament in support of the various bills had the objective of justifying legislation. The politicians concerned selected figures which were best suited for that purpose. The figures, therefore, were those most likely to state the problem in its strongest terms.

> Legislation has frequently been related to relatively isolated incidents and has often reached beyond the scope of an incident to affect people in no way concerned with that type of event.

> A recurring factor in the passage of (gun control) legislation is that, in most cases, the sponsors have claimed only limited objectives for their bills. In all cases, during the debates, it was accepted that the legislation would have only limited effects. Yet, as soon as each act had been passed, everyone appeared to have been surprised that the problem to which it had been addressed did not disappear overnight. The acts were very

quickly criticized for failing to be completely effective when everyone had accepted that they could not be. The failure of a particular act to have a marked affect on the problem simply lead to further legislation and not to research to determine the reason for the failure.

To continue with the process of attempting to deal with the criminal use of firearms by placing more restrictions on legitimate users is not likely to achieve anything. The great danger lies, not in the ineffectiveness of such restrictions, but in a belief that they will solve the problem. Whilst this mistaken belief persists, the real problem will not receive the attention and actions it clearly and urgently requires.

Rather than make comparisons of different countries, it might be more appropriate to compare different parts of this country. Vermont allows concealed pistol carrying. Puerto Rico, which requires a police permit for the possession of any kind of firearm, has a homicide rate of more than five times that of Vermont. Considering the United States as a whole, the average homicide rate in the 39 relatively non-restrictive states is lower than the average in the 11 restrictive handgun control states.

How About a Trip Up the River?

Mandatory sentencing is frequently proposed for persons who use firearms in the commission of a felony. In many respects, this is an excellent idea, but it does have at least two problems. One is the question of the constitutionality of such legislation since it interferes with the discretion of the courts. This question has not yet been settled. Another problem is the hesitation of some juries to bring in guilty verdicts on mandatory sentence cases. Some jurors do not wish to be responsible for anything further than their verdict.

Other objections have been raised, some of which appear to be rather peculiar. One editorial recently declared that "mandatory sentences were useless because they are imposed only after the crime and have no preventive value". Do we, or should we, have sentences which are imposed *before* the crime? Such a tactic makes even prior restraint look rather mild.

The U.S. Conference of Mayors, which has gone on record as opposing gun ownership, has addressed the question of mandatory sentencing in a recent booklet:

> Consequently, it is doubtful that the incarceration of violent offenders will significantly reduce the level of serious crime.

If that is the case, we can save a tremendous amount of tax money by simply closing up the prisons. What would the mayors suggest we do with violent offenders? Leave them free to rape, pillage, and murder?

Most importantly, mandatory prison legislation diverts attention from the failure of our laws to curb the availability of handguns, and places all of the blame for 'recidivism' and gun-related crime on individual offenders.

In truth, I have thought for years that the primary blame for crime belonged on the individual offenders. Now, to my most considerable astonishment, I learn that the tens of millions of honest Americans who own handguns for any of a number of legitimate reasons—including defense of their homes, families, and businesses—are ultimately responsible for the actions of the criminals.

Connection—French or Otherwise

Have there been any legitimate studies to suggest that a violent society such as ours would fail to realize any benefits from handgun restriction? According to a study completed in 1975 at the University of Wisconsin, the answer is, surprisingly, yes.[7]

Wisconsin researchers examined every state's gun laws in relation to demographic, economic, and other variables which could be statistically quantified. In the end, they found no correlation between handgun owner-ship—legal or illegal—and the rate of homicide in any state of the union. The conclusion of that report is, inevitably, that gun-control laws have no individual or collective effect in reducing the rates of violent crime:

> Societies more peaceful than our own have not gained that enviable status because they restricted handguns more severely. Indeed, attacking the easily identifiable gun is a way of avoiding this painful possiblity: That America's level of violence can never be reduced without radically al-tering many of the social forces shaping our collective personality. Without such radical change the problem of violence in the U.S. is insoluble and we must, therefore, learn to live with it.

The study concludes:

> If the law cannot control such highly visible criminal activities as drug traffic, gambling, and prostitution, with their continuing sales of com-modities and services to the general public, then it seems unlikely that it could control the one-time sale of an item that can last for generations.

A Government of Laws?

In the March 21, 1978 issue of the *Federal Register,* the Bureau of Alcohol, Tobacco and Firearms proposed regulations of sweeping effect, claiming that they were well within their prerogative to do so. Space does not permit a detailed exposition and analysis of the proposal and the reactions it caused, but a few highlights should be considered.

On April 4, 1978, Congressman Robert E. Bauman of Maryland summed up the feelings of many:

> What we are witnessing is a deceitful, treacherous and dastardly attempt by a bureaucracy to circumvent, obviate and overrule the repeatedly expressed public intent of the Congress of the United States by instituting, through bureaucratic fiat, a gradual, step by step process of sliding firearms registration.
>
> . . . . Furthermore these proposed regulations conflict directly with public sentiment on the issue of firearms registration. In a public survey reported on April 7, 1977 by Decision Making Information, only three percent of the American people indicated that any form of gun control was a desirable step that should be taken to reduce crime.
>
> . . . . This survey (GMA Research Corp. survey of American Chiefs of Police) revealed that two-thirds of them felt firearms registration would have no effect on crime and 86 percent indicated that if they were ordinary citizens, they would keep a firearm for the protection of their family and property.

By May 22, more than 175,000 letters had been received at BATF headquarters. Of some 37,000 already screened, nearly 35,000 opposed the regulations.

BATF had originally stated that no new funds would be required to implement their proposal—the $4,200,000 for the first year could be shifted from other Treasury Department funds. The House Appropriations Subcommittee on Treasury, Postal Service and General Government then cut the Treasury Department budget by $4,200,000. On May 22, the full Appropriations Committee reaffirmed the subcommittee action with a 38 to 3 vote.

On June 3, Rex D. Davis, Director of BATF, announced his retirement effective July 1. He stated, ". . . My decision to retire was made before this subject became controversial."

On June 7, 1978, an attempt to reinstate the deleted appropriation was rejected by the House of Representatives, 314 to 80. A leading anti-gun congressman characterized the vote as "punitive" and said it was a 'signal' to BATF that it "better not try to enforce the regulations or we'll cut your legs off."

Heard Any Good Gun Laws Lately?

As a matter of fact, yes. One of the best is probably that of Georgia, effective July 1, 1976. A license is required to carry a concealed handgun anywhere other than at home or business. The license applies to the person, not his guns; it covers all his handguns and authorities are prohibited from requiring information that could be used as de facto registration. The law does NOT require that the applicant justify why he wants the license, nor must he show any need for it. Minors, fugitives, felons, addicts and other categories of persons generally barred from gun ownership may not be granted a license. (There is a records check.) The issuing authority has limited discretion in denial.

When proposed, antigun people argued that it would mean death and destruction because everybody would start carrying guns and shooting each other. However, Gwinnett County Judge Alton Tucker points out that since he has been on the bench he has never heard of an individual with any kind of Georgia pistol permit being convicted of shooting someone. Many citizens who previously carried a concealed handgun illegally, rather than run the risk of being robbed, raped, mugged, or murdered, are now, again, honest citizens who can protect themselves legally.

Discussion Questions

1. There are certain segments of society in which, despite stringent proscriptions, a significant portion of the population is armed, while the enforcement segment is unarmed. These areas are prisons, and armed assaults are frequent. In view of the difficulties faced in disarming these special populations, what problems might be envisioned in an attempt to disarm the general public?

2. In spite of recent congressional actions, the BATF has suggested that it will move ahead anyway with its registration regulations, even if it must wait for "a more favorable Congress". What actions might reasonably be taken to restrain this, and other regulatory agencies, from deliberately attempting to thwart the will of Congress?

3. Antigun proponents frequently claim that an armed homeowner is more likely to shoot himself or a family member rather than a burglar. Since many instances in which a gun gave protection or prevented an assault, but shooting was not required, go unreported, what kind of research might be done to ascertain the real benefit/disaster expectations to the armed homeowner?

4. What are some of the distinct cultural differences between the United States and England that can help account for the differing attitudes of the public toward firearms regulations?

5. Assume the general public does become disarmed. If, as many would suggest, armed crime then still continues to increase, what might be the response of the antigun coterie, and what might be their possible future suggestions?

Notes

1. George Mason, on June 16, 1788, before his fellow Virginians then debating the ratification of the Constitution.

2. United States Code (10 USC † 311(a) 1970).

3. Eldridge Gerry of Massachusetts, circa 1776.

4. Chapter 44 of 18 U.S.C. was amended by Title 1 of P.L. 90–681, The Gun Control Act of 1968. Quotes are from sections 922 (g1, g2, g3, and g4), and (h1, h2, h3, and h4), (i) and (k).

5. Greenwood, Colin. *Firearms Control.* Boston: Routledge and Kegan, 1972.

6. Most of the quotes and much of the data in this chapter have been obtained from second sources, and not original material. The author has no reason to believe there are any inaccuracies in the material quoted. Sources include recent issues of *The American Rifleman, Guns Magazine, Guns and Ammo, Shooting Times, and Point Blank* (published by the Citizens Committee for the Right to Keep and Bear Arms, Washington, D.C.).

7. Murray, Douglas. *Handguns, Gun Control and Firearms Problems.* Master's Thesis, University of Wisconsin. Vol. 23, A193, October, 1975.

9

Conflicting Images of Organized Crime

FREDERIC D. HOMER

Introduction: Connection & Society

THERE ARE TWO IMAGES OF ORGANIZED CRIME in the public mind. Each image is represented by a work of fiction recently made into a major motion picture. In *The Godfather* organized crime is seen as a *society;* people in the crime family have formal titles such as Don, Consiglieri, and Capo. They think of themselves as a closeknit group, and very little is mentioned about their relationship with other groups. In other words, they are a single *society,* set apart from other groups; and they have a code of behavior all their own.

The contrasting image of organized crime is in *The French Connection.* Here the emphasis is not on a society or a crime family, but several groupings of people who have a business connection in narcotics traffic. Turks deal with Corsicans who in turn may deal with Italians but altogether they do not think of themselves as belonging to a name group or society. In fact, they want to keep at a minimum what they know about one another.[2]

Interestingly enough both books may be describing the same reality. *The French Connection* is concentrating on criminal groups, not on their inner workings, but on their business relations. *The Godfather* is focusing on the inner workings of a society but ignoring or playing down the connections itself and other groups and individuals.

The analysis of organized crime by students and experts alike usually follows either the perspective of *The French Connection* or *The Godfather.* The emphasis on one or the other perspective results in two very different views of organized crime. Those who would consider organized crime as the work of a *secret society* see a single group which is isolated, distant, and highly organized. Leadership is hierarchical in that power flows from the top to the bottom of the organization: The Godfather's orders are final and transmitted through a chain of command. The leaders know and can control everything that is going on within the group. Finally, there is a constant effort to bring all criminals under the central leadership. In contrast, a *connection* suggests that we define organized crime as a diverse activity rather than as a unified society. Organized crime involves illegal activities which continue to occur over time and are carried out by a number of people or groups. Although the activity may be highly organized, there is no central leadership or administrative hierarchy. The connection rests on mutual interests and an agreed upon division of labor.

Historical Images

The two images, *secret society* and *connection* highlight different parts of the same reality. Historically, however, the image of organized crime as a society has been predominant. At the turn of the nineteenth century there was widespread talk of an organized Italian secret society in the United States called the *Black Hand.* As proof of the society's existence, people pointed to the extortion notes that individuals in the Italian Ghetto would receive with a picture of a black hand on it. It was assumed that a single secret society thrived by carrying out with dispatch extortion as well as all other illegal activities. Subsequent investigations found there was not a single society but many groups, each using the sign of the black hand, for they knew it would strike terror.[3]

Secret criminal societies gained great notoriety during the era of prohibition which officially lasted from 1920 to 1933. Gang wars were seen as examples of attempts by individual societies to build an organization under the control of one big boss. Publicity centered on personalities like Al Capone, the purported leader of a secret society in Chicago, and his bloody clashes with other gangland bosses.

When a gang of men in Brooklyn were found to have committed murders on a nationwide basis, their colorful names—Blue Jaw Magoon, Kid Twist Reles, for example—and the grotesque crimes they committed made them subject of national headlines. For instance, one man who ran a juke box concession in the Catskill Mountains in New York was caught withholding some of the profits. They killed him, tied a jukebox to his leg, and threw him in a lake. On another occasion, they dragged a victim kicking and screaming into a gang member's home. One of the killers nonchalantly asked his mother-in-law for an ice pick and a rope. She promptly brought them, and the victim was efficiently dispatched.[4] Unfortunately, a reporter erroneously dubbed this group a *society* and called it *Murder Incorporated.*[5] It actually was a loosely organized group that sometimes killed on contract. Its members were of several ethnic groups and took orders from different bosses. Murder was a sideline to the more profitable gambling enterprise this group ran and was not the real reason for the organization. If the group had been described as a *connection,* more of the details of their operations, other than the sensational ones about murder, might have come to light.

Organized crime often comes to the attention of the public through congressional committees. In 1963, Joseph Valachi, an underling in a New York organized crime family made a series of startling revelations about organized crime. He told of a secret society called "our thing" or "cosa nostra" that ran much of organized crime in this country.[6] Senators ignored the business connections of Valachi and concentrated on the name of the society and its inititiation procedures, secret rites, and formal titles. They tended to brush over the fact that many of Valachi's activities did not follow rigid organizational lines.

Valachi's revelations of a *secret society* tended to stick in the public mind and were reinforced by past unsubstantiated claims that there was a nation-wide Mafia, Honored Society, or Black Hand in the United States. This view became more firmly fixed with the publication of *The Godfather* and the popularity of the screen version. However, *The French Connection* portrays the other image and if we look carefully there is much evidence that this view is needed. How else do we explain the extensive gambling activities in service clubs of the U.S. army, directed and supervised by army personnel in cooperation with corporation executives? Or how do we explain the variety of nationalities of individuals arrested for the manufacture of distribution sale of narcotics?

Dominance of Society Image

Nevertheless, the notion that organized crime is the work of a secret society remains dominant. One basis for the continuing popularity of seeing organized crime as a single secret society is that this view is simple and complete. It explains everything as a conspiracy and every event can be linked to that conspiracy. Even if no evidence exists linking two events together, the holder of the conspiracy theory may assume that the conspirators were able to conceal such links. Not only is it comprehensive in explaining events and economical in using a few principles to link events, but it is difficult to refute. The secret society has done a good job of keeping its secrets and that is why we cannot find the links.

The tendency to see conspiracies is a part of American life. Several times during this century the Communist party has been viewed as a serious internal threat. The Panthers, Ku Klux Klan, and the Weathermen in recent years have been viewed as secret societies. In organized crime we have had the Black Hand, Mafia, Cosa Nostra, and one writer even suggests there is a National Crime Syndicate, a society more powerful than the Mafia. This organization thrives because public attention is riveted on the Mafia while the National Crime Syndicate works silently behind the scenes.[7] In each case, the groups are viewed as secret societies, deviant from existing societies, and a threat to American life. Explanations of *their* behavior need not rest on laws that govern *our* behavior. Indeed they are usually portrayed as organized, efficient, and single-minded. It is true that the societal explanation may tell of the existence of collectivities which do, in fact, operate, but this explanation also fabricates the existence of societies. Even if a secret society really exists, adherents to the conspiracy theory often give an exaggerated view of the society's influence, prowess, and determination to destroy others which in turn obstructs inquiry into the group's real nature.

As a corollary to conspiracy theories, people are often looking for the behind-the-scenes leader who is making all the decisions. Over the years dozens of candidates have been suggested as "Mr. Big" in organized crime.[8] It is easier to understand a conspiracy if we can locate the dominant man behind it. In reality, it is incorrect to suggest that any one man dominates a confederacy, which is usually a political arrangement where member groups and not some solitary figure retain the power.

Another basis for holding the "secret society" view may be the prevalance of ethnic prejudices. It is easy to impute organized crime to one ethnic group. For instance, some infer that organized crime is purely Italian crime. If Italians were to disappear from the scene, there would be no more organized crime. This is clearly at odds with the realities of organized crime. As sociologist Daniel Bell has suggested, various ethnic groups have participated in organized crime as a means to achieve social and economic advancement.[9]

The "secret society" view is useful to public officials because it can mobilize public opinion behind enforcement programs. By pointing to a secret enemy (organized and efficient) government officials can expect to generate more funds than by trying to explain complex interrelationships between groups and individuals in crime. At Attorney General Robert Kennedy's insistence, Joe Valachi appeared before a Senate committee to talk about the inner workings of Cosa Nostra. Kennedy wanted to prod the FBI into investigating organized crime more thoroughly and to get the public opinion behind a drive against organized crime.[10] Government agencies have also been known to use the notion of a "secret society" to direct public attention away from their failure to prevent crime. Government agencies sometimes pursue certain criminal groups while leaving others alone to carry on their activities.

Finally, the notion of secret societies allows people to see in a relatively simple manner, usually through the use of organization charts, how one organization works. For example, Joe Valachi testified to formal titles, such as Boss, Underboss, Capo, and Consiglieri, to indicate how his group operated. These titles had been grafted on to already existing relationships by a man named Salvatore Maranzano as early as the 1930s. In reality, however, the interrelationships are much more complex than as described by a table of organization.[11]

In sum, the society view tends to look at organized crime as a secret society, purposeful, unified, and inalterably opposed to the purposes of legitimate government. It is an easy, comprehensive and economical explanation of organized crime in this country. If this view is oversimplified, it also contains important elements of truth. There is not a single group, but there are individual groups whose makeup resembles and has the characteristics of those described in the "secret society" image.

Basically, the theory of a single powerful society, bent on destruction of the American government does not fit the facts. In many sectors of the country there is a small, or non-existent, Italian population, yet organized crime exists. Italian groups may be heavily represented in the East, but in many sections of the South, non-Italians are and have always been in power. Criminal groups arose from neighborhood grass-roots organizations and not from the plans of a national society or syndicate. When consolidation took place it began with local alliances and local groups who made their own decisions.

Finally, and most important, the image of organized crime as a society leads us to accentuate the differences between our own behavior and the behavior of organized criminals. This image focuses on organized crime as a "secret society" tied together by loyalty and blood oaths: organized crime is a government within a government and organized criminals are all bad. This is then contrasted with an equally exaggerated image of our nation as a place where openness and not secrecy is a virtue, interest groups openly and fairly lobby for what they believe and citizens are infused with virtue. Therefore, when organized crime is looked at as a society, its behavior is often placed in sharp contrast to the behavior of Americans not involved in organized crime. While differences between organized criminals and the rest of society should be mentioned, this type of analysis tends to obscure similarities in behavior common to all facets of American life. Perhaps differences between criminal and non-criminal actions are not as great as they appear to be under the societal image. For example, we look with horror upon the killings that take place in organized crime. However, governments also officially sanction and often encourage kiliing in wartime situations. Both criminal groups and governments view war as justifiable in order to protect and enhance their own interests. Many other parallels between organized criminals and the rest of us should be explored, but unfortunately the societal image does not encourage this type of investigation.

Organized criminals usually see themselves as American citizens taking advantage of the "system" as ordinary citizens do every day. They argue that they are less hypocritical than policemen and politicians who take from them and then claim moral superiority. This may all be part of an elaborate rationalization, but it is more than that. Organized criminals see no need to alter existing society to bring it in lines with their own values. Politically, they are one of the most conservative groups in the country; they like the present system and can use it to their own advantage. Rather than looking at organized crime as a secret society totally different from other groups, we can look at it as a group of people who use the same fundamental processes the rest of us do and work with the cooperation and often complicity, of policemen, politicans, and ordinary citizens.[12]

The Connection: A New Perspective

This leads us to the seldom explored image of organized crime, the *connection,* as a way of understanding organized crime as a part of the American experience. The "connections" image focuses on the actual activities of criminals, as opposed to organization charts, political titles, and formal power arrangements. The reader must be careful of the "connection" image taken to its extreme. It would be a mistake to think that there are *only* connections of individuals and that there is no basis in fact for speaking of societies. Often this can be a way of denying that any one ethnic group participates more than its share in organized crime. Nevertheless, the "connection" image uncovers a different slice of reality from the societal approach.

Origins of Organized Crime in the U.S.

Organized crime in the United States and for that matter, in the world, is not merely an Italian import. In France in the early 1300s a group of criminals called the Gueux or Beggars formed a criminal subculture. Similarly, in Elizabethan England wandering beggars engaged in criminal activities. Each local district had its petty chiefs known as Upright men. Any beggar, thief, horse stealer, or criminal in the district paid a tax to the Upright Man in exchange for permission to operate in the district alone or in connection with other criminals.[13]

Of course nineteenth century organized criminal activity was not limited to Europe. In the 1900s the "Thugs" of India roamed the countryside robbing and often killing travelers on the open road. Like the organized criminals we are familiar with today, they often held some menial job (legitimate front) to serve as an alibi for their criminal activities.[14] In Singapore, an offshoot of a Chinese revolutionary society, the Triad, ran illegal activities. Gambling, opium trade, and prostitution were their staples, much as they are in the United States today.[15]

In the United States, as well, organized crime predates the Italian participation. Well known are the criminal groups in the nineteenth century, such as the Reno Brothers of Indiana and the Jesse James-Cole Younger gang from Missouri.[16] Crime in urban areas also has a long history. In every city there were groups, usually around the waterfront, who extorted money from laborers, ran gambling establishments, houses of prostitution, and pushed opium. Clearly, organized crime in the United States or elsewhere was never the special province of Italian societies.

Some have suggested that American organized crime may have been imported directly from Italy because of the Italian terms used in crime. But this is misleading. Analysts have noted that words such as Mafia and Cosa Nostra have two distinct meanings. When Mafia or Costra Nostra are used as adjectives, the words describe men who are brave, loyal, and willing to stand up for their friends. When used as a noun, these words may refer to a criminal organization. The culture of Mafia or Cosa Nostra may be imported but not necessarily the organization. Words such as Mafia, Cosa Nostra, and Black Hand and their double meanings have perplexed enforcement officials for a long time.[17] For some the Cosa Nostra, the term Valachi first introduced to the public, indicates the existence of a nationwide conspiracy while for others the term is applied only in New York and refers to a local organization. In fact, in different cities organized criminals refer to their cohorts by different names — the outfit, the syndicate, the organization, the mob, or Cosa Nostra. Use of words does not necessarily prove the existence of an extensive network of organized criminal groups. Even if every group used the same word, we still could not deduce a single organizational entity.[18]

The number of years it took for Italians to gain a foothold in organized crime suggests that the culture, but not the organization of mafia was transplanted to this country. Most Italians immigrated to the United States from 1900–1910 when 2,045,877 entered the country, and about half as many came from 1910–1920. Subsequently, immigration slowed and only about 330,000 Italians have entered this country since 1930.[10] Italian success in organized crime was by no means immediate which suggests that either they started on a small scale, or more likely it was Americanized Italians who had adapted to American ways who were first successful in criminal activities.

Spread of the organizational Mafia organization to the United States would be plausible if the Mafia from Sicily had previously exhibited imperialist tendencies toward other countries or provinces of Italy. To the contrary, Mafia did not spread to Northern Italy, nor even to the eastern end of the Island of Sicily. The Mafia was always suspicious of outsiders, and has tended to keep within the confines of the extended family in their business activities. Commentators talk of Mafia organizations in the plural. For instance, Gaetano Mosca, a famous Italian political analyst, suggests that Mafia as an organization signifies a number of small criminal bands.[20] It is, therefore, difficult to see how Mafia as an organization can have been transplanted from Sicily.

Not all of the Italian criminals in the United States, or their ancestors, were from Mafia strongholds in Sicily. Two important organized crime figures of the past, Vito Genovese and Frank Costello, were from Naples and Calabria respectively. Italians in organized crime in this country came from at least three different regions, each supporting separate criminal cultures: Camorra from Naples, Mafia from Sicily, and the Onorata Societa from the province of Calabria. These cultures and the groups they spawned had no affiliations with one another in Italy and indications are that Italian organized criminals in this country were steadfast in their former region loyalties. Many of the early battles in organized crime were between Italians of different regional origin. Before the advent of prohibition, criminal groups remained small and fragmented. Language barriers made it difficult for one group to deal with another and in pre-prohibition days, most groups were local, confining their activities to a single ethnic neighborhood.

Prohibition

Prohibition of alcoholic beverages profoundly altered the structure of criminal organizations and their relationships with the public because of the "nationalization" of the distribution of illegal commodities. Sales of alcohol were often made between cities and alcohol and alcoholic beverages were frequently smuggled in from other countries. Criminal groups in various localities had to cooperate to keep the public supplied. In pre-prohibition days such cooperation was unnecessary because illicit activities were usually a neighborhood service, as gambling or prostitution, or protection rackets. The only exception was the occasional transfer of criminal labor from one region to another. For example, imported hired killers were less easy to identify, and imported prostitutes were necessary to keep houses of prostitution supplied.

The nationalization of distribution systems took place at a time when there were many competing groups in the illegal alcohol industry. Profits were high, risk was low, and widespread public acceptance of bootlegging activities, encouraged many individuals to become involved in the "criminal" process. As with the distribution of marijuana today, the sources of supply could not be monopolized easily by large criminal groups. Every tenement was a potential source of supply. People formerly engaged in legal enterprises of the alcoholic beverage industry, as well as those engaged in making industrial alcohol, became potential suppliers in the now illegal trade.

The "nationalization" of distribution along with the proliferation of new criminal groups helps to explain the violent character of the prohibition era. There was a wildly competitive market with few established businesses; conditions that exist in most infant industries. Violence, not governmental intervention, resolved irreconcilable disputes that arose. In an unbridled free enterprise system, violence is the final arbiter. Eventually, as a result of gang wars, threats of violence, and finally negotiation, connections were made between groups to monopolize production and distribution on a larger scale. No longer did the neighborhood groups suffice for the delivery of goods or services. Much the same solution has been used by other American industries in the 20th century. Size of business is often a way of gaining competitive advantage in a free market system. In illegal, as well as legal enterprises, the larger enterprises can cut costs by dealing with mass markets and can gain political favors because of increased resources. For instance, in many cities larger gambling operations can afford to pay police substantial protection money. When the public clamors for arrests, the police close down the small independent operators.[21]

In conjuntion with the change in the organizational structure of criminal groups which resulted from Prohibition, the public began to glorify the exploits of these groups. People wanted the alcoholic beverages they could no longer purchase lawfully. When the laws of a country are not in line with its citizen's desires, groups organize with the tacit support of the population to provide the now illegal goods and services. Because the public accepts these illegal activities, public officials are reluctant to enforce the laws. Therefore criminal groups need not depend on guile for survival; indeed, it is difficult to fail if the public and enforcement agencies are indifferent or support you.[22]

One can only speculate as to why this country tends to be puritanical in its laws and permissive in its tolerance of illegal behavior. Hypotheses range from contrasting the permissiveness of the American frontier with the puritancial ethics of New England, to the conflict between laissez-faire economics and the welfare state. Regardless of the explanations, organized crime has continued to thrive on such discrepancies between morality and law. Gambling is a good example. In New York State, one can place a bet at the state lottery, but not with the local numbers runner. Some gambling is sanctioned and some is not. For example, churches are allowed to play bingo. Policemen have no real urge to crack down on gambling. The people in the neighborhoods would be so incensed as to give them no cooperation in dealing with other police matters. One large metropolitan police department, recognizing low public support for anti-gambling laws and the great potential for police graft, has ordered policemen not to make arrests of low-level personnel involved in gambling.[23]

Since the laws covering such things as gambling, prostitution, or marijuana are frequently not respected, the gangster is apt to be glorified and the officer of the law falls into disrepute. For example, during prohibition Al Capone became something of a folk hero. Seven books were published about Capone from 1929 to 1931 and the gangster movie came into Vogue. Capone and other bootleggers openly bragged about providing the people with quality alcoholic beverages. Their competitors served inferior brew. Capone did colorful, attention-getting stunts like taking a boy scout troop to a Northwestern football game. The crowd responded with periodic cheers of "Yea Al". The policemen and politicians in contrast, were the subjects of laughter and derision. Legend has it that Capone coined the phrase "Vote early and vote often," a testimony to democratic government in Chicago at the time. In one precinct, virtually all of the policemen were on Al Capone's payroll. The public was aware of this and it became all the more ludicrous when police overextended their greed. The precinct captain asked Capone's group for the name and badge numbers of all patrolmen on the payroll. The captain suspected policemen of collecting double and triple their payoffs by using false names and by borrowing the badges of others. Capone was a legendary character and the Chicago police were depicted as inept and corrupt. The same process occurs whenever police are compelled to enforce laws not respected by the people.[24]

Castellamarese Wars: The Americanization of Organized Crime

After the era of Prohibition, the next event which helped to shape organized crime was the Castellamerese War. The conflict could simply be viewed as an underworld power strugle that pitted the personal ambitions of one ambitious leader against another. In 1930, a man named Joe "the Boss" Masseria declared himself as the "boss of all bosses" of the Italian underworld in the United States. He tried to unite the various Italian groups that had come to prominence during Prohibition, but he had a rival for that position, one Salvatore Maranzano. Groups took sides and gangland killings took place in many cities around the country. In a single two-day period 30 to 40 individuals were killed. This phase of the war ended in typical gangland fashion. Masseria was shot and killed in a restaurant, betrayed by his allies. One of them reportedly went to dinner with Masseria and conveniently left him to go to the men's room just before the killers entered the restaurant. Maranzano took over as boss of all bosses and met a similar bloody fate. In September of 1931, Maranzano was shot and stabbed in his office by four unknown men posing as police officers. Shortly after Maranzano's death, the title of boss of all bosses was abolished and peace reigned for many years in the Italian underworld.[25]

The war is more significant than merely a clash between ambitious leaders trying to personally control organized crime. The "americanization" of organized crime took place during and shortly after this conflict. The end of the war brought decreased hostility and increased cooperation between formerly conflicting groups in organized crime. Originally, the conflict was aggravated by the fact that Masseria and Maranzano came from different regions in Italy. Groups divided upon the basis of origin in the old country, Neopolitans on one side and Sicilians on the other. The younger men who finally dominated after the war, tended to minimize these regional differences and were even willing to cooperate with other ethnic groups. Ironically, this is symbolized by the fact that the younger Italian leaders allowed non-Italians to pose as policemen and kill Salvatore Maranzano.

Americanization also included the substitution of profit for power as the major motivation in criminal organizations. In the old country, gang wars would often be fought on the basis of maintaining or enhancing power or avenging a personal breach of honor. In the early days in this country wars were fought for similar reasons even though groups stood to lose a great deal economically by gang war. In a war, the group cannot collect on their loans, run their gambling establishments or even be seen on the streets for fear of being killed. Police in time of gang warfare are forced to come up with arrests and publicly harass crimnal businesses. During the Castellamarese war, men of the old country ways were eliminated and a new breed of leader took over. They were more interested in profit than power, much as is true with their fellow American businessmen at the time. War was to the detriment of their business so they attempted, most often successfully, negotiation as opposed to war as a way of settling disputes.

Finally, Americanization meant that the quest for a centralized, nation-wide organized criminal group was abandoned for a confederation or alliances between major criminal groups. The centralization of power in organized crime was ushered in with and ended with the leadership of Salvatore Maranzano. Maranzano proceeded to reorganize the Italian families under his command and attempted to dominate the various families by the formation of his own personal staff. It appears that Maranzano's big mistake was his erroneous assessment of the structure of power in organized crime. Clearly, power lay with individual family heads, many of whom formed their crime families from scratch. By giving up his power base in an individual family and trying to establish a palace guard more powerful than the combined organizations, he misunderstood his limitations. From this time on, no one attempted to assert himself as the top man in the manner of Maranzano. The family structure survives him as does communication between the various groups, but the title, "boss of all bosses" has been abolished.

The Castellamarese wars were fought between those trying to establish a single society based upon ethnic loyalty, and those who saw economic opportunities and connections with other groups as the more realistic way to operate. The high watermark of those who promoted the notion of society was the reign of Salvatore Maranzano. A great admirer of Julius Caesar, he deliberately gave individuals formal roles and titles, organized them into families and tried to superimpose a dictatorship over the whole super-structure. In Italian culture, the emphasis was on power, bravery, and loyalty, while in the United States the profit motive was stronger. Crime had become big business.[26]

Even before the end of Prohibition, some of the more perceptive criminal groups had begun to diversify into other business, much like any business-man diversifies to spread his risk to major business losses. Gambling, prostitution, loansharking, extortion, and penetration of labor unions, all were distinct possibilities. In some cases larger combines swallowed up businesses run by smaller groups during the prohibition years. For instance, Dutch Shultz, a New York mobster, took over the Harlem lotteries from the blacks who had been running it.[27]

World War II

Much of post-prohibition organized crime can be understood when the inverse relationship between the American economy and crime is recog-nized. If business is bad, as it was during the depression and later downturns of the business cycle, many opportunities open up for organized criminals. People are known to gamble more in hard times; the possibility of getting rich quick by a "big score" is tempting. Also, in hard times, loan sharks became the only source of money for those who have come upon bad times and have no credit rating. Other economic dislocations are similarly advan-tageous for the criminal.

World War II, despite the return of prosperity, was a bonanza for organized criminals. A host of new regulations were passed necessitating price controls and rationing. This meant that organized criminals could steal and sell a commodity the public wanted—gasoline or sugar, for example. One gang broke into the Office of Price Administration: others counterfeited ration stamps; others bought gasoline stamps from corrupt OPA officials, while some stole from centers responsible for collecting the used stamps. The stamps ended up in the hands of the consumer who was willing to pay a price to criminals for the privilege of buying more than his share of gasoline.

Kefauver Hearings

Until 1950, organized criminals enjoyed unprecedented prosperity with little governmental interference. Only the revelations about Murder Incorporated and the trial and sentencing of a powerful underworld figure, Charles "Lucky" Luciano, on a charge of organizing prostitution, received much publicity. This changed abruptly in 1950 when the Kefauver hearings brought many criminal operations to the public's and law enforcement agencies attention. Senator Estes Kefauver, spurred on by complaints of big city mayors, chaired a special committee to look into the participation of criminals in activities which involved interstate commerce. The committee investigated a nationwide wireservice which provided the bookies with information from the country's major racetracks. It also traced the interactions among the major organized criminals that the committee had identified. The committee found at least two *connections* of major proportions in the country, although these connections were erroneously considered to be secret societies. For example, when they mentioned the Costello, Erickson, Marcello axis, it was as though they were describing men at the head of a single society when in reality they were describing members of different criminal societies who conspired together to install slot machines in New Orleans. The Kefauver committee had described as a society (axis) what was in fact an economic connection.[28] Since the Kefauver hearings there have been continual revelations about organized crime, but a paucity of legislation and few convictions have followed, due in part, at least, to the fact that the public condones many of the activities which sustain organized crime even when it is appalled by the scope, extent, and nature of the criminal organization.

Unions and Organized Crime

In 1955 when the Democrats took control of the Senate, John McClellan became chairman of the Senate Permanent Subcommittee on Investigations and Robert F. Kennedy became chief counsel. Their investigation began by looking into improprieties in the clothing procurement program of the

Armed Forces. They found some purported East Coast gangsters, Albert Anastasia, Johnny Dio and his brother Tommy, and others were involved directly or indirectly in the manufacturing or trucking of uniforms.[29] This suggested that organized criminals had muscled into the labor movement, and subsequent investigations were made into the relationships of organized crime to labor, especially with the Teamsters union. Investigations were focused on connections between union officials and criminals. Unions pension funds often can serve as a bankroll for criminal activities, for by law they rested beyond the scrutiny of government auditors. Union elections can be rigged or voters intimidated by organized criminals in order to control the union. Once in power there are a variety of ways to make money from putting jukeboxes in the union halls to entering "sweetheart" contracts with management. In the latter case, the union leader gets a kickback from management for settling on a contract favorable to management. Sometimes business gets a little rough. One union organizer tried to move into San Diego to organize juke box operators. He ignored a threat on his life but was knocked unconscious. When he woke up he had terrible abdominal pains. The doctors extracted a cucumber from his rectum. He was warned that next time, if he returned to San Diego, it would be a watermelon.[30]

Focus on Organized Crime as A Society

On November 14, 1957, in the small town of Apalachin, New York, a group of men gathered together at the house of Joseph Barbara, who was a beer and soft drink distributor in this upstate New York community. The police surrounded the grounds and the guests fled in panic. Those caught were known by the police in various cities as leaders of various crime families. The specific ties these men had with one another and the nature of the organized crime society they belonged to remained a mystery. Nevertheless, the government decided to prosecute these men for conspiracy, a charge finally thrown out by the courts upon appeal. Despite the lack of concrete evidence organized crime was regarded as a single society.[31]

Joseph Valachi's revelations in 1963 before the McClellan committee continued to fix attention upon the existence of a criminal society, one which he called Cosa Nostra. According to Valachi, the meeting in Barbara's house had been called by Vito Genovese to deal with the charge that he had attempted to kill the man who had become the boss of his family in his absence, Frank Costello. Valachi added that Genovese also wanted the blessings of the council for the murder of Albert Anastasia, a family boss who had died of an overdose of lead in a barber's chair three weeks earlier. Anastasia accused Genovese of selling memberships in the organization.[32]

The public, as well as enforcement agents, once again, viewed organized crime as a society and not as a connection even though police chiefs told the McClellan committee that they did not know of any overall structure.

From the early 1960s to the present, attention continues to be focused on societies and not connections, in part because of "family" disputes that have taken place in organized crime. Publicity or notoriety has centered on the clash of personalities in organized crime families rather than on their economic activities and interconnections. A close look at the disputes shows that they are not merely personality clashes, but are generated by the conflicting loyalties a criminal feels for his criminal society as opposed to his economic connections. For instance, in the early 1960s in a dispute known as the Gallo-Profaci wars, Profaci, an old time criminal boss whose command dated back to the Castellamarese wars, tried to maintain complete control over his criminal society. Members had to pay him monthly dues for the service of his organization, but a group of younger members led by the Gallo brothers, tried to abolish this tax. They felt more loyalty to the economic connections they worked with, such as gambling rings, loanshark groups, and narcotics networks, than to Joe Profaci and his society. The Gallo brothers felt they were receiving little or no benefits from the family and should not be taxed for membership. One of the reasons for open conflict was that other bosses had realized a long time ago that times had changed and had abolished practices such as the taxing of members. Profaci refused to change his ways.[33]

Joseph Colombo, a relatively young man for an organizational leader, took over the reins of the Profaci family in the early sixties. No more was heard publicly about the family and its disputes until the spring of 1970 when Colombo began picketing the FBI which had accused his son of melting down silver coins into ingots. At this juncture, the Italian-American Civil Rights league was formed and received Colombo's full support. By the end of the year, membership was said to number 45,000.[34] They held two rallies in New York City, one in 1970 and the second on June 28, 1971. These and other factors of the Italian-American Civil Rights League were aimed at taking police pressure off of Italian Americans and diverting attention away from Italian participation in organized crime. The words Cosa Nostra were deleted from the picture *The Godfather* and John Mitchell, then Attorney General, ordered his department to discontinue use of this phrase. The League won the battle but lost the war. These phrases were deleted, but their public pressure only drew attention to Italian criminal societies, and the mysterious name Cosa Nostra and drew attention away from the activities of other groups and connections.[35] As a post-script, while participating in the second rally of the Italian-American Civil Rights league, Joseph Colombo was shot by one, Jerome Johnson, who was immediately killed by an unknown assailant. Colombo, though eventually released from the hospital in the care of his family, suffered extensive wounds. Joey Gallo, who had recently gotten out of jail, was questioned by the police as to his role in the killing.[36] In 1972, Joey Gallo, celebrating his birthday with some friends in Umberto's Clam House, was shot and killed.[37]

Today, the society image of organized crime still predominates, yet more and more one hears about the complex sale of narcotics, and other economic connections and often involving non-Italians. Although these activities are easily explained as organized crime connections, most analysts still cling to the idea that organized crime involves only societies of Italians. Unfortunately, for most analysts, organized crime involves only societies of Italians. Unfortunately, for most analysts, organized crime is only the Italian criminal society depicted in *The Godfather*. These other activities are not categorized as organized crime nor treated as such by investigative agencies.

Changes in Organized Crime

The superstructure of organized crime has changed little since the Castellamarese wars. In 1930, for the first and last time, the attempt to establish a single society failed. Ever since, power has resided with local groups. There still is a Commission which has representation from some of the larger criminal groups (heavily overrepresenting Eastern interests), but its powers should not be overestimated. The Commission has no soldiers or treasury of its own, meets very infrequently and cannot compel powerful member groups to go along with its decisions. Its lack of power explains the fluid relationships that exist between all organized criminal groups, Italians and Non-Italians: a set of interlocking alliances formed on the basis of common business concerns often, but not always, cemented by common ethnic bonds and marital ties. Alliances are fluid, and conferences attended by various criminals should not be mistaken for formal representative bodies vested with lawmaking powers. At most, they can arbitrate disputes between consenting parties. The Commission and similar groupings are more like the United Nations or a series of peace conferences than a unitary government.[38]

Perhaps, beneath this superstructure, changes in the nature of organized crime are occuring. Violence often is an excellent indicator of organizational strains and changes. From 1914 to 1971 there were 1008 known gangland murders in Chicago. But over the years the number of such murders has been declining. From 1919 to 1930 there were 519 murders; from 1931 to

1940, 226 murders and in the last 3 decades only 70, 52, and 61 respectively. These figures would suggest there is relative peace and unity in organized crime, at least in Chicago, today. Other cities show the same decline.[39]

Superficially, it appears that criminal groups are not relatively stable and the drastic decrease in one form of violence (client-centered) hides an increase in another form (inter-organizational) which often indicates organizational instability. Client-centered violence, violence done to customers, has decreased. For example, fewer establishments are bombed if protection money is demanded and not forthcoming. More subtle means are used. For example, one group persuaded a series of beauty parlors to pay protection by hiring black women to frequent the beauty salons and frighten away upper and upper middle class trade. Although hidden in the overall figures, inter-organizational violence has increased in recent years. Not only are there wars in and among Italian families; blacks, Puerto Ricans, and other ethnics have been fighting white groups for the control of business in many cities. Increasingly, deaths from these conflicts are being reported.

The instability of criminal groups of late, as indicated by an increase in inter-organizational violence, may be the result of some problems which criminal groups face today. Generally, in pursuing economic opportunities (continued economic growth and the taking on of the trappings of the modern corporation), cohesiveness of local criminal societies has been weakened as well as has their ability to deal with potential competitors. Economically based connections continue to increase in importance while the power of nuclear societies has decreased.

Specifically, the pursuit of economic opportunities often means working with people who are not part of the nuclear society. To survive and prosper, criminals take advantage of any opportunity, legal or illegal. They may run a bar and grill, a dice game, steal securities, hijack trucks, loan money at exorbitant rates, or counterfeit money. The criminal's business connections are more important to him than his ties with a nuclear crime family.

In the 1920s, criminals worked and lived in the same neighborhood and continuously interacted (in business and social affairs) with the same individuals. Now expanded economic opportunities have taken the group outside neighborhood confines. The same group now may run enterprises in Las Vegas, Florida, and New York. Increasing prosperity has allowed them to live in the suburbs, apart from their place of work. Hence, interaction between nuclear group members has increased and surveillance of their activities by the leaders has become more difficult. This weakens the nuclear criminal society.

Another change comes with the death of dynamic leaders. Many of them in organized crime are now dead and the transition must be made, as it has been in other businesses, to people with managerial as opposed to charismatic skills. The transition often brings conflict and violence. Many of the elders came into organized crime with the original charismatic leaders and show scorn for the younger generation. It remains to be seen how smoothly the transition will be made from organizations where loyalty resided in the individual to an organization. The decline of charismatic authorities has tended to weaken the small nuclear societies and has strengthened the many connections that do exist.

Economic opportunities—some of them quite legitimate—can be exploited only with additional personnel. As the number of such activities increases and as the activities become more specialized, the greater the need for expert personnel. The old fashioned nuclear crime family was made up of generalists who could perform a variety of tasks—killer, gambler, loan-shark, and so forth. These people could be counted on more for personal loyalty than can the new specialists—the lawyer, the accountant, the stock analyst, or the business manager.

Often the strength of the nuclear criminal society was based upon ethnic identification. It may be asked whether these ties continue to be maintained through successive generations. Does the grandson or great grandson of the immigrant still maintain his ethnic allegiances? There seems to be a waning of ethnic allegiances in criminal groups as in the rest of society. Some criminal groups, no longer able to recruit members of sufficient loyalty and skill, have tried to bolster their organizations by illegally smuggling aliens into this country. It is difficult to ascertain how much ethnic loyalty has declined, but no doubt its partial demise has contributed to the weakening of the nuclear criminal societies.

In sum, then, organized crime faces the pressures involved in their becoming economic connections as opposed to nuclear political groups. We can find this theme suggested in the *Godfather*. On the surface, after the death of the old leader, the family retains many of the old virtues. Work, friendship, and family and a feeling of community among the members seems to remain. Yet there are signs of strain. For instance, some family members showed more fealty to a narcotics group than to their nuclear family. Fredo, the second of three sons of the Godfather fell under the sway of a non-member business partner in Las Vegas. In fact, as well as in fiction, as we have seen criminal groups are faced with the transition to modern business practices where in some of the very strengths of the nuclear criminal society are in danger of being lost. This tendency will probably accelerate in the coming years.

Organized Crime and Law Enforcement

The two images — organized crime as a society and organized crime as connections — have allowed us to explore organized crime as an integral part of American society. The two perspectives or images also help to judge law enforcement policies toward organized crime. If the societal view prevails, law enforcement efforts will be focused on a criminal society and its leaders rather than on a particular activity such as narcotics, prostitution, or stolen securities. The connections perspective would suggest that police decide priorities in terms of activities. Do we strike at the most morally reprehensible (murder or narcotics), most profitable (gambling), or the most deleterious to public morale (corruption)?

The connection perspective is preferable to the societal perspective for the purpose of law enforcement. The continued attack on a single society and its leaders which emanates from the societal perspective tends to be destructive of civil liberties. Our tendency is to laugh off, or ignore, intensive police pressure on selected organized criminals. We rationalize by suggesting they deserve to be harassed. However, we cannot prejudge someone as guilty and subject him to continued harassment because we do not like him or think he is a criminal. In our system, the presumption is always one of innocence until proven guilty and that maxim applies to citizen, politician, policeman, and purported criminal alike.

The societal image by focusing attention on a single society and its leaders may drum up considerable public support for a "war" on organized crime. The public's knowledge of secret societies is dependent to a great extent upon information and propaganda the government releases. A particular society may be singled out for attack while others as culpable are left alone. This can often be convenient for politicians who, for one reason or another, would like to confine their investigations to a single group. The same questions arose in the past whenever the government suggested there was a danger from a conspiracy, whether it be the Cosa Nostra, the Communist Party, the Weathermen, or the Black Panthers. By singling out a particular society, the government can prey on the worst instincts and fears of the American public and can create enemies to distract the public from more pressing public issues, or to raise appropriations for the public agency responsible for fighting the created menace.

Law enforcement under the connections image can be more comprehensive and imaginative. Enforcement under the societal image is often limited to tactical considerations, for example, mobilizing greater numbers of policemen, more extensive use of wiretaps, and more police discretion in cases of search and seizure. On the other hand, the connections image raises the possibility that widespread gambling, prostitution, and addiction are more a function of the discrepancy between a restrictive law and the desires of the people, than of poor police tactics. Perhaps we should make legal some of the activities, such as gambling and prostitution, whose prohibition cause the law enforcement problems in the first place. Or we might want to devise public agenices that would provide loans to people without financial standing in order to drive the criminal loanshark out of business. The connections image focuses attention on the fact that organized crime owes its existence to more than the machinations of an evil society of men different in character and disposition from the rest of us. Organized crime cannot exist without the complicity of ordinary citizens and cannot be understood and dealt with apart from the American experience.

Discussion Questions

1. Before you read this chapter did you think of organized crime as a connection or a society? Why?

2. What is the difference between a connection and a society?

3. Do we tend to perceive groups as conspiracies more in the United States than in other countries?

4. Is the Americanization of organized crime continuing to take place today? If so, how is it taking place?

5. If criminal organizations are connections, how should this alter our law enforcement policies?

Notes

1. Mario Puzo, *The Godfather* (Greenwich, Connecticut: Fawcett Publications, 1969).

2. Robin Moore, *The French Connection* (film starring Gene Hackman and Roy Scheider also starring Eddie Egan, the "real" Popeye Doyle).

3. See, for example, Arthur Train, *Courts and Criminals* (New York: Charles Scribner's Sons, 1925), pp. 285–286.

4. See Frederic D. Homer, *Guns and Garlic: Myths and Realities of Organized Crime* (Lafayette, Indiana: Purdue University Press, 1964), pp. 40, 48. 59, for more extended discussion of Murder Incorporated.

5. According to Burton Turkus, Harry Feeney of the *New York World Telegram*

came up with the name Murder Incorporated. Burton Turkus and Sid Feder, *Murder Incorporated* (London: Victor Gollancz, 1953), p. 19.

6. Peter Maas, *The Valachi Papers* (New York: Bantam Books, 1968).

7. Hank Messick, *Lansky* (New York: G.P. Putnam's Sons, 1971), pp. 7, 31–32.

8. See for example, *Inside the Mafia* Vol. 1, No. 1 (New York: Swinton Publishing Company, 1972).

9. Daniel Bell, *The End of Ideology* (Glencoe, Illinois: Free Press, 1960), pp. 121, 130–133.

10. Victor S. Navasky, *Kennedy Justice* (New York: Atheneum, 1971), pp. 49–50.

11. Maas, *Valachi,* pp. 103–113.

12. Homer, *Guns and Garlic,* pp. 12–15.

13. John Heron Lepper, *Famous Secret Societies* (Sampson, Low, Marston Company, Ltd., 1938), pp. 196–199.

14. Lepper, *Famous Secret Societies,* p. 296.

15. Arkon Daraul, *A History of Secret Societies* (New York: Citadel Press, 1961), p. 244.

16. Hugh D. Graham and Ted R. Gurr, eds. *Violence in America, A Report to the National Commission on the Causes and Prevention of Violence* (New York: Signet Books, 1969), p. 44.

17. Francis A.J. Ianni, "The Mafia and the Web of Kinship," *Public Interest* 22 (Winter 1971) also Francis A.J. Ianni, *A Family Business* (New York: Russell Sage Foundation, 1972).

18. Maas, *Valachi,* pp. 260–265.

19. Joseph Lopreato, *Italian Americans* (New York: Random House, 1970), pp. 12–15.

20. Gaetano Mosca, "Mafia" in Edwin R.A. Seligman, *Encyclopedia of the Social Sciences,* Vol. 10 (New York: MacMillan Company, 1933), p. 36.

21. For a more complete description of prohibition and organized crime, see John Kobler, Capone (New York: G.P. Putnam's Sons, 1971) or Kenneth Allsop, *The Bootleggers and Their Era* (New York: Doubleday and Company, 1961).

22. For a more extended discussion of the "nationalization" of organized crime, see Homer, *Guns and Garlic,* pp. 32–36.

23. *Summary and Principal Recommendations: Commission to Investigate Allegations of Police Corruption* (New York), 3 August 1972.

24. Kobler, *Capone.*

25. Maas, *Valachi,* pp. 103–113.

26. *Ibid.,* pp. 111–113.

27. Richard "Dixie" Davis, "Things I Couldn't Tell Till Now," pt. 2, *Colliers,* 104 (29 July 1939): 21.

28. *Second Interim Report of the Special Committee to Investigate Organized Crime in Interstate Commerce* (Washington: U.S. Government Printing Office, 1951).

29. Robert F. Kennedy, *The Enemy Within* (New York: Harper and Row, 1960), p. 6.

30. *Ibid.,* p. 20.

31. Frederick Sondern, *The Brotherhood of Evil* (New York: Farrar, Straus and Cudahy, 1959), pp. 3–4.

32. Maas, *Valachi,* pp. 260–265.

33. Ralph Salerno and John S. Thompkins, *The Crime Confederation* (New York: Popular Library, 1969), pp. 133–142.

34. "Columbo: A Man with Several Roles." *New York Times,* (29 June 1971), p. 20.

35. *Ibid.,* p. 20.

36. "Suspect in Shooting of Colombo Linked to Gambino Family," *New York Times,* (20 July 1971), p. 21.

37. Eric Pace, "Mafia Members Said to be Hiding," *New York Times,* (13 April 1972), p. 40. Joseph Colombo died in 1978 never having fully recovered from his wounds.

38. For more extended discussion of the power structure of organized crime, see Homer, *Guns and Garlic,* chapter 4.

39. Data from mimeo obtained from the Chicago Crime Commission, Spring, 1972, entitled *Gang Murders, Chicago Area, 1919–.*

Part II
Issues in Law Enforcement

1

The Mythology of Law Enforcement

DON BRADEL

A MYTH IS A BELIEF GIVEN UNCRITICAL ACCEPTANCE by the members of a group especially in support of existing or traditional practices and institutions.[1] The study of myths is applicable to law enforcement because there are few other governmental organizations in the United States that are as given to believing myths as are police agencies. The police do not use the term "myth" to describe these beliefs, but refer to them as policies or procedures. In reality, these procedures are myths because they are given uncritical acceptance by most police administrators. Recent research into various aspects of police administration has focused national attention on several of these procedures.[2] The findings of these studies have called into question particular police procedures which appear to be influenced by unquestioned myths about what ought to work, rather than by appropriately organized facts and theories. How valid are the operating assumptions of most law enforcement agencies? What are some of the most contested issues, and what are the reasons behind the perpetuation of these myths?

Preventive Patrol

Perhaps the most widely debated and fundamental police procedure is based on the myth of preventive patrol. Preventive patrol is the distribution of police officers, either on foot or in a patrol car, who, when not answering a citizen's request for assistance, are preventing crime by their high visibility to the public. Thus, patrol cars are distinctively painted and identified and police officers are dressed in distinctive uniforms. O.W. Wilson, the foremost proponent of the use of preventive patrol describes how preventive patrol should work:

> The apparent likelihood of arrest influences the degree to which the potential offender is convinced that the opportunity for successful misconduct is absent. (Preventive) Patrol provides this favorable influence

151

more completely than any other branch of police service. An impression of omnipresence is created by frequent and conspicious patrol at every hour and in all sections of the community. Suitable patrol succeeds in effecting immediate apprehensions; and since nothing succeeds like success, a reputation for quick and certain apprehension is spread by press, radio, and word of mouth. The potential offender is thus persuaded without the necessity of personal experience that the patrol is invulnerable.[3]

Thus, Wilson advocates preventive patrol as a crime deterrent in a seemingly logical way. It makes sense for law-abiding man to attribute his law-abiding behavior to the watchful eye of the police, so it follows that criminals, too, should be deterred. Zimring and Hawkins point out the fallacy of this reasoning in their discussion of deterrence:

> The official's personal experience is in most cases likely to lend support to his belief in deterrence. Having worked hard to achieve the regard of his fellows, is more sensitive than most to the threat of social stigma . . . He remembers slowing down when seeing a police car on the highway, remembers considering the possibility of audit when filling out his income tax return. He is less likely to recall deviations.[4]

Is the non-law-abiding person affected at all by preventive patrol? The now famous Kansas City Preventive Patrol Experiment, conducted by the Police Foundation, set out to answer that question. This year-long scientific evaluation of preventive patrol sought to determine the effectiveness of this police procedure. The experiment employed a methodology of dividing Kansas City, Missouri, into various controlled areas. These areas consisted of reactive beats which received no preventive patrol, proactive beats which received two or three times the usual level of preventive patrol and control beats which maintained their normal level of preventive patrol. The experiment was geared to measure a number of variables in regard to the preventive patrol concept; would the level of crime increase or decrease with variations in patrol density? Would the proactive beats increase the public's feeling of security and decrease the citizen's fear of crime? If the views of O.W. Wilson are correct, then the proactive beats should have had a substantial positive effect in both of these areas. However, they did not, and the summary of the experimental findings concluded:

> Given the large amount of data collected and the extremely diverse sources used, the overwhelming evidence is that decreasing or increasing routine preventive patrol within the range tested in this experiment had no effect on crime, citizens fear of crime, community attitudes toward the police on the delivery of police service, police response time or traffic accidents.[5]

Although these findings were published in 1974, they have had little or no effect on the preventive patrol practices of most police departments. The report met immediate resistance from police administrators who criticized it as not applicable to their situations. The real issue is: what can a police department substitute for preventive patrol?

Police Productivity

Law enforcement has been plagued by the inability to accurately measure the productivity of its agencies since the advent of modern policing. With the British Metropolitan Police Act of 1829, the police were told that the absence of crime will provide the best measure of efficiency for law enforcement. Since that time, the main indicator of success has been the rate of crime in the jurisdiction of the particular law enforcement agency.

This practice has continued in the face of overwhelming evidence against its validity.

> The rate of certain crimes is determined to a significant but unknown degree by factors over which the police have little control. Street crimes are affected by the weather, crimes against property by the prevailing economic conditions, crimes against the person by the racial and class composition of the community, delinquency by the nature and strength of family and peer group controls.[6]

By continuing to use crime rates as a measure of police efficiency, other abuses often result. These abuses include the dishonest reporting of crime by police officers, crime clearances by variances in charging practices which take the form of always charging an offender with a more serious crime than is actually applicable, and the unnecessary use of arrest by police officers. If the Uniform Crime Statistics as published by the F.B.I. are used, one way police can control the crime rate is to not report or misreport a criminal incident. Thus, a burglary becomes trespass to property and a battery becomes an assault. Clearance rates can be manipulated simply by charging a person arrested for auto theft with all auto thefts of similar nature which occurred in the area. If crime rates are used to measure the individual officers performance, it only follows that police will be more likely to use the arrest process, even though a non-arrest referral may be more appropriate. Thus a simple domestic disturbance may result in an assault arrest.

In spite of the evidence against the validity of using crime rates to measure efficiency and the drawbacks and abuses it fosters, these methods are still the most generally used in law enforcement today. The Uniform Crime Report published by the F.B.I. is still the benchmark law enforcement agencies use to judge their success.

Criminal Investigation

Probably no other function within the modern police organization is as riddled with myths as the criminal investigation function. Television series have glorified this police role and all patrolmen know this position is the steppingstone to bigger and better things within the police agency. A basic text on police administration describes this role as:

> Criminal investigation is the keystone of police service. The detection and apprehension of the criminal offender and the production of evidence against him, all depend on it. It is the point at which society brings the forces of law and order in sharp focus in its approach to the problems of crime and the criminal. The detective function—criminal investigation —is a basic feature of modern police work.[7]

Common sense would indicate that a person who spends all his time tracking down criminal offenders would be more effective at solving crimes than an officer who must answer citizen calls and spend time on preventive patrol. The evidence available, however, indicates that this is not the case. A study conducted by the Rand Corporation to assess the effectiveness of the criminal investigation function reported some interesting conclusions. This study used data from various sources which included a comprehensive literature review, a survey questionnaire, a detailed study of 25 police agencies, data from the Federal Bureau of Investigation, and interviews with crime victims. Some of the major findings of this study are:

> Differences in investigative training, staffing, workload, and procedures appear to have no appreciable effect on crime, arrest or clearance rates.
>
> The single most important determinant of whether or not a case will be solved is the information the victim supplies to the immediately responding patrol officer. If information that uniquely identifies the perpetrator is not presented at the time the crime is reported, the perpetrator, by and large, will not be subsequently identified.
>
> Our data consistently reveal that an investigator's time is largely consumed in reviewing reports, documenting files and attempting to locate and interview victims on cases that experience shows will not be solved.
>
> Of those cases that are ultimately cleared but in which the perpetrator is not identifiable at the time of the initial police incident report, almost all are cleared as a result of routine police procedures.[8]

Police Training

Police training is included as a myth in law enforcement because it reflects the role and function of law enforcement officers as they themselves will perceive it to be. Most police training curriculums consist of a limited number of courses which attempt to teach the recruit particular mechanical skills (firearms, first aid, arrest techniques) or the application of particular rules (criminal law, departmental policies, traffic law). These skills and rules reflect a strict law enforcement orientation. Very few training curriculums address the areas of interpersonal relations, the use of discretion or the community service functions performed by the police. Research relating to the police role has revealed that a majority of an officer's time is spent dealing with non-enforcement activities. In a review of these studies Roberg concluded:

> The research establishes that the actual amount of time a police officer devotes to even minimal law enforcement duties is not more than 10–30 percent; the remaining 70–90 percent of police work is related either to maintaining order or providing various community services.[10]

The emphasis on law enforcement in the training academies leads to additional problems for the recruit after he leaves the academy. The recruit finds himself ill-equipped to deal with the situations encountered in the field. An example of this is the recruit who must confront a violent emotionally disturbed person. The training this officer has received has not properly equipped him to deal with this type of behavioral problem. This issue was addressed by the National Advisory Commission on Criminal Justice Standards and Goals in their discussion of training program development:

> Great care must be taken to distinguish between the actual duties of the policeman and the way the policeman, the agency, or the public frequently envisions them. Many police employees graduating from police academies are shocked by reality. They often find the training they receive in the academy has little relationship to what happens in the field.[11]

These realities do not coincide with the collective wisdom of the past. Faced with a choice between change and the status quo, most administrators choose the status quo. Little headway has been made in changing outdated academy training curriculums.

Reasons for Lack of Change

The reasons for the lack of change in police agencies are for the most part structural in nature. These structural problems refer mainly to law enforcement's position in the political system, the closed administrative system within law enforcement and the structure of roles defined by the social system in which the police find themselves. These structural problems are all interrelated with their focal point being the police executive. Since the police executive is held fully responsible for the operations of his department, it is important to focus on the fundamental structural pressures exerted on the administrator which prevent change from occuring.

The Political System

The police are a part of the executive branch of government. Owing his position in the police organization to the generosity of the elected official usually means that the police chief must "keep his nose clean" and "not rock the boat". These mottos tend to form the basic operating philosophy for the police department. Thus the police administrator becomes a political animal, strongly influenced by partisan politics. The place law enforcement occupies in the political structure is under the realm of the local chief executive officer, usually the mayor of the municipality. Because most of these chief executives are elected, the appointed police executive position may become a political patronage appointment. In many cities throughout the country, each time a new mayor is elected, a new police chief is appointed.

The police administrator does not want to lose his acceptability to the elected official, and thus relies on past policies and procedures which have served his predecessor well. Innovation always involves the possibility of failure. New procedures which do not work may expose the chief to unfavorable publicity or adverse political repercussions. It is easier to live with an inefficient police department than to risk losing a hard earned administrative position. In a recent speech, Robert diGrazia, then Police Commissioner of Boston, characterized the nation's police chiefs as the "pet rocks' of politicians, unable to change or innovate.[12]

An example of just how powerful the political influence is in law enforcement is the case of Chief Robert McNamara. While Chief of Police in Kansas City, McNamara made many changes which resulted in that department becoming a national model for progressive police agencies. The Kansas City Department had virtually eliminated police corruption, improved relations with the minority communities, improved standards and the self-image of officers within the department, and was involved in many innovative research oriented experiments. There were some politicians, however, who were not in favor of these policies. As a result when a police salary raise was awarded, Chief McNamara was excluded. McNamara's response to this step was reported in a national publication: "I won't tolerate interference with my policies. I told them to go to hell. When the day comes when I can't run a department on a professional basis, I'll leave."[13] McNamara did leave and is now the Chief of Police in San Jose, California.

Internal Obstacles to Change

All formal organizations are resistant to change, this is especially true of police organizations. The police occupation fosters the development of a certain outlook which Skolnick has labeled the "Police Personality." The components of this personality include suspiciousness, social isolation, and police solidarity. These components combine to produce an intergroup climate that is especially resistant to change. Thus, if the police chief attempts to innovate and institute change within the organization, he may meet stiff opposition from the patrolmen ranks. The administrator's power is viewed as a threat and his ability to initiate change must be controlled. Wilson points out the dilemma of the police chief: "The power of the administrator is to be checked because the administrator, if he is a strong man, is 'out to get us' and, if he is a weak one, is 'giving way before outside pressure.'"[14]

A recent example of this phenomenon occurred in Madison, Wisconsin. David Couper was appointed Police Chief of the Burnsville, Minnesota police department, where he turned a typical suburban police agency into a progressive, efficient organization. Because of his innovative ideas, he was selected as Chief of Police in Madison, a much larger agency. Shortly after taking office, Couper met with a great deal of resistance on the part of his subordinates. This resistance was aimed not only at innovations he proposed, but also at Couper himself. The patrolmen attempted to oust him as police chief through legal action. Subsequent to this resistance, the rate of change in the Madison Police Department has slowed to a standstill.

The Closed System

Most police agencies are closed systems, that is, each officer must serve an apprenticeship as a patrolman before moving up the ranks. Administrators are developed through the promotion process, with very few lateral entry opportunities available in law enforcement administration. What this means is that contrary to business practices where the best possible person for the position is sought, police agencies get administrators from within. For the most part, the man promoted is a police officer, not an administrator. This inbreeding results in limited opportunities for professional growth and development. Ill-equipped to deal with the problems and strategies of innovation, the police administrator relies on the traditional system of policies and procedures with which he is familiar. This results in the perpetuation of outdated and non-productive police procedures. Referring to this myth, Menlo Park Police Chief Cizanckas sums up the situation by stating: "Instead of examining what is being done and why, the emphasis is on how to do it. And how to do it, in the final analysis, turns out to be the way it has always been done."[15]

Public Image of the Police

One of the most powerful influences on police policy and procedures are public expectations. Priorities regarding the police role are established by the community the police agency serves. Although the police have no control over the crime rate or various other community problems, the public expects the police administrator to "do something" about these problems. These public attitudes are constantly conveyed to police officers in their everyday interaction with the community. The traffic violator who tries to avoid a citation by telling the officer to "go catch real crooks" is just one example of how this image is perpetuated. In reponse to this pressure, the police create an impression of themselves as crime fighters. More officers may be dispatched to a particular area, detectives may be urged to clear more cases, and crimes that are solved receive extensive publicity. This activity reinforces the image of the police as law enforcers not only with the public, but also with the police officers themselves. As Wilson points out: "Because of the law enforcement orientation of the administrator, or because of what he believes to be the orientation of the public, the department will be organized around law enforcement rather than order maintenance specialties."[16]

Changing the orientation of the police agency from law enforcement to order maintenance would involve the risk of losing this public support and the public's perceived reliance on the police.

Summary

In summary, the police myths regarding preventive patrol, productivity measurement, criminal investigation and police training, have a common thread which runs through each. This common thread is history, with the procedures discussed all having a long record of use in police departments.

These police proposals are arrived at without the scientific knowledge to support them. Relatively few experimental or controlled studies on the effectiveness of these particular policies are conducted by police agencies. The major reasons for the perpetuation of these myths were identified as political concerns, internal organizational resistance and procedures, and the public's perceptions of the police role. The political concerns revolve around the position that law enforcement agencies occupy in the executive branch of local government. Internal organizational resistance results from the traditional give and take between labor and management. The patrolmen fear any change which may result in the loss of their power within the police organization. The public's perception of the police role as strictly law enforcement and their expectations of police performance were also found to inhibit change in law enforcement agencies.

Conclusion

The myths discussed in this review and the reasons for these myths being perpetuated place the police administrator in a curious dilemma. The answers involved in correcting these outdated procedures lie mainly in more empirical research and the improved ability to apply this research in a practical way. Innovations have proved successful. Team policing, a more adaptive organizational style, allows for more responsiveness to the community and more responsibility for the patrolman. Better means for measuring productivity and evaluating personnel have been developed. Improved training approaches have been instituted and are currently being developed. The police administrator does have answers to these problems available to him, however, the dilemma arises when trying to deal with the reasons for not instituting change. How does the administrator deal with the political, internal and community pressures resisting change? This is the critical issue for law enforcement in the coming years.

Discussion Questions

1. Describe the utility of preventive patrol in light of recent research findings.

2. What are the main problems with using the crime rate to measure police productivity?

3. From a police administrative standpoint, briefly explain the three main impediments to instituting change within a law enforcement agency.

Notes

1. Webster's Third New International Dictionary (Springfield, Mass.: G & C Merriam Co., 1971), p. 1497.

2. Two of the most recent are:

George Kelling et al., *The Kansas City Preventive Patrol Experiment A Summary Report* (Washington, D.C.: The Police Foundation, 1974).

Peter Greenwood and Joan Petersilia, *The Criminal Investigation Process Volume 1: Summary and Policy Implications* (Santa Monica, California: Rand Corporation, 1975).

3. O.W. Wilson and Roy McLaren, *Police Administration* (New York: McGraw Hill Book Company, 1975), p. 320.

4. Anthony Guenther, *Criminal Behavior and Social Systems* (Chicago: Rand McNally Company, 1976), pp. 93–94.

5. Kelling, p. 39.

6. James Q. Wilson, *Varieties of Police Behavior* (New York: Atheneum, 1974), p. 60.

7. V.A. Leonard and Harry More, *Police Organization and Management* (Mineola, N.Y.: The Foundation Press, Inc., 1974), p. 408.

8. Greenwood, pp. vi–vii.

9. President's Commission on Law Enforcement and Administration of Justice, *The Challenge of Crime in a Free Society* (Washington, D.C.: United States Government Printing Office, 1967), p. 248.

10. Roy Roberg, *The Changing Police Role* (San Jose, California: Justice Systems Development, Inc., 1976), p. 90.

11. National Advisory Commission on Criminal Justice Standards and Goals, *Police* (Washington, D.C.: United States Government Printing Office, 1973), p. 389.

12. Law Enforcement News, June/July, 1976, p. 1.

13. The Wall Street Journal, February 10, 1977, p. 1.

14. James Q. Wilson, p. 73.

15. Victor Cizanckas and Donald Hanna, *Modern Police Management and Organization* (Englewood Cliffs, N.J.: Prentice-Hall, Inc. 1977), p. 18.

16. James Q. Wilson, p. 69.

2

Professionalism at the Crossroads: Police Administration in the 1980's

SAMUEL WALKER

CONSIDER THE FOLLOWING INCIDENT: it is 11:30 on a hot Friday night. A police officer is dispatched to an apartment on the basis of a complaint about a domestic disturbance. The officer arrives on the scene to find three adults, two men and one woman, in the midst of a heated argument. The situation looks potentially dangerous. One of the men has a gold club in his hand and appears to have threatened one of the others.

Let us stop at this point. We don't know what will happen, but we do know that the police officer will have to exercise considerable discretion in handling the situation. He might leave quickly after giving a warning. Or, he might stay longer and attempt to resolve the dispute. He might make an arrest or he might not. If he does, he could be very selective about who he arrests and on what charge. Either way, his actions could have a major impact on subsequent events. If he leaves too quickly, the argument might continue and eventually result in serious injury or even death. If he makes an arrest, there could be serious consequences for the person arrested (a criminal record, etc.). Or, if he effectively resolves the dispute, he might help to avert further trouble.

This type of situation—a typical incident and one of the most difficult that the police are asked to handle—dramatizes the problem of achieving police professionalism. The basic problem is this: how can we guarantee that the officer on the scene will be prepared to handle the situation effectively? It is a simple question but one with no simple answers.

For more than seventy years experts have answered the question by saying that we should make the police "professionals." The following essay discusses the meaning of police professionalism today. It begins by defining professionalism and tracing the origins and development of police professionalization since 1900. Then it analyzes the problems with traditional-style professionalism and discusses some of the new ideas and progress that have appeared in recent years.

161

It is the central thesis of this essay that police professionalism stands at a crossroads. The choice is between two different approaches to the improvement of police performance. One alternative is the traditional style of professionalism that emphasizes managerial efficiency and bureaucratic centralization. The other alternative, the new aproach, involves bureaucratic decentralization and the direct participation of rank and file police officers in the police policy-making process.

The choice between the two alternatives is not an easy one. Neither approach is all right or all wrong. Rather, both approaches deal with important problems. Yet, each one is filled with certain hazards—the hazard of creating new problems or reintroducing old problems. This is a dilemma that confronts all of us—police administrators, patrol officers, elected officials, criminal justice experts and students, concerned citizens—who seek to achieve a democratic and professional police in America.[1]

Police Professionalism: A Definition

Everyone talks about a professional police, but few people agree on what it means. Some people equate professional status with higher levels of education for police officers. Others believe that professionalism involves equipping the police with the latest technology: new patrol cars, sophisticated communications and information systems, a wide range of lethal and non-lethal weaponry, etc. And for many people professionalism is nothing more than a cliche, a slogan that means something/anything better than what exists at present.[2]

To bring some clarity to this discussion it is useful to consider what sociologists of occupations have said about the meaning of professionalism. This can help to illuminate what police professionalism is and is not. The sociologists generally agree that a true profession has three characteristics: professional knowledge, professional autonomy, and a service ideal.[3]

A profession involves an area of activity about which there is a complex body of scientific knowledge. This knowledge can only be mastered through a long period of study, usually in a university or professional school. Professions also have a great deal of autonomy. Through their own organizations (i.e. the American Medical Association) they take the responsibility for recruiting and training new members, for running the professional schools, for generating new knowledge, and for disciplining its members. In return for this autonomy, members of the profession accept the third aspect of professionalism. a commitment to a service ideal. They agree to serve their clients, consistent with the latest expertise; they are not to serve their own self interests.

In light of this definition of professionalism, it is clear that the police are a long way from achieving that status. There is only a limited body of scientific knowledge about policing. Most officers learn the essentials of their work on the job not in formal training. There are some professional organizations, such as the IACP, but they do not have much direct control over the profession. Finally, there is no tradition of a self-enforced code of ethics among the police. Some experts go as far as to say that the police can never become a true profession. James Q. Wilson, for instance, argues that policing is essentially a craft rather than a profession.[4]

Yet, in a number of respects, the American police have achieved a degree of professionalism. Let us now examine briefly the history of the development of police professionalism in the United States. This is a key to understanding the current dilemma in police administration.

The Development of Police Professionalism

The idea of policing as a profession emerged around the turn of the century as a reaction to the corruption and inefficiency that pervaded the American police. Through the nineteenth century, police officers were recruited mainly on the basis of their political connections, not any proven aptitude for police work. Once appointed, they received no formal training. A few police departments established police academies (Cincinnati in 1886; New York in 1896) but formal police training did not become a reality until well into the twentieth century. There was no concept of a "police science;" no textbooks on police administration; and little thought given to how the police might carry out their assignments better.[5]

Political corruption was the rule, not the exception. Police departments participated in a systematic pattern of payoffs for overlooking illegal drinking, gambling, and prostitution. On patrol, officers were almost completely unsupervised; there were no radios to permit continuous contact with headquarters. They spent a great deal of time evading their official duties and, apparently, spent a lot of time in saloons. The administration of most departments was also inefficient. Police chiefs were usually figureheads. The real power lay with the Captains in the precincts. Many departments were run by boards of police commissioners which were divided by political factionalism. Everything, then, conspired to make the police corrupt and inefficient.

This sad state of affairs became the object of attack by a new generation of reformers beginning in 1900. The movement for professionalism was led by such men as Major Richard Sylvester (Superintendent of the Washington, D.C. police and President of the IACP for fifteen years), August Vollmer

(Chief of the Berkeley, California police and the leading advocate of police education), and Raymond B. Fosdick (a professional social worker and author of one of the most important early books on police administration). These men, along with many others, led the movement for professionalization. It was a painfully slow process, but between the 1900's and 1960's it succeeded in transforming the nature of policing in America.[6]

The reformers sought to do four things: first, to eliminate political influence; second, to secure expert leadership; third, to modernize the structure of police organizations; and, finally, to raise the quality of the rank and file police officers. To achieve these goals the reformers preached the gospel of administrative efficiency. Police departments should be run like corporations, they argued. They also put great emphasis on education, both for police executives and for the rank and file. August Vollmer was most famous for his pioneering work in establishing police training programs at the college level.[7]

The struggle for professionalism was long and difficult. Some departments professionlized early (Cincinnati in the 1880's); some departments underwent reform but quickly slipped back into the old ways (Philadelphia, 1912–1920's); still other departments seemed to resist every effort at reform (Chicago).[8]

By the late 1950's and early 1960's the Los Angeles police had a reputation as the most professional department in the country (an image cultivated by the popular *Dragnet* television show). Even the department's severest critics (and there were many) admitted that corruption was almost non-existent. The Los Angeles police had the most modern equipment, one of the best training programs, and an aggressive crime-fighting effort. But there were problems. As the 1965 Watts riot demonstrated, they had very bad relations with the black community. It was also the most militaristic police department in the country. In short, it represented the best and the worst of police professionalism: an efficient, militaristic bureaucracy, isolated from the public, hostile to the black community, and dominated by a conservative "law and order" ideology.[9]

The Limits of Professionalism

In Los Angeles and across the country, the violent racial disturbances of the 1960's focused national attention on the police. "Police-community relations" became the most critical aspect of the whole urban/racial crisis. Four presidential commissions examined the police during the 1960's. Their reports, and the work of many other individuals and groups, forced many experts to rethink the nature of police professionalism.[10]

The President's Commission on Law Enforcement and Administration of Justice (the President's "Crime Commission") in 1967 pointed out that "the needs of good community relations and of effective law enforcement will not necessarily be identical at all times." Aggressive law enforcement tactics, such as frequent stops and frisks, were often viewed by the black community as a form of harrassment. In 1968 the Kerner Commission (appointed by President Johnson to study the causes of the riots) reached a similar conclusion. It argued that "many of the serious disturbances took place in cities whose police are among the best led, best organized, best trained and most professional in the country." The emphasis on automobile patrol, for example, was efficient in terms of law enforcement but served to remove police officers from the sidewalks and from direct contact with the people.[11]

The isolation of the police appeared to be a serious problem. There was much discussion of the so-called "police subculture"; it was said that the police were both isolated from and hostile to the public. An early warning about the police subculture had been sounded by William A. Westley in 1950. Studying the Gary, Indiana police he found that police work seemed to encourage secrecy and violence. Because professionalization had led to the creatin of large police bureaucracies it was partly responsible for the emergence of the police subculture.[12]

In the early 1960's Jerome Skolnick identified some related problems in his study of the Oakland, California police. The emphasis on crime fighting and on getting "results" (i.e. arrests and a good "clearance rate") often conflicted with the values of a democratic society. In order to make an arrest, obtain evidence, or secure a confession, a police officer might violate an individual's constitutional rights. The values of the department encouraged "results" rather than respect for the constitution. The need for useful information, so important in vice work, also meant that the police had to enter into agreements with informers, many of whom were themselves criminals. This, of course, compromised the integrity of the police.[13]

Skolnick pointed out that police professionalism had taken a different form than in other recognized professions. The police had emphasized managerial efficiency, with a centralized bureaucracy that could monitor and control rank and file officers efficiently. The recognized professions had gone in a very different direction. They encouraged the independent judgement of the individual practitioner. They sought to instill a sense of professional commitment during the long training period. In the most professional police departments, however, just the opposite situation existed: the individual officer was subject to tight regulations and expected to do his job "by the book." In order to control officers effectively, police organizations had become centralized and militaristic. Many experts began to recognize, however, that this military structure stifled rather than enhanced the professionalism of the individual officer. [14]

In response to the police crisis of the mid-1960's, many reforms were proposed. Some of those ideas represented a continuation of the traditional approach to professionalization. In effect, some experts were saying that the police simply needed "more of the same." Others, however, began to take a very different approach to professional development. Let us consider first the traditional approach before we examine some of the new ideas. Each one takes a different approach to the problem of guiding and controlling the actions of the officer on the beat.

Traditional Professionalism Reaffirmed

The 1967 report of the President's Crime Commission contained many different recommendations concerning the police. Some of them represented the traditional approach to police professionalization: greater administrative efficiency, more expert leadership, and higher qualifications for police officers. It is important to remember the context in which this important report was written. By 1967 there had been three straight summers of urban racial violence and the worst was yet to come that summer. There were widespread charges of police misconduct. And in fact, most of the riots had been ignited by some incident involving the police, either an arrest or a shooting. The problem of controlling police conduct, then, was an immediate issue.

The Crime Commission made a strong recommendation that patrol officers be given specific written guidelines: "Police departments should develop and enunciate policies that give police personnel specific guidance for the common situations requiring the exercise of police discretion." The Commission also pointed out that "In most cities police officers receive too little guidance as to when firearms may be drawn and used." It recommended more extensive training and the development of written guidelines on the use of deadly force. [15]

To control corruption, another important form of police misconduct, the Crime Commission recommended that "every medium- and large-sized department should have a well-manned internal investigation unit responsible only to the chief administrator." This was consistent with the traditional approach to police reform: rely primarily upon a strong executive who would develop a cadre of subordinates loyal and responsible to himself. Both this proposal and the recommendation of written guidelines for police actions indicated that reform could be brought about through centralization, by concentrating power and responsibility at the top. [16]

With regard to the rank and file officers, the Crime Commission made the traditional recommendations: higher standards for recruitment and more intensive education. The Commission suggested that "the ultimate aim of all police departments should be that all personnel with general enforcement powers have baccalaureate degrees." It also recommended a minimum of 400 hours of classroom training for recruits and the development of statewide standards for all law enforcement personnel. With the establishment of LEAA in 1968, the federal government began to pour millions of dollars into college-level police training programs. [17]

Finally, the Crime Commission recommended a more professional level of management for police departments. It stressed the importance of research and planning, together with the application of modern technology to police problems. Sophisticated communications systems received particular emphasis and in the next few years, LEAA funds helped many departments to acquire them. Most of the recommendations of the Crime Commission were subsequently endorsed by the National Advisory Commission on Criminal Justice Standards and Goals (1973). [18]

New Problems, New Directions

By the late 1960's and early 1970's, an increasing number of criminal justice experts were dissatisfied with the traditional approach to police reform. Even the Crime Commission itself had mixed feelings. For example it gave a tentative endorsement to the idea of "team policing," about which we will say more shortly. Experts began to identify new police problems and to propose new directions for reform. The new approach emphasized *de*-centralizing police departments. It recognized the need to involve the rank and file patrolman in the policy-making process. And, finally, it put greater emphasis on the non-criminal, social service duties of the police rather than the law enforcement functions.

Where did these new ideas come from? There were two main sources. The first, of course, was the police-community relations crisis. It was an entirely new problem and one that demanded fresh thinking. As the Crime Commission and the Kerner Commission suggested, the traditional approach often served to worsen rather than improve the problem. The second source of new ideas was the research undertaken about the police. Partly because of the public concern about the police and partly because of LEAA funds, there was an upsurge of research on the police. As a result we have today a very different view of what the police do than we had only ten years ago. Many of the new ideas on police reform are based on the findings of this research. [19]

The new research, for example, indicated that the police actually spend only a small portion of their time (about 20%) on criminal matters. Most of their duties involve non-criminal *service* activities. The domestic disturbance described at the beginning of this essay is typical: it is a difficult assignment but it usually does not result in an arrest. Albert Reiss's study, *The Police and the Public,* was the most extensive documentation of what police officers actually do. The new group of reformers began to suggest that police departments be reorganized to emphasize the service activities than consume the bulk of police duties.[20]

Research also confirmed that police officers were extremely alienated. Not only were they alienated from the public, but from their superiors and the department as well. Police work was not a satisfying career that encouraged and rewarded commitment and creativity. Rather, the paramilitary structure seemed to encourage putting in your time and keeping your nose clean. In order to overcome this alienation and to make careers more attractive to people of talent and ambition, experts began to develop ideas about involving officers more directly in the policy-making process. After all, other professionals enjoyed that right.

The new direction in police reform, then, began with three objectives: (1) to bring the police closer to the public, in the hope of improving police-community relations; (2) to emphasize the service functions of the police, and to reward officers for doing well in that area; and, (3) to "democratize" police departments by involving rank and file in the policy-making process. All of these concerns were very different from the traditional approach to achieving professionalism.

The most significant attempt to implement these objectives is the idea of "team policing." A number of cities across the contry have experimented with this concept. Team policing originated in England in the 1940's and was tentatively endorsed by the Crime Commission in 1967. What is team policing? Basically it involves reorganizing patrol assignments so that a "team" of officers is permanently assigned to a specific geographic area. Also, the distinction between patrol and investigative officers is eliminated. A patrol officer who encounters a serious crime would follow up on the investigation rather than turn it over to a detective. Finally, the members of the team are to work together, as a task force, sharing experiences and ideas and formulating policy.[21]

The objectives of team policing are clear. By assigning officers permanently to an area, hopefully they will get to know the area and the people better and this will lead to improved police-community relations. By decentralizing the department and bringing the team closer to the community, hopefully the police will be more responsive to the community's needs. The involvement of rank and file officers in team decision-making would hopefully reduce alienation and allow individual officers to develop their own ideas and interests.

How well does team policing work in practice? The Police Foundation studied seven cities that had experimented with the idea (Dayton, Detroit, New York City, Syracuse, Holyoke, Los Angeles, and Richmond, California). The results were not clear. In many cases the experiment was undertaken too hastily and without proper preparation. In many cases it was not a true team policing experiment. It is also clear that team policing requires special training and committed and capable leadership if it is to work. Also, the fears of established interests within the department and in the community need to be addressed.

It is too early to reach a final judgement about team policing. But it is clear that police departments will have to incorporate many of its ideas. One of the major problems in contemporary society is the "bureaucracy problem:" the fact that our society is filled with large and often unresponsive organizations (both government agencies and private corporations). Team policing attempts to deal with this problem by *de*centrailzing, by bringing the delivery of services closer to the community.

Team policing also addresses itself to the question of police officer alienation. It seeks to give them a more direct involvement in the creative, policy-making process. There have been other attempts to accomplish the same goal by means of police officer "task forces." Two of these experiments, one in Kansas City and one in Oakland, deserve our attention.

The Kansas City task force is more famous for the result of its work. It led to the Kansas City Preventive Patrol Experiment, co-sponsored by the Police Foundation. This was one of the first attempts to scientifically test the effectiveness of routine police patrol. The results were extremely controversial for they challenged many assumptions about the value of routine patrol. But we are less concerned about the experiment here and more concerned about the *process* by which it developed.[22]

Under Police Chief Clarence Kelley (who was later appointed Director of the F.B.I.) the Kansas City Police Department began experimenting with police officer task forces as early as 1970–1971. In 1972 the department received an additional 300 men and began to discuss ways of using them most effectively. The South Patrol Division task force was able to list five major community problems, but had to admit "We don't know anything about existing patrol procedures, or the effectiveness of preventive patrol." Together with the Police Foundation, then, they designed a patrol experiment.[23]

How did the task forces operate? According to one participant, "The majority of the patrol task force members are patrolmen. They are provided with funds for travel and consultant assistance. They have been provided with private offices, generally away from Division stations. They have committed men full time to following up and working on task force projects. They have been given the authority to implement their recommen-dations and designs." In short, they were acting like professionals in other occupations, with much of the power, freedom and autonomy to make changes in their own work. This approach was very different from the usual style of innovation in policing. The old style usually did not involve the rank and file; instead a reform-minded police chief took charge and announced changes he had decided on. The result, usually, was more officer alienation.[24]

How well did the task force approach work? It lead to an experiment of national significance, but it was not without problems. Many officers opposed the project and there were often angry clashes between officers. One participant said that "We were all uncertain about what we were doing. This at times was a good deal frightening." But he also argued that "The task oriented groups are a potentially powerful approach to organizational change. We feel that they are a learning environment . . . and encourage innovation and creative thinking." It is certainly a different approach to professionalism and one with great potential for the future.[25]

In Oakland, California the police department under Chief Charles Gain tried a somewhat different approach to the use of task forces. In cooperation with the noted pyschologist Hans Toch, the department attempted to do something about the problem of violence. This was a new approach to an old police problem: what to do about officers who become involved in violent clashes with members of the public. The traditional approach, of course, had always been to wait until someone filed a complaint, investigate the incident, and if the charges were sustained, to discipline the officer involved.[26]

The new approach was based on the idea that you had to involve the individuals who seemed to be violence-prone in the process of change. Psychologist Hans Toch had been working on these ideas for some years. As a result, the department created a task force to work on the problems of violence; it was called the Violence Prevention Unit (VPU). Members of the VPU included officers who had been involved in a number of violent incidents. The task force went about its work by discussing and analyzing the details of specific incidents of violence. This too was a very different approach to the question of police discipline. It was similar to the approach used by established professions, a system of self-discipline which involves the members of the profession itself.

How well did the Oakland Violence Prevention Unit work? The results were mixed. Many problems were encountered along the way and there was some conflict within the department over the project. Also, it is difficult to measure the long-run effectiveness of the idea: did it really make a difference in terms of the incidence of violence? Nonetheless, it did establish a new approach to the old problem of disciplining police misconduct. And in this respect it deserves to be studied carefully for possible application in the future.

Police Professionalism at the Crossroads

The alternatives for police reform are clear. In one direction lies the traditional style of reform. It puts the greatest emphasis on mangerial efficiency, in centralizing the bureaucratic apparatus in order to give the police executive firmer control over the rank and file. In the other direction lies a very different style of reform. It seeks to decentralize the bureaucracy in order to involve police officers in policy-making and in order to bring the police agency closer to the community it serves. One defines professionalism in terms of an efficient organization. The other defines it in terms of an involved police officer, a "professional" who is committed to continuing self-development and who assumes responsibility for the conduct of fellow professionals.

The choice between these alternatives is not an easy one. The traditional approach has led to bureaucratization and police officer alienation. But it does have a positive side, one that is not to be ignored. Centralization has lead to greater uniformity in police practices. This is crucial to the law enforcement function, for the U.S. Constitution guarantees to all citizens the equal protection of the laws. In a democratic society it is unacceptable that the police treat similar situations in different ways, or treat different groups in different ways. This is the main problem with the new approach to police reform. If full decentralization were carried out, it might result in very different law enforcement policies in different parts of town. It might mean that the police chief, or public safety director, had no control over what patrol officers were doing. This is inconsistent with the need for accountability on the part of government agencies.

The choice between the alternative routes toward professionalism dramatizes the problem facing all large organizations in our society today. The problem faces private corporation as well as government agencies. It is the problem of maintaining the efficiency and accountability of the large organization while allowing for flexibility in policy and participation by those who carry out policy. In various ways those of us who are concerned with police administration will wrestle with this problem through the rest of the 1970's and into the 1980's.

Discussion Questions

1. What are the attributes of a profession? Give a brief definition, applicable to the full range of professional and semi-professional occupations.

2. Police professionalism emerged at a particular time period in the history of American police. Indicate the time period and the major problems that the reformers sought to deal with.

3. By the 1960's many experts were critical of the dominant style of police professionalism. Briefly summarize those criticisms.

4. Describe the main characteristics of the alternative approaches to police professionalism that have emerged in recent years.

Notes

1. The best summary of the state of policing in the United States today is Herman Goldstein, *Policing a Free Society* (Cambridge, Mass.: Ballinger, 1977).

2. The different definitions are analyzed in Samuel Walker, "Police Professionalism: Another Look at the Issues," *Journal of Sociology and Social Welfare*, III (July 1976); 701–710.

3. The best summary is W.E. Moore, *The Professions: Rules and Roles* (New York: Russell Sage, 1970).

4. James Q. Wilson, *Varieties of Police Behavior* (New York: Atheneum, 1973), pp. 29–30.

5. This material is drawn from Samuel Walker, *A Critical History of Police Reform: The Emergence of Professionalism* (Lexington, Mass.: Lexington Books, 1977).

6. For a valuable statement of police reform objectives, see Raymond B. Fosdick, *American Police Systems* (New York: The Century Co, 1920).

7. See August Vollmer, *The Police and Modern Society* (Berkeley: University of California Press, 1936).

8. Walker, *A Critical History of Police Reform*.

9. See the critical account in Paul Jacobs, *Prelude to Riot* (New York: Vintage Books, 1968).

10. President's Commission on Law Enforcement and Administration of Justice, *The Challenge of Crime in a Free Society* (1967); National Advisory Commission on Civil Disorders, *Report of the National Advisory Commission on Civil Disorders* (1968); National Commission on the Causes and Prevention of Violence, *To Establish Justice, To Insure Domestic Tranquility* (1969); President's Commission on Campus Unrest, *The Report of the President's Commission on Campus Unrest* (1970).

11. President's Commission on Law Enforcement and Administration of Justice, *The Challenge of Crime in a Free Society* (New York: Avon Books, 1968), pp. 258–259; *Report of the National Advisory Commission on Civil Disorders* (New York: Bantam Books, 1968), p. 301.

12. William A. Westley, *Violence and the Police* (Cambridge, Mass.: MIT Press, 1970).

13. Jerome Skolnick, *Justice Without Trial* (New York: John Wiley, 1966).

14. *Ibid.*, pp. 235–239.

15. *The Challenge of Crime in a Free Society*, pp. 267, 300–301.

16. *Ibid.*, p. 294.

17. *Ibid.*, pp. 280, 286.

18. National Advisory Commission on Criminal Justice Standards and Goals, *Police* (Washington, 1973).

19. For a summary of research, see Lawerence W. Sherman, "The Sociology and the Social Reform of the American Police, 1950–1973," *Journal of Police Science and Administration,* 2 (1974), 255–262.

20. Albert Reiss, *The Police and the Public* (New Haven: Yale University Press, 1971).

21. Lawrence W. Sherman, et al., *Team Policing: Seven Case Studies* (Washington: The Police Foundation, 1973); Peter B. Bloch & David Specht, *Neighborhood Team Policing (Washington: U.S. Department of Justice, 1973).*

22. *George L. Kelling, et al., The Kansas City Preventive Patrol Experiment: A Summary Report* (Washington: The Police Foundation, 1974).

23. National League of Cities, *Changing Police Organizatios: Four Readings* (Washington, D.C., 1973). pp, 16–17.

24. *Ibid.*, p. 16.

25. *Ibid.*, p. 21–22.

26. Hans Toch, et al., *Agents of Change: A Study in Police Reform* (Cambridge, Mass.: Schenkman, 1975).

3

Why the Police Cannot Stop Crime:
A Call for Police Reorganization

JAMES A. FAGIN

Introduction

THE FEAR OF CRIME is the number one public concern. Gallup polls, Presidential Commissions, and studies by the Law Enforcement Assistance Administration (LEAA) have concluded that Americans are fearful of becoming victims of crime both in the streets and in their homes. The Police are in the spotlight as Americans attempt to combat the "crime wave" (Crime Wave, 1975). Traditionally the police and public have viewed the primary mission of the police as the prevention of crime (Wilson, 1963) and historically the overwhelming majority of the police officer's time, emphasis training and resources has been dedicated to the catching of criminals and the prevention of crime. The strong emphasis upon the police as crime fighters is evident in that one of the original guidelines posited by Sir Robert Peel, father of modern policing, was that the best test of police efficiency was the absence of crime. The police have retained the responsibility for rising crime rates and unsafe streets and police officers and police departments have aspired to fight crime.

Unfortunately there is serious question as to the success of the police in combating the crime wave. Public confidence in the police is low. Preiss and Ehrlich (1966:8) affirmed that "the police suffer from a rather unilaterally negative image." The National Advisory Commission on Civil Disorders (1968:83) reported that public dissatisfaction with the police was one of the most serious complaints of citizens. Finally, the National Advisory Commission on Criminal Justice Standards and Goals (1973) has concluded that many of those whom the police serve have lost all confidence in the ability of the police to maintain law and order in the community. Why are the police failing to stop the crime wave?

Sir Robert Peel charged that the best test of police efficiency was the absence of crime; however, the American police officer is not like a specialist

174

or technician in that his exclusive function is to combat crime. The police are significantly affected in their ability to reduce crime by the resources they must expend to perform non-law enforcement or community service activities. Crime fighting is not the only responsibility of the police. The patrol officer finds that he must be proficient at a variety of tasks which have little if anything to do with crime fighting.

Upon first examining the activities of the police patrol officer it appears that there is no order to the seemingly endless variety of tasks that he performs. The police direct traffic, catch stray animals, catch criminals, escort officials and citizens, deliver babies, patrol business and residential premises, take crime reports, administer first aid, assist in natural disasters, patch-up domestic disputes, etc. However, the President's Commission on Law Enforcement and Administration of Justice (1967) after a comprehensive analysis of the activities of the American police officer concluded that his role could best be comprehended as divided into two major types of activities or roles which the Commission labeled law enforcement and community service. The law enforcement role is that role in which the police enforce the criminal laws and perform activities related to the enforcement of criminal laws such as the prevention of criminal activity and participation in court proceedings. The community service role is that role in which the police provide essentially a social service to the community, performing in a non-criminal, service capacity such as controlling traffic, providing assistance, and resolving of day-to-day conflicts among friends, family or neighbors. Investigations by the National Commission on the Causes and Prevention of Violence (1969) and the National Advisory Commission on Criminal Justice Standards and Goals (1973) also concluded that these two major roles, law enforcement and community service, constitute the totality of police activities in the community.

This division of time between law enforcement and community service has significantly reduced the effectiveness of the police as a deterrent to crime, called into question the legitimacy of their function, and eroded public trust and confidence. The primary reasons for this calamity are: (1) Community service activities dominate the demand for police service resulting in reduced resources and manpower to combat crime. (2) The police are inadequately trained to perform a number of community service activities such as conflict resolution which results in the police officer and the public being needlessly and recklessly exposed to potentially dangerous situations. (3) Finally, the two roles contain role expectations which are incompatible. The resulting role conflict results in frustration and attitudinal and behavioral problems for the police officer and the public.

Demand for Community Services

The police perform a great number of community services which are also provided by a proliferation of different governmental and community agencies. Although these services are provided by other agencies the police are the agents who are most frequently contacted because they are accessible around-the-clock, they have high mobility, and because often the citizen does not differentiate between the police and these various other agencies (National Advisory Commission on Criminal Justice Standards and Goals, 1973:10; hereafter referred to as National Advisory Commission). The role of the police officer has become so ubiquitous that to most citizens the police officer is the government (Greater Egypt Planning and Development Commission, 1971:1). The public has come to regard the police as a gigantic surrogate agency for the community, handling all the needs of all the people all the time. As a result of this perception by the public the police officer finds that the demand for his time is dominated by calls for community service.

In studies which have established quantitative measures of the division of time between law enforcement and community service the conclusion of all studies has been that the majority of the policeman's time is devoted to the performance of community service activities rather than law enforcement activities. James Q. Wilson (1968:18), for example, reported that according to his survey of the Syracuse Police Department (New York) sixty-seven percent of the calls requesting police service were requests for community service or order maintenance assistance; whereas, only one percent were requests for law enforcement or crime fighting assistance. In a summary of their findings the President's Commission on Law Enforcement and Administration of Justice (1967:13) concluded that police patrol officers spent considerably more time ". . . handling non-police items such as family disputes, calls for assistance or information, or order maintenance." Even in the large cities where one would expect that the police would be preoccupied with fighting crime the statistics still indicate that the police officer primarily performs community service rather than crime fighting. In a study of a Baltimore police district, for example, Wallach (1970:20) found:

> The bulk of police activity . . . does not relate to . . . the crime control function. The vast majority of police activities . . . do not involve crime and most of the crime related contacts are really after-the-fact report taking from crime victims. The vast majority of all resident's requests sampled was related to the maintenance of order, the settling of interpersonal disputes, and the need for advice and emergency assistance. Overall crime related calls constituted less than one-fourth of . . . police calls.

Similar studies of other cities indicate that in some cases as much as eighty percent of the policeman's committed activity is spent in performing community service activities (Garmire, 1972; Sterling, 1972; and Wasserman, 1973).

The resources and manpower of police departments are seriously strained by this large demand for community services. Most police departments have budgetary constraints which have reduced their manpower to near critical or critical levels. The time necessary to perform the community services demanded has in some cases exceeded the capacity of the police and it has become necessary to queue all requests for services. When requests are queued some citizens resort to deceit to obtain police services. Citizens who need assistance, perhaps to light a furnace that has gone out or retrieve a pet from a difficult situation or arbitrate a dispute with neighbors, give the police dispatcher fraudulent information to hasten the arrival of the police. They falsely report that they are being victimized or have observed a crime committed. For example, one elderly citizen who was unable to relight her gas furnace pilot light telephoned the police dispatcher and reported that a man was breaking down her front door. Several police units traveled at high speed across the city to respond to the scene only to be met by the citizen who informed them of her deceit. She admitted that she knew that if she informed the police dispatcher of her true circumstances it would be hours before the police would arrive, if they would arrive, and she did not want to go that long without heat so she reported the fictional intruder. Another citizen reported to the police dispatcher his neighbors were fighting and several appeared to be armed with knives and pistols. Upon arriving at the address of the "fight" the police found only a loud party in progress. The complaining citizen confessed his lie. His rationale was that he had called the police several times in the last hour complaining about the loud party and no one had yet arrived to "take care of the problem." He, therefore, reported the fight to hasten the arrival of the police.

More serious problems can result when citizens become impatient and attempt to resolve situations themselves in their own manner. One citizen, for example, telephoned the police dispatcher and reported that his eleven year old white son had been chased by a group of black juveniles who threw rocks at him. The report involved no report of injuries or present danger to any party so the call was queued. The dispatcher next received a call reporting a gun fight. The angered citizen, too impatient to wait, had returned to the scene of the alleged attack and had become engaged in an argument with the parents of the black juveniles which ended in gun shots being exchanged. The inability of the police to provide requested services can result in deterioration of trust and confidence by both the citizens and the police.

Excessive demands can have more direct effects upon the ability of the police to fight crime. The ability of the police to investigate crimes can be curtailed. The police find that they have inadequate manpower to properly investigate major crimes or to commit personnel to the investigation of specialized crimes such as white collar crime, organized crime, youth crime, etc. Overworked detectives and patrol officers can also be hampered in the investigation of "routine" crimes. Unable to respond to all the demands of citizens patrol officers devote time only to "major" problems. The police distinguish between "little stuff" and "real crime" and concentrate only on "real crime" (Wilson, 1969). Citizens are quick to realize the overworked patrol officer cannot or will not bring the criminal to justice and lose faith in the police. Citizens become apathetic and fail to report even "minor" crimes to the police or crimes which they "think" the police cannot or will not solve. This public apathy promotes increased crime rates in burglary, robbery, theft, rape and other crimes against persons and property.

Inadequate Training

Statistics indicate that approximately twenty percent or more of all police activity is directly involved in conflict management. These statistics, however, do not adequately reflect the fact that for certain population groups the police are the adjudicative agency for arbitration and peace keeping services (Wasserman, 1973:43). The police perform this community service not because of their desire to do so or the special training they receive or even a legal responsibility to resolve such conflicts. The police traditionally are not and do not consider themselves as an element of the helping service system but because they are usually the first summoned when conflict erupts, they have a highly organized mobile response capability, and they have legal and symbolic power, the public expects them to act as mediators or counselors.

The public looks to the police officer to provide authoritative, on-the-spot remedies to a great variety of situations without the use of arrest or violence (Shah, 1973:112). Legally speaking the involvement of the police in interpersonal conflicts is usually narrowly limited to the enforcement of laws. The police have the authority to arrest any party to the dispute who violates the law. That is to say, the police may arrest the disputants for acts of assault, disorderly conduct, drunkenness, etc., but the police have no clearly defined legal or moral responsibility to act as marriage counselor, psychologist, mentor, A.A. counselor, etc. This ambiguity is reflected in the organizational policy and the training the police officer receives. For most of the police departments there is no policy as to the handling of "domestic disputes," training in social service techniques or counseling, or organizational reward or recognitions for effective performance in what is essentially a social service.

The police officer is not trained and in some cases is not capable of delivering the community services demanded by the public. Police officers in general receive only minimal training. Seymour Lipset (1969) aptly pointed out the deficiency of police training by comparing it to training received in other occupations. While physicians receive a legal minimum of 11,000 hours of training, embalmers receive 5,000, barbers receive 4,000 and beauticians 1,200 hours of training; the policeman receives less than 200 hours of training. "The vast majority of policemen begin carrying guns and enforcing the law with less than five weeks training of any kind." Lipset concludes that society treats the policeman's job like a semiskilled position which requires, at best, a few weeks of training. Of the general training that police officers do receive little has to do with service. The National Advisory Commission (1973) in evaluating police training concluded that training in subjects other than law enforcement, e.g., order maintenance, psychology, interpersonal communication skills, sociology, etc., comprises only from five percent to twenty percent of the training curriculum. This is inadequate to prepare the police officer to perform the role skills expected of him.

Most of the training the police officer does receive in order maintenance skills is on-the-job training. This training usually emphasizes that the law enforcement officer is to control and direct people. Thus, the "natural" tendency is for the officer in interpersonal interactions to assume a position of superiority, control, suspicion, and neutrality. These characteristics are counterproductive in order maintenance (Barb, et al., 1975; Gibb, 1971; Johannesen, 1971; Mills, 1973). More seriously the "natural" response of the police officer frequently results in needless injuries and deaths. The "working personality" (Skolnick, 1966) of the police officer is such that in the "pacification of a routine domestic quarrel, the officer will behave in a suspicious, brusque and challenging manner" (Reiss, 1972:51; Steadman, 1972). The interaction of police and citizen in conflict situations where citizens are agitated and antagonistic is likely to produce hostilities and even combat between the two.

On-the-job training does not teach the police officer complex counseling skills and often the legal authority of the police officer to arrest the disturbing party is useless in solving disputes. At times a police officer who tries to exercise his legal authority of arrest only makes matters worse. When arrests are made as a means to settle interpersonal disputes often the officer finds that all parties to the dispute become uncooperative, hostile and resentful toward him for his actions. For example, if an officer arrests a husband for assaulting his wife, often the officer finds that the "victim" will fail to testify against her husband in court. This can happen even though at the time of the arrest the wife demanded, even insisted, upon the arrest of her husband. In some cases the wife (or husband) can even turn upon the arresting officer attacking him and defending the individual who just a few moments ago she was belligerently assailing.

Frequently the difficulty of the police officer's task in order maintenance is hard to appreciate. For example, in reaction to observations of police work in handling interpersonal and family conflict the general comment from a group of psychological consultants of New York City University (Barb, 1970:14) was:

> I had no idea how difficult the policeman's job is. . . . A clinician would take days of tests and interviews to make the decisions that these guys have to make under pressure, often at the risk of their own skin.

The mythology of police work is that law enforcement activities, catching criminals, are dangerous while community service and order maintenance, helping people, is safe. This simply is not true. Family fights are second in frequency only to motor vehicle accidents as incidents involving police action and there is always the potential of serious violence or even homicide resulting from such disputes. There are numerous studies which support Durkeim's observation that while family life has a moderating effect upon suicide, it rather stimulates murder. Wolfgang (1961) in studies of homicides committed concluded that "homicides committed during robberies receive much publicity but do not represent as great a number of killings as do marital discord and quarrels between friends." For example, according to Federal Bureau of Investigation crime statistics approximately seventy percent of the victims of homicides are related to, friends with, or knew their attacker. Of all murders reported approximately twenty-five percent occur between family members. Seven percent occur during "lover's quarrels," and approximately forty-one percent as the result of other arguments. Additionally, a large number of assaults and attempted homicides are committed upon relatives, neighbors or acquaintances rather than strangers.

The picture that clearly emerges from these statistics is that family quarrels and disturbances are a very hazardous assignment. Police officers surveyed in the Midwest indicated that they considered responding to a disturbance call as one of the most dangerous tasks they do (Fagin, 1977). This perception by the police officer is supported by statistics. In 1971 nine police officers were killed in the line of duty responding to disturbance calls. In 1972 the figure nearly doubled to seventeen and for 1973 again nearly doubled as thirty officers were killed responding to disturbance calls. This figure again nearly doubled for 1974, substantially increased in 1975 and remains a major cause of police deaths in 1978. The Federal Bureau of Investigation (Law Enforcement Officers Killed, 1973) warned:

> More officers were killed in responding to disturbance calls than any other type activity. Deaths resulting from responding to disturbance calls have increased more than deaths due to any other cause since 1971.

These figures do not record the additional danger the police officer faces in the numerous assaults that officers have suffered during disturbance calls. Due to inconsistent and inaccurate record keeping this figure cannot be known. However, it is surmised that over fifty percent of the days of work lost in the City of New York due to injury were due to injuries sustained responding to domestic fights and disturbances (Barb: 1973). The resulting loss of police officers due to death, the loss of days off due to injuries, and the time expended by the police office acting as marriage counselor, psychologist, etc., detracts from the ability of the police to combat crime.

Role Conflict

The performance of community service and order maintenance causes serious strain upon police resources and the inadequate training of officers further depreciates the quality of police services. However, there is even a more serious problem than excessive demand for police services and inadequate training that results from the division of the patrol officer's responsibilities between crime fighting and community service. This is the problem of role conflict.

Role conflict in general is the simultaneous occurrence of two or more role sendings such that compliance with one would make difficult compliance with the other (Katz and Kahn, 1966:184). A role sending is the transmission of the characteristics, attributes, attitudes, behaviors, etc., an actor is expected to exhibit in a defined role. Role sendings can be transmitted formally and informally by numerous means such as peer groups, mores, reference groups, rules, media, etc. For example, a common role characteristic expected of a police officer is that he or she be proficient in the use of firearms. This role expectation is transmitted formally by departmental regulations specifying minimum skills proficiency with firearms and is transmitted informally by peer pressure and to some extent by the image of the police officer represented in the media.

In the extreme case of role conflict the two expectations in conflict are mutually contradictory in that compliance with one expectation would exclude completely compliance with the other. For example, a police officer is expected to protect the public and at the same time the officer has expectations regarding his own personal safety. The situation can arise, however, in which these two are in conflict. In certain exigencies a police officer might have to jeopardize his own personal safety, even risk death, in an effort to prevent harm to others.

The expectations of the community service role and the law enforcement role are a case of extreme role conflict. To fulfill the expectations of one role would exclude compliance with the other. No amount of training, additional resources or skills can reduce the conflict between the two roles. The expectations for each role are sharply different and the skills necessary for each role conflict. Garmire (1972:4) argued that the two roles are so sharply different and conflicting that "one person simply cannot reasonably be expected to master both roles intellectually and jump psychologically from one to another in an instance's notice." The psychological, emotional and intellectual attributes and skills required to perform crime fighting and service are different. The crime fighter is suspicious, controlling, threatening, more responsive to danger cues, and more abrasive with the public. The crime fighter emphasizes the skills of self-defense, pistol shooting, alertness, legal knowledge, common sense and investigative skills. On the other hand service requires cooperation with the public, problem orientated interpersonal communication skills, empathy and trust. A police officer is expected to be a peace maker for domestic disputes and investigate a murder with equal skill and proficiency and demonstrate proper role behavior in each duty. This expectation by the public is unrealistic.

The problems generated by role conflict are complicated by the fact that police officers have not accepted the service role. Police officers have not desired to acquire the skills necessary for service and order maintenance. Police officers prefer to think of themselves as crime fighters. They strive to fulfill the role expectations related to law enforcement and develop emotional, psychological and intellectual skills that would enhance their abilities and skills as law enforcement officers. The police self image is one in which the police officer "pictures himself as the crime fighter standing alone against the Mongol hordes" (Police Need Help, 1968:26). There is much emphasis and importance placed upon the law enforcement role as reflected by the metaphor of "the thin blue line" used both by the police and the public and the police are committed to maintaining this self image. Preiss and Ehrlich (1966) reported from their observations of the Central State Police that one of the major themes of the culture was that the "department could be described as a masculine culture with sports and physical prowess among the main avenues of personal identification." They reported that despite the general recognition of "the largely honorific and artifact character" of competitive pistol shooting, boxing, and judo such skills were emphasized in the department. Shooting ability Preiss and Ehrlich (1966:14) observed "was considered by part of the training staff as one of the best criteria available for predicting success in the police role. Obviously this training stresses the importance of crime fighting skills. Service skills such as interpersonal communication, psychology, conflict resolution, etc., are often neglected. Training in "non-punitive orientation to social deviance" would lessen the self-image of the police as crime fighters and, therefore, has not received acceptance by the police (Trojanowicz, et al., 1975:155–156). There remains a residue of conviction by police officers that community service is a social function that is discrete from the "real" work of policing and is simply unappealing to most police officers (Fagin and Hogan, 1974).

The police officer's penchant for crime fighting and disdain for service is a characteristic of the police officer's "working personality" (Skolnick, 1966) that is developed over time in interaction with the elements of "danger" and "authority" which are inherent in the police role. Data from Sterling's (1973) longitudinal study of the development of the police officer's role perceptions concluded that the more experienced the officer became, the more his or her attitude shifted toward fulfilling the expectations of the law enforcement role and the less the officer valued attributes which would enable him to fulfill the service role. For example, Sterling reported that the experienced police officers tended to value formal education and its relevance to police work less than they did at the time they entered police work. The more experienced an officer became the more he reflected in his response to questionnaires a view of pragmatic realism or a sense of expediency in accomplishing his duties. Sterling summarized that the attributes which the officer saw as essential for the enactment of the police role were the general qualities of common sense, alertness, and job knowledge. Sterling (1973) concluded that personality development in the police officer generated extreme role conflict.

> The underlying tone of danger which pervades the police role appears to have the potential to detract in a number of ways from the effective performance of their duties. Considering the role demand upon the officer for the performance of community service activities and his desire for law enforcement and his subsequent personality compatibility with the latter and incompatibility with the former, it appears that as the officer becomes more experienced his personality becomes less suitable for the performance of community service activities which constitute the majority of his duties.

The desire of the police officer to perform crime fighting is frustrated. The public has come to expect even demand that the police provide social services such as marriage counseling, juvenile counseling, order maintenance, etc. (Klyman, et al., 1974). The performance of these service activities does little to strengthen the police officer's self image as a crime fighter and thus generates conflict (Taft and England, 1964) resulting in frustration, job dissatisfaction, poor role performance, and police community relations problems. This conflict cannot be solved or circumvented simply by rules, regulations or orders. The National Advisory Commission (1973:35) warned that in attempting to elicit changes in the attitude and behavior of police officers it must be remembered that "the police officer's attitude cannot be altered by administrative decree. The way an officer views his role depends upon many factors and the desire to achieve his agency's objectives is only one of them."

Conclusion

Due to social, institutional, and organizational changes the police role has undergone change. The police have become emersed in community service and order maintenance to the detriment of law enforcement. The result has been excessive demand for non-essential, non-law enforcement police services; exposure of the police officer to potentially dangerous situations for which he is not adquately trained; and the generation of role conflict which has further deteriorated the quality of policing. It is necessary to correct these problems.

It is not possible or desirable to suspend all service and order maintenance activities performed by the police; however, the law enforcement efficiency and effectiveness of the police must be increased. The problems of policing discussed are inherent in the present organization of police agencies rather than with the personalities of the individual officers (Broderick, 1977). Thus, to accomplish this goal there is the need to reorganize and redefine policing. Toffler (1971) has warned that the individual will have to become infinitely more adaptable and capable than ever before. "He must search out totally new ways to anchor himself, for all the old roots—religion, nation, community, family, or profession—are now shaking under the hurricane impact of the accelerative thrust." There is no reason whatsoever to believe that the profession of policing has not been subjected to and will not continue to be subjected to the "impact of the accelerative thrust of change." The reality is that the police role has undergone change but without the necessary individual, organizational, and social reorganization. The police role has undergone change but there is a lag between the new role expectations and the ability of the police to perform these new responsibilities.

It is beyond the scope of this paper to deliver the details of the necessary reorganization. This is a separate question for study. However, some possible changes to promote law enforcement efficiency which appear to have promise will be briefly highlighted. Briefly presented three major changes advocated by this writer are:

1. Reduction of police responsibilities in community service and order maintenance.

2. Major organizational changes in police agencies.

3. Education of the public to accept realistic responsibilities concerning the services, including law enforcement that the police can deliver.

Reducing Non-Law Enforcement Responsibilities

The police perform many duties which are the responsibility of other agencies or institutions. It is necessary to reduce the numerous non-essential function performed by the police to promote the crime fighting effectiveness of the police by returning the performance of these services to the proper agency or institution. There are several steps that could be taken to perform this. First, the resources and services of other agencies should be increased. Often the police handle the work of other agencies only because the proper agency is not open around-the-clock, does not have adequate resources, or does not have the mobility of the police. There is the special problem of strengthening the resources of the family, as the weakening of this institution is a major reason for increased police activity and responsibility in both service and law enforcement (National Advisory Commision, 1973).

Reorganization of Police Agencies

The police should be given new authority to deal with order maintenance problems, the most time consuming non-essential activity. This new authority would permit police officers to compel disorderly parties to submit to some form of professional arbitration or counsel. Presently police officers can only suggest that the disputants seek professional arbitration or counsel, or police officers can arrest the disturbing party. This approach is inadequate. The parties rarely ever seek professional help as suggested and to arrest the disturbing party at best can only provide temporary treatment of the symptoms of the problem.

Some police departments presently have analogous powers in handling intoxicated persons. Instead of arrest the police have the authority to deliver intoxicated persons to clinics or agencies especially prepared to treat the individual. Likewise, the police could be given the authority to compel disturbing parties to seek assistance from an adjudicative agency. Some communities have already established voluntary adjudicative agencies such as "neighborhood courts," "domestic affairs units," etc. The expansion of these existing adjudicative agencies combined with police authority to compel their use could be fruitful.

An innovative approach would be to create a new agency to handle community service and order maintenance activities. This agency would handle requests for service presently handled by police. Individuals in this unit would receive special training in the skills necessary to handle service calls and would have the authority necessary to complete the calls by themselves. A modification of this proposal would be to develop specialized units within the police department to provide services. This unit could be discrete from "law enforcement" units thus having different personnel recruitment, supervision, goals, role definitions, and reward structures. The establishment of such a specialized unit could be publicly or privately financed or the cost might be financed by charging appropriate fees for services rendered.

Major organizational changes within police agencies should be made to result in increased law enforcement effectiveness. Major reorganization to adopt such concepts as participative management, proactive policing, team policing, etc., could result in improved crime prevention and better crime clearance rates. Major reorganization would also require higher educational standards and more professional and role training for police officers in the process. Present police standards for education are inadequate as the majority of departments require only a minimum of high school graduation and the average police officer does not get needed skills training. The consideration of consolidation of police services or a centralized police would also be a major organizational change that could permit the necessary changes and growth to maintain law and order in the community. The concept of a centralized police would provide several significant advantages in combating crime.

Realistic Expectations

To restore dynamic equilibrium to the process of maintaining law and order it will be necessary to educate the public to accept realistic expectations concerning the services, including law enforcement, that the police can deliver. Presently public expectations are highly unrealistic. Police are underpaid, inadequately trained and overworked and yet the public expects the police to provide services requiring the mastery of complex learned psychological and intellectual skills on demand and without fault. Failure by the police to fulfill public expectations causes public hostility and distrust. Research (Police Community Relations Program, 1967:10) indicates that police-community relations problems are not so much the result of police brutality or corruption as citizen indignation over what is perceived as "clumsy manners, insensitive and rude communication and thoughtless indignities." While the cause of these problems sometimes is the responsibility of the police often this perception is due to unrealistic expectations by the public as to who the police are and the services they provide.

The public must also recognize that the police are not solely responsible for crime prevention. Numerous social and economic phenomenon beyond the control or influence of the police are causes of crime and disorder. It is necessary to attack the causes as well as the symptoms of crime and all responsibility for crime cannot be put upon the police.

Change and improvement can often be dangerous. Unfulfilled anticipated rising expectations can generate frustration, backlash and abandonment. Westley (1972:41) has pointed out that it is not in the nature of Americans "to make the policeman and the police objects of love and endearment" regardless of their professionalism, efficiency or effectiveness. Expectations of a pandemic cure for all police-community relations problems and law enforcement problems must be avoided. The primary mission of the police is to protect the public and to provide law and order in the community. A return to this primary mission is a reasonable goal. The police role has become so diversified and contradictory as to preclude a concentration of effort to provide law and order at a time when it is desperately needed.

Citizens and police need to enact change immediately as many police departments have already lost their ability to effectively combat crime. Wilkins (1973) warned that major change in the American criminal justice system is necessary immediately or the system will "suffer a complete breakdown before the year 2000." Maintaining law and order is a major problem in the latter years of the 1970's but it is not a police problem. It is a public problem. Extensive cooperation and support is necessary to solve what DeWolf (1975) termed "America's most pressing moral problem."

Discussion Questions

1. The majority of the police officer's time is spent handling community service and order maintenance activities but many of the services the police presently provide could or should be provided by other institutions or agencies. How can these waning or ineffective institutions and agencies be strengthened to reduce the demand upon the police for non-law enforcement services?

2. The police will probably always perform some non-law enforcement services; however, the present training and socialization of the police officer emphasizes almost exclusively the importance of law enforcement and law enforcement skills. What changes in the police role, police training, police recruitment, and educational standards for police would result in the police officer being able to perform community service and order maintenance more effectively and yet retain his or her identity and self image as a law enforcement officer?

3. A number of authorities report that police officers become cynical and frustrated over the apparent lack of efficiency of the criminal justice system, including police agencies, in dealing with the criminal offender. This phenomenon most likely depreciates the quality of policing. How can police agenices be reorganized so as to increase the effectiveness with which they apprehend and process the criminal offender? How can the criminal justice system be reorganized?

References Cited

Barb, M. *Training police as specialists in family crisis intervention.* Washington, D.C.: GPO, 1970.

———. *Family crisis intervention: From concept to implementation.* Washington, D.C.: GPO, 1973.

Barb, M. *et al. The function of the police in crisis intervention and conflict management: A training guide.* Washington, D.C.: U.S. Department of Justice, 1975.

Broderick, J.J. *Police in a time of change.* Morristown, New Jersey: General Learning Press, 1977.

The crime wave. *Time,* June 30, 1975, pp. 10–24.

DeWolf, L.H. *Crime and justice in America: A paradox of conscience.* New York: Harper and Row, 1975.

Fagin, J.A. *The effects of police interpersonal communication skills on conflict resolution.* Unpublished Ph.D. dissertation. Southern Illinois University, 1977.

Fagin, J.A. and Hogan, E.J. Integrating the Policeman into the Community. *Police Chief,* December, 1794.

Garmire, B.L. The police role in urban society. In R.F. Steadman (Ed.), *The police and the community.* Baltimore: The Johns Hopkins University Press, 1972.

Gibb, J.R. TORI community. In D.A. Kolb, I.M. Rubin and J. McIntyre (eds.), *Organizational psychology: A book of readings.* Englewood Cliffs: Prentice Hall, 1971.

Greater Egypt Regional Planning and Development Commission. *Police relations handbook.* Springfield, Illinois: Illinois Law Enforcement Commission, 1971.

Johannesen, R.L. The emerging concept of communication as dialogue. *The Quarterly Journal of Speech,* Volume LVII, Number 4, December 1971, pp. 373–382.

Katz, D. and Kahn, R.L. *The social psychology of organizations.* New York: John Wiley and Sons, Inc., 1966.

Klyman, F. and Kruckenberg, J.M. Preliminary report of citizen responses to a survey of perceptions of police-community relations. In F.I. Klyman, et al. (Eds.), *Police roles in a changing community.* Wichita, Kansas: Wichita State University, 1973.

Law Enforcement Officers Killed Summary. Washington D.C.: Federal Bureau of Investigation, 1973.

Lipset, L. Why cops hate liberals: And vice versa. *Atlantic.* April, 1969, pp. 76–83.

Mills, P. *Crisis intervention resource manual.* Vermillion, South Dakota: South Dakota University Press, 1973.

National Advisory Commission on Civil Disorders. *The Kerner Report.* New York: Bantam Books, 1968.

National Advisory Commission on Criminal Justice Standards and Goals. *Police.* Washington, D.C.: U.S. Department of Justice, 1973.

National Commission on the Causes and Prevention of Violence. *Law and order reconsidered.* Washington, D.C.: GPO, 1969.

Police community relations programs. *Management Information Service.* November 1967.

Police need help. *Time.* October 4, 1968, p. 26.

Preiss, J.J. and Ehrlich, H.J. *An examination of role theory: The case of the state police.* Lincoln, Nebraska: University of Nebraska Press, 1966.

President's Commission on Law Enforcement and Administration of Justice. *Task Force Report: The police.* Washington, D.C.: GPO, 1967.

Reiss, A.J. *The police and the public.* New Haven: Yale University Press, 1972.

Shah, S.A. Functions of police in modern society. In International Association of Chiefs of Police, *The police yearbook: 1973.* Gaithersburg, Maryland: International Association of Chiefs of Police, Inc., 1973.

Skolnick, J.H. *Justice without trial: A sociological study of law enforcement.* New York: John Wiley and Sons, 1966.

Steadman, R.F. *The police and the community.* Baltimore: The Johns Hopkins University Press, 1972.

Sterling, J.W. *Changes in role concepts of police officers.* Gaithersburg, Maryland: International Association of Chiefs of Police, Inc., 1972.

Sterling, J.W. Functions of police in modern society. In International Association of Chiefs of Police, *The police yearbook: 1973.* Gaithersburg, Maryland: International Association of Chiefs of Police, Inc., 1973.

Taft, D.R. and England, R.W. *Criminology.* New York: Macmillan, 1964.

Toffler, A. *Future shock.* New York: Bantam Books, 1971.

Trojanowicz, R.C.; Trojanowicz, J.M. and Moss, F.M. *Community based crime prevention*. Palisades, CA.: Goodyear Publishing Company, 1975.

Wallach, L.A. A new approach to solving the police dilemma. *Police*. September–October, 1970, pp. 58–61.

Wasserman, R.; Gardner, M.P.; and Cohen, A.S. *Improving police-community relations*. Washington, D.C.: GPO, 1973.

Westley, W. *Violence and the police: A sociological study of law, custom and morality*. Cambridge, Mass.: MIT Press, 1970.

Wilkins. L.T. Crime and criminal justice at the turn of the century. *The Annals of the American Academy of Political and Social Science,* Vol. 408, July, 1973.

Wilson, O.W. *Police administration*. New York: McGraw-Hill, 1963.

Wilson, J.Q. *Varieties of police behavior: The management of law and order in eight communities*. Cambridge, Mass.: Harvard University Press, 1968.

————. The police in the ghetto. In R.F. Steadman (Ed.), *The police and the community*. Baltimore: The Johns Hopkins University Press, 1972.

Wolfgang, M.E. A sociological analysis of criminal homicide. *Federal Probation Quarterly*. March 1961, pp. 48–55.

4

Police Discipline Management

RICHARD R. E. KANIA

THE CONDUCT OF ALL PUBLIC OFFICIALS rightly deserves public attention and scrutiny; the police all the more so. Law enforcement officers possess the rare, socially-bestowed sanction for the use of force and violence in the performance of their public duties. Assurance of the proper exercise of police power requires that standards be set for police conduct, and that these standards be maintained. Compliance with behavioral standards is the function of discipline. The term "discipline" has positive connotations when it denotes guidance and training toward self-control; the development of character, propriety and efficiency; and the acceptance of reasonable authority. More often, however, the term is used only in the negative sense of restraint or punishment. In the latter, more narrow sense, it is a topic of considerable interest to the students and scholars of public administration, personnel management, and law enforcement. The interest in the study of discipline did not develop within either the academic or professional communities, however. It was a product of the concern of the general public and the news media.

Police discipline is closely related to other recent issues receiving public interest, such as police ethics, abuse of civil rights, the use of excessive force, and overt brutality. Such public concern is not a recent phenomenon. It has had a history of rising to stimulate reforms and fading away into apparent dormancy, only to rise again in response to other related issues. In its prior manifestations, public interest in the conduct of the police has led to many reforms in law enforcement practices, policies and procedures. While court decisions have inspired many of the changes in recent years, the outcry of an outraged citizenry, provoked by a suspicious press, remains one of the principal causes of change.

The development of the early urban police departments was a response to public concern with corruption among elected sheriffs, marshals and wardens. The civil service reforms applied to the hiring and promotion practices of the police in many cities have also been the product of citizen involvement. More recently we have seen how popular pressure led to the creation of civilian review boards.[1] The growing popularity of internal affairs units is another development in this continuing trend.

While public interest and concern have inspired the formation of such units, their workings have not been known to the general public until just recently. The shroud of secrecy and mystery surrounding allegations of police misconduct was pulled away again by the critical press of the late 1960s. But the flesh and blood realities of these units have been exposed most vividly in popular fiction, notably Joseph Wambaugh's stories.[2] Although the "suspected cop" theme in fiction, as in real life, is not new, the attention that has been given to internal investigations procedures is. From the fictional dramatizations has come greater interest in how police manage, and should manage, discipline problems.

The development of the internal affairs unit has coincided with the rejection of the traditional approaches to internal discipline. However, even the most diligent search of the literature fails to discover any empirical data to indicate that this particular trend is having the desired effect of reducing police misconduct. For that matter, there is nothing to indicate that the traditional means of dealing with internal discipline were particularly defective. While it is reasonable to ask why the traditional approaches are being rejected, it is difficult to find an answer.

In 1976, as the culmination of a major study into the management of police discipline, the International Association of Chiefs of Police (IACP) released a comprehensive manual on this subject.[3] Brief mention is given to the traditional means of dealing with discipline. What the report has said about the traditional means is reserved and even somewhat negative.[4] In the IACP manual, and in much of the current literature, the older ways do not even warrant the assignment of a name. Hereafter, to overcome this deficiency in the IACP manual, it will be called the "chain-of-command" system of discipline in this presentation.

In the IACP manual the references to the use of specialized units for the management of police discipline are more extensive and are considerably more favorable.[5] The role of the line supervisor is downplayed. For example, the manual advises:

> When an allegation of a relatively minor nature comes to the attention of the agency, it should be the responsibility of the officer's immediate supervisor to investigate the truth or falsity of the allegation. Incidents of major proportion should be assigned to internal affairs for investigation. In either case the internal affairs unit should maintain staff control over all ongoing investigations.[6]

The conclusions of the IACP study minimizing the role of the line supervisors in managing police discipline, echo the recommendations of the President's Commission on Law Enforcement and Administration of Justice. Its Standard 19.3, "Investigative Responsibility," states:

> The chief executive of every police agency should insure that the investigation of all complaints from the public, and all allegations of criminal conduct and serious internal misconduct, are conducted by a specialized individual or unit of the involved police agency.[7]

Although the weight of professional opinion seems to follow the assumption that the chain-of-command system is deficient, a few scholars hold contrary views. After studying forty-six large police departments in 1970 and 1971, Robert Dempsey concluded that some departments do not need specialized units, and that the chain-of-command system "not only strengthens the authority of the direct supervisor, but also improves the morale of the officer in that he knows to whom he must answer on a regular basis for his trepidations."[8] N.F. Iannone, an expert on the supervision of police, came to a similar conclusion in his book on the subject. It is his determination that the line supervisor is, and should be, a key figure in effective discipline management.[9] In my own three-year study of disciplinary methods and procedures in a small urban police department in Virginia, I made the same findings. I could discover no justification to replace the existing system of line supervisor responsibility with specialization in the management of internal discipline.

For the police agency wishing to achieve effective control over the conduct of its officers, these conflicting views must present a bothersome dilemma. The standards promulgated by the President's Commission are a strong inducement for departments now lacking specialized units to form them, even if their current procedures utilizing the chain-of-command system may not be unsatisfactory. If police departments begin following these recommendations prematurely, however, the consequences may be adverse. The morale of personnel may decline, and supervisors may lose an important management tool by giving up control over internal discipline. At the very least, key department personnel will be diverted from more important duties to serve in specialized units for which no need may exist. If only because of the concern for efficiency in manpower utilization, this matter should be given more study. If there are situations in which the old system is inadequate, they need to be identified. If the use of specialized units is not clearly superior to the traditional processes of the chain-of-command system, however, this also must be made known.

Ideally, the way to resolve these questions would be to employ the comparative method, pairing similar departments serving similar communities and differing only in the manner in which discipline is managed. Once matched pairs are identified, the departments could be compared using both quantitative and qualitative measures. The results would then indicate the relative superiority of one system over the other.

To my knowledge, no such test has ever been attempted. Life does not lend itself to laboratory-type analysis easily. Every city and police department is unique. Matching departments in size, structure, local settings, and other variables that could affect police conduct is a difficult task. Because the potential for underestimating the significance of the uncontrolled variables is quite great, a comparative experiment of this type will always be problematical; and the results would be suspect.

Certainly other analytical methods could be used. The "before and after" technique is one of these that could be employed in this context. It overcomes many of the problems associated with locating matched pairs, because the department is paired with itself. But there are several serious problems inherent in this method. The "before" phase of this type of study rarely can be done adequately. Most "before and after" studies are done in situations where the change to the "after" condition already has occurred or is imminent. The time available, therefore, to study the "before" phase properly is severely limited or non-existent. Moreover, there are other forces biasing the results of this type of experiment. A transition from one system to another invariably results in some confusion and misunderstanding. Dissatisfaction with a new system may arise, attributable to initial unfamiliarity or reticence of persons affected; and not due to any deficiencies in the new system. Also affecting the results is the publicity often given to any innovation. Public and staff interest is far greater initially, and then gradually declines, distorting those quantitative measures related to citizen or staff participation in the transition phase. Qualitative data also may be biased by initial problems of acceptance, not related to the worth of the new system. The fate of civilian review boards provides an example.

Several studies have been done on the development and demise of civilian review boards, particularly in New York City[10] and in Philadelphia.[11] Based on these cases, it would be very difficult to come to any conclusions as to the effectiveness of these boards. They remained under hostile fire from their inception to their termination.[12] Under such attack, coming from the law enforcement officers these boards were intended to review, they could not be evaluated on functional merit.

The cases involving civilian review boards do give us some insight into a means for evaluating other disciplinary systems, especially the chain-of-command and internal affairs systems which concern us here. From the difficult times that civilian review boards have had, it becomes obvious that one of the key features of a workable disciplinary system is its acceptability to those subject to it. Without this acceptance, no matter how promising the system is in theory, it will be unsatisfactory in practice. Following this initial finding, we may proceed with evaluation, not by using quantifiable measures, but by applying sound sociological and managerial principles.

Discipline management is a form of that larger social phenomenon, social control. Sociologists have studied it extensively in the past via research and observation of occupational social control mechanisms. It has been recognized that an occupational group is a discrete subcultural unit. As such, it possesses its own ethics, values and norms. Thus, the first step in social analysis is the determination of the components of subcultural systems. Analysis then can proceed to explore how these components interrelate and function.

The values and norms which are part of the police subculture are determined and propagated by various institutions and social forces. These values and norms reinforce acceptable behavioral standards and discourage deviancy; from the point of view of the police, at least. That the police are part of our larger society does not insure that their values, ethics or norms will coincide precisely with those of society as a whole; or even meet the expectations that society has for the police.

The entry of persons into police subculture commonly begins with formal training, usually at police academies. These schools devote little time to conveying ethics and values to the new officers. Rules and regulations are reviewed as scholastic items, intended for rote learning. The internalization of these rules usually occurs during the on-the-job phase of police training, when the new officer is apprenticed to a senior partner. The integration of a new officer into the police subculture is a gradual and continuous process. Occasional refresher training sessions accentuate the department's emphasis on certain rules and regulations. Officers who run afoul of the rules are held up as negative examples to the other officers when their misconduct meets with adverse sanctions. Some input to the process comes from the general public as well. Police officers quickly learn the public's tolerance of, and even demand for, petty graft and impropriety in the exercise of police discretion. The perceptive police officer also becomes aware of the public's standards for police services. Although this public input is important, new officers learn the most from their fellow officers.

Determining how each disciplinary system fits into this structure should predict its suitability and, ultimately, its success. The chain-of-command system employs line supervisors to hear, investigate and adjudicate complaints against police officers. Because the supervisors are full members of the police subculture, having been promoted within it in most cases, they are fully aware of the values, ethics and norms of their departments. Therefore, a chain-of-command disciplinary sytem has the initial advantage of complete integration with the subculture. In Weberian terms, the authority of the line supervisor is both rational-legal and traditional. Moreover, an individual line supervisor possessing the intangible qualities of leadership can add the third Weberian attribute of charismatic authority. Given this potentially wide base of authority, a chain-of-command system has a clear advantage over other competing alternatives. At the other extreme, the generally discredited civilian review board approach has virtually no claim to a base with the police subculture. Civilians, no matter how aware they may be of police procedures, attitudes or problems, are always going to be perceived as outsiders. The actions of the civilian review board, even when supportive of the police, as they generally have been, are viewed as the impositions of one group upon another. The civilian review board's authority rests upon a narrow rational-legal base. Even time, Philadelphia's "experiment" lasted nine years,[13] could not widen the acceptance base. Thus, no traditional compliance has occurred. And since the interaction of police and board members occurred only in adversary situations, there has been little chance for charismatic authority to develop in the interface of the two subgroups.

The internal affairs unit has a greater chance of acceptance because internal affairs unit personnel are selected from the same police subculture as those whom they must regulate. However, prolonged assignment to an internal affairs unit gradually dissociates an internal affairs officer from his peer group. This potential problem was recognized by the President's Commission. Standard 19.3 states, "Specialized units for complaint investigation should employ a strict rotation policy limiting assignments to 18 months."[14] Prolonged specialization could make the dissociation from other police officers permanent. Internal affairs officers may develop a distinct subgroup identity, such as Wambaugh's "Headhunters." Eventually their relationship with other officers may rival the hostility existing between most civilian review boards and the police.

There is a trend for progressive police departments to adopt the internal affairs unit approach. Is this indicative of their greater worth? Or is the transition just a fashion with police administrators attempting to modernize their departments? Do internal affairs units overcome the deficiencies in the older chain-of-command system?

To learn the answers to these questions, we must discover the factors associated with the chain-of-command system that could make it inimical to good discipline. For example, if the norms, values and ethics of the subordinate officers and lower level supervisors are in conflict with those of the chief or the public, then problems will arise. The chain-of-command system can block the efforts of the departmental hierarchy at achieving needed reform. The qualities of lower level supervisors are key factors to be considered. Supervisors selected for popularity, seniority or political pull rather than objective merit may be unwilling or incapable of effecting discipline in their subordinates. The success of the chain-of-command system is based on the qualities of leadership and reliability that the members in the chain must possess. Poor line supervision can block an otherwise effective system.

The extent to which the failings of existing supervision have led to the development of internal affairs units has not been determined. I suspect, however, that the emergence of many internal affairs units can be associated with the hiring of a "Reform Chief." The need for reforms in a department's infrastructure requiring such a chief suggests a serious failure on the part of the line supervisors upon which a chain-of-command disciplinary system must rely. Or even worse, the standards maintained within the informal officer peer groups are too far out of harmony with the expectations of the command or the public for the internalized controls to function in support of the command's wishes.

In either case, an internal affairs unit may serve as a superior alternative to the existing condition. However, it is not the traditional chain-of-command system as much as the ineffective supervisors that is being supplanted. Thus, a internal affairs unit may be of some worth in propping up a weak police command organization.

As such, internal affairs units may not be needed everywhere. Where the personal code of the police officers reinforces the expectations of their commanders and the public, and where supervision is good, there exists little need for this specialization. An internal affairs unit is not a proper substitute for good supervision.

In Standard 19.3, it was advised that "every police agency" should have a "specialized individual or unit" to investigate all complaints from the public and all allegations of misconduct brought against law enforcement officers. I cannot agree. Therein lies the conflict, the issue that must be decided within each department considering the standard.

The objections to the absoluteness of this standard are widespread, although subtle. In a Virginia analysis of the Standard, it was said that, "In Standard 19.3, it was recommended that *larger* police agencies establish specialized units to investigate all complaints. . . ."[15] Relying upon common sense, that study exempted smaller agencies where the chief executive is the logical receptor for and investigator of complaints. But this responsibility of the small department executive cannot be considered as specialization. Virginia's analysis suggests that even if the Standard approximates wisdom, then there exists some point of definition at which larger departments should possess such units and smaller ones should not.

In all fairness to the Standard, it was followed with the statement that, "The existence or size of this specialized unit should be consistent with the demands of the work load."[16] Yet this statement is inconsistent with the preceding recommendation that *"every* police agency" should have this specialization. This leads to a paradox. If an agency has no unit because the workload of complaints does not justify it, then the agency fails to comply with Standard 19.3. But if the agency creates such a unit, though lacking the volume of complaints necessary to justify its existence, then the agency violates the second part of the Standard. Obviously too much revolves around the absolute nature of the word "every." If the President's Commission had added "larger," as did the Virginia analysis, the paradox would have been resolved.

But the issue would not! The existence of the paradox in Standard 19.3 suggests that it was not properly thought out. There is no reason to assume that there exists a point at which police agencies should specialize the management in internal discipline based on departmental size. The recent practices of larger departments, when examined by Dempsey, indicate that many of the largest departments function well without internal affairs specialization.[17] Brown's California data suggest the same is true there, since only 50% of cities of over 100,000 population had departments which specialized.[18] With as many agencies disregarding the recommendation as there are, we have little reason to believe that specialization of the discipline management function is required in all, or even most, cases.

As long as the existing chain-of-command system is functioning to the satisfaction of the command element and the community, the specialization of an internal affairs unit is an unnecessary luxury, possessing potential problems exceeding any potential advantages.

Even where deficiencies in supervision or the police peer group ethics exist to justify the need for the internal affairs unit, it functions only as an intermediate remedy. It may treat a symptom. But it is unlikely to cure the underlying deficiencies. The effort might better be directed toward weeding out the inefficient and corrupt that make a chain-of-command system less effective. When supervision functions as it should, so will discipline as managed through the chain of command.

Summary

The control of police behavior is a concern to law enforcement administrators and thoughtful citizens alike. Traditionally, police agencies have regulated their discipline through routine supervisory channels. This approach, known as the "chain-of-command" system, has declined in popularity in recent years. Increasingly, two reforms are being tried. The internal affairs unit is the more popular of the two. It is an in-house reform, with law enforcement officers investigating disciplinary problems within their own department. External control of police discipline management has been attempted in the other reform, using civilian review boards. While neither reform has been welcomed by the police officers in the lower ranks, only the civilian review boards have faced open rejection and hostility.

Neither reform has solved the problems of police misconduct outright. There is even some doubt that the reforms have done anything to improve the situation. This invites a reexamination of the older chain-of-command system in comparison to its reform counterparts. A thoughtful examination of the older system, and its proposed substitutes may reveal that the deficiencies of the former may not be corrected by the transition to the latter. The turmoil and expense of the transition are significant; and the merits of the three systems should be determined fully before any extensive departmental reorganizations are undertaken.

Discussion Questions

1. Does a low level of complaints from the public mean that the police are performing well; or that the citizens have little faith in the ability of the police to investigate themselves, and thus are not making complaints? How can a police administrator determine which explanation is more likely to be correct?

2. How will a shift from a traditional chain-of-command disciplinary system to one of the reform alternatives affect supervisors in a police department?

3. What are the advantages of a civilian review board, and the disadvantages, from the point of view of the citizens, and from the point of view of the police administrator?

4. What policies for an internal affairs unit will promote harmony and continuous integration of internal affairs officers with the other officers in the department; and what policies will dissociate them?

Notes

1. Lee P. Brown, "Police Review Boards: An Historical and Critical Analysis," *Police,* 10 (July–August 1966): 19.

2. Joseph Wambaugh, *The Choirboys* (New York: Dell, 1976); and the television series "Police Story" (National Broadcasting Corporation).

3. International Association of Chiefs of Police (IACP), *Managing for Effective Police Discipline: A Manual of Rules, Procedures, Supportive Law and Effective Management* (Gaithersburg, Maryland: IACP, 1976).

4. *Ibid.,* pp. 34–36.

5. *Ibid.,* pp. 37–41 and 60–62.

6. *Ibid.,* p. 59.

7. The President's Commission on Law Enforcement and Administration of Justice, *Task Force Report: The Police* (Washington, D.C.: U.S. Government Printing Office, 1967), pp. 193–197.

8. Robert R. Dempsey, "Police Disciplinary Systems," *The Police Chief,* 39 (May 1972): 53.

9. N.F. Iannone, *Supervision of Police Personnel,* 2nd ed., (Englewood Cliffs, N.J.: Prentice-Hall, 1975), pp. 284–321.

10. William H. Hewitt, "New York City's Civilian Complaint Review Board Struggle: Its History, Analysis and Some Notes," *Police,* Part I, 11 (May–June 1967): 10–21; Part II, 11 (July–August 1967): 14–29; Part III, 12 (September–October 1967): 20–33.

11. Brown, p. 28.

12. Sir Leon Radzinowicz and Joan King, *The Growth of Crime,* (New York: Basic Books, 1977), pp. 189–193.

13. Thomas F. McDermott, "Death of a Review Board," *Police,* 12 (September–October 1967): 4.

14. The President's Commisson, p. 193.

15. Division of Justice and Crime Prevention, Commonwealth of Virginia, *Law Enforcement: A Comparative Analysis of Virginia Practices and Procedures,* (Richmond, Va.: Division of Justice and Crime Prevention, 1974): 410.

16. The President's Commission, p. 193.

17. Dempsey, p. 53.

18. Lee P. Brown, "Handling Complaints Against the Police," *Police,* 12 (May–June 1968): 78.

The Police Training Dilemma

DONALD K. MCLEOD

THE NATIONAL ADVISORY COMMISSION on Criminal Justice Standards and Goals, provides valuable insight into the state of the art in police training throughout the United States. The Commission cites an I.A.C.P. survey from 1967 that indicates the average policeman received less than 200 hours of formal training. The study compared that to other professions and found that teachers received more than 7,000 hours, embalmers more than 5,000 hours and barbers more than 4,000 hours. The Advisory Commission comments, "No reasonable person would contend that a barber's responsibility is 20 times greater than a police officer's."[1] Incredible as it might seem, no State required basic police training until 1959. According to the Commission, thirty-three States had passed some form of basic police training standards by 1970. In 1977, the policy of appointing officers and permitting local jurisdictions 12 to 18 months before sending said officers for mandated basic police training still exists. In police work, society seems to accept the practice of hiring personnel, granting awesome police powers and arming the neophyte officer with a weapon without the benefit of even cursory training in the duties and responsibilities of enforcing the laws of the land. The horrendous practice of sending an officer for basic training after eight to twelve months of active police work in the field is analogous to permitting a professional, such as a doctor or lawyer, to practice before completing his studies and certification. Of course, one recognizes the fact that traits, habits and techniques which are developed early in one's career are difficult, if not impossible to eradicate after the initial learning process. The devastating results of such a practice must be borne by the police service and the community over a career span of twenty or more years.

A recent Census Bureau report indicated that $17.2 billion dollars was spent in the fiscal year 1975 on United States Criminal Justice Systems.[2] More than half the amount, 57 percent went for police protection. Traditionally almost ninety percent of a police budget is allocated to personnel expenses. It would seem ludicrous that as a nation, we are prepared to spend almost $9.8 billion on police personnel expenses and then overlook the responsibility to adequately train them to fulfill their role in society. The training vehicle that was appropriate for the past, no longer is viable and is as antiquated as the "Model T Ford." The residue of the pioneers work of the pasty twenty years must be utilized in order to fill the widening gap in police training. Are we to accept the fact that we will acknowledge the concept of periodic maintenance checkups for police motor vehicles, but deny the need to provide systematic and regular training for our most expensive commodity in police circles, namely our police personnel. The critical need for ongoing police training to meet the ever increasing demands of our society has been recognized by law enforcement authorities throughout the nation. The problem facing most agencies in this era of the austerity budget, is how to deliver training, in the most effective and economical fashion possible. Thus, the police administrators of large and small agencies face the dilemma of providing adequate training for their personnel in spite of limited financial resources. Frequently, the agencies that need police training the most can least afford it; there is no question that this is a major expenditure on the part of the agency and the jurisdiction they serve. The options available to the harried police executive range from little or no training through sporadic efforts to upgrade skills in a haphazard and incoherent manner.

A true appreciation of the laws of "supply and demand" can be garnered by the interested observer when perusing the proliferation of training programs in the law enforcement field. Numerous course offerings from public and private institutions purport to meet the needs of the police service. The sincerity of the various organizations is not questioned at this time; however, the relevancy to the actual needs of the police service must be addressed. The cost effectiveness of sending a limited number of police personnel to specialized courses, seminars and workshops should be a paramount concern to the administrator and the community. The overall benefit to the police agency and ultimately to the community must be the criteria by which police training will be measured. The acceleration of technological and social change over the past twenty years has had severe impact on the role of the police in society. Training and development are important management tools for changing and directing job behavior toward specified organizational goals. They may concentrate on improving present performance or preparing individuals for the future, depending upon managements' priorities. The problem facing the law enforcement community is how to harness the resources that are available in a coordinated and systematic manner. One major consequence of this complexity is the need for the same kind of planning that is applied to other demanding aspects of police work. A programmed approach is necessary for every level of the police service in order to promote efficient performance.

The massive effort of the Law Enforcement Assistance Administration over the past decade to upgrade and improve the police service should provide the catalyst for change in the traditional approach to police training. The professional police administrators of the United States should no longer be satisfied with the well intentioned but inadequate efforts of sporadic pre-packaged training programs offered by professional training organizations both public and private. In a sense, we have observed an evolutionary process where the past has served us well and prepared us to move to the next logical phase of police training in the nation. Over the last twenty years, billions of dollars have been invested in educating police personnel and developing innovative programs to enable law enforcement agencies to cope with the complexities of police work. The time has come where we must begin to harvest the fruits of the labors of the enlightened officials, who worked so diligently to improve the police service. This should not be construed as an exclusionary process that eliminates the outside consultant or educator; but, rather a collaborative process that reaps the benefits of the professional police expertise combined with the talents of the community professional. Implicit in this approach is a mutual recognition and respect for the skills and talents that are distributed throughout our society and a need for a "Declaration of Interdependence" to improve the quality of police service in the United States. The fragmentation of local law enforcement agencies and the snobbish academia attitudes toward police work must give way to a coordinated, collaborative approach to design and develop training systems that will meet the present and future needs of the police service. A system that will provide ongoing training, geared to the local needs and delivered by a local or regional faculty. The benefits of the resident faculty, in terms of supplying relevant and meaningful training, should far outweigh the value of the occasional "contract" training efforts of the past. The continuity and sequential development of programs that is so critical to the professional growth of the police service cannot be achieved under existing structures. The responsibility for developing a training system lies within the law enforcement community. The need for control, planned programs and cost effectiveness must be addressed by the police administrators of the nation; they must find ways to secure greater benefits from training while maintaining essentially the same costs.

A brief review of the National Advisory Commision's recommendations will serve to focus our attention on key issues. For example,

Standard 16.3 (1) of the Commission would require every police officer to have a minimum of 400 hours of basic police training and notes it should be given before an officer exercises police authority.[3] The problem of providing a viable in-service training program to keep police personnel up-to-date is addressed by the Advisory Commission in Standard 16.5, which states:

> Every agency should provide 40 hours of formal in-service training annually to sworn police personnel up to and including Captain or its equivalent.[4]

The chaotic state of in-service training is even more dismal than basic or recruit training. The lack of facilities, equipment, instructional expertise, and the constraints of manpower requirements are the major problems facing the police administrator in endeavoring to train personnel. The need for training to maintain, update and improve the necessary knowledge and skills of the police officers is not a controversial issue for the average police executive. The crux of the problem is how to achieve the goals and objectives that are so apparent and so necessary for the future of law enforcement in the United States? Once again we can review the recommendations of the National Advisory Commission and identify a practical solution to the problem. In Standard 16.7, the Advisory Commission offers:

> Every State should by 1978, guarantee the availability of State approved police training to every sworn police employee. Every State should encourage local, cooperative, or regional police training programs to satisfy State training requirements; when these programs cannot satisfy the requirements, criminal justice training centers including police training academies should be established by the state.[5]

These recommendations might not have been realistic twenty years ago; however, the evolutionary process in the world of law enforcement now makes the offering not only practical but also quite necessary. The vast reservoir of talent and expertise cultivated over the years by progressive police administrators and criminal justice educators of the nation mandates an effort to provide the opportunity to utilize the resources now available to improve the police service. Just as the maturation process moves one from childhood to adult status, the police of the nation are ready to move to a self-sustaining stance in the area of training and development. The supporting mechanisms for this change are present in virtually every area of the country. A collaborative program, incorporating the services of the professional educator, the psychologist and the social scientist can be blended with the police practitioner's expertise to

PARTICIPATING LAW ENFORCEMENT AGENCIES

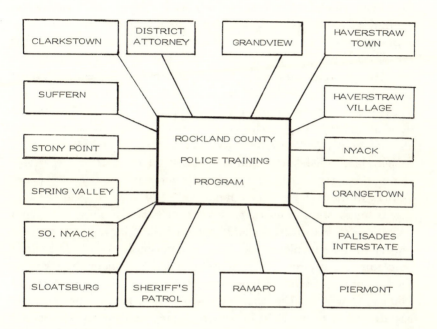

Fig. 1

provide a relevant and meaningful police training program. The basic difference from some of the efforts of the past would be an "equal partnership" status where the synergistic effort of available community resources would be devoted to provide the best police training possible. Consider for a moment the resources that are latent in most communities in the United States. Legal advice from the local District Attorney or State Attorney; the educational resources available in the community colleges and senior colleges; federal, state and municipal law enforcement resources; mental health resources from the professionals; community service agencies that handle almost every area imaginable; local training and management consultants; facilities that have been constructed to service community functions; and equipment that might be available for police use from both public and private organizations. The challenge is to weave the above resources into a functional structure for police training. The tremendous expense of duplicating existing structures and organizations can no longer be afforded by local jurisdictions. A far better approach would be use of the existing structures to maximize their capabilities. We need not re-invent the wheel, it already exists for our use. For example, most local community colleges possess audiovisual equipment and facilities that are available for use on a limited basis. Thus, police agencies should not have to bear the additional expense of developing supporting mechanisms for training when said structures are already present in the community. The approach mandates a spirit of cooperation, collaboration and willingness on the part of the various community resources to work together for the betterment of police services to the populace. Some might view this as a "Utopian Dream," that is unrealistic and unattainable. For the benefit of those who would doubt that such a structure could exist, we would like to briefly review a project that has employed the technique previously described. The real problems that confront police administrators throughout the nation in the area of police training brought forth a unique solution in Rockland County, New York. The following describes the efforts of a program that has attempted to meet the in-service training needs of the local police agencies.

Historical Background

An innovative resolution to the problem of providing advanced in-service training for the police personnel of Rockland County, N.Y. was initiated by the proposal of linking sixteen independent law enforcement agencies into one, cost effective training program (see fig. 1). Thus, a viable training system, so necessary to maintain and upgrade the skills of the professional police officer could be established and maintained within the County. A collaborative effort involving the County of Rockland, the Rockland County Police Chiefs' Association, the Sheriff of Rockland and Rockland Community College resulted in the awarding of a federal grant through the Division of Criminal Justice Services and the Mid Hudson Crime Control Planning Board (D.C.J.S. #1812 - C-86444) to establish an ongoing in-service police training program for the police personnel of the County. Several years of planning and the untiring efforts of the legislators and the law enforcement community culminated in the opportunity to improve police services to the populace of the County through training. The unrelenting pressure by those concerned with the program to ensure a wholehearted effort result in 6 months of pre-planning and screening of candidates for the Training Coordinators' role. Once again, the "team" approach was utilized as the police representatives collaborated with College authorities to lay out the basic design and select a training director. The operational phase of the program began in December of 1975 with the hiring of the Coordinator and preliminary meetings of the Advisory Board comprised of Police Chiefs, the Sheriff, and College representatives. It was resolved that all primary action and considerations would be subject to review by the Advisory Board. Thus, all aspects of the program would be governed by qualified professionals familiar with the complexities of police work. The Training Coordinator is directly responsible to the Advisory Board and the project director.

Management Planning

The goal of the project is to provide more effective police service for the populace of Rockland County through training. A strategy was developed by conducting a training needs analysis that involved the use of a questionnaire survey and interviews of the personnel participating in the program. The total commitment of the law enforcement community was demonstrated early in the program by active and supportive contributions from the various Chiefs, Sheriff and line personnel. Although the County is relatively small, a wealth of talent quickly surfaced and expressed a willingess to work for the success of the project. A few of the more notable facts disclosed by the survey are:

Educational Background

Attending/Some College Experience	148
Associate Degrees	100
Bachelor Degrees	49
Master Degrees	8

Police Biographical Data

Median Age	32.7 years
Median Length of Service	7.2 years

Training Needs

Law	162
Investigation	115
First Aid	111

The initial results of the survey were significant to formulating plans to achieve the objectives of the project. The Training Program services 508 law enforcement personnel in the County and the above excerpts indicate a relatively high educational level. The latent talent within the police organizations gave birth to the Training Cadre concept, whereby instructional expertise will be developed to provide for a completely self-sustaining faculty within the time frames of possible federal funding. The above figures fail to indicate the multiple qualities that are possessed by the resident police personnel such as certified range instructors, emergency medical technicians, and so forth. The biographical data indicates that we have fairly young and experienced police personnel within the County. A review of the training needs reveals the scope of police activity ranging from strict law enforcement functions (i.e., law, investigation) to the pure service function of first aid. The sincerity of the respondents to the questionnaire survey is best demonstrated by the inclusion of first aid as a training priority. The critical need of emergency first aid by the first officer on the scene reflects an intense desire by the Rockland police officer to provide the finest service available for the residents of the County. For sake of brevity, the training needs presented represent the top three areas identified by the police personnel. The requirements system of the program indicated the necessity for an organizational structure to address both common and specific training needs. Thus, the structure took the following form:

The Advisory Board oversees the program and maintains the integrity of the project in terms of relevancy and meaningfulness to the police personnel of the County. All courses of action are submitted to the Board for their recommendations, guidance and approval. The Training Director is directly responsible to the Board and is accountable for the design development and implementation of the program. Briefly, the mission, goals and objectives of the organizational components described above are:

CYCLICAL TRAINING

Mission: To provide ongoing in-service training for *all* police personnel of the County.

Goals: To conduct sufficient training sessions to expose *all* participating personnel to selected cyclical course content.

Example: In 1976, eighteen sessions of law were conducted.

Three hundred and sixty one officers attended the sessions for a total of 71.3% of the total population.

Objectives: To increase professional skills and job knowledge through training.

COMMENTARY: A total of 457 participants attended CYCLICAL training in 1976 for an in-service training hours commitment of 3,656 hours.

SPECIALIZED TRAINING

Mission: To conduct programs designed to meet identified training needs for *selected* personnel of participating agencies.

Goals: To design, develop and conduct courses to support field endeavors in specific areas of law enforcement.

Objectives: To increase professional skills and job knowledge through training.

COMMENTARY: A number of various courses were conducted in 1976 to accommodate the specific needs of the County personnel. The courses included narcotics training, a management workshop, training Cadre meetings, investigation, and so forth. A total of 328 participants attended the various offerings for a total of 3,705 in-service training hours commitment.

INTERNAL COMMUNICATIONS

Mission: To provide participating agencies with relevant written materials in the area of police training and to open the lines of communication concerning program development, progress and projections.

Goals: To promote a collaborative effort through the media of communication.

Objectives: To keep all program participants abreast of current developments regarding the programs and the general area of police training.

COMMENTARY: The Training Director published ten issues of the TRAINING NEWSLETTER in 1976 and three issues of a TRAINING BULLETIN which were distributed to participants at the Burglary, Robbery and Homicide Seminars.

TRAINING SERVICES

Mission: To provide support services for all components of the Rockland County Police Training Program.

Goals: To provide those services necessary to design, develop and conduct a viable in-service police training program.

Objectives: To develop resources within the County, such as from the participating police agencies, Rockland Community College and resident County professionals, to collaboratively research, design and develop materials, training aids and systems to support training endeavors. Ultimately, to develop a self-sustaining training effort in Rockland.

COMMENTARY: The strength of the program lies within this component of the organization. Most notable is the formation of the TRAINING CADRE, a staff of qualified instructors to meet the needs of the program. Legal education is under the aegis of the District Attorney's office; Social Science offerings are supported by professionals from the R.C. Mental Health complex. In 1976, the offerings included a "Behavioral Patterns" Cycle which dealt with crisis intervention, family disputes, alcoholism, youthful drug abuse, and so forth. The Criminal Justice faculty of R.C.C. assists in the development of all police science programs. Necessary support equipment such as visual aids, video equipment, etc. are being acquired as deemed necessary to complement the instructional resources within the County.

As part of the development system, we might address some of the concerns of a training director. The following briefly covers pertinent areas of the program:

Policy is developed by the Advisory Board and reflects the principle of combining education and training. The characteristic qualities of academic and theoretical principles will be linked to the methods, strategies and techniques of training to create an effective learning environment. While training may be viewed as teaching a skill or task or increasing job proficiency, it must also seek ways and means of developing and enlarging traits which will be increasingly important to satisfactory job performance.

Scheduling is administered by the Training Coordinator under the guidance of the Advisory Board. A training calendar has been developed and disseminated to all participating agencies. Submission of training rosters are confirmed by telephone from the Police Training Office. Adjustments are made as the situation arises. All participants attend during normal working hours and are in civilian clothes.

Methods and Techniques of Training are employed to elicit participation from the trainees. The traditional classroom structure has been discarded and replaced by a seminar/discussion format. Conference style classrooms are set up and a professional training decorum maintained. The use of audiovisual material, mainly videotape, will form an integral part of future programs. Dicussion and interaction is encouraged by the trainer/

facilitator as a matter of standard procedure. The use of the lecture method is held to an absolute minimum.

Evaluations are sought at the conclusion of every training program. A form is distributed to every participant to evaluate each session in terms of content and process. Open-ended questions permit the trainee to submit comments and recommendations regarding the session and the program. A form of ongoing needs analysis is conducted via the inclusion of a query as to the participant's top training need. The response is solicited to maintain an up-to-date perspective and to facilitate the management of a training cycle.

The validation system includes the administering and evaluation of the various training programs. Sessions are monitored by personal observations and review of evaluation forms. Feedback is distributed to appropriate parties such as instructors, the Advisory Board, and program participants. The most critical aspect of the validation system is the achievement by the participants of stated performance objectives. Currently, we are endeavoring to design a system whereby each participant will be expected to demonstrate his/her proficiency with the subject material. Thus, we will be able to measure our progress toward the goals of a particular session. The purpose of such an instrument has the twofold benefit of supplying the trainee with an indication of relative strengths and weaknesses, and also measures the effectiveness of the instructional staff.

In summary, we are attempting to install a training system concept. The three phases: requirement, development and validation systems are interdependent and interacting components of a total training system. The various organizational units and procedures are a product of our strategy to achieve the necessary objectives that will utlimately provide more effective police service for the populace of Rockland County through training.

Master Plan

The management planning of the Rockland County program recognized the need to systematically prepare for the future. The projected population growth in the County will rise from 246,000 in 1974 to 310,000 in 1980, and 370,000 in the year of 1990. These estimates mandate that the law enforcement officials prepare for future demands on the training system. In devising our "Master Plan," we attempted to keep the process simple, practical and flexible. Working within the time frames of possible federal funding, we set up a broad seven step program

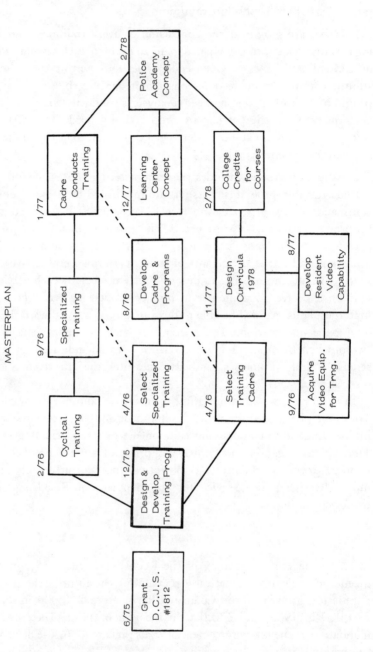

ROCKLAND COUNTY

POLICE TRAINING PROGRAM

MASTERPLAN

Fig. 2

to establish a self-sustaining training program by February of 1978 (see fig. 2). Basically, we set milestones to be achieved by specific dates that would sequentially develop our in-house capabilities. The plan is a combination of human and material resources, including organization and procedures required to coordinate their functioning to achieve the stated goal of the project. The focus of the plan is to develop those resources necessary for the institutionalization of a Rockland County Police Academy to service the training needs of the police personnel.

The Learning Center concept has been incorporated into our basic design for the purpose of providing the opportunity for self-development of County police personnel. It is envisioned that videotapes, cassettes, programmed texts, films and slides will be made available to police officers at the Learning Center. The resources available at the College Media Center will complement acquired training materials and provide an avenue for further study. Research is currently underway to secure college credits for some in-service training programs. Consideration of cutbacks in educational funds for police dictated that some provisions be established for the policeman of the future. While small of stature at this juncture, the Learning Center concept may be vital in the police training of the 1980's.

Program Perspectives and Commentary

In essence, we have discussed the model training system that Rockland County is endeavoring to achieve under the terms of a federal grant. A realization that no small independent agency can support a viable training program brought forth a collaborative effort in the County to design and develop a system that will benefit the police personnel and the community. In the spirit of the times, Rockland County has issued a proclamation entitled "The Declaration of Interdependence." The old adage of the fragmented law enforcement agencies and inherent evils therein has dissipated and a solid team concept of police training has taken its place. Needless to say, numerous meetings and discussions preceded the acceptance of the training system design and operational program. Monthly meetings are scheduled to keep all participants informed of the progress of the program. The moot question of where to conduct training was solved by the Advisory Board when consent was granted to use the magnificent facilities of the Rockland County Fire Training Center. The complex is located on 16 acres and possesses both classroom space and outdoor facilities for practical exercises. Once again the sense of community support and cooperation was demonstrated by effectively linking the public safety components of the Fire and Police services. An upshot effect of this liason was to further develop the warm relationships among the emergency service agencies of the county including the ambulance services which share use of the facilities for training.

The quest for available resources, both human and material, brought about unexpected bonuses for the neophyte program. The Bureau for Municipal Police, a subdivision of New York State Division of Criminal Justice Services, offered complete support and cooperation. Through their efforts contacts were established with other trainers throughout the state to share information and experiences. Federal agencies such as the F.B.I. and the D.E.A. not only offered advice, but volunteered qualified instructors to assist in training. On the local level, the Rockland County District Attorney has provided instructional staff for the law session and is assisting in the development of a Criminal Investigation course. The Consultation and Education unit of the Mental Health Complex is supplying professionals to cover such critical areas as crisis intervention, family disputes, handling abnormally ill persons and juvenile problems. The ever available resources of Rockland Community College have enabled the program to blend the academic world with training. Programs are being developed to offer home study materials and audio cassettes in such areas as management, languages and police science to the police personnel of the county. The incredible support and enthusiasm of local, state and federal agencies has resulted in the granting of every request for assistance.

The performance of the Rockland County Police Training Program is best demonstrated by a review of the achievements of the project in the 1976 period. The following is presented to indicate the impact of the program on the County police personnel in the first twelve months of its existence:[6]

TRAINING	PARTICIPANTS	IN-SERV. TRAIN. HRS. COMMITMENT
Cyclical Training	457	3,656
Specialized Training	302	3,618
Training Cadre	26	87
TOTAL	785	7,361

(As of December 15, 1976)

An appreciation of the effort of the police personnel can be culled from a perusal of the 1976 statistics. The growth potential of the program can be measured by the fact that the first three months of 1977 accounted for another 7,230 hours of training. The results of the program speak for themselves. An incredible effort was exerted by every person involved in the project. No one individual could claim responsibility for the initial success of the program. One can sense a tremendous pride in the many milestones achieved in our first year of existence. The unwavering support of the Chiefs of Police, the Sheriff and the line personnel of the various agencies accounted for a fantastic training year in 1976. The team effort involving resident County professionals gives high hopes for an institutionalized program in the future. The unquestioning support of the Rockland County legislators provided an opportunity for the police personnel to demonstrate their dedication to improve police services to the community. The police response was gratifying and mandates a continuation of the in-service training concept.

Summary

The deplorable state of the art in police training no longer has to be endured by the police and the community. The sporadic, uncoordinated efforts of the past in police training must be replaced by a systematic program to develop personnel in the most efficient and economical fashion possible. The responsibility for demanding a new approach to resolving the problems of providing adequate training lies with the police administrators of the nation. This should not be viewed as a regression to the isolationist policy of the past; rather, it should be viewed as a new, fresh approach on the horizon. It is one that would capitalize on the talent cultivated within the law enforcement profession over the past twenty years and link it to the numerous human and physical resources available in most communities.

The Rockland County program identified and utilized resources from the local, state and federal level. The skepticism of the past regarding collaborative projects with law enforcement agencies seems to have disappeared. Perhaps, it is a sense of urgency in the war against crime or a new respect for the complexity of the police role in society that accounts for this willingness to assist in the training and development of police personnel. Possibly, it might be the rather sophisticated attitude of the police in recognizing that there are many resources available that can facilitate the professional growth of the service. Whatever the reason might be, the key issue to address is that the time has come to institute major changes in the area of police training.

As with any change, one can anticipate dissonance. The fragmentation of and spirit of independence exhibited by local agencies must be adjusted to achieve organizational goals. Training police personnel is an expensive proposition; however, by working together, perhaps on a regional basis as recommended by the National Advisory Commission, smaller police agencies can provide their personnel with the necessary training to function effectively. By sharing resources within the organizations and those of the surrounding community, a relevant program can become a reality. The major contribution of proper planning and coordination can improve the opportunities for success in these ventures. The cost effectiveness of this approach cannot be denied. The overall benefit to the police and the community can only be measured in terms of improved performance and efficiency. The Rockland County program services agencies that range from a one man department to the largest comprised of ninety-six men. The total program budget for the year of 1976 was $53,000. For that sum, over 7,361 hours of training were achieved, a system for training and development was designed, support equipment including video playback and camera equipment was purchased, liaison with community agencies was effected and plans for eventual institutionalization of the program were implemented.

The potential in a program, such as the one described, cannot be truly appreciated at this time. One would not be so foolish as to prematurely judge the success of the Rockland County Police Training Program. However, we should analyze the relative achievements of the program in light of the recommendations of the National Advisory Commission on Criminal Justice Standards and Goals. The dire need for a planned, coordinated and systematic approach to police training advocated by the Advisory Commission is not a Utopian dream. The pilot project in Rockland County demonstrates that a collaborative effort is both feasible and practical. It provides the opportunity to create an environment that is conducive to the professional growth of the police service. It establishes a framework that ties training objectives to organizational performance. It provides for executive decision making on the part of the police administrator to develop true professionalism in the service. It reduces the friction of fragmentation among law enforcement agencies and promotes the harmony and collaboration so necessary for the reduction of crime in our society. The question remains; are we to accept the chaotic state of the art in police training, or are we prepared to accept the evolutionary process that has provided us with a model for future training systems?

Discussion Questions

1. In 1967, an I.A.C.P. survey indicated that the average policeman in the United States received less than 200 hours of formal training.

Although the national average of formal training hours may have increased in the past decade, a serious gap still remains between the police and other "professions," in the certification area. Discuss the multiple responsibilities of a police officer and the adequacy of training to fulfill this critical role in society.

2. The ever increasing demands of society upon the police service mandates the design of an efficient, effective and economical training and development program to equip police personnel to cope with their responsibilities. Identify and discuss the critical issues confronting the police executive in attempting to establish a viable training program.

3. The role of training and development toward the achievement of organizational goals has been recognized by management authorities throughout the world. The proliferation of high cost and low relevancy police training programs provides sporadic and unrelated attempts to fulfill this mission for the police service. Discuss the weaknesses of this approach and the resultant effects on performance.

4. The combined economic constraints of inflation and recession preclude the development of quality training programs by many medium and small police agencies in the United States. Discuss the options available to the police executive desirous of providing adequate training for the police personnel of the department.

5. Identify the resources in your community that might be available to assist in the development of a viable police training program. Discuss the potential problems inherent in a collaborative approach to a training project. Design a strategy to successfully cope with the identified critical issues.

Notes

1. National Advisory Commission on Criminal Justice Standards and Goals, *Police* (Washington, D.C.: U.S. Government Printing Office, 1973), p. 380.

2. New York Times, March 27, 1977, p. 15.   3. National Advisory Commission on Criminal Justice Standards and Goals, *Police* (Washington, D.C.: U.S. Government Printing Office, 1973), p. 392.

4. *Ibid.,* p. 404.   5. *Ibid.,* p. 417.

6. Rockland County Police Training Program, *1976 Annual Report* (Pomona, N.Y.: 1977), p. 5.

6

Origins of Police Misconduct

RICHARD J. LUNDMAN

IN DEMOCRATIC SOCIETIES police departments are commonweal organizations serving the public at large.[1] As compared to business organizations responsive to owners, labor unions serving members, or service organizations with specific clients, police organizations ostensibly function to protect and promote the best interests of the public at large.

However, recent research suggests that individual police officers frequently fail to protect and promote the interests of the public at large. Specifically, a large body of evidence suggests that police misconduct is far from uncommon. Thus, several researchers have reported that police exercise of arrest discretion is routinely influenced by variables *such as* demeanor, social class, race, and age.[2] Others have reported that some degree of corruption is present in nearly all police departments.[3] Still others have demonstrated that unnecessary police violence is not an infrequent occurrence.[4]

Attempts to explain these patterns of police misconduct have most frequently focused primary attention on the individual police officers involved in episodes of misconduct.[5] Moreover, the solutions proposed include better selection and training procedures and the suspension or elimination of experienced officers involved in misconduct.[6] Stated alternatively, existing images of the origins of and solutions for police misconduct are narrowly individualistic.

The purpose of the present chapter, however, is to suggest that routine police misconduct is largely organizational in origin. A second purpose is to consider certain of the prevention and control strategies which follow from an organizational understanding of the origins of police misconduct.

Origins of Police Misconduct

For police misconduct to be the property of police organizations rather than individual police officers at least three conditions or characteristics must be present.[7] First, the misconduct must be supported and encouraged by peer norms situated at some level within police organizations. This

218

support and encouragement can be active as is the case when all officers at a particular level engage in the misconduct or passive when the improper actions of a minority of officers are tolerated or covered for by the majority.

Second, for police misconduct to be an organizational phenomenon, there must exist mechanisms whereby new officers are taught the norms supportive of the misconduct. In addition, new officers must be provided opportunities to practice these actions. And, peer acceptance of new officers must be contingent upon adherence to norms learned and practiced during police socialization.

Finally, for police misconduct to be organizational in origin it must also be supported by police administrators. Administrative support may be active as police elites engage in improper actions or passive as adminstrators tolerate, cover for, or fail to undertake reasonable and routine investigative precautions.

Taken together, these three conditions specify the circumstances in which police misconduct is best understood as an organizational phenomenon. Although it will be clear that individual officers carry out the improper actions to be examined, the essential argument to be advanced is that they do so because of norms which are supported by peers and administrators and learned during police socialization. This can best be demonstrated by concentrating primary attention on one type of police misconduct: abuse of arrest discretion.

Police Abuse of Arrest Discretion

As noted, in democratic societies police departments are commonweal organizations serving the public at large. Among the norms surrounding police organizations there is an expectation that police officers be equitable or generally consistent in their treatment of citizens. In the case of police exercise of arrest discretion, the expectation is that police officers not discriminate against certain types of citizens.

However, social science study of the processes whereby police officers make arrest decisions suggests that police officers routinely violate norms emphasizing consistent treatment of citizens. Thus, my own research[8] and the research of others[9] demonstrate that variables or factors *such as* demeanor, social class, sex, age, and race routinely influence the arrest decisions of police officers.[10] If police officers are expected to be consistent in their treatment of citizens, then it is clear that police officers routinely violate this expectation.

In the past these actions were attributed to a minority of undisciplined and prejudiced officers. Consequently, ameliorative action was directed towards better selection procedures, more effective training programs, and in-service seminars. All of these efforts were intended to eliminate the prejudicial attitudes thought to be present within *individuals* seeking police employment or those already serving as police officers.

However, application of the criteria identified earlier reveals that police abuse of arrest discretion is best understood as an organizational phenomenon. Specifically, these recurrent patterns of discrimination in the context of arrest emerge as a consequence of norms supported by peers, learned by new officers during police socialization, and tolerated, if not encouraged, by administrative elites.

First, these recurrent patterns of discrimination emerge as a consequence of certain of the norms found in the patrol divisions of most large police organizations. Central to these norms are negative images or stereotypical images of minority citizens.[11] Similarly, negative images of relatively powerless citizens are generally contained within the norms of police organizations.[12] Finally, patrol colleagues indicate through their "war stories" that citizens who "bad mouth" police officers are to be treated differently than citizens who are polite and respectful.[13]

Peer adherence to these norms is buttressed by the uniquely solidary nature of the patrol subculture. Whether it be attributed to the concerns with danger, authority, and efficiency thought to be uniformly characteristic of the working personalities of police officers,[14] the occasionally dirty nature of police work,[15] or the simple facts of rotating hours and days off,[16] most individuals who have studied the police comment on the solidary nature of the patrol subculture.[17] This solidarity produces a high degree of attitudinal and behavioral conformity with the norms of the patrol subculture.

The available evidence, then, suggests that the first condition necessary for an organizational understanding of the origins of police abuse of arrest discretion—normative support—is present. Recall, however, that an organizational understanding also requires evidence of socialization in terms of these norms and administrative support of them. Available evidence with respect to these conditions is considered next.

Although police administrators and perhaps others would prefer to think of all police work as a science, it must be recognized that it is still very much an art, taught and learned on the street. During rookie school, therefore, new recruits are reluctantly[18] sent to observe and work with experienced officers. After completion of recruit training, the new officer generally spends a fixed probationary period under the guidance of an experienced officer.

As a consequence, new members of police organizations are exposed to patrol norms and encouraged to utilize the associated recipes for action against minority, lower class, and disrespectful citizens. Thus, during police academy training itself new recruits are exposed to norms emphasizing discriminatory arrest practices.[19] Once on the street, new officers are given a probationary period in which to practice actions in terms of these norms. Finally, peer acceptance appears to require either behavioral compliance or a demonstrated willingness to tolerate the discriminatory statements and action of colleagues.[20]

The available evidence, then, is also supportive of the requirement for an organizational understanding of police misconduct. Thus, new officers are taught norms emphasizing discriminatory actions, given structured opportunities to practice their enactment, and evaluated by reference to their active or passive support of them. The task that remains, therefore, is to determine whether evidence exists of administrative support of these norms. As is immediately clear, this requires a somewhat extended analysis.

To begin, it can be noted that most police organizations maintain a strict policy of promotion from within. Across all levels of police organizations, therefore, there exists a commonality of attitudes and actions reflective of the required street experience. James Q. Wilson, for example, observes that because "all officers of whatever duty or rank must first serve in patrol, the police organization develops its own special ethos: defensiveness, a sense of not being supported by the community, and a distrust of outsiders."[21] One consequence of this practice is that police administrators are typically well aware of the orientations and action of their subordinates; indeed, administrators either witnessed or were involved in these same actions while serving their compulsory period as patrol officers.

Therefore, it would appear that police administrators are in an especially effective position to eliminate patrol abuse of arrest discretion. This is, in part, because administrators possess an intimate knowledge of this problem. And, in part, because they occupy command positions in a quasi-military organization. For these reasons, the possibility of change through simple administrative command would appear to be present.

However, change of patrol norms by administrative action is beset by a number of problems. First, there is good reason to believe that change of patrol norms does not concern admnistrators. Specifically, the norms which guided the administrator on the street do not necessarily nor automatically become irrelevant simply because promotion has occurred. Second and equally important, the prerequisites for promotion include a willingness to be silent about police misconduct and loyalty to the organization.[22] Consequently, police administrators are generally organization people more concerned with the department (and their position in it) than the consistent or equitable treatment of citizens. Finally, police organizations are somewhat unique in that low level employees, street patrol officers, possess a great deal of behavioral latitude. To a great extent, the work of the patrol officer is unsupervised and, to a much lesser extent, it is unsupervisable. Police command , therefore, is at best precarious since subordinates can easily embarrass their superiors.[23] The result is that administrators exchange tolerance of patrol practices for infreuqent embarrassment and a modicum of departmental loyalty.[24]

In summary, then, the available evidence combines to suggest that police abuse of arrest discretion is an organizational rather than purely individualistic phenomenon. Although individual officers animate these actions, they do so because of norms learned as recruits and supported by peer and administrative colleagues. In a very real sense, therefore, the acting unit responsible for police misconduct is the department itself and not the individual officer.[25]

Preventing and Controlling Police Misconduct

If police misconduct is largely organizational in origin, then we are free to abandon the individualistic prevention and control strategies of the past. These strategies typically involved better recruitment and training procedures in an effort to eliminate the "bad apples" thought to be responsible for police misconduct. The experiences of George Kirkham illustrate their general ineffectiveness.[26]

Kirkham is a criminology professor at Florida State University who became a police officer for a short period of time. Prior to becoming a police officer, Kirkham reports that he was highly critical of the police and, insofar as he was aware, not racially prejudiced. Yet, Kirkham reports in a series of vivid articles the process whereby he learned and accepted patrol norms including those emphasizing the differential treatment of minority citizens. Despite extensive education and the apparent absence of personal prejudice, Kirkham observes:

> Like the patrolmen with whom I worked, I found myself moving gradu-
> ally from conscious fear and anxiety in my encounters with blacks toward
> a point where I became testy and abrasive, cocksure and aggressive in my
> dealings with them. The ubiquitous patrol car humor, the derisive jokes
> about 'niggers' and 'jitterbugs' became a mechanism on which I too began
> to rely . . .[27]

Stated alternatively, Kirkham, as is true of most police officers, was unable to resist organizational pressures towards compliance with departmental norms.

If individualistic strategies such as better recruitment and training are unlikely to be effective, what are the alternatives? In the remainder of this chapter one such alternative and several of its implications are considered.

To begin, it can be noted that if police misconduct is organizational in origin, then it should be clear that attempts at prevention and control must also be organizational in nature. Minimally, the prevention and control of police misconduct requires that would-be controllers work with an organizational rather than individualistic image of the actor responsible.

Effective prevention and control would also appear to require recognition of the relative powerlessness of individuals when confronted with improper *organizational* actions. As James Coleman has deserved, juristic or corporate actors such as police departments are wholly different from natural or individual persons.[28] Individuals, therefore, rarely have the resources or power to control organizational misconduct. Consequently, effective prevention and control of police misconduct must occur at the organizational level. Specifically, responsibility for the control of police misconduct must reside in other *organizational* actors whose sole function is the control of police misconduct. Put in a word, in contemporary society only organizations have the power and resources to control other organizations.

My first point, then, is that an alternative to individualistically oriented prevention and control strategies emerges when it is recognized that police misconduct is organizational in origin. This awareness sensitizes would-be controllers to the nature of the actor responsible for police misconduct and establishes the need for control of organizational misconduct by other organizations. In addition, a number of other prevention and control strategies emerge upon application of this understanding of the origins of police misconduct.

For one, an organizational understanding of police misconduct alerts us to the fact that the efficacy or strength of the organizational norms supportive of police misconduct does not necessarily require the personal commitment or endorsement of patrol officers or administrators. Thus, Kirkham's experiences as well as the reports of social scientists who have studied the police reveal that in conversation with *trusted* partners, outside observers, and occasionally citizens, individual officers are not as prejudiced, quick to condemn, or intolerant of disrespect as their actions or silent support of more vocal and active colleagues would appear to suggest. A reasonable question, however, is why do their actions suggest personal endorsement of the norms supportive of police misconduct?

Although the reasons are surely complex, it does appear that a useful answer can be developed by considering what individuals do in group situations. Sociologist David Matza has observed juveniles in "situations of company" and reported that they frequently support norms and enagage in actions contrary to their own inclinations.[29] Others have made similar observations of prostitutes[30] and student physicians[31] involved in group situations. Arnold Rose has labeled norms supported under conditions of mutual or pluralistic ignorance "pseudo-norms" and speculated that a concern with the maintenance of group membership fosters their perpetuation.[32] What these studies suggest is the existence of essentially similar pressures in group situations involving police officers. Specifically, it appears that in many police organizations officers are unwilling to openly challenge organizational norms for fear of being excluded from the patrol subculture,[33] lessening one's chance of promotion,[34] or fear of ineffective command for those already promoted.[35] What is being suggested, therefore, is that pseudo-norms essentially similar to those maintained by others in situations of company are among the factors responsible for police misconduct.

Parenthetically but importantly, the existence of pseudo-norms requires that the controller abandon the assumption that individual officers personally endorse the organizational norms supportive of police misconduct. Under an assumption of personal endorsement control is logically and inevitably directed towards identifying and sanctioning individual officers. If, however, attention is concentrated on police organizations and, therefore, towards the organizationally generated and maintained factors which help foster the perpetuation of these pseudo-norms, then the controller's approach to individual officers should be one of clarification and release from organizational constraints rather than mere punishment.

My second point, then, is that an organizational understanding of the origins of police misconduct cautions controllers to abandon an assumption that individual officers personally endorse organizational norms. Instead, it is likely that they possess doubts and questions regarding the ultimate wisdom and consequences of adherence to these norms. Consequently the controllers approach must be one of release and clarification rather than the identification and punishment of individuals.

Application of an organizational understanding of the origins of police misconduct also alerts would-be controllers to the need for change of a variety of common departmental practices. First, the existence of rotating hours and odd days off makes police officers highly dependent upon similarly situated colleagues for sociability. This in-group contact during off hours makes individual officers even more unwilling to openly challenge group norms. Therefore, even small changes such as lengthening the amount of time an officer is assigned a particular watch and increasing the predictability of off-duty time would presumably permit police officers to socialize with non-police others.

Second, adherence to pseudo-norms is also a function of the reward system of police organizations. Thus, peers reward patrol officers for their compliance with group norms while superiors evaluate officers in terms of easily codifiable criteria such as the number of tickets issued. Consequently most police officers have no choice but to be sensitive to organizational rewards since there are few, if any, meaningful rewards outside police organizations. Therefore, it is incumbent upon control organizations to provide individual police officers with meaningful rewards for effective and proper actions. Tenure for new officers and promotion for experienced officers should be rewards determined by factors other than adherence to discriminatory organizational norms.

Third, the perpetuation of pseudo-norms is also facilitated by the nearly universal policy of promotion from within. This policy insures that police supervisors are first tested on the street and found willing to comply with patrol norms. Therefore, it is incumbent upon control organizations to open administrative positions to qualified persons outside of police organizations. This is routinely done in many European countries[36] and there is no sound reason why this practice should not be instituted here.

Moreover, the benefits of opening administrative position to outsiders are severalfold. First and most importantly, because they are outsiders non-police administrators have not been exposed to organizational norms supportive of misconduct. Second, non-police administrators do not gain their position in exchange for a proven willingness to be silent about police misconduct. Finally, persons from outside police organizations bring *administrative* skills to administrative positions. Currently, administrators promoted from within bring police skills to essentially administrative tasks.

Fourth, controllers must prevent the perpetuation of pseudo-norms through frequent vocalizations. As noted, most urban police organizations abound in racial slurs, negative images of lower class individuals, and verbalized examples of how disrespectful citizens should be treated. These frequent vocalizations make individual officers even more unwilling to express disagreement or doubt and thereby contribute to an appearance of unanimity. Clear departmental rules forbidding these stereotypical vocalizations would help reduce this apparent unanimity.[37]

My third point, then, is that the effective prevention and control of police misconduct requires change of a variety of common departmental practices. These changes include more predictable work periods, external rewards and incentives, recruitment of non-police administrators, and clear departmental rules forbidding stereotypical vocalizations. Taken together these changes would reduce the apparent unanimity surrounding the organizational norms supportive of police misconduct.

The final issue to be addressed in this chapter includes specification of the nature of the organizations which would be responsible for the prevention and contorl of police misconduct. Clearly, this is a *critically* important issue.

The preceding analysis suggests that these organizations should evidence at least eight characteristics.

First, these control organizations must be *local* since police misconduct varies dependent upon area. Thus, in certain departments peer norms may emphasize the differential treatment of Native Americans,[38] while the norms of another department may emphasize the discriminatory treatment of Afro-Americans.[39] Consequently, local control organizations are inevitably more responsive to local control problems than state or federal organizations.

Second, these control organizations must be representative of the entire community served by the department being controlled. In the past, many similar organizations were dominated by powerful community members who, paradoxically, were least critical of police misconduct. This, of course, was because they were least likely to be the victims of discriminatory actions. Therefore, these organizations must include clear and forceful representation of the victims of prior police misconduct.

Third, these organizations must be *permanent.* In the past, citizen organizations have emerged in response to particular episodes of misconduct and then disbanded once the appearance of a problem had been eliminated. The long-run effects, therefore, were minimal since misconduct varied with the periodicity of citizen involvement. Permanent organizations insure constant monitoring and control.

Fourth, the citizens serving on these organizations must be monetarily *compensated* for their actions since the interests of volunteers tend to be episodic and short term.[40] Citizens whose jobs include the prevention and control of organizational police misconduct are likely to be considerably more effective.

Fifth, citizen control organizations must have a *professional* staff available to them. Police departments generally have their own legal staff and clearly have large numbers of investigative personnel. The professional resources of control organizations should be comparable.

Sixth, these organizations should have *budgetary* control over the department. In the past, similar groups have attempted to use publicity as the primary control mechanism and have not been particularly successful. Budgetary control makes the consequences of police misconduct significantly more meaningful.

Seventh, these organizations should review and be responsible for providing ultimate approval for the *tenure* and *promotion* of police personnel. Currently, these are internal decisions and they reflect the operation of organizational norms. External review insures that these decisions do not reflect adherence to organizational norms as a condition for tenure or promotion.

Lastly, the primary goal of these organizations is to insure that police departments serve *commonweal interests*. To accomplish this, however, these organizations must be local, representative, and permanent. Moreover, their members must be compensated and have professional staff to facilitate control over budgetary, tenure and promotion decisions. It is suggested that it is only when all of these conditions are met is it likely that police misconduct can be effectively prevented and controlled.

Discussion Questions

1. What are the likely points of resistance in viewing police misconduct as an organizational rather than purely individualistic problem?

2. Is it proper or "fair" to punish individual police officers for following and carrying out improper actions which are supported and encouraged by work group colleagues and superiors?

3. Given that police are opposed to civilian control is it likely that effective Civilian Review Boards will become a reality?

Notes

1. For a discussion of commonweal organizations see Peter Blau and W. Richard Scott, *Formal Organizations* (San Francisco: Chandler Publishing Co., 1962), pp. 42 ff.

2. For example see: Donald J. Black and Albert J. Reiss, Jr., "Police Control of Juveniles," *American Sociological Review,* 35 (1970): 63–77; Irving Piliavin and Scott Briar, "Police Encounters with Juveniles," *American Journal of Sociology,* 70 (1964): 206–214.

3. For example see Ellwyn Stoddard, "The Informal 'Code' of Police Deviancy: A Group Approach to Blue Coat Crime," *Journal of Criminal Law, Criminology and Police Science,* 59 (1968): 201–213; Julian Roebuck and Tom Barker, "A Typology of Police Corruption," *Social Problems,* 21 (1974): 423–437.

4. For example see Albert J. Reiss, Jr. "Police Brutality—Answers to Key Questions," in Richard Knudten (ed.) *Crime, Criminology and Contemporary Society* (Homewood, Illinois: The Dorsey Press, 1970), pp. 225–238; Rodney Stark, *Police Riots* (Belmont, Ca.: Wadsworth Publishing Company, 1972).

5. For a discussion of this approach see Stoddard, p. 202; Jonathan Rubenstein *City Police* (New York: Ballantine Books, 1973), pp. 403 ff.

6. *Ibid.*

7. For an expanded discussion of this see M. David Ermann and Richard J. Lundman, *Corporate and Governmental Deviance* (Unpublished Manuscript, The Ohio State University, 1977), pp. 1–19.

8. See Richard J. Lundman, "Routine Police Arrest Practices: A Common-weal Perspective," *Social Problems* 22 (1974): 127–141; Richard J. Lundman, "The Police Function and the Problem of External Control," in Emilio C. Viano and Jeffrey H. Reiman, *The Police in Society* (Lexington, Ma.: D.C. Heath and Company, 1975), pp. 161–166, Richard J. Lundman, "Police Work with Traffic Law Violators," paper presented at the annual meeting of the American Sociological Association, New York, August, 1976; Richard J. Lundman, Richard E. Sykes, and John P. Clark, "Police Control of Juveniles: A Replication," paper presented at the annual meeting of the American Society of Criminology, November, 1976.

9. See Egon Bittner, "The Police on Skid-Row: A Study of Peace Keeping," *Social Problems,* 32 (1967): 699–715; Donald J. Black, "Production of Crime Rates," *American Sociological Review,* 35 (1970): 733–747, Black and Reiss, pp. 63–77; Nathan Goldman, *The Differential Selection of Juvenile Offenders for Court Appearance* (Washington, D.C.: National Council on Crime and Delinquency, 1963); Wayne LaFave, *Arrest: The Decision to Take a Suspect into Custody.* (Boston: Little, Brown, 1965); David Petersen, "Informal Norms and Police Practices: The Traffic Quota System," *Sociology and Social Research,* 55 (1971); 354–362; Piliavin and Briar, pp. 206–214; Jerome Skolnick, *Justice Without Trial* (New York: John Wiley & Sons, Inc., 1975); James P. Spradley, *You Owe Yourself a Drunk* (Boston: Little, Brown, 1970): Robert Terry, "The Screening of Juvenile Offenders," *Journal of Criminal Law Criminology and Police Science,* 58 (1967); 173–181.

10. Not all of the studies identified above report on each of these variables. Rather it is routinely reported that variables *such as* demeanor and age influence police exercise of arrest discretion.

11. See George Kirkham, "On the Etiology of Police Aggression in Black Communities," in J.F. Kinton (ed.) *Police Roles in the Seventies* (Aurora, Illinois: SSSRC, Inc., 1975), pp. 167–163; Albert J. Reiss, Jr., *The Police and the Public* (New Haven: Yale University Press, 1971), p. 147; Skolnick, p. 256; William Westley, *Violence and the Police* (Cambridge: The MIT Press, 1970), p. 99; James Q. Wilson, *Varieties of Police Behavior* (Cambridge: Harvard University Press), p. 43.

12. See Reiss, p. 151, Wesley, p. 99; F.P. Williams, "Toward a Theory of Police Behavior: Some Critical Comments," in J.F. Kinton (ed.) pp. 133–147.

13. Reiss, p. 136; Rubenstein, p. 318; Skolnick, pp. 42ff; Westley, p. 119.

14. See Skolnick, pp. 42ff.

15. James L. Walsh, "Professionalism and the Police: The Cop as Medical Student," in Harlan Hahn (ed.) *Police in Urban Society* (Beverly Hills, Ca.: Sage Publications, 1971): pp. 225–246.

16. John P. Clark, "Isolation of the Police: A Comparison of the British and American Situations," Journal of Criminal Law, Criminology and Police Science, 56 (1965): 307–319.

17. Alan Edward Bent, *The Politics of Law Enforcment* (Lexington, Massachusetts: Lexington Books, 1974) p. 5; Egon Bittner, *The Functions of the Police in Modern Society* (Chevy Chase, Maryland: National Institute of Mental Health, 1970), p. 63; Eugene Eidenberg and Joe Rigert, "The Police and Politics," p. 293 in Hahn; Richard Harris, *The Police Academy: An Inside View* (New York: John

Wiley and Sons, Inc., 1973), p. 114; Reiss, pp. 150ff, Loyalty," in Hahn; Stoddard, p. 202ff.; Westley, p. 111; Wilson, p. 48.

18. For a discussion of the reasons for this reluctance see John Van Maanen, "Observations: the Making of a Policeman," *Human Organization,* 32 (1973): 407–418.

19. Bent, pp. 19–21; Harris, p. 127; Kirkham; Arthur Niederhoffer, *Behind the Shield* (Garden City, N.Y.: Anchor Books, 1969), p. 43; Westley, p. 154; F.P. Williams, "Toward a Theory of Police Behavior: Some Critical Comments," p. 137 in Kinton.

20. Bent, p. 36; Bittner, The Functions, p. 69; Eidenberg & Rigert, p. 293; Reiss, p. 150; Skolnick, p. 269; Westley, p. 186; Williams, p. 138.

21. Wilson, p. 138.

22. Rubenstein, p. 374.

23. David J. Bordua and Albert J. Reiss, Jr., "Command, Control, and Charisma: Reflections on Police Bureaucracy," *American Journal of Sociology,* 72 (1967): 68–76.

24. Bittner, *The Functions,* p. 59.

25. For a discussion of organizations as acting units see Ermann and Lundman; James S. Coleman, *Power and the Structure of Society* (Philadelphia: University of Pennsylvania Press, 1974).

26. Kirkham, pp. 167–173.

27. *Ibid.,* p. 172.

28. Coleman, pp. 1–6.

29. David Matza, *Delinquency and Drift* (New York: John Wiley and Sons, Inc., 1964).

30. James H. Bryan, "Occupational Ideologies and Individual Attitudes of Call Girls," *Social Problems,* 13 (1966): 441–450.

31. Howard S. Becker and Blanche Geer, "Participant Observation and Interviewing: A Comparison," *Human Organization,* 16 (1957): 28–32.

32. Arnold Rose, *Sociology.* Second Edition (New York: Alfred A. Knopf, 1965), p. 95.

33. Clark, pp. 309ff.

34. Rubenstein, pp. 374ff.

35. Bittner, *The Functions,* p. 69.

36. Stark, p. 227.

37. For an example of this see Skolnick, pp. 246ff.

38. Lundman, pp. 135–141.

39. Piliavin and Briar, pp. 208–212.

40. For an example of this see George Washnis, *Citizen Involvement in Crime Prevention* (Lexington, Massachusetts: Lexington Books, 1976).

7

"The Drunken Cop"

CHARLES M. UNKOVIC AND

WILLIAM R. BROWN

> He felt that the job was not particularly hazardous physically but
> was incredibly hazardous emotionally and too often lead to
> divorce, alcoholism and suicide.
>
> Joseph Wambaugh
> *The Onion Field*[1]

Introduction

DIVORCE AND SUICIDE AMONG POLICE OFFICERS are two major topics
which have been widely studied.[2] Research has shown that police have very
high suicide and divorce rates compared to the general public. But what
about the third area Joseph Wambaugh talks about—alcoholism? For a
variety of reasons, research concerning police and alcohol is sparse and does
not reveal convincing evidence as to the extent of alcoholism among police
nor any uniform policies to deal with the problem.[3] With more and more
research being done in the field of alcohol abuse, there is a need to research
the problem-drinking cop to see in what ways he or she may differ or be
similar to other problem drinkers. As we shall see, all police do not agree
that strenuous efforts should be undertaken to "mend" the drunken cop's
career; some feel a cop who succumbs to alcoholism demonstrates reason to
have his career ended.

It is necessary to define alcoholism prior to examining its prevalence and
possible seriousness among police. According to the legal definition from
Black's Law, alcoholism is ". . . in medical jurisprudence, the pathological
effect (as distinguished from physiological effect) of excessive indulgence in
intoxicating liquors."[4] Alcoholism as defined by Webster is "a complex
psychological and nutritional disorder associated with excessive and usually
compulsive drinking."[5] Alcoholism can also be defined in terms of the
percentage of alcohol in the body. It is generally agreed that alcohol
intoxication is a state of pronounced disturbance of function resulting from

the presence of alcohol in the central nervous system. An alcoholic exhibits a psychological and/or physiological dependency on alcohol; that is, the person cannot function normally without the assistance of alcohol. An enlightening discussion of definitions of alcoholism as they relate to various theoretical orientations and treatments can be reviewed in "The Rand Report."[6]

Alcohol is not a respecter of sex, race, education, age, or income; police *are* candidates for alcoholism. Since police are primarily responsible for the protection of the public, it is important to investigate to what extent they may have problems with alcohol and/or alcohol abuse. If police do have serious drinking problems, what is being done about it? This chapter examines local and national evidence concerning alcoholism among police and issues relevant to handling cops who are problem drinkers, information about who the drinking police are, what proportion are problem drinkers, why they drink, what they drink; it is not a judgment of police.

Research Design

The design employed for this research was three-fold. The preliminary phase was to search background reference material to determine the extent police had been studied concerning alcohol abuse. The second phase of the study involved writing directly to police departments in large cities for any information or unpublished reports readily available. Of the twenty cities contacted only three were able to provide significant data. The researchers also received information from the Department of Health, Education, and Welfare and the International Association of Chiefs of Police, Inc. The final phase of the study consisted of sixteen personal and/or phone interviews with police chiefs, policemen and ex-policemen. They were asked general information about the drinking patterns of police as well as specific information about the officers they knew to be alcoholics.

Background Literature

Numerous articles have been written concerning the alcoholics that police arrest and how the police handle these arrests. Nonetheless, only six journal articles and three books dealing with the alcoholic policeman per se were uncovered. The content of these articles and books are briefly summarized below.

Skolnick pointed out that police are by no means total abstainers from the use of alcoholic beverages.[7] Skolnick also noted that the "policeman who is arresting a drunk has probably been drunk himself; he knows it and the drunk knows it".[8] He reported that much alcohol is usually consumed at police banquets, often resulting in drunkenness, exchanges of loud insults, and plainly "letting oneself go". A main reason that police usually prefer keeping company with fellow officers is that the whole civilian world watches the police. The police feel more comfortable drinking with other police so civilians will not observe them just as college professors will drink when students are not present.[9]

In 1973, Hitz studied ten occupations commonly associated with heavy drinking.[10] From a sample of 765 white men in the San Francisco area, 165 were found to be heavy drinkers; ten of these were police officers. Hitz also found 24 salesmen, 24 postal workers, 7 firemen, 13 seamen, 15 printers and newsmen, 23 bartenders, 10 housepainters, and 39 cooks and restaurant workers in his sample who were heavy drinkers. According to the investigator, heavy drinking police were disproportionately over-represented in the sample. Recently, Dr. LeClair Bissell, Director of the Smithers Alcoholism Treatment and Training Center in New York City, estimated that "10 to 12 percent of the 360,700 physicians in the United States are now or will become alcoholics".[11] No career is immune to alcoholism . . . especially those whose members endure more stress.

J.A. Dunne, a New York City Police Department Chaplain, discussed the rehabilitation program he initiated in 1966.[12] Msgr. Dunne established an aggressive hunt for heavy drinkers to be placed in the N.Y.C.P.D. Rehabilitation Program. His insistence that problem drinkers be treated (i.e., "shape-up-or ship-out") has resulted in his being referred to as "The Body Snatcher."[13] All seven cops on his staff are recovered alcoholics. Seventy-five percent of the program's clients return to full duty. Further information regarding this New York City Police Department program is presented in the next section.

Captain Leon Dishlacoff of the Denver Police Department stated in "The Drinking Cop" that alcoholics become uncomfortable where there is no alcohol available.[14] He cited as an example an officer at roll call who was impatient to make the street so he could get a drink from a friendly bartender or from a bottle hidden in his private vehicle or briefcase. Dishlacoff also discussed various ways to help the alcoholic. He suggested intensive individual, group, and family counseling in a "Care Unit" program as well as out-patient seminars and group therapy for all former patients and their families on a regular basis. Dishlacoff stressed that it is the responsibility of the individual police agency and its administrators to recognize alcoholism as a disease and to set up in-house preventative and treatment programs for alcoholics. Some ways to detect the alcoholic, even those adept at credible alibis, excuses, and rationalizations, are listed by Dishlacoff:[15]

One or more of the following may be tell-tale symptoms in detecting employee alcoholism: (1) visibly uncontrolled drinking at company, agency, or public functions, (2) increasing absenteeism, particularly following weekends, or leaving work early and pleading illness; (3) uneven or progressively lower job performance; (4) repeated on-the-job accident, including vehicular accidents; and (5) intoxication during duty hours.

Heavy or excessive drinking is not necessarily synonymous with alcoholism, although it usually is indicative of impending, if not present, trouble.

Michael A. Graham, an investigator for the Wayne County Prosecutor's Office in Michigan wrote to the editor of *The Police Chief* to comment on Captain Dishlacoff's article.[16] He suspects that alcoholism is a greater problem for law enforcement than for most other professions. He attributed this to the stress and strain of the occupation, coupled with the constant exposure to the seamy side of life. An unknown percentage of police will become alcoholics. Graham noted that he had seen a lot of two-fisted drinkers in the ranks of police and prosecutors; they were fine human beings who were committed to their work, but did not realize they had a disease— alcoholism.

Several novels were found dealing with police and drinking. One such book written by Ray Toepfer depicted the policeman this way:[17]

> If you weren't a cop . . . it would be hard to understand that cops were people too. They got mad or drunk or violent, just like anybody else. Most forces tried to play it down. The cop is always cool, they said. He always thinks straight in any emergency. He never panics, never gets scared, never runs. He is the soul of honesty, and he never uses a gun or stick unless he has no other course of action open.
>
> It wasn't that way. A cop reacted to the same pressures as everybody else. He might be trained and disciplined, but he was still human, and sometimes he was apt to slip up.

Aaron and Shafter, authors of *The Police Officer and Alcoholism,* discussed the problem the Milwaukee Police Department has had with alcoholic arrests.[18] They reported that their Police Training School and the In-Service Training Program included curriculum concerning problems of alcoholism designed to help in the formulation of the attitudes of the police officers working in the field. Their program addresses mostly how to deal with the alcoholic the police officer is arresting . . . not the alcoholic within the department. Interestingly, the Milwaukee report does not mention that some of their own officers could be suffering from alcoholism, nor do they mention whether or not their own alcoholic program can include police.

A novel which deals directly with police and their drinking is *The Choirboys* by Joseph Wambaugh.[19] The title stands for the name the police gave themselves due to their getting together after work to drink in the park; they called this activity "choir practice". The setting for the story was Los Angeles. Even though Wambaugh states that none of the characters actually exist, he says that every incident mentioned had actually taken place. The reader may be shocked to learn of the incidents which purportedly occured. Wambaugh clearly implied that many policemen do drink regularly and that many of them are alcoholics.

No doubt a main reason for the lack of printed information concerning police and alcoholism is that it remains still a touchy subject for many departments. Only in recent years have progressive departments begun to address the issue as to whether the drunken cop is fair game for research and whether or not a drunken cop's career should be "ended or mended". Some additional information from two giant police departments are cited below.

Findings from Metropolitan Departments

The most useful and detailed information concerned two large city police departments: the New York City Police Department and the Philadelphia Police Department. Some points of interest concerning these programs are summarized below.

The most extensive program for alcoholic policemen is the New York City Police Department. Msgr. Dunne, briefly mentioned earlier, was the first to set up a program for the alcoholic policemen. His program was finally initiated in 1966, after many frustrating years of failing due in large measure to a Chief Surgeon who did not sympathize with alcoholics. After the Chief Surgeon's retirement, his replacement became very interested in helping Msgr. Dunne. The records of the "chronic sick" (ill five or more times a year), accident records, and disciplinary records were searched to detect policemen who might have a drinking problem. A staff was organized with recovered alcoholic policemen to function as members of a Counseling Unit. Each "suspect" had an initial interview with a member of this staff and then talked with Msgr. Dunne. If hospitalization was necessary, the policeman would be sent for a five day stay at a hospital in New Jersey. Next he would be asked to go to an Alcoholics Anonymous halfway house for a period of four to six weeks. Finally he would be given a 90 day program of "limited duty" (no firearms) which also required nightly Alcoholics Anonymous meetings and weekly rehabilitative sessions.[20]

In the first 13 months of the program, 216 men were interviewed; 79 men were subsequently hospitalized. Of the men who entered the program, 75% were returned to full duty; the unsuccessful were transferred to permanent limited duty and became eligible for retirement for physical disability after one year.[21] In a letter the researchers received from Msgr.

Dunne, he reported that for 1975 the New York Police Department Counseling Unit was able to restore 140 men to full duty with firearms.[22] Such a successful program should and has served as a model for other progressive police departments.

The City of Philadelphia Police Department also has an exemplary program for its employees with drinking problems.[23] The Counseling Unit was officially established in Philadelphia on March 26, 1971; a recovered alcoholic policeman was the first full-time counselor. In 1972, the Police Commissioner signed a memorandum which stated the Police Department's policy on employees with drinking problems. These guidelines are summarized as follows:[24]

1. All Command/Supervisory personnel are responsible for the early detection of problem drinking and prompt referral for assistance for this illness.

2. The primary purpose is to get the man into treatment before his problem becomes chronic, thus retaining a valuable employee. All information will be kept confidential.

3. The problem of drinking can affect all age groups and all ranks. (After this there was a list of symptoms to aid in early identification of problem drinkers.)

4. Referrals will be made on memorandum listing all pertinent information.

5. Problem drinking cannot be corrected by warning the employee or by "covering" for him or giving him another chance, as this is an illness and needs treatment or it will get worse.

6. If the employee refuses treatment or fails to cooperate with the departmental program, then the usual procedure for poor or unsatisfactory performance and violation of departmental orders and regulations should be followed.

Two "recovered" alcoholic policemen initiated the program on an informal basis. They then formed an Alcoholics Anonymous group with nine other policemen and firemen as well as a reporter. The formal program is available to approximately 10,000 persons; 8,000 of whom are uniformed officers. The program averages 13 to 14 new cases per month with an apparent recovery rate of 85 percent. Referrals come mostly from supervisors, but there are some self-referrals, medical referrals, and some who are referred by their family and friends. The Counseling Unit has had only two female alcoholics largely because of the relatively small number of women in the Department. The Counseling Unit also works with family members of officers on the force.

Some of the results that the Philadelphia Police Department Counseling Unit are of interest: the typical inpatient care was cut from 20.7 to 9.8 days per year; injury days were reduced from 4.2 to 2.2 per year; and suspension days were cut from 2.3 to 1.2 per year after they had been through the program. The outpatient results were similar.[25]

In a cost benefit study, the results show that the Department had recovered more than all of its costs as of March 31, 1974, for the group counseled before March 31, 1973. The expected future savings for this group were computed at $50,094 per year.[26]

The New York City and Philadelphia Police Department are large, progressive, and complete programs. We note, however, that their respective recovery rates for alcoholics of 75 to 85 percent is only slightly higher than the 71 percent attributed to Alcoholics Anonymous in the "Rand Report."[27] The recovery rate of untreated alcoholics is about 50 percent according to the "Rand Report." Some alcoholics are extremely difficult to treat effectively. In contrast to most data from police departments as well as other data, the Rand Report also raises doubt about the necessity of "total abstinence" for former alcoholics. This issue still rages.

Findings from Interviews[28]

With these larger programs in mind, we now turn to the personal interviews with numerous police chiefs, policemen, and ex-policemen from small and medium size departments. In order to assure anonymity to interviewers, no names and the cities are not identified.

One of the interviews conducted was with an assistant director of a Sheriff's Department of a Florida county. He did not believe that employees received much information during training concerning alcohol. He did note that only four or five people had been discharged in the last four of five years due to their being alcoholics or heavy drinkers. As a contrast with the NYC and Philadelphia PD's formal treatment programs, he added that his department would get rid of alcoholics or serious problem drinkers as soon as they were discovered, regardless of the type of duties performed by the police officer. This man did say that he would hire a recovered alcoholic, if he or she were qualified. One of the shift leaders in the department is a "recovered" alcoholic. The reason this policeman felt the rate of alcoholism is low among police is because of the high standards the department employs in selecting new applicants. He believes the alcoholism is higher in the populations of the lower educated and lower income. Apparently this man was not aware that alcohol is not a respecter of education or income, or of race and sex.

In a phone interview with the Chief of Police of a major Florida city, the Chief did not believe the younger police officers had an alcoholic problem, but he had noticed that the older officers sometimes have had a drinking problem. He stated that alcohol is a problem in the military, industry, and now it is obviously a problem with the police force; it should not be ignored. As a member of the disciplinary board, he had recommended to the previous chief of police that the alcoholic need not be disciplined but that the alcoholic should be treated. His recommendations were overruled.

A Major in this same Police Department stated that policemen do their fair share of drinking; there are few policemen who don't drink. This police officer said they drink mostly beer because they are on a beer budget. He knew of only three situations in the past 15 years of alcoholic police officers. Normally this Police Department would try to help the officer by taking some pressures off of him. Next they would send him to a psychologist as a means of helping him with the problem. If this did not work, they would send the policeman to the Chaplain. The Major said that the Police Department couldn't make the officer stop drinking; he had to do that on his own.

The Major described two of the alcoholic police he had known. The administration found out about an officer whose drinking had placed him in a very "compromising" situation. The officer admitted to having a drinking problem; they then sent him to the department psychologist who confirmed his drinking problem. The officer was ultimately transferred to an easier job with less pressure. He is still a member of the Police Department and will be retiring soon. The second incident involved another officer who had been drinking excessively while off duty. His work had not been affected and the administration was not aware of his problem. Subsequently the officer threatened a patrolman with a gun which brought the officer to the administration's attention. This officer was retired medically. The Police Department did not terminate him because of his alcoholism, but because of his conduct stemming from the alcohol.

The Major described another incident. A vice agent, while on duty, drank a little too much, became aware of this, and tried to drive back to the Police Department. He, the Vice Agent, couldn't make it back so he pulled over and went to sleep. He was found in the early morning hours and was suspended for five days. This Police Department has had only one instance of an officer drinking in uniform. Under normal circumstances, they view this as a felony.

The Major said he would not hire a recovered alcoholic. He said most of the people they hire are in their early twenties; he believes that there are not many alcoholics in this age cohort. The Major stated it was the older police who more likely would become alcoholics, especially single or divorced men over 40 years of age. He believes police drink together and tend to have mostly police for friends. Police can become alcoholics just like anyone else; he doesn't think problem drinking should be covered up. This officer also feels that there needs to be more understanding about alcoholism.

A Police Chief of a department with about 100 officers in a Florida city said alcoholism is seldom a problem in his department. He didn't know what he would do in the event the situation did arise where one of his officers was an alcoholic. There is not a set procedure to handle the problem. This Chief of Police also said he would not hire an admitted alcohoic to be a member of his police force.

In an interview with the Police Chief in another Florida city with over 100 police officers, the Chief reported that they had only three people in the past ten years who had been alcoholics. The one case he described was a divorced policeman who went to bars on his days off. This police officer would then flash his badge to gain special favors. The police officer received drinks from these bars for free in return for special protection. When the administration became aware of this man's drinking problem, they suggested that he seek help. When the police officer did not seek help, he was fired.

This same Chief of Police said he believed the reason alcoholism is not much of a problem for his department is that the police officers are highly educated. He noted that over 90 percent of the officers in his department had A.A. degrees, about 60 percent had a B.A. degree, five others either had or were working on their Master's degree. The Chief also said that he would hire alcoholics as long as they were "recovered." He stated that he would start them off with a desk job to observe their performance and then decide if they could be put on the road.

The Chief of Police and Assistant Chief of a Florida college campus were interviewed together. They had known policemen who drank but felt that alcoholism had no place on a police force. They would not consider hiring an admitted alcoholic. Their reasoning was to protect the public they serve. They felt there is always a tendency to go back to drinking. These two policemen did not think that police would drink due to pressure from their jobs, but rather due to personal problems.

An ex-Highway Patrol Supervisor also confirmed that most police do drink; what they drink depends on the situation. He stated that many of the police he knew would get off of work in the evening, drink a six-pack of beer while they watched television, eat dinner, and then start on another six-pack of beer. He noted the police are reluctant to go to bars to drink because they do not want to be recognized. This man felt that the police that were most likely to start drinking would be the ones out on the streets and the administrators. These police are under constant pressure; many times their escape is the bottle.

The ex-patrolman had experienced occasions when a policeman had been called in with alcohol on his breath. In these cases, he would send him home. He did not think alcoholic police would be more sympathetic to people who drank and were arrested. He noted the police are often under pressures from three sides: the administration (the hierarchy); his family as a result of some roles his job demands; and the public (the main source). This interrole conflict can be frustrating and may lead to many policemen becoming problem drinkers.

Case Study

A case study given by the ex-Highway Patrolman is presented below that illustrates many of the comments that were given to the researchers during this investigation:

This is a case study about Trooper C. He was fired for drinking in the early part of 1973. He was also fighting while he was drinking. Trooper C. at the time was 41 years of age. He was a white Caucasian, heavy set, with a ruddy complexion, a good fighter, and a heavy drinker. Trooper C. worked in a specialized area (in a small unit), but on holidays he worked the regular duty like everyone else. In his job he wasn't under very heavy stress. He had held this job for 1 1/2 years. He had been on the road before he held this job and he had been under stress during this time. Trooper C. was married and his wife worked in an office. He was very jealous and this created problems for them. Money and status were very important to him; this is what he strived for. He was the type of person who didn't want to work hard—he didn't want to kill himself with working too hard. He had two children and when this person met him for the first time he seemed to be very happy on the outside. This person noticed one thing about Trooper C. and that was he liked to go to Water Holes around town (he liked to go to booze joints to quench his thirst). This person began to notice a pattern that Trooper C. had gotten into. He quit hanging around with the guys after work, he began going home and would drink a six-pack of beer before supper. But the heavy drinking didn't start until after supper.

This person observed Trooper C. over a period of 2 1/2–3 years. He found out that Trooper C. was beating his wife. He came to know a neighbor of Trooper C. and found out more about their troubles. He also came to know Trooper C.'s boss and the rest of the information.

The information that the boss gave this person was that these people would fight until all hours of the night, maybe up until 4:00 in the a.m. Then he would get up and go to work in the morning. Trooper C. wanted money and since he wasn't getting it he was frustrated. This was his main problem. Since he wanted this money he started working on a loading dock (trucking) and he would load trucks and drive the trucks for four or five hours a night. He made as much money as a supervisor with all the years he had been employed. With this part-time job he brought in about

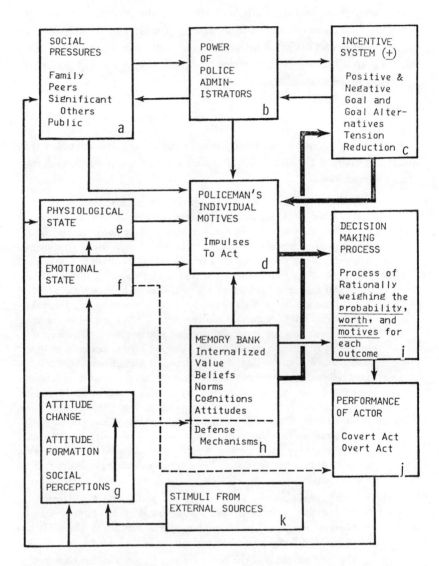

FIGURE I.   INTERACTION MODEL PORTRAYING SOURCES OF MOTIVES OF
POLICE OFFICERS THAT AFFECT THEIR DECISIONS AND PERFORMANCE.

$1450 a month before taxes. His wife worked in the courthouse and made about $450 a month. So they were living off of about $1900 a month. They lived in upper-middle class neighborhood. Even a few professionals lived in this area. So they were living the part of having a lot of money.

Trooper C. dropped out of association with friends. He began to get paranoid about his wife and thought that she was stepping out on him. So he began beating his wife even more.

In April of 1973 it all came to a head. He started drinking, the Sheriff's Department was called out and they didn't arrest him because he was a trooper. He would then continue to chase his wife and kids around the house. At 12:15 one night in April the Sheriff's Department was called out and he promised to go to bed and to quit fighting and tearing up the house. This didn't last for long because about 3:00 he woke up in a drunken stupor, knocked his wife across the floor (which gave her a broken nose, and multiple lacerations) and she somehow got out and called the Sheriff's Department and they came back out to get him. He (Trooper C.) made the mistake of running out into the front yard and trying to jump on the man from the Sheriff's Department. So they locked him up. When he woke up he was really out of it and was making a lot of noise. Trooper C. was immediately fired and he went to work full time for the trucking agency. His wife also filed for separation and took the children and left.

When Trooper C. went to court his background showed that drinking was the main reason for his acting as he did. The last this person heard Trooper C. had dried out, he was back working as a trooper, and his wife and kids were living with him. Trooper C. did have one slip and they sent him to a hospital to be an outpatient being treated for acute alcoholism.

Police administrators must thoughtfully consider various alternatives for early detection and intervention that likely would have prevented much of the above painful human episode. Were there not sufficient early warning signals as set forth by Dishlacoff?

Sources of Motives

Prior to concluding this chapter, a schematic model is presented that portrays various motives that can affect a police officer's decisions and performance. (Fig. 1). An inspection of this model clearly shows the complexity of human processes. A complete analysis of the model is beyond the scope of this chapter, but the model can be used to briefly illustrate and summarize some important points that are relevant to alcoholism among police officers.

Several interviewers and authors referred to the importance of social pressures (Cell "a" in the model), especially the constant surveillance of the public. With the exception of peer pressure (and sometimes family pressure), the officer is "expected" to be the "Mr. Right". His supervisors (Cell "b") also place strong pressures toward this "model" behavior. Yet other competing sources of motives such as his physiological (Cell "e") and emotional state (Cell "f") may at times compete with motive sources to be the cool, honest, polite cop he is always supposed to be. For example, he may be physically exhausted and/or emotionally drained (or emotionally frustrated) from earlier experiences of the day. Even more important, his own internalized value and belief systems (Cell "h") that have been developed from years of social experiences may not coincide with the expectations others have for him. We note that *his* value system determines which of the incentives available to him are important and worth pursuing or avoiding. Obviously shift work as well as income tend to limit, at least at times, the availability of some incentives that are more readily available to those in many other occupations.

One incentive that *is* available is the use of alcoholic beverages (or other escape modes) as a means of reducing the tensions of the day. Since he cannot readily drink in public places, he is more likely to drink with his peers . . . or at home. Note that should an officer's (or anyone's) physiological and/or emotional state be a more potent motive source at the moment than his rational processes (Cells "h" and "i"), he may act "irrationally." (Observe the dotted line from Cell "f" to Cell "j" that by-passes the rational processes). By definition, alcohol is dysfunctional to one's mental processes; the possibility of the drunken cop failing to perform his duties rationally is, therefore, real . . . potentially endangering both himself and those he is charged to protect. Lastly, note that should external constraining forces (Cells "a" and "b") be "cut off" due to anonymity in the situation, the relative force of other motives sources would be far stronger.

A further study of Fig. 1 can reveal other reasons and a great deal of insight as to why police officers with alcoholic tendencies should be identified early. What should be or can be done about their careers is still an open issue.

Conclusion

Voluminous research has been done in the area of alcoholism, but clearly relatively little empirical evidence has been systematically collected and analyzed in the area of alcoholic police. The literature search and interviews data in this report have shown that most police do drink moderately (mostly beer) and that there is an unknown proportion of alcoholic police. Officers' attitudes of tolerance toward police who drink excessively vary remarkably. Some administrators officers want to improve the ability to recognize and treat the police who are problem drinkers; others would ignore the potential problem . . . and immediately dismiss those drunken cops who could not be ignored. Police officers have many different ideas about the causes of alcoholism. The most important factor of all is that police do drink and the potential (and in some cases, real) problems of dysfunction by police officers is there.

The researchers of this paper feel they have only touched the surface concerning police and alcoholism. There needs to be further, extensive research done in this area. With more research, a better understanding of the problem would arise that could help the alcoholic police, their families, their employers, and the public *before* far more serious problems arose. In the process, the closet drinkers may be discovered and encouraged to come out of "hiding" so they *can* be assisted. The researchers urge more Police Departments to cooperate fully in this area of research.

The area of alcoholism is one of the country's major social problem areas. The first step in solving the problem should be the effective cooperation of all involved parties. As long as police alcoholics are ignored within departments and no one helps them with their problem, the problems will get worse . . . not better; the human and monetary costs will continue to soar. Cops are human beings and as such they are subject to the same frailties as others whose careers often engender unusual duress.

In sum, the first step is for more departments to *admit* that alcoholism among police can and does arise so that more preventive measures can be implemented and effective formal treatment programs can be directed toward problem drinkers. Why shouldn't all police departments encourage sophistication in this social problem area equally commensurate with their sophistication in their material equipment???

Summary

We have seen that police are indeed subject to problems of alcohol abuse. In view of the stress adherent in police work, (as well as other stress related occupations) it would be most surprising if some officers did not fall prey to the hazards of alcoholism. Fortunately we now live in a time when at least somewhat less stigma is attached to such problems. As described earlier, several successful programs have been developed throughout the nation that can serve as models for other departments to more openly and adequately cope with alcoholism among their officers.

While identification and treatment of alcoholics is the most urgent problem within departments, the obvious long-range goal is to prevent the abuse of alcohol. Alcoholism is the end product of a long process of contributing factors, as stressed in Figure 1. We need to give greater attention to the study of alcoholism (and other social problems) as on-going *processes* so that we can better determine where and when to more effectively intervene in this cybernetic process. We must also seriously study what structural changes within police organizations can best minimize the problems of alcoholism as well as other related problems. Systematically, openly addressing problems of alcoholism is the first step toward ameliorating this social problem.

Discussion Questions

1. Why has the problem of alcoholism among police officers been neglected for such a long period?

2. Do you believe a person who is an alcoholic can function adequately as a policeman? Discuss the pros and cons of this issue.

3. After carefully studying the factors and processes shown in Figure 1, compile a list of changes that could be practically implemented that would lessen the likelihood of alcoholism among police.

4. Select one of the changes from your list in #3 and follow the effects of this change through its process.

5. If you were a police chief, how could you handle cases of alcohol abuse by your officers? Discuss your policies and give your rationale for each.

Notes

1. Joseph Wambaugh, *The Onion Field* (New York: Delcorte Press, 1973), p. 4.

2. The authors wish to acknowledge the contribution of Joan Buchanan Scully as their research assistant for this study.

3. A search of the literature plus numerous letters to police departments failed to uncover even a dozen journal articles, reports or books (in total) directly related to alcoholism among police officers. The major sources reviewed are included below.

4. Henry Campbell Black, *Blacks Law Dictionary* (St. Paul, Minnesota: West Publishing Co., 1968).

5. Webster's Seventh New Collegiate Dictionary, (Springfield, Massachusetts: G. and C. Meriam Co., 1971), p. 21.

6. D.J. Armour, J.M. Pouch and H.B. Stanbud, *Alcoholism and Treatment* (Santa Monica, California: Rand, 1976), pp. 7–27.

7. Jerome H. Skolnick, "A Sketch of the Policeman's Working Personality," *Justice Without Trial, Law Enforcement in Democratic Society* (New York: John Wiley and Sons, Inc. 1967), pp. 57–58.

8. Ibid., p. 57.

9. Ibid., p. 58.

10. D. Hitz, "Drunken Sailors and Others; Drinking Problems in Specific Occupation," *Quarterly Journal of Studies on Alcohol* 34 (June 1973), pp. 423–424.

11. Donald Robinson, "The Menace of Drunken Doctors," *Ladies Home Journal* (April, 1977) p. 94.

12. Joseph A. Dunne, "Counseling Alcoholic Employees in a Municipal Police Department," *Quarterly Journal of Studies on Alcohol* 34 (June 1973), pp. 423–434 and *Labor-Management Alcoholism Newsletter* National Council on Alcoholism, May–June, 1974.

13. Michael Mok, "The Bow and Arrow Squad," *New York Sunday News* February 10, 1974, pp. 12, 36, 37.

14. Leon Dishlacoff, "The Drinking Cop," *The Police Chief* (January, 1976). pp. 32–39.

15. Ibid., p. 39.

16. Michael A. Graham, "Letters to the Editor," *The Police Chief* (March, 1976), p. 10.

17. Ray Grant Toepfer, *Endplay* (Greenwich, Conn.: Fawcett World Library) 1975, p. 149.

18. James E. Aaron and Albert J. Shafter, *The Police Officer and Alcoholism* (Illinois: Charles C. Tomas, 1973).

19. Joseph Wambaugh, *The Choirboys* (New York: Delcort, 1975).

20. Michael Mok, "The Bow and Arrow Squad," *New York Sunday News* February 10, 1974, p. 12.

21. Joseph A. Dunne, "Counseling Alcoholic Employees in a Municipal Police Department," *Quarterly Journal of Studies on Alcohol,* 34 (June, 1973), p. 434.

22. Letter form Rev. Msgr. Joseph A. Dunne, The City of New York Police Department, New York, New York (April 26, 1976).

23. National Council of Alcoholism, "Two Tales of One City," *Labor-Management Alcoholism Journal,* 4 (1975) pp. 1–16.

24. Ibid., pp. 2–4.

25. Ibid., p. 15.

26. Ibid., p. 12.

27. D.J. Armour, J.M. Pouch, and H.B. Stanbud, p. 97.

28. In order to assure the anonymity of interviewees, no names are used and the cities are not identified.

29. A detailed description of these processes are further illustrated in a paper by William R. Brown, Department of Sociology, Florida Technological University, Orlando, Florida, entitled "Integrating Attitude Formation and Attitude Change Into a General Behavioral Model." *The Florida Scientist,* Vol. 41, No. 3, 1978.

8

Citizen Participation in Policing: Issues in the Social Control of a Social Control Agency

GEORGETTE BENNETT-SANDLER

POLICE REPRESENT ONE OF THE FOREMOST AND FORMAL SOCIAL CONTROL MECHANISMS available for dealing with deviance. Their role as such, however, is complicated by the nature of their mandate as well as that of their constituency. The current approach for dealing with these complexities is the advent of citizen participation programs.

The impetus for the recent spate of efforts to secure citizen participation in government agencies derives from the policy of "maximum feasible participation" written into the 1964 anti-poverty legislation. This attempt at participation has found its way into a number of institutional spheres. These include welfare rights, urban renewal, and school decentralization. Efforts to solicit citizen participation in these spheres have resulted in varying degrees of success and failure. In the process, some hard lessons have been learned which are instructive as the police world embarks on its first serious efforts to encourage citizen participation.

The necessity for citizen participation in policing has been recognized since the 1950's, when the first image-building community relations program was installed in St. Louis, Missouri (1956). However, it took the social unrest of the 1960's for the need to hit home. Deterioration in community relations coupled with the increasing demand for service pointed to a link between the two variables. The link is the collaborative approach to policing which was highlighted in the 1967 *Task Force Report* on the Police—a police/community collaboration which would produce a greater flow of information, a reduction in police injuries, reduction in riots, and an improvement in general police operations.[1] As a partial response to this need, the Task Force recommended the establishment of specialized community relations units with clearly defined authority and responsibility.

Since the publication of the report, there has been a great proliferation of community relations units and related activities. These efforts at citizen participation have taken basically five forms.

The dominant mode is that of *public relations*. There is general agreement that most citizen participation programs have deteriorated into image-building endeavors. These tend to involve a one-way selling job in which police organization seek to "educate" the public about their agency. Such programs usually focus on noncontroversial issues and may involve school lectures, literature distribution, and visits to local civic associations.

Another type of citizen participation in policing—and one which has always existed—is *political pressure*. What makes this pressure different from the companion form which is emerging today, is that it is aimed indirectly at top police administrators via established political figures. Needless to say, in these circumstances, the media become important vehicles for pressure. However, the effectiveness of the approach is based on the vulnerability of those in appointive positions.

A more contemporary approach to citizen participation in policing is external control in the form of *citizen review boards*. These boards, while solely advisory in nature, nonetheless raise fundamental issues about the nature of police authority as well as the validity of laymen's post hoc judgements. What makes the review boards particularly controversial is that they function to receive and investigate citizen complaints against police.

By contrast, a more popular and less controversial form of citizen participation in policing is the *crime prevention program*. This generally includes citizens in the mechanics of reducing opportunities for crime and the immediacy of detecting crime. Such efforts include "block watchers," auxiliaries, Operation Identification, telephone relays, citizen patrols, and educational efforts.

What becomes immediately evident in the typology of citizen participation attempts described so far is that citizens' involvement occurs at a fair distance from their point of contact with police. It is here that the emerging citizen participation efforts differ from earlier attempts. There now exists an attempt to include citizens in policy making at the operational levels that deal directly with them. This means *intervention at the point of contact*.[2] Such interventions include advisory boards, community profiling, and collaborative development of police manuals.[4]

Despite all of these efforts, however, programs for citizen participation in policing cannot be declared a success. Twenty years since their inception, a variety of problems have emerged to which important lessons can be applied from similar efforts in other institutional spheres. The next section discusses some of these problems and then seeks additional clarification by examining issues deriving from the War on Poverty.

Lessons From The Past

Dilemmas of Citizen Participation—The Police

Citizen participation in policing is by no means a clear cut good or an unequivocal evil. It can range from being a catalyst to constructive change to nothing more than a search for petty patronage.[5] While it is an admirable goal, recent attempts to attain it have surfaced a number of problems and dilemmas which need to be addressed in future efforts. These include: the conflict between the openness demanded by citizen participation and the traditional secrecy of the police; the contradiction between police as an autonomous profession and a publicly accountable agency; the problem of the representativeness of the citizens who participate in policing as well as the agency which polices them; the mutual distrust that exists between police and segments of their clientele; and the marginal nature of the programs which have emerged to deal with these issues.

One of the fundamental dilemmas of citizen participation in policing is the confrontation of demands for openness with the traditional police norm of secrecy.

> Police should undertake to keep the community informed of the problems with which they must deal and the complexities that are involved in dealing with them effectively. Police agencies should cooperate with those who seek an understanding of police operations by affording opportunities for interested citizens to acquaint themselves with police operations and by providing access to the accumulation of knowledge and experience the police possess.[6]

While commendable, this ABA Standard nonetheless typifies a onesided approach to community relations. This aspect of it is not dealt with in the commentary, but the latter does recognize that the standard represents the antithesis of the most important norm governing police conduct—secrecy.[7] This norm is manifest in the Code of Silence which prevents brother officers from "ratting" on each other; strictures against airing departmental "dirty laundry" in public; and the belief that civilians constitute an outgroup which lacks the experience to evaluate police actions. It is at the heart of police resistance to civilian review and cannot be separated from philosophical considerations of the legitimation of police authority and the extent of police autonomy.

Central to this issue is the question of to whom police are ultimately accountable. If police indeed constitute a profession, as is currently argued, they are accountable to, and subject to review by, their peers. Even in a profession, however, clients sometimes organize and regulate the autonomy of the practitioner. Organizing of civilian review boards represents one such attempt. Their defeat is an indication that the occupational group is, in the case of the police, more powerful than the client. The client, for the police, however, is hard to define.[8]

One can only broadly define the client as "the community" or "society." Yet, what makes the police-client relationship unique is that, unlike the other professions, it is the client who gives the practitioners their mandate, while at the same time having no choice in practitioners. That is to say, police authority derives from the social contract. Members of society invest their private power to use coercion in a government body—the police. Hence, police authority over their clients is a perpetual loan. In contrast, the authority of other professions is based solely on special expertise.[9] While it may be argued that police also possess special expertise, they are nonetheless caught in a dilemma produced by their right to curtail freedom. Thus, whenever power of the police stops being public power and becomes their private power, the right is eliminated. Any attempt to remove the actions of police from external examination may be interpreted as an attempt to transform the power of police from a public loan to a private right.[10]

Herein lies the fundamental rationale for citizen participation in policing.

However, the question remains, which citizens should be considered representative of the community in the participation process? While patrol strategies such as team policing seek to reach down to the grassroots by contacting militants, gangs, and other hostile groups,[11] most attempts to solicit citizen participation avoid such contacts. Instead, many current efforts consist of creating non-controversial advisory panels or community councils made up of "responsible" citizens who have a stake in the community. "Responsible" often means agreement with the police and affiliation with some formal community organization. Thus, the very groups which need to be targeted are, in effect, further alienated.[12] Where a specialized community relations unit exists, member officers who have achieved a rapport with hostile groups may, as a result of the perception that they have joined the opposition, find themselves isolated within the department.[13] This provides additional discouragement of efforts to reach the roots of discontent in the community. Unfortunately, the most hostile groups are often the ones most affected by police policies, and at the same time, the ones with the least input into those policies. Hence, the "community" remains unrepresented.

Yet, when one talks about the "community," one is merely talking about a level of organization, and that level must be defined. Is it the voters? In Washington, D.C., a Pilot District Project (PDP) with a Civilian Board (CB) was instituted. The Board was resisted by the police on the grounds that low voter participation in the sanctioning of the project was indicative of low community support for that project. At the same time, the CB's mediator role was rejected because it had not been invited by the police. Thus, without community support and without requests by the police, the implementation of the PDP was experienced as political collusion.[14] Clearly, politicians, too, were considered to be unrepresentative of the community. What was not considered is that low voter turnout is often an indicator of great consensus around issues. The PDP may have been one such issue.

If formal organizations, voters, and politicians are not adequately representative of the "community," what remains? What remains is the whole range of random, unaffiliated members of that community. Their demographic characteristics vary from area to area, but with sufficient efforts, they can be tapped. While this will be discussed more thoroughly in a later section, it is appropriate to give an example here.

In developing a new police manual, the Cambridge Police Department sought to obtain inputs and support from all ranks within the department as well as those of local agencies and various citizen groups. The criterion for selecting the groups was that of having had recent problems with the police. Thus, rather than meeting with a single group assumed to be representative of the community, a number of separate constituencies were approached individually. These were: the Spanish speaking, public housing tenants, high school students, Blacks, and the business community. Inputs were solicited by holding one public meeting open to everyone as well as one meeting with each group. The issues raised in these meetings were then addressed and incorporated into the manual by the police committee.[15]

While it is generally accepted that the community (or some level thereof) does and should have some input into police policies, it is important to address the assumption which underlies the need for citizen participation. This assumption, baldly stated, is that police are a special group, separate from, and unrepresentative of, the community. Being exclusive, their perspectives are assumed to be limited and in need of broadening by the participation of "regular" people. It is this condition which underlies the emphasis on minority recruitment. Indeed, community relations usually means minority relations and it is assumed that representation of minority groups in the police service will ameliorate discontent in the community.

Here too, however, the issue is not clear cut. While it is true that the presence of minorities may create a broader base of community support by reducing some of the "colonialist" quality of an all white "occupying army" in the ghetto, it is also true that the minority officer is often viewed as a traitor by his people. This becomes particularly evident when he is paired with a white officer and given primary responsibility for taking action against other blacks. While this protects the white officer from charges of discrimination, it exposes the black officer to denouncement as a traitor. There does seem to be some indication that black officers take more severe actions against blacks than do whites (as do whites against other whites). His "protective coloration," however, does reduce some of the suspicion that would ordinarily exist and defuse the charges of discrimination that might otherwise prevail. In addition, there is no question about the benefits derived from the minority officer's access to information and rapport with citizens in the ghetto areas to which he is almost always assigned.[16] By assigning him in this way, it is assumed that the community has achieved some representation.

If, however, full representation of the community in policing were to be achieved, it would seem to obviate the necessity for citizen participation. Indeed, all community control/citizen participation efforts—whether attached to urban renewal, welfare rights, or schools—derive from the notion that institutional personnel are detached from, not representative of, their clients, and therefore not to be trusted. Hence, the need for clients' input. What it boils down to is a mutual distrust between practitioner and client—a distrust which is nowhere more vividly illustrated than in policing.

In the case of police, the mutual distrust is manifest with two groups—minorities and liberals. The former is particularly complicated because distrust is strongest among those groups which make the most use of police services. While more dependent on the police than the white middle class, minority clients experience themselves as being discriminated against. Conversely, police officers working in slum neighborhoods, find their negative cultural stereotypes confirmed. As they perceive it, they work in centers of crime, vice, and violence[17]—hardly recommendations for a trustworthy citizenry. Where this complicates the citizen participation process is that such efforts are viewed by police as reactive undertakings in response to external pressure by troublesome and unworthy groups.[18] For example, a major argument used in defeating the citizen review board in New York City (1966) was that such a board would result in abetting criminals. From the minority citizen's viewpoint, on the other hand, there is very little trust in obtaining a fair deal from police. The Community Alert Patrol of Watts bears testimony to the strength of this feeling. Here, citizens patrolled in cars equipped with two-way radios, armed with cameras and tape recorders. Their sole purpose was to observe and document police activity.[19] Even where channels for participation are established, as was pointed out earlier, the grassroots of discontent are seldom tapped.

Distinct from, though sometimes related to, mutual distrust between minorities and police, is that which exists between police and liberals. The source of this distrust derives partially from the blue collar socio-economic groups from which police are recruited, but also from the activities which have brought liberals and police in confrontation with each other. These include the civil right and peace demonstrations of the 1960's, culminating with the provocation of police by the New Left at the Chicago Democratic Convention. In this light, citizen participation efforts are seen by many police as coerced concessions to rebellion. They view it as deplorable to engage in negotiations with those who challenge the order police are charged to uphold.[20] Thus, liberals are not associated with programs that are popular with police. Nor are police associated with actions that are popular with liberals. One need only examine the line-up in the 1966 New York City referendum to repeal the law creating the Civilian Review Board. Pro repeal: Policeman's Benevolent Association, Conservative Party, John Birch Society. Anti repeal: Liberal Republican Mayor Lindsay, Robert Kennedy, New York Times, New York Post.[21]

All of these dilemmas have led to the problem which makes the efforts finally ineffectual—that is, the marginal nature of citizen participation programs have often been constructed and staffed in haste with broadly formulated mandates that lack clearly defined activities.[22] The Task Force on the Police recommendation that separate units be established and be answerable to the top administrator opened the way for making this function marginal. It is true that personnel without other full time responsibilities are needed to keep a finger on the pulse of the community. Yet, those assigned to such tasks are often isolated within the organization and not perceived as doing "real" policework. Their work has often consisted of giving talks, coordinating crime prevention programs, or establishing dialogue-oriented committees. Such community relations work is erroneously defined by some as social work. This partially accounts for some of the negative response of police. Social work, however, treats the individual while community relations changes the alignments among people.[23] Thus function is reflected in times of crisis when it is often the job of the community relations officer to go into the community and cool out emotions. Unfortunately, this has often been used as a substitute for dealing with the problem.[24] While the community relations officer should have sufficient local knowledge to anticipate many problems, this is hard to do if he is located centrally. If, on the other hand, he is commanded by a headquarters unit but assigned to a field unit, jurisdictional problems may emerge. In either case, the emphasis on a separate and central unit creates an excuse for the rest of the organization to default on its community relations responsibilities.

Some attempts to remedy this situation have been made. These consist of enrichment of the training process with sociology, psychology, human relations, and minority group history.[25] However, too much reliance is placed on the effects of training. And what is acquired in the training process cannot become and remain operational unless reinforced in all key organizational processes.

As an example, the San Diego Police Department (SDPD) has attempted to reinforce community relations training by using new performance evaluation criteria for an experimental group of officers. These include: beat knowledge, community involvement, and problem solving. The goal here is to get away from band-aid approaches to community problems.[26] The SDPD recognizes that traditional expectations discourage devoting time to beat and community knowledge, cultivation of community involvement and support, and development of appropriate responses to specific problems.[27] Hence, the need for an integrated, organization-wide approach to community relations and citizen participation.[28]

These, then, are some of the lessons learned from past efforts to secure citizen participation in policing. For police agencies, this is still a new and relatively superficial enterprise. In other institutional spheres, however, there exists a vast body of experience which serves to elucidate the very problems encountered by police. Some of these will be briefly reviewed below.

Dilemmas of Citizen Participation—The War on Poverty

The OEO mandated tenet of "maximum feasible participation" led to a proliferation of citizen participation programs directed at the poor. These included community planning boards, Mobilization for Youth, local school boards, and the like. As with the police, the chief advocates of such programs were the liberal middle classes.[29] (Unlike the police, however, those liberals were pitted against middle class professionals rather than a blue collar occupational group.[30]) Also, as with the police, problems emerged around issues of professional privilege, accountability, and representativeness. Where the experiences of the War on Poverty have elaborated on those of the police is in the area of community organizing and relationships to power structures. Indeed, it is in these two areas that many of the failures of OEO programs can be located.

Where the OEO failed to engage in adequate community organizing, it encountered the same lack of representativeness in participation as did police programs. As with the police, the establishment of community councils often served as the vehicle for citizen participation. These councils, however, were often "stooge" groups that were not threats to the status quo.[31] It is the fundamental dilemma of these councils that those who are able to hold their own in such a group, are unlikely to be still poor and uneducated. Such groups tend to attract those who are already on their way up and hence, not reflective of their communities. One of the lessons learned from the War on Poverty is that formal organization precludes the participation of unsophisticated people.[32] This is particularly true when the agenda is a technical one or when sabotage of the group takes place through information overload.[33] Those who survive are often coopted by the power structure with minor jobs or privileges, thus further separating them from, and making them targets of suspicion by, the community they allegedly represent. This was dramatically illustrated in the community rejection of their local school boards in the New York City decentralization controversy.[34] On the other hand, when such groups fail to align themselves with power, they are easily defused, as was demonstrated with Mobilization for Youth.[35]

What makes them vulnerable is the lack of a base. Without established powers for support, citizen groups are dependent on broad based community support. The community, however, is not represented. There is a direct relationship between income, social class, and civic participation. The higher the education and social rank, the more active in community organizations a citizen is likely to be. Hence, as the social rank of a community declines, involvement becomes less commonplace and control becomes concentrated among fewer and less representative people.[37] This produces the kind of distrust of local leaders which cripples citizen participation efforts.

Without a broad base, it is difficult to achieve independent power. A lesson of the War on Poverty is that the more fruitful alternative is to develop sufficient leadership skills within the community to enable co-participation (with the power structure) in program planning and administration.[38] In this way, planning becomes a two stage process in which concerned citizens define issues and the power structure implements them.[39]

Community organizing is the vehicle through which broad based citizen inputs are solicited. To be broad based, it is essential that efforts include the power structure, organized citizen groups, but especially those who have no formal organizational affiliations. The danger is that, in so doing, the real leaders become the professional community organizers.[40] The trade-off is that they may manage to secure some real inputs. Toward this end, some guidelines have emerged from the community organization literature.

    1. Organizing requires causes.
    2. For the poor, causes involving specific services rather than long run basic issues are more appealing.

3. Simple structures, such as ad hoc groups, invite better participation by the poor in these causes.[41]

4. Programs must be broad enough to attract most groups in the community, yet at the same time, they must be specific and immediately feasible.[42]

5. The client must be defined as the public rather than special interest groups or the power structure.

6. Staff ideas should be considered proposals for citizen discussion rather than master plans to be sold to the community.

7. Two-way communication is essential.[43]

That these guidelines can be enacted is demonstrated by the collaborative planning process utilized in Toronto. Here, upon completion of a proposal by the Planning Board, a summary is sent to every household and business in the district. Before becoming part of the official plan, it is discussed at small group meetings, amended in light of citizen comments, and reviewed by elected officials along with carefully recorded reports of citizen responses. The process is not without its problems. It requires additional time and staff and the synthesis of large amounts of data. The staff problem, at least, can be solved through the use of volunteers (students, retirees, etc.),[44] while the others are trade offs for a truly participative system.

This very brief review of major dilemmas of citizen participation emerging from the War on Poverty sheds some light on the problems encountered in parallel efforts in policing. For example, it becomes immediately evident that police citizen participation programs have suffered from a lack of community organizing. As a result, those who have most needed to be aligned with a power group—such as the police—that can act on their needs, have not been represented, while those least needing such ties have been the major recipients. Nonetheless, while community organizing is a clear deficiency in police programs, it is not at all clear that police are either functionally or politically suitable to undertake such a task.

The next section of this paper attempts to address this issue of feasibility by extracting from the dilemmas discussed above requisites for citizen participation and their "do-ability" by police.

Requisites for Programs of Citizen Participation in Policing

There are a number of requisites for citizen participation in policing. Some of them, however, are more feasible than others.

Two-way communication. Programs of citizen participation in policing require more than the one-sided selling job involved in police public relations efforts. While it is important for police to be open, so is it important for the community to be open. Equal opportunities must be created for the police to know their community and for the community to know their police. But two-way communication is hampered by the mistrust some citizen groups and police feel toward one another. As is demonstrated by the Washington, D.C. PDP, this distrust cannot always be overcome. Police are often defensive and citizens are often naive. The only sociologically sound way to deal with such distrust is through contact and communication. To this end, a number of promising programs exist. These include: group dynamics workshops, civilian patrol observations, and police participant observation in skid row and ghetto settings.

Accountability to the community. Citizen participation assumes police accountability to the community. Such accountability takes four forms: keeping the community informed; soliciting feedback on policies as well as giving feedback on responses to community inputs; external review by citizens; and shared responsibility for services with citizens.

With reference to the first two forms, a clear distinction must be made between crises and routine business. Clearly, police agencies cannot go through the cumbersome process of information sharing and feedback cannot occur after the crisis. This would be consistent with the requisite for two-way communication and would encourage ventilation of feelings as well. With more routine business, all policies which directly affect the local community ought to undergo this two-way process. What this boils down to is the inclusion of the community in the planning process. The Hartford Police Department is currently considering such a procedure for orders coming out of its Field Services Bureau. While it is true that such a process requires staffing, resources exist in the form of Community Service Officers, Community Relations Officers, and civilian volunteers.

The third form of community accountability, external review by citizens, is more complicated. External review may take the form of community response to service as part of a performance evaluation system, or citizen complaint review boards. While the first is desirable and indeed essential if citizens are to identify deficiencies in service, it is expensive and difficult to administer. It has been attempted in Dallas with some degree of success, but only with outside funding, and not as a measure of individual performance. Methods for such surveys include mail questionnaires, police delivered response cards, and follow up telephone interviews. The response rate for the first two tends to be low, and the third generates suspicion, particularly in minority areas where such measures are most needed.

Citizen complaint review boards pose another set of problems. While they do provide a forum for citizen complaints (in New York City, complaints jumped from 200/year to 100/week with the establishment of a board), these complaints are difficult to validate. Besides the problems involved in second-guessing police officers, validated claims must be weighed against myriad factors, such as activity level of the officer and activity level of his beat. By no means should outcomes be interpreted without reference to these other factors. Yet, they often are. Still civilian review boards are necessary, because management accountability is generally not sufficiently decentralized in policing to produce strong internal controls.

The last of the forms community accountability takes lies at the heart of citizen participation in policing. That is, responsibility of the citizen to work collaboratively with the police in law enforcement. It is a truism that police cannot do their job without cooperation from citizens. On the most basic level, this cooperation must begin with reporting of crimes and willingness to testify. Beyond this, however, the recent trend has been toward a more active role for citizens in crime prevention and detection activities.[45] Not only are these activities feasible, but they are essential. With the increasing demands for service, police must share their work. In this age of hiring freezes, budget cuts, and lay-offs, they cannot handle it all themselves. This fact in itself must stimulate a reassessment of traditional police-civilian distance and suspicion.

Representativeness of police. Although frought with problems (which require detailed exploration beyond the scope of this paper), citizen participation can be built directly into police organizations. This can be achieved by hiring personnel who represent a cross section of the service community. Such personnel include not only minorities recruited as sworn officers, but hiring of all kinds of people into civilian positions. Unfortunately, civilianization is generally concentrated at low level positions, in which personnel have little influence on policy.[46] Representation at higher levels is also required. (Boston, for example has a civilian director for its police academy, and four influential special assistants to the Commissioner. New York City has had a civilian director of police personnel.)

Representativeness of citizen groups. The foundation of any citizen participation effort is the representativeness of those involved. To be representative of a community, participation and planning must include political groups, other special interest groups, and ad hoc committees. The first two have always been heard and are the ones usually included in citizen participation efforts. It is the latter groups, however, that have the greatest chance of attracting unaffiliated community members and bringing in the multiple constituencies that must be represented. To be effective, these must be informal, issue-oriented, controversial, and short-range in their goals. Establishing such groups requires community organizing by the police. It is through such organizing that the grass roots of a community may be tapped. Yet, it is not feasible for police to engage in that very activity which would secure representative citizen participation. To begin with, the community organizer must be trusted. Yet, it is precisely the problem of distrust between police and citizens that most citizen participation programs are intended to ameliorate. Because he is not trusted by those he would organize, the police officer is not a good candidate for such a task. To build the necessary trust requires full time immersion of the organizer in the target community. It requires hanging out in local bars and becoming part of the street life of the area. However, most police officers, with the exception of some minority recruits, live outside their beat and are only too glad to escape when their tour is over. Furthermore, police have no on-duty time for community organizing. Nor can they be expected to organize citizens around controversial issues challenging the system police are sworn to uphold. Thus, it is simply not feasible for police to do community organizing. Unfortunately, without it citizen participation efforts are a sham.

Use of generalists and specialists. A partial solution to the above problems lies in making the securing of citizen participation the job of every police officer. Specialists can be used for guidance, data analysis, and follow-up work. But every officer needs to be utilized in collecting the data which represent the community's input. However, given the enormous range of tasks police officers perform, they cannot be expected to solicit citizen participation unless rewarded and recognized for doing so. This means structuring the total organization for a collaborative community orienta-tion. Recruitment and selection, training, performance evaluation, rewards, and management must be consistent with this orientation. The blueprint for doing so is outside the scope of this paper, but has been discussed elsewhere by the author.[47]

In sum, there are five requisites for citizen participation programs which emerge from lessons learned from prior efforts in policing and also those in the War on Poverty. These are:

1. Two-way communication
2. Accountability to the community
3. Representativeness of the police
4. Representativeness of citizen groups
5. Use of generalists and specialists

Prospects for the Future

The requisites cited above are met in varying degrees by several approaches to citizen participation which hold promise for the future. These include: ombudsman for police, police as community advocates, conscrip-tion of police, and full service neighborhood team policing.

Ombudsman. The concept of the ombudsman originated in Sweden in 1809. The ombudsman acts as an arbitrator between the government bureaucracy and the public. In so doing, he has the power to investigate, recommend, prosecute and publicize. In effect, by maintaining such an effective grievance procedure, the ombudsman serves to improve communications between all involved levels.[48]

The concept of an ombudsman for police has been proposed as an alternative to civilian review boards. However, legislation to create such positions has not generally been enacted. To some it represents a reversion to review boards,[49] and to others, it duplicates and weakens internal control mechanisms.[50] These objections notwithstanding, the concept of the ombudsman carries with it a very different connotation than a review board. It has the advantage of being truly independent of both police and public, while at the same time establishing a channel of communication between the two. In addition, because the ombudsman, as conceived in Sweden, is a highly respected public official, his access to high places enables him to act on mutual problems using power resources that would not ordinarily be available.

Community advocacy. Mutual distrust between police and citizens is one of the blocks to participation cited in this paper. In discussing community organizing necessary for achieving citizen representativeness, it became clear that trust in the organizer is an essential precondition for success. For a variety of reasons police were defined as an inappropriate source of leadership in this role. There is, however, a way in which police can appropriately bring pressure to bear on existing institutions, while at the same time building a handle for community trust and a vehicle for representative citizen participation. The means to these ends is the adoption of an advocacy perspective on the police role. In many ways, the role of community advocate is an ideal complement to the contemporary police role.

An advocate, like an ombudsman, acts as an intermediary between an agency of government and his client. Unlike an ombudsman, he is responsible solely to that client. It is his job to intervene if the rights of his clients have been denied or obscured. To intervene effectively, he must have a good knowledge of law and public agency administration. While he is responsible to his client and functions to plead his client's case, so is he also free to persuade his client and give the "adversary's" perspective.[51]

In the case of the police, the "client" may be defined as the members of the officer's beat. In the course of his work, the police officer encounters myriad occasions in which he finds himself between his clients and a government agency. These agencies include: social agencies to which clients are referred during service calls; domestic courts or small claims courts to which clients are referred during interpersonal disputes; criminal justice agencies through which criminals and victims are processed; and to the police department itself to which citizens turn for all manner of assistance in crises. Being the front line contact point between citizens and government agencies, the police officer is in an ideal position to communicate upward the concerns and circumstances of his beat while at the same time communicating downward the policies and constraints of government agencies—his own, in particular. Indeed, it is entirely feasible that each officer, at squad meetings, be called upon to "present the case" of his "clients." In this way, he is placed in a collaborative rather than conflict relationship with the community and the job of soliciting citizen participation in policing is reduced to do-able pieces.

In addition to facilitating communication and securing representation of ordinarily unorganized citizens, police in the advocacy role are in a position to use their knowledge of law and agency procedures to secure better services for their clients. Here, during slow periods—with the assistance of CSO's, community relations officers, and civilian volunteers—referrals could be followed up both with the client and the referred agency. Because of inexperience or disenchantment with bureaucracies, ghetto residents rarely follow through with referrals made by police. However, with some police assistance in securing services, agency response could improve and citizen utilization increase. In this way, citizens become aligned with an existing power group that can act on their inputs and problems. The ultimate product might actually result in a reduced reliance on police for non-essential services, while simultaneously yielding an increased trust in those same police. Hence, the additional investment of time and personnel might well be worthwhile.

Conscription of police. Most of the problems associated with citizen participation in policing relate in one way or another to the separation of police from the community. Piliavin[52] suggests conscription of police as one radical solution to this problem. Such a procedure, he argues, produces better representation of race and class within policing. By reducing self-selection of recruits, it further eliminates one source of community suspicion about personality traits which predispose them to policework. Conscription reduces the isolation of police from the community and reduces the debilitating effect (e.g. cynicism) of policework by limiting tours of duty.

Problems which need to be reckoned with in considering such an alternative are: the inexperience of recruits; an unwillingness to take risks in such a limited liability situation; and avoidance of the Selective Service experience in which privileged youths gained deferments while the less privileged were drafted.

Full Service Neighborhood Team Policing. It is this approach perhaps more than any other that combines the benefits cited above and incorporates all the requisites for citizen participating in policing. It does so by emphasizing a total systems approach to dealings with the community.

Broadly defined, team policing is a decentralized mode of policing in which a team, continuously assigned to a neighborhood and handling most calls within that area, takes 24 hour responsibility for its beat.[53] The concept requires that generalists handle as many police functions as possible within the team. The emphasis is on more effective policing through improved community contacts and adjustment to local needs. To these ends, team members are provided with flexibility in assignment, decision-making, resource allocation, and mechanisms for two-way communication within and without the department. Combined with the Full Service Model, this becomes a blueprint for total organizational change based on development of a professional, human relations, community relations, and law enforcement oriented style of policing.[54] In this context, each requisite for citizen participation in policing is met.

To begin with, two-way communication is built into the approach. Team members are encouraged to interact with community members both informally and by attending local meetings. Community members may likewise be brought into the policy making process by inclusion in departmental ad hoc task forces. The trust necessary for two-way communication develops as the community comes to define the police teams as "their" team, with the consistent contact between citizens and police establishing a basis for mutual identification.

Accountability to the community is similarly built into the Full Service Neighborhood Team Policing concept. Information sharing and feedback are achieved via team members' intensified contact with the community. External review by citizens occurs in their participation in the performance evaluation of their team as well as their ready access to the team commander. Finally, responsibility for policing is shared with citizens by using them as conduits of information and volunteers who act as translators, clerks, trainers, and other roles.[55]

Full Service Neighborhood Team Policing also takes into account the need for representativeness of policing. Because it is a model of policing oriented to local needs, staffing is done according to those needs. Thus, the characteristics of the community determine, to an extent, those of the personnel assigned there. At the same time, because there is a focus on reduction of police/civilian distance, there also exist more opportunities for utilization of civilians, both salaried and voluntary.

As for the representativeness of citizen groups, each police officer has the responsibility for comprehensive knowledge of his beat. In this context, he is expected to make contact with all key constituencies and see to it that policing is tailored to their needs. Finally, in the regularly scheduled team meetings and feedback sessions, he is provided with a forum in which to report on his findings and share information with other team members. In addition, Full Service Neighborhood Team Policing provides for sufficient organizational flexibility so that a team can pull together its community knowledge and create necessary structures to assure representativeness in citizen participation.

Full Service Neighborhood Team Policing also meets the generalist/ specialist requisite for citizen participation in policing. This model of policing defines community relations as a department-wide task, even though, where needed, there is room for the development of functional specialties within the team. Indeed, the entire program is community-oriented—and this orientation is reinforced at all key points in the organization. Recruitment efforts target on minorities, women, college education, and social service backgrounds. Entry procedures attempt to screen out those prone to aggression and test for a full service orientation to policing. Training stresses alternatives to force, human relations skills, cultural awareness, community dynamics, and related topics. Performance evaluation emphasizes team work, communications skills, community relations skills[56] and includes community response to service measures. The award system rewards for activities beyond gun runs and felony arrests. It recognizes community involvement and sensitive handling of service calls. Management supports the flexibility necessary for adoption of policing to local needs with a non-authoritarian participative, supportive style. Hence, the total organization is structured for a Full Service Neighborhood Team Policing approach to the community.

Needless to say, all of the above describes an ideal type. However, elements of it exist in many police departments and there currently exists a NILECJ project which attempts to integrate the whole in six demonstration sites across the country. The many problems of implementation notwithstanding, Full Service Neighborhood Team Policing represents the most comprehensive approach to meaningful citizen participation in policing to date.

Summary

This paper has sought to examine the issue of citizen participation in policing from several interrelated perspectives. First, it has described the various forms that programs of citizen participation in policing have taken. The experiences acquired in implementing these forms have yielded a variety of dilemmas—dilemmas which are clarified by looking at parallel developments in another institutional sphere. By combining the citizen participation lessons learned from the past in both policing and anti-poverty programs, a set of five requisites for future efforts were extracted. Future possibilities for citizen participation in policing were then examined in light of these requisites.

The overall focus of the paper reveals that efforts to secure citizen participation in policing require a reduction in police/civilian distance. The most successful programs are likely to be those in which participation takes the form of representative input into policy making rather than the establishment of independent power groups Whatever form such programs take, until police themselves become more representative of the communities they serve, citizen participation is a requirement which must be met.

Discussion Questions

1. In what ways can the representativeness of citizen groups be promoted?

2. How can one reconcile the conflicting trends of police professionalization and community accountability?

3. Select a local police/community relations program and critique it using the five (5) requisites for citizen participation outlined in this chapter.

4. Discuss the relationship of minority recruitment efforts to citizen participation in policing.

Notes

1. Task Force on the Police. *Task Force Report: The Police.* (Wash. D.C.: U.S. Government Printing Office), 1967, pp. 144-15

2. William Cassella, Jr. "Civic and Citizen Groups and Public Service Professional Associations," in Don Bowen (ed), *Public Service Professional Associations and the Public Interest* (Philadelphia: American Academy of Political and Social Science), Feb. 1973, p. 223

3. John Boydstun & Michael Sherry. *San Diego Community Profile—Final Report* (Wash. D.C.: Police Foundation), 1975

4. Lloyd Macdonald, "Preparing a New Police Policy Manual: The Cambridge Experience," Unpublished, Harvard Law School, 1972

5. Cassella, p. 224

6. American Bar Association. *The Urban Police Function* (New York: American Bar Association), 1973, Standard #9.4, Openess by Police

7. Ibid. p. 274

8. Muriel Cantor, "Social Control and Police Autonomy," in Jack Goldsmith & Sharon Goldsmith (eds), *The Police Community* (Pacific Palisades, Calif.: Palisades Publishers), 1975, pp. 277-288

9. Jeffrey Reiman, "Police Autonomy vs. Police Authority: A Philosophical Perspective," in Goldsmith & Goldsmith, pp. 225-233

10. Ibid. p. 231

11. Peter Bloch & David Specht. *Neighborhood Team Policing* (Wash. D.C.: U.S. Government Printing Office), 1973, p. 6

12. Egon Bittner. *The Functions of the Police in Modern Society* (Wash. D.C.: U.S. Government Printing Office), 1972, p. 115 and Robert Wasserman, et al. *Improving Police/Community Relations* (Wash. D.C.: U.S. Government Printing Office), 1973, Ch. 1

13. Bittner, p. 115

14. Kenn Rogers, "Group Processes in Police-Community Relations," in Goldsmith & Goldsmith, pp. 154-171

15. Macdonald

16. Nicholas Alex. *Black in Blue*. (New York: Appleton-Century-Crofts), 1969, pp. 18-19, 25, 205-208

17. Seymour Martin Lipset, "Why Cops Hate Liberals—and Vice Versa," *Atlantic Monthly* (March 1969), p. 81

18. Bittner, p. 114; Irving Piliavin, "Police-Community Alienation: Its Structural Roots and a Proposed Remedy," *Warner Modular Publications* (M114, 1973), p. 17

19. Lee Brown, "Handling Complaints Against the Police," in Harry More, *Critical Issues in Law Enforcement* (Cincinnati: W.H. Anderson Company), 1972, p. 251

20. Bittner, p. 114

21. Lipset, p. 80

22. Bittner, pp. 114-115; Wasserman, Ch. 1

23. Bittner, p. 116

24. Wasserman, Ch. 1

25. Ibid.

26. Boydstun & Sherry, pp. 83-84

27. Ibid. p. 75

28. For one such total systems approach to police change oriented in a community relations direction, see Ellen Mintz and Georgette Sandler, "Instituting a Full Service Orientation to Policing," *The Police Chief* (June 1974)

29. Arthur Hillman & Frank Seever, "Elements of Neighborhood Organization," in Cox, et al (eds) *Strategies of Community Organization* (Itasca, Ill: P.E. Peacock Publishers), 1970, p. 284

30. Welfare rights advocates in New York City consisted of social workers whose main weapon came to consist of serving notice on their counterparts in the Welfare Department, eventually leading to increased antagonism to the advocates and their program. See Richard Cloward & Richard Elman, "Advocacy in the Ghetto," in Cox, et al., pp. 211-212

31. Saul Alinsky, "Citizen Participation and Community Organization in Planning and Urban Renewal," in Cox, et al., p. 217

32. Peter Marris & Martin Rein. *Dilemmas of Social Reform* (New York: Atherton Press), 1967, Ch. VII;

33. Cassella, p. 223

34. Georgette Sandler, "Reneging on the Redistribution of Power in the New York City Public Schools," *Growth and Change* (January 1975)

35. Marris & Rein, Ch. VII: Lyle Fitch, "Social Planning in the Urban Cosmos," in Cox, et al, p. 335

36. Hillman & Seever, p. 283

37. Scott Greer. *The Emerging City* (New York: Free Press), 1965, "Social Types & Local Polity"

38. Fitch, p. 335

39. John Bodine, "The Indispensable One-hundredth of 1 Percent," in H. Wentworth Eldredge (ed) *Taming Megalopolis—Vo. II* (Garden City, N.Y.: Anchor Books), 1967, pp. 956-971

40. Marris & Rein, Ch. VII

41. Hillman & Seever, p. 284

42. Alinsky, pp. 219-220; David Godschalk, "The Circle of Urban Participation," in Eldredge, pp. 971-979

43. Godschalk, pp. 971-979

44. Ibid.

45. National Advisory Commission on Criminal Justice Standards and Goals. *Community Crime Prevention* (Wash. D.C.: U.S. Government Printing Office), 1973, pp. 13-14

46. Where utilized in these positions, interview findings in 13 police departments show that results have been good. See Alfred I. Schwartz, et al. *Employing Civilians for Police Work* (Wash. D.C.: U.S. Government Printing Office), 1975, pp. 8-10

47. See Georgette Bennett Sandler & Ellen Mintz, "Implementation of Full Service Model," in Public Safety Research Institute, *Full Service Neighborhood Team Policing: Planning for Implementation* (Wash. D.C.: U.S. Dept. of Justice), 1975, pp. 63-87

48. Frederick Ilfred & Richard Metzner, "Alternatives to Violence," in David Daniels, et al (eds) *Violence and the Struggle for Existence* (Boston: Little Brown), 1970, p. 142

49. Brown, p. 225

50. Paul Whisenand & George Felkenes, "An Ombudsman for Police," in More, p. 277

51. Cloward & Elman, p. 210; Paul Davidoff, "Advocacy and Pluralism in Planning," in Eldredge, pp. 596-615

52. Piliavin, p. 20

53. Bloch & Specht, p. 6

54. See Mintz & Sandler

55. Bloch & Specht, p. 101

56. See Public Safety Research Institute, Appendix B 1-10

9

Police Volunteers:
Are They Really Necessary?

MARTIN GREENBERG

THE ISSUE OVER THE UTILIZATION OF CITIZEN-POLICE VOLUNTEERS in order to augment police services has only recently surfaced. It arose because very few law enforcement agencies claim to have sufficient manpower due to local budget restrictions. Significantly, since personnel salaries take up the largest share of the police budget, the use of unsalaried police volunteers appears to offer a solution to this problem.

Generally, on the affirmative side of this critical issue we find many city planners and citizens groups, while on the negative are the many police who see volunteers as an attempt to rob them of employment and prestige. We will approach this debate by means of a brief review of some historical matters, the clarification of terminology and an analysis of advantages and disadvantages.

Historical Perspective

A few years ago, the modern American poet Richmond Lattimore wrote:

> Wearing some kind of iron hat,
> Armed to the teeth with whatever
>   weapons are latest,
> He has stood in some square
>   from occupied Troy to now . . .[1]

Lattimore was describing the trappings of the historic soldier. If this phraseology also seems to fit a depiction of some historic policeman, it is not surprising, since the military model was only slightly modified for the purpose of organizing the Metropolitan Police of London in 1829. This agency has been traditionally regarded as the first highly organized and centralized police system. Prior to that time, the responsibility for the maintenance of law and order throughout the Western World generally fluctuated between the use of military troops and unpaid citizen's watches. The early success of Peel's police system[2] served to focus all efforts on their upgrading, with very little energy diverted to the objective of reinstating civilian patrols.[3]

266

The outbreak of war in Europe brought an abrupt end to the foregoing era. Significantly, the threat of a World War stimulated the enrollment of over 8,000 persons in New York City into an organization called the "Citizens Home Defense League."[4] They were recruited under the leadership of Police Commissioner Arthur Woods. Simultaneously, in the City of Berkeley, California, Chief August Vollmer organized a special volunteer police force. The former body was to serve as an emergency reserve force in case of a manpower shortage due to the war effort and the latter force was organized for the specific purpose of enforcing local traffic regulations.[5]

In many communities throughout the world, part-time police volunteers are currently performing a variety of functions. These tasks include: neighborhood security patrols, traffic control, emergency rescue work, and such specific assignments as searching for missing persons and the reporting of public hazards. The volunteer police usually serve in units called "reserve" or "auxiliary" police. Members and teams of these civilian units may be observed at work on the streets of New York, Honolulu, Philadelphia, Washington, D.C., Dallas,[6] Los Angeles, St. Louis, Phoenix, London, Berlin and Moscow. The precise number of persons involved is unknown, but one source has estimated that throughout the entire criminal justice system in the United States there are about one million adults and teenagers performing volunteer work.[7]

Terminology

Citizen involvement in police work can take many forms. We will restrict our discussion to those police volunteers labeled reserve and auxiliary police. Either term shall be used interchangeably to mean a nonregular police representative who may or may not possess regular police powers or be compensated for his or her services.[8] However, there is a definite trend in the United States to provide these volunteers with peace officer status after each reserve or auxiliary recruit has passed a background investigation and completed a primary training period or course of instruction. All auxiliaries and reserves under our definition are required to wear uniforms while on duty, conform to the stated rules and regulations, and to participate in agency activities on a regular basis.

Many people may mistakenly assume that anyone wearing a police-type uniform is or has the authority of a sworn police officer. Therefore, it is vitally important to distinguish auxiliary and reserve police volunteers from the employees of the private security industry, "special police" personnel, community service officers (CSOs), police cadets, Explorer Post members, tenant and youth patrols, as well as the contributions made by various mobile citizen-observer patrol organizations.

Most security personnel are employed by contract-guard agencies, who are in turn hired by businesses and public institutions. These "rent-a-cops" may be observed throughout the shopping districts of many of our nation's cities. They deter shoplifting, employee theft, vandalism, and safeguard the transportation of payrolls and the company's daily receipts. Generally, security workers do not possess police powers unless such authority has been delegated to them through legislative enactments. Some institutions may employ their own "in-house" guards, but their legal status is not greater than that of an ordinary citizen or contract-guard employee.

Various commercial businesses require extra police protection; however, many municipal budgets cannot afford the additional costs. Consequently, many jurisdictions have enacted legislation authorizing the deputization of private citizens. This has been done for the express purpose of granting a limited peace officer power to employees engaged in security work. In general, the statutes also invest each employee with the title of "special police officer." The precise scope of the authority conveyed varies from state to state, but the practice has led to the creation of dual roles. Each employee must protect the assets and interests of his employer, as well as enforce the penal law. In many jurisdictions, the enabling legislation may or may not have provided for selection qualifications, effective supervision and training. However, with respect to the issuance of badges, the wearing of uniforms, and the need to take an oath, there has been a greater pattern of consistency.

In 1967, the President's Commission on Law Enforcement and Administration of Justice visualized the need for creating the position of community service officer. The President's Commission primarily viewed this position as a means of counteracting the isolation of the police from the community and as a way for affording minority group members the opportunity to serve in law enforcement. The duties of the uniformed CSOs would include: the referral of citizen complaints to appropriate agencies; emergency aid for the sick; the investigation of minor property losses; assistance to families encountering domestic problems; and other assignments of a purely service nature.[9]

Closely aligned to the community service officer, but belonging to an earlier origin, is the police cadet system. Typical police cadets are between the ages of 17 and 21. They are usually recruited for police work upon high school graduation. Selection is usually based upon the regular police screening process and its competitive examinations. The cadets are considered paid civilian employees of the police agency until their 21st birthday, whereupon they assume full police officer status and responsibilities. During the interim period, they may be required to attend the agency's training

Figure I

1969 Reserve Police Survey—Arlington County (Virginia) Police Department

	Manpower						Profile of Reserves							
		Auxiliary						Background Investigation						
Jurisdiction	Full-Time Regular Police Officers	Total Aux. Force	Other Officers	Capt.	Lt.	Sgt.	Min. Age of Recruit	Local	State	FBI	Other	Avg. Length of Service in Years	Avg. Hours per Man/Mo.	Min. Hours Req./Mo.
Akron, Ohio •	393	50					30	X	X	X		12	10	8
Arlington, Va.	226	12		1	1	1	25	X	X	X	X	8	36	15
Birmingham, Al.	520	69					21	X	X	X		3	16	8
Buffalo, N.Y.	1,425	1149		20	60		21	X	X	X	X	19	.5	0
Charlotte, N.C.	394	98	1 ea. Col. Lt. Col. Maj.	1	5	10	21	X		X		5	45	12
Cleveland, Ohio	2,161	500					21	X		X		11	4	
Columbus, Ohio	807	101	1 Maj.	4	8	8	21	X			X	5	13	8
Dallas, Tex.	1,504	248		8	16	42	19	X	X	X	X		10	8
Dayton, Ohio	427	100											16	16
Denver, Colo.	936	50					21	X	X	X	X		20	0
Detroit, Mich.	4,647	1200					23	X		X	X	1	16	8
Fort Worth, Tex.	580	105		1	7	7	21	X	X	X	X	3	30	24
Honolulu, Hawaii	786	103					30	X		X			32	32
Indianapolis, Ind.	1,023	70	1 Maj.	5	2	6	21	X	X	X		15	1	0
Long Beach, Ca.	660	90		2	4	12	21	X	X	X	X	10	22	16
Los Angeles, Ca.	5,927	200					21	X	X	X			32	16
Memphis, Tenn.	1,007	41		1	3		21	X	X	X	X		30	10
New Orleans, La.	1,377	137	3 Maj.	3	9	17	21	X		X		12	32	8
New York, N.Y.	29,939	3433		87	158	178	21	X				3	16	7
Newark, N.J.	1,379	487		8	12	25	21	X	X	X		5	5	4
Oakland, Ca.	651	70		1	2	6	21	X	X	X	X	2	16	16
Philadelphia, Pa.	7,319	265		14	15	38	21	X	X	X		8	30	0
Phoenix, Ariz.	774	81	Chief	2	5	8	21	X		X	X	8	21	12
Portland, Ore.	722	150		8	12	21	21	X		X		3	8	4
Rochester, N.Y.	573	44		3		2	21	X	X	X		5	5	0
Sacramento, Ca.	449	50					21	X	X	X		5	40	0
San Diego, Ca.	875	275		3	7	26	21	X	X	X	X	5	20	8
San Jose, Ca.	456	160		5	5	20	21	X	X	X		2	10	7
Seattle, Wash.	1,025	50					21	X	X	X	X	5	13	16
St. Louis, Mo.	2,016	91					21	X	X	X		3	18	18
St. Paul, Minn.	460	145		6	5	15	21	X		X		15	8	4
Tampa, Fla.	522	41		2	4	4	21	X	X	X	X	5	8	8
Washington, D.C.	3,220	650		1	27	71	21	X		X		8	10	12
Wichita, Kan.	333	100		6	6	12	21	X	X	X	X	10	40	16

	Duties Performed												
	Types of Patrol			Duties on Patrol						Other Assignments			
Jurisdiction	W/Reg. Officer	Two Aux.	Foot Patrol	2nd Man in Cars	Radio	Direct Traffic	Escort Prisoners	Drive on Occasion	Forms & Reports	Clerical	Radio Dispatch	Ident. Section	Switchboard
Akron, Ohio •	X		X	X	X	X	X	X					
Arlington, Va.	X			X	X	X	X		X	X	X		X
Birmingham, Al.	X			X	X	X		X	X				
Buffalo, N.Y.						X							
Charlotte, N.C.	X			X	X	X	X	X	X				
Cleveland, Ohio	X		X			X							
Columbus, Ohio	X			X	X	X	X	X	X				
Dallas, Tex.	X		X	X	X	X	X	X	X	X	X	X	X
Dayton, Ohio					X	X	X	X	X				
Denver, Colo.	X			X	X	X	X	X	X		X		
Detroit, Mich.										X			X
Fort Worth, Tex.	X	X		X	X	X	X	X	X		X		
Honolulu, Hawaii	X			X	X	X	X	X	X				
Indianapolis, Ind.	X			X	X	X		X	X				
Long Beach, Ca.			X	X	X	X	X	X	X	X	X	X	
Los Angeles, Ca.	X			X	X	X	X	X	X	X			
Memphis, Tenn.	X			X	X	X	X	X	X		X	X	
New Orleans, La.	X			X	X	X	X	X	X				
New York, N.Y.	X		X	X		X			X	X			
Newark, N.J.		X	X		X	X		X					
Oakland, Ca.	X			X	X	X		X	X			X	
Philadelphia, Pa.	X		X	X	X	X							
Phoenix, Ariz.	X	X		X	X	X	X	X	X	X		X	
Portland, Ore.		X	X			X							
Rochester, N.Y.	X			X	X	X		X			X		
Sacramento, Ca.			X			X							
San Diego, Ca.	X			X	X	X	X	X	X	X			X
San Jose, Ca.	X	X	X	X	X	X	X	X	X	X	X	X	X
Seattle, Wash.	X	X	X	X	X	X	X	X	X				
St. Louis, Mo.	X		X	X	X	X	X	X	X	X			
St. Paul, Minn.	X			X	X	X	X	X	X	X	X	X	X
Tampa, Fla.	X			X	X	X	X			X	X	X	
Washington, D.C.	X		X	X	X	X	X		X	X	X		
Wichita, Kan.			X	X	X	X		X	X				

	Working Conditions												
				Training				Equip. & Uniform Same as Reg. Man					
					Qualify								
Jurisdiction	Insured	Sworn In	Police Powers on Duty	Classroom	.38	Shotgun	Other (gas)	Uniform	Patch	Badge	Equip.	Sidearm	Shotgun Available in Cars
Akron, Ohio •	X	X	X	X	X	X		X	X		X	X	
Arlington, Va.	X	X	X	X			X	X			X		X
Birmingham, Al.		X	X	X	X			X			X	X	X
Buffalo, N.Y.	X			X							X		
Charlotte, N.C.	X	X	X	X	X						X	X	X
Cleveland, Ohio				X					X	X			X
Columbus, Ohio	X	X	X	X								X	
Dallas, Tex.				X	X	X		X	X		X		X
Dayton, Ohio	X	X	X	X		X							X
Denver, Colo.		X	X	X	X		X	X		X	X	X	
Detroit, Mich.				X		X							
Fort Worth, Tex.		X	X	X	X	X	X	X	X	X	X	X	X
Honolulu, Hawaii	X	X	X	X	X			X	X	X	X	X	
Indianapolis, Ind.	X	X	X	X	X	X		X	X	X	X	X	X
Long Beach, Ca.	X	X	X	X	X	X	X	X				X	X
Los Angeles, Ca.		X	X	X	X	X	X	X	X	X	X	X	X
Memphis, Tenn.		X	X	X	X	X	X	X	X	X	X	X	X
New Orleans, La.	X	X	X	X	X			X		X	X	X	
New York, N.Y.	X			X				X					
Newark, N.J.	X	X	X	X							X		
Oakland, Ca.	X		X	X	X	X	X	X	X	X	X	X	
Philadelphia, Pa.	X	X	X	X				X					
Phoenix, Ariz.	X	X	X	X	X	X		X			X	X	Sgts.
Portland, Ore.	X	X	X	X	X			X			X	X	
Rochester, N.Y.	X			X	X	X	X				X	X	X
Sacramento, Ca.	X	X		X	X	X							
San Diego, Ca.	X			X	X			X			X	X	
San Jose, Ca.	X	X	X	X	X	X	X	X	X	X	X	X	X
Seattle, Wash.	X	X	X	X	X	X		X	X		X	X	
St. Louis, Mo.	X			X				X			X		X
St. Paul, Minn.	X	X	X	X	X	X					X	X	X
Tampa, Fla.				X	X			X			X	X	
Washington, D.C.		X		X				X			X		
Wichita, Kan.	X	X		X	X	X	X	X			X	X	X

program, perform clerical duties, and/or attend a local college which maintains a program in the administration of justice.[10]

Explorers are young adult members of the Boy Scouts of America. There are approximately 30,000 young men and women participating in 1,300 law enforcement Explorer posts throughout the nation. Their activities range from supervised traffic control to various kinds of community crime prevention projects.[11]

Tenant, youth and community observer patrol associations are strictly a phenomenon of the nineteen sixties and seventies. The rise of these groups often stemmed from racial fears, a crisis situation or incident, and/or a desire to oppose crime in ghetto and other urban neighborhoods. Police support and encouragement towards these organizations varies tremendously. Members of such patrols often use citizen band radios and their own vehicles in order to deter crime and summon assistance. Since it is extremely boring to be watchmen and nothing more, many of these groups have a tendency to disband after a year or two of operation.

Unfortunately, very few studies have been devoted to the nature and extent of citizen involvement in crime prevention. Figure I indicates the results of a volunteer police survey conducted in 1969 by the Arlington County (Virginia) Police Department. Questionnaires were sent to all U.S. cities with a 1960 census of over 250,000.[12]

In 1976, George Washnis presented the findings of a study undertaken by the Center for Governmental Studies. The study financed by the National Institute of Law Enforcement and Criminal Justice, involved 37 different police-community crime prevention projects in seventeen cities. Washnis concluded:

> Police and city planning officials need to assess their own city's total crime prevention requirements; furthermore, community organizations should be involved in initial and continual planning stages . . . It is not enough that police officials alone be involved in planning; block leaders and other residents should also participate.[13]

(Figure I about here (camera ready)

In 1975, a team of researchers from The Rand Corporation identified a total of 850 active neighborhood patrols in cities throughout the United States. Their findings included that:

> Patrols last on the average of 4 to 5.5 years. Patrols are found in neighborhoods of all income levels, both white and racially mixed. Building patrols seem to prevent crime effectively. Patrols are occasionally susceptible to vigilantism.[14]

The Disadvantages of Volunteer Police

If one were set on scheming to disrupt the morale of a particular police agency, it would be a simple matter. Merely, have the chief announce that tomorrow a group of private citizens would be arriving to service in a police reserve or auxiliary unit! Most likely such news would be greeted by the following comments:

> I hate to play wet nurse to a bunch of cub scouts!
> It's tough enough looking out for yourself, let alone a taxpayer in uniform!
> These reserves only take the place of regular officers. What the city needs are more full-time men, not 'four hours a week' men. [15]

Several police commentators have also expressed their concern about the use of police volunteers:

> Some join because of patriotism, but others join for 'thrills' a 'night out,' to have an excuse for wearing a police uniform, or carrying a pistol, or for the 'benefit' derived from carrying an identification card near their operator's license. [16]

Moreover, agency administrators have reported that while they have to invest time and resources for volunteer training, the volunteers may discontinue their gratuitous services at any time.

Perhaps a more fundamental objection exists to forestall the deployment and recruitment of numerous police volunteers. This problem concerns their use as sources of police intelligence. How much surveillance will members of a free society accept?

The Advantages of Volunteer Police

The advantages of volunteer police may be divided into two categories. The first category consists of objective gains and the second, of less measurable subjective gains.

Primary Advantages

1. Provides additional manhours for extended periods of preventive patrol work.
2. Provides a trained pool of personnel for use in the event of emergencies.
3. Provides necessary manpower in the event it becomes necessary to police a special event without draining a precinct of regular personnel.
4. Provides an opportunity for individuals contemplating a law enforcement career to learn about police work.
5. Provides the foregoing advantages at very slight cost. [17]

Secondary Advantages

1. Provides an avenue for establishing mutual respect between the people and the police through joint participation in crime prevention activities.

2. A uniformed presence may provide an environment of less fear and greater security in those neighborhoods actively patrolled.

3. Provides a meaningful role for citizen's wishing to fulfill their civic obligations.

4. Fosters and encourages positive police performance and accountability due to the presence of citizen volunteers.

5. Provides the foregoing advantages at very slight cost.

Summary

There has been varying experience with volunteer police units ranging from highly successful to out and out failure. Perhaps, the two most valid objections to the utilization of volunteer police relate to their surveillance functions and to the economic and job security threat they seem to present to the regular members of the police agency. All the remaining disadvantages might also appear among regular officers and are usually handled through careful selection standards and continuing in-service training sessions.

Surely, when a local legislative body turns down a request for additional police personnel on the grounds that a sufficient combination of full-time and part-time volunteer police is available, the morale of both groups suffers. Nevertheless, it is precisely this type of savings which may result from the use of volunteer police. Consequently, the objection is without merit, although it may obviously serve as a source of ill-feelings between some members of the two groups for some time to come.

The degree to which a free society will tolerate police interference should be of constant concern to all persons within our nation. Traditionally, a complex set of relationships has existed between the police and citizens. The police have viewed civilians in adversary, bystander, complainant, informant, offender, suspect, victim and witness roles. Some of these unique interactions have been described by Albert Reiss, Jr.:

> Citizens may be found as adversaries of one another when some, the victims or complainants, charge others with violations and call the police. Or, citizens may call the police when they believe a crime has occurred, although a violator is not known. In these situations, the citizen is generally seen by the police, in the role of complainant, suspect, or offender.[18]

Undoubtedly, the primary function of volunteer police is to augment the scope or extent of police surveillance and to provide useful information for effective crime control. This purpose is the legitimate responsibility of law enforcement. Significantly, any citizen who chooses to openly identify with these goals should be applauded and not condemned as an obstacle to our freedom. In this way, citizens may undertake a new role with respect to their ordinary civic duties — that of a "helper." Moreover, by assuming the role of police helper, the volunteer agrees to abide not only to the laws of the land, but to the same rules and regulations which control the conduct of our regular police representatives. This undertaking should provide the necessary protections for our freedoms.

Furthermore, where auxilary police programs have existed, bonds of mutual respect have developed between the police, their helpers and the community. However, the institution of a program does not automatically guarantee successful results. In fact, where auxilary police volunteers and regular police have been kept separate and isolated from one another, unsatisfactory results have occurred. Consequently, community and police planners should examine several existing volunteer police programs before embarking on their own adaptations.[19]

Discussion Questions

1. Many officers feel that volunteers are a "pain in the neck", etc. Take a position for or against this belief and defend your views.

2. Assume that you are a regular police officer and have just been assigned to coordinate a local precinct's auxiliary or reserve police unit in a major city. What do you believe will be your main problems? Why?

3. What measures would you take to overcome the problems you identified in answer to question 2?

4. Discuss the kinds of activities volunteer police engage in in your community.

5. Contrast the role of the volunteer police officer from that of others who may be recruited by police departments.

Notes

1. Richmond Lattimore, "The Roman Soldier," *The New Republic*, 141 (1959): 22.

2. Sir Robert Peel, The British Home Secretary in 1829, is generally acknowledged as the founder of the first regular police force.

3. During the Gold Rush era, various citizen groups were formed to combat the lawlessness of the pioneers. Significantly, some early "vigilante" efforts actually served as the forerunner to the organization of the first official police forces in Los Angeles and San Francisco. See Frank R. Prassel, *The Western Peace Officer* (Norman: University of Oklahoma Press, 1972), p. 130.

4. See *New York Times,* April 27, 1916, p. 8 and July 6, 1916, p. 9.

5. "A City's Volunteer Police Force," *American City,* 16 (1917): 201.

6. For one of the few published reports available on the subject of the reserve police officer, see: Edward J. Brown, Jr., "The Police Reserve Officer in Dallas, Texas," *Texas Police Journal,* 24 (June 1976): 5–8, 15.

7. "Volunteerism: Key to Fighting Crime," *LEAA Newsletter,* 6 (March 1977): 5.

8. Historically, the "auxiliary" designation has signified a unit's origin from the Korean War civil defense era. For a set of guidelines on the topic of the selection and assignment of reserve police officers see The National Advisory Commission on Criminal Justice Standards and Goals, *Report on Police* (Washington, D.C.: Government Printing Office., 1973), pp. 263–269.

9. President's Commission on Law Enforcement and Administration of Justice, *Task Force Report: The Police* (Washington, D.C.: Government Printing Office, 1967), p. 123. The CSO idea has been utilized in several cities. For a view of how it has been placed in operation in New York City, see James M. Erikson, "Community Service Officer," *Police Chief,* 40 (June 1973): 40–46; *Police Chief* 42 (March 1975): 36–40.

10. V.A. Leonard and Harry W. More, *Police Organization and Management* 3rd. Ed. (Mineola, New York: Foundation Press, 1971), p. 139. Also see: James E. Rice and Henry C. Zavislak, "Police Paraprofessionals in Jackson, Michigan," *Police Chief* 44 (January 1977): 47–49.

11. John Renyhart, "Law Enforcement Explorers Get Involved," *Police Chief* 42 (December 1975): 54.

12. This table appeared on page 4 of the document entitled: *Special-Purpose Public Police, Vol. 5,* National Institute of Law Enforcement and Criminal Justice (Washington, D.C.: Government Printing Office, 1972). It is one of a series of five reports describing the results of a study undertaken by The Rand Corporation on the private police industry.

13. George J. Washnis, *Citizen Involvement in Crime Prevention* (Lexington, Mass.: D.C. Heath and Company, 1976), p. 133.

14. "Citizen Crime Patrols Active in Urban Areas," *Target,* 5 (September 1976): 3. (*Target* is a newsletter of innovative projects funded by The Law Enforcement Assistance Administration (LEAA) and published by The International City Management Association.) See R.K. Yin, M.E. Vogel, J. Chaiken, D. Both, *Patrolling the Neighborhood Beat: Residents and Residential Security* (Santa Monica, Cal.: The Rand Corporation, 1976), 154 pp.

15. W. Cleon Skousen, "What About A Civilian Police Corps?", *Law and Order* 21 (March 1973): 10.

16. A.C. Germann, Frank D. Day, and Robert R.J. Gallati, *Introduction to Law Enforcement and Criminal Justice* (Springfield, Ill.: Charles C. Thomas, 1970), p. 158.

17. Skousen, p. 15.

18. Albert J. Reiss, Jr., *The Police and The Public* (New Haven: Yale University Press, 1974), p. 65.

19. A very useful reference for guidance in the organization of an effective auxiliary police program exists. It is a very practical and well written book on the subject. The author goes into the "why" as well as the "how". Topics include: financing and staffing; recruiting; training; stimulating interest; and regulation and discipline. See Everett M. King, *The Auxiliary Police Unit* (Springfield, Ill.: Charles C. Thomas, Publisher, 1961).

10

Citizens' Initiative Crime Prevention

ORDWAY P. BURDEN

CITIZENS' INITIATIVE CRIME PREVENTION EFFORTS are new only in their attempt to recover part of what has been lost. For until very recent times people assumed that protecting oneself, and watching out for one's neighbor were duties belonging to every able-bodied citizen. The sense that the responsibility for preventing crime and apprehending criminals is solely that of the police, who, after all, are paid to do it, is a very modern idea, and one whose time, fortunately, is about to run out.

In colonial America law enforcement was largely a community responsibility, undertaken by individual citizens by turns or as the need arose. Preserving order in the boroughs and towns were members of the free, adult male citizenry, who rotated in the positions of constable and watchman. The sheriff, principal keeper of the peace for the county, was chosen from among wealthy landowners.

From this distance it seems to have been an easy task to maintain order in the earliest colonial settlements. So homogeneous were these communities in culture and religion that moral and religious behavior standards were enforced along with criminal. Blasphemy and adultery as well as theft or disturbing the peace brought punishments which were swift, severe, and took the form of public spectacles intended to stand as warnings to any future offenders. Generally, a labor shortage combined with public inability and unwillingness to support the construction of jails and the maintenance of prisoners caused punishments to take the form of physical abuse, floggings, duckings, brandings, or, for the most serious offenses, execution. [1]

As towns grew into cities in the 18th and 19th centuries, police work changed from communal self-protection to professional law enforcement. When American cities and towns became mixed religiously and culturally it was no longer defensible not to mention practical, to enforce sumptuary laws against drinking or blasphemy, for example. [2]

Although the Americans in early 19th century cities saw a rise in the number of assaults and other crimes, the first police departments dealt with crime as only a secondary problem. In 1823 Boston's Mayor Josiah Quincy created the post of Marshal of the City, a kind of super constable who headed a department of internal police and reported directly to the Mayor and Council. The first to serve in this post was a Harvard graduate, Benjamin Pollard, who had at his disposal a total contingent of two deputies and a horse. During the 1820's and early 1830's criminals posed a far lesser threat to public welfare than poor sanitation and unsupervised traffic in crowded streets. So this early police officer acted mainly as a Board of Health, handling fire inspections, traffic control as well as issuing summonses.[3]

With the notable exception of controlling the upheaval which accompanied the Civil War, the policemen throughout the nineteenth century dispensed social services at least to the same extent that they fought crime, and probably more. The officer was an integral part of his neighborhood community, one who benefited from the ward system of city government dominated by ethnic politicians. His job had been awarded to him by one of his own kind, and he, in turn, took care of the newest arrivals. Operating soup kitchens, finding jobs and homes for the destitute were among his most important duties.[4]

Today, agencies abound to perform the welfare duties of yesterday's policeman. He is now expected to concentrate on matters more pertinent to crime control.[5] Here he has had his work cut out for him for the past decade, when the crime rate has increased drastically each year, and went up a total of 180% from 1960 to 1975, according to F.B.I. reports.

The crime wave of the sixties and early seventies was due to a confluence of many circumstances. Among them was the migration in the 1950's from the rural South to Northern cities of a large population of unskilled blacks. Also, the period 1965 to 1975 saw the coming of age (crime age, that is) of the post war baby boom.

Another possible reason lie in institutional changes within city governments. Daniel Moynihan, in *Maximum Feasible Misunderstanding,* which dealt with the problems of the anti-poverty campaigns of the Johnson administration, pointed out that acts aimed at reforming corrupt city government, passed with the best of intentions to erase the sordid dealings of Tammany Hall, had in fact the effect of blocking Blacks and Puerto Ricans from participation in public affairs.[6]

This last list of the causes of crime is not intended to give an explanation of the problem, but simply to set the stage for the movement beginning in the 1960's to recreate a lost or diminished sense of local responsibility. This movement, begun throughout the country in response to growing crime, has been given greater impetus lately by federally sponsored programs.

While not strictly speaking a citizens' initiative program, auxiliary police departments should not go unmentioned. The San Joaquin County,

California, Sheriff's Department, under the direction of the late Sheriff Michael Canlis, has had an unusually effective auxiliary system for nearly 25 years. There auxiliaries undergo an intensive training course to be ready for emergency work. The force has grown to more than 100, and has contributed many thousand man hours each year. On an annual February weekend the auxiliaries assume total operation of the department for a 24-hour period.

In New York City auxiliaries are sent out on patrol in limited numbers. The auxiliary force was born during the Korean War, begotten by the State Defense Emergency Act of 1951. The civilian force then numbered 20,000, but is now confined primarily to the area near Central Park, and to guarding fire alarm boxes throughout the city.[7]

In a recently published study compiled by the Rand Corporation under a $108,980 grant from the Law Enforcement Assistance Administration, it was estimated that there are between 800,000 and 900,000 resident patrols in the United States. The study, encompassing 226 patrols in 18 cities, classified resident patrols into four broad groups: building patrols in high rise and apartment complexes; neighborhood patrols in suburban and city residential areas; social service patrols that perform additional services such as emergency medical aid and rescue; community protection groups which patrol against alleged police harassment as well as criminal activity.[8]

In 1968 the New York City Housing Authority established a Tenant Patrol Program to improve protection for approximately 600,000 apartment dwellers. At first the program employed full-time, around the clock uniformed guards, but as it became apparent that the costs were prohibitive, tenants turned to volunteer efforts. By 1975 there were more than 12,400 volunteers working in 746 buildings and 118 developments. These volunteers, who can be teenagers or senior citizens, patrol with walkie talkies, keeping an eye out for loiterers and other suspicious persons, discouraging vandalism and mischief by children, and escorting elderly persons. Joseph Christian, chairman of the Housing Authority, has contended that major crime within public housing projects is about one-fourth that of New York City as a whole.[9]

The Bromley-Heath housing project in Boston experienced a drastic improvement in the crime rate following a change of management in 1972. Prior to this time the development, 90 percent of whose 4,500 tenants were black, was a dumping ground for a ring of car thieves. When Bromley's new landlords, the Tenant Management Corporation took control under a contract granted by the Boston Housing Authority, a community security force of 8 unarmed tenants paid under a federal grant were appointed to patrol the hallways, guarding for suspicious persons, watching as children returned from school. In the first three months robberies dropped 75 percent; assaults, 20 percent; purse snatchings, 78 percent; according to Captain Joseph Cummings of the Boston Police Department.[10]

The Rand Corporation Report concluded that the building patrols, of all the resident patrols, are the most demonstrably effective.[11] But they are only a small part of the citizens' initiative ventures.

In New York approximately 10,000 of the city's 39,000 streets are organized into block associations. An organization called Citizens Committee for New York wants to organize all of them.[12] There are an estimated 3,000 block associations in Los Angeles and another thousand in Oakland.[13]

The function of block associations is simplicity itself. Citizens are encouraged to take common sense precautions against crime, and to develop enough civic spirit to give some thought to others' well-being. Mort Berkowitz, chairman of the Federation of West Side Block Associations in Manhattan describes these groups as "a return to an earlier age when we had small communities."[14]

Following a widely publicized incident in which a Greenwich Village housewife successfully employed a police whistle to alert neighbors and police to a would be burglar on her fire escape, other communities have issued police whistles wholesale. In Chicago, one community of 46,000 has been saturated with 19,000 whistles, and reports that purse snatchings have been cut by 41 percent, auto thefts by 37 percent. The Bronx Borough Chamber of Commerce reported that the distribution of police whistles to 16,000 elderly residents has resulted in less street crime.[15]

Some of the block associations are very specific in their purposes. In Indianapolis and Chicago groups have been formed solely to help women protect themselves against rape. In Prince Georges County, Maryland, and in New York City, parents have joined forces to make children secure on their way to and from school.[16] On Manhattan's wealthy Upper East Side members of Parents League patrol in bright orange ponchos, and while guarding children from crime, make reports on other hazards, such as out of order traffic lights, messy traffic patterns, and unusually large potholes.[17]

The better the purpose of a citizens' crime prevention group is defined the less likely it is to get into trouble. Most of the block associations and apartment house patrols in New York have the unqualified support of the police. In the case of the Bromley-Heath housing development in Boston, one police officer observed that before volunteer patrols had been instituted, kids had counted on the fact that they were strangers to the police; this camouflage was no longer possible against volunteers who saw them daily.[18]

As the duties of civilian groups have moved away from the essentially private space of the housing project into the domain of public streets and neighborhoods, police-community relations have often become more strained. One of the most successful New York based citizens' anti-crime efforts, that of the orthodox Jewish community in Brooklyn, brought the repeated criticism of police authorities.[19] Triggered by assaults on Yeshiva students by black youths, young men of the Hassidic community formed an auto patrol group called the Maccabees, (or Bagel Lancers, to local kids) inspired by a Biblical group of the same name. The group remained in force from 1964 until 1971 and had the effect of greatly reducing crime in the area (also of increasing the number of police assigned to the neighborhood).[20]

The success of the Brooklyn Hassidic community is atypical, probably lying more in the close-knit nature of the existing community than in any effective formula for civilian patrol. Another of the few well defined communities in New York, Little Italy, has also been able to maintain order without constant police intervention. A New York Times article noted that drug pushers with Italian surnames could be found in black or Puerto Rican neighborhoods, but never in their own.[21]

Other neighborhoods have been far less successful in preventing crime. In the 1960's frequent attempts were made by Harlem community leaders to do something about crime in that black ghetto. One such leader, The Rev. Oberia Dempsey of the Upper Park Avenue Baptist Church carried a revolver, and established "Operation Interruption", a service to escort parishioners to church, and women to market. The group claimed 200 armed members.[22] Mr. Dempsey defended his actions, saying, "We don't advocate taking the law into our own hands, but the emphasis of the law is placed on protecting the rights of the criminal, not the decent citizen."[23]

Nearly a decade after the Rev. Dempsey began "Operation Interruption" a march was organized in Harlem to protest crime and drug addiction. In June 1976, some 250 citizens belonging to CASH, Citizens' Action for a Safer Harlem, gathered on Eighth Avenue one Saturday in an effort to galvanize community sentiment. One of the leaders of the demonstration was Charles Kenyatta, a former bodyguard and close associate of the late Malcolm X. Mr. Kenyatta described Harlem's problem:

> In no other time and in no other place has our community been in so much trouble, because, now, we're killing each other. The drugs and the murders are all around and Harlem—after losing three generations to the dope—has become like a leper colony. And it's not just being blacks in a white society; the black man in the cities was poorer and didn't have any jobs at all 40 years ago—and there wasn't any heroin. And you never had it in the South or in the rural areas. You never had blacks who needed to have a march in their own neighborhoods to stop us from killing us.[24]

According to CASH director Eddie Waith there are somewhere in the neighborhood of 30,000 drug addicts in Harlem.[25]

An experiment in Harlem in community patrol pointed out the dilemma of police work in a ghetto. In 1968 Mayor John Lindsay formed a committee including New York Police officials to train a group of corpsmen for a one-week pilot project in patrol. Many of the young men chosen were members of Afro-American groups, and some had criminal records. They ranged in age from 17 to 31, with a median age of 20.[26]

The Community Patrol Corps was welcomed eagerly by Harlem residents. Their fellow ghetto dwellers were greatly pleased when action was taken to remove an abusive drunk from the streets. This kind of person, offensive but otherwise harmless, is considered by residents to be degrading to the community, but is often ignored by police for practical reasons.[27]

The enormity of the problem of controlling crime, particularly drug-related crime, in the ghetto, had led to the formation of vigilante groups in some cities. In Chicago's Woodlawn section an organization of young blacks, 22 of whom are Viet Nam veterans, have been patrolling, armed, late at night and early in the morning, meting out such punishments as breaking purse snatchers' hands, and beating drug dealers.[28]

Baltimore has seen assassinations of suspected drug pushers, whose bodies were discovered surrounded with leaflets reading, "These persons are known drug dealers. Selling drugs is an act of treason. The penalty for treason is death." Other ghetto residents described the killers as "ghetto warriors against genocide."[29]

Unfortunately for this country vigilante activities have a long and colorful history, and as strong a tradition as community self-policing. Beginning with the Regulator Movement on the South Carolina frontier in the 1760's and extending through the next two centuries, lawlessness has had a powerful appeal in folklore. An article in *The History of Violence in America: A Report to the National Commission on the Causes and Prevention of Violence* cited an 1872 incident at the Kansas City Fair. Three mounted men rode up to the ticket seller, firing several shots, one of which hit a small girl in the leg. Their total take was less than $1,000. Reporting on the incident, a Kansas City Times editorial stated, "so diabolically daring and so utterly in contempt of fear [was this act] that we are bound to admire it and revere its perpetrators."[30]

Even Wild Bill Hickock made his reputation by accidentally shooting from behind a curtain a man who had come to collect a debt.[31]

Explaining the transition from 19th to 20th century vigilantism, Professor Joe Frantz of the University of Texas writes,

> The Pioneer was beyond the reach of regular justice; he had to fill the vacuum. Sometimes he filled it with grave concern for the decencies of human relations. More often he moved in a state of emotion, even as

modern society would like to have done following the deaths of the two Kennedys, when the identities of the assassins were suspected.[32]

Full-fledged vigilante groups seem to be few and far between in America today. One such group is the movement in the West and Midwest called the Posse Comitatus, founded in the misguided belief that the sheriff is the only legitimate law enforcement officer, that the county is the largest allowable area of jurisdiction, and that local government alone is legitimate. In the summer of 1974 one member group assaulted and briefly held prisoner an IRS agent. In May, 1975, the Klamath County, Oregon Posse threatened to hang a state senator if he failed to work for the repeal of the Land Conservation and Development Commission Act of 1973.[33]

In South Boston, where judicially mandated busing to achieve school integration has encountered deep resentment in the white, Irish Catholic community, both blacks and whites have formed paramilitary squads to bolster the city's police force. The Irish neighborhood boasts 200 members in a night-time patrol group, which cruises in 31 cars and vans equipped with CB radios. White residents see the patrol as a last-ditch effort to keep from losing everything; Edmund Redd of the Boston NAACP has termed the movement "a vigilante organization with no real purpose but to keep South Boston exclusionary."[34]

Another indication of vigilante sentiment in the country may be the revival of street gangs in the inner city. Formed by boys to protect themselves from one another, the gangs tend to develop their private code of behavior. There is evidence to link them with executions of drug pushers and suspected criminals.[35]

Few, however, of the citizens' patrol groups formed in the past decade have been dangerous, or even armed. And some of those who have taken up firearms do not appear to pose a grave threat to society. For example, in Orlando, Fla., 2,400 women formed a "Pistol Packing Posse," after a series of rapes in beauty parlors, motels and apartments. In the first month of its existence, the Posse reduced the number of such crimes to zero. And in Detroit, grocers banded together for firearms instruction.[36]

Most of the more militant neighborhood patrols are formed in response to recent crime waves and many disappear just as quickly. According to the Rand Corporation Report, the average life span of all patrol groups is between four and five and one-half years, with 90 percent dying out before a decade lapses.[37]

In his foreword to the Rand Corporation Report, Gerald M. Caplan, Director of the National Institute of Law Enforcement and Criminal Justice, maintains, "A common concern about [citizens patrols] — the threat of vigilante activity — is not borne out in this study. It appears only an occasional problem, one that can be minimized by careful planning and review of patrol operations."[38]

In an effort to achieve this careful planning and review, and to enhance the chances for success of citizens' patrols, the federal government has in the past few years begun to bolster citizens' crime prevention programs.

The Department of Justice funds some of the most impressive citizens' initiative projects, among them the Crime Resistance Program of The Federal Bureau of Investigation; and under the auspices of the Law Enforcement Assistance Administration, the Neighborhood Watch Program of the National Sheriffs Association and numerous others across the country. Another extensive crime prevention effort being promoted on a national level is the Crime Prevention Programs for Senior Citizens of the International Association of Chiefs of Police.

Like the block associations and genuine community initiative projects which preceded them, the federal programs rely heavily on simple, common sense. The literature distributed by the Neighborhood Watch Program of the National Sheriffs Association emphasizes fairly elementary precautions which can be taken by a homeowner to protect himself and his property. Booklets and pamphlets available free to the public give advice on locks, and proper lighting. They urge foresight and encourage citizens to take an interest in the welfare of the people who live around them.

Neighborhood Watch works through the local sheriff who in turn contacts organizations, such as the PTA, Kiwanis, Rotary, Lions or Woman's Club. Through these clubs the sheriff can obtain speaking engagements, and forums to publicize the necessity for crime prevention.

In Rochester, N.Y. Sheriff William Lombard has implemented the National program with great success. There he instituted a two-part program in the town of Pittsford, one pilot concentrating on the commercial and business district, the other on the bedroom community. The program began in January, 1975 with publicity in weekly papers, and through written invitations to official, social and fraternal organizations.

In the first four months of operation, Sheriff Lombard spoke to 5,000 members of the community and distributed information house-to-house through the good graces of an Explorer Post.

In July, 1975, the Sheriff's Department was able to announce that there had been an 18 percent reduction in burglaries in the commercial district, and a 35 percent drop in the residential community.[39]

The Crime Resistance Program of the FBI is actually several distinct experimental programs in separate cities. Again, much of the emphasis is on common sense and public awareness. The focus of this program, as of most of the new citizens' crime prevention efforts, shifts the focus from the criminal to the victim. In his introduction to the first report on the Crime Resistance Program, FBI Director Kelley stated,

> Our nation has spent a great deal of time and energy attempting to keep people from becoming criminals; and often failing there, we have repeated the process in what, to date, has been a largely abortive effort to rehabilitate those who have become criminals. We must, of course, continue to make these efforts. However, what we have not done, and what we must do in every community in this country, is to spend a commensurate amount of time and energy in an effort to prevent our citizens from becoming victims of crime.[40]

Working closely with the Birmingham, Ala., Police Department, the Crime Resistance Program there concentrated on trafficking in stolen property. Birmingham is an industrial city of 280,000 where the median income is $8,692. The crime prevention campaign began with marking personal property. Birmingham is divided into 84 districts each with elected officers. Presidents of these districts conscripted block and street captains who proceeded door to door armed with etching tools. Concomitantly the Birmingham Police Department tried to improve the recovery rate of stolen property, first by establishing a special fencing detail and property hot line which allows citizens to call in with anonymous information about stolen property and to check whether goods they have purchased are stolen; and second, by enlisting the cooperation of owners and workers in high volume repair shops, which are very likely to receive many stolen goods.

Projects in De Kalb County, Georgia were directed against crimes against youth. De Kalb County is a residential suburb of Atlanta where the mean income is $17,016.

The task force selected one area of the county in which to organize a strong block parent program. Supervision of the block parent program was left in the hands of the PTA Safety Chairman or a designated block parent chairman. Block parents were instructed to be on guard for suspicious behavior, and to be at home during after-school hours so that their homes would be places of refuge for children.

The DeKalb County project also included a campaign to register and mark bicycles and to educate high school students about the criminal justice system.

Norfolk, Va. directed its efforts on crimes against women. Norfolk is a seaport city where the average family income is $8,984. One of the first suggestions urged upon the police department by the task force was an expansion of incident reports to include more information on victimization history, lighting at a crime scene, activities of the victim just before the crime, and precautions taken, or not taken, by the victim.

The police assigned two police officers, a husband and wife team — to conduct workshops for girls on personal safety and awareness of street crimes. These workshops were conducted in the high school (a high proportion of victims are very young), and were also given to city employees.

In Wilmington, Delaware, the task force directed its efforts against street crimes against elderly women. Here again, simplicity was a key to the approach. Since purse snatching is the most common offense these women, encouraging them not to carry purses will greatly decrease their risk, both of being robbed, and of suffering injuries during the crime. Elderly women were instructed to sew deep inside pockets in their coats.

The Wilmington program also included escort services for these elderly women. Experiments were made with teenage volunteers and scouts, but it was decided to limit the escort service to volunteers from service clubs and to persons 50 years of age and over.

That most of the people involved in the Wilmington project, as in the other test cities, were volunteers is important. One Wilmington volunteer, speaking of the role of the federal government in crime prevention, said, "Don't give us money. If you put money into the program, you'll kill it. Everybody quits working and gets on the take."[41]

In February, 1977, Philip Gross, a researcher for the International Association of Chiefs of Police, published a final report, "Crime, Safety and the Senior Citizen, A Model Project on Aging."[42] The study was underwritten by the Administration on Aging of the Department of Health, Education and Welfare.

The project began by gathering information on current police practices in dealing with crime against persons over 60, including characteristics about the perpetrator and the victim, the type of crime committed, place, time of day, circumstances, and any material available on why the particular victim was chosen. To date, information on 50 projects in 44 cities has been compiled into a volume intended as a handbook for other communities interested in starting crime prevention projects for the elderly.

Many of today's federally sponsored programs which attempt to nurture citizen initiative in a fight to prevent crime are still in their early stages. The push to recover a sense of local, cooperative responsibility has just begun.

In the nineteenth and early twentieth centuries, as cities increased in population, so did the tendency toward specialization. When American communities were very young everything was left to the individual citizen — he was responsible for disposing of his own garbage, obtaining heat and water. Even transportation was left to private initiative, in the sense that "use at your own risk" was the prevailing philosophy of road maintenance. Under these circumstances it was only natural that the responsibility for crime prevention be left to the individual.

The growth of a standing, professional police force, although an obvious necessity, may well have given people a false sense of security. Yes, the police can do much to prevent crime and apprehend criminals that ordinary citizens are unable and unwilling to do. But they cannot operate in a vacuum and require community cooperation and support.

When crime became one of the most pressing issues in the 1960's and many city dwellers felt that their very lives were threatened, many of them tried cooperative ventures in prevention and patrol. As we have seen, most of these efforts were short-lived. Created as an immediate response to local crime waves, they tended to disband as the problem disappeared or the original leadership abdicated. But viewed from a national perspective, the collective effort was impressive, encompassing as it did more than 800,000 separate building, neighborhood or block associations.

The entrance of federal agencies into the background of citizens' initiative crime prevention programs is welcome. The Law Enforcement Assistance Administration, the National Sheriffs Association, the Federal Bureau of Investigation, the International Association of Chiefs of Police and others may give local crime prevention programs the essential ingredient they lack — not funds, but the ongoing support of a well established agency, able to provide encouragement and sustenance when local leadership flags. The federally sponsored crime prevention programs are off to a hopeful start, but will require at least another ten years to prove themselves.

Summary

Citizens' initiative crime prevention programs in their present forms— block associations, building patrols, and community groups — were created in response to the rapid increase in crime in the 1960's and early 1970's. Their origins, however, date much further back, to an earlier, simpler age when each citizen bore responsibility for protecting himself and his neighbors.

There have been a few instances of vigilantism in the United States, in Boston, Baltimore, Chicago and Detroit, for example, but not many in comparison to the 900,000 resident patrols estimated by an LEAA-funded report by the Rand Corporation. This report also classified the patrols into four broad groups: building patrols in high rise and apartment complexes; neighborhood patrols in suburban and city residential areas; social service patrols that perform services such as emergency medical aid; and community protection groups which sometimes guard against alleged police harassment as well as criminal activity.

In general, the most successful and least trouble-prone patrols have been those with a well-defined purpose. Building patrols with a small patrol area have done better than groups charged with the responsibility of guarding several city blocks; civic groups who patrol the streets for specific reasons— to guard children going to and from school, for instance—also seem more successful than groups with broader objectives.

Patrols which guard a neighborhood against a danger from outside the community, such as the Hassidic Jews and Italian-Americans in New York City, have fared better than those which have had to guard against criminals from among their own.

Federal programs have been designed to strengthen local crime prevention efforts by supplying them with money and with a body of "how to" literature offering common sense advice to individual citizens as well as to project organizers.

Although judgment is premature, the federal presence in citizens' crime prevention programs may ensure their survival, not only because of the considerable infusion of funds, but because the government can provide a continual source of support and encouragement to what have been largely *ad hoc* and short-lived programs.

Discussion Questions

1. Under what conditions do vigilante movements seem to arise?

2. How have municipal reforms damaged communities within the city?

3. What will be the lasting effects of the federal backing of citizens' initiative crime prevention programs? Can the programs continue if the initiative and drive cease to be local?

Notes

1. Carl Bridenbaugh, *Cities in the Wilderness,* (New York: The Ronald Press, 1938), p. 74.

2. This has not prevented legislators from trying.

3. Roger Lane, *Policing the City* (Cambridge, Mass: Harvard University Press, 1967), p. 211.

4. Ordway P. Burden, "Community to City: A Perspective of American Law Enforcement," *Journal of Social and Political Affairs,* 2 (1976): 136.

5. I sometimes wonder how many people consider the wealth of duties performed by a police officer which are totally removed from the area of crime control, viz., emergency health care in the home and at the scene of automobile accidents, recovering stray children and giving directions.

6. Daniel Moynihan, *Maximum Feasible Misunderstanding* (New York: The Free Press, 1970).

7. New York Times, June 3, 1964.

8. Robert K. Yin, Mary E. Vogel, Jan M. Chaiken, and Deborah R. Both, *National Evaluation Program, Phase I Summary Report: Citizen Patrol Projects,* (National Institute of Law Enforcement and Criminal Justice, LEAA, U.S. Department of Justice, Washington, D.C., January, 1977).

9. Voluntary Action News, (Washington, D.C.: Institute for Voluntary Action, June, 1975).

10. Wall Street Journal, (New York: Dow Jones Company), April 18, 1973.

11. Yin, p. 22.

12. *New Yorker Magazine,* May 31, 1976.

13. *Changing Times Magazine* (Editors Park, Md: Kiplinger Co.), November, 1976.

14. Jack Shepherd, "A West Side Report," *New York Magazine,* October 15, 1973.

15. David L. Fortney, "Blowing the Whistle on Crime", *Good Housekeeping,* April, 1976.

16. *U.S. News and World Report,* "More and More Vigilantes—Legal and Illegal," Feb. 4, 1974.

17. Jane Geniesse, "Blockwork Orange," *New York Magazine,* October 15, 1973.

18. Wall Street Journal, April 18, 1973.

19. New York Times, Jan. 1, 1965 and September 1, 1971.

20. *Ibid.,* Feb. 14, 1971 and October 31, 1971.

21. Richard Severo, "Addicts' Victim Turn Vigilante," New York Times, September 23, 1969.

22. Malcolme W. Browne, "Pastor Organizes Militia to Combat Crime in Harlem," New York Times, October 21, 1967.

23. *Severox.*

24. Peter Kovler, "Harlem Marches Against Drugs," *Progressive,* November, 1976.

25. Tom G. Alkire, "The Posse Rides Again," *Progressive,* Oct. 1976.

26. George Nash, "The Community Patrol Corps: A Descriptive Evaluation of the One Week Experiment," (Columbia University Bureau of Applied Social Research), prepared for the Community Patrol Corps Committee of Mayor's Criminal Justice Coordinating Council, May, 1968.

27. *Ibid.*

28. "Vigilantes: Fair Means or Foul?" *Time,* June 30, 1975.

29. *U.S. News & World Report,* Feb. 4, 1974.

30. Joe B. Frantz, "The Frontier Tradition: An Invitation to Violence," *The History of Violence in America: A Report to the National Commission on the Causes and Prevention of Violence,* (New York: Frederick A. Praeger, 1969), p. 128.

31. *Ibid.,* p. 130.

32. *Ibid.,* p. 138.

33. *Alkire,* p. 48.

34. "Boston: Marshals of Southie," *Newsweek,* May 24, 1976. p. 30.

35. William L. Claiborne, "New Yorkers Fight Back: The Tilt Toward Vigilantism," *New York Magazine,* Oct. 15, 1973.

36. Wall Street Journal, March 23, 1967.

37. *Yin.*

38. *Ibid.,* foreword.

39. William M. Lombard, "National Neighborhood Watch Program Again Proves Its Effectiveness," *The National Sheriff,* February–March, 1977, pp. 8, 17.

40. Clarence Kelley, "Message From the Director," *Crime Resistance,* Federal Bureau of Investigation, Washington, D.C.

41. *Ibid.,* p. 10.

42. Philip J. Gross, International Association of Chiefs of Police, unpublished material. See also *The Police Chief,* February, 1977.

1

The Law and the Legitimacy Crisis: A Critical Issue for Criminal Justice

DAVID O. FRIEDRICHS

A Fundamental Critical Issue

WHEN WE SPEAK OF THE CRITICAL ISSUES confronting the criminal justice system today we recognize that such issues may be defined in a variety of ways. Ordinarily a critical issue is thought of as a problem perceived to affect a relatively large number of people, directly or indirectly, with negative or disputed consequences amenable to human intervention or policy reform. Of course there is no formula for identifying such issues to everyone's satisfaction; some issues, such as capital punishment, police brutality, and gun control, will be the object of considerable public awareness and interest, whereas other issues, such as the validity of crime data, the evaluation criteria for correctional program effectiveness, and the relationship of higher education to police role performance, will be of concern primarily to professional students of the criminal justice system.

While such obvious critical issues as the indeterminate sentence, the overreach of the criminal law, the plea bargaining system and community-based corrections require the attention of all people concerned with crime and justice in contemporary society it is argued here that it is critically important to understand the basic principles and assumptions upon which both the criminal justice system itself and the study of it are predicated. Some basic critical issues, going to the very roots of our criminal justice system, would include the following: How much *discretion* in our criminal justice system is desirable? To what extent is the *prediction* of criminal behavior possible? What are the most effective means of *deterrence* of illegal activity? These issues are not easily resolved by a straight-forward policy choice, as some issues might be, because they are broad and complex. And the interpretation and resolution of these as well as the conventionally defined critical issues is in turn rooted in an implicit or explicit understanding of the *most* fundamental critical issues: Is human behavior determined or freely chosen? Is human society best described as an integrated system or as a battlefield of conflicting interest groups? Is law as we know it primarily a force of good or evil? Now these are, of course, questions which have been pondered, discussed and debated in one form or another for centuries, and they are unlikely to be resolved to everyone's satisfaction in the near future, if ever. But an *awareness* of such primary or fundamental critical issues should be an essential element in the study of the criminal justice system. Students of this system in America have traditionally tended to take the meaning of the criminal law and the legitimacy of the legal order (the axis and the framework of the criminal justice system) for granted. This traditional or *conventional* perspective (essentially structural functionalist in sociological terminology) has tended to consider the law as a necessary and inevitable force of good, and the legal order (or state) as basically justifiable and broadly supported (or legitimated); in effect, society is an integrated system, bound together by consensus.

Direct and indirect challenges to the perspective or assumptions outlined above clearly surfaced in America in the 1960's, both within the larger societal context and ultimately within the professional discipline of criminology. This new or *radical* perspective (rooted in conflict theory) implicitly or explicitly rejected the authority of the law and the legal order; society, then, becomes a battlefield of opposing interest groups, with the powerful attempting to impose their will upon the powerless.

The critical issue which concerns us in this essay is thus a very fundamental issue: namely, the paradigmatic debate on the meaning of the law and the causes and consequences of the legitimacy crisis, and the relevance of this debate for understanding crime and the criminal justice system.

Conceptions of the Law

How to best define "law" has been a subject of formidable scholarly research and debate.[1] Law has meant many different things in the course of Western history.[2] F.S. Cohen's dictum represents one position: "A definition of law is useful or useless. It is not true or false . . ."[3] It must be recognized, then, that law manifests itself in a number of different ways and on a number of different levels. "Law" may be regarded as an institution common to virtually all human societies, it may be considered in terms of a particular legal order, or state, it may be used to refer to a written code and the many specific provisions of that code, or it may refer to the apparatus—administrative or judicial—constituting a justice system.[4] Although law will always be defined as a means of social control there has been an ongoing debate, especially among anthropologists, on the question of what specific attributes distinguish a system of law from other systems of social control. Some of the attributes commonly ascribed to law as a legal system have been: it is formal; it is external; it has sanctions (or "teeth"); it is specific; it has duly-appointed and recognized officials; it is political; it is regular, an on-going enterprise. Law is always *social* (and not individual), it always incorporates certain *values*, and it always involves the exercise of *power* in some form.[5]

If law may be defined in many different ways and for different purposes the search for its "essence" goes on. One basic dichotomy on the essential reality of the law distinguishes between *abstract* conceptions of the law (the law as rule) and *concrete* conceptions of the law (the law as human action). Harvard's Lon Fuller has stated the question here quite simply: "Does the reality of law lie in words on paper or in human behavior?"[6] It may be argued that the more traditional conception is of law as rule, and it is probably true that even today most people would define law in this way. But in relatively modern times the development of legal realism and sociological jurisprudence has provided an alternate conception of law, in terms of experience and not logic, and what the courts do in fact, as Oliver Wendell Holmes, Jr., expressed it.[7] The relevance of this distinction for understanding the relationship between law and legitimacy may be clarified somewhat by examining various conceptions of the origins or sources of the law and the functions of the law.

A long list could be compiled of the original sources attributed to law, including among other origins God's will and sovereign commands.[8] Law may be considered to have a natural origin (Aristotle), it may be considered the imperative of the powerful (John Austin), or it may be seen as originating in the crystallization of cultural mores (de Savigny). Andrew Hopkins has recently utilized a three-fold typology relevant to the fundamental sources of the criminal law: value-consensus, value or interest conflict, and rational interests.[9] For our purposes an even more basic division, a dichotomy between functionalist and conflict interpretations of the origins of law, developed by W.J. Chambliss, may be utilized.[10]

In noting that theories of the criminal law parallel quite closely general theories of society Chambliss contends that: "The chief division is between those who see the state as being controlled by and reflecting the interests of particular social classes and those who see the state as responding to the views of the general public."[11] Although Chambliss acknowledges the possibility of intermediary positions, and concedes that a literal attribution of exclusive law-making influence to the ruling class is exaggerated, he argues that law is far more likely to originate as a result of a conflict of interest rather than as a product of broad value consensus.[12] In examining vagrancy laws, theft laws, drug laws, procedural laws, prostitution laws and prohibition law Chambliss identifies some of the various elements involved in their formulation; where the *manifest* influence and interests of the powerful and rich is not evident their latent influence and interest can be discerned.[13] Thus we have two contrasting paradigms for understanding the sources and origin of the law. On the one hand the law may be seen as a product of consensus, rationality and necessity, a fundamentally inevitable and desirable development in human society (the functionalist or conventional view); on the other hand the law may be seen as a product of conflict, calculated interests and arbitrary will, a reflection of an inequitable and socially stratified society, the radical view).

The dichotomous conceptions of law suggested above can be elaborated upon in terms of the perceived functions of the law. The *conventional* conception perceives law in a positive light: law is the instrument whereby a human civilization is secured and even enhanced, and law reflects either the universal good or a democratic consensus.[14] The law settles disputes, maintains order, defines relationships, keeps records, creates and advances social values, symbolically defines normative boundaries, and provides a means for social catharsis.[15] In this conception the law has an organizational and educational function, providing opportunities and promoting desirable behavior.[16] The law, it is believed, articulates, promotes and protects the idea of justice, in the eyes of many thinkers who have seen it in a positive light.[17] Law is not merely a desirable dimension of a civilization, it is absolutely necessary to maintain order and insure smooth social interaction.[18] In the words of the one contemporary philosopher: "Law is the process by which an orderly society exists. 'Lawless society' is a contradiction in terms."[19] Such is the view officially advanced by the establishment in our society, and it is a point of view which has been integrated into the socialization process.

The *radical* conception has challenged the positive perspective just given; inspired by Marxist theory and rooted in the assumptions of the conflict paradigm, it casts the law in a negative light: law is an instrument of oppression whereby the interests and values of an elite class are advanced and protected, and law reflects the coercion of the powerless by the powerful. The law is an instrument which is designed to preserve the institution of private property and the *status quo*; law is a tool of the ownership class and a means of maintaining domestic order in a Capitalist society.[20] Even those without a specifically radical outlook recognize that the law supports the existing system of social stratification and legitimates special interests.[21] Furthermore, since the law acquires a special mystique of its own what it ordains tends to be accepted, simply because it is law.[22] Rather than the law being an instrument to suppress violence it has been argued, by Marcuse, that the law legitimates and institutionalizes its own violence.[23] The law may serve also as an instrument of "social engineering", of controlling human consciousness in the interest of the elite class.[24] Rather than being seen as a means of conflict resolution the law should be seen as the source of conflicts.[25] The law prohibits behavior and activities which a large part of the population indulges in—victimless crime—thus generating conflict between citizen and state.[26] Laws developed to advance selfish interests will necessarily generate conflict,[27] as will the inequality of access to legal resources.[28] Law perpetuates injustice rather than justice, in this interpretation.

We have noted earlier that all students of the law would agree that it is a form of social control. But social control may be seen as a passive means of ensuring the general welfare, or it may be seen as repression, whether or not this repression is manifest.[29] The law has commonly been regarded in the Anglo-American tradition as a provider of security and guaranteer of certain freedoms, but it may conversely be regarded as an oppressive hindrance to freedom.[30] Thus it is clear that law—its definition, essence, origins and functions—may be perceived in very different ways. A proper understanding of crime and criminal justice should begin with an appreciation of this fact. Why people fail to comply with the criminal law is a basic question in the study of crime, and at least part of the answer must be rooted in understandings of and attitudes toward the law itself. Conversely, an understanding of the law serves as a basic point of departure for understanding how certain activities and individuals come to be labelled criminal. And every study of the criminal justice system which implements the law begins with an explicit or implicit assumption of what the law is and what it should be doing. Although the student of crime and criminal justice may not feel compelled to commit himself to one or the other opposing perspective on the criminal law, and may indeed recognize elements of both perspectives as valid, he ultimately must at the least be aware of the controversy and take it into account, if only indirectly.

Those who advocate and subscribe to the conventional perspective are interested in demonstrating the universality and inevitability of the law, whereas those who advocate and subscribe to the radical perspective are interested in demonstrating the oppressive bias of the law and the possibility of an alternative, socialistic normative order. If popular conceptions of law in America correspond more closely to the conventional perspective, it is also evident that people are increasingly and conspicuously exposed to critical contradictions and characteristics of the law. This development in American society can be explored further within the context of the legitimacy crisis confronting the whole legal order. This will provide a larger framework for understanding how the law manifests itself and how it is understood and responded to by members of society.

The Legitimacy Crisis and the Law

It is frequently claimed today, by social scientists as well as politicians, that American society is in the throes of a "legitimacy crisis."[31] Such a claim is ultimately based upon relative perceptions, but for our purposes a crisis may be said to apply to a situation in which dramatic changes, conflicts, and tensions are perceived and active responses are called for. "Legitimacy" itself is a concept with a long history. Legitimacy has been used to describe both a state of affairs and a process; legitimacy is attributed to various sources; legitimacy is generally considered at the very least a wholly desirable, and at the most an absolutely necessary, element of a stable and effective legal order, or state. Ultimately it involves explicit or implicit justifications for the authority of an order on the one hand and the development of a concomitant sense of obligation on the part of subjects or citizens on the other hand. On another level we may say that legitimacy involves the generation of expectations relating to the official order and the support necessary for their successful fulfillment.[32] A legal order makes a claim of legitimacy, and legitimation and de-legitimation refer to the acceptance and rejection of such a claim, respectively. A legitimacy crisis refers to a situation of serious challenge to the legitimacy claims of the legal order; we are interested in the relevance of this situation for an understanding of crime and criminal justice.

Upon what specific grounds may it be said that a "legitimacy crisis" exists? A number of factors may be cited. First, polls have indicated a significant erosion of faith in the governing institutions and leaders.[33] Secondly, a significant amount of citizen participation in riots, protests, voter apathy and illegal behavior emerged in the 1960's and concomitantly was met with increasing reliance upon repressive measures by the political leadership of the legal order.[34] Thirdly, it has been widely alleged that the legal order, or state, has failed to effectively and properly fulfill its responsibilities as a democracy.[35] Thus, a legitimacy crisis may be said to have a *perceptual, behavioral,* and a *structural* dimension. The focus of the crisis, as Daniel Yankelovich has pointed out, may be *moral* (involving disillusionment with the quality and integrity of the leadership), *ideological* (disillusionment with the core values of the system), or *functional* (disillusionment with the effectiveness of public institutions).[36] Insofar as a legitimacy crisis may exist there is some disagreement over whether it is a response to "the system" itself, the fundamental principles upon which the system is based, or the leadership of the system.[37] With specific relevance to crime and justice Charles Reasons has attributed the "increasing erosion of the legitimacy of the state" to:

> (a) The belief that law and legal institutions are illegitimate as well as unresponsive; (b) a condemnation of the bureaucratic delays, judicial indifference and overt racism of most courts; (c) a rejection of, and in many instances a contempt for, establishment officials—police, judges, and lawyers, and (d) an affirmation of individual rights and an identification with group, class, racial and sexual liberation.[38]

Some general qualifications relating to the above characterization of the legitimacy crisis: Such a crisis is obviously a matter of degree, it is relative; not only are the perceptions listed above held by only a part of the citizenry, but in addition this part may not constitute a majority. It should be obvious, as suggested earlier, that it is possible to challenge some aspects of the legal order or criminal justice system without subscribing to a monolithic rejection of the legitimacy of the order or system as a whole. Finally, it is also obvious that a legal order and a criminal justice system can and does continue to operate despite such dissension, but its effectiveness is inevitably compromised. Having made these points one can turn to the question of the basic causes to which the legitimacy crisis, such as it is, has been attributed by those subscribing to conventional and radical perspectives.

The conventional perspective tends to attribute the legitimacy crisis to the emerging consequences of a modern mass society, including the disintegration of an effective socialization process. Some thinkers, including historian J.H. Plumb, argue that a worldwide crisis of authority is evident as a consequence of modernization.[39] A modern mass society is characterized by industrialization, urbanization, bureaucratization, (mass) communication and much geographic mobility.[40] Anomie (the breakdown of traditional norms) and alienation are some of the consequences of such characteristics, with de-legitimation and illegality inevitable by-products. In effect, such related characteristics of modern mass society as impersonality, anonymity, impermanence, a diversity of values and a loss of community are considered correlates of de-legitimation and illegality. Traditional assumptions of the sanctity of law erode,[41] and tensions arise because of conflicts between different sources of authority.[42] From a conventional or functional perspective the problem of crime in a modern mass society must be dealt with by repression, or by developing more successful and uniform control over the socialization process, or by eliminating the more blatantly alienating features of the criminal justice system.

An alternative interpretation of the basic cause of the legitimacy crisis focuses on the capitalist character of a modern mass society. A legitimacy crisis, from this radical perspective, is one facet of the inevitable crises of a capitalist system which Marx predicted. A crisis becomes inevitable in a capitalist system, according to German sociologist Jürgen Habermas, if the evolution of a subcultural subsystem raises expectations which can no longer be fulfilled by rewards in conformity with the system.[43] Whether the various contradictions and inconsistencies which are attributed to "late-capitalism" are peculiar only to this type of economic system has been a subject of debate.[44] But those who consider the legitimacy crisis a problem of American capitalism would argue that widespread illegality and an ineffective criminal justice system and the legitimacy crisis which they reflect require a fundamental transformation in the social and economic system.

Finally, those with a radical perspective as well as those subscribing to the conventional perspective recognize that special events, circumstances and actions may play a significant role in precipitating a legitimacy crisis. If legitimacy involves certain expectations upon the part of citizens with regard to the policies of the official order and the actions of its personnel, a legitimacy crisis may be provoked when such expectations are not met. The *nature* of expectations will vary considerably among citizens and constituent groups, with ideological principles subscribed to, pragmatic interests, idiosyncratic biases and preferences, past experiences and situational factors all playing a role in their formulation. Michael Barkun, assuming that diffuse *original* legitimation of the legal order takes place, argues that a legitimacy crisis occurs when individuals withdraw from such commitments to which they were once socialized.[45] It implicitly follows from this that some event, circumstance or consciousness-raising process must occur to "cancel" the commitments assumed in the course of original socialization. Although such developments may have a highly personal basis, or may emerge out of an intersubjective process, they may also be at least partially precipitated by external events and circumstances occuring in the larger social context. Such events as the Civil Rights revolution, the Vietnam War, Watergate, Attica, Kent State, the FBI & CIA Senate hearings, the Knapp Commission and the like—all of which revealed either ineffectiveness, corruption, hypocrisy and other undesirable characteristics of the legal order, or divisions and personnel of that order—may help bring about the legitimacy crisis.

In general it may be said that the conventional interpretation of the events cited above would be that they are aberrations or deviations in a fundamentally sound system, whereas the radical interpretation is that they are usually manifestations of the inherent corruptness of the capitalist system. Responses to such events, as well as the other precipitants of the legitimacy crisis, are complex and varied, however, and must be explored in more depth in terms of the consequences of the legitimacy crisis.

Consequences of the Legitimacy Crisis

An official order which is unable to generate a diffuse degree of legitimation (i.e., recognition of the validity of the state and a sense of obligation toward it) is likely to be in a continuous state of crisis. Those with a conventional perspective tend to see this crisis as resulting in a proliferation of various types of illegal behavior, including crime, riots, and revolutionary activity; those with a radical perspective tend to emphasize the increasing use of coercive and repressive measures by the state as a response to such a crisis.[46] The *effectiveness* of a legal order is widely conceded to be dependent in substantial part upon the extent to which its norms are legitimated and it has succeeded in inspiring respect.[47] With specific reference to the criminal law and the criminal justice system a "crisis of law observance", as Law professor Paul Freund puts it, is so commonly acknowledged as to virtually constitute a cliché.[48] This crisis of law observance, or crime, can be attributed to many factors, of course, but the role of an erosion of legitimacy must certainly be considered among them. Philadelphia Judge Lois Forer has argued:

> What is unusual and significant today is the fact that the average, decent citizens of all ages and both sexes have little regard for law. Few Americans believe that law binds them in their conduct or protects them from misdeeds of others. The restrictions imposed by law are treated as inconvenience to be avoided, circumvented or ignored. It is common knowledge that the law will not prevent crimes nor provide civil redress for wrongs suffered. Neither the indigent nor the working poor look to the police, lawyers or the elaborate structure of courts to secure their rights. People of moderate income are discouraged by exorbitant costs and long delays. The motto "Equal Justice under Law", engraved onthe marble portico of the United States Supreme Court building is a cruel lie to all Americans who are poor, on nonwhite, or young, or old, or female, or who differ from the common consensus in their beliefs and life-styles.[49]

The increasing sophistication of citizens, their growing awareness through education and the media of what would be possible and what actually prevails, the conspicuous and well-publicized hypocrisies and failures, create a situation in which legitimacy, as a National Commission recognized, "has to be earned, almost daily, and earned in the face of everincreasing standards of performance.[50] During the 1960's many minority group offenders as well as white militants began to redefine conventional acts of illegal behavior into specifically political terms.[51] One interpretation of a series of studies of violent, illegal protests of the 1960's designates the development of distrust (an aspect of delegitimation) as a major precipitant of such law violation, rather than social pathology or failures in the socialization process.[52] The role of ideology and attacks upon the legitimacy of the legal order have also been regarded as significant factors in events such as the Attica uprisings.[53] Thus the failures of the state and the legitimacy crisis have been linked to riots, rebellions, demonstrations, and assassinations;[54] in addition, research has suggested that there is a positive correlation between negative assessments of the legal system, or some of its principal components, and conventional criminal behavior.[55] Rejection of the legitimacy of the legal system, with a concomitant lack of a strong sense of obligation to comply with its laws, would logically be most evident among those groups which have been most dicriminated against, and historically disenfranchised by this system (e.g., black people in America).[56] Although lower class and minority groups may be more affected in *absolute* terms by both the ordinary and the abusive use of legal powers by this system and other problems of the modern capitalist state Claus Mueller claims that the middle class may be *relatively* more affected by such phenomena because (1) they are better situated to be aware of and understand implicit or explicit abuses and contradictions, and (2) they are today being affected by various structural developments which in the past they could often avoid.[57] The nature of response to this situation may vary greatly, but it could be argued that one significant deterrent to illegality will have eroded.

The complex of possible responses to the various possible precipitants of the legitimacy crisis may be further explored by examining reactions to the celebrated Watergate affair. It has been suggested that a critical event such as Watergate contributes to a legitimacy crisis, although it may also be seen at least partly as a symptom of such a crisis. The term "Watergate" is used here to refer to the whole series of illegalities attributed to the Nixon administration and campaign of the early 1970s, including acts of burglary, bugging, fraud, extortion, tax evasion, bribery, sale of influence, misuse of funds, destruction of criminal evidence and obstruction of justice. The significance of Watergate and the related scandals is not simply in the commission of such offenses by government officials (a common enough occurrence in American history) but rather in (1) the documented involvement of the government officials of the very highest rank, including the President and Vice President, (2) the massive publicity involved, including the hearings of the Senate Committee on Watergate and the House Committee on Impeachment, (3) the widely diffused allegations of socioeconomic inequities relative to the handling, prosecution and ultimate disposal of these cases, and (4) the involvement of an administration which had strong symbolic identification with a "law and order" stance. On a most basic level the Watergate affair and the various responses to it raised the question, as Sociologist Jack Douglas put it, of: "What is legal and illegal? The claims and counterclaims raging on all sides in this controversy have been beautiful examples of the problematic and conflictful nature of the meanings and uses of social rules in our society."[58] Those who initially held a *conventional* view of American society, in the broad sense that they were not committed to overthrowing the "system" as such, responded in one of the following ways: (1) *Apathetic or Cynical Indifference*—Many citizens were simply indifferent to Watergate, either because it didn't strike them as having any significance, or because they were genuinely apolitical, and didn't personally perceive any harm as having resulted from Watergate.[59] This group would probably include the thousands who protested to the media when Watergate hearings preempted soap operas, and dominated newspaper space.[60] In addition there are the cynics who view politics as corrupt in any context, a "dirty business" which will always and everywhere involve such violations of law, making Watergates inevitable; (2) *Reactionary*—this response perceived the Watergate crimes as means to the achievement of desirable ends. A man in a Queens, N.Y., bar put it this way during a period of considerable exposure of Watergate matters:

> We're at virtual war right now. War against anarchists and subversives, revolutionaries and Maoists who arm their members and urge them to kill policemen. Stirrers in ghetto neighborhoods who hurl missiles at authorities. We need a man who can exercise firm control over our enemies. If it means bugging the other side or breaking into a file, I say God bless him.[61]

Such rationales were, of course, used by Watergate defendants themselves, including former Attorney General John Mitchell.[62] The reactionary "law and order" position subscribed to by such people is not support for legality *per se*, but rather selective and instrumental support for rigorous enforcement of laws against anti-social and revolutionary violators, and disregard for laws impeding political gains. (3) *Reform & Prosecution*—Blame in a third type of response is directed at social or individual morality. The social aspect is that Watergate crimes are a symptom of and reflection of an undesirable but widely diffused set of general norms. The distinguished

American historian Henry Steele Commager writes that "A . . . possible explanation (for Watergate) is that . . . our crisis is rooted in changes in the American character, the American mind, American habits or traits—use what term you will—over the past quarter century, changes reflected in Mr. Nixon and his associates and in the current style of American politics."[63] In a similar vein the journalist Vermont Royster, in an assessment of Watergate, writes: "It has been a sorry spectacle. But not the least disturbing thing about it is the gnawing thought that the attitude it represents may be a reflection of the current public morality."[64] This perspective implies a broad social responsibility for Watergate, but it does not directly challege the legal order as such; rather, it suggests the possibility of moral reformation for society.

The individual aspect of this perspective takes the form of condemnation of specific individuals or groups involved, with corresponding attribution of blame. The Washington, D.C. columnist Hugh Sidey, in a lecture to educators, labelled Watergate "a failure of men, not of a system".[65] Psychiatrist Robert Coles, a student of political consciousness among children, quotes a nine year old Boston girl:

> The President made a mistake. Its too bad. You shouldn't do wrong; if you're president, its bad for everyone when you go against the law. But the country is good.[66]

This type of response calls for prosecution of the individuals or groups involved, but again does not challenge the legal order or system itself; in fact, this response may be viewed as a reaffirmation of a system which can expose and prosecute such offenses with democratic checks and balances.[67]

The alternative to the conventional responses to the Watergate affair which are discussed above would be a *radical* response. Such a response perceives Watergate, in the final analysis, as an inevitable manifestation of an oppressive system. In certain respects, as is so often the case, the perspective of the far left has features in common with the reactionary, or far right, response. Leftist writer Michael Myerson agrees with the reactionary blue-collar worker quoted earlier that the Watergate offenses were a reaction to developing patterns of domestic disorder, but he attaches different values to this perception: "The growing disaffection of the poor . . . and the powerless . . . was seen as a wave of lawlessness by the powerful, those of 'the law'. So the law resorted to a true wave of lawlessness . . ."[68] This is a recognition of the relativistic relationship between law and lawlessness. Noam Chomsky puts this even more directly in his analysis of Watergate: "It is clear that those who have the power to impose their interpretation of legitimacy will so construct and construe the legal system as to permit them to root out their enemies."[69] The Watergate crimes in this perspective are seen not as isolated acts but, as Criminologist Richard Quinney puts it, "a conspiracy led by powers within the United States."[70] Furthermore, these crimes are not simply to be considered the conspiracy of an elite group happening to hold power at the present time but rather, as leftist philosopher Herbert Marcuse sees it, as the inevitable struggle of the capitalist order in a changing world.[71] This radical conception, then, sees Watergate as a product of the legal order rather than a deviation from it.

The various Watergate scandals were massively publicized, and much attention was given to such inequities as the Agnew plea bargain deal, the million dollar Mitchell-Stans defense, the alleged "country club" imprisonment of some defendants, and the Nixon pardon. Relatively little empirical research has been undertaken on the specific impact of Watergate on conceptions of the legal order, but there have been indications that attitudes have been affected. Various polls and studies have revealed a steady erosion of confidence in national institutions;[72] while it is clear that this erosion or decline of confidence precedes the Watergate affair it also appears to be true, as Harvard political scientist James Q. Wilson points out (citing relevant national polls) that:

> Watergate exacerbated that decline. Note . . . that the decline in trust in government that occured between 1964 and 1970 was *not* accompanied by any growth in the belief that politicians are crooked; it was the *behavior* of government, not the motives of its officials, that was the object of increased public cynicism . . .[73]

The middle class has become disillusioned with the government's ineffectiveness in dealing with conventional crime on the one hand; on the other hand, Watergate created considerable distress at high-level illegalities and inequities.[74] One study found that middle class conservatives were more likely to experience a loss of faith in the political leadership as a result of Watergate than lower-class people, who even seem to have acquired an enhanced regard for the system as a response to the way in which the situation was handled.[75] A 1973 study involving 367 children in Boston indicated considerable awareness of the Watergate affair, and a significantly negative conception of executive leadership in the government.[76] Since studies of political socialization commonly suggest the importance of Presidents on the political socialization of children it is not unreasonable to hypothesize the liklihood of some impact of Watergate on ultimate conceptions of the legal order.

The complexity of possible responses to Watergate has been indicated, but it can be suggested that Watergate and like developments contribute to the growth of an anomic situation, or an erosion of traditional normative assumptions. Thus the legitimacy of the legal order is affected by Watergate insofar as the forms of justification, the sense of obligation, the degree of compliance with the law and expectations of the legal system may all be influenced by it.

Finally, the *positive* responses the state or legal order can make to the consequences of the legitimacy crisis must be considered. It is suggested that three basic types of positive responses would be *educational, repressive* and *reformist*.[77] The first is addressed to the perceptual or attitudinal aspect of the crisis, the second is directed toward the behavioral aspects, and the third claims to deal with the structural aspects.

The state endeavors to educate and socialize (or *re*-educate and *re*-socialize) the public toward a respectful, supportive and compliant orientation toward the legal order and the legal system. In the conventional view this is a proper and necessary enterprise, one which promotes the existence of an orderly society. It is specifically carried out by designing curriculums for public schools which foster a positive orientation toward the law, by developing such public relations programs as police community relations offices, and by controlling the release of information to the media as well as cooperating with entertainment ventures (such as the TV show "The FBI") which cast the criminal justice system in a positive light. In the radical view such efforts are seen as propaganda, as image management, designed to manipulate the consciousness of the public by projecting a falsely benevolent image of the state. The state is seen as cynically promoting its own legitimacy through its control of the media and the principal institutions of socialization.[78] There are growing indications today, however, that the public is becoming increasingly sophisticated, and has various contrary sources of information and ideals, and cannot be so easily manipulated in this way.[79] The many failings of the state become increasingly obvious in a modern mass society but, as law professor Paul Freund put it quite bluntly to a group of educators: "How do you deal with the disparity between the ideals of the law and the legal order and the reality?"[80] This dilemma is not easily resolved by the state.

The second type of response which the state can make to a legitimacy crisis is the invocation of directly repressive measures and actions and the increasing use of such tactics as covert surveillance. Responses to anti-War demonstrations (e.g., Kent State) and prison riots (e.g., Attica) would be examples of the first; revelations of the activities of the FBI and the CIA, in hearings and investigations during the mid-1970s, illustrate the extent of covert repressive actions. In addition, with regard to the criminal law and the criminal justice system, other types of repressive instruments are developed by the State. The criminal code revised by the Nixon justice department and considered by the U.S. Senate as S-1, called for extending investigative powers of the state, outlawing many forms of protest, and inflicting harsh penalties on lawbreakers. Such measures as these, as well as authoritarian interpretations of discretionary powers by the Criminal Justice system, may be seen in one version of the conventional perspective as necessary and justified to re-establish order; in the radical perspective the order being maintained is an unjust and unequal one which ought to be overthrown. It is widely recognized, however, that this type of response may aggravate the legitimacy crisis more than it controls it. This is the dilemma for the State identified by Isaac Balbus: to contain revolutionary violence and at the same time to maximize legitimacy by minimizing the use of force.[81] Repressive action by the State may have a short-run effectiveness, but in the long run may create more problems for the legal order and the criminal justice system than it solves.

The third type of response which the State can make to the legitimacy crisis is broadly subsumed under the heading of "reform", or the alteration of specific or institutional conditions which have been instrumental in bringing about the crisis in the first place. Such reform could involve the withdrawal of the State from certain areas where its role may be perceived as having done more harm—in terms of maintaining legitimacy—than good.[82] For example, State enforcement of victimless crime laws (e.g., marijuana laws) may compromise the legitimacy of other realms of the legal order with significant segments of the public. The state can undertake reforms by making laws and institutions more responsive to democratic input, realizing more closely espoused principles of equality and justice, and fulfilling basic needs in a humane and effective manner. Non-repressive reform of the criminal law usually takes the form of amendments or rulings which eliminate conspicuously provocative laws or add specific laws for which there has been a strong demand, but which do not revise the law in a fundamental way; with regard to the criminal justice system, the police may be professionalized, court procedures may be revised, and prison conditions may be modified. A conventional perspective will tend to view such reforms as authentic, but a radical perpective is likely to see such reforms as part of that State's image management campaign. Thus the State may alter superficially or camouflage some of the more blatantly offensive elements of its operation, prosecuting the conspicuously corrupt. It may also give the appearance of responding positively to crisis-provoking situations by appointing investigatory commissions, restoring some legitimacy with the direct or implicit promise of implementing recommended reforms.[83] Liberal and enlightened reforms may well extend rather than limit the power of the State.

We can conclude this long section, then, by noting that it has been suggested that American society has been in the throes of a "legitimacy crisis", and that this crisis has various causes, symptoms and consequences which are relevant for an understanding of crime and criminal justice.

Conclusion

The basic argument of this essay is that students of the criminal justice system cannot take conceptions of the law, or the legitimacy of the legal order, for granted. What the criminal law is and should be becomes increasingly problematic in a heterogeneous and sophisticated mass society, which is also capitalistic and relatively democratic. In such a society citizen expectations cannot be easily met and citizens are constantly exposed to conflicts and contradictions in the legal order. In the relatively benign period of the mid and late 1970s it is quite easy to forget the political and social turmoil of the 1964-1974 period, but it can be argued that the long range impact of this period and its ultimate effects may yet emerge. Various claims have been made that illegal activity is diffuse and even growing among both the powerless and the powerful. Although crime rates are difficult to validate, and the ultimate reasons behind illegal behavior are often complex, understandings of the legal order and the law itself must be taken into account. The powerless and the poor have been exposed to many challenges to a conventional conception of law as an even-handed instrument of order and justice; rationalizations of illegal behavior, and even ideological justifications of it, become more viable in such a situation. If exposure of crimes in high places and prosecution of those involved may reaffirm some faith in the legal order it remains true that its inequities and contradictions remain conspicuous for the powerless.

The middle classes experienced much confusion and disillusionment at either the ineffectiveness of or the abuses of the law by those in power which became so evident in the 1960s and early 1970s. Although the diversity of responses to this perception are many, as indicated, resorting to extra-legal measures or developing cynical disregard for the law are two significant responses for a segment of society traditionally considered committed to compliance with the law. One popular film in the early 1970s portrayed a middle class liberal who has taken the law into his own hands to avenge crimes against his family ("Death Wish"); another involves a middle-class couple who turn rather casually to bank robbery after the husband loses his job ("Fun with Dick and Jane"). While it is not suggested that such patterns of behavior are common among the middle class they may reflect potential paradigms for rejecting the sense of obligation to the law.

The "powerful" is not a wholly unified elite in our society, but is rather made up of individuals and groups of varying interests and principles. In general it may be said that the powerful view law as an instrument to maintain the *status quo*, or to modify it in a positive direction. If the powerful inevitably tend to uphold the legitimacy of the legal order it is also true that they may do so selectively. In other words, an instrumental or hypocritical legitimation of the legal order makes it possible for the powerful to violate laws conflicting with political or personal interests while still professing a commitment to "law and order".

Students of the criminal justice system cannot simply focus upon the concrete, immediate critical issues confronting that system. It is of fundamental importance to understand what is meant by law, and what determines orientations towards law and legal order. We have sought to demonstrate that the meaning of the law and the legitimacy crisis confronting the legal order can be interpreted in very different ways. The responses of the legal order to the challenges of the legitimacy crisis must be understood in terms of such different perspectives on the ultimate meaning of law. It cannot be conclusively demonstrated that a conventional perspective or a radical perspective is "correct", since ultimately an ideological choice and commitment is involved. But students subscribing to either perspective, whether they essentially believe the existing legal order should be maintained or destroyed, must understand what might make either of those objectives possible. An understanding of the criminal justice system must begin with an understanding of the law and the legal order which produces it. The issues confronting the criminal justice system must ultimately be understood within the framework of the critical issue of what the law is and what upholds the legal order.

Discussion Questions

1. Can the concept "legitimacy crisis" be quantified? What kind of index would you use to identify the existence or persistence of a legitimacy crisis?

2. What is *your* orientation toward law? In what sense do you regard the legal order as legitimate—or illegitimate?

3. What types of responses may the state make to challenges to its legitimacy? Which types of responses are most effective? What are the basic limitations of each of these types of responses? Is widely diffused, authentic legitimation of the legal order an unrealistic goal for a complex, heterogenous mass society? An unnecessary goal?

4. Do you agree that a consideration of the meaning of the law, the basic sources of support for the law, and an understanding of the assumptions incorporated by a system of law is a necessary or a desirable point of departure for considering critical issues in Criminal Justice? Why? Why not? Can we simply take the meaning of law for granted; can we assume that cognitive and normative orientations toward the law are not especially relevant for delineating and interpreting critical issues such as the future of juvenile justice, the persistence of police corruption or the impact of restoring capital punishment?

5. A dichotomy of "models" of the law (broadly conceived) might include: Principles vs. Practices; Natural vs. Positive; Restitutive vs. Repressive; Statutory vs. Case; Criminal vs. Civil; Adversary vs. Inquisitorial; Substantive vs. Procedural (and Crime Control vs. Due Process). Define these different types of law or legal systems. Can an argument be made that certain "models" of law have a more natural affinity with a situation of legitimacy than their counterparts? What is the relationship of these different "models", and the tensions between them, to a legitimacy crisis?

Notes

1. Paul Bohannon, "Law and Legal Institutions", *International Encyclopedia, of the Social Sciences*, 9, David C. Sills, ed. (USA: MacMillan Company, 1968, p. 73; see also Jack P. Gibbs, "Definitions of Law and Empirical Questions", in M. Barkun, ed. *Law and the Social System*, (New York: Lieber Atherton, 1973, pp. 16-17; and Lawrence Friedman, *The Legal System: A Social Science Perspective*, (New York: Russell Sage Foundation, 1975, p. 1.

2. Carl J. Friedrich, *The Philosophy of Law in Historical Perspective* (Chicago: The University of Chicago Press, 1958, 1963), pp. 3-153.

3. F.S. Cohen, "Transcendental Nonsense and the Functional Approach", in F.S. Cohen & M.R. Cohen, ed. *Readings in Jurisprudence and Legal Philosophy*, (Boston: Little Brown & Co., 1951), p. 429.

4. Roscoe Pound, *Social Control Through Law*, (New York: Archon Books, 1968), p. 33.

5. Ronald Akers. "Problems in the Sociology of Deviance: Social Definitions and Behavior", *Social Forces*, 46 (1968): 455-465; Lon Fuller, *The Morality of Law*, (New Haven: Yale University Press, 1964), pp. 33-94; E.A. Hoebel, *The Law of Primitive Man*, (Cambridge: Harvard University Press, 1967), pp. 18-28; E.H. Sutherland & D.R. Cressey, *Principles of Criminology*, (Philadelphia: J.B. Lippincott Co., 1966), pp. 5-9; Ehrlich, Eugen, *Fundamental Principles of the Sociology of Law*, (New York: Russell & Russell, 1962), p. 53; Edwin Schur, *Law and Society* (New York: Random House, 1968), p. 85; Bohannon, p. 77.

6. Lon Fuller, *The Anatomy of the Law*, (New York: Mentornal, 1969), p. 18.

7. Oliver W. Holmes, Jr., "The Path of the Law" (1897), quoted in Cohen, p. 429.

8. Friedrichs, pp. 3-153.

9. Andrew Hopkins, "On the Sociology of Criminal Law" *Social Problems*, 22 (1975), pp. 610-611.

10. W.J. Chambliss, "Functional and Conflict Theories of Crime: The Heritage of Emile Durhkeim and Karl Marx" in W.J. Chambliss & M. Mankoff, ed. *Whose Law? What Order? A Conflict Approach to Criminology*. (New York: John Wiley & sons, Inc., 1976), pp. 7-16.

11. W.J. Chambliss, "The State and Criminal Law", in ibid, pp. 66-67.

12. W.J. Chambliss, "Funtional and Conflict Theories . . .", p. 15.

13. W.J. Chambliss, "The State . . .", pp. 68-100, p. 101.

14. Hopkins, pp. 610-611; Pound, p. 49.

15. Friedman, pp. 17-20.

16. Adam Podgorecki, *Law and Society*, (London: Routledge Kegan & Paul, 1975): pp. 218-219.

17. Friedman, p. 9.

18. Kenneth, Carlton, *Law and the Structure of Social Action*, (New York: Columbia University Press, 1956): p. 156.

19. Samuel Thompson, "The Authority of Law", *Ethics*, 75 (1964), p. 16.

20. Karl Marx & Friedrich Engels, "The German Ideology", in T.B. Bottomore & M. Rubel, ed., *Selected Writings in Sociology & Social Philosophy*, (New York: McGraw-Hill Co.: 1956), p. 225; for other Marx & Engels references on law and crime see W.J. Chambliss, "Toward a Political Economy of Crime," *Theory & Society*, (2 1975): 168-169; see also: Kenneth Cloke, "Law is Illegal", in J.P. Black, ed., *Radical Lawyers*. (New York: Avon, 1971), p. 41; Kenneth Cloke, "The Economic Basis of Law and State", in R. Lefcourt, ed., *Law Against the People*, (New York: Vintage, 1971), p. 79; Richard Quinney, "A Critical Theory of Criminal Law", *Criminal Justice in America—A Critical Understanding*, (Boston: Little Brown & Co, 1974), pp. 8, 23; Richard Quinney, "The Ideology of Law: Notes for a Radical Alternative to Legal Oppression", *Issues in Criminology*, 7, (1972): 2-5; Richard Quinney, *Critique of Legal Order*, (Boston, Little Brown & Co, 1974).

21. Friedman, pp. 17, 20; Perfecto Fernandez, "Law and Polity: Towards a System Concept of Legal Validity", *Philippine Law Journal*, 46 (1971): 377: Gray L. Dorsey, "Law and the Formative Process of Social Order", in Barkun, p. 98.

22. Fernandez, p. 403.

23. Herbert Marcuse, "Ethics and Revolution", in Richard T. DeGeorge, ed. *Ethics and Society*, (New York: Ancho-Doubleday, 1966), pp. 133-148; W.J. Chambliss, *Crime and the Legal Process*. (New York: McGraw Hill, 1964) pp. 3, 4.

24. W.J. Chambliss & Robert Seidman, *Law, Order and Power*, (Reading, Mass.: Addison Wesley Co., 1971) pp. 8-9.

25. Austin Turk, "Law as a Weapon in Social Conflict", Social Problems, 23, (1976): 276.

26. Schur, pp. 82-84.

27. Stanley Diamond, "The Rule of Law versus the Order of Custom", in D. Black & M. Mileski, ed., *The Social Organization of Law*, (New York: Seminar Press, 1973), p. 332.

28. Turk, p. 284.

29. R.J. Michalowski & E.W. Bohlander, "Repression and Criminal Justice in Capitalist America", *Sociological Inquiry*, 46 (1976), pp. 97.

30. Zenon Bankowski & Geoff Mungham, *Images of Law* (Boston: Routledge & Kegan Paul, 1976), p. xi.

31. Richard Barnet, "The Twilight of the Nation-State: A Crisis of Legitimacy", in R.P. Wolff, *The Rule of Law,* (New York: Simon & Shuster, 1971), p. 222; Walter D. Burnham, "Crisis of American Political Legitimacy", in H.I. Safa & G. Levitas ed., *Social Problems in Corporate America*, (New York: Harper & Row, 1975), p. 494; Jurgen Habermas, *Legitimation Crisis*, (Boston: Beacon Press, 1973); J. Van Doorn, "The Military and the Crisis of Legitimacy", in G. Harries-Jenkins & J. Van Doorn, ed. *The Military and the Problem of Legitimacy*, (Beverly Hills, Sage, 1976) p. 18; D. P. Moynihan, quoted in Claus Mueller, The Politics of Communication, (New York: Oxford University Press, 1973), p. 5; E.G. Brown, Jr., quoted in Joseph Kraft, "A Day with Jerry", New York Post, March 22, 1975, p. 28.

32. James Hurst, "Problems of Legitimacy in the Contemporary Legal Order", Oklahoma Law Review, 24 (1971): 224-225; Dolf Sternberger, "Legitimacy", in David L. Sills, ed., *International Encyclopedia of the Social Sciences*, IX, (USA: MacMillan Co., 1968), pp. 244-24; Peter G. Stillman, "The Concept of Legitimacy", *Polity*, VII (19740: 32; Van Doorn, pp. 17-26.

33. Daniel Yankelovich, "A Crisis of Moral Legitimacy", *Dissent*, Fall, 1972: 526; Louis Harris, "Lawmen's Rating Dips", New York Post, October 22, 1973, p. 6.

34. Stanley Aronowitz, "Law, the Breakdown of Order, and Revolution", in Robert Lefcourt, ed., pp. 150-182.

35. Barnet, pp. 222, 226.

36. Yankelovich, pp. 528-530.

37. Alexander M. Bickel, "Watergate and the Legal Order" *Commentary*, 57 (1974), p. 23; John H. Schaar, "Legitimacy in the Modern State", in R. Quinney, ed. *Criminal Justice . . .*, pp. 63-64; Burnham, p. 499.

38. Charles Reasons, "Social Thoughts and Social Structures: The Criminologist, Crime and the Criminal", *The Criminologists: Crime and the Criminal*, (Pacific Palisades: Goodyear Publ Co., Inc., 1974), p. 5.

39. J.H. Plumb, in Burnham, p. 499.

40. David O. Friedrichs, "Mass Society: A Comparative Analysis of Sociological and Existential Perspectives" (Unpublished Master's Thesis, New York University, 1970), pp. 1-60.

41. Ronald Glassman, "Legitimacy and Manufactured Charisma", *Social Research*, 42 (1975), pp. 615-636; Schaar, pp. 63-64, 92.

42. Roberto Unger, *Law in Modern Society*, (New York: The Free Press, 1976), pp. 70, 174, 176.

43. Jurgen Habermas, in Boris Frankel, "Habermas Talking: An Interview", *Theory and Society*, 1 (1974), p. 51; Habermas, *Legitimation Crisis*, p. 73.

44. Stanford Lyman, "Legitimacy and Consensus in Lipset's America: From Washington to Watergate", *Social Research*, 42 (1975), p. 732.

45. Michael Barkun, "Law and Social Revolution: Millenarianism and the Legal System", *Law & Society* Review, 6 (1971), p. 132.

46. John Fraser, "Validating a Measure of National Political Legitimacy", *American Journal of Political Science*, 18 (1971), p. 119; Friedman, p. 118.

47. Podgorecki, pp. 254, 256.

48. Paul Freund, "Law in the Schools: Goals and Methods", *Law in American Society*, 1 (1972): 10.

49. Lois Forer, *The Death of the Law*, (New York: David McKay Co., 1975), p. XIV.

50. J.S. Campbell, J.S. Sahid & D.P. Stang, *Law & Order Reconsidered,—National Commission on the Causes and Prevention of Violence*, (Washington, D.C.: U.S. Gov't Printing Office, 1969), p. 9.

51. Ibid, xxi.

52. Phillip Worchel, P.G. Hester & Philip Kopala, "Collective Protest and Legitimacy of Authority", *Journal of Conflict Resolution*, 18 (1974): 54.

53. New York State Special Commission on Attica, *Attica* (New York: Bantam, 1972), pp. 106-107, 114-141.

54. John Schaar, "Legitimacy in the Modern State", in R. Quinney, ed. *Criminal Justice . . .*, pp. 62-63.

55. A. Mylonas & W.C. Reckless, "Prisoner's Attitudes Toward Law and Legal Institutions", *Journal of Criminal Law, Criminology & Police Science*, 54 (1962): 479.

56. John Davis, "Justification for no Obligation: Views of Black Males toward Crime and Criminal Law", *Issues in Criminology*, 9 (1974): 69-831.

57. Mueller, pp. 159-160, 170.

58. Jack D. Douglas, "Watergate: Harbinger of the American People", *Theory & Society*, 1 (1974); 90.

59. J.H. Perkinson, "Watergate: The Failure of the Educators", *New York University—Education Quarterly*, 5 (1974): 2.

60. Ibid.

61. Gail Sheehy, "Watching Watergate in Archie Bunker Country", *New York Magazine*, August 12, 1973: 40.

62. John Mitchell, quoted in New York Times, *The Watergate Hearings*, (New York: Bantam Books, 1973); p. 390.

63. H.S. Commager, "The Shame of the Republic", *New York Review of Books*, july 19, 1973; 12.

64. Vermont Royster, "The Public Morality—Afterthoughts on Watergate", *The American Scholar*, Spring (1974): 256.

65. Hugh Sidey, "Watergate and the Classroom", *Today's Education*, January, February (1974): 23.

66. Robert Coles, "The Politics of Middle Class Children", *New York Review of Books*, March 6, 1975: 13.

67. Dennis H. Wrong, "Watergate: A Symbol of What Sickness", *Dissent*, Fall, 1974: 501.

68. Michael Myerson, *Watergate—Crime in the Suites*, (New York: International Publishers, 1973), p. 26-27.

69. Noam Chomsky, "Watergate: A Skeptical View", *New York Review of Books,* September 30, 1973: 3.

70. Richard Quinney, *Criminology—Analysis and Critique of Crime in America.* (Boston: Little Brown & Co., 1975), p. 160.

71. Herbert Marcuse, "When Law and Morality Stand in the Way", *Society*, 10 (1973): 23.

72. Yankelovich, "A Crisis . . .," p. 526-32.

73. James Q. Wilson, "The Riddle of the Middle Class", *The Public Interest*, 39 (1975): 126.

74. Louis Harris, "The Harris Survey: Big Majority Faults White House on Handling of Watergate", *Staten Island Advance*, April 30, 1973: 11.

75. R.G. Dunham & A.C. Mauss, "Waves from Watergate", *Pacific Sociological Review*, 19 (1976): 469-487.

76. F. Christopher Atherton, "The Impact of Watergate on Children's Attitudes Toward Political Authority", *Political Science Quarterly*, June, 1974: 272.

77. Amitai Etzioni, *Social Problems* (Englewood Cliffs: Prentice Hall, 1976), pp. 103-105.

78. Samuel Bowles, Herbert Gintis & Peter Meyer, "Education, IQ and the Legitimation of the Social Division of Labor" *Berkeley Journal of Sociology*, 20 (1975-1976): 233-264.

79. Mueller, whole book.

80. Freund, p. 14.

81. Isaac Balbus. *The Dialectics of Legal Repression.* (New York: Prentice Hall, 1973), p. 3.

82. E.M. Schur, "A Sociologist's View", in E.M. Schur & H.A. Bedau, ed., *Victimless Crime* (Englewood Cliffs: Prentice Hall, 1974).

83. Anthony Platt. *The Politics of Commissions*, (New York: MacMillan, 1971).

2

Is It Time to Abolish the Exclusionary Rule?

JACK M. KRESS

WHILE IT IS RELATIVELY EASY TO RECOGNIZE A WRONG, it is often difficult to fashion a remedy. When the police act unconstitutionally—whether the violation is an illegal search, a coerced confession, an improperly suggestive line-up, etc. —what is the court to do? What consequences will flow from the recognition of such behavior? In recent years, the primary sanction applied by the courts has been the exclusion from use at trial of evidence obtained through improper law enforcement behavior of virtually any sort. It will be the purpose of this commentary to make the case against present judicial reliance on the Exclusionary Rule.

The "Exclusionary Rule" states that various kinds of evidence of guilt (e.g, weapons, drugs, confessions, eye-witness identifications) are excluded from jury consideration, on the issue of guilt or innocence, where a law officer has not fully complied with a judicially enforced rule of conduct. "The central thesis of the exclusionary rule is that police will be compelled to comply with the substantive commands of the law if the penalty for failure to comply is the exclusion, from a criminal trial, of evidence of guilt which is otherwise relevant and competent."[1]

The history of the Exclusionary Rule as a judicial control device has been a relatively recent one, beginning primarily in the early Twentieth Century. In 1914, the United States Supreme Court first adopted the Exclusionary Rule, as the primary judicial remedy for misconduct by Federal law enforcement officials, in the case of *Weeks v. United States*, 232 U.S. 383. The Court at that time did not require the Exclusionary Rule to be used by state courts, and, indeed, from time to time expressed serious misgivings about ever doing so.[2] In 1961, the Supreme Court reversed itself and declared the Exclusionary Rule to be constitutionally mandated in state court criminal proceedings. The Court's decision was influenced both by the growing number of states that had adopted the Exclusionary Rule on their own and also by a finding that the existence of other remedies was largely imaginary: "To hold otherwise is to grant the right but in reality to withhold its privilege and enjoyment" [*Mapp. v. Ohio*, 367 U.S. 643, 656 (1961)].

312

Recently, however, the shortcomings of the rule have become glaring and disenchantment with the practical effects of the Exclusionary Rule has been widely expressed.[3] Indeed, within the Supreme Court itself, the cries for abolition of the rule have grown more insistent. The scope of the rule's application, for example, was somewhat limited in two recent decisions.[4] It is quite possible that the rationale Chief Justice Warren Burger expressed in a 1971 dissent may soon become the majority view of the Supreme Court:

> I do not question the need for some remedy to give meaning and teeth to the constitutional guarantees against unlawful conduct by government officials. . . . But the hope that this objective could be accomplished by the exclusion of reliable evidence from criminal trials was hardly more than a wistful dream. Although I would hesitate to abandon it until some meaningful substitute is developed, the history of the Suppression Doctrine demonstrates that it is both conceptually sterile and practically ineffective in accomplishing its stated objective. [*Bivens v. Six Unknown Named Agents,* 403 U.S. 388, 415 (1971)].

The Exclusionary Rule in Theory:

Many of the negative aspects of the Exclusionary Rule were foreseen long ago, but it was felt necessary to adopt it as a last resort. The courts did not regard the rule as something good in and of itself; quite to the contrary, it was viewed as a necessary evil. Its adoption was urged not on the basis of lofty claims of principle, but rather on grounds of expediency: a feeling that nothing else had worked in the past and therefore this remedy should be tried. At the time of its adoption, there was no thought of its being indispensable, but rather it was hoped that the Exclusionary Rule *would* eventually be replaced by a workable alternative. It was just another of those "temporary" stopgap measures which seem to last forever. It is said that criminals laugh at the law because of it, and shyster lawyers get rich on it. As United States Supreme Court Justice Robert Jackson observed: "It deprives society of its remedy against one law-breaker because he has been pursued by another" [*Irvine v. California,* 347 U.S. 128, 136 (1954)]. In other words, and in short, two wrongs *here* make a right.

In opposing the adoption of an Exclusionary Rule in New York State, New York's Chief Judge (later Supreme Court Justice) Benjamin Cardozo argued that, although the courts are always forced to strike a balance between the rights of society and the rights of the individual, the Exclusionary Rule goes too far. He perceptively foresaw two major drawbacks in one succinct phrase: "The criminal is to go free because the constable has blundered" [*People v. Defore,* 242 N.Y. 13, 15 (1926)].

"The criminal is to go free"

The Exclusionary Rule frees the guilty criminal, but does nothing for the innocent person. Of all the remedial rules fashioned by the courts, this is perhaps the only one that makes no pretense or claim that a potentially innocent person may be involved. When we exclude confession by torture, we feel that even an innocent defendant may have made an admission in such circumstances. Not so here. *Only* guilty criminals are aided; the violated innocent person is left without a remedy by application of the Exclusionary Rule.

As one example, think of the recent situation in East St. Louis where an unauthorized search and entry was conducted by some unknown narcotics officers. The people involved were terrorized. Unfortunately for them, they committed no wrong; they were *innocent* of any wrongdoing. Therefore, the Exculsionary Rule offered them no protection at all, and hence they were seeking money damages—the kind of money damages which those who argue against any substitute for the Exclusionary Rule have repeatedly said are "inadequate." However, if the people involved *had* been narcotic whole-salers or kidnappers, then they could have availed themselves of the Exclusionary Rule and been set free.

As one more example, let us assume that police see a number of known narcotic addicts go into a building from which they soon emerge. The police station themselves outside the building and see that all of the addicts go up to the fourth floor. They observe this much but can't get any closer without being observed themselves. They realize that the fourth floor has six apartments in it, but they can't tell from which one the drug seller is operating. This is not a wholly implausible fact situation. Let us now assume that, acting on this information, the police engage in a raid (later deemed illegal) on every apartment on the fourth floor. Under the present practice of the Exclusionary Rule, the occupants of the five apartments where no crime had been committed, where only innocent people resided, have *no* remedy. Only the guilty occupant does. The five innocents whose homes have been torn apart, whose privacy has been invaded, have no practical recourse. The criminal, however, does.

"The constable has blundered"

Justice Cardozo's second point is equally important in practice. The word "blundered" is an altogether appropriate one for the Exclusionary Rule does not distinguish between honest error and intentional misconduct on the part of an "offending" police officer. An unintentional blunder, sloppy typing on a search warrant, an honest mistake as to the time limits of its execution; any of these will render a search and all of its fruits inadmissible in evidence against the assorted murderers, rapists and muggers who go free because of it.

Deterrence

And now let us deal with the crux of the argument in support of the Exclusionary Rule: "It is *necessary*." But why is it necessary? "Because it will work." How will it work? "Because of its deterrent effect." "The purpose [of the *Mapp* decision] was to deter the lawless action of the police" [*Linkletter v. Walker,* 281 U.S. 618, 637 (1965)].[5] Lawless police action is the wrong to be corrected; the Exclusionary Rule is the pragmatic means by which the correction is to be achieved; a belief in deterrence is the philosophical underpinning of the means chosen.

Let us speak of deterrence. Criminologists have performed countless studies in this area and have unfortunately reached the somewhat inconclusive conclusion that they cannot find much of a specific deterrent effect in most of the criminal laws of this country. (In fact, it is both a curious and interesting fact to note that among those who most strongly support the continuance of the Exclusionary Rule we find those who, when the issue was the abolition of the death penalty, strongly argued to the Supreme Court that there was no such thing as any deterrent effect in that case.)

Without going through all the literature on deterrence, let us say only this: To be an effective deterrent, it would probably be agreed that the remedy should be — at least — certain, direct and immediate. However, even California's respected Chief Justice Roger Traynor, in *adopting* the Exclusionary Rule, conceded that there was no proof that the Exclusionary Rule had *any* deterrent effect whatsover [*People v. Cahan,* 44 Cal. 2d 434, 437 (1955)]. Mr. Justice Jackson once declared that the "disciplinary or educational effect of the court's releasing the defendant for police misbehavior is so indirect as to be no more than a mild deterrent at best" [*Irvine v. California,* 347 U.S. 128, 136 (1954)].

Not only is its effect indirect and not immediate (often coming months after an arrest — or even *years,* particularly if the decision is made on appeal), often it is not even *known,* usually not even by the offending officer, but almost certainly not by his supervisors.

Ask any police officer this question: When is a case marked "closed" in police files? He will tell you that the answer is: At the point of arrest — not after court disposition, not after a motion to suppress, not after the invocation of the Exclusionary Rule — at the point of arrest.

Ask any police officer this question: In how many of the arrests which you make, do you ever tell your story in a court of law? He will tell you that, because of the prevalence and predominance of plea-bargaining, he doesn't go to court very often after the arrest and rarely does he do so to testify.

Ask any prosecutor or judge this question: If a police officer testified in your court and he and you were present when a case was lost on a motion to supress issue—when the Exclusionary Rule was put into effect—would the police officer be told that it was because of his illegal behavior? Almost universally, the honest answer would have to be "no." Judges and district attorneys work with police officers; they see no profit in insulting them. Besides, as overworked as they are, they rarely have time for detailed explanations, or to give solace to offended police officers or victims.

Ask any police commander the following question: If a case were thrown out of court due to the action of a police officer, on a motion to suppress evidence, how would such a case be reported back to you? His answer, almost invariably, would be that someone in the court messed up—the district attorney goofed, the judge gave the courthouse away, etc. And those answers would be given only in those few situations in which the police officer would even report the fact back to his command, since there is no such reporting requirement in any police force in the country. Furthermore, there is no requirement that a district attorney report a situation of improper police behavior to a police commander. There is no such requirement upon a judge or upon a defense attorney either. And such reports are almost never volunteered by anyone.

Ask any police officer the following question: If any of the arrests you made—where you *succeeded* on a motion to suppress, or at a trial, on the issue of the propriety of your behavior—were appealed, would you know about the appeal? The answer, of course, is a very loud "no." The officer would not even know *whether* any case of his was ever appealed, much less the result of such an appeal—and, of course, the officer would never know whether or not the legal language of the appeal meant that his actions had been proper or improper, even if it had been communicated to him.

On the basis of these questions and these answers, can one seriously call the 'disciplinary or educational effect" of the court's invocation of the Exclusionary Rule merely "indirect" or "mild"? One would be more honest if one called it non-existent."

Moreover, the very concept of impropriety cannot be said to be a clear-cut one. The application of the Rule is uncertain, varying markedly from case-to-case and court-to-court. Supreme Court Justices frequently divide 5–4 on narrow issues that a high school-trained police officer is supposed to clearly understand and apply in an emergency situation. "Enough is enough. These processes would not deter or enlighten a policeman in Gary with a Ph.D. who was going to law school at night."[6]

And finally, in practice, the hopes of the proponents of the Exclusionary Rule have, unfortunately, not been realized. Respect for judicial integrity has not increased; rather, cynicism toward the law enforcement process has been enhanced. The police have not in fact been deterred from misconduct; if anything, even *additional* abuses have occurred. For example, recent studies show that police perjury has apparently increased since the *Mapp* decision.[7] "Most disturbing is the argument that if the police are subject to the restrictions of the exclusionary rule they cannot obtain the convictions necessary to carry out their law enforcement function, and it they cannot obtain such convictions they will be tempted to harass suspects, to inflict extra-legal punishments."[8]

Mens Rea

Now let us examine the very concept of police "misbehavior" at which the Exclusionary Rule purportedly aims. In our society's penal laws, we speak of the concept of *mens rea,* which gets at the question of the mental state of the criminal. Usually, the criminal punishment is reserved only for those who have intentionally transgressed the law. Is this the case with regard to the Exclusionary Rule? Or, to put it another way, which police officers does the Exclusionary Rule aim to deter: the "good" police or the "bad" police?

If it is the "good" cop, then a model police officer may do all in his power to do right and conform with proper police procedure and behavior, but find his case thrown out of court due to his inadvertent error. This may very well cause the "good" cop to become quite cynical indeed about our criminal justice system, and the profusion of such results has indeed created systemic disaffection on the part of many honest law enforcement officials.

If it is the "bad" cop at which the Exclusionary Rule is aimed, then clearly there can be no deterrent effect whatsoever. The police officer who would intentionally make an illegal search, and therefore violate his oath of office on purpose, will also quite obviously have no compunction about coming to court and violating his oath as a witness by lying as to the circumstances of the search.

Thus, we can see that the Exclusionary Rule protects only the criminal and not the innocent person, and that it is also geared to affecting the behavior of the "good" police officer and not the person at whom its supporters claim it is aimed: the intentionally offending police officer.

Judicial Integrity

It should be clear by now that the effectiveness of the Exclusionary Rule as a deterrent is open to very serious question. We should note that the courts have sometimes stressed a second, subsidiary function of the Rule—a function of propriety, what the *Elkins* Court called "the imperative of judicial integrity" [*Elkins v. United States,* 364 U.S. 206, 222 (1960)]. "Courts which sit under our Constitution cannot and will not be made party to lawless invasions of the constitutional rights of citizens by permitting unhindered governmental use of the fruits of such invasion" [*Terry v. Ohio,* 392 U.S. 1, (1968)]. Historically, indeed, this rationale, now paid scant attention to in recent decisions, was first expressed in the *Weeks* case in terms of the impropriety of judicial sanctioning of governmental participation in illegal conduct. Justice Brandeis once argued: "If the Government becomes a law-breaker, it breeds contempt for law . . ." [*Olmstead v. United States,* 227 U.S. 438, 484 (1928)]. The point made is that it is morally repugnant and completely inconsistent for the courts to declare police misconduct unlawful on the one hand, while simultaneously accepting the fruits of the unlawful conduct into evidence in a court of law. This is analogous to what lawyers refer to as the equity doctrine which requires a party to come into court with "clean hands."

Such again is the claim, but what is the reality? The criminal goes free and public respect for the law is lessened, not increased. And what about "judicial integrity" of another sort—corruption? There is this one further, practical objection to the Exclusionary Rule, and that is the fertile ground it has given to the corrupt: the bribed police officer's lie need not be so blatant today, for he may immunize a criminal from prosecution by appearing *overzealous,* by purposely overstepping legal bounds in obtaining vital evidence; the corrupt prosecutor or judge may blame the decision on a "legal technicality"; and, since appeal by the State is so rare in America,[9] corruption of the lower judiciary is all the better masked by the presence of an Exclusionary Rule. If anything, contempt for the law by the public has *increased* since the decision in *Mapp v. Ohio.*

It is fair to ask, "Are there any better methods of controlling improper police activity than the enforcement of an Exclusionary Rule?" The major criticism leveled at proposed alternatives has been that they have been tried in the past and they have been found to be wanting. However, it is not unreasonable to think that, in the almost two decades since uniformity was imposed upon the United States, there have been some social and economic changes that have made past solutions more viable today, and furthermore, there have been new solutions proposed. Let us list some of the potential remedies, many of which could certainly be applied in addition to an Exclusionary Rule.

Preventive action is, of course, the very best, and, although only briefly alluded to here, that is not meant to diminish the potential significance of controlling illegal activity before it ever occurs. In this realm are such sanctions as statutory and/or judicial prohibitions, including "the law" by definition. Various administrative regulations, such as internal police department procedural rules, might be better geared toward encouraging more appropriate police behavior.[10] Better training within the police department; more training sessions in conjunction with local district attorneys, etc.; more communication between the various judicial agencies and the police department to provide feedback to the police department as to present police activities in court: all of these would help.

However, assuming the worst, that all preventive measures have failed and police misbehavior continues (an unfortunately not unreasonable assumption), then we must look more carefully at potential alternative sanctions which will occur after the event of police misbehavior. The most often referred to measure is the common law sanction of tort damages.[11] This civil remedy has been called ineffective for a number of reasons. State rules have previously allowed a broad defense of privilege, juries have been unwilling to convict, plaintiffs have usually been viewed as undeserving, and actual recovery of damages has been difficult. However, this does have the signal advantage of providing relief to non-criminals. Tort damages are primarily termed "inadequate" for two reasons. First of all, the individual offending police officer doesn't have much money and therefore is too poor to pay damages or, as the lawyers so euphemistically put it, the officer is judgment-proof. This argument, however, fails for four reasons: (a) police officers are not so poorly paid today as they once were; (b) a police officer could very well take out the equivalent of medical malpractice insurance so that future damages *would* be recoverable;[12] (c) it is very possible that a liability-sharing program, perhaps sponsored by the Patrolman's Benevolent Association, might come into effect, were such tort damage suits to be *really* instituted;[13] and, (d) liability could go to the entire police department, or even the City, as well as to the offending officer, in addition to the liability now imposed upon the officer himself" [Justice Spense, dissenting, *People v. Cahan*, 44 Cal. 2d 434, 444 (1955)].[14]

A second argument terming tort damages "inadequate" is usually based on a belief that juries will not convict police officers. However, this argument also fails: (a) the climate of the times has clearly changed and jurors no longer simply accept on faith whatever a police officer says to them — the many allegations of police corruption, the story of New York's Knapp Commission — all have gone to undermine the once unshakable faith of the populace in the veracity of the police; (b) in any event, even were this argument to have any merit, it would only occur when a heinous criminal would be the plaintiff in such an action. Petty offenders often evoke sympathy and the argument is of course inapplicable in the situation of an innocent person who has been aggrieved.

Another post-illegal behavior sanction would be a series of statutory penalties which might include periods of imprisonment or a fining system. Were there to be a set fine, for example, for a particular unauthorized breach of privacy — perhaps paid out of a patrolman's own pocket — then we might actually see some deterrent effect. Again, however, the spectre of jury sympathy for the police is raised; but since it is also argued so often that the *real* menace of police misbehavior is that it destroys citizen faith in the court system and brings the entire judicial process into disrepute, a quite simple analogy may be at hand. It might be very easy to think of such police misconduct as being a form of "contempt of court." "Another recent suggestion would have courts enforce individual rights by citing offending law enforcement officers for contempt of court, but thus far there has been virtually no experience with this remedy."[15] Using the contempt procedure, a *judge* would make such a ruling on police misbehavior, therefore obviating the potential danger of jury sympathy.

Criminal prosecution cannot be ruled out if the misbehavior is gross enough.[16] The argument has been that criminal prosecution of law enforcement officials who themselves violate the law would generally be ineffective: prosecutors would be unwilling to prosecute and juries unwilling to convict. However, in today's climate, not only is there less inherent faith in police officers or government agents as such, but the Watergate situation has made more plausible the concept of a special independent prosecutor, with an investigative arm distinct from that of the officers to be investigated. Certainly, it is not inconceivable, when we think of the varied forms official corruption takes, for our society to support an independent staff of investigators to look into these matters — and police misbehavior of the sort that the Exclusionary Rule should really aim at cannot be treated any differently.

Departmental discipline is not an absurd possibility. The argument is made that police cannot police themselves. However, there have been many successful, independent and *open* police review boards throughout the United States. When necesary, civilian review boards, reviewing various other forms of police misconduct, have proven somewhat successful.[17] Why could they not be instituted as a substitute for an Exclusionary Rule?

The injunction is another viable alternative. This would be just as difficult to enforce as any other statutory sanction, but in those cases of continued and persistent violation of rights, this remedy might prove as useful as it has been in the area of civil rights.

Another suggestion has been a variant of an ombudsman. An independent investigator or judge would handle such a matter perhaps as traffic violations are handled, on an administrative basis with a review not having the time-consuming and possibly disastrous effects of jury trials. [18]

All or Nothing?

One further comment would seem to be in order. Should *all* police misconduct be punished or only some? Is there a valid distinction to be drawn between the malicious and the mistaken? And are there degrees of maliciousness? In short, even were we to continue the Exclusionary Rule in some form, should it at least be modified to abandon the all-or-nothing nature of it? Our legal system is called an adversary system. We speak of wrong or right. The decision is guilty or not guilty. Only rarely do we have some form of in-between result. But should things be so black and white? Are all the rationalizations the courts have made in the various cases applying and not applying the Exclusionary Rule really an attempt at accommodation, of equity in a sense? Are differential sentences, plea-bargaining, parole boards, and all those countless extras that keep the criminal justice system from being so neat, really societal attempts at alleviating the all-or-nothing statements in the law? We can at least think the alternative.

There are many other possibilities. This list of alternatives is not exhaustive, but merely illustrative. Unfortunately, however, our thinking on this matter has been stultified by the uniformity of the Exclusionary Rule throughout the country. Justice Jackson frequently remarked that each time we federalized a particular principle and wrote it into constitutional scripture, as it were, we decreased the possiblity for reform. The United States contains 50 testing grounds. These testing grounds are shut down whenever the Supreme Court says that one, uniform, federal rule is required in every one of them. Mr. Justice Brandeis once cogently expressed the case for experimentation: "It is one of the happy incidents of the Federal system that a single courageous State may, if its citizens choose, serve as a laboratory" [*New York Ice Company v. Liebmann,* 285 U.S. 262, 311 (1931)]. [19] Once the Exclusionary Rule was uniformly required throughout the United States, judicial innovation ceased. But the process is not irreversible.

Indeed, only recently, the National Advisory Commission on Criminal Justice Standards and Goals suggested that a reconsideration of the Exclusionary Rule be accorded a priority: "Use of the exclusionary rule as a means of attempting to compel compliance by police and others with judicially promulgated rules of conduct should be studied and modification and alternative courses of action should be recommended as appropriate." The Commission further contended: "The effectiveness of the exclusion of resulting evidence as a deterrent to others who might engage in the prohibited conduct is open to question; the cost of the exclusionary rule in terms of court time and case delay and confusion is not."[20]

Summary

The Exclusionary Rule of Evidence calls for even trustworthy and convincing evidence to be barred from use at the trial of a criminal defendant if the evidence was secured through the illegal activity of law enforcement officials. The Exclusionary Rule became applicable to all the states through the 1961 Supreme Court decision in *Mapp v. Ohio.* Recently, the rule has come under strong attack and there are many who feel the Supreme Court may soon abolish it. Supporters of the Exclusionary Rule argue that it will deter improper law enforcement procedures, preserve the integrity of the courts, and, furthermore, that there is no viable alternative to it. Opponents of the Exclusionary Rule contend that it hinders the search for truth, prevents reliable evidence from being considered by jurors, shackles law officers in their efforts to prevent and detect crime, fails to deter illegal activity, and, moreover, that there are viable alternatives to it.

Discussion Questions

1. State the arguments in favor of the Exclusionary Rule.

2. State the arguments against the Exclusionary Rule.

3. Analyze the concept of deterrence as it relates to illicit police behavior.

4. Discuss the possible alternatives to the Exclusionary Rule.

Notes

1. Inbau, Thompson, and Sowle, *Criminal Justice: Cases and Comments* New York: Foundation Press, 1968), p. 2.

2. See, e.g., *Wolf v. Colorado,* 338 U.S. 25 (1949).

3. See Harvey Wingo, "Growing Disillusionment with the Exclusionary Rule," *Southwestern Law Journal,* 25 (1971): 573.

4. *United States v. Calandra,* 414 U.S. 338 (1974); *United States v. Janis,* 428 U.S. 433 (1976).

5. See also *United States v. Calandra, supra, United States v. Janis, supra,* and *Stone v. Powell,* 428 U.S. 465 (1976).

6. Burns, "Mapp v. Ohio: An All-American Mistake," *DePaul Law Review,* 19 (1969):80.

7. Comment, "Effect of *Mapp v. Ohio* on Police Search-and-Seizure Practices in Narcotics Cases," *Columbia Journal of Law and Social Problems,* 4 (1968):87.

8. Monrad Paulsen, "The Exclusionary Rule and Misconduct by the Police," *Journal of Criminal Law, Criminology and Police Science,* 52 (1961): 252, 257. See also Comment, "Police Perjury in Narcotics 'Dropsy' Cases: A New Credibility Gap," *Georgetown Law Journal,* 60 (1971):507.

9. Wayne R. LaFave, "Search and Seizure: 'The Course of True Law . . . Has Not . . . Run Smooth.'" *University of Illinois Law Forum,* 1966:255, 387–389.

10. See Carl McGowan, "Rule-Making and the Police," *Michigan Law Review,* 70 (1972):659.

11. See Caleb Foote, "Tort Remedies for Police Violations of Individual Rights," *Minnesota Law Review,* 39 (1955):493.

12. See Edward J. Horowitz, "Excluding the Exclusionary Rule—Can There Be An Effective Alternative," *Los Angeles Bar Bulletin,* 47 (1972):91.

13. Harvey Levin, "An Alternative to the Exclusionary Rule for Fourth Amendment Violations," *Judicature,* 58 (1974):74.

14. See Walter E. Dellinger, "Of Rights and Remedies: The Constitution as a Sword," *Harvard Law Reivew,* 85 (1972):1532; and Note, "Municipal Assumption of Tort Liability for Damage Caused by Police Officers," *New Mexico Law Review,* 1 (1971):263.

15. Dallin Oaks, "Studying the Exclusionary Rule in Search and Seizure," *University of Chicago Law Review,* 37 (1970):655, 674. See also, Alfred Blumrosen, "Contempt of Court and Unlawful Police Action," *Rutgers Law Reviews,* 11 (1957):526.

16. Richard A. Edwards, "Criminal Liability for Unreasonable Searches and Seizures," *Virginia Law Review,* 41 (1955):621.

17. See Peter G. Barton, "Civilian Review Boards and the Handling of Complaints Against the Police," *University of Toronto Law Journal,* 20 (1970):448; and Note, "Grievance Response Mechanisms for Police Misconduct," *Virginia Law Review,* 55 (1969):909.

18. See note, *Harvard Civil Rights Law Review,* 5 (1970):104.

19. See the argument by Stuart S. Nagel, "Testing the Effects of Excluding Illegally Seized Evidence," *Wisconsin Law Review,* (1965):283.

20. National Advisory Commission on Criminal Justice Standards and Goals, COURTS, Recommendation 4.1 (Washington, D.C.: United States Government Printing Office, 1973).

3

Determinate or Indeterminate Sentencing — The Changing Scene

LAWRENCE A. BENNETT

IN RECENT YEARS A STRONG SENTIMENT HAS EMERGED for the elimination of the indeterminate prison sentence approach to assessing penalties for serious felonies. California, Indiana, Illinois and Massachusetts have all abandoned the indeterminate sentencing system in favor of fixed terms, with narrow limits within which judges can modify the standard penalties. Wisconsin and Minnesota are considering adoption of a more determinate form of sentencing. A variety of factors can be identified that played a part in causing the desertion of the long-held and highly cherished policies and beliefs supporting the indeterminate sentencing model. One of the primary factors appears to be a need to punish; there seems to be emerging an almost archetypical need to express public vengeance. As noted by Dershowitz[1] punishment as a mechanism of crime control is older than recorded history. Even the 1870 National Prison Congress which gave impetus to the rehabilitative ideal with its Declaration of Principles, noted that punishment served both "in expiation of the wrong done" and as a remedy for the "moral disease" of crime.[2]

It would appear that there is an increasing acceptance of Immanuel Kant's view of penal law as a categorical imperative. His approach is that the imposition of punishment is necessary as a part of public responsibility for justice, even if the imposition of punishment serves neither to deter or to rehabilitate. Expressed in a somewhat more benign manner, James Q. Wilson states:

> We also want, or ought to want, sentences to give appropriate expression to our moral concern over the nature of the offense and to conform to our standards of human conduct.[3]

and

> Humanity and a sense of proportion require us to make the penalty commensurate with the gravity of the offense . . .[4]

Areas of Discontent

A study of some of the influences in shaping the thinking of many legislators has been that of Fogel, which resulted in the State of Illinois introducing in 1975 a plan for a return to a determinate sentencing policy, ". . . to achieve 'fairness' in sentencing and establish an atmosphere of certainty among prisoners."[5]

The concept of certainty about the future, needless to say, is definitely a prisoner concern. Studies of prison violence have often noted[6] the tensions created by inmates not knowing when they will be able to gain their release for return to society. The usual pattern has been for individual inmates to be reviewed for parole consideration at least once a year. From the inmates' point of view this hearing is a specially stressful version of Russian roulette. A person might make a sincere effort to fulfill the demands and requirements set out for him at a previous hearing only to learn that something quite different is now expected of him. He is then postponed for another year. Unfortunately, it was often the case that he had not served sufficient time to fulfill society's expectations about appropriate punishment, a decision cloaked in the guise of rehabilitation.

Mixed in with the concerns about fairness and certainty was the lack of accountability—the wide latitude of discretion exercised by the parole boards. The 1969 procedures of the U.S. Parole Board, for example, were strongly criticized by Davis, who stated,

> . . . the board makes no attempt to structure its discretionary power through rules, policy statements of guidelines;. . .
>
> The board has never announced rules, standards, or guides. The most specific standard is the statutory provision, repeated by the board's regulations, that the board "may in its discretion" release a prisoner on parole if the board finds "a reasonable probability that such prisoner will live and remain at liberty without violating the laws" and that "such release if not incompatible with the welfare of society." The board has not publicly listed the criteria that are considered.[7]

The description is very apt and fits well the operations of parole boards across the nation during the '50's, the '60's and up into the early '70's, in some cases.

Why hasn't some reform come about earlier? Despite the strong criticism of the autonomous and arbitrary manner in which paroling authorities operated, the courts, until very recently, upheld the notion that the policies of the board and the decisions based on those policies are not reviewable if they were in accordance with the law.[8]

An additional concern has to do with a basic fairness that would insure that the basic human rights of the individual are met. A number of writers

have decried the trampling of the rights of inmates by the prison system but
have often singled out the paroling authority as a heavy contributor in this
area.[9] When reforms are implemented by modified procedures and some
sense of balance is presented a different picture emerges. Philip Selznick has
characterized this state of affairs as "justice is therapy."[10] Glaser expands on
this in the following manner:

> Another proposition on reduction of recidivism, applicable to all
> branches of the criminal justice system, is the commonsense assumption
> that: I. *Commitment to criminality is increased if offenders perceive their treat-*
> *ment by a criminal justice agency as unjust* . . . offenders almost always seem
> to collect injustices and become censorious toward the criminal justice
> system as a normal defense.[11]

An additional force reducing the support for the indeterminate sentencing approach has come about because the concept of rehabilitation, upon
which the indeterminacy was based, has fallen into disrepute. To illustrate
this point it will be necessary to outline some of the implicit assumptions
("implicit" because the philosophical or logical basis for the various policies
are seldom articulated and even less often presented in written form)
associated with the emergence of the indeterminate sentence.

Earlier the view was held that inmates were misguided, inadequately
trained and uneducated individuals who could be assisted to take their place
in society if only the correctional system could "straighten them out" by
providing vocational training, spiritual guidance, educational opportunities and inspirational messages. Such a view persists in the minds of a
large segment of the public and a fair proportion of prison officials.

Growing out of these views, and sometimes operating in parallel with
them, came the idea that those who transgressed against society were
emotionally maladjusted, had psychological problems, were in a word,
"sick." To modify inmates suffering from the kinds of conditions outlined
there needed to be specially trained professionals. Psychiatrists, social
workers, psychologists and, more recently, behavior modifiers trooped
through the prisons. Individual therapy, group therapy, therapeutic communities, group counseling and peer counseling have had their turn at
assisting individuals to develop "insight," integration, to improve understanding of their problems or to change behavior.

The role of the indeterminate sentence in this "medical" model (based on
the concept that the inmate is "sick" and can be treated for and, perhaps,
cured of his criminality) was related to the view that anxiety or concern
about one's problems seemed a necessary basis of motivation for treatment to
have an effect. Many inmates (perhaps most according to the belief of some
professionals) have sociopathic tendencies. Sociopaths, in turn, have the

reputation of being anxiety-free and treatment resistant. It was felt, then, that if their release was contingent upon an improvement in their self-understanding, in their psychological adjustment, these inmates might become motivated to participate in treatment. It was recognized that the distress aroused might be less the concern of an individual about his emotional maladjustment than a dissatisfaction with the predicament in which he finds himself.

While there continue to be stalwart adherents for the various therapeutic intervention strategies[12] the recent work of Lipton, Martinson, and Wilkes[13] as well as the earlier efforts of Robison and Smith[14] has dashed considerable cold water on the idea that corrections really corrects. Lipton et al. reviewed selected evaluation studies of correctional programs and concluded that few corrective efforts had the kind of impact hoped for and promised by correctional administrators. While far from decisive, the conclusions were widely accepted as demonstrating that "nothing works" in corrections. The findings, however, when examined in detail, point out that some programs have a positive influence on certain kinds of offenders. Further, as pointed out by La Mar Empey, "the finding of no difference in outcome between two or more correctional alternatives does not demonstrate that correctional programs have no effect."[15] Despite the limitations of Martinson's review, correctional administrators have adopted a negative view as uncritically as they had earlier embraced the positivistic philosophy inherent in the hopeful new treatment programs.

An additional part of the disenchantment on the part of the public was a feeling that they were not being protected — that dangerous inmates were released when they should not be. Thus, a part of the responsibility of parole authorities is to determine "readiness for release." Improvement in a treatment program might be indicative of readiness to be considered for release. But in no case should a man be released if any maladjustment remains in evidence. It is becoming apparent that the coherent application of the treatment model and "readiness for release" concept cannot be easily achieved. While predictive devices[16] can help determine the likely percentage of a given group that will succeed on parole, there is no instrument or technique that can predict how a given individual will behave. The futility of this effort has been amply critiqued by Robison and Smith.[17] Statistical outcome measures suggest that assaultive inmates, especially murderers, represent a group with a high potential for success upon return to society. Of murderers released from prison, less than one half of one percent of the cases are returned to prison for new offenses involving violence within two years.[18] Despite their "readiness for release" at an early date, the public would not accept such a decision, reaffirming that punishment may be playing a major part in societal reactions.

Along similar lines society is quite disturbed when protection is violated by the release of an individual who subsequently reoffends by becoming involved in some particularly vicious act or series of such acts. Thus, the demand is placed upon parole boards to predict violence. The fact that they fail should not be too surprising; it is an impossible task. While knowledgeable judgment can and probably does prevent the release of some individuals so maladjusted that they are unsuitable for return to society, there is no known method for determining, in advance, who will engage in acts of violence. A number of studies[19] amply illustrate that neither judgment nor predictive devices nor a combination of both can predict with any degree of accuracy. Because of the statistical problem of predicting the rare event, the usual outcome of such efforts is the designation as dangerous a rather large group, most of whom are nonviolent. In our democratic society we usually come to some point where we reaffirm that it is unfair to punish an individual for what he *might* do rather than for what he has done.

Impossible Demands on Corrections

What is only beginning to become clear is that punishment should be recognized as the basic rationale for incarceration. However, the matter is not that simple and never has been. As Milton Rector pointed out a number of years ago, four main themes can be discerned in present day corrections:

(1) the aim of punishment . . . retribution for the crime;

(2) the aim is deterrence—to teach the offender not to repeat and to teach others not to follow his example;

(3) the aim is rehabilitation (whether by punishment or other treatment) and, in the meantime, the protection of society from the danger the offender presents;

(4) the aim is vengeance.[20]

Part of the difficulty confronting both prison officials and the judges and parole board working with them was the attempt to meet all of these demands simultaneously. When the treatment approach was in its ascendancy (more recently "reintegration" has become a more acceptable catch word that "rehabilitation")[21] no one dared mention punishment.[22] While it seems healthy to acknowledge that punishment is a central factor in sending people to prison[23] it is quite another thing to suggest that prison programs be abolished and that prison be reserved for punishment alone.

But what about deterrence? Deterrence is currently being given great weight in the discussion of what kinds of penalties should be imposed. Carlson[24] urged criminal justice personnel to admit that one of the real purposes of prison is deterrence. Others, including Zimring,[25] recognize the deterrent effects of the imposition of punishment but note that the extent of influence is unknown. However, there is almost no evidence that the length of prison sentence (severity of punishment) is in any way related to the deterrent effect.[26] In the words of Leslie Wilkins, " . . . the pressures to be offset are not invariant"[27]—namely that if some punishment deters it does not necessarily follow that twice that amount will have double the effect or even any greater effect, at all. All of which suggests that public policy may be based upon assumptions without strong supportive evidence.

Differing Models for Determinate Sentencing

Perhaps one of strongest statements favoring the determinate sentencing is that of Fogel in his "justice model."[28] He feels that the penal sanction should *only* mean a temporary deprivation of liberty and that it should be experienced justly, reasonably and constitutionally. Within this model therapeutic treatment programs would not be eliminated but would be participated in on a voluntary basis.

These views are strongly supported by Wilson:

> . . . suppose we abandon entirely the rehabilitation theory of sentencing and corrections—not the effort to rehabilitate, just the theory that the governing purpose of the enterprise is to rehabilitate . . . we would view the correctional system—namely, to isolate and to punish. It is a measure of our confusion that such a statement will strike many enlightened readers today as cruel, even barbaric. It is not. It is merely a recognition that society must impose some costs . . . on criminal acts . . .[29]

There continues to be confusion about exactly how flat sentencing would operate. Fogel and McGee note the varieties of indeterminate sentencing with some states allowing judges to fix sentences between legislatively established limits, some using the judges to set the length of incarceration with the parole board given the authority to make modifications, while others placed almost the entire responsibility on paroling authorities, falling just short of the application of a fully indeterminate model.[30] Similarly the newly adopted statutes and proposed legislation for determinate sentencing fall far short of the certain impositions of exact, fixed sentences. The study of the Council of State Governments on definite sentencing[31] examined the developing programs in four states—California, Illinois, Maine, and Minnesota, noted that sentencing discretion is divided in the new systems between judges and parole boards within minimums and maximums legislatively defined. Similarly they prefer the term "definite" since the judge sets a *definite term of imprisonment* from a range established by legislative action. The study found the four states considering definite sentencing for varying reasons. Some felt the need for reducing sentencing disparity while other states seemed to be reacting to alleged capriciousness of parole boards. As noted earlier, critics felt that parole board decision-making took place without regard to human dignity, was based on limited information, was guided by ill defined procedures, was marked by unpredictability and provided no means for redress because of a lack of accountability. Other states felt that predictability of length of prison stay was essential if the bitterness of inmates was to be reduced sufficiently to avoid prison riots and other outburss of violence.

Let us look for a moment at some of the underlying assumptions associated with the determinate, or definite, sentencing approach. Based on the classical view of man such as that of Beccaria,[32] "let the punishment fit the crime" there is the assumption that man is a rational being and crime is a volitional act.[33] If this be so then it follows that individuals will behave in a manner to avoid punishment. But the punishment should be only as severe as necessary to achieve that end for anything beyond that would be vindictive and cruel. The imposition of punishment then is to deter both the individual and those who might consider committing a similar offense. While the authors of the Council of State Governments report contend that the deterrence effects are minimized by the advocates of determinate sentencing, it seems obvious that such views have a great deal of appeal to the public and will be used politically to "sell" the concept.

Similarly the Twentieth Century Fund Task Force on Sentencing report assumes deterrence by such statements as,

> . . . the ineffectiveness of today's sentencing system in conveying the message that violations of the criminal law will be punished, thus weakening the deterrent value of prison sentences.[34]

That report rejects the flat-time approach as going too far by eliminating all flexibility.[35]

The concept of a mandatory minimum sentence is also viewed with disfavor based on much the same reasoning. As a substitute "mandatory sentencing" is presented for selected offenses with the length of incarceration set by the nature of the offense as in any other case.

The plan presented by this group, called "presumptive sentencing" is nearly indistinguishable from "definite sentencing." Guidelines would be set by legislative action and judges would give the "presumptive sentence"—the usual punishment for the usual offense. Extent of deviation from this would be within narrowly defined limits and would require justification of mitigating, or aggravating factors, such as extent of culpability or other extenuating circumstances.

A reduction in length of prison terms is also advocated on the basis that the *fact* of incarceration is probably as effective in terms of punishment as length of incarceration.

The Values of Determinate Sentencing

It seems likely that some of the less desirable features of the procedures associated with the indeterminate sentencing system will be improved by the determinate sentencing approach. There should be, for example, somewhat greater *predictability* — an increase in certainty on the part of both the offender and the public. *Accountability* will be enhanced inasmuch as marked deviations from expected sentences can be clearly seen and the decision-maker required to justify the basis for the sentence given. Those most affected by process, the offenders, should view the system as providing more equitable *justice* in that the basis for decision-making will be more nearly explicit. The certainty of sentences will be greeted with enthusiasm by law enforcement personnel and prosecutors. Further, the public will believe that crime is being controlled by sure and just punishment.

Dangers, Drawbacks and Deficiencies of the Fixed Time Approach to Sentencing

Most writers have been so busy extolling the great gains to be anticipated as a result of determinate sentencing approaches that possible shortcomings are seldom discussed.[36]

First there is the matter of deterrence. While the report from the Council of State Governments suggests that proponents do not stress this aspect, "The rhetoric . . . appears to be more modest and restrained compared to the optimistic expectation of the indefinite sentence as it has developed. . ."[37] there seems to be strong belief on the part of the public that flat sentences will cause people to avoid becoming involved in criminal behavior. Zimring, who has studied the matter of deterrence extensively notes:

> . . . the nature of evidence which is available for study . . . is ambiguous and susceptible of various interpretations, there are also bodies of evidence which move observers to two clearly antithetical conclusions.[38]

Thus, there is little evidence that the manner in which the criminal justice system operates exercises any sort of consistent or measurable deterrent effect, whether sentences to prison are indeterminate or definite. As a justification, then, deterrence has little value in the argument.

How about the equity of punishment? Here we see considerable confusion. First the public gains a sense of security because of a belief that by a system of fixed sentences every offender will receive equal punishment. It simply does not nor will not happen that way. The changes affect only that portion of the cases *sentenced to prison*. While the percentage varies from jurisdiction to jurisdiction most offenders convicted of serious felony crimes are not sent to prison. Illustrative of this is the report of Dershowitz[39] based on a recent study in Ohio noting that some judges made use of a prison disposition four times as often as other judges in the same jurisdiction for similar offenses. McGee similarly notes that sentences to prison are applied to only a small fraction of those involved in crime.[40]

Further confusion ensues, based on the belief that fixed sentences somehow are mandatory. The establishment of mandatory sentences for certain offenses is quite another matter, however, usually enacted only in relation to highly select offenses. Much of the current legislation being considered would eliminate the mandatory aspects of sentencing except in a few isolated instances.

The idea of consistency of sentencing is seriously questioned. Here the assumption is made that if legislative intent is codified in the form of statutes that courts will of necessity carry out that intent in specific action.

The cold facts of the matter are that there are few jurisdictions, if any, that have the statistical data collection capability to determine with any accuracy the current state of affairs. Many individuals who should have been granted lowered sentences based upon mitigating or extenuating circumstances will not be given an opportunity to explore these possibilities. Others who should have been given longer sentences may not have received such additional time because of the pressure of crowded court calendars. Who is to know? Even with the limited discretionary power extended to the court under definite sentencing there can be inadvertent abuse unless actions are closely monitored. However, such monitoring is extremely difficult considering the usually wide geographical distribution of the court system and the reluctance of most courts to subject themselves to accountability to anyone.[41]

A significant consideration, however, is the placement in the hands of the legislature the responsibility for developing a set of standards that will define not only the penalties but each and every kind of mitigating or aggravating factor. Beyond this are the many matters of plea bargaining, prior offenses, concurrent and consecutive sentences plus the motivation of the individual. It might be analogous to asking for legislative action to establish truck rates or the price of farm produce. It is unreasonable to expect any legislation to be enacted that can serve well all segments of society during a period of rapidly changing conditions and values. Dershowitz recognizes this point, but discounts it.[42] The legislation enacted in California in 1977 has undergone constant revision. In the process of dealing with these political pressures the tendency is often to attempt to control crime by the imposition of stiffer penalties. While there has been a suggestion that in the past shorter prison sentences have been associated with definite sentencing procedures,[43] other studies support the notion that legislators, especially freshmen legislators, work toward increasing prison terms.[44]

What happens when these "corrective" actions are taken when the definite sentencing procedures are in operation? Estimates suggest that the prison population would skyrocket and the cost to the state to deal with the larger number of inmates would require a very large budget increase. Yet there is no indication that the increase in length of prison stay in any way effects subsequent behavior.[45] Thus, despite the hopeful view of Fogel, ". . . we believe that knowledge in this case *can* guide a legislature,"[46] the process must be viewed with grave caution. While the initial legislation may achieve a balance of sentences among offenses and offenders, subsequent adjustments are sure to create inequalities, negating the positive aspects of the definite sentencing approach so conscientiously sought.

A Modified Procedure

While several alternative approaches have been developed[47] what is presented here is believed to be a better way to achieve the desired goals of justice, certainty, fairness, balance among offenses, consistency and account-ability in sentencing.

The compromise model would incorporate features of the definite sentence approach but would also retain the flexibility of the indeterminate sentencing system. Under the suggested approach, legislation would be required to provide the philosophical base for operation plus requiring the parole board to adopt regulations and operating procedures to place that philosophy into operation. Within this framework the paroling authority could outline suggested rules and regulations and conduct public hearings before adoption of any procedures. Given this structure, the details of how long a prison stay should be imposed for a first time armed robbery as compared to a second time unarmed burglar could be established. Such an effort seems much more appropriately managed at an administrative level than at a legislative level, for details will obviously require adjustment as the program is tried out in practice. Some individuals have dubbed this model the "public utilities model"[48] because of its seeming parallel to how charges for gas and electricity would be arrived at in an idealized society. The other feature that suggests a similarity is the possibility of modification in response to public pressures. If after a year's trial it became apparent that the public, law enforcement, court personnel, correctional officials and ex-offenders felt that assault upon a child, for example, should be punished more severely than armed burglarly when in the past it might have been viewed as of equal seriousness, changes could be achieved without disrupting the total system in that balance among offenses could be maintained by minor shifts in regulations. Under the determinate model all changes would have to undergo the full legislative process. The tendency is to deal with each offense separately. Should this occur, the relationships among offenses in terms of severity of sanction would be destroyed. The alternative would be to pass a revised penal code each year — a process so cumbersome as to be beyond reasonable expectations.

Relationships similar to that suggested between legislatures and parole boards exist in a variety of areas. Congress, for example, enacts laws regarding health, welfare, and education. Included in the law is the requirement that the appropriate agency develop the specific regulations guiding the direct application of the laws.

The guidelines, recommendations and procedures developed within the limits established by the legislature (which should also encode philosophy and policy), should be quite specific so that all reasonable individuals can grasp their meaning and so that the procedures can be easily applied. With such carefully defined guidelines all concerned can see how much time is added for prior criminal behavior, how much is added for consecutive sentences and how much should be deducted because of reduced culpability. Specificity to this level is essential to insure accountability. If more than the specified time is added in a category, the decision maker can be called upon to explain the basis for the deviation. If the reasons presented are not adequate, the condition can be readily corrected by an internal appeals procedure. If such a correction is not forthcoming there is an identifiable set of facts upon which a judicial appeal can be based. Here the contrast with the old, uncontrolled indeterminate approach is most evident. Earlier an inmate might feel that he had received a disproportionately long sentence but had a difficult time in finding a basis for challenging the outcome, for the parole board could always say that the decision was based on a totality of the factors considered.

Clear depiction of each aggravating or mitigating factor also serves to permit total accountability. It is one thing to issue a policy but quite another to be certain that the implementation is in accord with expectations. Accountability is an essential element of any satisfactory system. With a group as small as a parole board, it is possible to establish statistical reporting procedures that can provide a monthly analysis of the extent to which the group is conforming to set procedures.[49] Of equal importance, deviations and the extent of variance can be easily discerned, including any individual departure from the rules. Lack of adherence can arise for a number of reasons in addition to a tendency to maintain a high degree of discretion—lack of understanding of rules, simple clerical and mathematical errors and inappropriateness of the procedure. But a clear identification of deviance can lead to correction. As noted earlier, if the fixed sentence is adopted and judges determine the mitigating and aggravating factors, the possibility of ascertaining to what extent the law is actually implemented would be extremely difficult. One court might be encouraging the consideration of mitigating factors while another may look only for aggravating aspects of the offense or in the offender's history. A legalistic review might well show that both are operating quite legitimately within the fixed sentencing law but in reality exercising considerable discretion with a resultant inconsistency in length of prison incarceration—an inconsistency unlikely to be revealed in the ordinary course of events.

What about the uncertainty on the part of inmates? With minor modifications in the law to eliminate the dependence on rehabilitation as a basis for release consideration, the determination of the period of incarceration can take place within a few weeks after induction into the prison system. This procedure not only alleviates the anxiety and uncertainty of the inmate, it also removes the calculation of time to be served from the emotionally laden court scene with its adversary proceedings. In the calmer setting of the board hearing where the inmate no longer has to avoid revealing his guilt, issues can be objectively discussed.

Can such a system really work? Both the U.S. Parole Board and Oregon operate under a similar system. One such model, in most of its essential details, was tried in California from February 1975 through March 1976. Based on carefully prepared statistical data, a system was developed under the leadership of the then Chairman of the Adult Authority, Raymond Procunier. Designed to establish release dates early and with understandable certainty it was planned to be accomplished without significant increases or decreases in length of incarceration as compared to a previous four year based period.

Although over thirty decision makers were involved, an amazing degree of consistency was attained within a three or four month period because feedback results were provided each month on a timely basis. Where deviation occurred it was usually because of a misunderstanding of the policy. On one or two occasions, however, when a large segment of the group were off target in a consistent direction , it became apparent that the procedures were in need of modification.

A general description of the system is provided elsewhere[50] as well as a discussion of the value and impact of statistical feedback.[51]

As outlined thus far this suggested solution sounds very much like the determinate sentence approach. The difference lies in the flexibility with which the additive factors can be adjusted and the fact that not *all* individuals have to be forced into the same mold. Those seen as seriously emotionally disturbed or unusually vicious can be dealt with administratively and retained in the institution until some change can be observed. When the condition of concern is ameliorated, the individual can be shifted back into the determinate mode. Under the totally definite sentence system an individual at time of release may be observed to be dangerously disturbed or potentially homicidal but must be released according to a sentence imposed years before, assuming a not too serious commitment offense. It is felt that the public will have little patience with the new law after a few such individuals are precipitously released back into society.

Alan Dershowitz in an often quoted statement outlines the gains to be realized and the limitations of the determinate sentencing approach:

> In the end, neither this nor any other solution to the sentencing dilemma will prove to be a panacea. Discretion and disparity will not be eliminated. Police will still decide whom to arrest, prosecutors will still engage in plea bargaining and governors will still pardon and commute. But a major source of unfairness will be regulated.[52]
>
> The question must be raised, however, if the locking of detailed sentences into the concrete of legislated statutes may not create problems greater than those for which the cure is being designed—especially when the less drastic measures proposed in this section have demonstrated the capability of achieving most of the same objectives with greater effectiveness.

Summary

In this chapter the matter of the determinate/indeterminate prison sentencing controversy has been discussed. Historical shifts of prison philosophy have been explored as they relate to the present day confusion. The shift from rehabilitation toward punishment was noted and interrelated with the disenchantment with treatment programs. Another basis for the dissatisfaction with the indeterminate approach to establishing length of prison incarceration has been the abuses of discretionary powers of the parole boards. The value and gains to be derived from the court setting definite sentences were pointed out along the dangers of the systems being proposed or adopted. A middle-ground approach has been presented that would deliver the advantages of the fixed sentence program without a total loss of flexibility of the indeterminate system that was once seen as having great value. The advantages of the proposed procedures become even more pronounced when compared against the serious dangers anticipated by the determinated sentence approach—a cure that may cause more problems that the evils it was designed to eradicate.

Discussion Questions

1. Outline how serving time under the determinate sentence system will affect the motivation of inmates to participate in treatment or training programs.

2. Describe why it would be difficult to control discrepancies in sentencing under a determinate sentencing approach.

3. Discuss the values to be gained from a determinate procedure for establishing sentence length.

4. Give your reaction to the phrase, "To provide equal justice, unequal sentences sometimes must be imposed."

Notes

1. Alan Dershowitz. "Criminal Sentencing in the Unites States: A Historical and Conceptual Overview" *Annual of the American Academy of Political and Social Science,* 423 (1976): 117–132.

2. E.C. Wines (Ed.), *Transactions of the National Congress on Prisons and Reformatory Discipline* (Albany, N.Y.: Weeds, Parsons & Co. 1871; reprinted by the American Correctional Association, 1970).

3. James Q. Wilson, *Thinking About Crime* (New York: Basic Books, Inc., 1975) p. 164.

4. Ibid, p. 178.

5. David Fogel, *". . . We Are the Living Proof," The Justice Model of Corrections* (Cincinnati: Anderson, 1975).

6. Albert Cohn, George Cole and Robert Bailey (eds.) *Prison Violence* (Lexington, Mass.: Heath & Co., 1976); John Irwin, *The Felon* (Englewood Cliffs, N.J.: Prentice Hall, 1970); A. Nassi "Therapy of the Absurd: A Study of Punishment and Treatment in California Prisons and the Roles of Psychiatrists and Psychologists," *Corrective and Social Psychiatry,* 21 (1975): 21–27; Harold Ransford, "Attitudes and Participation in the Watts Riot" in Edward Margargee and John Hokanson (Eds.) *The Dynamics of Aggression* (New York: Harper & Row, 1970).

7. Kenneth Davis, *Discretionary Justice* (Shreveport, La: Louisiana State University Press, 1969) p. 126.

8. See, for example, *People ex rel. Slofsky vs. Agnew,* 326 NYS 2nd 477–1971 cited in Vincent O'Leary and Jane Nuffield, "A national survey of parole decision-making," *Crime and Delinquency,* 19 (1973): 178–383.

9. John Conrad, "Citizens and Criminals," (paper presented at the Western Division of the American Society of Criminology, February 1976) as well as Davis; Irwin; and Nassi.

10. Philip Selznick, "Justice is Therapy" in Eliot Studt, Saul Musinger and Tom Wilson, *C-Unit: Search for Community in Prison* (New York: Russell Sage, 1968).

11. Daniel Glaser, *Strategic Criminal Justice Planning,* (Rockville, Maryland: National Institute of Mental Health, Center for Studies of Crime and Delinquency, 1975).

12. Robert Hosford and C. Scott Moss (Eds.), *The Crumbling Walls—Treatment and Counseling of Prisoners* (Chicago: University of Chicago Press, 1975).

13. Douglas Lipton, Robert Martinson and Judith Wilks, *The Effectiveness of Correctional Treatment—A Survey of Treatment Evaluation Studies* (New York: Praeger, 1975).

14. James Robison and Gerald Smith, "The Effectiveness of Correctional Programs, *Crime and Delinquency,* 17 (1971): 67–72.

15. La Mar Empey, Book Review of *Effectiveness of Corrections Treatment in Contemporary Sociology: A Journal of Reviews* 8 (1976): 582–583.

16. Dean Babst, James Inciardi and Dorothy Jaman, "The Use of Configural Analysis in Parole Prediction Research," *Canadian Journal of Criminology and Corrections,* 13 (1971): 1–9.

17. Robison and Smith.

18. See *Uniform Parole Reports* (Davis, California: NCCD Research Center, 1955).

19. Ernst Wenk and James Robison, *Assaultive Experience and Assaultive Potential,* (Davis, California: NCCD Research Center, 1971); Ernst Wenk, James Robison and Gerald Smith, "Can Violence be Predicted?" *Crime and Delinquency,* 18 (1972): 393–397.

20. Milton Rector, "Corrections: Punishment or Treatment?" (Paper presented at Corrections Institute, University of Southern California, Los Angeles, February 1963) p. 3.

21. Robert Culbertson, "Punishment vs. Rehabilitation: A Case for the Reintegration Model," (Paper presented at the Annual Meeting of the Academy of Criminal Justice Sciences, San Mateo, California, March 1977).

22. Ernest van den Haag, *Punishing Criminals* (New York: Basic Books, 1975) and von Hirsch.

23. See, for example, James Q. Wilson.

24. Norman Carlson, "Search for the Role of Prisons" address at the dedication of the Federal Youth Center, Miami, Florida, March 26, 1976, noted in *Delinquency and Rehabilitation Report,* May 1976.

25. Frank Zimring, "The Medium is the Message," *Journal of Legal Studies,* 1 (1972): 97–123.

26. Robert Lamson, Carol Crowther, Betty Stacy and Veronica Crump, *Crime and Penalties in California,* Assembly Office of Research, Sacramento, California, 1968; even in the case of the ultimate punishment, execution, clear deterrent effects are not clearly in evidence—Ezzat Fattah, "The Deterrent Effect of Capital Punishment: The Canadian Experience," in Edward Sagarin and Donald MacNamara (Eds.) *Corrections: Problems of Punishment and Rehabilitation* (New York: Praeger, 1973): 106–109.

27. Leslie Wilkins, *Social Deviance* (Englewood Cliffs, N.J.: Prentice Hall, 1964) p. 118.

28. David Fogel, *". . . We Are the Living Proof," The Justice Model of Corrections* (Cincinnati: Anderson, 1975).

29. Wilson, pp. 172–173.

30. Richard A. McGee, "A New Look at Sentencing," *Federal Probation,* June and September, 1974.

31. Foster, *et al.*

32. Cesare Beccaria, *On Crime and Punishment* (Reissued, Indianapolis, Indiana: Bobbs-Merrill, 1963); Elis Monachesi, "Cesare Beccaria" in Hermann Mannhein (Ed.), *Pioneers in Criminology,* (London: Stevens and Sons, 1960).

33. John Bowring, *The Works of Jeremy Bentham* (New York: Russell and Russell, 1843).

34. *Fair and Certain Punishment,* pp. 6–7.

35. Ibid, p. 39.

36. See, for example, David Fogel, *Flat-Time Prison Sentences—A Proposal for Swift, Certain, and Even-Handed Justice* (Chicago: Illinois Law Enforcement Commission, 1975).

37. *Fair and Certain Punishment,* p. 38.

38. Frank Zimring and Gordon Hawkins, *"Deterrence—The Legal Threat in Crime Control"* (Chicago: Univeristy of Chicago Press, 1973) p. 3.

39. Alan Dershowitz, "Let the Punishment Fit the Crime," *New York Times Magazine,* December 28, 1975, and Cy Shain, "The Indeterminate Sentence Concept: A Reexamination of the Theory and Practice," *Resource Series No. 12 Journal* (Tokyo, Japan: United Nations Asia and Far East Institute, October, 1976).

40. McGee.

41. See, for example, Gerald Robin, "Judicial Resistance to Sentence Accountability," *Crime and Delinquency,* 21 (1975): 201–203.

42. Dershowitz, "Let the Punishment Fit the Crime."

43. Sol Rubin, "Long Prison Terms and the Form of Sentence," *National Probation and Parole Journal* 2 (1956): 344–347.

44. Lamson, *et al.*

45. Lamson, *et al.,* Lawrence A. Bennett, "The Psychological Effects of Long Term Confinement," *Proceedings, Third National Symposium of Law Enforcement Science and Technology* (Chicago: ITT, 1970), Dorothy Jaman, Robert Dickover and Lawrence Bennett, "Parole Outcome as a Function of Time Served," *British Journal of Corrections* 49 (1972): 5–34.

46. Fogel, *. . . We Are The Living Proof,"* p. 259.

47. McGee, "A New Look at Sentencing"; John Conrad, "Citizen and Criminals: Model-Changing Instead of People-Changing," paper presented at the Western Division of American Society of Criminology, San Diego, California, February 1976; Jack Foster and David Ashley, "A Social Contract Approach to Sentencing," paper presented at the Annual Meeting of the Academy of Criminal Justice Sciences, San Mateo, California, March 1977.

48. I am indebted to James W.L. Park, Assistant Deputy Director for Planning, California Department of Corrections for suggesting this title.

49. Lawrence Bennett, "Evaluation, Feedback, and Policy," paper presented at the National Conference on Criminal Justice Evaluation, Washington, D.C., February 1977.

50. Lawrence Bennett, "California Parole," *Parole Bulletin,* 1 (1976): 3–11.

51. Bennett, "Evaluation, Feedback, and Policy."

52. Dersowitz, "Let the Punishment Fit the Crime," p. 27.

4

Plea-Bargaining in Some of the Largest Cities in the United States

RAY H. WILLIAMS

Introduction

FROM TIME TO TIME AN INVESTIGATION MUST BE MADE into the social institutions of America to determine if they are working, if they still exist and if they are in need of repair. This article reports upon a study and review of pertinent literature that was made concerning the effect that "Plea-bargaining" has had upon the constitutional right to a trial-by-jury for those accused of crimes. What is Plea-bargaining?

> It is the process of disposing of a criminal prosecution without a trial. The accused through negotiations with the prosecutor and sometimes the court agree upon the amount of punishment that he will take in consideration for his plea of guilty. As a result of the agreement or bargain, the accused is required to waive his constitutional right to a trial-by-jury.

It was found that out of slightly over 100,000 felony prosecutions that were started in 1975, in the responding jurisdictions, that there were 7,783 trials or only 7% of those persons charged with crimes received trials. Based upon the study including the literature review, it seems that career criminals commit multiple crimes and by virtue of the plea-bargaining process plead guilty to all but only pay a penalty for one. Through the dropping of charges by the prosecutor, as a concession for the guilty plea, the criminal is able to reduce the measure of his punishment.

The results of the study and the literature reviewed over all indicate that the criminal justice system is evaporating under the heat of heavy caseloads into a sick non-system that seems to encourage and promote lawlessness. Doses of Plea-bargaining are used as the primary medicine for the cure. However, the medicine actually spreads the disease. As an urban resident with two decades of practice in the criminal justice system, I am very concerned about the deterioration of the system, and the errosion of constitutional rights.

Over the Summer and part of the Fall, 1976, a study among one-hundred prosecuting officials in the largest cities, by population, in the United States, was conducted to determine: if there is uniformity in the plea-bargaining process; how plea-bargaining is defined from jurisdiction to jurisdiction; the number and percentage of felony cases disposed of by this process as opposed to dispositions by trial for 1975, in each jurisdiction; what roles are played by the prosecutor, the defense lawyer, the judge and the accused in the plea-bargain process; and should a national conference be convened to discuss and/or resolve the many constitutional issues that have been raised by the plea-bargain process.

The questions posed in the study questionnaire resulted from a review of pertinent literature on plea-bargaining; discussions with a jury of criminal justice practitioners and my own twenty years of experience as a practitioner in the criminal justice system.

The results of the study coupled with the literature review on the subject of plea-bargaining gives strong evidence from which an inference can be drawn that the quality of criminal justice court services have diminished in the urban centers of America. This must be changed. The need for practicing plea-bargaining, the reduction of caseloads, causes criminal justice practitioners, including the courts, to take an ambivalent attitude toward its practice. Moreover, the practice causes the urban dweller to be continually victimized by recidivists who when caught, are able to negotiate for their freedom. Plea-bargaining must be considered as a factor in making the urban resident feel that laws are inequitably administered and that the assertion of constitutional rights—in the courts—are not effectual.

What follows is a presentation of plea-bargaining and the facts thereon in a concise manner. The problem, issues and concerns raised must be recognized by every citizen, but more particularly, the duty of salvation rests entirely upon the governmental structure of America. It is noteworthy at this point, however, to say that 73% of the respondents to the study questionnaire want a national conference convened to discuss and solve the concerns that plea-bargaining has caused.

Discussion: Plea-Bargaining

The United States Constitution commands that in all criminal prosecutions, the accused shall enjoy the right to a speedy and public trial, by an impartial jury,[1] and that the accused cannot be compelled in any criminal case to be a witness against himself.[2] Moreover, the Fifth and Fourteenth Amendments forbid both the Government and the States from depriving any person of life, liberty or property without due process of law. Trial-by-jury is the method by which the founding fathers of America felt guilt or innocence should be decided—trial is the fountain-head of due process of law.

Yet, the study results and literature review show that the "trial" as a method of determining guilt or innocence in criminal prosecutions has all but disappeared. It seems that the accused not only picks his crime but the punishment as well, that the prosecuting attorney and defense attorney are no longer adversaries, but are negotiators and that the judge's duties have been reduced to a mere recorder of the negotiated plea. This process called plea-bargaining, is supposedly for the sake of reducing prosecutorial and court caseloads. But in fact the plea-bargaining process has destroyed the dignified roles of participants: the prosecutor, the lawyer and the judge. Invariably the rights of the accused are abridged and the rights of the victim are completely forgotten. According to the study, the process has detrimentally and destructively metastasized throughout the entire body of the Criminal Justice System in America leaving the citizen with constitutional rights but with no healthy method of asserting the same.

As demonstrated by the study findings 106,841 prosecutions were started in the responding jurisdictions in 1975. Of that number only 7% were disposed of by trial. Less than 10% were disposed of by dismissal. Slightly less than 60% of the total number of prosecutions that were started were disposed of by guilty pleas (plea-bargain). But slightly more than 20% (or, 27,463 cases) were unaccounted for or undisposed of at the close of 1975. These cases were probably carried over into the next year. It follows that of the felony prosecutions that were started in 1975 and disposed of in 1975, that better than 80% of the cases were disposed of by pleas of guilty or the plea-bargaining process. It further appears that there is no uniformity in the plea-bargaining process and many prosecutors and judges disclaim aggressive participation in it, or to say the least, their roles are confusing; further there is no standard definition for it, nor is there a standard method of practicing it. For instance, composite answers and random excerpts to responses to the study quesionnaire show:

> This jurisdiction does not have a definition for plea-bargaining; there is no formal definition; it has no statutory definition; it is a process of give and take; it is called plea-negotiation: it is called plea agreement; it varies from court to court and prosecutor to prosecutor; and this jurisdiction no longer participates in plea-bargaining.

And,
> Usually, the defense counsel initiates the discussions. Either the prosecutor or defense counsel will initiate the discussions.

And,
> Judges ordinarily remain aloof from plea-bargaining. The Judge plays no role whatsoever. Some judges willingly become a party to the negotiations.

Under the law, however no disclaimer on the part of prosecutors or judges can stand. Their roles are clearly defined in the foundations of our law. Heavy caseloads have caused the honorable roles of judges and prosecutors to become obscured. Furthermore, of 1600 felony prosecutions that were started in 1975 in Hartford, Connecticut, only 39 were disposed of by trial which means that only 2.4% of those accused of crimes were able to assert their rights to "trials". In Atlanta, Georgia, there were 6,140 prosecutions started, 541 trials or 8.8% of those accused of crimes were able to assert their rights to trials. In Bridgeport, only 2.8% of those accused were able to receive trials. In Louisville, Kentucky, only 3.6% of those accused were able to have trials. In St. Louis, Missouri, 5,779 prosecutions were started and only 5.9% were able to receive trials. Akron, Ohio started 1,662 prosecutions; there were 78 trials. Tulsa, Oklahoma started 3,087 prosecutions; there were 93 trials, and in Houston, Texas, 15,000 prosecutions were started with 3.3% being disposed of by trial. In Manhattan, New York County, New York, eight courtroom are kept extremely busy trying five percent of the cases.[3] Negotiations between prosecutors and defense counsel have become institutionalized.[4] The attitude of the United States Supreme Court has gone from being solidly for trial-by-jury as the means of disposing of criminal prosecutions,[5] to sanctioning the plea-bargaining process as a necessary evil of an overworked court.[6] The Court in announcing sanction of the plea-bargaining process said:

"Properly administered, it is to be encouraged . . ." But can plea-bargaining be properly administered? Many knowledgeable commentators think not; they consider the process to be a sham, a charade that rivals the original charge in many instances;[7] that innocent persons find it more to their advantage to plead guilty to get their time in jail awaiting trial declared by the Judge's to be their punishment,[8] that truly guilty persons persuade the prosecutor to press concurrently all charges filed against them so that the sentence on each will run concurrently rather than run consecutively,[9] that the legal roles involved change radically as plea-negotiations become institutionalized, that the Judges role has become warped,[10] that the Administration of Justice practitioners have been condemned for not showing courage in the face of the plea-bargining process,[11] that the ambivalence of the Criminal Justice System has likewise been condemned[12] and more shocking, that juveniles are even being encouraged to plead guilty for very much the same reasons as adults.[13]

Plea-bargaining has illegitimately become institutionalized displacing and destroying the constitutional right to trial-by-jury in all criminal prosecutions. Likewise, it has destroyed the justiciable roles of its practitioners. Criminal Justice practitioners must now come together to develop strategies to abolish the plea-bargaining system and resolve to restore trial-by-jury as the only constitutional method of disposing of criminal prosecutions in the United States.

The Supreme Court's reasons for sanctioning the "Plea-bargaining Process" in the *Santabello Case*[14] are not justified and are contrary to the public policy that the Court set a few years earlier in *Duncan v. Louisiana*, 390 U.S. 570, when it clearly encouraged trial-by-jury for all persons accused of serious crimes. But the Court reasoned in *Santabello*:

> . . . The disposition of criminal charges by agreement between the prosecutor and the accused, sometimes loosely called "plea-bargaining", is an essential component of the Administration of Justice. Properly administered, it is to be encouraged. If every criminal charge were subjected to a full-scale trial, the States and the Federal Government would need to multiply by many times the number of judges and trial facilities.

> Disposition of charges after plea discussions is not only an essential part of the process for many reasons. It leads to prompt and largely final dispositions of most criminal cases; it avoids much of the corrosive impact of enforced idleness during pre-trial confinement for those who are denied release pending trial; it protects the public from those accused persons who are prone to repeat criminal conduct even while on pre-trial release; and, by shortening time between charge and dispositions, it enhances whatever may be the rehabilitative prospects of the guilty when they are ultimately imprisoned.

> However, the Court's contention are disputed.

According to the New York Joint Legislative Committee on Crime, headed by Senator John H. Hughes, a report on Plea-bargaining, a few years ago:[15]

> The final climate act in the plea-bargaining procedure is a charade which in itself has asepcts of dishonesty which rival the original crime in many instances. The accused is made to assert publicly his guilt on a specific crime, which in many cases he has not committed, in some cases he pleads guilty to a non-existing crime. He must further indicate that he is entering his plea freely, willingly and voluntarily and that he is not doing so because of any promises or consideration made to him.

The Hughes Committee went on to warn,

> . . . that no program of rehabilitation can be effective on a 'prisoner who is convinced in his own mind that he is in prison because he is the victim of a mindless, undirected and corrupt system of justice.

Moreover, the role of judge in the plea-bargaining procedure has gone to something less than honorable, and Richard Quinney in *Criminal Justice in America*, reports:

> The Judge's role becomes warped as well. Despite the structures of the due process rules, the judges are completely aware that the pleas which

are solemnly asserted by defendants to be free and voluntary, made without coercion or promise of benefit, are almost invariably the result of a bargain struck in the hallway. In fact, sometimes one sees a judge solemnly approving a defendant's statement that his plea was not induced by threat or promise, when the plea-bargain was actually struck in the Judge's chambers![16]

When more than 80% and as high as 95% of those persons who are accused of crimes cannot have trials and are required to plea guilty, it follows that the honorable roles of functionaries of the justice system (i.e., judge, prosecutor, defense attorney) have diminished as upholders of constitutional values to roles abhorent to the constitution. Under the plea-bargain system they must do that which is forbidden by the constitution to wit, "encourage", "cajole", and "coerce" the accused into pleading guilty. Moreover, it would seem that the high rate of guilty pleas negates the idea that defendant's "waiver" of the right to a trial-by-jury is a voluntary act free from coercion. In fact, the practitioners of the system make a concerted effort to reduce caseloads by getting the accused to "cop-a-plea."

". . . We are running a machine", a Los Angeles trial assistant declares, "We know we have to grind them out fast". An Assistant States' Attorney in Chicago notes that there are more than 2,500 indictments currently pending in Cook County Circuit Court, the greatest number in history. He says, *"I'll do anything to the backlog."* A Houston trial assistant observes, "We moved more than 2,000 cases through six courts during the past three months; clearly the most important part of our job lies in making defendants think they are getting a good deal". A Manhattan (New York County, New York) prosecutor says, "our office keeps eight courtrooms extremely busy trying five percent of the cases. If even ten percent of the cases ended in a trial, the system would break down, [*Emphasis Added*]. (See footnote 3)

This might be effective in reducing caseloads, but it is most ineffectual in promoting constitutional values. When only a small percentage of persons accused of crimes (2.4% in Hartford, Conn.; 3.6% in Louisville, Ky.; 5.9% in St. Louis, Missouri; 4.3% in San Francisco, California) can receive trials because the Criminal Justice System would collapse if as many as 10% (according to a New York County Prosecutor a few years ago) had trials, then it is time to completely review the Criminal Justice System in America, and make the necessary repairs. Quite to the contrary of what the Supreme Court has said:

. . . it (plea-bargaining) avoids much of the corrosive impact of enforced idleness during pre-trial confinement for those who are denied release pending trial . . . it protects the public from those accused persons who are prone to continue criminal conduct even while on pretrial release; . . .[17]

For example, see Louis L. Knowles and Kenneth Prewitt, "Racism in the Administration of Justice" *Institutional Racism In America* at 72 (paperback edition) and on plea-bargaining generally from a Black perspective, Alex Swan, "Police Discretion, Public Defenders, Plea Bargaining and Black Defendants" The Journal of Afro-American Issues, Vol. II No. 2, May, 1974.

In my many years as a practitioner in the Criminal Justice System, the only persons that are denied release are those that cannot afford bail—the poor. The career criminal and the more affluent citizen are able to provide money for bail and thereby gain their release pending trial.[18] Plea-bargaining has corroded the entire Criminal Justice System in America. It has often made it attractive for innocent persons to plead guilty in order to have the time spent in jail awaiting trial declared as their punishment.[19] Another of the insidious aspects of plea-bargaining is the fact that it actually encourages recidivism and criminality. The career criminal is encouraged to commit more and more crimes because when he is caught he plea-bargains to receive one sentence or punishment for all of the crimes that he committed.[20] As a result, the law abiding citizen in the inner-city is left as repeat prey for a very small percentage of lawless individuals. Most crimes of violence are committed by a Black perpetrator on a Black victim in the inner-city.[21]

Moreover, juvenile offenders commit more and more muggings, burglaries and other violent crimes unabated by the non-system that our Administration of Justice System has become. And they too, are now even allowed to plea-bargain away responsibility for lawless conduct.[22] Needless to say, that the American social institution trial-by-jury for criminal prosecutions must be restored. A person can only be deterred from his criminal acts when he knows from the start that he will receive punishment for that criminal act. In other words, criminality can only be lessened if the career criminal receives his full measure of punishment instead of the part measure that he now receives under the plea-bargaining system. The poor Black law abiding citizen in the inner-city has a right with all other citizens to expect that the criminal laws will be administered by a set of rules that will discourage criminality instead of encouraging it as the plea-bargaining method of administering justice, in a very flexible way, now does. Flexibility is a necessary factor in a lawless society.[23] Justice can only occur, however, when it is administered through a fixed set of rules by concerned trained administrators. But more, the judicial branch of our government must arise again as an equal partner with the legislative and executive branches. If support from the executive branch and legislative action with sufficient financial appropriations are necessary, then our leaders must muster the courage to accomplish the task of restoring the proper partnership balance; to do less is to render one of the checks in the American governance balance a nullity.

What has been said here is not intended to give an iota of support to those who advocate doing away with such rehabilitative tools as parole and probation since society has never really substantially supported either with sufficient financial resources. I do intend, however, as a criminal justice practitioner and a citizen to share my concerns, my condemnation of criminal behavior, be it Black or non-Black behavior, and to express my condemnation of the "plea-bargaining process". The process encourages and promotes criminality. Professional criminals know from experience that additional charges are usually dismissed during the plea-bargain process. After an arrest for a crime of which he seems sure to be connected, a confirmed criminal will conclude that he has a license to commit additional offenses while on bond "for free".[24] His free ride must be stopped and his license, plea-bargaining, must be revoked.

There are a number of constitutional issues, questions and concerns raised by the plea-bargaining process. Here are some of them:

> The atmosphere in which the plea-bargaining process takes place is coercive.
>
> The accused right to a trial-by-jury in criminal prosecutions has been gravely impaired by the process.
>
> Does the accused still have a constitutional right to face his accuser?
>
> Is the waiver given by the accused prior to his plea of guilty free and voluntary?
>
> Has the traditional adversary proceeding been lost to plea-bargaining?
>
> Have heavy caseloads resulted in United States Constitutional values being sacrificed to the expedient—plea-bargaining?
>
> Has the role of the prosecutor in disposing of criminal cases changed to that of expeditors of as many cases as possible without just consideration for guilt or innocence of the accused or the rights of its victim?
>
> The career criminal—the multiple offender—benefits from the plea-bargaining system.
>
> Should juveniles be allowed to plea-bargain?
>
> Does the plea-bargain system pressure innocent persons into guilty pleas?
>
> The law abiding citizen is entitled to have the person who commits a crime against him arrested, tried and convicted for the crime that was actually committed—and no lesser crime.
>
> If the judicial branch of the government is to regain its place as an equal partner with the legislative and executive branches, then support from the executive branch and legislative action with sufficient financial appropriations must be given.
>
> Governmental leaders, Administration of Justice practitioners, Educators and Citizens must muster the courage to accomplish the task of restoring

the proper partnership balance; not to act is to render one of the checks (the judiciary) in the American governance balance a nullity.

Plea-bargaining should be abolished.

A conference and an action plan concerning the issues raised by the plea-bargain process is needed. Such a conference on the national level would go a long way toward re-establishing the Criminal Justice System and the judiciary as an equal partner in the governance of the United States.

Discussion Questions

1. Has the accused right to trial-by-jury in criminal prosecutions been gravely impaired?

2. Has the plea-bargaining process nullified the traditional adversary proceeding in criminal cases?

3. Does the multiple offender benefit from the plea-bargain process?

4. Does the plea-bargain process pressure innocent persons into guilty pleas?

5. Should plea-bargaining be abolished? If so, how do we relieve the over-burdened criminal court systems.

Notes

1. Sixth Amendment, United States Constitution

2. Fifth Amendment, United States Constitution

3. An article, written in the latter part of 1968, by Albert W. Alschulert that appeared in the *University of Chicago Law Review* (Vol. 36: 50).

4. Criminal Justice in America, Richard Quinney, Little Brown, p. 224.

5. *Duncan v. Louisiana,* 390 U.S. 570.

6. However, a few years after *Duncan*, plea bargaining seems to have fund sanction by the United States Supreme Court. Mr. Chief Justice Burger spoke for the Court in *Santobello v. New York*, 404 U.S. 257 (1971).

7. *The Law of Corrections and Prisoner Rights*, Shelden Krantz, West Publishing Co. (1973) at page 114 reports; and the author quotes in pertinent part as follows:

The New York Joint Legislative Committee on Crime headed by Senator John H. Hughes described the (plea-bargaining) process:

The final climatic act in the plea bargaining procedure is a charade which in itself has aspects of dishonesty which rival the original crime in many instances. The accused is made to assert publicly his guilt on a specific crime, which in many cases he has not committed; in some cases he pleads guilty to a nonexistent crime. He must further indicate that he is entering his plea freely, willingly, and voluntarily and that he is not doing so because of any promises or consideration made to him.

The Hughes Committee made a study of prisoner attitudes toward plea bargaining at Attica, Greenhaven, and Sing Sing prisons and found that almost 90 percent of the inmates surveyed had been solicited to enter a plea bargain. Most were bitter, believing that they did not receive effective legal representation or that the judge did not keep the state's promise of a sentence which had induced them to enter guilty pleas.

The Hughes Committee warned that no program of rehabilitation can be effective on the "prisoner who is convinced in his own mind that he is in prison because he is the victim of a mindless, undirected, and corrupt system of justice"

8. *Introduction to Administration of Justice*, James F. Adams, Prentice Hall (1975) at page 90.

9. *Justice in America*, Ed, Herbert Jacobs, Little, Brown, (1972) at page 1972.

10. *Criminal Justice in America*, Richard Quinney, Little, Brown (1974), page 245.

11. *The Harvard Law Review*, Vol. 84: 148 (1970), comments upon a series of decisions that the United States Supreme Court rendered in its 1969 term concerning plea bargaining.

12. *The Ambivalent Force*, Neiderhoffer and Blumerg, Rinehart Press (1973) at pages 280 and 281, Blumberg reports:

The overwhelming majority of convictions in criminal cases (usually over 90 percent) are not the product of a combative, trial-by-jury process at all, but instead merely involve the sentencing of the individual after a negotiated, bargained-for plea of guilty has been entered. Although more recently the overzealous role of police and prosecutors in producing pre-trial confessions and admissions has achieved a good deal of notoriety, scant attention has been paid to the organizational structure and personnel of the criminal court itself. Indeed, the extremely high conviction rate produced without the features of an adversary trial in our courts would tend to suggest that the "trial" becomes a perfunctory reiteration and validation of the pre-trial interrogation and investigation.

13. *The Washington Star*, October 26, 1976, wherein Diane Brochett reported:

Defense Attorneys have admitted privately that they sometimes use the backlog situation to free their clients, refusing to plea bargain with prosecutors in anticipation that the court will dismiss the charge if the youngster is kept waiting for trial too long.

But the Backlog also is having the opposite effect. I have plead several kids, one attorney admitted, because I knew I could get them out immediately that way and if we waited for a trial they would be locked up at least six more weeks.

14. Ibid, note 6

15. Ibid, note7

16. Ibid, note 10

17. Ibid, note 10

18. Foote, *Comment on the New York Bail Study—Forward,* 106 U. Pa. L. Rev. 685; In *Brady v. United States*, 82 Justice Douglass, said:

> To continue to demand a substantial bond which the defendant is unable to secure raises considerable problems for unequal administration of the law. We have held that an indigent defendant is denied equal protection of the law if he is denied an appeal on equal terms with other defendants, solely because of his indigence. Can an indigent be denied freedom,

where the wealthy man would not, because he does not happen to have enough property to pledge his freedom.

See also, Gayle C. Williams, "The Bail System: A Rich Man's Tool" *"Balsa Reports,* Spring, 1975, and the authorities therein cited.

19. Ibid, note 8

20. Ibid, note 3

21. President's Commission on Law Enforcement and Administration of Justice, *Task Force Report: Crime and It's Impact* (Washington, D.C. U.S. Gov't. Printing Office 1967); See also, Ramsey Clark, *Crime in America,* Pocket Book, 1971, pp. 34-35; Sue Titus Reid, *Crime and Criminology,* Holt, Rinehard and Wilson 1976, pp. 62-65.

22. Ibid, note 3

23. University of Chicago Law Review, Vol., 36-71

24. Ibid, note 3

5

Making the Offender Pay:
Revitalizing an Ancient Idea

BURT GALAWAY

EVIDENCE FROM ANCIENT LAW SYSTEMS[1] as well as contemporary tribal law[2] indicates that a frequent pattern for dealing with wrongdoing has been to require the offender to redress the harm which was done by making some payment to their victim. Restitution is an ancient idea. But its use in modern criminal justice was largely lost, except as a peripheral condition of probation, until a resurgence of interest in the concept occurred in the 1970's. This chapter will examine some of the forms which modern restitution programming is taking, consider the advantages of this criminal justice practice, and conceptualize some of the issues which require resolution as restitution is further developed and operationalized.

The term restitution is used to refer to a sanction imposed by an authorized official of the criminal justice system in which the offender is required to make a monetary and/or service payment to either the direct victim of the offense or to some substitute victim. This is a broad definition including service as well as monetary payment and provides for restitution to individuals or organizations other than the actual victim of the crime. Restitution, to be consistent with this definition, requires approval of an official of the criminal justice system and this excludes informal settlements which may occur prior to the involvement of the criminal justice system. Many neighborhood disputes and other matters may be quite appropriately settled informally, without necessity for resorting to the criminal justice sanction; repayment may sometimes be made and many of these informal settlements may be considered restitutive sanctions. Suggestions have been made, however, that some types of wealthy and organized offenders may make restitution to buy off victims and avoid prosecution;[3] this latter type of behavior is highly undesirable; this, the definition of restitution is narrowed to exclude settlements made without knowledge of an official of the criminal justice system. The two variables of type of restitution (service or monetary) and type of victim (direct or substitute) permit the development of a restitution typology which emcompasses most of the present restitution practices.

FIGURE I

TYPOLOGY OF RESTITUTION

Recipient of Restitution

Form of	Victim	Community Organization
Restitution Monetary	Type I Monetary-Victim	Type II Monetary-Community
Service	Type III Service-Victim	Type IV Service-Community

Type I restitution consists of monetary payments made by the offender to the direct victim of the crime. This is the most frequent form of restitution and is usually the referent when people initially speak of restitution programming. Type I restitution has apparently been imposed frequently as a probation condition. This practice has also been found in a number of specialized restitution projects including the Minnesota Restitution Center[4] and the Georgia Restitution Shelters.[5] Both of these programs involve adult offenders who live in residential community corrections programs, work in the community, and make payment to the victims of their crimes.

Type II restitution refers to monetary payments made by the offender to some community organization. Both the Georgia and Minnesota restitution programs have reported situations in which victims did not wish to receive restitution, could not be located, or who had not sustained any damages. In some of these situations offenders were required to make restitution payments to a non-profit human service organization. A similar practice can be found in the juvenile and youth courts in West Germany[6] in which one of the corrective sanctions available to courts is to order the young person to make a payment to a charitable community organization. Type II restitution is distinguished from a fine because the monetary payment is made to a charitable organization rather than to a level of government.

Type III restitution occurs when the offender makes a payment in service to the victim of the crime. This type of restitution is undoubtedly used less frequently than other types but a number of interesting examples are occurring in the reports of various restitution programs. The Pilot Alberta Restitution Program described a case situation in which a sixteen year old who had burglarized the home of an elderly woman made partial restitution by shoveling snow from her sidewalks during an Alberta winter.[7] Similar cases are recorded from British Columbia:

> In Nanaimo, boys who were caught vandalizing a mechanic's car at a service station were required to work there, repairing the car and learning the trade. When the work order ended the garage asked to hire the boys as regular employees.
>
> In Prince George some boys broke into an old folks' home. They were required to repair the damage and perform house repairs. After this the elderly people called the boys back in whenever they needed help around the place, and the boys are reported as being well-behaved.[8]

The Victim Offender Restitution Project in Kitchner, Ontario, regularly brings victims and offenders together to work out a reconciliation which frequently takes a pattern of the offender providing a service to the victim.[9] Cases are recorded in which offenders work for businesses which they had victimized, have done home repairs, etc. Probation officers occasionally report, verbally, that they from time to time try out Type III restitution especially with juvenile offenders. Vandalism may be an offense particularly suitable for requiring youth to make amends to the victim by cleaning up the mess caused by the delinquency. To date little systematic recording use has been made of Type III restitution; this is an area which might be very fruitfully explored.

Type IV restitution occurs when the offender is required to make a service payment to the community. This type of restitution appears to be used quite frequently as a condition of probation and in some jurisdictions as an alternative to probation. Special projects can be located in this country in which service requirements are imposed upon misdemeanment offenders,[10] juvenile offenders,[11] and even adult felony offenders.[12] The Community Services Order program in Great Britain is the most widespread and developed example of Type IV restitution. In that program adult offenders are ordered to make from 40 to 240 hours of community service restitution as an alternative to custodial sentences.[13] The program was initially started in 1972 in five probation districts and has now been made available throughout Great Britain.

All four kinds of restitution are being utilized in a variety of settings. Restitution programming has been receiving active support from the Law Enforcement Assistance Administration and is enjoying increasing popularity among criminal justice staff. Reasons for the use of restitution will be discussed followed by analysis of ways in which some practical issues can be resolved as restitution is operationalized in the criminal justice system. Reasons to support increased use of restitution include the need for increased sentencing options which restitution provides, the possibility of restitution resulting in victim offender reconciliation and the opportunity restitution provides for victim involvement in the criminal justice process.

Reasons for Use of Restitution

Restitution will increase sanctioning options. The American criminal justice system is caught in a sanctioning dilemma. The system vacillates between the extremes of failing to impose any meaningful sanction on large numbers of offenders and, alternatively, over punishing a comparatively few. The sanctioning alternatives in use are usually limited to probation and imprisonment. The large majority of convictions lead to a sentence of probation which, in practice, is a fairly meaningless sanction.[14] Usually, offenders report infrequently to a over-worked, allegedly harrassed probation officer who dutifully notes the reporting date in a case record and offers little in the way of supervision, limitation on freedom, or other requirements that might be effectively enforced as a sanction against the offender. At the other extreme, a comparatively small number of convicted persons are sent to prison but, those imprisoned, tend to be sentenced for substantial lenghts of time. Additional sanctioning options are necessary to bridge the gap between these two extremes.

One largely unexplored area is whether there are types of offenses (or offenders) for which restitution might appropriately be the only penalty imposed. Karl Menninger, in arguing *The Crime of Punishment*, suggested, for example, that check offenders were a group of offenders for whom the only necessary action would be an order of restitution which should also include a payment to the state to partially compensate for the cost of apprehending and processing the offender.[15] The British Community Service Orders Program involves the use of Type IV restitution with adult offenders as an alternative to custodial sentences, fines and probation.[16] Jurisdictions within the United States appear reluctant to test the use of restitution as a sole sanction. Recently established programs in Georgia[17] and Oklahoma[18] are moving in this direction; in both states a population of property offenders will make restitution with minimal additional obligations to the criminal justice system.

Restitution can, of course, be combined with other sanctions. The widest application is as a condition of probation; more systematically attaching a restitution requirement to probation would make the probation sanction a more severe, and perhaps appropriate, punishment. The State of Georgia is currently managing four restitution shelters in which residents, most of whom are probationers, are required to reside while working in the community and completing court ordered restitution.[19] Kathleen Smith has developed a proposal in which offenders would pay restitution plus a discretionary fine both of which would be set by the sentencing judge; the offenders would serve a custodial sentence but work at prevailing labor rates. Upon completion of the restitution and fine they would be released from custody.[20]

Restitution might also be used to reduce the severity of penalties imposed against some offenders when the only choice is probation or imprisonment. The Minnesota Restitution Center was developed to test the notion that a group of property offenders could be managed in a residential community corrections center from which they would make restitution as an alternative to prison. While the persons coming into the center did serve significantly less time in prison than a control group, both groups having been randomly selected from a defined population, preliminary follow up of the two groups indicates that the restitution group was subjected to a longer period of state supervision (four months imprisonment, residence in a community corrections center, plus parole supervision) then the control group which experienced imprisonment and parole.[21] Further, members of the restitution group were somewhat more probable of having their parole revoked because of a technical violation.[22] Whether a shorter period of time in prison and a longer period of time on parole is less harsh than a longer period of time in prison and a shorter period of time on parole may be a matter in which individuals disagree; nevertheless restitution made from a community corrections center was substituted for imprisonment for a group of property offenders. Recently this potential role for restitution within the sanctioning system was suggested by Minnesota's leading legislative proponent for determinate sentencing.[23] The likely impact of the determinate sentence on prison population, the resulting need for new construction, and the high cost of new prison construction, lead the legislator, a deputy police chief in a large urban center, to suggested the use of restitution shelters for property offenders as an alternative to imprisonment in order to provide sufficient prison space for offenders who commit crimes of violence without the need to invest substantial capital funds in prison construction.

Restitution offers an additional sanction alternative for the criminal justice system. Restitution can be used solely, can be combined with other sanctions such as probation to make this a more meaningful punishment, and, under some circumstances, might be used as an alternative to harsher sanctions such as imprisonment.

Restitution may lead to victim-offender reconciliation. Restitution, as a punishment, holds considerable potential for the reconciliation of offender and victim. In this sense, restitution punishments will contribute to a more cohesive, integrative society by reducing the sense of separation which the offender may feel and by engaging the offender in socially acceptable behavior which is likely to result in offenders' receiving a higher degree of acceptance from victims and other members of the community.

Dockar-Drysdale has commented on the importance of restitution in assisting disturbed children and making amends for their wrong-doing.[24] Albert Eglash offers creative restitution as a rehabilitative procedure for offenders by providing them with an opportunity to enhance their self-esteem as they engage in restitutive acts.[25] August Aichhorn in his psychoanalytic treatise on the treatment of delinquents, suggests rectification as a disciplinary technique.[26] More recently, R.M. Foxx and N.H. Azzin have developed restitutive procedures, based on learning theory, for the reduction of aggressive and disruptive behavior on the part of retarded and brain damaged patients.[27] The use and importance of restitution in self-help organizations such as Alcoholics Anonymous is well known and has been offered as a useful treatment tool by O.W. Mowrer.[28]

Brickman analyzes procedures for handling rules violators in sporting events vis-a-vis procedures for handling rules violators in criminal proceedings. He suggests the greater use of restitution as a means of dealing with law violators in order to place greater emphasis upon the restoration of fairness and minimizing the disruption of relationships between law violators and the rest of society.[29] Brickman's work draws from equity theory, a social-psychological orientation of particular relevance to the impact which restitution might have as a sanction for offenders.[30] Equity theorists postulate that a sense of social equity existing between offender and victim is upset as a result of wrongdoing. The condition of inequity in the relationship creates distress on the part of both victim and offender. Two type of strategies are available to the offender for reduction of distress. The wrongdoer can reduce distress through the use of justification strategies including derogation of the victim, minimization of the victims suffering, and denial of responsibility for the act. The justification strategies are similar to the neutralization techniques Sykes and Matza theorized are used by delinquent youth to neutralize guilt and shame experienced from wrongdoing; techniques of neutralization include denial of responsibility, denial of injury, and denial of the victims and are rationalizations which follow the delinquent act and protect the youth from self-blame and the condemnation of others.[31] Wrongdoers may also restore equity by conpensating the victim for harm done, i.e., restitution. Restoring the victim through restitution will reduce the offender's need to make use of justification strategies and should reduce the sense of psychological alientation between victim and offender.

The idea that the restitution sanction may result in integration of victims and offenders rests largely on clinical and laboratory evidence and still awaits field testing in the criminal justice system. Theoretical work is sufficiently well developed, however, to suggest that restitution as a sanction may lead to increased integration of victim and offender, victim and community, and offender and community.

Provides for Victim involvement in the Criminal justice system. The crime victim's role in the criminal justice system is largely limited to the decision of whether or not to precipitate the process by reporting the victimization to the police. Apparently large numbers of victims (well over half in many types of crimes) choose not to involve themselves at all.[32] Those victims who do decide to precipitate the system have a very limited role except the occasional giving of evidence or serving as pawns in machinations of the defense or prosecuting attorneys as they attempt to get the victims in or out of the courtroom as is in the best interests of their case.[33]

Proposals have been advanced to give the victim a more meaningful role. Marvin Wolfgang has recommended a system of accountability in which information regarding disposition of a case would be routinely reported back to the victim.[34] LeRoy Schultz advocates the inclusion of information secured from the victim in the presentence investigation report prepared by probation officers.[35] More recently a number of victim assistance programs have been advocated by the National District Attorneys Association and funded by the Law Enforcement Assistance Administration. These programs, however, appear quite varied as to program and aims; programs directed towards providing remedial services to victims seem to be much more acceptable than programs directed towards providing the victim with an opportunity for input into criminal justice decision-making.[36]

The closed nature in which many criminal justice decisions are made, the lack of opportunity for the victim to have any input, and the failure to provide the victim with even the most sketchy information concerning the outcome of the proceedings may well lead to a sense of frustration and dissatisfaction with the criminal justice system. Public support for the criminal justice system would be enhanced if victims had more opportunity for systematic involvement in the process.

Restitution programming provides a mechanism for victim involvement in the criminal justice process. Laura Nader notes that in small scale societies the victim is a key part of the reparation process; she suggests that if a society does nothing to compensate innocent crime victims, the social control system is unlikely to be respected.[37] Restitution provides a way for the victim to express their point of view as to the proper disposition, and, of course, to become familiar with the actual disposition of the case.

Restitution will, of course, provide redress to some crime victims. Occasionally advocates of restitution argue for the program on the basis of its potential for restoring the losses experienced by crime victims. This argument is on very shaky grounds; advancing restitution as a victim assistance program is likely to result in considerable community disillusionment. Restitution is a very inefficient program to accomplish a public policy of restoring crime losses because restitution requires the apprehension of an offender before the victims losses are restored. The vast majority of crimes are not solved through an arrest of an offender (usually less than 20% clearance rate for property crimes). Victim compensation programs provide greater potential for meeting victim losses and are preferred programs for accomplishing the social objective than restitution. Victim compensation is a publicly administered social insurance in which a level of government (presently state government in the United States) compensates certain classes of victims (usually victims who were injured as a result of a violent crime) for the financial losses sustained as a result of the victimization.

Dealing with the practical issues

Several practical problems are likely to be encountered as restitution is operationalized in the criminal justice system. Some of the problems will be identified in this section and possible direction for their resolution suggested.

Determining the amount of restitution. A number of problems are associated with assessing the amount of restitution. These include the problems of victim overestimation of losses, whether the victim should receive restitution for nonmonetary losses such as pain and suffering, whether the offender should be required to make restitution in excess of victim losses, and the appropriate procedures for determining the amount of restitution. Many of the presently operating pilot restitution programs report some concerns that victims may inflate loss claims and, in effect, attempt to victimize the offender. No evidence exists as to the extent to which this occurs and an equally plausible and theoretically sound rival hypotheses is that in many cases offenders may underestimate the extent of damage done.[38] The neutralization strategies hypothesized by Sykes and Matza[39] as well as the justification strategies formulated by the social equity theorists[40] suggest that offenders may frequently deal with their own sense of guilt and distress by minimizing the extent of damages caused to the victim. Additionally, many offenders are unlikely to have an experience base from which to make realistic estimates of repair costs and damages done to property and thus may tend, from their own lack of knowledge and experience, to underestimate the damages resulting from their criminal behavior. Differences between victim and offender estimates of damages resulting from the criminal offenses may be as likely to result from offender underestimation as the victim overestimation of losses.

Most pilot restitution programs have developed workable procedures for resolving this problem. Two clear models, an arbitration and a negotiation process, are presently in use to arrive at the amount of the restitution obligation. In the arbitration model a neutral expert (usually officially a judge but frequently operationally a probation officer) receives information from victims and offenders and arrives at a restitution amount which is then binding upon the offender (the amount is not necessary binding upon the victim, however, who does have the recourse of civil suit available). The negotiation model is operationalized by the Minnesota Restitution Center[41] and several other projects which bring the victim and offender together with a staff member of the restitution project to negotiate a restitution agreement. Both of these approaches appear to be workable procedures for arriving at a restitution amount. The arbitration model may have the advantage of efficiency and will involve minimal criminal justice staff time at arriving at a restitution decision. The mediation model is more likely to produce a restitution decision which is acceptable and perceived as just by the parties involved due to their own input into the decision-making process. This model further has the advantage of bringing the victim and offender into direct communication and should reduce stereotypes which they may have held of each other.

To what extent should victims receive reimbursement for nontangible losses such as pain, suffering, emotional distress, etc.? The predominant pattern among present restitution programs is to limit restitution to out-of-pocket losses sustained by the victims. For the most part, restitution is used with property offenders; with property offenses nontangible losses are sufficiently rare and, if present, extremely difficult to quantify, which may account for their omission from present restitution schemes. The future development of restitution programming should build on past experience and not attempt to include pain, suffering, and other nontangible losses in restitution agreements. If victims feel strongly that they should be reimbursed for these damages they should, of course, be free to pursue the matter in civil proceedings.

Another set of questions center aound the issues of partial and excessive restitution. Partial and excessive are relative to the damages experienced by the victim. Partial restitution occurs when the offender is required to make less restitution than the damages experienced by the victim and excessive restitution occurs when the offender's restitution obligation exceeds the amount of damages experienced by the victim. The experience of restitution programs indicates the full restitution can be made in most cases without creating an unjust hardship on the offender. This experience tends further to be confirmed by available data indicating that the losses sustained in most victimizations are sufficiently modest that offenders can reasonably be expected to make full restitution.[42] Unusual situations may, of course, occasionally occur when offenders actions may result in inordinately high losses to victims. In these rare cases questions may be raised about the appropriateness of requiring full restitution; when this occurs the decision-making process used to arrive at the restitution amount (either arbitration or negotiation) would involve a consideration of the extent of the loss in relation to the nature of the crime and might arrive at a less than full restitution obligation. This contingency reaffirms the desirability of using a negotiation rather than an arbitration process. Situations in which the victims have negotiated and accepted a less than full restitution agreement are much more likely to be accepted as fair and just situations than those in which the amount is determined by an arbitrator leaving the victim with only the recourses of accepting the amount or attempting a civil suit. Further, laboratory research testing the equity theory formulations suggests that full restitution is more desirable than either partial or excessive restitution because full restitution is more likely to be voluntarily made by the wrongdoer.[43]

Questions around the issue of excessive restitution are much more complex. Obviously the community incurs considerable costs in solving a crime, apprehending the offender, and arriving at a determination of guilt. Should offenders be reasonably expected to share in these costs? Unless attempts are made to attach restitution obligations to concepts such as pain, suffering, mental anguish, etc. many serious crimes may involve comparatively minor damages in which restitution for out-of-pocket losses may be a very mild penalty. To a large extent, this problem could be controlled by limiting restitution to property crimes. Further, without the possibility of excessive restitution, major class injustices may occur in which wealthy offenders might easily make restitution whereas poor offenders would find the restitution obligation much more burdensome. This problem has led a number of restitution scholars to accept the notion of excessive restitution. Kathleen Smith proposes that offenders be sentenced to pay restitution as well as a discretionary fine set by the judge and based on the seriousness of the offense.[44] Stephen Schafer, one of the most consistent modern advocates of restitution, thinks that restitution must be combined with other penalties to avoid class injustices.[45] Most presently operating restitution programs do, as least indirectly, require excessive restitution inasmuch as obligations such as probation or residence in a community corrections center are imposed in addition to restitution. Programs in Georgia[46] and Oklahoma[47] are moving away from this pattern and are attempting to demonstrate the use of restitution as a sole sanction. Offenders in these states are technically on probation status while making restitution; they have very few other obligations, however, and will be discharged from probation upon the completion of the restitution requirement. The problem of excessive restitution might well be resolved by beginning to find types of crime (predominantly property crimes) in which restitution might be the sole sanction and identify other more serious crimes (predominantly crimes against person) in which restitution might reasonably be required but in which the offender would also be subject to other criminal justice sanctions. The concept of court costs might also be expanded by establishing a set fee based on the type of crime which all convicted offenders should be required to pay to partially reimburse the community for the costs of their apprehension and conviction. Parenthetically, the converse of this would also be reasonable. Persons who are subjected to criminal charges which are later dismissed or for which they are acquitted should receive compensation from the community for their legal costs and other losses.[48]

The questions of determining the amount of victim damages for which restitution is to be made, assessing whether or not restitution should be made for intangible damages such as pain, suffering, mental angush, etc., and the issues of partial and excessive restitution are all practical problems which must be resolved; present experience clearly indicates that they are resolvable. Two procedures—arbitration and negotiation—are being employed to resolve these issues on a case by case basis. Generally the negotiation procedures hold greater promise for arriving at resolutions which will be accepted as fair by all parties to the victimization.

Enforcing the obligation. A second set of issues centered around the question of how to enforce restitution requirements. There are two aspects to this problem. One aspect is that of the indigent offender (how-to-get-blood-out-of-a-turnip) aspect and the other is enforcing a restitution sanction against the solvent offender who may be reluctant to give up resources. The problem of the indigent offender may be overstated. The experience to date is that the restitution amounts are quite modest; the vast majority of restitution contracts negotiated by the Minnesota Restitution Center, for example, have been under $200.[49] With the aid of installment payment plan, most offenders will be able to handle their restitution obligations. In some situations other resources may need to be made available to the low income offender. These resources could include assistance with job finding or the use of short term public service employment by which the offender would be put to some useful public work in order to earn sufficient money to meet the restitution obligations.

One occasionally expressed fear is that indigent offenders will steal in order to make their restitution obligations. While this is certainly a possibility, there is no evidence from current restitution programs that it occurs except in isolated instances. This, admittedly undesirable contingency, could certainly be controlled with even minimal monitoring of the offenders' sources of income as they complete the restitution requirement.

Another alternative is personal service Type III restitution, in which the offender completes restitution by working for the victim rather than making a cash payment. Several restitution projects report examples of this type of restitution,[50] although to date there has been so systematic study of the use of personal service restitution. This does appear to be a viable option which might be explored and used with some indigent offenders. If restitution decisons are made through a negotiation process the possibility of personal service restitution could be discussed and considered as one of the alternatives under consideration.

There will be some offenders who will willingly agree to a restitution obligation to avoid harsh outcomes of the criminal process. Some will then attempt to avoid completing the obligation even when they have income and resources to do so. In view of these problems, the criminal justice system must maintain the possibility of imposing a more severe sanction if the offender fails or refuses to meet the restitution obligations. While many offenders will undoubtedly meet their obligation out of a sense of duty, some will be evasive and means must be available to coerce those who wish to evade their responsibility. This, of course, is a current practice when restitution is made a condition of probation; failure to make the restitution obligation can then become grounds for violation of probation or imposing th original penalty.

The Cost of restitution. Will the more systematic use of restitution in the criminal justice sysem increase the costs of administering criminal justice programs? This depends upon the role restitution is to play vis-a-vis other criminal justice sanctions. If restitution is simply added to the present panoply of sanctioning and correctional programs then the cost is likely to increase. If, on the other hand, restitution can be used in lieu of existing criminal justice programs then the cost will be decreased. Less staff time will be necessary to establish a restitution agreement (even using negotiating procedures) and in monitoring the implementation of that agreement than is now being used in probation services to develop presentence evaluations and to carry out probation supervision. Substituting restitution for probation will lower cost; the cost savings will be even greater if restitution can be used as an alternative to incarceration which, of course, is an extremely expensive sanction and effectively penalizes the victim twice—once by the offender and secondly through taxes to support the incarcerated offender. Another alternative which would reduce costs is to use less restrictive incarceration and restitution in lieu of traditional imprisonment. The Minnesota Restitution Center retained offenders who had previously been in a maximum security prison in a community corrections center where they completed their restitution obligation at less per diem cost and that required to operate the prison.[51] Likewise the Georgia restitution shelters are providing a degree of incarceration and restitution at considerably less costs to the tax payers in Georgia than would be incurred if the offenders in the shelters were placed in a more traditional prison.[52] If restitution can be substituted for the concept of coerced counseling and therapy, sanctioning will become a less labor intensive and thus less costly undertaking. On the other hand, there is considerable danger that restitution will simply be added to the present range of criminal justice treatment sanctioning activities which would increase the overall cost. Restitution, to save money, must result in a reduction in other types of correctional programming, and requires an identification of types of offenses for which restitution would be a suitable sole penalty along with systematic exploration of the use of restitution alone without other types of sanctions.

Victim culpability. An additional practical problem centers around the question of victim precipitation of their own victimization. There is an increasing body of evidence to suggest that in many situations crime victims either actively or through carelessness engage in behavior which partially precipitates their own victimization.[53] If the victim is partially at fault should the offender be required to make full restitution for the victim's losses? This is an issue which has not been addressed explicitly in most present restitution programs. Most appear to operate on the assumption that the offender was fully responsible for the victim's losses and should, therefore, make full restitution.

There are two directions by which this issue might be resolved. One direction would be to develop a procedure by which the offender could request a reduction in the amount of agreed upon restitution based on evidence that the victim was partially at fault. This would be similar to the concept of contributory negligence in civil suits. Such a procedure would, of course, involve additional legal costs. A similar process which might accomplish the same ends would be to permit the issue of victim culpability to be considered in either the arbitration or negotiation processes designed to arrive at a restitution amount. The offender might be permitted to try to negotiate a lesser restitution amount based on contentions that the victim contributed to the victimization or, perhaps, the arbitrator might award less than full restitution to the victim on the same bases.

A second approach is to assume that even in situations of high provocation, an individual has more than one alternative way of behaving. Persons who select an alternative which leads to damages to another person, even if provoked, should be held accountable for the damages which flow from their decision. This approach would suggest that so long as noncriminal alternatives are available, offenders should be held accountable for their acts even if provoked. This alternative response to the question of victim culpability has some distinct advantages. First, basic human dignity of the offender is protected because the offender is perceived as a responsible person who has the power and obligation to make decisions. Conversely, an offender is not perceived as a sick or helpless person who, in a deterministic manner, responds criminally in provocative situations. Secondly, the interests of the community are better protected by a policy stance which expects and demands responsible behavior from persons. To permit easy rationlizations is simply to encourage irresponsible behavior.

Summary

Over the past few years the use of restitution as a sanction for offenders has received renewed attention. Restitution refers to a sanction imposed by an official of the criminal justice system in which the offender makes either a monetary or service payment to the actual victim or to some substitute victim. Contemporary restitution practices can be classified into one of four types. Type I restitution involves the offender making a monetary payment to the victim of the crime. Type II restitution involves the offender making a monetary payment to some substitute victim such as a community charity. Type III restitution involves the offender making payment to the direct victim in the form of service. Type IV restitution involves the offender providng a service to some community organization.

There are several reasons for the increasing interest in restitution. Restitution provides an additional sentencing option for courts. Present sentencing options to courts are generally limited to probation or imprisonment. Restitution provides an additional option which can be used alone, in conjuction with probation, or as an alternative to imprisonment. Restitution practices are also consistant with the emerging interest in the crime victim. The use of restitution as a criminal justice sanction provides an opportunity for facilitation of victim offender reconciliation. Additionally, it provides a mechanism whereby the victim might be brought into the criminal justice proceedings at least at the dispositional stage when issues regarding restitution are decided.

Administering a restitution program involves resolving a number of practical issues. These center in the areas of determining the amount of the restitution obligation, inforcing the restitution obligation, justifing the cost of carrying out a restitution program, and resolving issues of victim culpability. Both arbitration and negotiation procedures are being used to determine the amount of the restitution obligation. Generally restitution is used for property offenders who are held responsible for losses stemming from damage or lost property but generally not damages resulting from pain and suffering or other intangible losses. Issues of payment for intangible damages, partial restitution, and excessive restitution, must all be addressed. Restitution obligations appear enforceable so long as installment payments are authorized, implementation of restitution agreements is monitored, and judicious use is made of job finding services, public employment and personal service restitution, and more severe sanctions can be imposed if the offender refuses to complete the restitution obligation. If restitution can be used as an alternative to present correctional programs the overall cost will be reduced. This requires addressing attention to the types of offences or offenders for which restitution might reasonably be used as a sole penalty. The issue of victim culpability might be addressed by either providing the offender with opportunities to request a reduced restitution amount based on a finding that the victim was partially responsible for their own victimization or by operating from the assumption that even in provocative situations, persons have alternative courses of actions they can take. Given this assumption, the person who selects an alternative which harms other persons might reasonably be held accountable for this choice.

The renewed interest in restitution in the United States remains in a very preliminary phase. Major projects, however, are being funded by the Law Enforcement Assistance Administration for both adult and juvenile offenders and are being studied by a national evaluation team. As these studies and pilot projects become known, criminal justice experts will be in a better position to assess the extent to which issues such as those raised in this paper can be resolved and to make decisions concerning further development of restitution programing.

Discussion Questions

1. What are the advantages and disadvantages of type I (Monetary restitution to victims) compared to type IV (Community service) restitution?

2. What are the major limitations and problems in efforts to implement a restitution scheme in which the offender makes a direct monetary payment to the victim of crime?

3. Do you think that there are types of offences or offenders for which restitution (any of the four types) might reasonably be used as the sole penalty imposed against the offender? If so, what types of offences or offenders? What is your reason for believing that restitution would be a sufficient penalty in these situations?

4. Do you think victim culpability should play any part in determining what penalty is assessed against a convicted offender? Why or why

not? If so, how would you take account of victim culpability in making decisions concerning sentences to impose against offenders?

Notes

1. Stephen Schafer, *The Victim and His Criminal* (New York: Random House, 1968), pp. 7-20.

2. E. Adamson Hoebel, *The Law of Primitive Man* (New York: Atheneum, 1970); Laura Nader and Elain Combs-Schilling, "Restitution in Cross-Cultural Perspective," in Joe Hudson and Burt Galaway (eds.), *Restitution in Criminal Justice* (Lexington: D.C. Heath Lexington Books, 1977), pp. 27-44.

3. Edwin Sutherland and Donald Cressey, *Criminology* (Philadelphia: J.B. Lippincott, 1970), p. 318.

4. Joe Hudson and Burt Galaway, "Undoing the Wrong: The Minnesota Restitution Center," *Social Work* 19 (May, 1974): 313-318; Robert Mowatt, "The Minnesota Restitution Center; Paying Off the Ripped Off," Joe Hudson (ed.) *Restitution in Criminal Justice* (St. Paul: Minnesota Department of Corrections, 1976), pp. 190-215.

5. Bill Read, "How Restitution Works in Georgia," *Judicature* 60: 7 (February, 1977): 329-311.

6. Federal Republic of Germany, Ministry of Justice, "The Treatment of Young Offenders in the Federal Republic of Germany" (Unpublished report in English, n.d.).

7. Pilot Alberta Restitution Centre, "Progress Report: The Pilot Alberta Restitution Centre, September 1, 1975-February 29, 1976" (Unpublished report, 1976), pp. 28-36.

8. Patricia Groves, "A Report on Community Service Treatment and Work Programs in British Columbia," *Community Participation in Sentencing* (Ottawa: Law Reform Commission of Canada, 1976), pp. 130-131.

9. Mennonite Central Committee, "A Proposal for Victim-Offender Reconciliation" and "Victim/Offender Reconciliation Project-Progress Report, November 13, 1975" (Unpublished materials, Kitchener, Ontario).

10. Sylvia Sullvan, "Convicted Offenders Became Community Helpers," *Judicature* 58: 8 (March, 1973): 333-335; Donald E. Clark, "Community Service: A Realistic Alternative for Sentencing," *FBI Law Enforcement Bulletin* (March, 1976): 3-7.

11. David Larmon, "The Arbitration Experience: Improving the Process of Intake Screening" (Unpublished paper, Maryland Department of Juvenile Services, Annapolis, Maryland, n.d.); Maryland Department of Juvenile Services, "Community Arbitration Programs" (Unpublished materials, Annapolis, Maryland, n.d.).

12. Pima County (Arizona) Adult Probation Department, "Annual Report, 1975" (Unpublished report), pp. 2-4.

13. John Harding, "Community Serive Restitution by Offenders," in Hudson and Galway (eds.), *Restitution in Criminal Justice*, pp. 101-130.

14. James Q. Wilson, *Thinking About Crime* (New York: Basic Books, 1975).

15. Karl Menninger, *The Crime of Punishment* (New York: Viking Press, 1968), pp. 67-68, 251.

16. Harding, pp. 105-106.

17. Read, 329.

18. Mark R. Arnold, "Making the Criminal Pay Back His Victim," *National Observer*, April 2, 1977, p. 1.

19. Read, 324-328.

20. Kathleen Smith, *A Cure for Crime: The Case for the Self-Determinate Sentence* (London: Duckworth, 1965); Kathleen Smith, "Implementing Restitution Within a Penal Setting," in Joe Hudson and Burt Galaway (eds.) *Restitution in Criminal Justice* (Lexington: D.C. Heath/Lexington Books, 1977), 131-146.

21. Minnesota Department of Corrections, "Interim Evaluation Results: Minnesota Restitution Center" (Unpublished report, St. Paul, Minnesota, 1976), p. 50.

22. *Ibid.*, p. 39.

23. Minneapolis *Star*, January 14, 1977, p. 1.

24. B. Dockar-Drysdale, "Damage and Restitution," *Bristish Journal of Delinquency* (July, 1953): 4-13.

25. Albert Eglash, "Beyond Restitution-Creative Restitution," in Hudson and Galaway (eds.), *Restitution in Criminal Justice*, pp. 91-99.

26. August Aichhorn, *Wayward Youth* (New York: Viking Press, 1935).

27. R.M. Foxx and N.H. Azzin, "Restitution: A Method of Eliminating Aggressive-Disruptive Behavior of Retarded and Brain Damaged Patients," *Behavior Research and Therapy*, 10 (1972): 15-27.

28. O.H. Mowrer, "Loss and Recovery of Community," in George M. Gazeda (ed.), *Innovations in Group Psychotherapy* (Springfield: Charles C. Thomas Publisher, 1968), pp. 130-148; *The Crisis in Psychiatry and Religion* (Princeton: Van Nostrand, 1961).

29. Philip Brickman, "Crime and Punishment in Sports and Society," *Journal of Social Issues.*

30. Elaine Walster, Ellen Berscheid, G. William Walster, "New Directions in Equity Research," *Journal of Personality and Social Psychology*, 25 (1973): 151-176.

31. David Matza and Gresham Sykes, "Techniques of Neutralization: A Theory of Delinquency," *American Sociology Review*, 22 (1957): 664-669.

32. Phillip Ennis, *Criminal Victimization in the United States: A Report of a National Survey* (Washington: U.S. Government Printing Office, 1967), pp. 41-51; United States Department of Justice, *Criminal Victimization in the United States: A Comparison of 1973 and 1974 Findings* (Washington: U.S. Government Printing Office, 1976), pp. 40-42.

33. William McDonald, (ed.), *Criminal Justice and The Victim* (Beverly Hills: Sage Publications, 1976), pp. 17-55.

34. Marvin Wolfgang, "Making the Criminal Justice System Accountable," *Crime and Delinquency*, 18 (January, 1972): 15-22.

35. LeRoy Schultz, "The Pre Sentence Investigation and Victimology," *University of Missouri at Kansas City Law Review*, 35 (Summer, 1967): 247-260.

36. Fredrick L. Dubow and Theodore M. Becker, "Patterns of Victim Advocacy," in McDonald (ed.), pp. 147-164.

37. Nader, p. 40.

38. Burt Galaway and William Marsella "An Exploratory Study of the Perceived Fairness of Restitution as a Sanction for Juvenile Offenders," (Unpublished paper presented Second International Symposium on Victimology, Boston, Massachusetts, September, 1976).

39. Sykes and Matza.

40. Walster, Berscheid, Walster.

41. Hudson and Galaway, "Undoing the Wrong"; Mowatt.

42. United States Department of Justice, *Crime in the United States, 1974* (Washington: U.S. Government Printing Office, 1975), 29-31; Burt Galaway and Joe Hudson, "Issues in the Correctional Implementation of Restitution to Victims of Crime" in Joe Hudson and Burt Galaway (eds.) *Considering the Victim: Readings in Restitution and Victim Compensation* (Springfield: Charles C. Thomas Publisher, 1975), 351-360: Minnesota Department of Corrections; Roger O. Steggerda and Susan P. Dolphin, *Victim Restitution: Assessment of the Restitution in Probation Experiment* (Des Moines: Polk County, Iowa, Department of Program Evaluation, 1975).

43. Walster, Berscheid, and Walster, p. 158; Ellen Berscheid and Elaine Walster, "When Does a Harm-Doer Compensate a Victim?" *Journal of Personality and Social Psychology*, 6 (1967): 435-441.

44. Smith.

45. Schafer.

46. Read, p. 329.

47. Arnold, p. 1.

48. Richard Moran and Stephen Ziedman, "Victims Without Crimes: Compensation to the Not Guilty," in Israel Drapkin and Emillio Viano (eds.), *Victimology: A New Focus; Volume II Society's Reactions to Victimization* (Lexington: D.C. Heath/Lexington Press, 1974), pp. 221-225.

49. Galaway and Hudson, "Implementing Restitution"; Minnesota Department of Corrections.

50. Burt Galaway, "The Use of Restitution," *Crime and Delinquency*, 23: 1 (January, 1977): 57-67.

51. Mowatt, p. 8.

52. Read, p. 327.

53. Lynn A. Curtis, *Criminal Violence* (Lexington: D.C. Heath/Lexington Books, 1974), pp. 81-100.

6

Should Heroin use be Decriminalized?

Gerald F. Uelmen*

NOW THAT "DECRIMINALIZATION" OF MARIJUANA USE is being tried in state after state,[1] the suggestion is heard with greater frequency that we should try a similar approach to heroin. Instead of jailing the heroin addict, why not make heroin available, so the addict does not have to rob and steal in order to acquire the money to purchase heroin in the "black market?" This suggestion is both simple and seductive, especially when viewed from the perspective of our prior unsuccessful attempts to deal with the problem of heroin addiction.

Previous Approaches

About ten years ago, it was estimated we had 250,000 heroin addicts in the United States. Heroin addiction was viewed as a major social problem, and we adopted some dramatic and expensive measures to deal with it.

First, we attempted to eradicate the supply. Through international cooperation, we broke the famous "French Connection," cutting off the flow of heroin from Turkish opium fields. Just as fast as we closed the front door by disconnecting the "French Connection," however, the "Mexican Connection" was put together, and brown heroin began flowing through the back door.[2] We are now supplying helicopters and chemicals for eradication of the Mexican poppy crop at a cost of millions of dollars, while several new sources of supply loom on the horizon, including a resurgence of Turkish opium production and increased imports from the "Golden Triangle" of Southeast Asia. The strategy of eliminating supply has confronted us with a hydraheaded monster which grows two new heads to replace each one we chop off.

Second, we undertook a major treatment program, utilizing methadone as a substitute for heroin. While the verdict is not yet in, we have learned that programs of addiction maintenance may create as many new problems as the old ones they resolve. These problems include a high rate of diversion of methadone to the illicit market. In New York, for example, they have been averaging 1,000 drug related deaths a year. The leading cause of these deaths is overdose on methadone, which currently outruns heroin deaths two to one.[3] We've also undergone a rather subtle transformation. Metha-

370

done is no longer viewed as a "cure" for heroin addiction, but rather as a "substitute." Most of the 135,000 addicts currently enrolled in methadone programs expect to stay there indefinitely,[4] at a cost averaging $2,000 each per year.[5]

Finally, some jurisdictions adopted a "get tough" stance by dramatically increasing the criminal penalties for drug offenses. The most notable example of this approach was New York, which adopted laws in 1972 mandating life sentences for sale of heroin. After two years of experience under the new law, a recent evaluation cosponsored by the Association of the Bar of the City of New York and the Drug Abuse Council concluded that none of the key indicators of successful implementation are evident: offenders face no greater risk of punishment, the number of offenders sentenced to prison has not increased significantly, and the speed with which cases are processed has not improved.[6] More dramatic evidence of the failure of New York's approach is readily available. As Mayor Abraham Beame recently discovered, all you need to do is call a cab and drive through Harlem, and someone will offer to sell you heroin or methadone before you have travelled six blocks.[7]

Today, after ten years of these efforts, it is estimated we have 500,000 heroin addicts in the United States. I'm reminded of an experience I had several months ago shopping for a gift for our four-year old son. I found a box of oddly shaped plastic parts, depicted on the cover was a gleaming flying saucer. I asked the clerk whether it didn't seem a bit complicated for a four-year old to put together, and she assured me it was an educational toy designed to equip a child for life in today's world: no matter *how* he put it together, it was wrong. That pretty accurately summarizes our experience with the heroin problem in the United States; no matter how we've put it together, it seems to have turned out wrong. In this setting, the arguments in favor of decriminalizing heroin deserve careful consideration. Proposals for heroin maintenance programs are being seriously discussed in at least seven states right now, and a grand jury in San Diego, California included a recommendation in favor or heroin maintenance in its report last year.

Arguments for decriminalization

The arguments in favor of heroin Decriminalization can fairly be summarized as follows:

First, we cannot eliminate the black market by cutting off the supply of narcotics, so we should eliminate it by competition. By providing a legal source of heroin, we can drive the illicit supplier out of business. This argument is similar to the argument successfully used to establish legalized gambling in many states. Since the bookmaker was operating underground without paying taxes, it was suggested that the obvious remedy was for the state to go into the bookmaking business.

Second, we apparently can't cure addicts, so at least we should minimize the crimes which addicts commit to support their habits. A "normal" habit costs about $40 a day to maintain. Since a "fence" pays about one-third of what stolen property is worth, an addict needs to steal $120 worth of property every day to buy heroin on the black market. If that heroin were available from a legal source, it would cost less than $1 a day.

Third, it is suggested we look to England, where they've been supplying addicts with heroin for many years. The success of the British system is offered as an example for us to emulate in establishing heroin maintenance programs in America.

Fourth, our experience with marijuana decriminalization is cited to establish that use of a drug will not increase simply because criminal penalties are repealed.

Each of these arguments, however, rests upon assumptions which require greater scrutiny.

Elimination of Black Market

The argument that the creation of heroin maintenance clinics would eliminate the black market in this country contradicts all of the accumulated experience we have to draw upon. Our experience with methadone has taught us that maintenance programs may augment the black market rather than eliminate it. Ten years ago, there was virtually no black market in methadone; today, in New York, 15% of the addicts seeking treatment are addicted *not* to heroin but to methadone, which they've acquired on the black market.[8] Nor has the British system eliminated the existence of a heroin black market in England. Close to 1,000 convictions every year for unlawful possession or sale of heroin indicate a very active black market. And British drug experts concede the source of most of the heroin on the illicit market is the heroin being dispensed through the maintenance clinics.[9]

There are at least two reasons why government distribution of heroin will not eliminate the black market. First, many of the addicts enrolled in maintenance programs will not be satisfied with the dosage level which the physician at the clinic is willing to prescribe, and will seek to supplement their supply with illegally acquired drugs. This has been a perennial problem in methadone programs in this country, and is apparently a serious problem in the English heroin maintenance program as well. One 1970 survey disclosed that 84% of the British addicts on heroin maintenance had obtained drugs from sources other than the clinic in the preceding 3 months.[10] Secondly, many heroin users are not addicts, and would not even qualify for heroin maintenance programs. A recent study undertaken by the Drug Abuse Council concluded there may be more than two million occasional users of heroin in the United States who are not addicted.[11] The existence of these "chippers" insures the continued existence of a black market.

The proponents of heroin maintenance argue that the illicit diversion problem can be dealt with by strict controls: all heroin would be administered by the clinic; no "take home" dosages would be supplied. The difficulty with that argument is that it is self-defeating. The stricter the controls over distribution, the less attractive to addicts will heroin maintenance programs be. The addicts will prefer to hustle on the streets, rather than put up with the strict regimen of reporting to a clinic four times a day. It's reminiscent of what happened to New York's off-track betting corporation. Most gamblers are either very social characters, who like to nurse a drink or two while waiting for the results after placing a bet, or very busy characters who want to let their fingers do the walking and place their bets by telephone. The off-track betting offices set up by the state are about as warm and social as the local office of the Internal Revenue Service, and just about as hostile over the telephone, insisting all bets be made in person. Thus, the illegal book-makers continue to thrive, simply because they try harder. Now the off-track betting corporation is seeking to outdo the bookmakers in providing all the comforts of home to their customers. The lesson is an obvious one. If we want to compete with the black market for heroin addicts, we may end up having to offer more than we really care to.

Minimizing Crime

The relationship between addiction and crimes against property is well documented:

In 1971, the Santa Barbara, California Police Department undertook an extensive sweep arrest of known narcotic addicts, and discoverd that during the brief period of time they succeeded in holding the defendants in jail, the burglary rate dropped 50%.[12]

In 1972, the Los Angeles Police Department undertook an analysis of the records of all those arrested for crimes against property, and discovered 40% had prior drug arrests. In reversing the process, they discovered 87% of those convicted of narcotic offenses had prior arrests for propery crimes.[13] Similar studies in New York have revealed even higher correlations.

A soon to be released project of the Rand Corporation gives even more dramatic evidence. They undertook a study of the careers of fifty "career criminals." An average of 39 years old, they had spent an average of 10 years of their adult life in prison, the other 10 on the street, where they committed an average of 200 crimes. Two-thirds reported being under the influence of drugs or alcohol at the time of committing their crimes, and one-third reported that money for drugs or alcohol was the main reason for their illegal activity.[14]

But saying drug addicts commit a lot of crimes does not necessarily mean they will stop committing crimes when supplied with heroin. There are several reasons to question this argument.

One, most addicts have a record of criminality which *predates* their addiction.[15] Seen in this light, the relationship between addiction and crime begins to resemble the relationship between the chicken and the egg, each of whom has an equally plausible claim to being the cause of it all.

Two, most long term follow-up studies of addicts receiving treatment show that criminality returns to previous levels *after* treatment stops.[16] This suggests that a reduction in criminality during a period of treatment may have more to do with involvement in the treatment process than the alleviation of the addiction itself.

Finally, even the impressive statistics collected by early methadone programs showing dramatic decreases in criminality *during* treatment may not be transferable to heroin maintenance programs. Other more recent studies suggest that a reduction in criminality may have more to do with the age of the patients or the availability of counseling than the supplying of methadone.[17] In the British heroin maintenance programs, it was reported that one-third of the addicts enrolled admitted committing some crime other than drug law violations during one three month period.[18]

The British System

The argument that heroin maintenance has worked well in England is difficult to refute. Although England has a black market drug problem, and continuing involvement of addicts in criminal activity, it must still be conceded that the size of the addict population has stabilized over the past few years and the average age of addicts is slowly increasing, indicating that few are being initiated into the rank and file of narcotic addiction in England today. However, legal distribution of heroin in England is on a very limited basis. Only confirmed addicts are allowed any dosage whatsoever and that dosage is prescribed at the professional discretion of specially licensed doctors. At last count England had less than 3,000 narcotic addicts, most of whom were being maintained on methadone, rather than heroin. British doctors have found it so difficult to stabilize addicts on heroin that they have stopped prescribing it in favor of methadone in all but 87 cases![19] Hence, heroin maintenance in England is a program of rather miniscule dimensions and the success of the British battle against narcotic addiction is as much attributable to other factors as it is to heroin maintenance.

The above considerations notwithstanding, there are several good reasons why the British System would be unworkable in the United States. The most obvious reason is the sheer enormity of the problem in America. The 500,000 Americans hooked on narcotics make the problem of 3,000 addicts in England seem almost inconsequential. In New York City alone, there are an estimated 150,000 narcotic addicts. A duplication of the British model in New York City would require 1500 clinics, 2300 qualified psychiatrists, 4000 nurses and up to 8000 additional social workers. Such a force of manpower is neither practicable nor available.[20]

Even if the sheer size of the American addict population did not create an insurmountable barrier to a duplication of the British system, the sociological differences between American and English addicts give ample reason to ponder the advisability of our adoption of the British System. England's current addict population grew largely out of the white working and middle class, many of whom hold jobs in the mainstream of society. By contrast, a significant portion of the addict population here is derived from the hard core unemployed of the ghettos.[21] Many of these individuals are without hope of ever entering the mainstream of society and their lives have become inextricably intertwined with a narcotic sub-culture. The heroin dispensing clinic cannot totally supplant that lifestyle, and may merely function as a supplement when street supplies are low. Recent research has suggested the relationship between heroin addiction and social stress.[22] Supplying free heroin in the ghetto would not eliminate that stress.

Another troublesome aspect of the heroin problem here is the nature of our black market. Illegal narcotic sales in England consist mostly of diversion of prescription drugs by addicts stretching their dose, hoping to bring in a little extra cash.[23] By contrast, the black market in America is a highly lucrative business supplied by organized smuggling operations.[24] It would be foolhardy to assume the sellers of illegal heroin would discontinue their efforts merely because the government began supplying the heroin to addicts in limited quantities. On the contrary, since heroin maintenance would be available only to the addicted, the pushers may concentrate their sales efforts on unaddicted users and create an ever growing burden on the government clinics.

Finally, the attitude of the average American toward heroin is such that the necessary acceptance of heroin maintenance by the general public may presently be impossible. One of the reasons the British System has succeeded is that the British population takes a more lenient view of addiction than do most Americans. Rather than considering heroin addicts to be morally reprehensible the British attitude reflects a genuine concern with addiction as a medical problem, to be dealt with in the same way with which other public health problems are dealt. Should heroin maintenance be attempted in the United States, the predictable moral fervor and emotionalism might be counter productive, driving the addicts who need help even further underground.

The Marijuana Experience

The greatest risk of embarking on a program of heroin maintenance is that we may actually increase our problem by creating even more heroin addicts. Thus, the experience in states that have decriminalized marijuana is being closely watched. Earliest reports from these states suggested no dramatic increase in the use of marijuana,[25] but a recent California survey indicated 14% of adults polled considered themselves "current users" of marijuana eleven months after the new law took effect, as compared to 9% in a previous poll taken ten months before the new law took effect, an increase of 55% in "current users."[26] Comparing marijuana to heroin, however, leads us nowhere. The two drugs are totally different both in their effects and the patterns of use. Marijuana has become a recreational "youth" drug, used across the whole socio-economic spectrum.[27] Heroin, although the pattern is changing somewhat, is largely an "inner city" drug problem, with a large proportion of racial minorities among its users.[28] Thus, whatever pattern of marijuana use emerges after decriminalization may not repeat itself if heroin were decriminalized.

But there is an even more significant difference between the approach we are taking to decriminalization of marijuana, and proposals for heroin maintenance programs. In decriminalizing marijuana use, we have not established a legal source of supply. Sale or distribution of marijuana remains a serious offense even in states which have decriminalized possession. Thus, we officially acknowledge the existence of a consumer demand for marijuana estimated at four billion dollars per year, at the same time we abandon that market to the underworld, untaxed and unregulated except by the enforcement of criminal sanctions for sales. The proposals for heroin maintenance programs, however, may or may not be accompanied by repeal of criminal penalties for illicit possession or use. In fact, stiff criminal penalties for *illicit* possession may help in implementing heroin mainte-nance, by encouraging addicts to seek their supply only from the legiti-matized source. This, in fact, is a major feature of the "British system," where unauthorized possession of heroin is punishable by seven years imprisonment. Thus, we would "decriminalize" heroin only to the extent it is dispensed by an authorized maintenance program.

The extent to which such limited decriminalization may create the risk of additional addicts being produced is difficult to assess. The most important variable may be how it is dispensed. Since the effects of heroin last only six hours, the demand for some sort of "take-home" dosage will be great. If we insist on the addict reporting to his clinic four times a day, the program may be impossible to administer. In England, the addict is permitted to pick up his heroin at a pharmacy, and inject it himself. Utilizing that approach in this country could be disastrous in terms of the possible diversion of drugs to the black market and an increase in the number of addicts. Thus, a real dilemma is presented: the goals of limiting illicit diversion and encouraging accessibility are irreconcilable.

Balancing the Cost

Even if we accept all of the claimed benefits of heroin maintenance at face value, and concede that it will eliminate the black market, reduce crime, and produce no increase in the number of addicts, the other side of the equation remains unexamined. What will it cost? The British system now costs an average of the equivalent of $2,400 per addict per year.[29] Assuming we can rise to the same levels of efficiency that the British government has achieved, heroin maintenance for our 500,000 addicts comes to 840 million dollars a year. Costs are likely to be much higher if we adopt a more tightly controlled model, where heroin is dispensed only at the clinic. Confronted with a possible bill of $1 billion each year, John Q. Public will probably echo the sentiments of John Mahar, founder of the Delancy Street drug rehabilitation program in San Francisco:

> "To me, the addicts are a rather boring subgroup of humanity who have received far more attention than they deserve. They're the last on my list to cry about. I'd rather see our society start worrying more about crippled children, or our senior citizens who have to eat dog food to stay alive."[30]

Summary

While the arguments in favor of heroin decriminalization are simple, an examination of the assumptions underlying those arguments reveals the complexity of this issue. The elimination of the black market is highly unlikely, while the reduction of crime cannot be safely assumed. The risk of creating new addicts is a real one, while the projected costs are astronomical. Neither the British experience, nor our own experience with marijuana are of much relevance. Still, there are those who will say, "we can't do much worse than we're doing now, so why not give it a try?" I think we can do a lot worse. The nine million alcoholics in this country should serve as a grim reminder of just how badly we can do. To borrow the words of Los Angeles Chief of Police Ed Davis, this solution makes about as much sense as throwing gasoline on a flash fire.[31]

Discussion Questions

1. Is the experience gained in decriminalization of marijuana applicable to heroin? How will differences between the two drugs require different approaches to decriminalization?

2. How does the "British system" of heroin control really differ from the American system? What differences between the British and American legal systems and cultures should be considered in assessing whether the "British system" could be implemented in America?

3. Will "decriminalization" eliminate the heroin black market? Why?

Notes

*. J.D., L.L.M.; Professor of Law, Loyola Law School, Los Angeles California. Co-author, *Drug Abuse and the Law* (West Pub. Co. 1974). The author wishes to acknowledge the assistance of Allan Ides (J.D. Loyola Law School, 1979) in the preparation of this article.

1. Alaska (Alaska Statutes, §17.12.110); California (California Health & Safety Code, §11357); Colorado (L75, P437, Sec. 9); Maine (Health and Welfare, M.R.S.A., §2383); Minnesota (M.S.A. §152.15); Ohio (Ohio Revised Code §2925.11); Oregon (O.R.S., §167.217); South Dakota (S.D. Compiled Laws §39-17-96).

2. James Q. Wilson, "The Return of Heroin," *Commentary*, (April, 1975), pp. 48-50.

3. See Report of Doctor Dominick J. Di Maio, New York City's Medical Examiner, cited in *People v. Duryea*, 82 Misc. 2d 1049, 371 N.Y.S. 2d 555, 557 (1975).

4. Peter G. Bourne, *Methadone: Benefits and Shortcomings*, (Washington, D.C.: Drug Abuse Council, Inc., 1975), p. 3.

5. James V. DeLong, "Treatment and Rehabilitation," from *Dealing With Drug Abuse*, Wald and Hutt, ed., (New York: Praeger Publishers, 1972), pp. 202-203.

6. Staff Report of the Drug Law Evaluation Project of the Association of the Bar of the City of New York, "The Effects of the 1973 Drug Laws on the New York State Courts," (August, 1976), Section 2, pp. 1-5, 7-9.

7. *New York Times*, January 30, 1977, p. 1.

8. Bourne, p. 15.

9. Horace Freeland Judson, *Heroin Addiction in Britain*, (New York: Harcourt Brace Jovanovich, 1974), pp. 38, 42.

10. Gerald V. Stimpson and Alan C. Ogborne, "A Survey of a Representative Sample of Addicts Prescribed Heroin at London Clinics," Bulletin on Narcotics 22, (October-December, 1970); 13-22.

11. Leon G. Hunt and Norman E. Zinberg, *Heroin Use: A New Look,* (Washington: D.C.: Drug Abuse Council, Inc., 1976), p. 5.

12. Harold L. Votey, Jr., "Which Drug Policy is Least Costly: Addict Control or Control of Supply," *Journal of California Law Enforcement* 10, No. 4 (April 1976), pp. 148-153.

13. George Aliano and Lyle Knowles, "The Addict as Non-Victim: Narcotics Crimes Versus Property Crimes," *Journal of California Law Enforcement* 10, No. 4, (April 1976), pp. 154-157.

14. Rand Corporation, Study of Career Criminals, "The Roles of Drugs and Alcohol," Section VII, (Unpublished project, 1977).

15. H.L. Voss and R.C. Stephens, "Criminal History of Narcotic Addicts," *Drug Forum* 2, (1973), pp. 191-202.

16. Frances Rowe Gearing, "Methadone Maintenance Treatment Five Years Later—Where are They Now?" *American Journal of Public Health*, 64, Supp., (December, 1974), p. 49.

17. Michael Alexander and Catherine McCaslin, "Criminality in Heroin Addicts Before, During, and After Methadone Treatment," *American Journal of Public Health*, 64, Supp., (December, 1974), pp. 51-56.

18. Stimpson and Ogborne, pp. 13-22.

19. News Release, British Home Office, "1975 Statistics of the Misuse of Drugs in the United Kingdom," October 7, 1976.

20. Judson, p. 95.

21. Patricia M. Wald and Peter B. Hutt, "The Drug Abuse Survey Project: Sumary of Findings, Conclusions and Recommendations," from *Dealing with Drug Abuse*, Wald and Hutt, ed., (New York: Praeger Publishers, 1972), pp. 4-6.

22. Griffin Edwards, "Relevance of American Experience of Narcotic Addiction on British Scene," *British Medical Journal* 3 (1967), pp. 425, 428.

23. Judson, pp. 372, 379.

24. Leroy C. Gould, "Crime and the Addict: Beyond Common Sense," from *Drugs and The Criminal Justice System,* Inciardi and Chambers, ed., (Beverly Hills: Sage Publications, 1974), p. 61

25. Erich Goode, "Sociological Aspects of Marijuana Use," *Contemporary Drug Problems* 4, (Winter, 1975), pp. 397, 438-43.

26. Drug Survival News, March-April, 1977, p. 8.

27. David P. Ausubel, "The Psychology of the Marijuana Smoker," from *Marijuana*, Goode, ed., (New York: Atherton Press, 1969), pp. 17-19.

28. Wald & Hutt, pp. 4-6.

29. Judson, p. 115-117.

30. Los Angeles Times, April 11, 1976, Part V, p. 1.

31. Los Angeles Times, April 11, 1976, Part V, p. 14.

7

Narcotic Addiction and Criminal Responsibility:
A Current Controversy in the Courts

R. V. Phillipson and L. J. Striegel

The national institute on drug abuse estimates that there are between 350,000 and 700,000 addicts in the United States, with an additional number of persons—variously estimated at between 2–3 million—who use illegally obtained narcotic drugs on an occasional, recreational, or experimental basis. Congress estimates that drug-related programming and research reached $.75 billion in fiscal year 1977. Physicians, attorneys, and legislators continue to debate the issue of what constitutes society's proper response to the problem. In spite of humanitarian efforts to help narcotic addicts through increased access to treatment facilities, researchers continue to report disturbing increases in inner city crime rates presumed related to illegal drug use. In New York City, for example, researchers found that a 10 percent increase in the price of heroin led to a 3.6 percent increase in robberies, a 1.8 percent increase in burglaries, a 2.0 percent increase in larceny under $50, and a 2.5 percent increase in auto theft.[1] The necessity to resort to crime in order to support heroin addiction has been noted by both expert and lay persons. Statistics have also suggested that there is a corresponding decline in criminal behavior when heroin use decreases.[2]

The medical and legal professions have adopted different perspectives on the problem of heroin addiction. Medical experts have concentrated on developing treatment alternatives for the addict so as to alleviate the *causes* of criminal behavior. Federally supported methadone maintenance programs, as one example, currently offer the addict a controlled-dosage substitution for the use of heroin which provides a lasting effect of twenty-four hours. The accessibility of methadone decreases the need to obtain heroin every six hours to maintain a narcotic habit, and therefore permits an opportunity for the addict to stabilize his/her lifestyle and gradually withdraw from narcotic dependence.

The legal profession, on the other hand, has been faced with the *effects* of drug addiction seen in the increase in street crime associated with acquiring heroin. In attempting to conform the legal approach to the medical approach, Federal and State laws have provided for noninstitutional diversion programs for the addict convicted of nonviolent heroin crimes, such as possession of heroin and possession of the implements of a crime (i.e., syringes and needles, etc.). However, the courts have been faced with the added problem of protecting society from violent crimes against persons and property committed by the addict.

I. The Legal Perspective

The results of the legal system's attempt to recognize the special medical problems of the drug addict have been conflicting. It must be recognized that the basic premise of the criminal justice system is founded upon the maintenance of the social order and the criminal justice system will only go as far as society in general will allow. What is criminal behavior today may be non-criminal behavior tomorrow. To complicate the legal approach even further, the legal system is a bifurcated one, dealing with both Federal and State laws concerning heroin use. Federal laws attempt to define a coherent body of offenses that will apply to all the States. State laws can be vastly different both in providing for treatment alternatives and in prescribing punishment for persons who violate their criminal codes. Sentencing under Federal laws is therefore often more uniform than it is under the different State laws.

In spite of all of these problems with the legal approach to heroin addiction, the United States Supreme Court, in the case of *Robinson v. California,* 370 U.S. 660 (1962) has provided the legal system with some guidelines on the issue. In this landmark decision, the Supreme Court held that drug addiction was an illness and that a California State statute making an individual who was addicted criminally punishable for the addiction was unconstitutional. The Court held that any punishment of an individual *solely* for being addicted to narcotics amounted to cruel and unusual punishment, violating the Eighth Amendment of the Constitution. Under the California statute that the Court reviewed in *Robinson,* a person could have been criminally punished for the "status" of addiction, even though no criminal act might have been committed by the person in the State. While the Court specifically stated that any State could enact laws to punish persons for the criminal behavior of possessing narcotics, selling or manufacturing narcotics, or possessing the implements of a crime, it was held unconstitutional to inflict punishment for an illness without a showing of other related criminal behavior.

While the Court did find that narcotics addiction was not, in itself, criminal behavior, the *Robinson* case has raised more questions for the courts than it has answered. The issue for the courts today is whether the addict can be held criminally liable for violating any law. If addiction is an illness, the argument runs, how can the addict be said to be responsible for his/her behavior at any time?

Since the Robinson case, addicts have attempted to broaden the Supreme Court's holding by raising the issue of whether the illness of an addict removes responsibility for not only narcotics-related offenses such as possession, but other criminal behavior such as larceny, robbery, and shoplifting used to generate money to feed the narcotics habit. After the *Robinson* decision, in 1962, three types of arguments have been made to the courts concerning the issue of drug addiction and criminal responsibility:

> *The 8th Amendment Argument:* that all laws making possession of narcotics a crime should be declared unconstitutional as cruel and unusual punishment.
>
> The M'Naghten Rule, Durham Rule, and Model Penal Code Argument: that addiction should be seen as a type of insanity, so that addicts accused of criminal behavior could raise addiction as a defense.
>
> *The Drug Compulsion Defense Argument:* that an addict charged with a nonviolent crime should be entitled to argue that s/he is not criminally responsible.

All of these arguments are based on the Supreme Court's holding that drug addiction is an illness and not a crime. Each type of argument has attempted to make the law's response to drug addiction more flexible.

The 8th Amendment Argument

The cases arguing that State statutes which punish individuals for nonviolent narcotics crimes are unconstitutional, as cruel and unusual punishment, have not been upheld in the courts. It has been argued that the addict has been compelled by the disease of addiction to commit narcotics-related offenses, such as possession of heroin, so that any State punishment for these offenses is the same as punishing an addict for being an addict. The courts, however, have held that the States have a constitutional right to punish any persons for violating narcotics-related prohibitions to insure the public safety and well-being of their citizens.

Recent State decisions, therefore, have upheld punishments of five years imprisonment for the sale of heroin; 1 1/2 to 4 years imprisonment for self-administration of heroin; 15 years imprisonment for unlawful possession with intent to sell; 10 years imprisonment for possession of heroin; and one year in jail for unlawful possession of narcotics paraphernalia, (i.e., the implements of a crime). It can be seen from these examples that the length of sentences imposed for similar crimes varies widely among the States concerned. This, in itself, has led to further controversy among judges, attorneys, and addicts. In May, 1977, for example, a Federal District Court judge in Virginia ruled that a sentence imposed by a jury for 40 years and a $20,000 fine for possessing and selling nine ounces of marijuana was cruel and unusual punishment. Under Virginia law, the power to fix sentences is in the hands of juries, not the judges. The decision is the first one to hold a sentence unconstitutional because of its length. It may very well be that if the decision stands, a new precedent may be set involving the Eighth Amendment and drug-related sentencing that will bring new appeals and result in some conformity among State decisions.

The M'Naghten Rule, Durham Rule, and Model Penal Code Argument

The most widespread argument that addicts have used with regard to criminal responsibility is that the addict is not liable for criminal action by reason of drug-induced insanity. The insanity defense is particularly troublesome to the courts since it directly involves the courts with psychiatric testimony by expert witnesses that is often inconclusive. First articulated in the famous *M'Naghten* case of 1843, the insanity defense has undergone great changes in recent times. Although M'Naghten remains the legal definition of insanity that can be found in all jurisdictions. The *Durham rule* and the *Model Penal Code* definitions of insanity have altered our perceptions of what constitutes criminal responsibiilty. Each different definition of insanity has a direct bearing on the amount and type of proof required to be established by the defendant. The law presumes that a criminal defendant is sane or competent to stand trial. That is a rebuttable presumption, however, and an accused can raise the issue of insanity as a defense to any criminal charge. If the accused meets all the requirements of the particular test applicable in the State, the burden of proving that the accused is competent shifts to the prosecutor. Once insanity is established by the evidence, the accused can no longer be charged with the crime, since the intent to commit a crime, or *mens rea,* is lacking and the accused is therefore not criminally responsible. As a result, the insane person is held not to be competent to stand trial and is committed to an institution for treatment until such time as competency can be established and the trial can be resumed.

Addicts have attempted to use the insanity defense when charged with narcotics-related offenses and other types of criminal behavior, arguing through drug compulsion the addict has lost the capacity to commit criminal acts. It has been argued that the overwhelming need to possess drugs has been such a compulsion as to render the addict insane at the time of committing the criminal act (at "material times").

Under the M'Naghten definition of insanity, in order for the accused to be relieved of criminal responsibility, the accused must have been laboring under such a defect of reason, from a disease of the mind, as not to know the nature and quality of the act done, or — if that was known — as not to know the wrongfulness of the act done. This right-wrong test requires that the addict show addiction and such drug-induced disease that s/he is incapable of exerting a reasoned choice as to whether or not to commit criminal acts. M'Naghten is considered to be the strictest type of insanity definition and addicts claiming an insanity defense in M'Naghten States have not been successful. This lack of success is attributable to the controversy over whether drug influence constitutes a disease of the mind and abrogates free will. Juries have looked to the expert testimony of psychiatrists and physicians to resolve this problem. Since the opinion of the experts is often conflicting, the jury has been left to determine whether the accused was capable of knowing right from wrong at the time of the crime. Generally, lay definitions of insanity tend to be predicated on complete madness. Unless the accused is found unable to distinguish right from wrong, the insanity defense is of little utility under the M'Naghten definition.

The Durham insanity rule, first adopted in the District of Columbia in 1954 and later overruled there, has posed an equally difficult test for an accused. Under Durham, an accused is found not guilty by reason of insanity if the unlawful act was the product of a mental disease or defect. Mere proof of addiction is not sufficient. The addict must show that the unlawful act was a product of the disease. While the accused need not prove that s/he cannot distinguish right from wrong under this test, the accused must show that drug addiction is a mental disease or defect. Again, the medical experts in the field of drug addiction have not resolved this question: the resolution of the problem has been left to the jury. In the face of statistics that drug addicts can voluntarily give up the addiction and choose treatment, and in view of the fact that treatment alternatives are often readily available to the addict, it has been difficult for juries to find that addiction is a mental disease. Thus, the Durham insanity test has not been of much assistance to the addict.

The most recent insanity definition is found in *the Model Penal Code* rule written in the late 1960's, which has been adopted in a minority of jurisdictions. Under this rule, an accused in not responsible for criminal conduct if, at the time of such conduct and as a result of a mental disease or defect, the accused lacks substantial capacity to appreciate the wrongfulness of the conduct or to conform the conduct to the requirements of the law. The courts which have used this test have usually accepted the premise that addiction is a mental disease or defect. Thus, jury conflict over this issue is reduced and the problem for the court is whether the addiction has resulted in substantial deprivation of the ability to conform personal conduct to the law. This test is generally regarded as the broadest insanity definition, since there is no need to prove total incapacity because of addiction, but only substantial incapacity. The Model Penal Code definition has been used by the courts in dealing with the drug addict's claim of drug compulsion. The accused must show addiction and must demonstrate that the need to possess narcotics was so overpowering that the accused was unable to substantially conform his/her conduct to the law. The courts have cautioned that the Model Penal Code test specifically excludes antisocial or repeated criminal behavior. Under this test, the courts must decide whether the criminal acts committed are examples of antisocial behavior or whether they are done involuntarily under a type of compulsion that could not be prevented by the addict.

The cases brought under this definition of insanity have met with some limited success in the courts. However, conflict in the medical profession has led experts in the field of drug abuse to argue that drug addiction is voluntarily induced and that any addict committing acts under the influence of drug compulsion bears criminal responsibility. Due to the lack of consensus among the experts as to the voluntariness of drug-induced compulsion, this test of insanity has met with the same result as the other tests explained above: the resolution of conflicting expert testimony is left up to the judge or the jury to decide. Traditionally, juries have tended to opt for a conservative approach to the insanity issue and, thus, even under the more liberal Model Penal Code definition of insanity the defense of drug compulsion-insanity is not often upheld.

The Drug Compulsion Defense Argument

A third and much more forceful legal approach used by addicts involves the argument that the addict cannot help but commit the specific crime of heroin possession and should be able to raise this drug compulsion as a defense to any nonviolent heroin crime charge. This approach narrows the scope of the argument to crimes of possession and implements and is a combination of cruel and unusual punishment argument with the drug-compulsion insanity defense. The case of *U.S. v. Gorham*, 399 A. 2d 401 (District of Columbia, 1975), sets out the arguments for a drug compulsion defense for nontrafficking addicts.

In the *Gorham* case, addicts attempted to raise the affirmative defense of drug compulsion to crimes of possession of implements of a crime. Simply put, the accused persons argued that the heroin dependent individual is compelled to commit the crimes of possession of heroin and the paraphernalia necessary to administer it because of their addiction. Thus, they sought to maintain the argument that a drug dependent person has no criminal responsibility in relation to narcotics-related offenses not involving manufacturing or selling drugs.

The court, in an exhaustive opinion, looked to the intent of Congress in establishing the Federal narcotics laws and to the expert testimony of psychiatrists to determine whether such a defense could be raised. It was held in *Gorham* that the Federal court has no power to recognize this defense which, if allowed, would constitute a new common-law rule of criminal responsibility to insulate drug users from punishment. In effect, the court said, recognition of the drug compulsion defense would legalize or sanction the possession of heroin and the possession of heroin paraphernalia. The court looked to the intent of the Narcotic Addict Rehabilitation Act of 1966, the Drug Abuse Office and Treatment Act of 1972, and the Drug Control Act of 1970, and found that although these acts provided for treatment alternatives for the addict, none of these legislative enactments was intended to relieve the addict of criminal responsibility or prosecution.

The Court also looked to the testimony of psychiatrists, one of whom, Dr. R.V. Phillipson, stated that addicts were responsible for their actions at material times unless there was clearcut evidence of insanity. If addicts were legally viewed as being under compulsion at the time of committing the criminal acts of possesion, Dr. Phillipson testified, then how could any addict exercise free will sufficient to choose a treatment alternative, as many addicts had? And further, without the threat of criminal prosecution for these acts, why would an addict choose a treatment alternative?

The *Gorham* court decided that the efforts of Congress showed no intent to allow this defense and thus legalize possession of narcotics, and that Congressional efforts to provide treatment alternatives to criminal prosecution would be seriously hampered by the removal of the prosecution deterrent. The result of the *Gorham* case is to emphasize that drug dependence alone does not remove criminal responsibility from the addict. The only way for the addict to legally maintain a claim of drug compulsion today, then, is within the context of the insanity defense.

The Legal Perspective Summarized

The courts have defined addiction as a legal illness. Faced with a huge proportion of drug-related criminal activity, however, the courts have held that addicts, as other persons, are responsible for the commission of criminal actions. The fact that addicts must often commit crimes in order to raise the money needed to support their addiction, and that these crimes work great harm on victims for whom the law must provide protection, has tended to fortify the legal argument that criminal sanctions must be maintained.

The law has provided a place for the drug compulsion defense and this has been within the context of the insanity claim. It is certain that addicts will continue to attempt to broaden the *Robinson* holding so as to remove criminal sanctions for the possession of heroin and heroin paraphernalia. However, it is the opinion of the authors here that the Supreme Court is not likely to hold State statutes making possession of heroin or parapernalia a crime unconstitutional. For, no matter how the medical experts resolve the dispute as to addiction and criminal responsibility, there is a clear threat to society from the criminal behavior of drug addicts. It is society that must provide treatment alternatives to the addict, and it is the place of the law and the courts to provide protection for all citizens, including the addict, in the best and most humane way possible.

The critical issue for the law, then, is to set an objective standard by which all citizens can be measured and yet provide enough flexibility for subjective arguments about drug addiction to be raised within that context. To what extent the law has succeeded in achieving this compromise is the point at issue here. It is clear, however, that until the medical experts achieve some consensus about addiction and its effects on behavior, the law and the legislators cannot formulate new rules by which the members of society can exist. The ultimate statement about the law's response to the question of drug dependence and criminal responsibility is that the law, with *Robinson,* has recognized the problem.

II. The Medical Perspective

When a member of the medical profession is called upon by the courts to give expert testimony for the benefit of the lay jury, difficult questions are raised. Since psychiatry by definition is not an exact science, medical opinions will vary. Under the M'Naghten Rule, medical experts have been required to answer the right-wrong test in terms of an accused pleading insanity. To the layman, M'Naghten more closely conforms to a complete madness or incurably insane test, and the law has almost confined psychiatric testimony to this observation. Unless the accused is suffering from a complete inability to make a reasoned choice about his/her actions, according to the M'Naghten Rule, the accused will be held responsible under law.

The problems for the medical profession under this strict test stem from the fact that the right-wrong issue requires moral and not scientific answers. Further, the M'Naghten Rule applies only to cognitive features of the accused's behavior, and will not allow for the introduction of testimony concerning environmental factors that could affect the situation. In 1843, of course, the M'Naghten Rule may have provided an objective test by which the psychiatrist could define and the courts could understand insanity. Developments in the field of psychiatry have correspondingly increased psychiatric criticism of these legal tests. Under the Model Penal Code, there is more room for psychiatric observation of the accused in the environment. However, psychiatrists accustomed to studying the causes of addiction have encountered great difficulty in conforming their observations to even the most lenient objective legal requisites, like the Model Penal Code test.

Psychiatrists dealing with drug addicts have additionally been confronted with recent scientific breakthroughs that the brain, itself, produces morphine-like substances called Endorphins, which raises the difficult issue of whether addiction may have biological or genetic concomitants. What impact further research into this area will have on the drug addiction-insanity defenses is yet unknown.

In addition to the problems of adapting medical opinion to fixed legal definitions, the experts who have been involved in treatment of addicts have consistently cited the need for treatment as an alternative to incarceration. This presupposes that addicts are treatable and that their compulsiveness can be removed or re-directed. Development of long acting drugs that function as heroin substitutes have given experts more data on the process of recovery from narcotic addiction.

In view of the fact that the society has addicts who have participated in treatment and who have made a reasoned choice to seek treatment, legal arguments over drug compulsion-induced "insanity" become moot. Once addicts become responsible enough to choose treatment, the medical profession can probably not continue to define addiction in terms of the addict lacking criminal responsibility. Under M'Naghten, the mere fact that any addicts in a State using the test had chosen treatment would sufficiently destroy the argument that addicts lacked criminal responsibility while under the influence of heroin. Under the Model Penal Code test, data on recovery rates of addicts would have a substantial impact on the issue of responsibility. In fact, few studies have been conducted by the medical profession using data from recovered addicts on the issue of whether or not the addicts believed themselves to have been responsible while under the influence of heroin. Dr. R.V. Phillipson conducted one such preliminary survey in 1971, using questionnaires circulated to twelve narcotic treatment centers. Sixty-seven percent of the recovered addicts, responding to the issue of criminal responsibility, agreed that their motivation for cure would have been removed if the law ruled that heroin addicts were not responsible for their actions at material times.

Clearly, there can be no solution to the problem of drug dependence and criminal responsibility without a closer working definition of addiction, itself. Until addiction is defined by the medical profession in the context of mental disease or defect, or until the legal profession changes the laws to include the addict's special type of illness, the controversy will continue to divide the courts, anger the medical profession, and punish the society.

The Medical Perspective Summarized

Most legal tests require a psychiatrist to conform subjective evaluation to objective fact. Due to the inexactness of the science, it is almost impossible to comment upon psychiatric disorder in anything but the most general terms. Hypothetical questions asked of a psychiatrist in a courtroom, while beneficial for a lay jury, often result in superficial responses not applicable to the facts of an individual's case.

Since the causes of addiction may vary from psychological stress to physical dependence and chemical insufficiency, the discovery of these causes can be a particularly time-consuming process. Of course, such discovery could bear directly on the issue of criminal responsibility, and is not amenable to the type of instant analysis required of psychiatrists in court. The often contradictory testimony of defense and prosecution experts is the result not only of differing individual opinions but of time constraint. It is proposed, therefore, that the psychiatric and legal communities coordinate their efforts to provide the services of independent experts to judge and juries. While many courts already permit judges to call upon such experts, there has been no attempt by the medical profession to assist the courts in assembling a body of expert information upon which the courts may rely for some consistency of approach. Further study by the medical community into drug dependence is certianly required, but in view of the alarming effect on society of growing drug dependence, action in such a direction is required now.

III. Conclusion

This article has attempted to point out the difficulties inherent in the legal and medical approaches to drug addiction and criminal responsibility. Until it is understood that the different perspectives stem from approaching the causes of addiction on the medical side and effect on the legal side, the professions will never reach agreement on the addict's responsibility to society and society will suffer from continued confusion and controversy over the issue.

Discussion Questions

1. Do you agree with the hypothesis that legal recognition of "uncontrollable impulse" is counterproductive for the addict in that it would remove the motivation to become drug free?

2. In the absence of established insanity, would you agree that each individual is fully responsible for his actions at material times?

3. Suppose a non-addicted person commits murder while under the influence of PCP, a drug which some medical evidence suggests induced psychotic reaction. You are the judge or jury called upon to decide the case. How would you answer the following questions:

   A. Is there any criminal intent here?

   B. Would you take the type of drug into account in making your decision?

   C. Would you make a distinction between violent and non-violent criminal actions?

   D. How should society punish the murderer or vindicate the family of the victim?

   E. What evidence would you want to see or hear from the defense and the prosecution?

Notes

1. G. Brown and L. Silverman, *The Retail Price of Heroin: Estimation and Applications* (Washington, D.C.: Drug Abuse Council, Inc. 1973).

2. Tinklenberg, "Drugs and Crime," *Technical Papers of the Second Report of the National Commission on Marijuana and Drug Abuse* 242.262 (Washington, D.C.: 1973).

8

Prostitution and the Criminal Justice System— An Analysis of Present Policy and Possible Alternatives

STEPHEN ROWE

Introduction

THE CRIME OF PROSTITUTION lies in an area continually marked by controversy. Laws against prostitution are enforced on an often erratic basis, largely affected by changing political winds. Prostitution, often called "the world's oldest profession," has remained where many a civilization has fallen.

It will be the scope of this chapter to discuss prostitution as it relates to the criminal justice system. Some of the specific topics to be covered are: the prostitute in society, the present law-enforcement policy toward prostitution enforcement, the role of ancillary crime, and finally, the policy alternatives of decriminalization and legalization.

The Crime of Prostitution, an overview

The Prostitute in Society— "the world's oldest profession"

Prostitution is an institution which has existed in ancient as well as modern times. In ancient Greece, the hetarea played a valued role in the religious ceremonies, often living in the cities' finest homes. During the crusades, King Louis IX of France had prostitutes making up his entourage when setting out for the Holy Land. The term "hooker" is believed to be derived from the camp followers who affiliated themselves with a division of Civil War General Joseph Hooker's soldiers.[1]

From ancient times to the present, prostitutes have been classified by themselves, and researchers, into three specific groupings. Lowest on the social scale is the brothel worker. She is looked down upon because the brothel is seen by her peers as a form of incarceration; furthermore, she has no choice in the selection of customers. The next step up the ladder constitutes the intermediate (and largest) group of individuals— the streetwalkers. The streetwalker, with her typical brightly colored hot pants and high boots represents the most visible aspect of prostitution. She can often be seen walking the city's seamier streets. At the apex of the prostitutes' status ladder is the call girl. Normally white, sometimes affiliated with a pimp (though more often not) they seek the white collar end of the business. They can most commonly be found around the conventions and high-class hotels. Call girls are rarely arrested, and as a result can easily make $1,000 per week.

Recently there has been a trend, especially in New York, for a "daytime" crowd of housewives and working women who use prostitution as a means of supplementing the family budget. New York police estimate that as many as ten percent of the prostitutes in Times Square during the weekends are housewives from suburban Long Island and New Jersey.[2]

Beside housewives, there has been a trend for a younger crowd to involve themselves in prostitution. These are teenagers from the suburbs who engage in prostitution either as runaways or just looking for a means to make extra cash. These newcomers, as a result of their inexperience, fall prey to both vice officers and pimps. The pimp attempts to strike up a conversation with the juvenile with recruitment into his own "stable" as his ultimate goal.[3]

The pimp fills a special role in the prostitute's life. He handles the financial aspects of the business, such as holding her money, bailing her out in case of arrest, supporting her children, and so forth. Furthermore, he often supplies strong-arm protection against potentially violent customers.

In addition, the prostitute's life contains much isolation and loneliness, and thus the pimp supplies the emotional support or caring that they need. Therefore, in many cases, the relationship between the prostitute and her pimp will be one of lovers:

> . . . because I love him very much. Obviously, I'm doing this mostly for him. . . I'd do anything for him. I'm not just saying I will, I am . . .[After discussing his affair with another woman] I just decided that I knew what he was when I decided to do this for him and I decided I had two choices—either accept it or not, and I have accepted it, and I have no excuse.[4]

Ancillary Crime

Prostitution is illegal in every state of the union with the exception of rural counties in Nevada. Law enforcement officials often argue that prostitution must remain illegal so that they can control the crimes associated with it. These crimes include larceny, robbery, assault, drug addiction, and occasionally even murder.

The most common offense reported, supported by both field research and police statistics, is larceny. Larceny is normally committed by some prostitutes while the customer is distracted during the sexual act. Many prostitutes see no difference in committing an act of larceny along with an act of prostitution. Often they have found that, in some jurisdictions, committing an act of prostitution will carry a higher penalty than committing larceny.[5]

Another form of larceny occasionally committed in association with prostitution is a confidence game known as the "paddy hustle." This ploy occurs when the customer leaves his wallet and valuables with a trustworthy third party (who often is the pimp), only to find both possessions and "friend" gone when he returns.[6]

The role of drugs in the prostitute's world is often cited as another ancillary crime. Indeed, many prostitutes, streetwalkers in particular, are often addicted to heroin. And yet, a distinction can be made between the addict-prostitute and the professional prostitute. The addict-prostitute normally uses prostitution only as a means of acquiring fast money, for she often commits other petty crimes as well. The professional prostitute tends to dissociate herself from narcotics usage in general. Furthermore, many pimps double as drug pushers. Besides dealing drugs, some pimps use narcotics as a means to keep control over the girls in their stable.

Some assaults also occur in association with prostitution. Assaults to the customer and the prostitute are not uncommon. Pimps will occasionally beat their women to maintain discipline. The customer may be attacked, robbed, or murdered as a result of his being in an area with a high criminal element.

It is often assumed that organized crime is involved in prostitution. However, this may not be true, for the President's Crime Commission reported in 1967 that prostitution plays ". . . a small and declining role in organized crime's operations."[7] Nevertheless, organized crime can be defined in terms other than Mafia involvement. For instance, what about the common ownership of massage parlors? As one big-city vice officer put it: "Two or three individuals are the owners of approximately 60–75% of the massage studios (in this city) and some prostitution occurs in these studios."

To be sure, the relationship between prostitution and ancillary crime is complex, and an area lacking in solid research and evidence. Even the police are unsure of the connection, in the words of the previous vice cop: "(We have) no way of telling, since there is a reluctance to report crimes of theft, assault, because of the stigma prostitution attaches to the crime." Nevertheless, some are more convinced, as one urban deputy district attorney relates:

> Well, there is a lot of ancillary crime associated with (prostitution); because a lot of prostitutes are drug addicts, there is a dependence on pimps for their bail money, and pimps tend not be very nice people. . . . In any event, it's a seedy, seedy world, and there are robberies, there are

extensive amounts of drugs, venereal disease; these are most of the problems associated with prostitution.

Community and Business Interest in Prostitution

A point briefly touched upon by the preceding deputy district attorney's remarks is the widely held belief that prostitutes are a significant source of venereal disease. However, public health officials report that prostitutes, even though they have numerous sexual contacts, account for approximately only 5% of the cases nationwide.[8] Increasing promiscuity and changing sexual mores of the young people account for 84% of all reported cases of venereal disease.[9] Thus, community fears that prostitution is a health menace are largely based on misinformation.

Another aspect of prostitution which concerns members of the community and business districts is the occurrences of public solicitation. As an illustration, many streetwalkers not satisfied by having the customers coming to them, seek to "drum up" extra business by flagging down cars and grabbing the coattails of pedestrians. Many citizens and tourists alike are offended by such behavior. Furthermore, many individuals consider such flagrant solicitations as an indication of increasing lawlessness. They believe this to be one of the many indications that the criminal justice system is failing to protect them and this produces a growing fear in the citizenry.

Moreover, many small businessmen complain that large groups of streetwalkers outside their shops are deterring customers from entering and, as a result, they lose business. Hotel managers are also quite vocal in regard to the presence of prostitutes in their hotels. "Not a night goes by," explained Daniel C. Hickey, president of the Hotel Association of New York City, "that security guards in reputable hotels are not compelled to eject numbers of prostitutes who solicit customers in its halls and public rooms."[10]

Finally there is a sizable segment of the community which feels that the present enforcement policies against prostitutes are discriminatory, both racially and sexually. This group is made up of feminists, lawyers, liberal reformers, as well as many in the minority communities. They feel that there should be alternatives to the present enforcement policies of the criminal justice system.

Present Law Enforcement Policy Toward Prostitution

Role of the Vice Squad

Nowhere does law enforcement policy appear more susceptible to changing political whims than in the area of prostitution. Arrest statistics will climb one year and fall the next. When pressure to "clean up the streets" gets too hot, a street sweep is often put into operation. The sweep merely removes the prostitutes from the streets temporarily (often until they are bailed out), gets a lot of publicity, and enlarges the arrest statistics. Normally, the arrests from such a campaign will not hold up in court due to lack of evidence, resulting in dismissal of the charges. Therefore, street sweeps are not very productive for the resources expended.

Another method for achieving a prostitution arrest is for the crime of solicitation. Any citizen can report that he had been solicited. However, few have the time to spend going to police headquarters, filling out a complaint, and testifying in court. Furthermore, customers naturally do not want to be involved with a prostitution arrest. If a police officer arrests a prostitute and customer on the street, the customer is apt to produce false information, be released (since many jurisdictions do not detain customers) and thus, eliminates the prospects of locating him when the case comes to trial. If the customer should produce correct identification, few appear in court to testify anyway.

Therefore, since the police have learned that the customer's testimony cannot be relied upon, they have resorted to the use of plainclothes officers, who pose as customers and await a solicitation. If contact is made with a suspected prostitute, the officer must let the woman set the price and mention the act involved, for any overt action on his part would be considered entrapment. The girl, unless she is a novice, would be wary of any man playing coy, because she would assume him to be a police officer. This verbal skirmishing results in consuming police time and energy toward a futile objective. Finally, the plainclothes officer's identity would soon spread through the street grapevine, making his future use worthless.[11]

A third method is to hire civilian agents, who have sex with the prostitute and later testify in court against her. Often many acts must occur before the arrest is made; in each case, the city pays for the service. If the civilian agent is married, he would be breaking adultery and sodomy laws in order to facilitate the prostitution arrest.[12]

Female agents are also used to arrest the customers. Female agents and decoys (who may be policewomen or policemen's wives) normally are solicited, lure the customer to where he thinks the act will take place, and finds vice officers waiting to take him into custody.

Present in any discussion of the vice squad is their high potential for corruption, due to the nature of the work. Their lack of accountability (many departments have the vice squad accountable only to the chief), type of investigative procedures, use of informants and civilian agents allow for corruption to gain an entrance into a police department. Some examples include not arresting a prostitute or inspecting a tavern or hotel where prostitution is known to occur, as a result of a payoff.[13]

A final example of the vice squad effectiveness can be found on the West Coast where prostitutes are thought to travel a "circuit." They start in San Diego, then San Jose, next San Francisco and Oakland, then Portland on to Seattle, then back to San Diego again.[14] They work a particular city until they have accumulated enough charges to where they must stand trial. They will then leave town, change their identity, and start again in a new city.[15] In short, vice officers often succeed in only "displacing" prostitution from one area to another.

The Prosecution of Prostitution

Bringing a prostitute to trial is not an easy task either. The first item of business for the prostitute's attorney is to demand a jury trial. The asking for a trial date accomplishes two points. First, if the case centers upon a customer's testimony, the case will probably be dismissed due to the fact that few customers appear to testify.

If the customer turns out to be a vice cop, then the tactic is to ask for repeated continuances, until the prosecution offers a better plea-bargain deal. Both tactics succeed in tying up further an already overburdened court system. The end result is often dismissals or suspended sentences arrived at through plea bargaining. As one urban deputy district attorney explains it:

> If a case goes to trial, the defendant probably has a large number of suspended sentences hanging over her head anyway, so she'll probably be facing a lot of jail time . . .
>
> The practice [in this city] is to try to get high suspended sentences on the first, second or third disposition . . . But it doesn't necessarily follow that the defendant's first time through the system will be a conviction for [prostitution]. The evidence may be bad or in several cases kicked out, or there may be a lesser offense on the first charge. In any case, the practice is to get a suspended sentence of some duration . . .

Limited Jail Space

If the prostitute is sentenced to a term in the local jail facility, she merely burdens the criminal justice system even more. Most jurisdictions have inadequate jail space accorded for female prisoners. Consequently, many female prisoners are "boarded" at facilities in other counties, resulting in higher detention costs.

Rehabilitative Potential

What is the potential for rehabilitating a prostitute while in jail? Not much. Prostitutes are quite hostile to the prospect of rehabilitation. As one prostitute interviewed for a study in prostitution law stated quite clearly:

> Why do I have to be rehabilitated? I have no education, no skills . . . Is
> there a job I can have that will give me the freedom and the money that
> this (prostitution) can? . . .
> The longer you're in the business, the more you become professionali-
> zed, and it becomes too big of an effort and expense to change careers and
> turn to a new life.[16]

Indeed, society has to find employment alternatives for poor, young,
uneducated women. Prostitution is the only occupation offering affluence
and glitter in the midst of poverty.

The present manner in which prostitution is enforced results in valuable
criminal justice resources being utilized toward a futile goal. In fact, the
arrest and bailing out, infrequent trial, and occasional fine, probation or
short jail sentence are viewed by many prostitutes as a "license fee" for doing
business.[17] Moreover, it has been estimated that various law enforcement
agencies spend between $600 and $1,200 to arrest, try, and incarcerate a
single woman charged with prostitution.[18] As one crime commission stated
it: "One thing is clear. Present law enforcement practices have not worked,
and we can do little worse by trying something different."[19]

Policy Alternatives Within the Present Criminal Law Framework

Many law enforcement officials feel that their state's prostitution laws are
inadequate to meet the problem. However, their complaint lies with the
present system for administering justice. The courts are overcrowded with
the delays vice (and other) crimes cause. Therefore, what these individuals
advocate is a massive infusion of resources to increase efficiency in the
administration of justice. This will result in the increasing of the number of
courts, as well as the construction of new jails. Unfortunatley, most urban
dwellers are already overtaxed, and to increase the tax rate for these additional resources would not go unchallenged.

Another method is to use the existing criminal law statutes more effectively by making prostitution a citable offense. Police officers would issue
citations, like traffic tickets, for violations of prostitution. The citation
would then be treated like any other traffic ticket in court. The offender
would be, by paying a fine, eliminating the need for a court appearance,
thereby greatly reducing court costs. This procedure has been used effectively with other misdemeanor crimes in the past, and awaits the application
to the crime of prostitution. A side benefit of the citation procedure would
be the diminishing of the prostitute's reliance on her pimp for bail money.

A final method for controlling prostitution is to zone certain areas in the
city whereby prostitution can be practiced freely and to increase the
penalties for those working outside the area. Most law enforcement officials

oppose the idea, for it would concentrate the criminal element into a small area, thus causing an increase in crime for that area, an increase in police resources into the area, and a decreasing of police services throughout the rest of the city. The city of Boston's now infamous "Combat Zone" is pointed out, by police officials, as an example of the impracticality of this solution. A variation of the zoning technique applying especially to massage parlors is to zone them apart, thereby preventing a "combat zone" collection of establishments to occur.

Innovative Policy Alternatives — Decriminalization and Legalization

The policy alternatives of decriminalization and legalization involve major modifications in the criminal code. Hence, any attempts toward the institution of these policies would have to originate in the legislative sector. One law enforcement official stated that any policy change of this magnitude should be nationwide, so as not to overburden specific states.[20] As an example, suppose New York or California legalized prostitution. It would be natural to assume that out-of-state prostitutes would gravitate toward those states.[21]

Decriminalization

Decriminalization involves the total removal of criminal sanctions toward the crime of prostitution. This alternative is one held by individuals who feel that it is not the law's function to regulate the private morals of its citizens. Furthermore, many feel that legalization would in fact legitimatize the exploitation of women. As Margo St. James, Chairmadam of COYOTE (Call Off Your Old Tired Ethics), a San Francisco group advocating the decriminalization of prostitution, succinctly put it:

> I prefer the decriminalization over legalization or the total criminalizing of (prostitution), because if you have it legal or illegal, history shows us that women are exploited, no matter what way it's run, unless you let them run it themselves, which decriminalizing would do.

Just how would prostitution be run under the atmosphere of decriminalization? Supporters believe that since it is basically an illicit occupation at present, simply treat it like any other business. Again, in the words of Margo St. James:

> If it is treated just like any other business, they (prostitutes) can go downtown, get a small business licence, stick to whatever requirements are set up to obtain and keep that license, file income taxes as independent contractors, even have cooperatives with each other . . . What this does is make prostitutes feel that there is a regulatory system protecting them and their rights . . . that their status is raised to that of ordinary people

who offer their services for a living . . . that in their work can be a sense of pride for doing a service that there is a market for, for doing it well and for getting paid well for their work. Then there is no stigma attached to their occupation. . .[22]

Law enforcement officials are quite opposed to the prospect of decriminalizing prostitution. The reason for their objection is quite simple. Decriminalization would remove prostitution from police control, and subject it to ordinary business regulation. They point out that under decriminalization the amount of ancillary crime will largely increase. As one vice officer summarized it:

I think decriminalization is highly impractical. With some controls, perhaps we are not too successful with them, but there is still a chance that an arrest will be made. Decriminalization will open the door to more prostitution and pimps. If we went carte blanche, there will be a tremendous increase in related crimes of credit card thefts, assaults, and narcotics.

Naturally, the supporters of decriminalization would have to counter this forceful argument to further their cause. Margo St. James sees the law enforcement belief that ancillary crime will increase as:

. . .total hogwash, because keeping it illegal is what forces the prostitute into the criminal element in the first place. She is usually the victim of those crimes and often keeping it illegal makes it possible for people who are really theives to pretend to be prostitutes. . . The customer commits all kinds of crimes against the prostitute which you never hear about . . . They're encouraged to commit crimes against each other by the illegality and the fact that they are both outside the law.

Therefore, it would be logical to separate the ancillary crimes from the crime of prostitution. Indeed, if there was no stigma or fear of arrest, customers would be more apt to come forward to testify. The presence of prostitution-related crimes could therefore be best controlled by the allocation of police resources directly to these crimes. In addition, proponents of decriminalization suggest that the addict-prostitute could now seek legitimate medical help due to her diminishing need for a pimp as a protector against the criminal justice system. Also, since she would not need to be bailed out, the pimp's role is further diminished. In short, if the coercive aspects of pimping were to remain illegal, the decriminalized prostitute could decide to remain with a pimp by choice, not by necessity.

Public solicitation is another point used by law enforcement officials as a reason for keeping prostitution illegal. In the words of one prosecuting attorney:

> The issue really is: if there is no restriction against the solicitation of sex for money, then you're going to have lots of whores on the streets, and then you're going to have lots of johns running around soliciting women they think to be whores. That, to an awful lot of people, is offensive. That is something decriminalization couldn't deal with.

COYOTE, and its affiliates, contend that public solicitation should be allowed, though encouraged to be done through discreet ads in newspapers or at special bars. If a citizen has been offended, he or she would go to the police headquarters, sign the arrest report, and then the police could take action. The offense could then be classified as a public nuisance. The punishment for this offense would be a citation or a fine. [23]

To briefly summarize, the decriminalization of prostitution would allow the greatest personal freedom from government interference for a conduct of a private nature. Regulation would be done in a business atmosphere, incorporating health requirements and zoning with the unlicensed prostitute being prosecuted. Solicitation would be controlled as a public nuisance only if someone, not the police, complained. Finally, ancillary crime can best be fought by the allocation of police manpower to those specific crimes.

Legalization

> Because you don't have enough resources, you have de facto legalization in private, we can't make the government Big Brother, so it's not so anything will change.
>
> A Law Enforcement Official
>
> . . . decriminalization . . . in my opinion is not a workable alternative, and what I advocate is . . . that the legislature should explore alternatives to the present system, and before I would support any alternative, there would have to be a comprehensive study leading to regulation of what would become a regulated, but legal, industry. There would have to be health regulations, there would have to be standards of where and what circumstances (the activity) concerned about would take place, would be a taxable, commercial activity like any other commercial activity.
>
> Joseph Freitas, Jr.
> San Francisco District Attorney

Legalization[24] requires that sexual conduct be regulated by the government. This system is usually characterized by the institution of brothels or houses of prostitution. Under legalization, prostitutes will work in these houses and be supervised by a madam or foreman. The customer would come to the house, select a prostitute, and conduct his activity there.

As mentioned in section one, most prostitutes would not enjoy working in brothels. As one researcher has written:

. . . Most prostitutes do not want to work in controlled houses where they cannot choose their customers and must make excessive payments to the madam or foreman. Many customers do not like the closed, commercial atmosphere of a house and still prefer to meet women on the street or through a call girl system. . . . The only women who would actually work in state-run brothels would be those who are now frequently arrested: the poor, minority, and less-able women who have limited opportunities or alternatives. They would be forced to exchange one form of incarceration for another.[25]

Supporters of legalization contend that it would control the time and place of prostitution; hence, offensive street solicitation would be eliminated. The need for a pimp would be eliminated. The usage of drugs and violent ancillary crime would be reduced. Venereal disease would be easily controlled through periodic in-house medical checkups of customers and prostitutes. Finally, the customer would know what to expect ahead of time in terms of prices and acts to be conducted via a printed brochure.

Nevada is the only state of the union allowing legalized prostitution with some limitations, to occur. However, regulation is left only to rural counties, for counties with a population of 200,000 people or more are disallowed by Nevada statutes from legalizing prostitution.

Opponents of legalization point out that the Nevada procedure of allowing local licensing of brothels can create a monopolization of the prostitution in a single area. The infamous Mustang Ranch near Reno is a prime example, being the only brothel in Storey County. Opponents state that a legal scheme of this type invites involvement by organized crime, as well as the possibility of public officials being corrupted.

Summary

The crime of prostitution is a controversial one. This chapter has discussed the prostitute in society, the present criminal justice system policy toward the crime of prostitution, policy alternatives within the present criminal law framework, and the innovative alternatives of decriminalization and legalization

Prostitution is a subject of many perspectives. Historically, the prostitute belongs to "the world's oldest profession." Currently, she can be a brothel worker, streetwalker, runaway, or high-class call girl. Her world is a violent one, where assaults and drug addiction are commonplace. Her pimp may act as her protector from the criminal justice system, with bail money and lawyer fees, or he may be her pusher, supplying the illicit drug to which she is addicted. Finally, she works in a community where mixed messages concerning prostitution enforcement occur. One segment feels that prostitutes are a bane to business and a source of disease and crime, while another faction feels that since prostitution is a victimless crime the police should be directing their efforts in other directions.

The criminal justice system has been largely ineffective in enforcing the laws against prostitution. Vice squads spend much of their time producing little in the form of concrete results. Hundreds of dollars are spent with the end result often being only the displacement of prostitutes from one area of the city to another. The prostitute who has been convicted and sentenced merely burdens further the system and the taxpayers.

If the only goal of the legislature is to recognize prostitution as the social reality that it is, then there is basically no difference between decriminalization and legalization. The major difference lies in the amount of governmental intervention each alternative would allow. Decriminalization would require a minimum level of involvement by the government, whereas legalization would result in an intensive regulation of prostitution by the state. Furthermore, where decriminalization would "tolerate" or "condone" prostitution, legalization would be giving it a stamp of approval.

It is because of the prospects of governmental regulation into what is basically a private matter that this author supports the decriminalization of prostitution (operated as previously described) with strict laws against public solicitation as a feasible alternative. By keeping public solicitation illegal, the prospects of minimizing the public affront caused by streetwalking can occur while allowing the greatest measure of personal freedom possible for both the prostitute and the customer.

Conclusion

The issue of prostitution enforcement is one which invokes a wide range of discussion and dissent within our present system of criminal justice. There are those who feel "business as usual" to be a proper and efficient course of action. In contrast, there are individuals who consider the present enforcement policy toward prostitution to be a waste of resources which could be allocated to more serious crimes.

A major problem facing any researcher trying to discuss prostitution and the criminal justice system is the lack of solid research on the subject. Further research toward the inter-relationship between prostitution and ancillary crime, as well as the effectiveness of the present policy, needs to be done. One law enforcement official remarked that a comprehensive study would have to be done before any major policy alternative is made. Furthermore, current policies should be written down, ideally with input from the community concerning its values on victimless crime. In any case, the present enforcement policy toward prostitution has been largely ineffective for the resources expended, and ". . . we would do little worse by trying something different."

Discussion Questions

1. Is prostitution really a victimless crime? If not, then who are the victims?

2. Discuss the vice squad's role in the suppression of prostitution in your community. Do you believe they are effective in regards to the time and money spent in the course of a vice investigation?

3. How would ancillary crime be controlled by the police if prostitution was decriminalized or legalized? How can it be more effectively handled under current circumstances?

4. Many vice officers emphasize that it is the pimp, not the prostitute that law enforcement agencies seek to apprehend. Discuss the reality of this view.

5. What would be some of the problems of a prostitute who attempts to leave the profession, and how might this be changed under decriminalization or legalization?

Notes

1. Adler, Freda, *Sisters in Crime—The Rise in the New Female Criminal.* McGraw-Hill Book Co., New York. 1975. pages 55–56, and 57.

2. Adler, page 65.

3. Lindsay, Mary K. "Prostitution—Delinquency's Time Bomb," *Crime and Delinquency.* Vol. 16, No. 2 (April, 1970). page 152.

4. Bryan, James H., "Apprenticeships in Prostitution," *Social Problems.* Vol. 12, No. 3 (Winter, 1965). page 289.

5. James, Withers, Haft, and Theiss, *The Politics of Prostitution.* Social Research Associates. November, 1975. page 56. (hereafter cited as James).

6. The San Francisco Committee on Crime., *A Report on Non-Victim Crime in San Francisco, Part II.* 1971. page 29.

7. President's Commission on Crime and Administration of Justice, *The Challenge of Crime in a Free Society.* Government Printing Office, Washington, D.C. 1968. page 189.

8. James, page 50.

9. ibid.

10. Adler, page 78.

11. San Francisco Committee on Crime, pages 21–22.

12. James, page 54.

13. Goldstein, Herman, *Police Corruption—A Perspective on its Nature and Control.* Police Foundation, Washington, D.C. pages 16–17, and 19.

14. Kalmanoff, Alan, *Criminal Justice: Enforcement and Administration.* Little, Brown, and Company, Boston. 1976. page 99.

15. ibid.

16. Megino, Gloria R., *Prostitution and California Law.* California Leglislature, Senate Committee on the Judiciary. February, 1977. page 26.

17. Kalmanoff, page 99.

18. James, page XV.

19. San Francisco Committee on Crime, page 37.

20. San Francisco District Attorney Joseph Freitas, Jr. in an interview in April, 1977. All quotes not footnoted were the result of interviews by this author for this article.

21. New York City has been a recent example of prostitutes moving to what they perceive to be a more lenient atmosphere. See footnote 1 in Lindsay, (1970) footnote 3 above.

22. Megino, pages 16–17.

23. Margo St. James, telephone conversation of May, 1977.

24. Megino, pages 29–30.

25. James, page 62.

Part IV

Issues in Corrections

1

Can Corrections Correct?

Leonard J. Hippchen

Introduction

ONE OF THE MOST HEATED CONTROVERSIES raging throughout the country today concerns the question of correctional effectiveness. Critics of corrections have cited evidence that corrections doesn't work.[1] Others are urging a return to a more punitive handling of criminals, and a moving away from correctional approaches.[2]

This current emergence of controversy can be seen merely to be an outbreak between the proponents of two different criminal justice concepts: punitive vs. corrections. This is a deep, long-standing conflict in philosophy concerning the proper method of handling criminals. The punitive attitude towards criminals, of course, is centuries old. The basic philosophy is summed-up in the Mosaic Code by the statement: "an eye for an eye and a tooth for a tooth."

This punitive philosophy through many years has been an advocate of capital punishment, corporal punishment, long sentences, incarceration in gothic-like, impenetrable prisions, and a revenge-like handling of prisoners within the walls and cages of the prison.

About 100 years ago, a new philosophy of corrections was introduced. It emphasized not only the more humane handling of criminals, but the idea that prisons should be designed to assist the criminal to reform his anti-social lifestyle. Ever since the introduction of this new approach to the handling of criminals the controversy has raged. Those advocating the punitive philosophy have continued their efforts to maintain ascendancy over the correctional approach. Every move forward by the correctional model was derided and challenged by those supportive of the punitive model.

The forces supportive of the punitive model have been very strong, drawing on the powerful instinctive demands for revenge. In more recent years, the argument has been changed to a call for justice: justice requires retribution by the offender for the wrongs committed against society. The corrections model, still in the infancy of its development, has been vulnerable to attack because its methods have not yet reached maturity. But the arguments against corrections appear more to be philosophical than factual. Proponents of the punitive philosophy use their highly selective facts to downgrade corrections, but they really want to attack its philosophy, which is growing in strength. The basic question still remains: What is the proper way today to handle prisoners, punitively or correctionally?[3] Further, if the critics say that corrections isn't working, neither has the punitive method!

This chapter will review the main themes of current critics of corrections, discuss the limitations of these arguments, and present evidence to support the contention that corrections can be effective when undertaken in a manner consistent with true correctional philosophy.

Main Themes of Contemporary Critics

The contemporary literature contains five major areas of criticism against corrections: 1. Recidivism rates are too high; 2. Corrections can't correct; 3. The medical model is inadequate for correctional treatment; 4. Correctional management is ineffective and inefficient; and 5. That the main purpose of sentencing should be for punishment, not for rehabilitation.

Recidivism Too High. Sheldon and Eleanor Glueck conducted what was probably one of the earliest follow-up studies of inmates concerning recidivism. This was in the 1930's. They reported that recidivism was 80 percent after 5 years of release, basing their findings primarily on their studies in New York and Massachusetts.[4]

During the 1950's some observers and prison officials maintained that about two-thirds of released prisoners returned again to prison. These estimates were based upon studies of prison populations which showed that two-thirds of the inmates were repeaters in crime.

These findings were challenged by Glaser in the 1960's, following his study of several State prisons. Glaser's data showed that only about one-third of all inmates were returned in the first two to five years after release.[5] Glaser used follow-up studies of specific groups of inmates to arrive at his conclusions, as had the Gluecks in their earlier studies.

Then came the major study of Martinson. Martinson's review of 3,005 studies of recidivism rates from the years 1967-75 indicated the following:

> 1. The data appear to indicate that the general recidivism rate in the U.S. in the last several decades is below the "one third" rate previously estimated by Glaser.

2. The mean recidivism rate in the 1970's (23.26%) was lower than it was in the 1960's (33.17%).

3. The recidivism rate for imprisonment plus parole (25.35%) is lower than those discharged without parole supervision (31.55%).

4. Reduced-custody residential establishments appear to have a high rate (41.67%) when introduced prior to a sentence of imprisonment, but a lower rate (22.07%) when introduced following incarceration (halfway houses).

5. The mean recidivism rate for standard processing of offenders (24.22%) does not differ from the rate for "standard plus special treatment." (24.73%).[6]

This reported decrease in recidivism rate over the past 35 years from 80 per cent to 25 per cent appears to contradict the notion that corrections isn't working. It may be that the recidivism rate studies are not completely accurate. Or, it may mean that something which is being done, indeed, is working!

Corrections Can't Correct. In the mid-1960's, Bailey conducted one of the first literature reviews in an attempt to evaluate correctional effectiveness of specific treatment programs. He reviewed 100 reports of correctional programs which appeared in research journals between 1940-60.[7] He concluded that the results were not encouraging. But of the studies he reviewed, most had poor evaluative controls, which made it difficult to draw conclusions. Actually, of the 22 studies which used experimental designs, 9 showed that treatment was effective.

In 1967, Adams reviewed 22 experimental studies of probation and parole in California. Thirteen showed a reduction in recidivism or a cost benefit.[8]

In 1971, Robinson and Smith reviewed the outcomes of several studies in California, and concluded that "there is no evidence to support any program's claims of superior rehabilitative effectiveness."[9] They indicate, however, that adequate measures of effectiveness were not used in most studies they reviewed, and also that most rehabilitation takes place in a punitive environment, which is inappropriate to effective treatment.

In 1975, Martinson, reported on the results of his review of the evaluative literature between the years 1945-67.[10] Accepting only those studies which included experimental controls of treatment evaluations, Martinson concluded that the 231 studies he reviewed provided little evidence of correctional effectiveness. However, he explained that he did find a number of individual studies in which experimentals did better than control groups, but that they were in the minority. These effective programs, he said, tended to use probation, skill development, individual psychotherapy and milieu therapy with youth, and milieu therapy and medical therapy with adults. He also emphasized that treatment programs tended to have a number of important additional advantages than just lower recidivism: 1. Teaches illiterates to read; 2. Improves vocational skills; 3. Improves institutional climates; 4. Probation and parole are cheaper than is imprisonment.

In responding to Martinson's earlier charge that nothing works in corrections, Glaser has stated that the primary contribution of past research is not in its answers to the questions that were investigated, but in its guidance to more fruitful questions.[11] He also pointed out that in more than 40 per cent of the correctional evaluation studies summarized by Martinson in his article (What Works?) he indicates distinctly positive results for some progams for some types of offenses in some circumstances.

Palmer also has made a similar rebuttal in his reaction to Martinson's charge.[12] Palmer argues that it is unsound to expect that a single service or procedure will strikingly reduce recidivism. Rather, he says, we should ask: What works best for what subjects under what circumstances, and why?

Wright and Dixon in 1977 reported on their review of 6,000 abstracts dealing with correctional projects for juvenile delinquents.[13] Only 8 per cent of these studies included some form of empirical data concerning project effects. Their analysis of 96 projects concluded that: 1. Individual and group counseling showed some effectiveness; 2. Social casework was useful only with juveniles who had less serious problems; 3. Community treatment programs are at least as effective as incarceration and cheaper; 4. Educational and vocational training programs are helpful but they don't tend to reduce recidivism. They did not find volunteers or street corner workers to be effective in reducing recidivism.

Finally, Adams summarized the findings of seven literature reviews and evaluations as follows: 1. Three of the reviews conclude that corrections is not effective. But, he says, the reviews are skeptical and polemical in tone. They question the integrity of correctional administrators and they clearly ignore some impressive evidence of program effectiveness; 2. Four of the reviews indicated that consideration of a wide range of evaluative studies will disclose some good research and some effective programs; 3. Studies using experimental designs show that about half of the programs have important treatment or cost benefits. He concludes that correctional effectiveness appears to be about the same as that which can be found in other fields of human services.[14]

In summary, the studies of correctional effectiveness appear to indicate that most of the evaluative attempts have been plagued with poor research design. Many of the programs which may be working thus do not have a basis upon which to demonstrate their effectiveness. Also, the studies which do incorporate good research design appear to suggest that some correctional programs have been effective with some types of offenders under certain conditions.

These global-types of reviews have offered an excellent overview of some of the problems and limitations of current research and correctional programs. But, as Glaser has noted, their greater contribution lies in the fact that they have clarified the important questions that yet need to be investigated. We still need to know much more about which types of programs can work best with what types of offenders in which types of environment settings.

Limitations of the Medical Model. A number of contemporary critics approach the problem of correctional effectiveness by attacking its assumed treatment method. These persons are critical of the use of what is called the "medical model" of corrections. Typically, this term is used to refer to treatment approaches that consider the commission of a crime primarily as the result of an emotional disturbance in the individual offender.

Lehman, for example, describes what he feels has become the standard treatment in correctional settings—Freudian psychoanalytic therapy.[15] He feels that we should not try to reform the offender, but to stop criminal behavior. He suggests that we use a mosaic of treament alternatives rather than rely on any one model.

Clendenen claims that the medical model takes the blame off of the individual criminal and puts the fault on a "sick" society.[16] He feels corrections should hold the individual fully responsible for his antisocial acts and that treatment should consist primarily of training in responsibility. Balch feels that the medical model assumes that only professionals trained in abnormal psychology can treat offenders.[17] This approach, he says, ignores the social forces in delinquency development and the social aspects of treatment environments.

Conrad says that we have "disabused ourselves of the notion that criminality is a disease to be cured by the psychiatrist."[18] He feels that the medical model approach to criminals has caused them considerable frustration by the demands that they somehow become better before they become free.

These criticism of correction's use of a medical model appear to be more of a theoretical disagreement between two disciplines than they are supportable in fact. Much of this type of criticism tends to come from academic sociologists who are arguing for more consideration of social factors as opposed to psychological factors in the etiology and treatment of criminals. But a presentation of the importance of social factors does not mean that it is necessary to downgrade the psychological and/or psychiatric aspects of the problem, as Barrington has emphasized.[19] Furthermore, the supplying of therapeutic services by psychiatry or psychology in corrections has been meagre. The medical model really has not been implemented in prisons, so how can it be considered a failure? The relatively few therapists in the prison systems of the country are required primarily to provide diagnostic and screening services, not therapy. Thus, this charge by the academic community is not based upon fact, but appears rather to be a dispute over whose theory is best!

As far as the argument that corrections needs a multi-disciplinary approach to treatment, corrections *has* emphasized a multi-disciplinary approach in institutions where professional staff are used at least since the 1930's. Again, the critics do not seem to know the facts of the situation in attacking the "medical model" in corrections.

The Failure of Correctional Management. Considerable criticism has been leveld at correctional management as the source of the problem of correctional ineffectiveness. Mangrum, for example, says that all of the blame for correctional failure cannot be laid at the door of public apathy, lack of budgetary support for facilities, and inadequate staff. He sees the additional factors to include management's focus on mistaken punitive goals and in being entrenched in punitive traditions which hamper innovation. He also accuses management of yielding to vested interests.[20]

Thomas lays the blame for failure in inadequacies of the organizational structure of the prison.[21] This structure, he claims, leads to conflict between treatment and custodial staff, development of an inmate subculture, and a routinization of daily procedures, all of which work against treatment goals. Bennett also calls attention to some of the organizational problems in corrections, and suggests the use of a "management by objectives" to make the system's input-output more efficient.[22]

Cohn questions whether the rehabilitation ideal ever has been significantly implemented. He suggests that custody and control have been the primary goals of management, whereas rehabilitation, while espoused, has only been dealt with to a superficial degree.[23] Cohn states that his study of the problem led him to conclude that correctional failure can be attributed primarily to the inadequate managment and leadership of correctional executives.

He says that the correctional executive tends to cherish security, avoids taking risks, is not strong or forceful enough to mold his beliefs into progressive policies and programs, and serves primarily as an apolitical bureaucrat (one who is highly influenced by public attitudes and political groups). Cohn says they also tend to compromise and avoid conflicts or confrontations, that they have insufficient management and treatment education, and that they tend to follow rules and regulations mechanically.

He says that management reports contain many irrelevances to correctional goals.

These charges represent an extensive indictment of correctional management, to say the least! If true, they easily could account for the low degree of correctional effectiveness claimed by the critics. It is true that the top correctional leader in each State system typically is a political appointee of the Governor. Many of these appointments do not represent professionally-trained leadership. Even if professional, these leaders are subject to extensive pressures from the Legislature and other government officials, from pressure groups, and from other forms of public opinion, such as the mass media.

Upon taking office, most of these managers inherit on on-going prison or training school system which has been operating along punitive lines for many decades. They inherit a large, undertrained staff, who were hired primarily for punitive purposes. They have few treatment personnel, or funds with which to hire additional treatment staff. Proposed change also might bring attacks from internal quarters, since staff may be threatened by any move in the direction of treatment.

Most professionals, confronted with these problems, tend to move cautiously toward improvements in the system. However, outside funding in recent years from the Federal Government has stimulated the introduction of many treatment innovations in correctional systems throughout the country. But these improvements, too, bring problems with their blessings! If the manager moves for change too quickly, or if modifications in the system are too extensive, negative political/public reaction can result in his removal from his position. Few professional managers have been successful in implementing broad changes and improvements while still being able to remain in their jobs!

It might be conceded that the criticism of correctional managers is true in many cases. But it also is true that many other correctional managers are well-trained, are courageous in dealing with internal and external pressures, and that they have been effective in vastly improving a system which is very resistent to change. Certainly, research has shown that many of these managers are achieving effective results even against often overwhelming odds. But by defending these specific courageous leaders we should not overlook the validity of the critic's charges where they are appropriate!

Should We Sentence for Punishment? A number of critics in recent years have been saying that confinement should be for punishment purposes only, not for rehabilitation. Others have said that sentencing should be primarily for punishment, but that we should have some programs for those criminals who volunteer for and can profit from treatment programs.

Morris, for example, has stated that rehabilitation must cease to be the claimed purpose of a prison sentence. He says that we should imprison criminals as punishment for what they have done. He sees it as a cruel injustice to cage them for what they are in order to remake them.[24] Pierce[25] and Amos[26] feel that with the present state of correctional knowledge that only some but not all offenders can be rehabilitated. Thus, they suggest that criminals should be imprisoned for punishment and its deterrence value and for the protection of society, and that we should treat only those who are open and amenable to treatment.

Brantingham and Faust[27] approach the problem of criminal behavior from a slightly different perspective. They feel that much criminal behavior can be prevented by early intervention and by taking steps to correct injustices in the physical and social environment. But they, too, would reduce recidivism by imprisoning incorrigibles and treating only those who are amenable to treatment.

The move toward harsher treatment of criminals has been developing rapidly over the past decade. This trend has been accelerated by the fast-rising rates of crime throughout the country during this period. Some have felt that judges have been too liberal in their use of probation, and that this has placed many criminals out in the street to continue their criminal ways. Others have felt that parole boards have been too lenient in releasing offenders early from prison, which also produces additional crime threats on the street. Others have decried the dangers of institutional programs such as furloughs, work release, and pre-release for the same reasons.

Together with the cries of correctional failure because of the advertised high recidivism rates, many have begun to advocate a return to a "get tough" policy. Mandatory sentencing of all criminals and long sentences for incorrigibles have been recommended. These suggestions, however, appear merely to be a return to the punitive attitude toward criminals, rather than a true solution to the criminal problem. In reality, the people on the streets are scared. They want the criminals off the street, and they have made this clear to our political leaders, who, in turn, are putting pressure on the criminal justice system for more effective remedies. But the return to punitive methods is the most simple of all possible solutions only to the uninformed!

To further complicate the problem, our nation's correctional institutions currently are facing an extensive overpopulation problem. We have 280,000 men and women in prison and an additional 250,000 in jails, a new high in America. Anthony Travisono, executive director of the American Correctional Association, recently has said that no other nation on earth can claim such a terrible achievement! It is evident that solutions other than tougher sentencing must be found.

Evidence That Corrections Can Be Effective

There have been an increasing number of innovative projects undertaken during the past two decades in corrections. Much of the impetus for these efforts has been given by establishment in 1967 of the Law Enforcement Assistance Administration. Federal funds have greatly increased the intensity of correctional developments throughout the country since that time.

Most of these correctional efforts have involved relatively small demonstration projects, where the attempt has been to develop and test new correctional ideas. Many of these efforts have shown great promise of effectiveness. The following section will report on the results of four of these promising new approaches to correctional effectiveness; 1. The therapeutic community organizational approach; 2. Implementation of treatment teams; 3. Social education programs; and 4. Biochemical approaches to offender rehabilitation.

Therapeutic Community Approaches. Development of a therapeutic community involves a vast change in organization from the prisons of the past. It represents an attempt to organize all aspects of the facility primarily for treatment purposes, although some degree of security is maintained.

The institution basically is "open," without walls, bars or cages. If segregation or control of certain offenders is needed, they are placed in rooms temporarily behind locked, guarded doors. Most offenders selected for this type of program, however, would not represent a serious assault or escape risk.

All staff are selected, trained and used for treatment goals. The assumption is that all offenders who enter the program are interested in improving their ability to function effectively on a social basis. The staff is professionally prepared to guide them in this task.

The program includes all of those elements needed to assist in the therapeutic goals of the institution. These include, for example, medical, psychiatric, psychological, social therapy, religion, academic and vocational education and recreation. Each offender is studied for deficiencies and a specialized program of treatment is developed to assist him in overcoming these deficiencies. An important part of the therapeutic effect of community life are the growth-stimulating interrelationships established between staff and offenders and between offenders and offenders. This new approach has been so effective in treatment compared with earlier prison organization that the American Correctional Association in 1963 approved a position statement supporting its further use.

The prototype of a therapeutic community for offenders is the Air Force's 3320th Retraining Group.[28] This program began on an experimental basis in 1952 at Amarillo AFB, Texas. Because of its outstanding success in offender rehabilitation, both cost-wise and in effective correction, the Air Force continued the program on a permanent basis. The program was moved to Lowry AFB, Colorado, in 1968 where it continues to operate to this time.

Prisoners are sent to the Retraining Group from Air Force bases all over the world. They include every kind of criminal offense typical of civilian prisons, although those who have committed the most serious crimes (about 5 per cent) have been screened out. The Group typically is able to see sufficient progress within 120 days to restore to full-duty status about 75 per cent of the offenders processed through the program. The remaining 25 per cent are discharged, although somewhat improved. Follow-up studies conducted on all airmen six-months after restoration from the Group show that about 90 per cent of them are successful. About 80 per cent are able to successfully complete the remaining part of their enlistment, which averages 2½ years.

Implementation of Treatment Teams. The idea of using treatment teams in correctional institutions was originated about 1960. This idea was introduced operationally about this time both in the Air Force's 3320th Retraining Group and in selected Federal prisons, principally at El Reno, Oklahoma.

Treatment teams developed out of dissatisfaction with classification committees, which typically are used in most prisons today. Classification committees have the responsibility of diagnosing the offender's problems and of developing with the offender a suitable rehabilitation program. They follow the offender in his program, making any changes needed, until he is ready for release or parole. Hopefully, progress will be sufficient to allow parole at his first hearing.

Classification committees typically are made-up of departmental heads, not treatment staff. They may include, for example, the Assistant Warden, the Chaplain, and the heads of Social Services, Custody, Academic and Vocational Education, and Classification. Committees may see offenders on an average of three to six months, and the meetings tend to be formal and brief.

In 1962, the 3320th Retraining Group replaced its classification committees with treatment teams. This action resulted following a study which showed that the committees were too inefficient in accomplishing their tasks. Their formality was not conducive to therapeutic goals, their lack of daily contact with offenders severely limited them in observing important behavioral changes, and the limited data they had available caused them to make too many poor decisions.[29]

The teams were organized to include nine treatment staff members on each team. None were department heads. Each team was assigned to work with a group of 50 offenders, from entry to release from the program. They even were housed together. Meetings were frequent and could be arranged almost spontaneously as the need arose. The meetings were conducted on an informal basis. Thus, the team not only could be more therapeutically helpful, but they also had more observational information on behavior with which to make their decisions.

A three-year study of the comparative effects of the two operational approaches was conducted from 1962-65. The criteria used for measuring change included rate of restoration to duty, and six-month follow-up success rates. The team showed a 21 per cent improvement over the classification committees in rate of restoration, and a 2 per cent increase in six-month follow-up success rates.

Social Education Programs. Social education represents a direct attempt to help the offender improve his social attitudes through education. Small group instruction and a variety of action-oriented educational techniques are used.

One form of social education, known as Emotional Maturity Instruction (EMI), was developed and first applied successfully in 1967 in a maximum security prison in Georgia. More recently, EMI has been used successfully in a county juvenile and adult court, in a community residential treatment center for probationers, in a medium security prison, and in a training school for girls.[30] EMI was developed by the Social Research Laboratories, Inc., of Atlanta, Georgia.

Instruction in the EMI program begins with the teaching of important principles related to personal growth and to social relations. Then the student is introduced to a series of experiential exercises to allow him to test his ability to practice these basic principles in his behavior. After a week of practice on a limited number of principles, his new behavioral experiences are presented and discussed in small-group meetings. Errors are detected and new correctional devices are taught to aid the offender in developing his new behavior patterns. When these few principles are appropriately incorporated by him in his behavior, new principles and behavioral exercises are introduced. The total program typically will run from 12 to 15 weeks.

All of these applications of EMI have been studied to determine their effectiveness in correcting offender attitudes and behavior. In general, EMI appears to be effective in helping selected offender groups at the rate of 70 per cent. About 70 per cent of all offenders who volunteer to participate appear to able to considerably profit from the program. An additional 15 per cent show some improvement. Follow-up studies have been conducted on most of these projects. The follow-up success of those completing the program successfully has ranged from 90 to 96 per cent.

Biochemical Approaches to Offender Rehabilitation. Recent research in the biochemistry of the functioning of the brain suggests findings which challenge our current total emphasis on psychosocial explanations of criminal behavior. Biochemical theory suggests that behavior associated with delinquency and crime can be caused by chemical deficiencies or imbalances in the body or by brain toxicity. These problems can originate from genetic factors or they can be induced especially during the birth process or in early childhood by improper nutrition of the mother and/or child.[31]

The major symptoms which may accompany biochemical disorders in the brain include perceptual disorders and hyperactivity. A child with bio-chemical imbalances or brain allergies may suffer from a variety of blockages and distortions in seeing, hearing and speech. In addition, or separately, the child may react with behavior which is seen as over-activity, restlessness, destructiveness, or tantrums. As the child becomes older, these "anti-social" forms of behavior are less tolerated by parents, teachers, and friends, and a pattern of action-reation may begin to set behavior in this form of lifestyle. Later, truancy, juvenile delinquency or criminal acts might emerge and bring the youngster into the criminal justice system with its typical repressive and punitive reactions. This tends further to insure continuance of the anti-social lifestyle.

Over the past decade a number of programs have emerged throughout the country which take a biochemical approach to treatment of deviant and offender groups. The biochemical approach typically uses large controlled doses of vitamins and minerals, and highly nutritious diets. They are not used as exclusive treatment agents, but along with other programs which deal with the psychosocial aspects of the problem.

For example, the North Nassau Mental Health Clinic in Long Island has reported extensive use of megavitamin therapy in treatment of alcoholics, suicides, drug addicts, and schizophrenics. They have been successful in remission of symptoms for an average of 75 per cent on more than 7,000 persons. Also, a drug center in Phoenix, Arizona, has used megavitamins with drug addicts and alcoholics, and they claim an 80 per cent success rate.

Children with learning and behavior disorders also have responded well to megavitamin therapy in a number of programs. Dr. Allan Cott of New York City, for example, has reported successfully treating more than 500 such children. Dr. Bernard Rimland, director of the Institute for Child Behavior Research in San Diego, also has reported considerable success with this approach.

Drs. Abram Hoffer and R.J. Green, Canadian psychiatrists, both have reported 85 per cent success in treating a wide-variety of disorders with megavitamin therapy: alcoholism, drug addiction, delinquency, institutionalized criminals, and schizophrenics.

Although the biochemical approaches have shown impressive success in dealing with a variety of deviant/criminal forms of behavior, their greatest potential resides in the area of prevention. If the perceptual and hyperactive disorders early can be identified and treated, much delinquent behavior could be prevented. And if proper nutritional care were given to mothers during pre-natal and early nursing periods to children in early developmental life, still more of the problems could be prevented.

Summary and Conclusions

This writing has addressed the question of correctional effectiveness. Contemporary critics maintain that recidivism rates are too high, and that correctional programs where used have not been shown to be effective. They feel that much of the blame for this ineffectiveness can be laid at the door of correctional management, and because corrections has adopted the limited medical model for rehabilitation. With the charge that corrections doesn't work, many criminal justice spokesman are calling for longer and mandatory sentencing, and for a return to a more punitive handling of criminals, especially repeaters. They say that the main purpose of imprisonment should be for punishment, not for rehabilitation.

A review of some of the facts of the situation, however, suggests that much of the current criticism of corrections is not justified. For example, recidivism rates have shown a dramatic improvement in the past several decades. Reported studies of innovative programs have shown effectiveness with some types of offenders in therapeutic types of settings.

In regard to the criticism of correctional management and the medical model of rehabilitation, it also can be seen that the case largely has been overstated. Correctional management cannot reasonably be criticized as a whole. Some managers may be inefficient and ineffective, but many are not. A better understanding of the pressures under which these managers operate may lead to a lessening of the criticism of their efforts. The medical model criticism, on the other hand, appears to be considerably outdated. This model, initiated in the 1920's, long since has been expanded to include a wide range of interdisciplinary programs in most correctional settings.

The current criticism seems more to be a throw-back to the earlier philosophical conflicts of the 19th Century. It was at that time when enlightened correctional leaders challenged the long-standing inhumane and punitive approach to criminals. The conflict today, however, no longer is merely philosophical, because the social and behavioral sciences have produced considerable additional evidence to show the superiority of the correctional model in today's world. Enlightened humanitarianism also has seen the folly of the punitive approach and the fact that society best is not served nor protected by the cruel treatment of deviants, deliquents and criminals.

Modern correctional philosophy also is aware of the fact that practically all criminals today, regardless of their crimes, are returned to society. It behooves society, therefore, to provide means for helping even the worst criminals to correct their behavior and to prepare for useful, constructive lives once released from prison. This not only is humane, but it rationally serves best to protect society from further harm!

But the new philosophy also would put more emphasis on early intervention and prevention efforts in the community. Our most effective efforts in reducing crime probably will not emerge until we find a way of reorganizing our basic social institutions. Building strong families, developing good moral characters in our children, providing equal educational and work opportunities for all people, and strengthening ties and unity in action between diverse groups all are ways of improving the social life of the community. Only an improved social life for all in the community will have the effect of dramatically lessening the criminal elements!

Our final effort in challenging the idea that corrections can't correct has been to present four new approaches which in recent years have shown great promise in increasing our correctional effectiveness. Development of therapeutic communities and utilization of treatment teams have been shown to be much more efficient organizational/procedural approaches to corrections. The treatment approaches of biochemistry and social education also have shown considerable effectiveness in correcting certain groups of offenders, including even the most dangerous.

In conclusion, we can say that there is considerable evidence to support the contention that corrections *can* correct! In the least, it has been demonstrated that certain offender groups, given the right treatment programs in the right environment, can be treated in a highly effective manner. Thus, rather than return to the archaic realms of the punitive model, we should continue our efforts at more humane and rationally-sound methods of dealing with offenders.

Criminals should be corrected in the community, if possible. If they can't be corrected there, they should be institutionalized, especially if they are a threat to the community. But their incarceration should be *as* punishment, not *for* punishment. The primary purpose of a prison should be for correction and for successfully reintegrating the criminal back into the community. More efforts should be directed toward early diagnosis and intervention with children and youth. But, most importantly, true preventive means must be found to rid society as much as possible of those crime-breeding elements of prejudice, political corruption, uncontrolled spread of vices, and family disintegration.

Discussion Questions

1. Differentiate between the punitive philosophy of handling criminals and the philosophy of modern-day advocates of corrections.

2. Evaluate the contemporary charges against corrections that recidivism rates are too high and that correction can't correct.

3. Discuss the question of whether or not we should sentence criminals primarily for purposes of punishment.

4. What are the advantages of therapeutic community and team treatment approaches to the correction of criminals. Why do you feel that these approaches are not more widely used in corrections?

5. Evaluate social education and biochemical techniques as promising new approaches to offender corrections. What do you see as their strengths and weaknesses?

Notes

1. Robert Martinson, "What Works? Questions and Answers About Prison Reform," *The Public Interest*, 1974, 22-54.

2. See James Q. Wilson, *Thinking About Crime* (New York: Basic Books, 1974), Ernest van den Haag, *Punishing Criminals: Concerning a Very Old and Painful Question* (New York: Basic Books, 1975); and David Fogel, *We Are The Living Proof: The Justice Model for Corrections* (Cincinnati, Ohio: W.H. Anderson Company, 1975)

3. According to the *Manual of Correctional Standards* of the American Correctional Association, the essentials of a modern correctional program include: 1. Scientific classification and program planning for each offender based upon a complete case history and thorough medical and psychosocial testing; 2. Adequate medical services: medical and psychological; 3. Use of psychological services as related to placement for education, work assignment, treatment and parole; 4. Correctionally-oriented use of disciplinary measures; 5. Facilities, staff and correctional services and processes consistent with therapeutic community and team treatment concepts; 6. Adaquate individualized correctional training and correctional training and correctional programs in the areas of psychology, social casework, psychiatry, medical, and academic education and vocational training; 7. Competent correctional and training personnel; 8. Adequate library services, religious programs, and recreational programs; and 9. Adequate buildings, equipment, and food services.

4. Sheldon and Eleanor Glueck, *Criminal Careers in Retrospect* (New York: The Commonwealth Fund, 1943)

5. Daniel Glaser, *Effectiveness of a Prison and Parole System* (Indianapolis, Ind: Bobbs-Merrill Co., Inc., 1964) pp. 19-24.

6. Robert Martinson, *Preliminary Report* (New York: The Center of Knowledge in Criminal Justice Planning, 1976).

7. Walter C. Bailey, "Correctional Outcome: An Evaluation of 100 Reports," *Journal of Criminal Law, Criminology and Police Science*, June (1966), pp. 153-160.

8. Stuart Adams, "Some Findings From Correctional Caseload Research," *Federal Probation*, (Dec.) 1967, pp. 48-57.

9. James Robinson and Gerald Smith, "*The Effectiveness of Correctional Programs*," 17 (Jan.) 1971, pp. 67-80.

10. Robert Martinson, "The Effectiveness of Correctional Treatment: A Survey of Treatment Evaluation Studies," *Proceedings*, American Correctional Association annual meeting, 1975. Also see study report of the same name, co-authored with D. Lipton and J. Wilks, (New York: Praeger Publ., 1975).

11. Daniel Glaser, "Achieving Better Questions: A Half Century's Progress in Correctional Research," *Federal Probation*, 39 (Sept.) pp. 3-9.

12. Ted Palmer, "Martinson Revisited," *Journal of Research in Crime and Delinquency*, 12 (1975).

13. William Wright and Michael C. Dixon, "Community Prevention and Treatment of Juvenile Delinquency," *Journal of Research in Crime and Delinquency*, 14 (Jan., 1977) pp. 35-67.

14. Stuart Adams, "Evaluation Research in Corrections," *Federal Probation*, 38 (March, 1974) pp. 14-21.

15. Paul E. Lehman, "The Medical Model of Treatment: Historical Development of an Archaic Standard," *Crime and Delinquency*, 18 (April) pp. 204-212.

16. Richard J. Clendenen, "What's the Matter With Corrections?" *Federal Probation*, 35 (Sept.) pp. 8-12.

17. Robert Balch, "The Medical Model of Delinquency: Theoretical, Practical, and Ethical Considerations," *Crime and Delinquency*, 2 (April) pp. 116-130.

18. John P. Conrad, "We Should Never Have Promised a Hospital," *Federal Probation*, 39 (Dec.) pp. 3-9.

19. Robert Barrington, "Corrections—Victim of a Self-Fulfilling Prophecy," *Proceedings*, 1975 annual meeting, American Correctional Association.

20. Claude T. Mangrum, "Corrections's Tarnished Halo," *Federal Probation*, 40 (Mar.) pp. 9-14.

21. Charles W. Thomas, "The Correctional Institution as an Enemy of Corrections," *Federal Probation*, 37 (Mar.) pp. 8-13.

22. Lawrence A. Bennett, "Should We Change the Offender or the System?" *Crime and Delinquency*, 19 (July) pp. 332-343.

23. Cohn, Alvin W., "The Failure of Correctional Management," *Crime and Delinquency*, 19 (July) pp. 323-331.

24. Norval Morris, "Keynote Address," *Proceedings*, annual meeting, American Correctional Association, 1975; also see: Norval Morris and Gordan Hawkins, "Rehabilitation: Rhetoric and Reality," *Federal Probation*, 34 (Dec.) pp. 9-17.

25. Lawrence W. Pierce, "Rehabilitation in Corrections: A Reassessment," *Federal Probation*, 38 (June) pp. 14-19.

26. William E. Amos, "The Philosophy of Corrections: Revisited," *Federal Probation*, 38 (Mar.) pp. 43-36.

27. Paul Brantingham and Frederic L. Faust, "A Conceptual Model of Crime Prevention," *Crime and Delinquency*, 22 (July) pp. 284-296.

28. Leonard J. Hippchen, "The Air Force's 'Therapeutic Community' Concept in Treatment of Selected Military Offenders," *American Journal of Corrections*, 25 (Jan.-Feb.) pp. 14-19.

29. Robert F. Hart and Leonard J. Hippchen, "Team Treatment of Air Force Offenders," *American Journal of Corrections*, 1966 (Sept.-Oct.) pp. 40-46.

30. Leonard J. Hippchen, "EMI—A New Approach to Social Education," *Proceedings*, annual meeting, American Correctional Association, 1974.

31. Leonard J. Hippchen, "Biochemical Approaches to Offender Rehabilitation," *Journal of Offender Rehabilitation*, 1 (1976) pp. 115-124.

2

The Failure of Prison Rehabilitation

FRANKLIN GOULD

EVERYBODY ASKS TOO MUCH OF PRISONS. From the invention of the penitentiary nearly two hundred years ago to the present time, the goals that have been suggested have been multiple and contradictory. As originally conceived, the prison was expected to offer little more than a solitary opportunity for the criminal to contemplate his crimes and repent his sins. In addition, it was also seen as a substitute for the harsh and cruel punishments that were being regularly meted out to convicted miscreants. To many reformers, prison took the place of stocks, pillories, gibbets, branding, whipping trees, and even impressment and transportation. In general, it could be said that the Pennsylvania system, designed by the Quakers of that state, emphasized repentance, whereas the competing Auburn system in New York State was concerned with establishing less severe standards of punishment.

This term "punishment" contains two essentially different concepts. The psychologist's definition of punishment as aversive or negative re-inforcement has little application in the prison setting. Most laymen and many professionals do not look on imprisonment in terms of correcting the behavior of the convict but rather in terms of what the criminal deserves. The outcry following President Ford's pardon of Nixon grew not out of any public desire to improve the ex-President's attitude or to teach him that crime doesn't pay, but to clobber him, to make him suffer. When Patty Hearst or Claudine Longet get sentences that are popularly believed to be incommensurate with their crimes, no one suggests that either woman is losing an opportunity to have her behavior modified. Punishment, as usually thought of in discussing prisons, has much more to do with retribution and revenge than it has to do with the learning process that the psychologist studies in the laboratory.

Punishment as an aspect of the learning process, if it is considered at all, is usually lumped under the heading of deterrence, another term that is ambiguous not only to the layman but even to many of the experts. When a convict is put in a prison (1) the punishment is expected to deter him from continuing his life of crime. Also (2) the threat of punishment is expected to deter others from entering the field. These are two considerations, quite distinct, but even after writers on penology spell out the difference, they frequently use the term "deterrence" as if it had only one meaning; i.e., to stop further criminal activity.

The kind of deterrence that results from punishing an individual has been widely investigated by psychologists. A subject can be punished either by withholding a positive reinforcement (this process is called extinction) or by administering an aversive stimulus (negative reinforcement). Both methods are used conjointly when a convict is assigned to a prison term. Extinction has been shown in laboratory experiments to be highly successful in stopping unwanted behavior, but prison terms are poorly designed to make the maximum use of this powerful method.

Negative reinforcement, however, is what prison terms are all about, and research has shown that even under the most ideal circumstances this method produces very ambiguous results. In the first place, the effectiveness of negative reinforcement deteriorates very rapidly as the time increases between the behavior which we want deterred and the punishment. A burned finger quickly deters touching a hot stove. When the punishing stimulus is not linked closely both spatially and temporally to the unwanted behavior, it is impossible to predict the result. The unwanted behavior may stop, but more likely something else will happen varying all the way from an autistic withdrawal from society to a proliferation of the undesired action. The possibility of an unwanted pregnancy is only mildly inhibiting as far as illicit sexual activity is concerned. Prison sentencing more closely resembles the nine month waiting period than the burned finger.

It has been found in the laboratory that punishment is a very tricky element in the process of learning. You can "bump" a rat back into a pathway of a maze by an electric shock. You can regain the attention of a child in school by taking a switch to his legs. But unless you follow these aversive stimuli with some goal-directed opportunity, you lose both the rat and the child. Other uses of punishment for training purposes beyond this simple bumping technique seem to be limited.

Punishment can be defined only in terms of the victim. What is punishing to one may not effect another for many reasons: differences in physical attributes, past experiences, expectations, associated stimuli, etc. Simply to be exposed as a criminal would be amply punishing for most human beings. Others, however, welcome notoriety and even public condemnation adds to their feelings of self-importance. These people, popular belief holds, need to be punished more directly by fines and imprisonment. Yet, occasionally, there are individuals who need the security of prison and even commit crimes to attain it. Even assuming that we could make punishment work as a deterrent, we cannot make much use of it until we can define it.

What one learns mostly from punishment is to avoid it. Ideally, the criminal would learn through punishment to stop doing the crime society is punishing him for. More frequently his desire is to learn how to continue the positively reinforcing crime without running the risk of being caught. While prison authorities are theoretically instilling social virtues into an inmate, his cell-mates are busy teaching him what he would regard as the more valuable skill—how to avoid the penalty. Penalties can be avoided by more careful execution of the crime, by deceiving the police and other authorities, and by discovering all the esoterica of the criminal's rights under the law. Classes in such fields are being run by the convicts simultaneously with the formalized rehabilitation program. Each semester I teach a weekly mini-course in Adolescent Psychology at a nearby correctional facility for young men. To each class I bring a group of undergraduate students from my Criminal Behavior course to assist me. The last half hour of the two-hour session is given over to socializing, letting individuals from the two groups get acquainted with one another. At the end of a class last semester I found that one of the inmates had organized a small group and was giving my students instructions on how to hot-wire a car and the safest procedure for fencing a stolen vehicle.

There has been little, if any, research into an even more important effect of incarceration: the deterring effect of observed punishment. If one man sees another being punished for some undesirable behavior, does this make the first man less likely to undertake that behavior? When there is a threat of a $25.00 fine for violating the speed limit—particularly when we know our neighbor was caught and fined—does this knowledge cause us to control our speed? Common sense tells us that it does. But common sense also tells us that the world is flat. For several years I have been asking audiences about their speeding convictions and have found that they can be roughly divided into two groups: a large number who have never been arrested and a few who have been arrested several times. This would seem to indicate that there is something more than the fear of the arrest behind the validation of the norm of safe driving, probably a value system formed early in life.

Unlike direct punishment, observed punishment seems to have no effect on the behavior of animals, so laboratory research on rats and pigeons is useless. Experimentation on human beings, even when ethical, is difficult to design because of many extraneous variables. Relevant research has been conducted with children in the areas of attitude formation and role modeling, but the part played by observed punishment in these areas is almost always ambiguous and frequently negligible. Albert Bandura and others, have shown, for example, that children will not imitate as readily the aggressive behavior of an adult when the adult is punished, but much the same result occurs when a second adult model simply expresses outright disapproval of the aggression.[1] As far as I can determine no one has investigated what happens when the aggressive adult model shrugs off the punishment or accepts it heroically, as when the ex-con struts in front of younger brother and friends.

Before the modern prison was designed, exile, impressment or transportation were traditional methods of ridding the community of undesirables, whether criminal or political. Even in my childhood, I recall the rumor that the local trial justice had ordered a putative child molester to "get out of town and stay out." Whether the rumor was true or not, he disappeared. When the penitentiary was instituted it was found to be ideal for isolating from the community those who had been designated as public dangers or even nuisances.

To keep a man isolated from the community we must make sure that he does not escape and this raises the problem of control—an aspect that is not necessarily inherent in the other previously mentioned goals of prisons. This means that prisons must be designed for containment rather than living. It means obedience and conformity to iron-clad rules. Constant surveillance replaces all freedom and self-sufficiency. When a prisoner attempts to escape from his isolation, he can be punished only by deeper isolation, which grants the guards an implied invitation to respond with violence and unmitigated force.[2] Zimbardo's experiment at Palo Alto showed that even pseudo-guards quickly learn to tyrannize pseudo-prisoners.[3]

Unfortunately, a concomitant of isolation is corruption. Since society is frequently kept out more effectively than the prisoners are kept in, guards easily decide that any method that works is acceptable. Deals are made with convict cliques in exchange for the maintenance of order. Drugs, alcohol and sex, used mainly for control, are available in many, if not most prisons.

The final, and currently most popular, goal of prisons is "rehabilitation". In the last couple decades or so, all states and the federal government have started referring to their prisons as correctional facilities or by some similar euphemism to indicate the change in orientation from punishment or reformation to preparation for a successful return to society. Emphasis is now on education and training (or re-training), on counseling and therapy, on behavior modification and even brain surgery. Rehabilitation has been made the principal goal.

"The prisons have failed", has been the cry for a number of years, because they have not taken the dregs of society[4] and so indoctrinated them according to some planned program that they will become useful citizens. (Some reformers word that last sentence, "that they will *again* become useful citizens," but such silliness can be ignored.)

Obviously, rehabilitation has not succeeded. The recidivism rate has not changed significantly either up or down. The crime rate continues to rise. At this moment the goal of rehabilitation has divided the penologists into two camps. One group says that the concept is a failure and our legislatures would be foolish to spend any more money on it. Robert Martinson says that the implication is clear that if we can't do more for (and to) offenders at least we can safely do less. The other group is convinced that all our efforts in this direction have been half-baked and poorly funded and only by doubling our enterprise can we begin to make inroads on the present criminal population.[5] (There is a third group who want to tear down the prisons, but I will not deal with them here.)

Up to this point I have examined briefly the multiple goals of the typical prison system. As I have pointed out, the following list overlaps: 1. Penitency, 2. Retribution and revenge, 3. Punishment, 4. Deterrence, 5. Isolation, 6. Rehabilitation.[6] All of these goals seem to fall far short of attainment. In my own investigations, which I shall discuss later, I have found that prisons succeed best with the repentant wrong-doer. Sometimes this repentance takes the shape of a religious or ethical experience, while in others it is merely the recollection of a stable childhood, but a number of ex-cons who have made it in society speak—sometimes directly, but more often indirectly—of learning to face their guilt in the solitude of prison. In general, it is safe to say that none of the other goals mentioned above either hinder or facilitate this outcome.

With this exception, each of the goals can be said to hinder all the others. Retribution, for example, must satisfy the victim of the crime, while punishment, to be effective, must be controlled. The father who beats his son in anger for blowing bubbles with his meerschaum (retribution) is quite different from the father who says, "this hurts me more than it does you", as he paddles his son for teasing his younger sister (rehabilitative punishment).

If punishment is going to deter others, then it must at least be publicized if not directly observed. In the former days when the pickpocket had his hand cut off, he was a constant reminder to his fellows on the street of what might happen to them if their own hands strayed into other pockets. Today the convicted pickpocket is isolated and if his fellows miss him at all, they are apt to lionize him as a member of that somewhat exclusive club—men who have served time. Actually, dangerous criminals cannot be isolated because of all the other goals set for prisons. They must be housed with the grass users, draft dodgers, and other mild offenders whom they not only endanger but also corrupt. On the other hand, sometimes the zeal for isolation precludes the deterrence of others entirely. Recently, a man who heisted a bank in upstate New York was caught in California, tried and sentenced in the federal courts of that state and no one in the bank area even knew of it for some time.[7] His fellows thought he was off enjoying the fruits of his labors. The goals of retribution, punishment, isolation and deterrence certainly interfere with one another, even where they are not mutually exclusive.

The contradictions between these goals and rehabilitation, however, are total. It is impossible to teach a man to integrate into a society by isolating him from the society. You cannot teach a man to have self-respect—obviously so necessary for successful re-entry—by using him as a horrible example for the deterrence of others. Revenge breeds revenge, and whatever deterrent effect punishment might have is diluted to the degree that the convict feels the retribution he has suffered is unfair.

When these insurmountable difficulties are considered, it seems not unreasonable to suggest that perhaps we are not failing in the goal of rehabilitation. It depends on how one defines success. The recidivism rate—by which most authorities measure the failure of prisons—hangs somewhere around 70%. Statistics on prisons are apt to be inaccurate and in disagreement. In most prisons about 70% of the inmates have served time previously. Studies have shown that about 70% of those released from prison during any period of time will show up again in other prison populations. As disparate authorities as former Attorneys General Ramsey Clark[8] and John Mitchell[9] each have quoted comparable percentages. (A number of penal programs boast of lower recidivism rates, but a careful reading of their data usually shows that they were dealing with a highly selected population, or that the cost of the program would make it prohibitive for general use or that they were playing games with their statistics.[10] Those who regard 70% a failure ignore the raw material the prisons receive. I suggest that grateful emphasis should be placed on the 30% who seem to make it.

A few years ago I started interviewing ex-cons, who had successfully re-integrated into society, in the hope that I could discover some commonality that might indicate the right direction for the prison reformers to take. I looked for those who had been in a penal situation for at least three years and had either been out for five years without involvement with the law or were now in a position of such stability that it would be safe to say they had made it. It is almost impossible to find these people. One of the first things an ex-con has to do in order to make it is to get lost. Neither prisons, police nor parole departments have much information on their successes. Through bartenders and other chance sources, I finally found and talked with somewhat more than fifty ex-cons in four major sections of this country (Northeast, South, Southwest, and Far West).

At an interview, which can last up to three hours, progresses, I frequently learn that for one reason or another the ex-con does not meet my criteria. Some, I discover, are still engaged in illicit activity and have just not yet been apprehended. Some failed to mention at the beginning that they were picked up last month in a drug raid or for some similar violation because they didn't think it very important. Others, like civil rights activists, were never criminal and society should only be grateful that prison did not destroy their inherent decency. I tried to avoid the "professional" ex-cons— the ones who speak to Rotary Clubs on the evils of our prison system—but a few of them slipped through.

Now that I have apologized for the shoddy quality of my random sample, I can safely say that my interviews have produced some interesting material. What, for instance, are some of the reasons why a few ex-cons succeed? As I mentioned above, a few actually used their prison time to contemplate their past mistakes, to consider their options and to repent in much the way that the benevolent Quakers expected them to do. Most simply matured. Even those who gave credit for their reformation to a special individual or organization or an inspirational book, usually revealed during the interview that they had been confronted with several similar opportunities in their youth and had simply not been mature enough to take advantage. Former Attorney General Saxby's callous remark on a TV interview that to stop all crime all we have to do is to identify the young criminal and lock him up until he is thirty-five years old is not without some merit even though Saxby's methods of identification smacked of totalitarianism.

The part that maturity played may be debated, but many of my ex-cons did report that they had met someome who had a powerful, positive influence. Frequently these statements sounded more like an obligatory ritual than a sincere attempt to explain the reformation. It was hard to take seriously the ex-con who gave all the credit for his success to the lovely woman he met and married after he got out and then later in the interview told of cheating on her, beating her up and of her constant nagging. Or another who gave great praise to the director of the prison hobby shop and then couldn't remember the man's name. Despite these caveats, there can be no question that a personal interaction with a decent individual may be a big factor for an ex-criminal in establishing a new goal. It is not, however, a method that society can depend on.

Probably of more importance than individuals are the organizations which exist throughout the country dedicated to the rehabilitation of convicts and ex-cons. They use many different methods. Each of them experience a tremendous number of failures. Many of them appeal only to a certain type of personality. Some are manipulated by convicts to obtain brownie points with the Adult Authority or with some other parole board. But after everything has been said to belittle them, it cannot be denied that they offer tremendous assistance to those ex-cons who want to help them-selves, assistance that can be found nowhere else in society. I am speaking of such groups as Delancey Street in San Francisco,[11] the Fortune Society in New York City,[12] the Seventh Step in many areas, the Jay Cees, the many centers sponsored by the Quakers and other religious organizations throughout the country. There are many more.

Only a few of the ex-cons with whom I have spoken failed to mention favorably at least one such group. In addition to the usually worthwhile programs they offer, such as training, counseling, employment, etc., they often permit the ex-cons to meet that one person who is later to be regarded as a turning point away from a life of crime. They also present an opportunity for ex-cons to work with other ex-cons, an experience that my interviewees assert is therapeutic both to the giver and the receiver. It would be difficult to commend one of the organizations over the rest. For most of them the success ratio is not nearly so high as their literature implies, but they do succeed in many cases. Society probably has no right to ask more than that.

I have yet to talk to an ex-con who gives credit to the rehabilitation program of the prison where he was incarcerated for his successful re-entry. Even those who spoke highly of individual counselors or instructors always added that those were exceptions who were bucking the trend. A few were grateful that they had been able to complete their high school equivalency while still behind bars, but even on this point most seemed to feel that they succeeded in spite of the prison. One ex-con, for example, who was a college student at the time of my interview, recalled that the prison instructor had turned the high school equivalency class over to him for tutoring. At the time of my interview, not a single ex-con was employed at a job requiring skills he had learned in prison, although some had worked briefly at such occupations while looking for more attractive work.

Critics of rehabilitation programs sneer at the license plate factories in most state's prisons and ask, "How many jobs are there outside making license plates?" It is true that most programs show little imagination, but the critics fail to recognize the enormity of the problem. Over the years a number of imaginative plans have been proposed. The ways in which a program can be shot down are numerous. The Governor fails to ask for money. The legislature refuses to raise money. Prison authorities see in the plan a new and more efficient method of control. Unions see the products from prison as unfair competition, which they are. Merchants see the products from prison as unfair competition, which they are. Many professions—undertakers, barbers, lawyers, bartenders, to name only a few—don't want ex-cons in their ranks and lobby for legislation against it.

But the biggest problem comes from the prisoners themselves. Governor of Georgia Lester Maddox was reported to have said that nothing could be done about the prisons of Georgia until they got a better class of prisoners. I don't agree that nothing can be done, but I do feel that his excellency recognized a problem. Nearly two-thirds of our State prisoners never finished high school and better than a quarter of them failed to finished the eighth grade.[13] These men have already rejected the educational system of a free society. Our very best educational authorities have failed to design schools that could enchant these men the first time around. To imply, as many prison critics do, that penal experts have failed in this area is pure fantasy and irresponsible. Educational opportunity must be offered to prisoners, but we must be realistic about the chances of success.

The same can be said for job training. Nearly two-thirds of the inmates of State's prisons were employed during the month previous to their arrest. (Over two-thirds, if part-time employment is counted.)[14] Of course, many of these were working at minimum wages, but the expectation that steady work, even at much higher wages, will prove attractive to them and win them away from the paths of crime is romantic wishful-thinking. Many convicts are imprisoned for crimes related only peripherally to their economic security—homocide, sex offenses, drugs, etc.—while the rest have found that crime pays much better than a nine-to-five job and is worth the risk. Anybody who has earned a living breathing welding smoke for eight hours a day has to have a strong moral fiber not to envy the man who can make a better living holding up liquor stores.

Job-training in prisons is essential, but society must expect minimal returns. No matter how effective a job-training program may be, only an extremely small percentage of the ex-cons will be able to take advantage of it after release because of a multiplicity of variables ranging from personality defects to widespread unemployment.

Many varieties of psychiatric counseling and therapy sessions have been tried in a number of penal settings; all with very little success.[15] The "medical model" for explaining criminal behavior has never worked very well although it still has many exponents. A young drug dealer told me that he couldn't understand society:

"They put me in a prison and they elect your dealer president of the Chamber of Commerce. Each of us is just supplying our customers with what they want." He was, of course, referring to the man from whom I buy liquor. A man who tries to apply the rules of logic to society may be somewhat out of touch with reality, but he is certainly not sick. The psychiatrist who believes he can "cure" this kind of thinking is probably more confused than his client. A small number of convicts are disturbed in the psychiatric sense and would benefit from therapy, but court-enforced treatment has a poor reputation for success and psychiatry has a miserable track record for predicting criminal behavior.[16] Individual and group therapies have real value in the penal setting, but it should be available rather than required and society should not be encouraged to expect more than minimal results from it. In most prisons today lack of funds keep psychiatric help from being available to those who desire it. Even trained counselors are in short supply.

Probably the most unfortunate development of the "medical model" approach to criminal reform is the indeterminate sentence which was designed with the idea that a criminal could be kept in prison until such time as an appropriate board indicated that he was ready to return to society. Although the concept originated in the 19th century it has been implemented in the last few decades and more recently has come under wide attack. Instead of decreasing the length of sentences, it has lengthened them. Instead of increasing the motivation of convicts, the effect of not knowing how long a term is going to last is depressing. Prison authorities have used it as a method of control rather than as a means of positively reinforcing rehabilitation.[17]

Those who still support indeterminate sentencing as a viable method assert that it has not been given an adequate chance, that insufficient funds have been appropriated to pay for the extra psychiatrists, psychologists, and counselors that are needed.[18] This is undoubtedly true, and there is some evidence to support the hypothesis that one-on-one counseling and support pays off in less criminal and more acceptable behavior. Nevertheless, unless a much higher success rate is established that can now be demonstrated, it is pure fantasy to imagine any state legislature raising the exorbitant sums that would be necessary to maintain such a program. In the meantime, the indeterminate sentence serves more to brutalize than to elevate.

So far my litany has been concerned not only with why prisons fail, but even more important, with why they cannot succeed. Society, of course will not accept this attitude. Penologists must be dedicated to making prisons work. What do we have to do? What changes must we make in the system or in society itself in order to get benefits from our penal program? The answer to such questions is: probably not very much is going to succeed. Here, however, are some of the areas where a beginning can be made.

First, there must be full employment. No matter how much we train a convict or change his attitude or pray for his salvation, unless he can find work when he gets outside he is bound to end up back inside. He is at the bottom of the employment barrel. A firm that hires ex-cons during a period of recession instead of other available applicants is not serving its community very well. No reasonable prison reformer could ask that an ex-con be given preference over a stable, family man. To have a job available for every ex-con would not stop crime by any means, but until that day arrives we are not going to make any inroads into recidivism rates. If there is full employment, we will not have to worry much about job training in prisons for in times of prosperity industries quickly find the money for on-the-job training.

Full employment, however, is a job for society as a whole. To change prisons the first problem is the sorting out of priorities. Since the current goals are all mutually, separately and in tandem, totally contradictory, every effort must be made to eliminate as many of them as possible.

It is doubtful that revenge will be eliminated, no matter how many penologists deny its importance. The general public demands it. They insist that a criminal must pay his debt to society. He must suffer the way he made others suffer. He must be treated as he deserves. That such vengeance (or retribution or restitution or punishment or whatever you may call it) is demonstrably of little value and of tremendous cost does not seem to be particularly impressive. Vengeance does so little to repay the victim and possibly may harm him. As a punishment, imprisonment is so delayed and frequently so unrelated to the crime that it cannot serve as an aversive or negative reinforcement. (Many criminologists demand *swift* and *certain* punishment, insisting that this will increase its effectiveness. However, psychological research seems to indicate that this is wishful thinking. No matter how efficient the courts become with extra judges, computerized communication and streamlined procedures, we cannot make punishment immediate. The efficacy of punishment deteriorates so rapidly with delay between the behavior and the aversive response, that after a few minutes the relationship is so negligible that further diminution over weeks or months is inconsequential. Without disastrous reduction in our civil rights, we cannot sufficiently speed up the trial or increase the certainty of the penalty to make any appreciable difference to the criminal. In order to guarantee deterrence society cannot give the police authority to punish immediately every law breaker they catch.)

While the evidence that imprisonment deters the imprisoned is skimpy, the evidence that it deters anybody else is non-existent. Social psychologists have done considerable investigation into the formation of moral codes. Although it is by no means a settled question, it seems likely that inter-nalized self-control—which is what we are looking for—is brought about more by positive than negative reinforcement. Our behavior is more for approbation than for fear of punishment. In fact, punishment and fear of punishment seem to eliminate the necessity of justifying our behavior to ourselves. Whenever we function under a state of threat, we don't have to say to ourselves, "This behavior is right or wrong", so when we perceive the threat as being removed we have no internalized code of ethics to guide our behavior. Most of the research in this area has been done with children,[19] for that is the period when moral codes are internalized, but there is no evidence to indicate that the findings do not apply to adults as well.

It is my belief that only a very small portion of the population have not during childhood internalized a set of values that were calculated to preserve the integrity of our society. Perhaps, only a fraction of one percent. It is only necessary to tell most adults that a certain behavior is undesirable and they shape their actions to incorporate this information into their value system. Murder is readily seen to be undesirable, that society would crumble if it were permitted. Committing murder is avoided for many reasons, but each reason seems to grow out of the individual's wish to preserve the culture and his position in it, not from the fear of punishment.

Punishment alone will not validate a norm. We were told that marijuana is undesirable and for many years most people accepted this restriction and internalized the rule. During the Sixties, however, many young people observed their peers smoking grass without harming either society or their position in it. A new rule was internalized: Grass is good. Punishment and the fear of punishment made no difference. Although those, who still believe that grass endangers society, keep laws on the books and keep upping the punishment, usage continues to grow.

Research is needed to find out whether social norms will be validated if the severity of the punishment is reduced. Society certainly must not allow the concept to be created that murder, robbery and rape have no social significance, but are the extreme penalties now administered really necessary? I wouldn't commit a murder if the penalty were reduced to a $5.00 fine, but I am not sure enough of my thesis—without a great deal of research—to extend this rationale to my potential enemies. The growing child must be convinced of the enormity of the crime of murder. However, the deterrence factor between life imprisonment and capital punishment does not seem to be significant.[20] Perhaps we might discover that the current murder rate would not increase if we only fined the convicted murderer half of his gross annual income. Consider how much this would save the taxpayer in prison support.

I do not intend this suggestion as frivolous. Through research it might be possible to divide society into two groups: (1) those who need little deterrence and (2) those who cannot be deterred. If it should be true that a small part of the population, who have not internalized any concern for the future of our culture, are not deterred by the fear of punishment then it is a foolish expenditure to maintain a prison system designed to deter them. Finding the answer will not be easy. Psychological experiments to test this hypothesis are hard to design, perhaps impossible. But until we know whether deterrence based on observed punishment really works, we are setting a goal for our prisons that they cannot possibly attain.

Finally, rehabilitation must be taken out of the prisons. It is my opinion (and I am not alone in this thought) that a man who is capable of rehabilitation should not be in prison to start with. If we can eliminate from the list of goals: revenge, punishment, and deterrence, then rehabilitation as a prison goal is no longer needed. When the courts (or whatever agency is authorized) decides that a convicted criminal needs job-training, it is foolish to send him to a poorly equipped prison workshop. (Prison reformers are always calling for better equipment for prison training programs, but they are whistling in the dark. No legislature is going to listen to them.) In times of full employment he can have a job in an industry that provides on-the-job-training.

When he needs counseling and directive therapy, a beefed-up parole and probation system can take care of him. Parole and probation do not appreciably change the recidivism rate one way or another, but they are a much cheaper way of handling the criminal population than imprisonment. (Unfortunately, a mistake is costly. When an armed robber continues to ply his trade while on probation or parole, the public outcry is great. So far, efforts to reduce this risk have not been productive.)

Many states have already made a start toward getting rehabilitation out of the prisons, but the idea that the two are compatible remains. Family days are scheduled, quarters for conjugal visiting are made available, work-release and study-release programs are designed. But as long as these programs are tied to prison life they cannot succeed. Typical, I believe, was the report of the veteran of Parchman, the Mississippi State Pen, where conjugal visiting is allowed. Whenever his wife was scheduled to visit him, that same morning his prison lover insisted on having sex relations. "After all," he told me. "She only showed up once a month; him I had to keep happy every day." Prisons are no less prisons because they have pretty programs.

It will not be easy to determine which prisoners are to be released for programs outside, but if society can forego the goals of punishment, deterrence, and particularly vengeance, the job will be that much easier. It is not within the scope of this article to describe or even enumerate the facilities where rehabilitation can be provided outside of prisons, but many types of half-way houses have been developed and most states are experimenting with new forms of probation and parole.

Of course, in this utopian prison, where only the dangerous are isolated, opportunities must continue to exist. Educational and training facilities must be available, but not as rehabilitation. The few prisoners who are left must be given every encouragement for self-improvement, but they must be informed that this effort is not preparing them for a return to the street. It is designed to make their incarceration more bearable.

If the general public can be convinced that they should forego vengeance, and perhaps they will when they understand the cost of it; if the concept of deterrence can be eliminated as psychologically improbable, if not impossible; if repentance can be left to the guilt-ridden conscience of the individual; if the promise of rehabilitation can be removed from the prisons and returned to the "street" where it belongs, then only isolation is left as a goal for prison authorities to worry over.

Summary

In general, it can be said that prisons cannot succeed because of the conflicting demands that society makes of them. Each expectation— rehabilitation, isolation, deterrence, punishment, retribution and repentance—presents the penologist with almost insuperable problems all by itself. However, to some degree each goal interferes with the attainment of each of the others. Prisons will continue to fail until the public demonstrates a willingness to forego a number of these demands and permits the prison authorities to concentrate on the only job they can reasonably be expected to do well: protect society from the dangerous criminal.

Discussion Questions

1. When we say that a person is "deterred by punishment" what do we mean? What evidence do we have that this is actually happening?

2. In what ways do punishment and retribution conflict? In what ways are they identical goals? Is this only a problem of definition?

3. What methods of rehabilitation have proved most effective? What evidence can you offer to back up your conclusion?

4. Federal grants through the L.E.E.A. have financed the construction of training workshops in many prisons. In what ways is this a good idea? A poor idea?

5. When did rehabilitation first become one of the goals of the modern prison system?

Notes

1. Albert Bandura, *Aggression a Social Learning Analysis* (Englewood Cliffs, N.J.: Prentice-Hall, 1973), pp. 221-230. An excellent overview of the research in this area.

2. Only prisoners who attempt to escape are punished. If one succeeds, this is obviously a blessing to the community since it no longer has to support him in prison.

3. Philip Zimbardo, et al, "The Mind is a Formidable Jailer: A Pirandellian Prison." *The New York Times Magazine*, (April 8, 1973) pp. 38-60. Philip Zimbardo et al, hired a group of college-age youths for a prison experiment. They

were divided randomly as guards and prisoners, but within hours the role-playing became real and the guards so tyrannized the prisoners that the experiment had to be called off before it was half completed.

4. And make no mistake about it. The inmates of our penal institutions are for the most part the dregs of society. It is possible to find a few who were framed or were victims of a mistake, but most convicts have had many brushes with the law, had multiple previous incarcerations and had effectively severed themselves from social intercourse long before the courts decide to put them away.

5. Robert Martinson, "What Works?—Questions and Answers About Prison Reform," *The Public Interest*, (Spring 1974), pp. 22-54. (This article has been combined with replies from Ted Palmer and Stuart Adams and published in a pamphlet by the National Council on Crime and Delinquency, 411 Hackensack Ave., Hackensack, N.J. 07601, entitled *Rehabilitation, Recidivism, and Research* 1976).

6. There are several other minor or subsidiary goals, but listing them would serve no purpose. "Justice", of course, is the problem of the courts and not the prisons.

7. Jim Flateau, "Tuttle Admits Richfield Bank Heist," *Daily Star*, Oneonta, N.Y., (Nov. 23, 1976). When the story of Tuttle's escape from a California federal prison came over the news wire, the local reporter investigated and found he was serving 15 years for a New York bank robbery he had committed five months earlier. Even the bank manager had not been informed that he had confessed to the crime and had been sentenced.

8. Ramsey Clark, *Crime in America* (New York, Pocket Books, 1971) p. 195. Actually Clark uses "80%".

9. John M. Mitchell, Keynote address at the National Conference on Corrections, (Dec. 6, 1971).

10. Cf. Martinson.

11. Delancey Street Foundation, Inc., 2563 Divisadero, San Francisco, CA, 94115.

12. The Fortune Society, 29 East 22 Street, New York, New York, 10010.

13. *Survey of Inmates of State Correctional Facilities, 1974, Advance Report*, U.S. Dept. of Justice, L.E.A.A., National Criminal Justice Information and Statistics Service. Page 24.

14. Ibid

15. A good survey of the various methods that have been tried in penal situations can be found in Martinson et al.

16. Joseph E. Jacoby, "Prediction of Dangerousness Among Mentally Ill Offenders," (Presented at the Annual Meeting of the American Society of Criminology, Toronto, Canada, Oct. 31, 1975.) Typical of findings in this area. Approximately 1/3 of those predicted to be dangerous turned out not to be, while 1/3 of those predicted to be not dangerous turned out to be.

17. Jessica Mitford, *Kind and Usual Punishment, the Prison Business*; Vintage Books, New York, 1974. Chapter 6, p. 87, contains a brief but cogent account of the indeterminate sentence.

18. Karl Menninger, *The Crime of Punishment*, Viking Press, Inc., New York, 1969. One of several books by Menninger calling for greater psychiatric involvement with prisoners.

19. Leon Festinger and Jonathan L. Freedman, "Dissonance Reduction and Moral Values", pp. 220-243 of *Personality Change*, ed. Worchel & Byrne, John Wiley & Sons, New York, 1964.

20. Isaac Ehrlich in the American Economic Review, June, 1975, offers a statistical demonstration that the death penalty deters. This is not supported by empirical evidence gained from many years of observing murder rates in juxtaposed states where laws on death penalty differ or in states where the death penalty has been abandoned or introduced. More research is needed.

3

Why The Problems in Prison Today?

Harry Rubenstein

IN THE EARLY MONTHS OF 1974, the State of New York decided to place a pilot project at the Attica Correctional Facility by creating a Psychiatric Unit inside its walls.

The opportunity was given to the Unit to do, more or less, what it wanted to, without much interference. The Staff was able to see things for themselves, maintain files and records, given a chance to work with both sides of the prison population, such as the officers and inmates, and generally initiate new procedures in a prison setting. They were able to sit back and examine the methods being utilized and introduce changes to administration with the hope that they would listen.

The biggest problem was to remember that Staff had to walk a narrow, straight line. The Unit did not take sides with the inmates or the officers; however, it had been accused of doing so.

Before going any further in this chapter, it should be understood very clearly that at times it will sound biased; however, there has always been an attempt to be honest and constructive in the observations to be found here. The following endeavors to illustrate some of the problems a person is confronted with upon being arrested, put in jail, tried in a courtroom, convicted, and finally, sentenced.

The problems in prison today begin at the time of arrest. For example; if the arresting officer (who today must follow a complicated process), does not make out the papers correctly, one word being out of place or misused, could result in such mistakes as to allow a man to go free, without ever facing prosecution. This certainly sets up problems for law enforcement. On the other hand, some charges are placed against the individual that do not adequately state the nature of the crime and are confusing to the lay person.

The arrest having been made, the individual then finds himself in the city or county jail. The problem is continued in the jail as here the inmate may be incarcerated for 24 to 48 hours before his (or her) family is even notified. This particular person could have been on medication prior to his arrest and it is possible for him to go many days without his prescription or medication. The inmate in the city jail sometimes may wait days before he sees an attorney.

All of this may not seem like much to anyone when discussing it; however, picture yourself in a 6' X 6' room, locked in, not being given any information or seeing anyone that you think could help your case. You can imagine the frustration. Indeed, those who cannot post bail may be forced to wait many months before going to trial. Combine this with an antisocial situation to begin with, and a lot of things could happen. This compounds the problem of what is going on in prisons today.

Probably one of the biggest problems is that of waiting for your turn at trial. Lawyers are busy, and material has to be gathered. This all takes time and, meanwhile, the arrested individual sits in a cell and waits. Most jails are small, as they are supposed to be areas where one sits for a short length of time awaiting trial and so there is not much room for any recreation. These overcrowded conditions make it necessary, at times, for prisoners to sleep out in the gallery on mattresses; tension mounts, and things begin to happen.

The solution to this is not necessarily psychiatry, or medicine. The solution is to improve the procedure, simplify the "paper-work", speed up the courts, and get things moving.

The time comes for the accused to actually have his "day in court". This "day" usually runs into *days* in court and, here is where the problem widens. It is unfortunate that many an inmate is illiterate or inadequate, or cannot comprehend the jargon of a court, let alone its rules, regulations, etc. Some of these people are told what to do by their attorneys to the extent that if they say this, or admit that, it could affect their case in various and specific ways. The outcome, therefore, can be quite different from that which was predicted. The defendant may sign certain papers, admit certain facts, feeling they will be resultant in a lighter sentence (and, indeed be told that such is a real possibility), when, lo! and behold, it does not happen; in fact, just the opposite may very well result. Lengthy sentences are given and after being placed in a maximum security institution, realization comes and he now wonders, "What did I say or do wrong in court . . . What happened?"

It is at this point that the Forensic Psychiatrist faces a very angry and violent individual who feels he has been "sold down the river" and, of course, this individual takes out his feelings on those around him, such as other inmates, and the officers.

There is also the process known as "plea bargaining" which is carried on between the judge, the district attorney, and the lawyer, which may affect the determination and length of the sentence. This is similiar to a "swap shop". "I will give you this, if you will give me that". Such "deals" made between the lawyer and the district attorney may result in the inmate being more confused than ever. In the beginning of his case, he was probably told that what he did was regarded as a horrendous crime and he has to be punished for it as provided by the law (the usual interpretation being that of a prison term). A few days later, a plea bargaining has been conducted and he is now told that he may plead to a lesser crime. This can certainly be more confusing to him than anything else. That is to say, if the crime was horrendous one day, it must still be considered horrendous the next day! At least, so far as the lay person's understanding of such is concerned, the passage of time does not change the nature of the crime committed.

Having been sentenced, the prisoner is sent first to a reception center for 30 days. The problem still goes on, as he is not told when he will leave for the reception center or where the center is located. Families are not given the courtesy of notification. The prisoner is simply packed up one day, put on a bus, sent to a reception center that the state has set aside for this purpose. After 30 days in "reception", where he is given various psychological tests, and where he may be examined by a psychiatrist or psychologist, he is then indoctrinated in what will be happening to him while serving his time in one of the correctional facilities.

While at "reception" he will be given a suit of clothes, a book of rules, and will await the end of his 30 days before knowing where he will serve his time. Most of the time in reception is spent in quarantine because he is a new inmate coming into the institution. Times goes very slowly, and idle men are potentially unpredictable men.

The individual is then sent to a prison (deemed appropriate for the nature of his crime) in accordance with the number of years of his sentence. Some men will go to minimum security prisons; some to moderate security facilities; others, to maximum security.

This chapter will address the subject of maximum security facilities, inasmuch as Attica (where these observations and experiences took place) is such an institution.

The problem in the prison now gets much larger as the individual has now arrived at the final stage of the process, or where he is going to do his so-called "time". It is now when everyone must make a decision as to what this correctional facility must do. Is it the facility's job to rehabilitate, or is it to punish? Merely changing the name from "prison" to "correctional facility" does not provide any guarantee of rehabilitation. There are many people who claim that the individual in the facility gets away with too much and should be punished for what he did. Others will say, "These men should be rehabilitated; they should be changed; they never had a chance".

Actually, both sides are right. Some inmates do get away with too much, and some could be rehabilitated. Two important points should be made at this time: (1) As far as rehabilitation is concerned, if the aim is to modify someone's behavior, the inmate must be sent to a place where he will not be babied, and where, because he will not like what is going on, the result will be in his not wanting to be there and certainly, once his time has been served, never to have to go back. In other words, he should not be made too comfortable. Some institutions are not like correctional facilities at all. In fact, the inmate does not mind coming back to what some seasoned criminals refer to as "country clubs". This sort of place certainly doesn't modify anybody's behavior or rehabilitate them. (2) Some men should be given the opportunity for rehabilitation; especially young men who have been caught up in a crime at an early age and are serving a first felony. However, to try to rehabilitate these men in the setting of a maximum security facility where there are seasoned, hardened, unmanageable individuals, is a physical impossibility.

To those of you who are novices on correctional institutions, it should be pointed out that the inmates of such a facility have their own government, their own rules, and "enforcers" who see that their rules are adhered to. In plain words, "if you don't do as you're told", and you don't go along with your peers, you are "taken care of".

It is very difficult to see a young inmate (that could be rehabilitated) having to live 24 hours a day on a cell-block with the kind of men just described. It has been said before, and bears repeating here, that there should be a "maxi-maximum" correctional facility for incorrigible, hardened, unmanageable individuals. In providing such a setting for the difficult-to-manage-prisoner, those in charge know what they are dealing with. Such men should be offered intensive therapy. If they refuse, at least they will not be endangering others, nor preventing them from receiving help.

In a previous paragraph, mention was made of the fact that some correctional facilities are regarded like "country clubs". This is not only this writer's opinion, but apparently the opinion of inmates who have been transferred into Attica from other state facilities and who have told me that the place they came from was "like a country club where you can get whatever you want". Things such as drugs, liquor, and other contraband can be bought.

Rules have been changed in answer to prisoner-organized demands: for example, inmates may wear their shirt-tails outside their pants. The average layperson will say, "So what if he wears his shirt-tails free?" The corrections officer will quickly answer, "Wearing a shirt outside the pants allows one to conceal a weapon, such as a knife, in the belt-line under the shirt."

In some institutions, a man can wear his hair as long as he wants. One would say, again, "What's wrong with long hair?" The officers will tell you, "Instruments such as knives can be hidden in an "Afro" or long hair." Also, the mere fact that men congregating in a prison setting where some inmates refuse to bathe or wash can certainly cause an epidemic of lice which like to live in long hair. One can readily see the havoc such relaxed attitudes can create.

The rules and regulations in these facilities should be made by the officers and guards who work there and who are charged with the responsibilities of keeping order. Once having reviewed the rules and approved them, government-appointed administrators should then support those they have entrusted with the job of enforcement.

People on the "outside" have no business trying to influence and run an institution they know nothing about. Correction officers should have the opportunity for more training and instruction and should be screened in order to make sure there are no sadistic individuals hired. They should be cool under fire and should understand the nature of their work.

At this point, I must say that during the time that I have been at Attica I have never witnessed an action by a correction officer that I would not call humane. These men have been seen to take abuse from inmates, without blinking an eye, and must be commended for what they do. However, it is impossible to see everything that goes on and there are some officers, no doubt, that do not belong in the institution. Still, there are some inmates who, just as certainly, are violent and dangerous men who make it impossible to be handled without resorting to some force. Resorting to force is often the only way to protect the officer, other inmates, and in so doing, protect the offender from himself.

One of the biggest reasons related to some of the problems we face in prisons today is the news media; newspapers, radio, television, etc. The writers who write "just to sell papers" are misguided and although may not have intended to be purposefully detrimental, nevertheless the effect can be harmful to carefully-designed facility programs. Television programs are designed to attract audiences; material used in newscasts are often gathered so quickly as to be pieced together and information reported may be out of context with the actual facts. Many stories are written, or beamed, before being properly and thoroughly investigated.

As a psychiatrist, I have a deep concern for the increasing number of mentally ill patients in a prison setting. Placing such persons in correctional facilities is partly due to the concept of "deinstitutionalization" of psychiatric centers (mental hospitals or institutions). These people, who commit crimes because of their mental illness, find themselves in a prison where they cannot cope in any way. The other inmates, in turn, cannot cope with them and feel threatened and scared. The officers are certainly not trained to handle them; lay people (prisoners) in the prison cannot handle the mentally ill. This, indeed, has become a severe problem that cannot and should not be handled in a prison setting.

If this chapter does nothing else but make people think about why there are problems in prison today, and forces people to talk about it, either pro or con, I would feel that I have accomplished something worthwhile.

Some things, which could be done to help chip sway at some of the problems, are as follows:

There should be definite sentencing for an individual. A man should be given time to serve for a certain crime and be able to work out the sentence by keeping a good record, thus reducing the time he serves. This would enable us to do away with the parole system, which, in my opinion, accomplishes nothing. The parole system, as it operates today, compounds the problems in prisons by causing more frustration than could ever be imagined.

For example: a prisoner who went before the parole board, was given one or one and a half years to serve, after which he was told to return to the board. Upon return to the board, he may then be told that he must serve two more months and again come before the parole board. At this point the inmate begins to think optimistically, "I was given one year, now I have only two months!" However, upon returning to the board he may be told he still must serve two more years. He does not understand why, nor does he know what he has to do to have a good record that will enable him to get out. In such a system, the man is constantly kept on his toes, he never knows what is going to happen. He may not see the same parole board he saw before, as the boards move around to the various facilities. The definite sentencing would do away with this anxiety and frustration. The inmate would know exactly when he was getting out by keeping a good record for the length of his sentence.

The counselling system in the prisons today also add to the problem. For instance, a man who commits a crime, such as a sex charge, may be told, "Because of the nature of your crime, you cannot go to a minimum security prison." Yet, I have done psychiatric evaluations for parole-eligible prisoners in minimum security prisons on men who have committed sex offenses. It is surprising that, on the one hand, a man *can* be placed in minimum security, while in the other case, the offender is told he cannot. This is indeed quite frustrating and causes a lot of unnecessary problems.

Another problem-causing factor in prisons today is the bureaucracy of the administration. Reference is made here to a bureaucracy of administrators and government attempting to run these institutions from hundreds of miles away. It is extremely frustrating to be asked for advice and input and to learn that nobody is listening. If, indeed, they do listen, nobody does anything. To be so close to a situation and to feel that there are things that could be done to improve or correct existing programs; to supply statements and written reports suggesting improvements, only to have them fall by the wayside, is discouraging, to say the least.

Administration has a duty to listen to those involved in the field work, such as the superintendants, the officers, the counsellors, the psychiatric units, the medical units, and the inmates themselves. It is surprising how many inmates want more discipline in an institution because, "I feel safer when I know I can walk the halls and I know there is some discipline here." Remember, this statement comes from inmates, not officers!

The administration (government) should not make the same rules for every institution and dictate that they all must do the same things. What might be good and advantageous at one facility, may not work well at another. Again, the solution here is to *listen* to the men in the field and hear what they have to say. What may work in one setting, may not work in another. An example of this is that most of the correction officers in the Attica Correctional Facility are men from small towns (mostly farms) in the surrounding area, with a different way of life than an officer who would work in Sing-Sing Prison and who comes from metropolitan New York City. The language, the tempo, the makeup is entirely different. All of these factors should be taken into consideration. We are dealing with individuals, not with sentences; we are dealing with individuals with feelings, temperaments, and different physical make-ups. We are dealing with different psychiatrists; different people in different institutions.

If one institution has a good system operating, there is no reason for it to be changed. Changes made because of political consideration should not be encouraged or tolerated. Only qualified persons should be permitted to hold such positions of responsibility.

The general staff people who work in the institution and must keep a job to make their living, apparently feel they have to keep their mouths shut in order to hold their job. One of the big problems is that these same people, who could effect changes for the betterment of all, confine their complaints to the lunch hour or the ride home in the car. Open and free discussion is essential in order to effect change. Sincere expression of ideas should be possible without fear of administrative reprisals, if we really want changes to take place.

If this chapter will provoke people to think, especially students going into this field, it will have served its purpose; hopefully, it will help to turn around some of the problems found in prisons today.

Suffix

The author of this chapter was asked late in 1973 to consider forming a Pilot Project, a Psychiatric Unit in a special area of Attica Correctional

Facility, just a few short years following the Attica Prison riot (September, 1971). The Unit was formed, comprised of two Psychiatrists, a Psychiatric Nurse-Administrator, and a Psychologist to do testing. The team was available upon request for the needs of various inmates of the correctional facility. Record-keeping was meticulously maintained and the Unit operated under strict guidelines as set forth by them and accepted by the Office of Mental Hygiene, State of New York. The Unit first became operational in March of 1974. The problems discussed in this chapter were direct observations of the author. Dr. Rubenstein was later asked to transfer back to the Buffalo Psychiatric Center (where he had previously headed the Alcoholic Unit and where he had received his residency training) to act as Unit Chief for another new program, the Intensive Treatment Unit, to deal with clients who are considered dangerous and a threat to other clients in treatment. Dr. Rubenstein set up the Intensive Treatment Unit in March of 1978. It is currently operating with 20 beds for short-term clients who return to the referring Unit following treatment.

Discussion Questions

1. Do you believe that a prison is a place for punishment? Rehabilitation? Discuss.

2. Discuss the role of the prison in relation to treatment of the mentally-ill, incarcerated individual and the setting you believe best for this type of prisoner.

3. How would you "speed up the courts" to free-up the docket and thus place people charged with crime in a more expeditious system?

4. Should, or should not, the news media be controlled?

5. Discuss the Parole Board as it functions today and what changes would you make, if any?

6. Please give your interpretation of discipline and how you would accomplish this in a prison setting.

4

Challenge or Trap?
Predicting Dangerousness in Corrections

LAWRENCE A. BENNETT

THROUGHOUT THE ENTIRE CORRECTIONAL PROCESS there is an increasing demand for methods to predict not only which individuals will adjust on probation or on parole but also who will fail in their adjustment attempts by committing a violent act. Citizens fear to walk city streets at night anticipating being mugged, robbed or violently assaulted.[1] While society would like predatory individulas locked up *before* they commit their crimes, the balance toward a sense of judgment prevents this safeguard. But with the person who has been caught and convicted there should be some protection—such an individual, it is felt, should be kept isolated until his tendencies toward violent behavior have been reduced or eliminated.

Thus, there seems to be a strong need to improve our ability to predict behavior inasmuch as there is clear societal demand which seems based on facts—the rate of violent crimes seems to continue to increase each year. With an increased knowledge of human psychology and with mammoth computers to augment the impressive statistic talents available, the task presented should be an easy one—but is it?

Certainly if a predictive tool could be devised there would be ample scope for application. The determination of who should be placed on probation would be made much easier if the judge could be informed which offenders were likely to commit acts of violence. Once probation is denied and the individual is placed in prison the decision about when to release to parole could be made with less difficulty if the parole board could easily tell which inmate applicants could be released without causing a public outcry by some vicious act. It should be noted that the problem of whom to release from prison and when is related to indeterminate sentencing systems where "readiness for release" is one of the criteria considered for placement on parole or discharge from prison. Under the determinate or definite approach now being adopted by several states and seriously considered by others, the length of prison stay would be based on the "just desserts" related to the offense committed rather than any tendency or lack of it to commit further offenses of a similar nature (see chapter on the indeterminate/determinate issue for more details).

But there are still other areas where knowledge of the potential for violent behavior would be most valuable. The need for custodial controls, for example, must be based upon some notion as to the extent to which a prisoner is likely to be a threat to other inmates.[2] Along similar lines, some individuals may not be likely to cause problems with other inmates but if it were known that that person had a high potential for harming others should he escape, it might not be wise to place him in a camp or other minimum situation.

Thus, it can be seen that there are pressing needs for the capability to predict violent behavior—a variety of settings for ready application. Can science and corrections meet the challenge to produce this capability? Then comes the question, should they?

Efforts to Predict General Adjustment

In an attempt to bring objectivity into the decision making process in corrections several efforts have met with considerable success in predicting the probability of successful completion of two years of parole supervision. Gottfredson[3] using a technique developed by Wilkins[4] developed the California Base Expectancy Scale which has been demonstrated to be highly reliable over time. That system places parolees of a release cohort into risk groups. Thus an individual might be in a group with a probability of success of 75 percent. Unfortunately no one can determine which individuals out of the group will fall into the 25 percent that fail. Similar techniques have been applied by others with varying levels of statistical accuracy.[5] The basic problem continues, however. That is, such techniques are adequate for group prediction and are helpful as statistical controls in evaluating program impact but they cannot be used for individual predictions.

When this dilemma emerges, the tendency is to reject the statistical procedure—most decision makers feel such techniques are too cold and analytical anyway—and turn to experienced judgment. Unfortunately, such efforts usually, when tested, reveal that human judgment is even less adequate to the task. There is even some question as to the entire selection process. The *Gideon Decision* in Florida, for example, on the basis of legal deficiencies in the commitment process, forced the release of a sizable number of inmates without benefit of a determination of their readiness to assume their normal responsibilities in society. This group which was released on essentially a random basis was compared to a group released after careful screening in terms of subsequent arrests. The two groups performed equally well.[6] Findings such as this raise serious doubts about the capability of making accurate judgments that can be of predictive value.

While the inadequacy of clinical judgment as a technique for prediction can be demonstrated in a variety of fields,[7] the fact of the matter is that in all phases of life many decisions must be made by one group that determines in some way the opportunities or restrictions placed on others. Supervisors rate employees, teachers grade students, banks evaluate loan applications. The field of corrections is certainly no exception. Supervisors determine intensity of parole or probationary supervision; prison classification committees decide what programs inmates may utilize and the level of custody to be imposed. Is there a way that statistical predictive devices can be of use in the decision making process? The work of Norm Holt[8] would seem to be a good example of making this kind of contribution. Correctional administrators were concerned about the rising number of excapes from the California camp system. Nearly 35 percent of the prison population was in minimum custody at that time, which meant that large numbers of inmates had to be found for camp replacements every month. Using a configural approach, Holt was able to identify groups with specified characteristics with clearly stated probabilities for escape, based on past experience. There are critics who will point out that decision makers do not feel comfortable with probability statements but only want to know if this inmate standing before them will or will not escape. However, as concerns about the mounting escape rate increase, any assistance is gratefully received. If two men are being considered for camp placement and one is carrying the probability of 0-5% chance of escape and the other is rated as having a 15-20% chance of escape, the prudent course is to choose the individual with the lower probability. Note that the chances of the second man are really not very high, but then most men placed in camp do not escape. Thus, scales of this type can *assist* decision makers. There is no pressure for slavishly following the results in every instance; there may be circumstances that warrant taking some slight extra risk, but the tool is available to use if desired.

The Enthusiasm for Predicting Dangerousness

If these techniques are so readily available, why can't they be applied to the problem of predicting dangerousness? Unfortunately, the problem is not nearly so simple. First, there is the problem of defining dangerousness. Is the individual who is continually involved in bar room brawls a dangerous person? Or is it only the individual *convicted* of several offenses involving harm to others? How about violent behavior that never comes to official attention? Are threats to be considered the same as assaultive behavior? All these issues must be faced and dealt with before we can begin to attempt to develop systematic ways to predict the behavior in question.

Despite the difficulties of dealing with these issues, a great deal of prediction goes on in the correctional continuum. Evaluators and decision makers take their responsibilities regarding the protection of society very seriously. Thus, if any doubt arises the decision comes down on the side of caution. Thus the probation officer, in his presentence report, is likely to lean toward denial of probation if there is a record of violence or if the individual is at all threatening in his demeanor. Judges are more likely to sentence to prison such individuals. Once such persons are in prison, the prison psychiatrist or psychologist is unlikely to recommend release. The parole board is not likely to order release, and so on. The cautious approach is sometimes made a matter of policy as was the case with the California Adult Authority, for example, in 1973. Their policy stated:

> The following priorities in order of importance are:
> 1. *The protection of society*
> 2. The punishment of offenders: to make the punishment fit the criminal rather than the crime.
> 3. The deterrence of the offenders (by the punishment imposed) and of others (by example of the punishment imposed on the offender).
> 4. To rehabilitate those who are amenable to and capable of it.
>
> Felons committed to prison should be kept there until there is reasonable cause to believe they can lead crime free lives in society. *Doubts should be resolved in favor of public protection.* Prisoners who make a career of criminal behavior forfeit their right to be treated leniently.
>
> Violent, dangerous criminals and those who make a career of stealing other persons' property will be confined until there is *adequate assurance they have been reformed*. (emphasis added)[9]

Steadman[10] in discussing psychiatrists tendencies to react in a conservative manner could just as easily be describing decision makers throughout corrections. He noted the constant pressure to overclassify toward the dangerous side for it only takes a few "false negatives" (persons released who later become violent) to cause a great deal of alarm. The other side of the coin is given little consideration, with the view expressed that even if a few people are misclassified and confined as dangerous when they actually are not, such a loss can be tolerated in exchange for greater societal protection. Others, Rubin,[11] Dershowitz[12] and Pasternach[13] reach similar conclusions about the overprediction of dangerousness.

Let us look at a group who feel that they can, within certain limits, predict dangerous behavior. Kozol, Boucher and Garufalo state, "dangerousness can be reliably diagnosed and effectively treated,"[19] but only given certain circumstances. Namely, "No one can predict dangerous behavior in an individual with no history of dangerous acting out."[15] They report on the outcome of 529 male convicted offenders, illustrating support for their claim by showing that of those recommended for release as not dangerous only 8.6 percent subsequently committed serious assaultative crimes while 34.7 percent of those considered dangerous were involved in such offenses after release which was against the clinical recommendation of the team. However, using their own figures[16] it is learned that if all those released after diagnostic study no matter what the recommendation, only 11.3 percent became recidivists. In contrast those diagnosed and treated and released, no matter the recommendation, 10 percent became recidivists. Such a finding might suggest that treatment resulted in a 1.3 percent gain, not a very impressive gain, considering the great expense of psychiatric diagnostic and treatment staffs. Of course, the contrast might be the difference between the total (11.3 percent) group and those treated and recommended for release— those who might be characterized as satisfactorily treated—which is 6.1 percent. Now we have a 5.2 differential, not usually large enough to be statistically significant nor impressive from a simple common sense point of view.

Others have attempted to predict violent behavior by an examination of the past history of the individuals involved in assaultive behavior.[19] While correlates can be found such as enuresis, pyromania and cruelty to animals and claims of a high degree of prediction made, the fact of the matter is that while such signs can identify violent individuals with 80 percent accuracy, the actual predictive accuracy is 45 percent when one takes into account the false positives and the false negatives (the 20 percent of the violent patients who were not so classified plus those characterized as violent who were not).

It is interesting to note that while a variety of decision makers must deal with the prediction of dangerousness in the criminal justice system the discussion takes on heavy emphasis toward psychiatrists making the key decisions in the area. While no where is it contended that individuals must be mentally ill to be dangerous and there are several studies that suggest that few mentally ill people are dangerous[18] both the courts and correctional custom tend to turn to psychiatrists to determine dangerous propensities within the individual. Let us now look more closely at the problem of making this most difficult prediction.

Can Dangerousness be Predicted?—And the Problem of Predicting the Rare Event

First, let us look at what experts feel about the present "state of the art" of prediction. Wenk and his associates[19] arrive at the conclusion that prediction, at this time, is simply not possible. Magargee explored the field from a somewhat different perspective and arrived at a similar conclusion:

> Thus far no structured or projective test scale has been derived which, when used alone, will predict violence in the individual case in a satis-

factory manner. Indeed, none has been developed which will adequately postdict, let alone predict, violent behavior.[20]

Similarly Stone is convinced that, ". . . neither objective actuarial tables nor psychiatric intuition, diagnosis, and psychological testing can claim predictive success . . ."[21]

Norval Morris, in looking ahead at how imprisonment may be employed in the future seems to want to eliminate the concept altogether:

> Despite the weight of authority supporting the principle of dangerousness, it must be rejected because it presupposes a capacity to predict quite beyond our present capability or foreseeable technical ability.[22]

With specific reference to the ability of psychiatrists to predict, Dershowitz, in reviewing the few studies available that have attempted to follow up the predictions made found evidence strongly suggesting that psychiatrists are rather inaccurate predictors. This view appeared to be true in the absolute sense, but also in comparison to other professionals or actuarial devices.[23]

What seems to be the problem? Certainly with all the reviews conducted to date, a variety of factors must have been isolated to assist in making the desired prediction. Indeed this is true but well controlled application of these diagnostic signs had disappointing results. In attempting to assist administrators in controlling violence within California prisons, of which there has been a fair amount[24] those designated as the aggressors in stabbing incidents were compared with the prison population from which they were drawn. While the sample was significantly different from the total in terms of age, ethnic background, nature of commitment offense and assaultive history, an attempted application of these characteristics correctly identified fewer than 5 percent of the sample.[25] Further, such a procedure incorrectly included a large number of inmates who gave no indication in their history of any sort of tendency toward violence.

The problem resolves itself to the dilemma of *predicting the rare event*. Rosen[26] seems to have been among the first to bring this concern to the attention of social scientists but, unfortunately, the word has not spread sufficiently to prevent repeated attempts at this impossible task.[27] To illustrate let us say that a scale could be developed that could detect 80 percent of the violent individuals in a group of 100 inmates made up of both aggressive and nonaggressive men. Further let us assume a very high rate of violent behavior of 10 percent. The device then would select 8 violent men and 20 non violent men, while losing two who could represent dangerousness. As noted earlier, violence in prison, violent assaults on parole, escapes all are fairly rare events. Less than 1 percent of murderers released commit another murder; fewer than 8 percent of those inmates placed in prison camp escape,[28] etc. So we see that we really are trying to predict the rare event. Meehl,[29] working with Rosen determined that the incidence of a given behavior must be nearly 50 percent to permit the development of a sound predictive device.

Well, what's so bad about false positives if we manage to control a fair percentage of those likely to cause trouble? One might make the argument that on a cost benefit basis the gains outweigh the unnecessary controls placed on a few more inmates. Andrew von Hirsch takes strong exception to this point of view.

> . . . *cost-benefit thinking is wholly inappropriate here.* If a system of preventive incarceration is known systematically to generate mistaken confinements, then it is unacceptable in absolute terms because it violates the obligation of society to do individual justice.[30]

He is also concerned that the inappropriate labeling of an individual as "violent" or "aggressive" may cause others to react toward him in a manner to bring the suggested behaviors into the open—the self-fulfilling prophesy. There is some indication that such labeling, however, does not inevitably lead to a negative outcome.[31]

Ethical Issues and a Suggested Approach

As can be seen, it seems extremely difficult if not impossible to predict dangerous, violent behavior. Given the high ratio of false positives generated—the number of individuals incorrectly identified as dangerous when they are not compared to those correctly identified as violent prone—it would also seem to be apparent that the application of prediction devices at this time would be quite dangerous for individual justice.

The ethical issue boils down to the extent to which efforts should be made to reduce the constant attempts to judge the potential of an individual to engage in dangerous assaultive behavior. The relationship to the problems confronting preventive detention is quite clear. The American system of justice places great emphasis upon societal sanctions being applied for what an individual has done, not what he is, not what he thinks but what he has done. The continued use of devices to predict assaultive violence almost insures a violation of individual justice and the principles just outlined.

There may be a way out of this dilemma. It is suggested that in each situation where the demand is made for the prediction of future violence a reverse prediction formula be developed. Thus, if the desire is to predict which individuals are too dangerous to be placed on probation the suggestion is made that a prediction be made as to which candidates are likely to handle probation in a safe manner. Such a procedure can actually be placed in operation.[32] Similarly, readiness for release from parole supervision,[33] removal from control units, all could make use of this approach.

But isn't this technique just the reciprocal of predicting dangerousness and lead to the same results? At first glance it would appear so but further review will reveal it to be quite different. First, the accuracy of prediction is consistantly quite high. As long as emphasis can be maintained on how well the system is working, support will be maintained. Most such efforts are around 90 percent accurate in their predictions. To illustrate how support might be generated the analogy of betting on horse races might be used— who would want to go to the track with someone who could pick winners 90 percent of the time. Unfortunately it sometimes only takes one or two individuals who fail spectacularly to eliminate all predictive devises and bring about a return to excessive controls as a means to gain control.

Second, when we look at the consequences of false predictions we see that no individual is penalized. Under present approaches those incorrectly classified have to undergo restrictions on their freedom, are subjected to treatment they neither need or want and are generally treated like second class persons. In the process of applying the proposed system, those not correctly categorized gain greater freedom, are placed in less restrictive settings and are considered to be free of the need for treatment intervention.

Third, as previously noted, there is a constant pressure for conservative decisions at all stages of the criminal justice system. Large numbers of individuals will be locked in controlled settings no matter what kinds of predictive techniques are employed. The proposed procedure would insure that at least some of these people would be afforded the opportunity to demonstrate their lack of threat to the prison population or to society. The application throughout the correctional continuum does not seem beyond consideration.[34]

This concept is of such importance that it might be well to consider the development of a policy statement that social scientists, researchers and others concerned with classification could adopt. Such a policy might read something like this:

> Efforts to improve classification and screening techniques should be limited to those instances involving the prediction of the individual's tolerance for lowered controls or lessened supervision including total freedom. The adoption of this proposition is to insure that the consequences attendant upon errors of classification will result in an increase in individual freedom and an improvement of the person's life situation rather than unwarranted deprivation of liberty.[35]

Summary

In this chapter the problems surrounding the prediction of dangerousness have been outlined. The need for the capability to predict is clear for almost every step of the way through the criminal justice system and particularly the corrections segment of it, decision makers are called upon to determine who requires tighter controls, closer supervision or total removal from society. Techniques seen as helpful in making these predictions were reviewed and their general lack of successful application was noted. Serious concern was expressed about the strong tendency to overpredict leading to the imposition of controls unnecessarily onto large numbers of people. Similarly the statistical problem of predicting the rare event was examined with the finding that the use of even seemingly accurate rating scales or procedures lead to high levels of misclassfication to the detriment of the nonviolent.

An alternate approach was presented—that of reshaping all predictions toward determining which individuals could manage satisfactorily with fewer controls, with less supervision or free from all restrictions. It was argued that such a procedure would function with a greater percentage of accuracy as well as not imposing upon any false postives in the system unjust restrictive measures. Further the possibility was presented that this type of orientation might be adopted by correctional researchers, planners and those in charge of classification systems as a code of ethics to help prevent the application of neutral tools toward ends that all too often, inadvertently, lead to considerable injustice in the field of corrections.

Discussion Questions

1. What are the dangers involved in predicting violence? In *not* predicting violence?

2. Suggest the number of variables that might be seen as optimal to predict violence and defend your position.

3. Discuss how you would handle a request from the top administrator for a device for predicting violence if you were a researcher.

4. In addition to the statistical problems involved in predicting violence what might be some additional resources that make prediction in this area difficult.

Notes

1. Donald T. Lunde, "Our Murder Boom—Hot Blood's Record Mouth," *Psychology Today*, July 1975: 35-42.

2. South Carolina Department of Corrections, Collective Violence Research Project, *Collective Violence in Correctional Institutions: A Search for Causes* (Columbia,

South Carolina, 1973); American Correctional Association, "Violence Statistics for 1972 and 1973," *ACA Survey* (College Park, Maryland, 1974); A.J. Huenther, "Violence in Correctional Institutions: A Study of Assaults,": paper presented at the Annual Meeting, American Correctional Association, 1974; Burt R. Cohen, Richard J. Gould, Sandra Felderstein, *Prison Violence in California: Issues and Alternatives* (Sacramento: California Department of Finance Program Evaluation Unit, July 1975).

3. Don M. Gottfredson "The Base Expectancy Approach" in N. Johnston, L. Savitz & Marvin Wolfgang (Eds.) *The Sociology of Punishment and Corrections*, 2nd Edition (New York: Wiley, 1970).

4. Hermann Mannheim & Leslie T. Wilkins, *Prediction Methods in Relation to Borstal Training*, (London: Her Majesty's Stationery Office, 1955).

5. Lloyd Ohlin, "The Stability and Validity of Parole Experience Tables", (Unpublished Ph.D. Dissertation, University of Chicago, 1954); Dean Babst, J. Inciarde & Dorothy R. Jaman, The Use of Configural Analysis in Parole Prediction Research, *Canadian Journal of Criminology and Corrections*, 13 (1971): 1-9.

6. *Impact of the Gideon Decision upon Crime and Sentencing in Florida*, (Florida, Department of Corrections, 1966).

7. Paul Meehl, *Clinical vs. Statistical Prediction*, (1954); and Michael Haheem, 'Prediction of Parole Outcome from Summaries of Case Histories," *Journal of Criminal Law, Criminology and Police Science*, 52 (1961): 145-155.

8. Norman E. Holt, *Escape from Custody*, Research Report No. 52 (Sacramento, California: California Department of Corrections, Research Division, 1974).

9. California Adult Authority Policy Statement No. 24, Adopted March 27, 1973, "Functions and Priorities for Term Setting and Revocation of Parole".

10. Henry J. Steadman, "The Psychiatrist as a Conservative Agent of Social Control," *Social Problems*, 20 (1972): 263-271; and Henry J. Steadman and Joseph J. Cocozza, "We Can't Predict Who is Dangerous", *Psychology Today*, January, 1975, 32-84.

11. Bernard Rubin, "Prediction of Dangerousness in Mentally Ill Criminals," *Archives of General Psychiatry*, 27 (1972): 397-407.

12. Dershowitz, "The Law of Dangerousness: Some Fictions About Predictions," *Journal of Legal Education*, 23 (1970): 24-27.

13. Stephan A. Pastornach, *Violence and Victims* (New York: Spectrum, 1975).

14. Harry L. Kozol, Richard J. Boucher and Ralph F. Garufalo, "The diagnosis and Treatment of Dangerousness," *Crime and Delinquency*, 18 (1972) p. 392.

15. Ibid., p. 320.

16. Ibid., p. 383.

17. Daniel S. Hellman and Nathan Blackman, "Enuresis, Firesetting, and Cruelty to Animals: A Triad Predictive of Adult Crime", *American Journal of Psychiatry*, 127 (1971): 49-54, Ernest A. Wenk and James O. Robison "Assaultive Experience and Assaultive Potential," (Davis, California: National Council on Crime and Delinquency, Research Center, 1971).

18. see Steadman and Cocozza, and Pasternach.

19. Ernest A. Wenk, James O. Robison and Gerald W. Smith, "Can Violence

be Predicted?" *Crime and Delinquency*, 18 (1972): 393-402.

20. Edwin I. Magargee, "The Prediction of Violence with Psychological Tests," in C. Spielberger (Ed.), *Current Topics in Clinical and Community Psychology*, (New York: Academic Press, 1970) p. 98.

21. Alan A. Stone, *Mental Health and the Law: A System in Transition*. (Rockland, Maryland: National Institute of Mental Health, 1975) p. 33.

22. Norval Morris, "The Future of Imprisonment: Toward a Punitive Philosophy," *Michigan Law Review*, 72 (1974), p. 1167.

23. Dershorwitz, p. 46.

24. Lawrence A. Bennett, *Crime and Violence on the Streets and In the Prisons*, (Sacramento, California: California Department of Corrections, 1974).

25. Lawrence A. Bennett, "Brief Analysis of Characteristics of Male Felon Inmates Designated as Aggressors in Stabbing Incidents" (unpublished report, Research Division, California Department of Corrections, Sacramento, 1974).

26. Albert Rosen, "Detection of Suicidal Patients: An Example of Some Limitations in the Prediction of Infrequent Events," *Journal of Consulting Psychology*, 18 (1954): 397-403.

27. Recently the Department of Corrections of Michigan developed a scale or series of characteristics that seemed to offer hope of identifying the violent men in prison. By creating subcategories the scale was able to identify 80 percent of the aggressive inmates in one group. Closer examination, however, revealed that this high level of accuracy could only be applied to a very small percentage of violent inmates, allowing the build up of large numbers of false positives.

28. Holt, and *Uniform Parole Reports* (Davis, California: National Council on Crime and Delinquency, Research Center, 1974).

29. Paul E. Meehl and Robert Rosen, "Antecedent Probability and the Efficiency of Psychometric Signs, Patterns, of Cutting Scores," *Psychological Bullentin*, 52 (1953) 194-216.

30. Andrew von Hirch, "Prediction of Criminal Conduct and Preventive Confinement of Convicted Persons," *Buffalo Law Review*, 21, (1972) p. 740.

31. A.D. Cheatwood, "Restrictive Labels in a Juvenile Correctional Setting" (Columbus, Ohio: Program for the Study of Crime and Delinquency, Ohio State University, 1972).

32. The study of the presentence diagnostic evaluation program of the California Department of Corrections is illustrative of just this approach. It is reported in Lawrence A. Bennett, "Evaluation, Feedback, and Policy," a paper presented at the National Conference on Criminal Justice Evaluation, Washington, D.C., February 24, 1977.

33. Lawrence A. Bennett and Max Ziegler, "Early Discharge: A Suggested Approach to Increased Efficiency in Parole," *Federal Probation*, September, 1975; and Dorothy R. Jaman, Lawrence R. Bennett and John E. Berecochea, *Early Discharge from Parole: Policy, Practice, and Outcome*, Research Report No. 51 (Sacramento, California: Research Division, California Department of Corrections, 1974)

34. Lawrence A. Bennett, "Should We Change the Offender or the System?" *Crime and Delinquency*, 19 (1973): 332-342.

35. Lawrence A. Bennett, "Risk and Supervision" (Carbondale, Illinois: Center for the Study of Crime, Delinquency, and Corrections, Southern Illinois University 1976) p. 14.

5

Individual Responsibility

CLAUDE T. MANGRUM

A BASIC PRINCIPLE underlying effective corrections is the concept of individual responsibility; that is, the idea that the offender is responsible for his actions and accountable for their consequences. This concept is at variance with much of the traditional rehabilitative ideal, and the lack of emphasis on individual responsibility helps to explain why corrections has not been more successful in its efforts.

One of the major tasks of correctional activity is to facilitate change of behavior on the part of the offender from that which is harmful—thus undesirable—to that which does no harm—thus is desirable; that is, from illegal to legal conduct. Unless the individual offender is caused to recognize and accept responsibility for his actions, corrections will not be able to fulfill its task of behavioral change. This makes the concept of individual responsibility a crucial issue in current correctional philosophy and practice.

The following discussion of individual responsibility should be considered in terms of a framework within which correctional activity takes place rather than as a specific method or technique of correctional treatment. The corrections practitioner can focus on holding the individual accountable while employing a variety of individual and group counseling approaches, work-sentence programs, restitution to victim plans, payment of fines, vocational and educational training efforts or other activities designed to deal with the offender's needs and behavior. Stress can be laid on individual responsibility whether the offender is incarcerated in a correctional facility, is a resident of some kind of half-way house or is residing freely in the community on probation or parole. This principle of individual responsibility is a philosophical or attitudinal stance which permeates whatever specific correctional approach is used to deal with offender conduct.

Some readers will feel that this discussion of individual responsibility as essential to effective corrections has a strong moralistic tone. In some measure this is true; however, without getting entangled in arguing the philosophy of the free will of man, it should be sufficient for present purposes to simply state that one foundational assumption on which the concept of individual responsibility is based is that the individual does have considerable choice in what acts he commits. Traditional correctional philosophy has projected the "blame" for criminal acts onto environmental factors and conditions completely outside the individual, thereby implying (and sometimes making quite explicit) that he is not to be saddled with responsibility for his actions. This is not a valid argument because nonoffenders are just as much "products of their environment" as are offenders—and few would seriously argue that nonoffenders are not responsible for their actions.

Social conditions do constitute the environment in which all actions take place; they serve both to restrain individuals and to provide opportunities for illegal behavior. There are, in fact, many conditions of emotional, cultural or economic deprivation (for example: poverty, lack of opportunity, social and legal injustices, discrimination, rejection, pressures of all kinds, misunderstandings and mistreatment) that are faced by many who commit crimes, as well as many who do not. Even if all these "unhealthy" conditions were eliminated and life was made more ideal for these persons, there remains the matter of choice: they can still choose to behave in ways injurious to others—that is, in ways defined as criminal—or they can choose to behave responsibly toward others.

The basic issue is not the nature of the deprivations or opportunities faced by an individual, but what choices he makes in responding to these conditions—this is what makes him accountable for his actions. More or less deprivation, temptation or opportunity does not excuse from responsibility; and, unless offenders are more subject to "determinism" than nonoffenders, there is no reason why they should be less responsible for their acts than the general population.[1]

Compassion for the offender as a person, or moral disapproval of the conditions under which he has lived or does live, must not cause us to excuse his actions or overlook the consequences of his choices. One must be aware that what explains does not necessarily justify; that is, the existence of certain social conditions may help one to understand the offender's motivation in the commission of a crime, but that does not justify the act. These social conditions are mitigating circumstances which may serve to temper the imposition of the penalty for an offense; and this is an appropriate consideration. But this is not to be confused with justification of the offense, a situation which would totally eliminate the penalty because then the individual would not be responsible. Unfortunately, traditional rehabilitative philosophy with its "medical model" orientation, has often confused these two issues of mitigation and justification.

A Central Issue

In theory, the criminal justice system is to identify responsibility for a criminal act, intervene to halt it and cause the actor to accept responsibility.

In practice, this is usually done in legal processes up to the point of conviction, then the system changes direction. In the earlier stages of proceedings the focus is on what the individual *did*, but in the correctioal stage the focus shifts to what he *is*. If the idea of individual responsibility is socially and legally sound up to the point of conviction for a criminal offense, why should it be thought unsound and generally abandoned when the question of sanctions is reached?[2]

> "It is one thing to exact a penalty for what a person *did*, quite another to do so for what he *is*. In the first instance, we say that the individual has incurred a debt and there is a finite price to be paid. In the second case, we say that he or she is a deficient person and must become a better one before being accepted by us."[3]

Corrections has often functioned at cross purposes to this very vital concept, focusing not on what the individual has done but on what is "wrong" with him as a person and trying to determine all the social and psychological reasons for his condition. That what he has *done* is what brings him within the purview of corrections is forgotten, and attention is focused on his *need* for whatever corrections has to offer him. As a result, both the causal and treatment emphasis has been on "he is" issues: he is from a deprived childhood; he is the victim of an unwholesome environment; he is socially or emotionally inadequate; or some other rationalization—all of which actually say that he is not responsible.

But he *is* responsible! Whatever his motivation or the surrounding circumstances, he chose the course of action which is defined as criminal. Short of the legitimate inability to know the consequences of his acts due to mental aberration or extreme youthfulness, every individual is responsible for his actions and their consequences. This is why the legal system stresses such concepts as choice, intent, willfulness of action, knowledge of the wrongfulness of an act, the capacity to knowingly act—in other words, culpability. The legal system is a carefully constructed process for determining responsibility; *who* did *what*. Thus, since individual responsibility is the foundation of criminal and civil law, it must also be the basis for correctional efforts if they are to be effective.

The major task of corrections is to deal with illegal and harmful behavior in ways designed to reduce the risk such conduct poses to others; that is, to facilitate change of behavior from that which is harmful or threatens harm, therefore is legally forbidden, to that which represents no risk, therefore is acceptable. It is impossible to bring about such necessary change in offender conduct unless he clearly understands that he is responsible for what he does. If he is led to believe, through whatever processes and for whatever reasons, that he is not responsible, he is in effect given free license to do as he pleases.

If he never has to be accountable for what he does, why should he bother to consider the life, well-being or possessions of others? Why not follow whatever whim strikes his fancy?

A Correctional Failure

Corrections' failure to hold the individual responsible for his own behavior has some very harmful consequences. First, it encourages excuses, rationalizations and projection of blame by the offender. He will try to avoid looking at his behavior because it makes him uncomfortable to be confronted with what he has done or failed to do. He will plead all kinds of excuses which he has learned might be accepted to absolve him of responsibility: I didn't mean to do it; It wasn't my fault; I was depressed or emotionally upset; I was misled; You didn't make it clear to me. The offender may try to manipulate the corrections practitioner by giving him what he seems to want, as evidence of development of "insight into my problems"—thus gaining control of and exploiting the relationship to his own advantage. If the offender cannot dominate through such means, he may try to put the counselor on the defensive by contrasting their respective "hard" and "easy" lives; or he may try to gain sympathy by asking, "Wouldn't you do the same thing under similar circumstances?"

All of these ploys are attempts to evade responsibility by shifting the limelight from himself to some irrelevant but nicesounding rationalization. The offender knows what he is doing and what will likely be the response to his alibis, and he usually expects to "pull it off" since it has worked so well in the past. The corrections practitioner must cut through this fol-de-rol and keep bringing the offender back to the central issue: what you did was illegal and you *are* responsible for your actions. If this is not done, most of the other things the practitioner may do will be ineffective for correcting offender behavior.

Second, failure to hold the individual responsible encourages the very irresponsible behavior corrections is supposed to correct. In normal social functioning, we expect people to behave in responsible ways and we relate to them based on whether their conduct is seen as responsible or irresponsible. There is no reason to set expectations for responsible behavior for offenders that are different from those for non-offenders; *everyone* is expected to behave responsibly. Such differential expectations for the offender and treatment based on them imply that he *is* different; that he is not quite "normal;" that he is less capable than others to behave and succeed in a normal manner— therefore, he needs to be given special consideration and/or concessions.

This is a "put down" of him which will cause him to be reluctant to assume responsibility or, perhaps, even to aggressively resist it. Most every person wants to feel worthwhile in his own right. Making him responsible for his own actions tells him that he *is* worthwhile and *can* behave as everyone is expected, or others would be forced to assume responsibility to act for him. Not allowing or not causing the person to accept responsibility for his own actions tells him he *is not* responsible. This tends to destroy any inclinations he may have in this direction and encourages him to place the responsibility on anyone or anything other than himself. Most certainly, this is not a state conducive to specific behavior change or general personal development.

Possibility of Change

A well-developed sense of individual responsibility is the primary source for the acceptable social behavior necessary to the orderly and safe functioning of a society; it is the first line of defense against the kind of harmful conduct which has been defined as illegal. Limitations and controls that are imposed on the individual externally are secondary and should be designed to support—not to supplant—the primary source of control. In this context, the task of corrections is to identify the behavior which brings the individual within its processes and which needs to be corrected, then apply methods capable of facilitating that change. If specific conduct can be sustained long enough to become a pattern, attitudes and feelings will also change in line with the new behavioral patterns.

That an offender has behaved irresponsibly in the past does not mean that he cannot learn to act responsibly in the future. Offenders *can* change behavior that is illegal, even when it has become a way of life.[4] The offender can and must learn from his experiences, just like all other persons. He *can* learn to look at the relationship between what he does and what happens to himself and others as a consequence. To do this, he must recognize and be held to his responsibility for his own conduct. Many offenders do need some help in this process, however, and this is one of the key functions of the corrections practitioner.

Principles for Facilitating Change

Individual responsibility is the foundation on which various approaches to facilitate change of illegal behavior must be based if the correctional effort is to be effective. Of course, permanent change in behavioral patterns must stem from within the individual, but there are some things the corrections practitioner can do to *facilitate* that internal change. Some of these are discussed below; however, it is important to keep in mind that they do not constitute a specific "treatment approach," but form a general philosophical and attitudinal framework within which correctional efforts are carried on.

One of the cardinal principles of stressing individual responsiblity is to focus on behavior; that is, deal with what the offender *did*, not what he *is*. Corrections has contact with and some jurisdiction over the offender because the judicial system had held him responsible for the violation of some legal restriction or requirement on behavior. Thus, he comes within the purview of corrections because of what he *did*—not what he thought, felt, believed, liked, disliked, was or is. So, the explicit task of corrections is to try to correct behavior, not to restructure personality, revamp beliefs or realign allegiances. This is not to imply that these things are unimportant or are to be neglected; it simply says that they are the primary province of activity of other fields, not corrections.

Obviously, something triggers the illegal behavior, but this "something" is not necessarily a personality deficiency or the result of some uncontrollable social force inpinging on the individual. It is more probable that the "trigger" is the indivdual's conscious or subconscious perception that the specific act will in some way provide the satisfaction he seeks at that moment: material gain, release of emotion, revenge, thrill, status with peers, control of the situation or some other satisfaction or relief. Traditional rehabilitative philosophy tends to focus on the offender's condition and away from his conduct, so that the central issue becomes not *what he has done* but what he is and *what he needs*. His need, rather than what he has done or what are the consequences of that action, usually determines the level and extent of correctional intervention. Correctional effectiveness can be greatly improved if the basic approach is to hold the individual responsible for the consequences of his behavior and apply sanctions and methods designed to facilitate change of that behavior rather than to try to "redeem" him.

Another basic principle of the concept of individual responsibility is the clear expression of behavioral expectations, because there can be no valid accountability unless the required behavior is clearly indicated. The consequences of failure to conform to the requirements of the criminal law are serious enough that it is unfair and morally indefensible to expect people to conduct themselves according to particular standards, but fail to fully inform them in understandable terms just what those standards require. Thus the correctional client must be clearly told how he is expected to conduct himself to ensure the kind of behavior necessary to the safe and orderly functioning of society. He must not be expected to "be like us" in terms of the usual middle-class values or standards of social conduct. While the corrections practitioner can hope that the client will act and/or change in ways which may make general social interaction smoother and more satisfying (if, in fact, such change is needed at all), expectations can only deal with behavior which is harmful and/or illegal or which directly relates to his previous illegal conduct.

A third important principle for establishing individual responsibility is the immediate confrontation of illegal behavior when it is known to have occurred. Failure to do so implies official disinterest, if not acceptance. This is most certainly not conducive to accepting responsibility or changing behavior. Confrontation serves to put a choice squarely before the offender—he can either do something to correct his behavior or he can ignore the issue and risk whatever consequences may result. In either case, the choice is his; and this *is* an exercise in individual responsibility. This underscores the necessity of *some kind* of response to the behavior and indicates that the *certainty* of response is probably more important than exactly *what* is done. Ignoring *known* incidents of illegal conduct dilutes the meaning and strength of behavioral requirements because it implies they are not important enough to enforce. If the issue is dealt with immediately upon discovery, there will be little chance of the offender missing the relationship between his illegal behavior and the sanctions imposed.

Confrontation is further enhanced if it is direct and simple. Like most others, the offender usually hears and perceives what is to his own advantage. Clear, unambiguous action in response to misconduct reduces the opportunities for the offender to rationalize or excuse his behavior in terms of the familiar, "I didn't know" or "You didn't make it clear." It is also necessary that confrontation be consistent in terms of sanctions realistically related to the offense and in terms of follow-through; that is, helping the offender to see that the santions imposed are the *result* of his illegal behavior. This process of confrontation serves to reinforce the basic idea that the individual is responsible for what he does.

Fourth, acceptance of responsibility is aided if the offender has to answer only for what he has done. In order to adequately and fairly deal with what he has done, it is important that the sanctions be sufficiently severe to avoid depreciation of the seriousness of the crime he has committed but not so severe that it imposes penalty beyond what is necessary to meet society's needs for protections.[5] This is the concept of "commensurate deserts;" that is, the principle that severity of punishment should be commensurate with the seriousness of the wrong.[6] Seriousness involves considerations of the harm done or risked by the illegal act as well as the culpability of the offender in terms of his intent, previous conduct, or other factors which indicate the degree to which he may justly be held to blame.[7] Thus, several proposals have been advanced for sentencing or penalty scales which relate sanctions to seriousness of the act.[8]

An important facet of sanctions which fit the conduct, in addition to seriousness, is the requirement that they be imposed equally—regardless of social or economic status or political connections. Conduct which is illegal is illegal for everyone, and everyone found engaged in such conduct must be brought to account. This applies to so-called "street crimes," white-collar crimes, crimes committed while trying to enforce other laws and those resulting from fraudulent "national security" rationalizations. Where one segment of society sees another segment committing illegal acts and "getting away with it"—for whatever reasons—the integrity of the law is undermined. This stress on equal application of sanctions does no violence to the principle of "individualized justice," as some may suppose. Various factors in mitigation and aggravation must be considered in fixing sentence for a crime, so long as those factors are consistently and objectively considered for *everyone* for whom they exist. Justice does not necessarily mean everyone must pay the *same* price; but it does mean that everyone must pay *some* price according to the principle of commensurate deserts.

Effective corrections through individual responsibility requires, in the fifth place, that offenders be treated in a lawful manner. The very thought of raising this issue is a sad commentary on the present process of administering criminal justice. There is no need to detail here examples of how offenders are unlawfully treated; numerous appellate court decisions on various aspects of due process attest that, in fact, such treatment occurs. The misuse or abuse of official position and selective law enforcement by agents of criminal justice are also indicative of this lack of lawful handling of offenders.

One of the major aims of the justice system is to ensure, as much as possible, lawful behavior by every citizen. If the justice process (or the agents of the justice system) does not treat violators in a lawful manner, the process loses its force and becomes something for citizens to circumvent or "beat" rather than to respect and obey. It is impossible to teach an offender individual responsibility when he is given such an inappropriate example to follow. Thus, the dramatic impact of unlawful treatment tends to negate, rather than reinforce, desired lawful behavior patterns. Whenever it is deemed appropriate to impose legal sanctions for illegal behavior, the justice system must be sure that both the application and the impact of those sanctions are lawfully made.

A sixth and final principle for stressing individual responsibility as a means of facilitating behavioral change has to do with reinforcement of the desired behavior. Positive reinforcing of desired conduct should be as much a part of correctional behavior change efforts as that of imposing penalties for undesirable conduct. To be sure, corections is usually not able to provide as many or as great a variety of rewards as it can provide penalties—that is the nature of its structure and process. However, practitioners must not lose sight of the viability of desirable behavioral change through the use of the positive rewards that are available. Thus, use may be made of such rewards as less restrictive conditions of parole as the individual demonstrates his ability to lead a law-abiding life, early release from probation as the result of extra-ordinary compliance with its terms, or greater privileges of many kinds in the institution because the inmate has cooperatively followed the rules.

Perhaps the most effective use of positive reinforcement of desired behavior is to fully restore the offender to the mainstream of social life and interaction after the necessary and appropriate sanctions have been imposed. As long as the offender is going to live in the midst of and interact with other people, the ordinary and legal pursuits of social existence should not be denied him. There is no valid connection between conviction for most criminal offenses and the all too common restrictions against possession of a driver's license, licenses for various occupations unrelated to the offense, the right to vote, or many other privileges denied the offender by law but enjoyed routinely by the nonoffender. These things can add meaning, dignity and stability to one's life; therefore, *no* individual should be deprived of them unnecessarily. Both formal statutes and general social attitudes should, once the necessary sanctions have been imposed and the offender has adjusted his illegal behavior, look on the matter as "debt paid and cancelled."

Conclusion

The discussion above is not intended to imply that to focus on individual responsibility will be the cure for all correctional ills. However, it does suggest a practical and feasible way to immediately improve the effectiveness of correctional efforts. The principle of individual responsibility could and should be a thread consistently running through all criminal justice processes. Not only would this help to tie the system components together in their joint mission, it would also establish a solid foundation on which to develop correctional efforts to facilitate behavioral change. The focus on individual responsibility brings the offender into the same realm of expectations, considerations and treatment as everyone else; it de-emphasizes differences, requires the same conduct of offenders and nonoffenders alike and protects the worth of the individual. Within the framework of individual responsibility concepts, and despite what many critics say about the system, corrections *can* correct.

Discussion Questions

1. Discuss the different impact on offenders of using environmental conditions to *explain why* he committed a crime as opposed to using those conditions to *absolve him* of responsibility for his conduct.

2. Choosing *either* the pro or con side, argue the merits of the state-

ment: the individual offender is legally and morally responsible for his criminal actions.

3. What evidence can you submit that shows it is possible for offenders to learn legally and socially acceptable behavior patterns?

4. Discuss some of the treatment implications resulting from the traditional rehabilitative stance of responding to offender *needs* rather than offender *conduct*.

5. Explain the importance of restoring the offender to the full array of his civil rights after the criminal sanction has been imposed.

Notes

1. van den Haag, Ernest, *Punishing Criminals: Concerning a Very Old and Painful Question* (New York: Basic Books, 1975), pp. 99, 108.

2. Harris, M. Kay, "Criminal Justice: Rehabilitation or Punishments?" (Speech at NASW, Washington, D.C., January 1975) Mimeo, p. 3.

3. Ibid., p. 7.

4. For example, see Mangrum, Claude T., "The Function of Coercive Casework in Corrections," *Federal Probation*, 35 (1971), pp. 26-29.

5. Morris, Norval, The Future of Imprisonment (Chicago: University of Chicago Press, 1970), pp. 73-80.

6. von Hirsch, Andrews, *Doing Justice: The Choice of Punishments* (New York: Hill and Wang, 1976), p. 66.

7. Ibid., p. 69 and Chapter 9.

8. For example, see von Hirsch, *Doing Justice*, Chapter 16; Fogel, David, "We are The Living Proof"—*The Justice Model for Corrections* (Cincinnati: W.H. Anderson, 1975); and Kress, Jack M., Wilkins, Leslie T., and Gottfredson, Dan M., "Is the End of Judicial Sentencing in Sight?" *Judicature*, 60 (1976) pp. 216-221.

6

Ex-Offenders as a Correctional
Manpower Resource

JERALD K.M. PHILLIPS and GARY R. PERLSTEIN

ONE OF THE MOST SIGNIFICANT DEVELOPMENTS in the field of corrections
during the past ten years has been the increased use of nonprofessionals in
the delivery of direct client services. This has evolved, to a large extent, from
a continuing servere shortage of professionally trained personnel coupled
with an increasing disenchantment with some of the professional treatment
models. The numbers show that there are simply not enough correctional
professionals to fill a minute percentage of the available positions now
existing in the field. Even if the manpower shortage were corrected, there is
little evidence to support any kind of belief in a marked increase in success
rates (using any available standards). We have already seen a number of
special projects of the intensive counseling variety fail to show a consistently
favorable result pattern even though they were the product of highly trained
professionals.

Few persons in the field of corrections would argue the point that
correctional work entails a rather wide variety of tasks aimed toward the
rehabilitation of a similarly wide assortment of social types in the person of
the offender population. While a certain number of these tasks and certain
offenders need the services of a competent professional to effect change,
others do not. In fact, it may be that certain tasks and certain types of
offenders may be more effectively served by nonprofessionals, i.e., ex-
offenders.

Correctional Manpower Needs

Manpower needs in corrections have been addressed by every august body
from the Wickersham Commission in the 1920s, to the National Advisory
Commission on Criminal Justice Standards and Goals in the 1970s. In
1965, for example, the President's Commission on Law Enforcement and
the Administration of Justice recommended increasing the correctional
work force eightfold. Phillips puts the actual absorption rate of probation
and parole in 1965 at 20,000 additional workers.[1] R.R. Korn put the
problem in perhaps a more realistic posture: "many of the present difficulties
in corrections stem no so much from deficiencies in the numbers of personnel

as from deficiencies in what personnel are doing."[2] This view of Korn is in concert with Loughery's observation that

> . . . probation must get out of the country doctor era and into the age of the clinic. We can no longer waste the training of probation officers on inappropriate tasks. We are less in need of extra probation officers than we are in need of a corps of auxiliary workers to spread the effect of the officers we already have. . . .[3]

The subscribing to theories of correctional rehabilitation which can only function under the guidance and implementation of highly educated professionals, while also recognizing that there never will be enough professional workers is, in Cressey's view, leading correctional workers down a most frustrating pathway. Instead, we should examine the large pool of untrained, unemployed, nonprofessionals who are trainable in the performance of significant roles in the field, given the proper professional guidance. Economically, it is more efficient because of the increased use of automation and the subsequent reaction of many people leaving production occupations towards the prospect of service in the rehabilitating of the "criminal."[4] This position concurs with Sigurdson, who believes the expansion of the role of the nonprofessional is the most realistic answer to the problem of correctional manpower shortages.[5]

The historical basis for nonprofessionals in corrections goes back to the volunteer efforts of John Augustus, a Boston cobbler, in 1841. Today, well over 200 courts in the United States, the majority being adult misdemeanor or juvenile corts, are now using part- or full-time volunteers to provide correctional services.[6] It has been found that a volunteer's usefulness depends on knowledge of the available community resources and opportunity. Citizen volunteers in the circuit court juvenile department in Eugene, Oregon have befriended juveniles with a goal of improved school performance, employment, family, and peer-group relations.[7]

Afact to consider at this point is the structural makeup of probation and parole, which, unlike some other countries, is based in the United States on financing and operation through and by governmental agencies. This has led us to suppose that officially appropriated budgets are to be the only source of funding, and that in any given jurisdiction the duly constituted governmental probation or parole agency has the total responsibility for the whole job of rehabilitation. This sense of exclusivity and "officialness," on the part of an agency impedes the use of volunteers. Judges, parole boards, and their agents have tended to assume that no one except the official staff members could truly be responsible for a case.[8]

We have seen that nonprofessionals can be used in a variety of useful and creative ways such as was previously mentioned about the juvenile court program in Oregon. The Oregon Division of Corrections has conducted an operation called "Project Most." State probation and parole officers are involved in the training of nonprofessionals to work in teams with professional field staff. A small number of ex-offenders have also beeen employed resulting in high optimism about the impact of the nonprofessional upon Oregon's correctional system. It's been shown that a well-organized program employing volunteers can extendt a staffs effectiveness, or, as in Royal Oak, Michigan, actually serve as the probation service where none existed otherwise.[9]

A Look at Other Professions

Other major professional fields have been served, and served well, by nonprofessional workers. Many careers are developing for this individual in all major service areas. The public school's use of the teacher's aide to perform many of the routine organizational and administrative functions, leaving the teacher more valuable time to prepare subject matter. The medical lab assistant, nurse's aides, dental and physicians assistants have shown that they can be a valuable resource. Social work has made progress in the use of nonprofessionals in areas of aging, welfare services, public school systems, ect. For example, Cain and Epstein went out and recruited a group of housewives to serve in the capacity of volunteer case aides in a state mental hospital. These volunteers were able to provide the needed one-to-one relationship for patients, helping them towards the reestablishment of interpersonal relationships and the making of more realistic release plans.[10]

The Helped-Into-The-Helper Concept

Probation and parole have for a number of years observed, and cooperated with, organizations such as Alcoholics Anonymous and Synanon. For the most part, however, the field of corrections has not adapted to its own setting the single most effective ingredient in both these programs. Simply, the insistence that as soon as a person begins to get his problem under control it is expected that he will work diligently to help others.

An understanding of the personality traits of the offender provides a rather solid basis for assuming success of a self-help program if it were used in the probation and/or parole environment. Social research has shown the offender, particularly the repeat offender, is a person in receipt of society's help or control most or all of his life. He has grown up in a welfare family, been disciplined by his teachers, hasseled by the police, and totally rejected by employers. In effect, there has been a great amount of punishment and a small amount of rewards, or "positive strokes." His only contact with being needed was probably for his criminal skills. It is in a setting such as this, that motivation for improving one's position seems such a farce. It causes the jails and prisons to be no threat, certainly no deterrent, and not materially worse than the life without future that it presently being lived. [11]

The use of earnest advice and other methods hold little promise for the probation officer in light of the aforementioned situation. Self-respect and enthusiasm for any improvement are extremely hard to generate by mere words to a person who brings a life experience that produces anything but self-worth. Thus the offender has to learn a new view of himself through the new experience of being os use and value. This is a focal point of any rehabilitative experiences that will provide a sense of competence and need.

In the juvenile setting there have been several experiments in providing success experiences for the client. The results of these experiments have provided enough groundwork to apply this to the adult offender population. Many adult offender/clients whose problems are rather simple could receive the probation effort in the form of a requirement that the process be one of regularly helping another. Is it possible that the repeater may gain all the strokes he needs by simply helping to stabilize another offender?

Turning the helped into the helper is not new to corrections. One example has been the hiring, by the New York State Division for Youth, of ex-offenders to work in the same programs in which they were helped. The New Jersey Highfields program presented the most systematic approach to the ongoing treatment model. Male or female members of those programs, plus variations in effect in Kenctucky, Minnesota, South Dakota, and Florida, are faced daily with the responsibility of helping their peers, as well as themselves, to improve. This is not a training school model, instead, it is an insistence that the client must take responsibility to provide change and growth in others, as well as themselves.

Social Class Recruitment

Much has been done in the last decade with regard to the recruitment of nonprofessionals from the same social class as that of the client being served. The majority of professional correctional workers now agree that the bulk of their clientele are apart from the societal main stream by virtue of norms, values, and general life style. These clients are the so-called hard-to-reach, unmotivated, untrustworthy, antiauthority types. In other words, there does exist a marked social distance between the middle-class correctional workers and the bulk of their lower-class clientele. [12]

If the social distance and acknowledged lack of rapport problem is not within a reasonable length of time, it will certainly inhibit productive development of a working relationship between the client and corrections professional to the point of the client dropping out of the total rehabilitative process. If the idea is the creation, by the professional, of an effective role model; then, perception by the client of a social distance will certainly shut down potential progress. The similar-class worker, however, has often experienced situations and problems common to the hard-to-reach client. The results of this relationship may just be the greater facility of developing a more productive atmosphere between worker and client.

Another way of looking at the social distance problem, is to understand that minority groups are usually overrepresented among ex-offenders and underrepresented among the corrections staff. An example would be Attica prior to the 1971 riot where 54 percent of the incarcerated population were black and 9 percent Puerto Rican, but only one black and one Puerto Rican were on the staff. Since 1971, more blacks and Puerto Ricans have been hired and trained, but racial disparity between inmates and staff still exists. [13]

New York corrections managers, among others, have recognized the importance of developing an institutional staff with the ability to achieve needed rapport with the offender. It is this offender who tends to be young, black, Puerto Rican, Chicano, or Native American; who tends to come either from the urban ghetto or the rural slum. It is for this population that a concerted effort must be made to recruit people from these social groups for careers in the field of corrections.

The points raised in community-based correctional programs focus on the needs and potentials for using minority group members in the probation and parole function. If we are to succeed with community-based programs, then minority staff personnel are probably the only way to begin to close the social distance problem. Intimate knowledge of neighborhood conditions unknown to while colleagues will enable the minority group staff member to locate potential help sources with much greater ease and success.

The Ex-Offender—The Manpower Shortage—A Solution

The logical extension of the discourse on paraprofessionals, minority group correctional staff members, volunteers, and the obvious need for knowledgeable corrections workers draws us to the use of the ex-offender as a correctional manpower resource. Drawing upon the previous experiences of Alcoholics Anonymous, Synanon, and many other self-help groups, it is obvious that those who have experienced and overcome a problem have a unique capacity to demonstrate the helped-to-helper thesis.

For points to the fact that ex-offenders have been working in corrections in perceptible numbers from the late 1960s to the present time. [14] Granted, many of this number had worked in the institutions and other programs for a greater period, but the numbers represented were quite small. Fox goes on to point out that the warden of a Georgia correctional facility was once a prisoner in the Georgia prison system; also the superintendent of a juvenile institution in Florida is also an ex-offender.[15]

Dr. J.D. Grant and his New Careers Development Organization branched from welfare and income maintenance, in 1967, into the field of corrections and achieved success in Oakland, California in 1969 by having New Careerists, themselves offenders, apply to the program. Dr. Grant's program took offenders who were still under supervision and identified as inmate leaders, and used them to counsel inmates at San Quentin as well as in the local community.[16] The advantage of experience is inescapable in the provision of service and facilitation of two-way communication. Few members of a correctional staff possess the expertise to maintain the needed rapport with the offender that is present in the ex-offender. The special skills aquired through "being there," gives the ex-offender special value. This value is voiced by Milton Luger, director of the New York State Division of Youth, who seconds the motion when he is quoted as saying that he wants offenders as part of the rehabilitative effort because he *needs* them, and not merely because he feels sorry for them.[17]

Since 1968, the New York State Division of Youth Services, the Los Angeles Probation Department, Florida Division of Corrections, and numerous other jurisdictions have followed the lead of the United States Bureau of Prisons in the employment of the ex-offender.[18]

Numerous private sector agencies have now begun to use ex-offenders in the functional areas previously reserved for the professional correctional worker. St. Leonard's House in Chicago is now staffed almost entirely by ex-offenders.[19] St. Leonard's is located in the large, poor, Black community and has used the New Careers Program to create significant impact on the community and the field of corrections. In using the ex-offender as the helper, St. Leonard's House creates a peer pressure on the offender that forstalls their claim of exploitation by a white, middle-class power structure.[20]

Summary

Ex-offenders, as a group, have traditionally experienced difficlties in the labor market, particularly in periods of rising unemployment. Evidence from existing manpower programs suggests that in slack labor markets, training, placement, and job development tend to be less effective when there are many unfilled jobs. Simply, employers are unwilling to talk to, or hire, ex-offenders as long as a pool of candidates without criminal records are available.

It is increasingly doubtful that the private sector can provide the needed jobs to produce satisfactory changes in the unemployment picture of the urban youth and the ex-offender. Even in the best of economic times, the public sector will have to provide meaningful employment to slow the rate of chronic unemployment among this target group.

Attitudes and practices concerning the employment of ex-offenders, and offenders, in correctional institutions and agencies has certainly improved in the last decade. Granted, the use of offenders in prison as teachers and supervisors has been, for the most part, out of economic need. In those institutions where sufficient funding allowed the hiring of civilian staff, this use of the offender did not occur. However, the 1970s have seen the use of offenders and ex-offenders in counseling capacities, technical capacities, as well as performing adminstrative tasks, increasing at a rate unforeseen several years ago.

The 1960s saw the university with a criminal justice program reluctant to accept the ex-offender, even though other major fields of study were open to them. Most major universities with criminal justice programs today, have ex-offenders as students and sometimes lecturers. The ex-offender is afforded practicums and internships in the field of corrections in many areas of the country, and many of these students are offered positions upon obtaining their degree. As Vernon Fox states, "The traditional distance between the keeper and kept in the field of criminal justice, especially corrections, has been significantly reduced."[21]

We are quite sure that most employers would not hire an applicant because he or she is an ex-offender without a proper selection process. We are not advocating this approach at all. We do advocate, however, the selection of the ex-offender if he possesses the acceptable capabilities and credentials and, in addition, has the experience factor as a bonus in terms of understanding and generating the communicative process on a common ground. Yes, careful selection is needed, as in all fields of a professional nature, however, corrections will have to get away from thinking only of high-risk and must concentrate on high-gain, if any significant impact is to be made in the manpower shortage race.

Finally, we cannot overlook the gains, by the offender and ex-offender, in the arena of political and social power. Granted, this power has been bestowed by a shifting of the courts' policy from the emphasis on prisons in the 50s, to a greater emphasis on the offender's rights in the 70s. The formation of identifiable ex-offender groups such as the powerful 7th Step Foundation and the Fortune Society and the prisoner union movement all signal new assertiveness through organization. The American Correctional Association, at it's mid-winter meeting in 1976, announced the formation of the American Association for Ex-Offenders.

Corrections can no longer be a self-perpetuating system grounded in the old-line institutional treatment models. If the system is sincerely committed to workable community-based programs, then the ex-offender will have to be the central source of manpower used in reaching the hard-to-reach. The performance can be volunteer, paraprofessional, fully trained, whatever; the idea is to make use of a most valuable resource—the ex-offender.

Discussion Questions

1. Discuss the various criteria that should be used in determining if an ex-offender should be hired by a correctional agency.

2. Discuss the idea that an ex-offender is a minority group and should be employed under affirmative action guidelines.

3. Discuss the concept that only an ex-offender can significantly communicate in an effective manner with an offender.

Notes

1. C.W. Phillips, "Developing Correctional Manpower," *Crime and Delinquency*, 15 (3), (July 1969), pp. 415-419.

2. R.R. Korn, "Issues and Strategies of Implementation in the Use of Offenders in Resocializing Other Offenders," *Offenders as a Correctional Manpower Resource*, Report of a seminar convened by the Joint Commission on Correctional Manpower and Training, (June 1968), pp. 73-84.

3. D.L. Loughery, Jr., "Innovations in Probation Management," *Crime and Delinquency* 15 (2), (April, 1969), pp. 247-248.

4. D.R. Cressey, "Theoretical Foundations for Using Criminals in the Rehabilitation of Criminals," *Key Issues*, Vol. 2, (1965), pp. 87-101.

5. H.R. Sigurdson, "Expanding the Role of the Non-Professional," *Crime and Delinquency*, 15 (3), (July 1969), pp. 420-429.

6. D.W. Beless, W.S. Pilcher and Ellen Jo Ryan, "Use of Indigenous Nonprofessionals in Probation and Parole," *Federal Probation*, Vol. 36, No. 1, (March 1972), pp. 10-15.

7. R.J. Lee, "Volunteer Case Aide Program," *Crime and Delinquency*, 14 (4), (October 1968), pp. 331-335.

8. R.E. Hardy and J.G. Cull (eds.), *Introduction to Correctional Rehabilitation*, (Springfield, Ill.: Charles C. Thomas, 1973), Article by P.W. Keve, "Probation and Parole," p. 85.

9. *Ibid.*, p. 86.

10. L.P. Cain and D.W. Epstein, "The Utilization of Housewife as Volunteer Case Aides," *Social Casework*, 48 (5), (May 1967), pp. 282-285.

11. Hardy and Cull, p. 83.

12. Beless, Pilcher and Ryan, p. 11.

13. *Attica*, Official Report of the New York State Special Commission on Attica, (New York: Bantam Books, 1972), pp. 24-28.

14. V. Fox, *Community-Based Corrections*, (Englewood Cliffs, New Jersey, Prentice-Hall, Inc., 1977), p. 175-177.

15. *Ibid.*, p. 175

16. R. Pruger and H. Specht, "Establishing New Careers Programs: Organizational Barriers and Strategies," *Social Work*, 13, No. 4, (October 1968), p. 21-32.

17. *Correctional Briefings*, Number 4, (Washington, D.C.: Joint Commission on Correctional Manpower and Training, 1969).

18. Fox, p. 175.

19. E.L. Durham, "St. Leonards House: Model in the Use of Ex-Offenders in the Administration of Corrections," *Crime and Delinquency*, 20, (3), (July 1974), pp. 269-280.

20. Fox, p. 177.

21. *Ibid.*, p. 181.

7

Prison Reform and Conjugal Visiting

DON EVANS

The mood and temper of the public with regard to the treatment of crime and criminals is one of the unfailing tests of the civilization of any country—Winston Churchill, 1910.

Introduction.

"IT'S A CINDERELLA WORLD OUT THERE," Mr. Noonan at the Atlanta Federal Penitentiary waved his hand and shook his head. "These people live under abnormal conditions! It's an artificial world in here. They don't work for a living, they don't pay grocery bills, hospital bills, etc.! They don't have to worry about insurance and taxes like we do. They're dependent wards of the state."

Unfortunately most of our prisons are so very abnormal that not only is rehabilitation virtually impossible but prisoners' personalities and family relationships are irreparably damaged. The following pages discuss ways to *normalize* prisons, ways to help rather than hurt inmates and their families. This is an issue of vital importance and we must act now. This paper presents current research findings and discussions of conjugal visitation and coed prison programs in the United States and, secondly, a discussion of prison conditions, rehabilitation practices, and conjugal visiting in Mexico.

I spent four weeks during the summer of 1974 gathering data from seven prisons in southern, central, and northern parts of Mexico. Interviews with inmates, wives of inmates, and administrators were recorded on cassette tapes and by detailed notes taken in shorthand. A third means of recording information was photography which was permitted in two prisons.

This chapter is not categorically opposed to punishment. Not at all. I am aware that punishment of offenders can be functional on a societal as well as an individual level. I am, however, opposed to at least two kinds of punishment: (1) that which is destructive and has no positive aim, and (2) that which is unnecessary (punishment merely heaped onto the pile—often in the name of retribution). Blanket refusal to implement conjugal visits—even in the face of positive research findings—constitutes both destructive and unnecessary punishment.

Why should we be concerned about conjugal visits for prisoners in view of the fact that "more important" reform efforts are underway or are needed?

Why? Because it is assumed by the writer that other dramatic prison reform such as extensive use of community-based programs and furloughs will not soon significantly reduce the number of people cloistered in the abnormal one-sex prisons of the Unitd States. It is urgent, therefore, and possible in many prisons to implement some of the practices discussed herewith. Urgent because human personalities and family relationships are at stake. Urgent because it is incumbent upon us to remove inhumane practices from our prisons. Urgent because, "The world is a dangerous place to live. Not because of those who do evil but because of those who stand by and let it happen!"[1]

A controversial issue. Like most new programs which are introduced into old systems, conjugal visiting for prisoners is presently an emotional and controversial issue. Although there are persuasive arguments both for and against the practice, it is decidedly clear that American society in general opposes the idea primarily on the grounds that a prisoner is to be *punished* and not "coddled" by privileges such as the granting of legal marital rights (are they rights or privileges?). Probably the second greatest objection to conjugal visits is that the monetary cost involved in the provision of facilities is too great.

Admittedly, there are real problems (attitudinal and financial) related to the implementation of conjugal visitation programs in prisons, yet these programs *are* working in other countries, in Mississippi and in California. Columbus Hopper who studied the Mississippi experiment concluded that

> Parchman's (Mississippi) experience does not prove that the objections to conjugal visiting are invalid; it suggests, however, that conjugal visiting, at least in some penal situations, cannot be ruled out as a possible adaptation in American penology.[2]

Again, the principal objection of prison officials and members of society to conjugal visitation programs for inmates continues to be that prisoners are to be punished, ergo, granting marital rights to law breakers is "being too easy," or "too good" to them. Is this true? Do people really want to deny marital rights to incarcerated people? Consider the following reactions of prison officials, police officers, and small town people: first, a recent survey of penal administrators (52 out of 73 responded) found that 56.0 percent opposed and only 13.4 percent favored conjugal visits for inmates.[3]

Next, a newspaper reporter was covering my field observations of Mexican prisons and their conjugal visitation programs and, during the interview, the reporter was noticeably worried that the story might not get past her editor "due to the nature of the subject matter'" which might provoke undesirable public reaction (I thought the press was free!). As we expected, reaction to the story from many readers was: "Don wants to set up a Holiday

Inn for convicts." Small wonder that Balogh decried our blinding passion
for retribution.

> Society's unwillingness to analyze and recommend even subjectively, is
> most difficult to understand. Since the principle of retribution is inherent
> in our philosophy of punishment as indicated by criminal law, the future
> can hardly be characterized by social optimism.[4]

I subsequently reported the Mexican research findings by indicating
various habilitative aspects of conjugal visits to a night class of criminology
students consisting of about forty percent police officers. Most questions and
responses were passionately negative and their overly-punitive attitudes can
be represented here by a question from an irate officer who fired away,
"What about mass murderers—do they get conjugal visits too?" From time
to time prison administrators in Georgia have found questions about
conjugal visits puzzling, bizarre, and maybe even "off-base" whenever I or
my penology students delved into this area of prison reform. "What is your
opinion of conjugal visits for prisoners?" we asked a young administrator in
one prison. He seemed momentarily stunned, then replied, "You must
remember that a man comes to prison to be punished!" In yet another
Georgia prison, whose ill-repute horrifies most new inmates, we asked a
counselor, "Don't you think conjugal visits for prisoners would help
normalize life conditions?" His inconceivable answer was, "I believe this
prison is as normal as can be right now."

Hopper, too, recognizes that the old philosophy of punishment rather
than treatment is pervasive among penal administrators:

> Although carefully disguised, the objections of most prisons adminis-
> trators to conjugal visiting seem, in large part, restatements of the old
> philosophy that criminals are sentenced to prison for punishment, not for
> treatment. For example, most penologists want to develop a furlough
> system rather than conjugal visiting. Although they realize that some-
> thing needs to be done about sexual problems in prison, their emphasis
> upon leaves rather than conjugal visits indicates that they do not want
> much change within the institutions themselves.[5]

Cavan and Zemans argue "that many countries hold a more humanitarian
attitude toward prisoners than do many groups in the United States. . . .
Deprivation of marital characteristics is less likely to be made a part of
punishment (in other countries) than in the United States."[6] Not only is this
an emotional and controversial issue for correctional workers and penologists,
but another serious problem hinders any intelligent analysis of conjugal
visits for prisons: ignorance.

Conjugal visitation for prisoners is an ignored subject. Few criminology and
penology textbooks deal with this practice which, I believe, has great

potential for creating prison conditions more conducive to rehabilitation. Many educators, professionals and correctional people simply are neither sensitive to, nor informed about existing programs. For example, my wife gave me Hopper's SEX IN PRISON, one Christmas and four years later I read it. Sex in prison? So what? The English drive on the left side of the road. Before I read the book, the significance and sensibility of the idea did not occur to me. After all, one seldom hears much discussion about conjugal visits for prisoners, and rarely comes upon articles written about it. Hence, the faces of unaware prison officials convey bewilderment and shock when penology students ask "What do you think of conjugal visits for prisoners— as they have in Sweden, for example?" One administrator admitted, "I don't know what they're doing in Sweden (a bad admission), but prisons are supposed to punish people." Of course academicians need more "practical" exposure to prisons, but more importantly, front-line practitioners must constantly acquire information about new research and new programs being implemented by other states and other countries.

Indeed, the concept of conjugal visiting is generally ignored, but worse than that is the intolerable ignorance that prevails about the success of existing programs. One incredible example will suffice: An inmate in the Atlanta federal penitentiary attempted to obtain conjugal visitation rights with his legal spouse but the United States Court of Appeals, Fifth Circuit, affirmed an earlier ruling* which denied such rights. Note that the court, in its appendix which follows, was ignorant of *any* existing conjugal visiting program in the United States:

> While other nations have experimented with the idea of 'sexual visita-tions' for prisoners in confinement, the *Court knows of no case which requires or permits such practices in United States institutions.*[7] (Italics mine.)

The court knows of no such practices in United States institutions! Yet conjugal visits for prisoners have been permitted in Mississippi at least as far back as 1918. And where is Mississippi? In the Fifth Circuit!

Another example: a California news writer, ignorant of the Mississippi program, mistakenly reported that the family visitation program of a California prison was the "first of its kinds."[8]

The need for change. Sir Winston Churchill once said the level of civiliza-tion attained by a society can be measured by the way it treats its criminals. Most Americans probably believe the U.S. penal system has "come a long way." Yet social scientists suggest that we have simply substituted one form of torture for another—psychological torture in the place of physical

---

*Tarlton V. Clark, 441 F.2d 384 (1971), *cert. den.,* 403 U.S. 934 (1971); United States Court of Appeals, Fifth Circuit.

torture. Awareness of this sorry condition at high levels is illustrated by Governor Askew's denunciation of the "alienation and the exile" of prison inmates at a Florida correctional conference. Years ago, Ervin Goffman observed tht prisons are "total institutions" signifying that inmates are so completely cut off from the wider society that "disculturation" occurs for those in such abnormal isolation.

In this context it recently occurred to me what a half-way house is. It is a relatively new institution devised to reintegrate inmates back into the stream of normal life (from prison: the abnormal life). Obviously, the first institution (prison) systematically devastates its residents psychologically and behaviorally to such an extent that a second "correctional/transitional" organization is required to undo the effects of "treatment" received from the first "correctional" institute. A patient leaves doctor "A" (prison) and must be hospitalized by doctor "B" (half-way house) in order to get over doctor "A's" treatment! Is this corrections for corrections?

Following a 1954 study of a New Jersey state prison, Gresham Sykes identified four "pains of imprisonment": (1) the loss of liberty; (2) the deprivation of goods and services; (3) the deprivation of heterosexual relationships; and (4) the deprivation of autonomy. Now there are several studies which reveal that the second and third "pains" are greatly diminished in Mexico and in other countries. *Why should they not be diminished in the U.S.?* In our society people incarcerated are stripped of personal belongings and are totally impoverished by imprisonment:

> Now in modern Western culture, material possessions are so large a part of the individual's conception of himself that to be stripped of them is to be attacked at the deepest layers of personality.
>
> But impoverishment remains as one of the most bitter attacks on the individual's self-image that our society has to offer and the prisoner cannot ignore the implications of his straitened circumstances.[9]

South of the border inmates can work for themselves on the inside of prisons, earn money, support their families, remain bread-winners and maintain their self-images as men (or women), not to mention the fact that the state is partly relieved of providing subsistence for them. If working for money is an incentive outside prison, why not permit it to some degree, to be an incentive on the inside? Is denial of such a practical human activity "reform" or mere punishment? What is the constructive outcome or intent of this arbitrary economic poverty?

Mexican prisons differ in another way: male and female inmates can have body contact with their spouses and children. Affection, intimacy and even sexual intercourse occur wherever conjugal visitation programs exist. In contrast, at many U.S. prisons (the New Jersey prison in 1958, for example) inmates "see" their wives or girl friends on the other side of a plate glass window.* Communication is often by means of a phone while under the scrutiny of a guard. I have seen one place in my state where visitors sit on the other side of a heavy mesh screen where not even finger tips can touch. A California inmate described the brutal and senseless deprivations of family affection:

> 'When I was in San Quentin,' Benito Arzaga remembers, 'we were allowed to visit with our families—if they stayed on one side of the table and we stayed on the other. My kids would reach out their hands to me to try to touch me. I'd look up at the guard, and he'd shake his head. The kids would start crying and yelling "Daddy." I couldn't do nothing. Just sit there and watch my kids crying.'[10]

Psychological torture? Is it necessary for society to reject, to impoverish, and even more, to figuratively castrate an inmate by imposing involuntary celibacy even when a person is legally married? Again, Sykes warns of the destructiveness of abnormal prison societies to the human psyche. He indicates that an essential component of a man's self conception—his status of male—is called into question:

> Yet as important as frustrations in the sexual sphere may be in physiological terms, the psychological problems created by the lack of hererosexual relationships can be even more serious. A society composed exclusively of men tends to generate anxieties in its members concerning their masculinity regardless of whether or not they are coerced, bribed, or seduced into an overt homosexual liaison.[11]

Under these adverse conditions a person's life goals, defense systems, self-esteem, and his sense of security are assaulted. "Such attacks on the psychological level are less easily seen than a sadistic beating, a pair of shackles in the floor, or the caged men on a treadmill, but the destruction of the psyche is no less fearful than bodily affliction . . ."[12]

A better approach: emphasis on family ties and normalization for rehabilitation. I recently addressed a group of law enforcement officers and one of them asked, "Will conjugal visiting rehabilitate prisoners? Will it reduce recidivism?" I don't know, I replied, but it will prevent them from "going backwards" into loss of self-esteem, into homosexual behavior, etc. And it can create conditions more conducive to rehabilitation by diminishing the abnormality of prison society and its current high level of mutilation to human psyches.

---

*This practice is changing in many prisons where inmates are allowed to meet their spouses and children in a visitation room. Some affection—hugging, touching—is permitted.

It is clear that the best approach to the subject matter at hand is to place emphasis on strengthening family stability and not to emphasize the mere provision of sex for offenders.* After all, an inmate is not an isolated entity and any treatment process must recognize this sociological fact as Alcoholics Anonymous has done. At a correctional conference in Tallahassee a speaker told how female prisoners "fall apart at the time of their release because their children don't know them." This family tragedy is less likely to occur in Mexico because some prisons have nurseries for infants and kindergartens for children of inmates. Mothers and young children may be together inside the prison until a child reaches age six. The Mexican culture places great value on the family system and will not allow imprisonment to greatly impair nor utterly destroy family relationships just because one member has offended the law.

In the Mississippi study inmates were asked what they believed was the most helpful result of conjugal visiting. Sexual release? No! *The Majority said they believe conjugal visits keep marriages from breaking up.* The second largest percentage thought reducing homosexuality was the most helpful result of conjugal visiting.

Like Mexico, California has developed a Family Visiting Program because of "deep concern over what was happening to the family man while confined in prison and what was happening to his wife and children at home." Lawrence Wilson, California administrator, told a Minneapolis workshop that field investigators "find deep cleavages and almost irreparable estrangements of wives and children toward the husband and father who is away in prison." He charged that permanent damage to marital relationships results from long separation of spouses. "It is our contention," he declared, "that we do not protect society by contributing to the dissolution of the family unit."[13]

Why does California want conjugal visiting? Wilson:

> California does not want conjugal visiting . . . California wants FAMILY visiting aimed at preserving the family relationship and helping families grow stronger. The fact that husbands and wives engage in sexual intercourse is incidental to our main objectives: the preservation and strengthening of the family.[14]

*In 1962 Hopper said, "In the United States the chief objection is that such visits would be incompatible with existing mores, since the visits seem to emphasize only the physical satisfactions of sex." But things changed by 1969 and Hopper told a workship in Minneapolis that it is now "unrealistic to reject them [conjugal visits] as being against current mores in America" since "the majority of American now accept sex as a natural part of human existence and do not object to married prison inmates having the privilege."

Conjugal visits for prisoners would significantly normalize prison life. It would help maintain family ties, preserve the inmate's self-image of masculinity or femininity, reduce the disculturation process, reduce the incidence of homosexuality and rape, and finally, create conditions more conducive to rehabilitation.

Governor Ronald Reagan recognized that family visitation for prisoners had goals far beyond the more physiological gratification of sexual needs: "The intent of the program (in California) . . . is to 'develop family strengths to sustain ex-inmates as they complete the transition from prison to a law-abiding society.'" Fred Long, a California inmate, agrees that "this thing will save a lot of marriages . . . Just knowing this [family visit] was coming up has helped mine. My wife and I didn't know each other too well."

Moreover, the U.S. Bureau of Prisons has awakened to the sensibility of normalizing conditions for incarcerated people and has responded by opening four coed facilities in the early 1970's. Sexual activity is banned but the goal is normalization for rehabilitation:

> The principal goal is to increase the chance that a prison sentence will reform a criminal rather than alienate him further from society. Explains Robert Vagt, deputy commissioner for community services in Massachusetts: 'Our whole thrust is to get incarcerated people into a more normal environment. If it's not coed, then we're preparing them for a situation that they are not going to meet in life.'[17]

Officials of those coed institutions say "that whatever their problems, coed prisons are clearly far more humane than their predecessors." They also believe that coed incarceration is a success. Warden Campbell of the Fort Worth coed prison reports these significant improvements in behavior: (1) no drug overdoses; (2) little violence; (3) a dramatic decline in homosexual activity. Also at a coed prison in Massachusetts homosexual activity declined "drastically," and in West Virginia "there has not been a single case of homosexual rape reported in the three years since the prison became coed."[18] Down in Mexico City an American inmate said of Lecumberri prison: "it's not much like a prison here—women and children are all over the place—normalization."

In short, there is a need to reduce unnecessary psychological torture of prisoners. Incarceration itself is punishment and there is no need to require a man's soul along with his loss of freedom; no need to destroy his personality. Neither does a society need to contribute to marital dissolutions nor to increase family suffering. Family visitation programs amount to some normalization of harsh and brutal prison conditions which, to repeat, is conducive to rehabilitation.

Research Findings: The Merits of Conjugal Visiting. Hopper's study of conjugal visiting at the prison in Parchman, Mississippi found: (1) Both inmates and staff members believe the incidence of homosexuality is reduced by conjugal visits. Camp size, however, was an intervening variable with a higher incidence of homosexual behavior occuring at larger camps ("The conjugal visit has not done away with the problem of homosexuality . . . but it has helped to reduce it . . . we cannot afford . . . to reject something which helps the problem even a little."[19]); (2) Inmates receiving conjugal visits (compared to those who do not) indicate a greater willingness to work at their penitentiary jobs; (3) are more cooperative with the staff; (4) believe that conjugal visits keep marriages from breaking up and, finally, (5) prisonization is reduced. This is indicated by the more favorable attitudes of those receiving conjugal visits. For example, they are more willing to work hard, to cooperate with staff, to trust staff and to view staff members as fair. Another important function of conjugal visiting is especially noteworthy, if not surprising:

> While most people who hear of conjugal visiting think of sexual release as the only function of the practice, those who participate in the program speak first of the freedom of visiting in private with their wives and of being able to talk intimately and frankly to them without fear of being heard by the prison authorities. They emphasize the emotional satisfaction rather than the *physical* satisfaction.[20]

These data make the arguments of some critics seem irrelevant, especially the argument that conjugal visits have little effect on the biological needs of inmates since most visitation programs in prisons do not permit visits to occur often enough to significantly reduce the sexual needs of participating inmates. Why must we belabor the point that sexual intimacy between spouses is far, far more than mere "biological release?" "What it would influence, however, is the image of a man. It would allow a man to keep his masculine image and reduce the need to establish it through homosexual conquests." Another merit of conjugal visits is suggested by Clinton Duffy, renowned former warden of San Quentin, who believes the program at Parchman explains why there have been so few riots at the Mississippi prison.

"I don't know of anything that's more important," a camp sergeant told Hopper. "It's a touching sight to see a man and his wife greet each other on visiting day. I believe it's the right thing to do."[21]

At Tehachapi, California conjugal visiting is working: Many wives "after having family visiting . . . were able to strengthen the marriage and have abandoned separation plans."[22] What has been the effect on the institution as a whole? "Very positive."[23]

Mexican prisons: family visitations and normalization. Prison uniforms were often ragged, unkempt. At Lecumberri there was no dining hall, and food was delivered in dirty looking oil drums. Here and there men ate their meals while squatted against a wall; the food was served on plastic plates, and handkerchiefs were bread holders. In several prisons work equipment was primitive, if not ancient. At one "jewelry shop" inmates used cow bones to make pieces of jewelry. The palms of human hands patiently rubbed the bone jewelry until a lustre was achieved. Nearby a cement mixer manufactured in 1900 was used to make bread in the bakery.

Many Americans would pity Mexican inmates for the manifest poverty of their prisons, yet there are human conditions which make incarceration less painful that U.S. prisons, and they far outweigh our modern equipment and painted walls.

Some sociological conditions which were outstanding and impressive are: (1) there were so many women and children inside some prisons that I actually felt as if I were outside on a small village street; (2) in prisons for women, nurseries and kindergartens are provided so that mothers can maintain normal relationships with their young children; (3) inmates work and earn money which helps them to continue to support their families; (4) staff-inmate relationships were noticeably good in some prisons.

Women and children: a heterosexual prison world. As I stepped past tall steel gates and khaki-coated, solider-like guards, I was literally stunned at the sight of numerous women and giggling children swarming the "streets" inside Lecumberri prison in Mexico City. Female employees work in almost every part of the prison. One inmate pointed toward a lone female crossing a plaza: "See the lady? She is a doctor and she goes any places she pleases and is safe," he boasted. "No one will harm her—women are safe here." Other female volunteers enter the prison to teach the mentally ill every week, and the hospital at Lecumberri was crawling with female attendants.

In almost every dormitory mothers, wives, girl friends (and probably some prostitutes) were visiting inmates.

One patio was crowded with inmates and their families, many of whom were sitting on sun-splashed, multi-colored tiles eating lunch together picnic style. Nearbly, a restaurant buzzed with couples who were eating, drinking, and socializing to Mexican music. Just outside, a fountain threw water skyward, and hungry pigeons stole crumbs lost by prisoners and their families. Sound a little romantic and rose colored? Perhaps, but I walked right through it (in two days I spent ten hours inside Lecumberri). The point is that male-female relationships seemed so normal in dramatic contrast to our dangerous, restricted, and sterile U.S. prisons.

In my home state, female students cannot accompany male students who "tour" prisons. Why? The danger is too great—it is completely out of the question, they say. Yet, in the Atlanta federal penitentiary female students are permitted to go any place male students go during a tour! What is the difference in the two prisons? Is the real difference in the nature of the inmates or is it in the way prison administrators *perceive* their prisoners? Are U.S. federal and Mexican state prisoners less violent, less dangerous than some Georgia state prisoners? If female visitors and employees were more common in a prison environment, it is conceivable that male inmates (like most males on the outside) would be adjusted to their presence to the extent that they would not be inclined to attack them.

In August 1974, there were 3,705 inmates at Lecumberri. Each inmate is allowed to have up to five visitors on Saturdays and Sundays. On a recent Sunday there were 7,000 visitors. Little wonder the teeming prison streets seemed as safe and normal as streets on the outside.

What about homosexuality in these prisons? *Every prison which had a conjugal visitation program reported that they had "virtually no homosexual problem at all."* That report is in pronounced contrast with the pathological situation found in U.S. prisons where homosexuality, fags, punks, wolves, knifings, lovers' fights, and gang rapes are pervasive.

In prisons with conjugal visitation programs I asked administrators why they favored the program. In Monterrey, the director of a prison smiled, shook his head, and responded with a question: "It's normal, isn't it?" Other reasons cited for favoring the program are: (1) inmates get along better with each other; they are easier to handle; (2) homosexual behavior is reduced; (3) inmates work better; and (4) inmates are easier to rehabilitate.

Hayne's 1967 findings are essentially the same. He asked what conjugal visits mean to them, and large numbers of Mexican prisoners "agreed that these visits 'help keep my family together,' 'make it easier to serve time,' 'keep me from fighting.' They agree with staff that conjugal visits 'keep homosexuality down.'"[24]

Indisputably, the Mexican culture is family oriented and will not allow even incarceration to interfere more than necessary with marital and family ties. The U.S. culture, in contrast, is punishment oriented. A law breaker is "evil" and deserves punishment which includes deprivation of family and marital rights. Because he has been wicked, from here on out his tortured personality must cope with incessant violence within a one-sex community which foments abnormal relationships. "Shut away from friends and families that are part of normal life, inmates are denied the sympathetic contacts that soften the grossness of the sex drive."[25]

Nurseries and kindergartens: emphasis on the family. In two of the Mexican prisons for women, infants and young children are not separated from their imprisoned mothers. These prisons provide nurseries and kindergartens which enable women to continue to be mothers by visiting, loving, and caring for their offspring twice or more each day. The idea seems to be that almost nothing should have the power to interfere with a mother-child bond, and prison does not!

Children may remain with their mothers until age six after which they must leave the prison and live with relatives until the mother is released. "Would this experience of living in prison cause children to become criminals later in life?" a police officer asked me. I have no data, but I have an opinion and some logic for response to that question: I do not believe the "criminal" (deviant) influence is so pervasive in prisons that a child would be criminalized by residing near its mother for six years inside a prison. I do not believe most mothers inside prisons differ greatly from mothers on the outside. My experience as a chaplain for thirteen months at a prison for women taught me that a large percent of incarcerated women love their children and love is what a child needs. It is true that in the U.S. a child who spent six years in prison with his mother would be stigmatized and might be called a "jail bird" in the first grade at school because American people have little heart for prisoners, ex-prisoners, and children of prisoners. At any rate, ask yourself, "Why won't U.S. prisons allow mothers to have their small children with them inside prison?" Because prison is a hell-hole? Because prisoners aren't people? Because . . .? Is it really humane and constructive to have mothers released from prison "fall apart because their own children don't know them?" "Constructive" or not, that is essentially what we now have.

Maintenance of the wage-earner status: inmates work and earn money inside prison. Why don't we remove manifest and unmistakable impediments to human rehabilitation? If you rob the American male of his sexuality and take away his economic status, what is left? Elmer Johnson notes the relationship between a prisoner's self-image and his work status:

> The self-esteem of the offender is undermined by his loss of the wage-earner status, which is a major element of male adulthood. The erosion of the prisoner's status as a fullfledged adult indicates the importance of economic factors as limitations on correctional reform.[26]

Many Mexican prisons consist of a complex of small shops and industries where inmates work, earn monetary profit, and (males) retain the status of wage-earner, of breadwinner, of "man." There is yet another incentive to work; for every two day's work, a prisoner's sentence is reduced by one day. I saw radio and television shops, auto mechanic and body shops, jewelry and art shops, hand and machine garment shops, wood and carpenter shops. Prison administrators told me that all profit earned went to the prisoner (except in one prison for women where 30 percent of the earnings was sent to the victim of the offender).

I was not able to learn how many robberies and killings occur over money; however, if this was a great problem, it seems likely that administrators would change the system. One wife of an American prisoner was of the opinion that most killings do occur over money. It is conceivable that, like the presence of females, the presence of money inside prison might become so common and natural that inmates (similar to people on the outside) might not constantly rob others. Furthermore, a man's wife could control his income if she sells his products on the outside, which is generally the case.

Staff-inmate relationships: inmates praise staff. In most of the prisons studied, there was a noticeable degree of positive staff-inmate relationships. At two institutions I found high level administrators playing soccer and basketball with inmates. In Mexico City at the Carcel de Preventiva de Coyacan, I met the sub-chief (number two man) as he walked off a soccer court with both arms around two inmates—all three men were drenched with perspiration, and I first thought he, too, was an inmate. At three of the seven prisons, inmates praised staff members even when they were not present: "The director is a good man;" "they try to help us, they are good to us here;" "I am free here. We are treated well." While passing through a hospital inside Lecumberri, the director shouted to sick inmates from room to room, "Any complaints?" "No complaints," they waved back. "This is the best general we have ever had," several inmates told me. "This is a good prison, it is very humane." It is, or course, difficult to say how genuine these compliments are and how many were simply brownie points. I can only say that I have never heard inmates praise staff members to this extent in our own prisons. It was impressive.

Conclusions. Are Mexican prisons better than U.S. prisons? I really have not tried to answer that question. I have selected "good" practices of Mexican prisons which might be considered for use in U.S. prisons—some programs are not culture bound, which means that they could be translated into U.S. prison systems. Admittedly, there are many "bad" things about Mexican prisons which are not set forth in this paper: long sentences are common, inmate cliques exert power and kill, some foreign inmates must pay for food, safety, and telephone calls. Guards "milk" U.S. prisoners of their money and so forth.

Few studies have investigated inmates and their family relationships. We need to know if conjugal visiting really maintains family ties because no society should have power to destroy family relationships. We need to know if family visiting and an opportunity to work for wages would significantly reduce the psychological torture which now exists for American men and women in prison. We need to know if these practices will preserve feelings of self-worth, if they will impede the homosexualization of heterosexual people. Finally, if I had to respond to Sir Winston Churchill's hypothesis quoted at the beginning of this paper, I would be inclined to say that poverty in Mexican prisons is greater (in terms of modern equipment), but that "civilization" is higher than my own country. We need to know.

Discussion Questions

1. Discuss and describe the ways U.S. Prison life is "abnormal." Tell how life inside these prisons could be more "normalized" in order to create conditions conducive to rehabilitation efforts.

2. State the arguments for and against conjugal visitation programs. Which argument seems to outweight the other?

3. Why are so many Americans punishment oriented? What is the cultural basis for this orientation? Why are Mexican prisons more lenient than U.S. prisons with respect to family relationships of inmates?

4. Discuss the pros and cons of allowing prison inmates to work and earn money during their prison sentence.

Notes

1. Attributed to Albert Einstein by the NBC movie, "King," aired in February, 1978.

2. Columbus B. Hopper, *Sex in Prison* (Baton Rouge: Louisiana State University Press, 1969), p. 142.

3. J.K. Balogh, "Conjugal Visitations in Prisons: A Sociological Perspective," *Federal Probation*, 28 (1964): 53.

4. Ibid., p. 52.

5. Hopper, pp. 144-145.

6. Balogh, p. 52.

7. Leonard Orland, *Justice, Punishment, Treatment* (New York: The Free Press, 1973), p. 371.

8. Louis P. Carney, *Introduction to Correctional Science.* (New York: McGraw-Hill, Inc., 1974), p. 340.

9. Gresham M. Sykes, *The Society of Captives* (Princeton: Princeton University Press, 1958), pp. 69-70.

10. "Penology," *Time*, August 9, 1968, p. 68.

11. Sykes, p. 71.

12. Ibid., p. 64.

13. Lawrence E. Wilson, "Conjugal Visiting and Family Participation in California," *Proceedings of the American Correctional Association*, (1969): 262.

14. Norman S. Hayner, "Attitudes Toward Conjugal Visits for Prisoners," in Don Evans (ed.), *Illustrative Readings in Sociology* (Lexington: Xerox Individualized Publishing, 1975), p. 177.

15. "Penology," *Time*, August 9, 1968, p. 68.

16. Ibid. p. 68.

17. "Coed Incarceration," *Time*, September 16, 1974, p. 84.

18. Ibid., p. 84.

19. Columbus B. Hopper, "Conjugal and Family Visitation in Mississippi," *Proceedings of the American Correctional Association*, (1969): 260.

20. Hopper, *Sex in Prison*, p. 104.

21. Hopper, "Conjugal and Family Visitation," p. 260.

22. Wilson, "Conjugal Visiting and Family Participation," p. 263.

23. Ibid., p. 264.

24. Hayner, pp. 174-175.

25. Elmer H. Johnson, *Crime, Correction, and Society*. (Homewood: The Dorsey Press, 1974), p. 461.

26. Ibid., p. 533.

1

Isolating the Condemnation Sanction in Juvenile Justice: The Mandate of In Re Gault

JOHN C. WATKINS, JR.

THE DISCORDANT VALUES interacting in the treatment process of juvenile law violators are hopelessly confused. Clearly, no single set of norms having a common denominator have yet emerged. Instead of consistency, we are faced with conflicting historical, ideological and emotional sources that continue to color our dispositional and rehabilitative philosophy in juvenile justice.

Treatments versus Custody: The Image Conflict

Research in social science denies that there are any fixed or inevitable sequences in the etiology of delinquency. The authoritative *Task Force Report: Juvenile Delinquency and Youth Crime,* published in 1967 as a part of a national crime study tells us, "As yet no behavior patterns or personality tendencies have been isolated and shown to be the antecedents of delinquency, and it is unlikely that they will be."[1] Although this remark was made some ten years ago, there is no reason to believe that the passage of time has affected its continued validity. Because of the diffuse character of the delinquency syndrome, it is questionable whether or not the juvenile court, *as a court,* has any business at all being either an agent of change or prevention in juvenile law. Garrett Heyns, formerly executive director of the Joint Commission on Correctional Manpower and Training, was probably correct when he said, "[I]t is not the primary function of the [juvenile] court . . . to prevent delinquency."[2] Rather, he adds, "It is their task to help the one already delinquent into acceptable behavior, and in this way to prevent the repetition of delinquent acts on the part of their charges."[3] It is believed that such a task will release for more profitable employment energies which would otherwise be dissipated in a fruitless attempt at prevention.

Granting the "helping" role of the juvenile court to be of paramount concern, we are immediately faced with a *non sequitur*. In order to properly correct the psychosocial antecedents of serious delinquent behavior, juvenile courts are more or less compelled to consider institutionalizing the minor. Institutionalization subsumes custody and custody is basically at war with the rehabilitative ideal.[4] It is truly remarkable that we have had any degree of success at all in juvenile corrections.

Correctional philosophy seeks, among other things, to create in the adjudicated delinquent the notion that old ways should be abandoned and new, more legitimate modes of behavior be substituted for former law-violating lifestyles. Korn and McCorke, although writing primarily about the adult correctional client, gives us a cogent insight into this general problem area when they state:

> Whatever the personality disturbances or problems of . . . offenders, it may be agreed that their social adjustment is most often characterized by exploitation of and devious dealings with other people. It therefore becomes the goal of treatment to assist them in abandoning these ways of dealing with people—ways that bring them into prison. This process of abandoning old ways and learning new ones involves repeated demonstrations of the failure of the old ways, and it is indispensible that the treatment situation be one in which those ways are made to fail.[5]

It is extremely difficult, nonetheless, when speaking to the issue of delinquency to infuse the delinquent minor with conduct norms of legitimate society when he knows full well that such norms are alien to his associational references. Legitimately conceived aspirations are culturally blocked, thereby reinforcing subcultural transgressions. The abandoning of "old ways" in many cases is merely held in abeyance under the custodial regime and treatment is often a mirage, not a reality. Furthermore, how can we treat the "disease" of delinquency without isolating the germ of socio-cultural breakdown? The medical analogy, of course, has only marginal utility in a field where scientific knowledge is far less precise than in the healing arts. Social pathology can rarely be treated or cured within the custodial clinic called a training school.

It is here that the image of treatment clashes head-on with the reality of custodial isolation of "warehousing" as some are inclined to call it. The treatment/custody dichotomy is thrown into clearer focus when we view recent United States Supreme Court decisions dealing with juvenile law. In 1967, the U.S. Supreme Court for the first time in its history took issue with some of the tenets held sacred by many in the juvenile justice field. It is believed that the decision in *In re Gault*[6] has begun to spur additional inquiry into the entire problem of juvenile incarceration and questions incarceration's ultimate worth as a corrective device. Proceeding now to adjudicate the minor more in accordance with the criminal procedure model calls for a reevaluation of our entire juvenile correctional structure.

Prior to the *Gault* case, the training or industrial school population in the United States was comprised of a host of offenders. Some were decidely dangerous and definitely in need of incarceration; others were merely the unlucky recipients of a benevolent despotism. The hard-core delinquent was routinely mixed with the truant, the wayward, the incorrigible and a number of other status offenders in a hodge-podge correctional milieu. Such a state of affairs more likely than not prompted the author of the majority opinion in *Gault* (Mr. Justice Fortas) to observe: "[T]he highest motives and most enlightened impulses led to a peculiar system for juveniles unknown to our law in any comparable context."[7] Fortas branded as "debatable" the theoretical basis for such a system of state supported intervention in the lives of children caught in the juvenile court net.

The theoretic bedrock, of course, was the unwavering assumption that delinquent children should somehow be "helped' in the correctional process and ultimately be returned to society as productive human beings. But, according to the late Dean John H. Wigmore, the promoters of juvenile court legislation "in their enthusiasm for its benefits and their determination to eliminate the condition of the usual criminal court, have gone to the borderline of prudence in their iconoclasm."[8] Certainly this "borderline of prudence" was reached when many untested social theories were pressed into the service of the state. But theory and practice, unfortunately, were far apart in the actual day-to-day operation of the system. Many theories of delinquency have thus reaped the whirlwind of contemporary criticism.

The English essayist, Aldous Huxley, has subjected to biting criticism the claim of some academicians that social science holds all the answers in this area. Says Huxley, "Like Sir Galahad's their strength is the strength of ten because their heart is pure—and their heart is pure because they are scientists and have taken six thousand hours of social studies."[9] Admittedly, recognizing the purity of one's heart certainly does not dispose of the problem. Pious rhetoric is not the answer because the "gulf between the State's treatment of the adult and of the child requires a bridge sturdier than mere verbiage, and reasons more persuasive than cliche can provide."[10]

As long as we have crime, society will attempt through various devices to isolate the dangerous offender, be he child or adult. In criminal correction, the constant interplay and resultant friction between custody on the one hand and treatment on the other is rather of the essence of the system. But sound policy dictates that we should strive to keep this friction to a minimum and isolate only those persons who are, in fact, a threat to community solidarity, not anyone and everyone who perchance violates a set of state-imposed sanctions of questionable merit. The "gulf" that Justice Fortas spoke of in his characterization of the hiatus between adult and juvenile correction is made all the more ludicrous by our present, all-encompassing statutory definitions of delinquency. *In re Gault,* however, does give us at least a possible legal justification for closing this gap. If some of its more explicit warnings are heeded by state legislatures, we will probably not see a wholesale legalization of delinquency adjudications. If, on the other hand, state legislative bodies fail to recognize the problem and act thereon, we can expect a further case-by-case mandate to constitutionalize the entire juvenile court process.

Gault's Potential Impact on the Differential Definitions of Delinquency

If a new proposition in delinquency legislation is to prevail, public opinion must be appealed to in order to convince appropriate law-making agencies to act. Such an endeavor, however, has not met with a greal deal of success in what can generally be called the post-*Gault* era. The *Gault* teachings are still viewed by many juvenile justice agents as a threat to their autonomy. This factor, along with others, precludes solid research findings insofar as those findings relate to empirical data on *Gault's* impact in a certain socio-legal constellation. Because of this fact, a need immediatley arises to take a second look at the posture of delinquency statutes in the United States. Perhaps some of the suggestions that follow can become effective fodder for the cannon of judicial reform.

One organization which certainly could exert a mobilizing effect on public opinion is the National Council of Juvenile Court Judges. At their Thirtieth Annual Conference held in Fort Lauderdale, Florida, on June 29, 1967, some forty-five days after the *Gault* opinion was handed down, this organization discussed at length both the virtues and the vices of the *Gault* decision. One question particularly disturbing to the assembled judges was how far the jursidiction of juvenile courts should be narrowed in light of the *Gault* case in order to secure the services needed for the treatment and rehabilitation of delinquent youth. Justine Wise Polier, judge of the New York State Family Court, stated in this connection that "Experience in the juvenile courts has alerted its judges to the fact that it is one thing to require procedural safeguards but that it is quite another to secure the services that demand far more from the community . . ."[11]

It is the securing of effective treatment-oriented community service agencies that have inhibited the long range goals of juvenile rehabilitation. In many cases, a juvenile court judge is left with the often sterile option of incarceration or probation. Incarceration, as previously noted, affords little real treatment, despite assertions to the contrary. On the other hand, probation means little more than a return to the self-same habits which predisposed these juveniles to judicial recognition in the first instance. Similarly, many non-judicial procedures are likewise inadequate to cope with our present problem. As the *Task Force Report* states:

> [T]he current procedures for non-judicial handling of putative delinquents . . . are inadequate and defective. Few formal guidelines are available to those who are responsible for exercising discretion in determining which youngsters should be sent deeper into the judicial process .
> . . Hampered by the unavailability of resources which can serve as alternatives to court referrals, youngsters are sent to court when they need not be, or referred to resources lacking the capacity to offer necessary help. [12]

The inevitable concomitants of those circumstances bode ill for a sophisticated refinement of either judicial or social service techniques in the handling of the delinquency problem.

In re Gault, however, is singularly instructive in at least one aspect of this dilemma. Although the Supreme Court set forth new procedural guidelines not heretofore recognized as universal in juvenile court procedure,[13] the holding itself involved *only* an adjudication of "delinquency" based on a violation of state law. The very same Arizona statute, if violated by an adult, would have been labeled a "crime". The wide-ranging majority opinion by Justice Fortas in *Gault* did not address itself to delinquency based solely on such diffuse categories of juvenile wrongdoing as truancy, waywardness, incorrigibility or other assumed delicts bottomed primarily on status. Unfortunately, however, the very same "dispositions are permitted for these youngsters as for those who may have indulged in more serious criminal conduct."[14] The real fallacy with this approach lies in its inherent wastefulness of community resources. When the *Gault* opinion was rendered on May 15, 1967, the *Task Force Report* on delinquency estimated that the number of juveniles in *status* categories who appear before juvenile courts comprised about one-fourth, or approximately 185,000 of the total number of children's cases classified as delinquent.[15] At that time, the *Task Force Report* informed us that

> A summary review of the population of nearly 20 correctional institutions for delinquent children indicates that between 25 and 30 percent of their population is composed of children whose offenses would not be classified as criminal if they were adults. [16]

In the intervening ten years, the problem of incarcerated status offenders in juvenile institutions has not materially lessened the need to closely examine this jurisdictional aspect of the juvenile court. For example, in June, 1975, the National Council on Crime and Delinquency reported that twenty-three percent of the males and seventy percent of the females held in juvenile institutions as of that date were incarcerated for offenses that were such only for children. It seems somewhat incomprehensible that all of these juveniles were in need of judicial incarceration! Surely we would have at our disposal a better tool to winnow out those clearly needing some form of judicial restraint from those needing a less restrictive form of community treatment. However, in order to segregate more appropriately those juveniles who do and those who do not stand in need of judicial handling, a problem of first moment presents itself. What are we to do about the expansive statutory definitions of delinquency on the state level? A close reading of *In re Gault* will, it is believed, force conscientious policy makers to re-think the wisdom of retaining statutory delinquency definitions that are largely the result of historical anachronisms in child welfare policy at the end of the nineteenth century. In short, the *Gault* case should serve as a conceptual stalking horse to rid the organic law of delinquency of legal constructs that serve only to further clog an already overcrowded and overworked system. The majority opinion in the *Gault* decision serves as an ideal predicate for the removal of many "status" and "condition" offenses from delinquency definitions. It is believed, furthermore, that these forms of social deviance (if, indeed, they can be called "deviant"), can be handled more appropriately by non-judicial processes. Neither juvenile courts nor juvenile correctional institutions are functionally equipped to handle a problem of this dimension.

Isolating the Condemnation Sanction

With the advent of the juvenile court structure in the United States in 1899,[17] legislation was drafted which separated the child from the adult offender in both the adjudicatory (guilt determining) and dispositional (sentencing) stages of the criminal process. At first, following the Illinois prototype,[18] statutes were passed in language clearly delineating the differences between delinquent conduct on the one hand, and dependency and neglect situations on the other. As time progressed and social casework philosophy became more dominant in the juvenile court repertory, many states automatically added statutory language to their delinquency definitions not found in the original acts or in penal legislation generally. The word "delinquent" became a mask behind which hid a number of euphemistic quasi-legal wrongs. Their incorporation into the legislative mold gave juvenile courts a jurisdiction over children far broader than the criminal court's jurisdiction over the adult offender. By virtue of such laws, many juvenile judges felt that had a roving commission to seek out and treat errant youth under the *parens patriae*[19] rubric. Inflated claims were made only to be realized, if at all, in theory, rarely in practice.

Few authorities would claim that the juvenile court has no proper function beyond its delinquency jurisdiction. In fact, the dependency and neglect jurisdiction of the court is where its real curative powers reside. But this question is present: "Does inclusion in the delinquency definition of children who are not offenders but may be in need of protection, complicate the concepts of the juvenile court?"[20] It is believed that it does. In our heady desire to rescue children from the more rigid and less sophisticated law of crimes, we have, in turn, failed to isolate the condemnation aspects of delinquency. Given the broad and omnibus definitions of delinquency, virtually any juvenile could conceivably be adjudicated. This adjudication often incorporates a category of offenses not closely associated with any legally-conceived wrong-doing in the criminal law. Sol Rubin makes an interesting observation when he writes, "If the child's behavior is dangerous to community well-being, delinquency is indicated. If, however, the child and not the community, is in danger, the child needs protection, but delinquency is not indicated."[21]

Indeed, more and more evidence is accumulating pointing toward the thesis that the label "delinquent" bears a stigma of some proportion. Long before sociologists became increasingly interested in labeling theory, the Supreme Court of Virginia in a 1946 case stated:

> The judgment against a youth that he is delinquent is a more serious reflection upon his character and habits. The stain against him is not removed merely because the statute says no judgment in this particular proceeding shall be deemed a conviction for crime or so considered. The stigma of conviction will reflect upon him for life. It hurts his self-respect. It may, at some inopportune, unfortunate moment, rear its ugly head to destroy his opportunity for advancement and blast his ambition to build up a character and reputation entitling him to the esteem and respect of his fellow men.[22]

The more recent *Task Force Report* reinforces statements such as those made by the Virginia court and others. It says:

> So long as the community's classification of a young person remains informal, the likelihood that it can be modified by changing circumstances remains possible. But the official labeling of a misbehaving youth as delinquent places him in a clear category which is difficult to escape.[23]

Are juveniles who commit acts deemed to fall within the status offense category to be condemned as delinquent with all the socio-legal connotations that word imports to the average mind? These terms are more expressive of psycho-cultural dysfunctions than ones denoting criminal pathology *per se*. They have no adult counterpart in the penal code. By institutionalizing expressions of distaste through such concepts, legislatures have wittingly or unwittingly failed to isolate the behaviors which they really seek to condemn. In this context, it is prudent to look to the criminal law's condemnation sanctions, not as standards of juvenile behavior necessarily, but as guides to what the community considers dangerous and intolerable.

Delinquency definitions are the classical paradigms of the overcriminalization of juvenile law. Legal policy makers have excessively relied upon juvenile justice to perform tasks for which it is ill-suited, and, in the process, have created acute problems of judicial administration. By condemning categories of activity that on the adult level lack criminalistic characterization, legislatures have handicapped the enforcement of the juvenile law against genuinely threatening conduct. This failure to isolate those acts in delinquency legislation which society truly seeks to condemn has created the unfortunate phenomenon which led, ultimately, to the *Gault* decision.

Gerald Stern, writing on the problem of public drunkenness in the November, 1967, issue of *The Annals,* made a statement that bears repeating in the present context. According to Stern:

> The effectiveness of the criminal justice system depends upon the respect it commands as an impartial forum. By failing to dispense due process in all cases, the entire system is weakened. Moreover, by handling cases which are regarded as non-criminal in nature, the system breeds disrespect for its institutions, thereby becoming less potent to deal with serious crimes.[24]

If we substitute the word "juvenile" for the word "criminal" in the above quotation, its admonition would still be relevant. In the same issue of *The Annals,* law professor Sanford Kadish writes, "One hopes that attempts to set out the facts and to particularize the perils of overcriminalization may ultimately affect the decisions of legislatures."[25] To date, professor Kadish's plea has largely been ignored.

It is our default "to particularize the perils of overcriminalization" that suggests the need to isolate the condemnation sanction in juvenile justice. We are inundated with delinquency legislation that has little conceptual utility in its present form. Being labeled a delinquent for what would be non-condemnatory conduct on the adult level serves only to increase the minor's self-conception of himself as an outsider. Continuing to perpetuate such a state of affairs is neither logical nor defensible.

Redefining Delinquency: The Condemnation Sanction Made Manifest

As far back as the year 1921, Judge Edward F. Waite warned:

> Has not the time arrived when no tribunal should claim the title of juvenile court, implying in its origin and major application a jurisdiction

and procedure followed wholly on the parental idea, without distinction in aim and essential method between delinquent, dependent and neglected wards of the state. . . .?[26]

Fifty-six years later we are still debating this issue and its resolution, as yet, eludes us. Definitions of delinquency have apparently slumbered too long under the addiction of *parens patriae.*

According to statutory authority modeled after reform legislation in the early twentieth century, a criminal charge lodged against a minor within a certain age range was dismissed, with several exceptions, on the ground of non-age. Such a dismissal, however, did not determine the matter. Such a person was then brought into juvenile court, adjudged delinquent and allegedly "treated" for his own protection as a ward of the state. "Juvenile delinquency", says Paul Tappan, "implies a special age range, a more or less distinct court jurisdiction, and a concept of status."[27] He then makes this crucial observation: "There is the further, most significant, and more difficult problem of the behavior denoted by that term. Here is real confusion in the purpose, philosophy, and the content of the law . . ."[28]

As noted earlier, juvenile courts have traditionally justified their use of the *parens patriae* power by assuming that a minor committing a proscribed act is the proper subject for state intervention. But, in order for the state to claim any legitimate right to intervene in a child's behalf as its parental *alter ego,* two subtantive conditions must be met. First, assuming incarceration is the treatment of choice, the juvenile training school or reformatory to which the youth is sent must be a parent surrogate in the strictest sense of that term. Secondly, the stigma of criminality must not attach to the juvenile as a result of his correctional sojourn. Neither of these two conditions have been realized on a national scale in the seventy-eight year history of the juvenile court. *In re Gault* stands as a constant reminder of our failure to even approach partial implementation of these dual objectives. *Parens patriae* has been the judicial shibboleth behind which the juvenile court failings have been hidden.

What is suggested here is that in those cases where a minor subject to juvenile court jurisdiction has committed an act violative of a delinquency statute, where that same act, if committed by an adult would not constitute a crime, common sense requires careful scrutiny of our dispositional alternatives. Roscoe Pound advises us that "[c]hild placement involves administrative authority over one of the most intimate and cherished human relations. . . . It is well known that too often the placing of a child in . . . an institution is done casually or perfunctorily."[29]

It is also interesting to note the position taken by the United Nations on this aspect of the delinquency issue. Its Advisory Committee on Delinquency stated:

> Many children, especially during the adolescent years, commit overt acts
> forbidden by the laws, mores and customs of the particular state of society
> in which they live. . . . Children who violate the law should not be
> subjected to a legal adjudication of delinquency merely to secure treat-
> ment of their problems.[30]

From this statement and others,[31] the United Nations takes the policy
position that juvenile delinquency should be defined strictly in terms of
violations of the criminal law, rather than in the sometime nebulous
parlance of civil litigation. This becomes an important distinction when we
approach the issue of the condemnation sanction in delinquency legislation.
"What distinguishes a criminal from a civil sanction," says Henry Hart, ". . .
is the judgment of community condemnation which accompanies and
justifies its imposition."[32] There is little overt community condemnation
inherent in the so-called status and conditions offenses which still comprise the great bulk of our juvenile jurisprudence. This raises the question
of whether we can conceptually square present status and condition
commitments of delinquents with criminal law theory?

Transgressions of the law of crimes represents the violation of a norm
calling for some sanction-producing result by a politically organized state.
Professors Michael and Wechsler suggest that

> . . . [T]he determination of the kinds of behavior to be made criminal
> involves three major problems: (1) What sorts of conduct is it both
> desirable and possible to deter; (2) what sorts indicate that persons who
> behave in those ways are dangerously likely to engage in socially undesir-
> able behavior in the future; (3) will the attempt to prevent particular
> kinds of behavior by the criminal law do less good, than harm, as
> measured by their other harmful results.[33]

Legitimate state force against the various depredations of the adult
criminal element finds expression in criminal law through the so-called
"principle of legality." The Latin rendition of this concept is *nullum crimen
sine lege,* which, when employed in its more restrictive sense, means "that no
conduct may be held criminal unless it is precisely described in a penal
law."[34] Professor Jerome Hall says this principle has two corollaries: "penal
statutes must be strictly construed, and they must not be given retroactive
effect."[35] The first corollary is particularly relevant to delinquency legislation.

As applied in both the penal statutes of Europe and in those of the
United States, the principle of legality represents the opposite of *carte
blanche* authority to punish deviant behavior generally. Its touchstone is
not an expansive jurisdiction, but rather a limitation on penalization
effected through the application of specific norms.[36]

At first blush, delinquency statutes in the United States have the outward appearance of draftsmanship with the principle of legality in mind. Certain conduct is made punishable by these laws if violated by a juvenile within a certain age range. Upon closer examination, however, one finds that the principle of legality in these statutes is only a facade. Engrafted upon one or a small group of condemnatory proscriptions, we find a host of *socially* distasteful conduct denominated as acts of delinquency. If assessed from the viewpoint of the substantive criminal law, many of these acts would not be criminal at all.

The principle of legality, if it existed at all in juvenile justice, withered away very quickly in the early 1900's under the bright lights of social defense, *parens patriae* and treatment concepts focusing on the socio-psychological problems of the "whole child". This was viewed as a major revolution in the name of progress! No longer would the somewhat myopic law of crimes fossilize the rehabilitation of the child in an archaic mold of legalism. The juvenile court was free, so the argument went, to promote the widest possible benefits throughout the widest possible juvenile population.

Under this enlightened aegis the delinquent was not in theory a criminal, hence, *nullen crimen sine lege* was not strictly applicable. Since 1899, however, fact has begun to overshadow theory. Via *Gault,* we have come to the somewhat belated conclusion that contemporary delinquency adjudications are distressingly similar, both in form and in content, to criminal trials. Nonetheless, their statutory base is still largely bottomed on a "double standard" of criminality not found on the adult level. This differential processing of juveniles at the hands of the juvenile court is at war with both the principle of legality and with the more modest correctional goals professed by those in juvenile rehabilitation.

Recognition must surely be given to the fact that it is most difficult to stigmatize conduct as criminal *per se* unless such conduct has, historically, ethically and socially, come to denote one of the more or less legally-recognized crimes in the traditional felony-misdemeanor category. It is not believed that the average man-on-the-street equates many of the delinquency proscriptions with "true" criminal conduct, yet the stigma is there and it is acted upon. Paul Tappan provided a clear insight into this dilemma when he wrote that "[a]n evolving jurisprudence of delinquency has been less sure of its ground in this issue of conduct to be made taboo, perhaps than any other branch of law."[37]

Since delinquency as a legal entity was unknown at common law and is wholly a creature of statutory formulation, it falls on the collective shoulders of state legislators to do something about these definitional deficiencies. Legislatures should very quickly come to grips with this reality: delinquency in its present context is nothing more than a euphemism for crime and delinquency proceedings are essentially criminal in their dispositional aspects. Therefore, the definitions of delinquency should be sharpened and honed under a re-vitalized "principle of legality" with all the theoretical and practical connotations that term implies. Legislation should be enacted to reinstate the *nullum crimen sine lege* doctrine in the organic law of delinquency to recognize that a youth charged with delinquency as such should be accorded all the protections of *In re Gault* and its progeny.[38] However, for those children classified as status or conditional offense violators, neither the condemnation sanctions of the adult criminal law nor the dispositional alternatives of that law should be legislatively mandated.

If such a statutory division were accomplished, we would then be on our way toward dealing more effectively with the real criminogenic child. This would, in turn, smooth the way for the further implementation of the *Gault* teachings, while, at the same time, give correctional attention to the juvenile client most in need of it. The dependency, neglect, CHINS and PINS jurisdiction of the juvenile court would not be emasculated; they would simply appear in another separate section of the juvenile code. In addition, greater flexibility in pre-judicial disposition would be effectuated by a more definitive statutory standard of delinquency.

These suggestions will certainly not foster unanimity in the current dialogue in juvenile justice issues. It is hoped, however, they will spur additional thought. Inherent in any system of justice worthy of the name are limitations upon official action. Although to some, the thesis suggested will appear restrictive and overly legalistic, seventy-eight years of trial and often egregious error in juvenile court law clearly demonstrate the need for tighter legislation regarding the delinquency jurisdiction of that court.

Summary

The juvenile justice system in recent years has come under strident attack from both practitioners and academicians alike. For nearly seven decades, juvenile courts in the United States operated a low-profile, non-adversarial system of juvenile adjudication that was often at odds with both the due process concept and the rehabilitative ideal. There seemed to be, indeed, a marriage of convenience between the early "child saver" concepts of non-punitive treatment with the correspondingly loose procedural devices advocated by juvenile court pioneers. This marriage, however, came to an abrupt end on May 15, 1967. On that date, the United States Supreme Court rule 7−2 in *In re Gault,* that certain constitutional rights must be afforded a juvenile in the adjudicatory stage of a delinquency hearing where loss of liberty was a real possibility.

The *Gault* decision has imparted additional due process safeguards into juvenile justice administration and has also impacted several areas of juvenile justice outside the traditional adjudicatory hearing phase. By virtue of the decision's expansive language, juvenile justice personnel and legislatures alike were sensitized to the need to revamp juvenile statutory law to comport with both the letter and spirit of the *Gault* case. As yet, there has not been what could be termed a wholesale restructuring of the organic law of juvenile courts, but both the federal government and the states are moving in that general direction. Thus, the *Gault* decision has provided the judicial backdrop for the implementation of a more effective public policy in both the juvenile adjudication and correctional fields.

Discussion Questions

1. How has the early English chancery doctrine of *parens patriae* been affected by the decision of *In re Gault* in your own state? Has it been completely overruled, only modified or left untouched?

2. Consult your state juvenile code to determine whether or not the prevailing definition of "delinquency" still includes some of the so-called "status" offenses committed by juveniles or only behavior considered to be criminal if committed by adults.

3. How has *In re Gault* affected the juvenile corrections field? Has it had only minimal impact or has it had substantial impact in the area of the *kinds* of youth committed to your state's juvenile institutions?

4. Do you believe that the juvenile justice system should revert to the pre-1889 handling of juvenile lawbreakers due to the alarming and continual rise in the juvenile crime rate? Discuss.

5. Why do you think the United States Supreme Court waited some sixty-eight years before correcting what many consider some serious constitutional abuses in the juvenile justice process? Discuss.

Notes

1. *Task Force Report: Juvenile Delinquency and Youth Crime,* The President's Commission on Law Enforcement and Administration of Justice, p. 93 (1967) (hereinafter cited as *Task Force Report*).

2. Garret Heyns, "The 'Treat-'em-Rough' Boys are Here Again," *Federal Probation,* 31 (June, 1967): 8.

3. *Ibid.*

4. A term popularized in criminal justice literature by Francis A. Allen in his book *The Borderland of Criminal Justice: Essays in Law and Criminology* (Chicago: University of Chicago Press, 1964), pp. 25–41.

5. Richard Korn and Lloyd McCorkle, *Criminology and Penology,* (New York: Holt, Rinehart and Winston, 1959), p. 475.

6. *In re Gault,* 387 U.S. 1 (1967).

7. *Ibid.,* p. 17.

8. John Wigmore, *A Treatise on the Anglo-American System of Evidence in Trials at Common Law* (Boston: Little, Brown and Co., 3rd ed. 1940) p. 145.

9. Aldous Huxley, *Brave New World Revisited* (New York: Harper Bros., 1961), p. 26.

10. *In re Gault,* pp. 29–30.

11. Justine Polier, "The Gault Case: Its Practical Impact on the Philosophy and Objectives of Juvenile Court," *Family Law Quarterly,* 1 (December, 1967), p. 47.

12. *Task Force Report,* p. 396.

13. The procedural guidelines to be applied in the adjudicatory stage of a *delinquency* hearing were the following: (1) the right to notices of charges; (2) the right to counsel; (3) the right of confrontation and cross-examination, and (4) the privilege against compulsory self-incrimination.

14. *Task Force Report,* p. 398.

15. *Ibid.*

16. *Ibid.*

17. For a thorough and thought-provoking review of the historical events leading to the establishment of the world's first juvenile court in Chicago, see Anthony Platt, *The Child Savers: The Invention of Delinquency* (Chicago: University of Chicago Press, 1969), ch. 5.

18. The original juvenile court Act of Illinois provided a clear-cut distinction between "delinquent", "dependent", and "neglected" children. Illinois Laws (1899), p. 131.

19. Harry Black states that *parens patriae* translates as "'father of his country', or more literally 'parent of his country'." *Black's Law Dictionary* (St. Paul: West Publishing Co., 4th ed., 1957), p. 1269. The *parens patriae* doctrine was an outgrowth of early English chancery practice involving guardianship of selected minor wards of the court. For a detailed history of the legal development of *parens patriae,* see Joseph Story, *Equity Jurisprudence* (Boston: Little, Brown, and Co., 14th ed., 1918).

20. Sol Rubin, "The Legal Character of Juvenile Delinquency", *The Annals of the American Academy of Political and Social Science,* 261 (January, 1949): 2 (hereinafter cited as *The Annals*).

21. *Ibid.,* p. 3.

22. *Jones v. Commonwealth,* 185 Va. 335, 341–42, 38 S.E. 2d 444, 447 (1946).

23. *Task Force Report,* p. 360.

24. Gerald Stern, "Public Drunkenness: Crime or Health Problem? *The Annals* 374 (November, 1967): 153.

25. Sanford Kadish, "The Crisis of Over-Criminalization", *The Annals,* 374 (November, 1967): 170.

26. Edward Waite, "How Far Can Court Procedure Be Socialized Without

Impairing Individual Rights?", *Journal of Criminal Law and Criminology,* 12 (November, 1921): 340.

27. Paul Tappan, *Juvenile Delinquency* (New York: McGraw-Hill, 1949), p. 15.

28. *Ibid.*

29. Roscoe Pound, *Criminal Justice in America* (New York: Henry Holt Co., 1930), p. 62.

30. "Juvenile Delinquency in the North American Region", United Nations, ST/SOA/SD/1 (1952): 115.

31. For example, *see* "New Forms of Juvenile Delinquency: Their Origin, Prevention and Treatment," report prepared by The Secretariat, A/Conf. 17–7, *Second U.N. Congress on The Prevention of Crime and the Treatment of Offenders,* London, August 8, 1960.

32. Henry Hart, "The Aims of the Criminal Law", *Law and Contemporary Problems,* 23 (1958): 404.

33. Jerome Michael and Herbert Wechsler, *Criminal Law and Its Administration* (Chicago: The Foundation Press, 1940), p. 11.

34. Jerome Hall, *General Principles of Criminal Law* (Indianapolis: Bobbs-Merrill Co., 2d ed. 1960), p. 28.

35. *Ibid.*

36. *See,* for example, Advisory Opinion, 1935, Permanent Court of International Justice, ser. A/B, No. 65 at pp. 53, 56.

37. Paul Tappan, *Juvenile Delinquency,* p. 16.

38. Since the *Gault* case was decided in 1967, the U.S. Supreme Court has delved even further into juvenile law in certain limited areas. For example, the following cases illustrate the continuing "selective incorporation" of the Bill of Rights into juvenile law: *In re Winship,* 397 U.S. 358 (1970) ("beyond reasonable doubt" doctrine must apply to juveniles as well as adults in adjudicatory hearing); *McKeiver v. Pennsylvania,* 403 U.S. 528 (1971) (juveniles have no constitutional right to trial by jury); *Ivan v. City of New York,* 407 U.S. 203 (1972) (This case accorded retroactive effect to the holding of *In re Winship*); *Breed v. Jones,* 421 U.S. 519 (1975) (prosecution of juvenile as an adult after an adjudicatory proceeding in juvenile court violates the Double Jeopardy Clause of the Fifth Amendment, as applied to the states through the Fourteenth Amendment).

2

Issues in the Diversion of Juveniles

RAYMON C. FORSTON

THIS CHAPTER ADDRESSES several issues which are related to the diversion of juveniles. Its purpose is not to describe characteristic and current examples of diversion but rather to state several issues concerning diversion, to provoke readers' discussion of the probable consequences of different positions on the issues, and finally to help readers resolve the issues sufficiently in their own minds to assume positions concerning them

Diversion is a relatively new correctional response, and whether its use increasingly diminishes or grows will depend on politicians' and criminal justice practitioners' stances concerning the most important issues regarding it. The chapter's primary purpose, then, is to raise issues about diversion and to provoke its readers to discuss them; its secondary purpose is to serve as a catalyst or inspiration for its readers to advocate (1) the widespread diffusion of various diversion procedures, (2) the abandonment of the diversion "experiment," or (3) some compromise position between ardent advocacy of diversion continuation and gloomy pessimism about the appropriateness or efficacy of diversion.

If diversion is broadly (and inadequately) defined as any behavior of a policeman, judge, or some other agent of the state which keeps an offender (an adult who violates the criminal law or a juvenile who commits an act of delinquency) from being inititiated into or processed further into the criminal justice system, then diversion is indeed as old as law enforcement itself. Examples of diversion would be (1) discretionary arrests which overlook perpetrators of minor offenses, (2) prosecuting attorneys' decisions not to press charges, grand juries' failures to return true bills of indictments, and petit juries' failures to find defendants guilty, if all of these actions were based not on the offender's presumed innocence but rather on the assumption that, for one of a variety of reasons, doing nothing against the offender might be in the best interests of both the state and the offender.

But it is currently common to define diversion as doing something rather than doing nothing, and the varying practices we now call diversion have a relatively recent origin. They are rooted in the 1967 recommendation of the President's Commission on Law Enforcement and Administration of Justice that entry of offending juveniles into the formal, structured justice system be superseded by their referral to local community and youth service bureaus which stress prevention and correction.[1] Such a referral, if successful, would keep a youngster out of the justice system. The definition of diversion which is probably the one most widely used at present is that of the National Advisory Commission on Criminal Justice Standards and Goals, which refers to diversion as "formally acknowledged and organized efforts to utilize alternatives to initial or continued processing into the justice system."[2] Observe that the definition has three separable notions which merit attention: (1) diversion is a *formally acknowledged effort,* not something a policeman or judge does and never reports, (2) diversion is an *organized* effort, not an isolated effort by someone disposed to divert, and (3) diversion prevents either *initial* or *continued* processing into the justice system, i.e., diversion may first occur before a formal arrest is made or may finally occur after the adjudication of the juvenile as a delinquent but before the execution of a disposition that would leave him under state correctional scrutiny such as probation or incarceration in a training school.

ISSUE 1: *What are the theoretical underpinnings of diversion and how useful or valid are they?* It is easy to identify three deviance/criminology perspectives or theories which buttress arguments for diversion, namely differential association, labeling, and anomie. The principle or theory of differential association posits that one learns how to and does indeed become a delinquent when he has been exposed to an excess of pro-delinquency norms from people who have high prestige with him over anti-delinquency norms from people of lesser prestige.[3] Diversion would presumably be of such a nature that a juvenile's contacts with definitions favorable to violation of the law would be diminished and that his contacts should be increased with people whom he could trust and respect and who would by precept and example unfavorably define law violation. Is diversion inherently implied in the theory as an effective means of control? It is difficult to empirically verify Sutherland's differential association theory, but as an organizing principle, it is more useful in explaining the etiology and epidemiology of delinquency than any other single theory.

Labeling theory, which distinguishes between primary (first) and secondary (subsequent) deviance, states that a society may react to an act of delinquency in such a way that it is in fact designating or labeling the juvenile as delinquent, that it will subsequently react to him in his new delinquent status, and that he may in turn see himself as a delinquent and act out his self-image of a deviant.[4] Thus may societal labeling cause secondary deviance. Diversion should either eliminate or at least greatly diminish the labeling effect on the juvenile.

A third theory should also be briefly considered. Robert Merton has postulated that when there is a disjuncture between the goals which people have and the means which they have for achieving them, then the usual conforming behaviors of a person might change to deviant or delinquent behavior as a means for achieving his goals.[5] If there are indications that delinquency is related to a lack of legal opportunity to reach a socially approved goal, could diversion put the offender in a position where access to legal means for achieving his goals was enhanced?

It seems appropriate that this first issue should concern the legitimacy of the theoretical underpinnings of diversion efforts. How valid or how useful are the three theories just mentioned? Do juveniles really commit delinquent behavior because they have learned it as Sutherland suggests? Does society's labeling of a juvenile force him or her into a deviant role, especially if the labeling caused the juvenile to be sent to a state training school where he would be in the constant company of others also so labeled? Labeling theory is useful in explaining some secondary deviance and is not inherently logically incompatible with the theory of differential association. The primary unanswered question about labeling theory is that it fails to explain why the labeling of some people leads to secondary deviance and the labeling of others does not. In like manner, anomie theory does not explain why some people without means for achieving their goals abandon their goals rather than use illegal means for achieving them. We can similarly ask if all delinquency is learned from association with pro-delinquency norms, or whether there is another source of the origin of delinquency.

What is being asked here is: (1) whether the three theories just discussed are adequate explanations of the etiology and epidemiology of delinquency and, if they are not, what theory(ies) is(are) and (2) if the three are the best theoretical statements we have for explaining delinquency, may it be logically deduced from them that diversion is (or at least sometimes is) the best societal reaction to delinquency we can make?

ISSUE 2: *How structured and formal should diversion provisions be?* This second issue is suggested by the definition of diversion. Should there be laws or at least guidelines on who can divert whom, or should diversion be informal and unstructured? Let us look briefly at some of the possible consequences of each alternative. A well organized diversion system (System A) working within formalized rules or laws would first of all restrict diversion to juveniles who had either violated the law, the law violation either admitted by the juvenile or determined by a juvenile court, or who had been legally found to be in need of supervision or assistance. The juvenile would agree to his being diverted. The extreme alternative to this (System B) would be diversion by some agent of the state of a juvenile whom that agent merely thought to be in need of assistance and without either legal prescription or the juvenile's permission for his diversion. The latter practice invites court action on whether the child's constitutional rights have been denied. In System A, the guidelines would state clearly the circumstances in which diversion either could or must be made by either the police, the probation officer, or the juvenile court. Without such guidelines, the amount of diversion and the sorts of juveniles diverted would be determined by the whims, emotions, prejudices, and punitive philosophy of various agents in the justice system. The guidelines would also state the boundaries of how, to whom, and for how long, a juvenile should be diverted. Without such guidelines, a juvenile's diversion could be more punitive than probation, could be of more benefit to the agency to whom diversion was made than to the juvenile, and could be for unreasonable lengths of time. Without such guidelines, unorganized and unofficial diversion may also discriminate against youngsters in poor or minority families and consequently aggravate the problems of equal access of all juveniles to justice. In summary, it is asked whether there should be formalized rules or legal provision which specify who may divert, when diversion can be made, and what will be done by the juvenile during his period of diversion.[6]

ISSUE 3: *Why do we divert? What is the purpose of diversion?* Let us assume that the following are goals which we hope to achieve by diversion: (1) enhance the chance of successfully socializing the juvenile in law abiding behavior by keeping him in the community where he can be with local peer groups and have access to presumably superior local resources, (2) avoid the stigmatization of the delinquent label by either keeping the juvenile out of the justice system or by minimizing his contact with it, and (3) save the state money by reducing probation case loads, numbers of juvenile court hearings, and diminishing the population of the state training schools (juvenile prisons). Are these three goals appropriate ones? Let us look at each of them in turn. The question regarding the first goal is not whether diversion is more effective than its alternatives (see Issue 7) but whether or not a juvenile deserves to be treated differently than an adult when he violates the law. If a juvenile has harmed a victim or his property, should he in turn be required to suffer and to learn early in life that "crime does not pay" and that his own suffering will be a consequence of any future law violations? In reference to the second goal, it can be asked whether a juvenile who has broken the law should be permitted to escape being labeled as a delinquent and subsequently stigmatized. Is it right that a society fail to punish a juvenile and label him as delinquent, allowing him to "save face," when an adult might be sent to prison for behavior for which the juvenile was diverted? Regarding the third named goal, the question again is not whether diversion saves money but whether economy should be an issue. We could grant momentarily that diversion is cheaper than probation or incarceration in a state school, but we must also note that excecution of at least young, if not old, offenders is also probably cheaper than incarcerating them. Many who would acknowledge the economy of execution would still remain execution prohibitionists. Is economy a manifest function of diversion or rather a latent function if and when it is more economical? Questions concerning these three general goals of diversions are not sociological or psychological (or scientific) questions but ethical ones. That the questions are not scientific does not make discussing or answering them any less important than if they were scientific in nature; it merely means that the arguments used to justify stances taken in reference to them will utilize more value judgments and less empirical data than one would use if they were scientific questions.

ISSUE 4: *Who should be diverted?* An early and often repeated recommendation was that diversion be used for all juveniles who commit status offenses. The assumption was that the court system, albeit a civil one, was an inappropriate agency for handling offenders whose offenses would not have been crimes had they been committed by adults and would therefore not have been a legal concern of a criminal court. The implication is that adjudicating delinquents for status offenses in civil courts is not sufficient "decriminalization" and that the offenders should be handled by other agencies such as Youth Service Bureaus, public school systems, etc. The early suggestions for the diversion of status offenders did not preclude the possibility of the diversion of others; they were merely arguments for taking status offenders out of the court system. Few who favor diversion would categorically exclude juveniles who violate the criminal code for adults; the question, rather, involves which offenders should be diverted. The National Advisory Commission on Criminal Justice Standards and Goals suggested that good candidates for diversion were offenders who were young, whose victims would not object to the offender's diversion, who had no history of violence toward others, and in whom there was no evidence of long established delinquency patterns which might show little prospect of change. The Commission also observed that the community might choose to prosecute rather than to divert in instances in which a need was felt to deter others from similar behavior, such deterrence being expected to be more easily accomplished by prosecution of the offender than by diverting him.

Since juveniles are, by definition, young, then by that criterion all of them would be likely candidates for diversion. Where resources are limited, should younger juveniles be given preferential consideration for diversion? Should diversion become more problematic when the offender approaches statutory adulthood?

Is diversion ever indicated even though the offender's victim opposes it? Can diversion of an offender without his victim's agreement to it jeopardize the community's acceptance of diversion? It is possible that a victim's opposition to a diversion that was made without his approval would be more likely to discredit diversion if (1) the victim is a prominent and politically powerful person or (2) if diversion failed to effect reformation of the offender. It is also possible that victims' opposition to diversion can be lessened if the successes of diversion are well publicized, protecting, of course, the identity of offenders. In discussing New Clinics for Kids in Trouble, *Time* Magazine reports: "A youth injured while chasing a purse snatcher turned out to be a former purse snatcher himself, rehabilitated through clinic-inspired counseling and work programs."[8] The same article also tells of an elderly man's twelve year old mugger, who, instead of being incarcerated, successfully worked part-time in an old folks' home. Victims' opposition to diversion may cause a judge's disposition of a juvenile case to be painfully made, regardless of whether his decision is for or against diversion, for diversion has a better chance of public acceptance when there is not victim resistance to it.

The Commission also observed that one was a poor candidate for diversion if he had a history of violence towards others or a history of undesirable behavior patterns which appeared resistant to change. But it was not the intent of the Commission to suggest that "hardened" offenders can be more effectively reformed in correctional (incarceration) schools than in diversion programs. The Commission's position reflects a realistic realization that when a judge has questions concerning what might most effectively reform the "serious" offender and what the consequences are for the community if the offender, while in the society in a diversion program, recommits the crime, then he is likely not to allow diversion. In such a case, it is highly unlikely that the community would tolerate diversion. Like the judge, it would opt for temporary safety from an incarcerated offender. Judges are characteristically reluctant to leave violent offenders in the community and the community is characteristically reluctant to retain them.

ISSUE 5: *When should diversion take place?* It has already been noted that diversion may occur so early that it prevents *initial* processing into the justice system; it may also occur later, sometime after arrest or even after detention and juvenile court hearing, in which case *continued* processing into or in the justice system is prevented. The basic question we face here is when diversion should occur. Does determination of the optimum time for diversion require consideration of the interests of others besides the juvenile? For example, is it not possible that some cases of delinquency with victimization are considered so severe by society or so heinous by the victim that an ounce, if not a pound, of flesh will be demanded? Would either or both society and the victim in such cases accept diversion from what they consider punishment, for example, training school incarceration and separation from parents, only after the juvenile had been arrested and perhaps even adjudicated delinquent? The implication of the questions is that it might be necessary sometimes, as a matter of expediency, to divert late rather than early because late diversion may be the only alternative to complete processing in the justice system.

If the interests of only the juvenile are considered, however, it would appear that early diversion is usually indicated. If really well planned and sophisticated diversion alternatives are available, then it might be argued that diversion is not only possible for juveniles with histories of violent behavior suspected to be resistant to change but that early diversion is recommended. Early diversion, indeed diversion of the violent juvenile at any step in the justice processes, *may* not be in the best interests of society, but it is difficult to make a good case that it is not in the best interests of most youngsters. In the case of juveniles with single offenses, minor offenses, status offenses, and offenses without victims, the theories of both labeling and differential association clearly imply that earlier diversion is preferable to later diversion. The earlier diverted juvenile is less likely to be branded as a delinquent by the courts, the police, his family and friends, and most importantly, by himself. Common sense, if not evidence, would suggest that the more society labels a person as a delinquent and behaves as if he were a delinquent, the more likely is the labeled one to develop a self concept of a delinquent and then act out a role consistent with his new delinquent status. The theory of differential association implies that for rehabilitative purposes the offender's contact with definitions favorable to delinquency should be minimized and definitions unfavorable to delinquency should be maximized. Surely the best way to accomplish the opposite of this is to keep the offender in close contact with other offenders. If we wanted to stop a child's learning to speak French, we would at the earliest possible time isolate him from French speaking people and surround him with non-French speaking people. The parallel for resocializing the offender is obvious.

On the other hand, early diversion raises several interesting and important legal questions. The fact that pre-trial diversion is non-punitive and meant to be in the offender's best interests does not change the fact that constitutional guarantees of due process or fair procedures may be omitted from diversion proceedings. Since a hearing ("trial") has been foregone, can and should the state prescribe intervention activities in the life of a juvenile without a legal determination that he needs it? Can a parent or guardian surrender a juvenile's right to a hearing? All of these and similar questions have not been fully resolved for adult offenders, therefore we have insufficient precedents to suggest what the logical extensions (as in the Gault decision) to juveniles would be.[9]

In summary, the principal questions concerning the best time for diversion involve whose interests are being primarily considered, what the nature of the offender and his offenses are, and finally, why we, in fact, divert.

ISSUE 6: *Who should pay for diversion?* If diversion is to consist of something more than mere release of the juvenile or a requirement that he periodically report to some designated person, then it is going to cost something, the cost varying with the type and amount of service provided and the salary level of the one or ones providing the service. That cost can be borne by the offender (or his parents), an agency of the state, or by a private agency. Regardless of who pays for diversion, it will be cheaper to the state than incarceration.[10] Figures are not available for the portions of total diversion costs in the U.S. which are borne by each of the three sources for paying, but it is probable that the major costs are borne by the state. Is it reasonable to expect that parents who can afford to do so be required to pay whatever costs are incurred in their child's diversion? If diversion services are provided by a non-profit agency, should the state underwrite the costs of diversion services or expect the agency to arrange for its own funding through charitable donations or sponsorship by another serviceminded organization with financial resources?

If the diverted one is required to work as part of his rehabilitation, should that work be an unpaid service to an organization or to the state, or should the offender be paid for his work? If he is paid, should he keep all of his earned money, or should he give some of it to the state or to a private organization which may be sponsoring him? If his offense had a victim who experienced monetary loss directly (e.g., theft) or indirectly (e.g., medical bills), should the offender, if working, be required to make reparation or restitution to the victim?

These important questions may be difficult to answer in the abstract, but if one posits cases in which something is known about the offender and his family, his victim (if there was one), and the nature of the diversion services provided for the offender or required of him, then resolution of the questions and speculations about the probable consequences of the resolution may be made more easily and more meaningfully.

ISSUE 7: *How should diversion be evaluated?* The efficacy of any correctional technique or resource should be determined by an assessment of the extent to which it accomplishes its general goals, assuming that the technique was competently used or the resource adequately exploited. When a diversion program has specifically stated goals, then the extent to which goals were met should be the measure of the success of the program. The goals may even be stated so specifically that a categorical "yes" or "no" answer may be given concerning whether the goals were met. Such a goal might be stated as: "The officially known and recorded recidivism rate of diverted youngsters will be less than fifty per cent."

In the discussion of the third issue, it was assumed that there are at least three major general goals of diversion programs, and the reader may have thought of additional ones or may have rejected some of the three stated goals. Let us look briefly at each of the three goals. The best way to determine the comparative efficacy of diversion with its three most common alternatives, release, probation, and incarceration in a training school, is to conduct an experiment in which there is random placement of juveniles in (1) diversion programs or merely releasing them, (2) diversion programs or on probation, and (3) diversion programs or in training schools. This was to some extent done in the famous Provo experiment.[11] Some jurisdictions might not approve of the conducting of an experiment on the groups that diversion is already thought to be superior societal response which juveniles should not be randomly denied. In such a case, the evaluation of diversion has to face the problems associated with determination of recidivism and resolve them in the best way possible. The layman's assumption here is that a correctional technique is good in proportion to the low percentage of its participants who are subsequent violators. The whole problem of recidivism has been a particularly difficult one to work with because (1) true recidivism rates, as distinguished from official recidivism is often difficult, for a variety of reasons, to determine. It is even more futile to try to determine true recidivism rates than it is to determine true delinquency rates, for since the former involves the specific identification of the offender, victim surveys do not help as they do in delinquency rate surveys.

Three methods commonly used to determine recidivism rates have been (1) self-reporting, (2) official records, and (3) peer reports. It is appropriate to ask here what the difficulties are in the use of each of the three methods. It should be noted that self-reporting is obviously reliable only to the extent that respondents answer honestly, and there are no morally or legally acceptable ways of ascertaining respondents' honesty when they are answering questions about their recidivism. The invalidity of official records is too well known to need elaborate describing here, but it may be briefly observed that it is assumed that the recidivistic offenses of the most serious and the most persistent offenders are the ones most likely to be officially known and recorded. The third method requires asking youngsters to report on the delinquent activities of other youngsters whom they know. The reliability of this method is superior to that of police record use, but there may be moral objections to it. How morally justifiable is it, in the name of science, to ask one youngster to reveal his knowledge of his peers' delinquencies?

In addition to the methodological difficulties and issues involved in determining how much recidivism there is, an even more basic problem lies in defining recidivism. It is simplistic to refer to recidivism merely as an offense occuring after diversion which followed a prior offense. Recidivism has at least three properties: quality, quantity, and timing. Quality refers to the seriousness of the recidivistic act. If a first offense assault occasions diversion which in turn is followed by minor vandalism, then the offender is a recidivist. But could we not agree that the offender had improved if his assaultive behavior had stopped but was followed by minor vandalism? By an absolute standard which defined recidivism as an offense following diversion, then as a repeat offender and a recidivist, he might be considered a failure in terms of what diversion had done for him. But in relative terms concerning quality of recidivism, he would not be considered a failure. Quantity refers to the number of recidivistic acts, and the suggestion here is that two youngsters who have both participated in diversion programs are not equal failures if, after diversion, one commits a single act of law violation and the other commits numerous similar acts. And finally, timing refers to when the recidivism occurred. There is surely a difference in two recidivistic acts, one of which occurs either during diversion or within a few days after the completion of a diversion program and the other which occurs a year or two after diversion. Can the second case be considered as successful as surgery on a cancer patient who lives a few years after the surgery?

And finally, it might be asked whether there are latent functions or unintended consequences of diversion which might be found to be socially desirable. There is a wide variety of possible latent consequences, some of which might not be highly visible and others which might be difficult to measure: improved public image of police, greater respect for the judicial system, increased social solidarity because of the feeling of the socially functional importance of participating agencies or individuals, better parent-child relationships, happier youngsters, etc.

ISSUE 8: *What is the effect of diversion programs on other aspects of the justice system?* We do not have a definitive answer to this question, but we do have relevant information and we can ask intriguing questions for which we can look for answers. Kai Erikson has argued that a society's definition of deviant behavior is related to its ability to process in its justice system the offenders created by the definitions. [12] If this is so, does diverting juveniles from or out of the justice system cause it to define additional behaviors as delinquent or indicative of a need for supervision of the child? Harold Pepinsky voiced this fear in a tape made for The Center for the Study of Democratic Institutions, [13] a tape in which he argues that new correctional institutions and devices increase the frequency and intensity of state supervision of people's lives. His reasoning is that new devices such as probation or diversion do not become substitutes for old institutions but merely additions to them. This is so, he argues, because new devices allow new kinds of people to be brought into the system and because the new devices do not empty the old institutions. Two questions are suggested here: (1) whether diversion has brought into the justice system kinds of youngsters who heretofore were ignored by the police and the courts and

(2) whether more time available to police, reduced probation loads, or shrunken juvenile court hearing dockets have, in fact, resulted in bringing into the system youngsters whose behavior would have been ignored had the various justice system officials had less time to process offenders. The implication is that the justice system is functioning according to Parkinson's law: definitions of delinquency and observances and processing of delinquents will broaden to consume the time available for it. The Massachusetts experience with the abandonment of detention institutions in favor of community programs and increased diversion would be one source of enlightenment on this intriguing and important question.

In summary, we ask: Does diversion of juveniles decrease probation case loads? Does diversion reduce the number of juvenile judges' hearings? Does diversion cause a greater variety of behaviors to be defined as undesirable or illegal? Does diversion change peoples' perceptions of who or what a delinquent is? Does diversion bring new kinds of youngsters (e.g., upper middle class) into the justice system?

Summary

Eight issues regarding the diversion of juveniles have been suggested. These issues involve questions about (1) the compatibility of diversion with the control implications of various theories of delinquency; (2) what diversion is, why we divert, whom we divert, when we divert, and how we divert; and (3) measuring the efficacy of diversion as well as its effect on the total justice system. There are surely others which could have been mentioned. Answers have not been given or suggested for all of the questions asked nor has a systematic attempt been made to foresee all of the consequences of different positions regarding the issues. It is important, however, that these issues be discussed and that we realize and evaluate the consequences of the position we take regarding them. The future course of juvenile justice in this country is related to the positions the power elite and the legal establishment take on these salient issues.

Discussion Questions

1. Diversion should be highly unstructured, with either no, or a minimum of, guidelines or restrictions on how diversion is to occur.

2. Diversion should be available only to juveniles who committed non-violent offenses.

3. When a juvenile's offense had a victim (in the *usual* sense of a crime with a victim), the juvenile should not be diverted unless the victim agrees to the diversion.

4. If a juvenile offense caused the victim to experience financial loss, the juvenile should not be diverted unless the victim has been compensated for his financial loss.

5. Diversion should not occur unless it simultaneously provides for some punishment of the juvenile.

Notes

1. President's Commission on Law Enforcement and Administration of Justice, *Task Force Report: Juvenile Delinquency and Youth Crime* (Washington, D.C.: U.S. Government Printing Office, 1967), pp. 19–20.

2. National Advisory Commission on Criminal Justice Standards and Goals, *Task Force Report: Corrections,* (Washington, D.C.: U.S. Government Printing Office, 1973), p. 73.

3. See Edwin Sutherland and Donald Cressey, *Criminology* (9th ed.) (Philadelphia: J.B. Lippincott Company, 1974), pp. 75–77.

4. See Howard Becker, *Outsiders* (New York: The Free Press, 1963), p. 9.

5. See Robert Merton, *Social Theory and Social Structure* (New York: The Free Press, 1957), p. 140.

6. For a provocative discussion of possible consequences of overformalization, see Ruth Cavan and Theodore Ferdinand, *Juvenile Delinquency* (3rd ed.) (Philadelpia: J.B. Lippincott Company, 1975), pp. 438–440.

7. William Sheridan, "Juveniles Who Commit Noncriminal Acts . . . ," pp. 599–605 in Rose Giallombardo (ed.), *Juvenile Delinquency* (3rd ed.) (New York: John Wiley and Sons, Inc., 1976), p. 602.

8. *Time,* April 18, 1977, p. 51.

9. A bibliography of related literature can be found in Louis Carney, *Corrections in the Community* (Englewood Cliffs, New Jersey: Prentice Hall, Inc., 1977), p. 70.

10. See *Ibid.,* p. 58 and LaMar Empey and Maynard Erickson, *The Provo Experiment* (Lexington, Mass.: D.C. Heath and Company, 1972), p. 201, for two interesting illustrations.

11. Empey and Erickson, pp. 25–27.

12. Kai Erikson, *Wayward Puritans* (New York: John Wiley and Sons, 1966), pp. 23–24.

13. The Center for the Study of Democratic Institutions, "Diversion Programs in Criminal Justice—Humane or Coercive" (tape), Santa Barbara, California.

3

Comprehensive Planning in the Juvenile Justice Systems

Nicholas A. Reuterman

COMPREHENSIVE PLANNING IN JUVENILE JUSTICE has become quite commonplace during the past decade. Virtually every state has a State Planning Agency (SPA) which plans and coordinates both crime and delinquency prevention and treatment efforts. In addition the vast majority of states have various regional planning bodies which serve the same purpose and function as the SPA's but for a more limited geographical area. These planning efforts are a direct result of a series of Federal Acts — the Juvenile Delinquency Prevention and Control Act of 1968, the Omnibus Crime Control and Safe Streets Act of 1968, and the Juvenile Justice and Delinquency Prevention Act of 1974 — which were intended to combat the perceived increases in both adult and youth crime. This and related Federal legislation recognized that attempts to prevent and combat crime and delinquency required significant efforts in the area of comprehensive planning. In principle there has been little real disagreement with the necessity of such planning. On occasion, planning efforts may be viewed as a form of procrastination, a means to avoid taking action against the problem, but on the whole the desirability of planning is widely recognized by individuals at all levels of the juvenile justice system.

Problems in Comprehensive Juvenile Justice Planning

While comprehensive planning is regarded as desirable, useful, and even necessary for the prevention and control of delinquency, in reality several general problems have arisen. After almost a decade of explicit planning efforts, delinquency and crime still appear to be increasing. According to the Uniform Crime Reports, there has been a 13.2 percent increase from 1970 to 1975 in arrests of persons under the age of 18. The increase in arrests for persons older than 18, however, is considerably smaller.[1] Juvenile gang activity, particularly gang violence, appears to be increasing both in terms of frequency and seriousness.[2] Various criminal victimization surveys also note a general increase in crime rates in many cities when selected years between 1970 and 1975 are compared. While there are exceptions for certain cities and certain types of crimes, the general pattern of increase is clear.[3] It is not this writer's intention to argue that the country is in the grip of a crime wave; however, it is important to emphasize that during the time parameters when comprehensive planning was accorded considerable importance, crime and delinquency certainly did not decrease and, in all likelihood, increased.

The reasons for this state of affairs are certainly numerous and complex. One distinct contributing factor, however, may well have been that comprehensive planning in any true sense of the concept was not taking place, or at best, occurring rarely. Some support for this suggestion may be seen in the introduction to the *First Comprehensive Plan for Federal Juvenile Delinquency Programs* which states that Federal programs are often "fragmented and inconsistent in philosophy, purpose, and method".[4] If such a situation exists at the Federal level, it is naive to expect better results from state, regional, and local planners.

Unfortunately, comprehensive planning activities are largely new and unfamiliar to those involved in either the criminal or juvenile justice systems. It is not surprising, therefore, that comprehensive planning efforts have often been relatively unsophisticated and, in many instances, relatively unproductive. Examples of such faulty efforts are numerous. One particularly disturbing example is illustrated in a comparison of the descriptions of failure in two programs relevant to the juvenile justice system, one initiated during the 1950's and one during the 1970's.[5] In the descriptions of both program efforts, mention is made of conflicting ideas concerning the attainment of goals, divergent operating philosophies and procedures, mutually exclusive priorities, protection of vested interests, lack of coordination, and ultimate program failure and disbandment. Ironically, residual effects of these conflicts appeared to be a reduction in services to a level below that which prevailed before the given program was initiated. Several conclusions may be drawn from this example. First, the program failures in both examples were largely due to inadequate comprehensive planning; second, poor planning may, in a sense, be more detrimental than no planning if the resultant program may ultimately fail and result in a reduction of the general level of services; and third, and perhaps most important for the present purposes, virtually the same planning related mistakes were made in both programs—programs separated by a twenty year time span. Thus, it would seem that individuals planning in the human services fields do not readily learn from previous mistakes in attempts to systematically plan for intervention in human problems.

The major difficulty which exists regarding comprehensive planning in the juvenile justice field is simply that such planning in any real sense is not taking place. The principal outcome of this lack of truly comprehensive planning may well be the chaotic situation which is readily apparent to an observer of the juvenile justice system. The net result of this chaotic situation, in turn, may be a major contributing factor to what appears to be an acceleration of youth crime.

The Meaning of Comprehensive Planning

Efforts in the juvenile justice system to conduct "comprehensive" planning often involve two types of errors. The first of these may be regarded as an error of exclusion, the second an error of inclusion. With regard to the first type of error, the juvenile justice system is usually viewed as consisting of law enforcement, proseuction and defense, courts, probation, corrections, and aftercare.[6] From a strictly definitional point of view, this is a realistic conception. However, from the point of view of comprehensive planning, it is somewhat incomplete. For planning purposes, the juvenile justice system should be conceptualized as additionally including those nonlegalistic agencies which have contact with significant numbers of delinquent or predelinquent youth, or which can provide supplementary services and programs which are not available through the usual juvenile justice agencies. The President's Commission on Law Enforcement and Administration of Justice notes the importance of joint planning involving both categories of agenices.[7] The most common nonlegalistic agencies include the schools, welfare departments, and mental health agencies. In addition, various specialized and unique agencies which exist in a given area should also be included in comprehensive planning efforts.

The inclusion in the planning process of all agencies which may potentially be effected by a given program can do much at the outset to reduce the probability of inter-agency conflict, the obstructionism of vested interests and similar factors which contribute significantly to program failure. In the actual process of implementation most delinquency prevention and rehabilitation programs require a considerable degree of support and cooperation from a variety of agencies. Such support can best be attained through initial coordinated planning efforts involving all affected agencies.[8]

The juvenile justice system, for purposes of comprehensive planning, should also be conceptualized as including the offender and his community.[9] The delinquent is obviously a most vital aspect of the system, and since he cannot be realistically separated from his community, planners must involve these factors in their considerations.

The second type of error, that of inclusion, is actually a geographical problem. All too often "comprehensive" is translated into system-wide planning where system is taken to mean the juvenile justice system of an entire state. Thus there occurs proliferation of State Planning Agencies and state plans to combat and prevent delinquency. The concept of state level planning per se is desirable and necessary, as long as it is not carried to the extreme.

The juvenile justice system of a given state can be conceived of as a relatively closed geographical system. Nonetheless, this system is made up of numerous geographical subsystems; regions, counties, cities. The current emphasis on state level planning should not preclude or discourage comprehensive planning in these various subsystems of the state. Obviously such efforts must be coordinated with state level agencies and organizations, but at the same time the state agencies should encourage regional and local planning efforts. Quite frequently local problems can best be handled at the local level with comprehensive planning involving all relevant agencies in the given geographical subsystem. In brief, state level planning should not preclude comprehensive planning efforts at lower levels; on the contrary, such efforts should meet with encouragement, cooperation, and assistance from the state.

Elements of Comprehensive Planning

Any comprehensive planning effort, whether at the state, regional, or local level, should include a number of aspects. Some of these aspects should be included since they are necessary to the planning effort per se, others because they will assist in reducing the potential for inter-agency conflict and in facilitating the implementation of programs and procedures which emerge from the planning process.

Resource Assessment

Any comprehensive planning effort should give immediate attention to the assessment of available resources to deal with the problem of delinquency. This should include all potential contributing agencies within the designated geographical area. A model for such resource assessment has been developed and applied at both state and regional levels.[10] The identification of resources is necessary to specify overlap and redundancies in services and to provide a basis for any reorganization of existing services and reallocation of resources.

Need Assessment

Attention should be directed toward identifying existing needs or demands for services. This should include needs perceived by the planning organization and also needs perceived by the relevant agencies. The previously mentiond model is useful in need as well as resource assessment. Comparisons of current resources and needs can enable the immediate identification of gaps in services. Several sources are available to assist in this process.[11] The comparison of resources and needs is also important in the setting of priorities for action. Most often establishment of priorities is unique to the particular location in which the planning efforts are taking place.

Need Projection

Beside identifying current needs, comprehensive planning must make an effort to project future needs and demands for services. Sigurdson, Carter, and McEachern have provided a detailed discussion of the importance of such projections and also suggestions as to how they may be developed and utilized.[12] Cartwright has discussed the adequacy of the prediction of delinquency rates based on population projections and current rates.[13] The anticipation of future needs, both in terms of quantity and type, is one of the most important aspects of any comprehensive planning effort and should be given considerable emphasis.

Agency Involvement

All agencies which may potentially be affected by any outcome of the planning effort should be involved in the actual planning process. This will assist in reducing inter-agency conflict and increasing multi-agency support for new or changed programs and procedures which may result from planning. An important basis for agency support of a given program seems to be beliefs regarding delinquency causation. Agency personnel are more likely to lend support to those programs which they consider most likely to alleviate the causes of delinquency. There appears to be considerable discrepancies in beliefs concerning delinquency causation among personnel from different agencies[14] as well as among personnel in different staff positions in a single agency.[15] Taking such attitudinal considerations into account during the planning process can be useful in several ways. First, it can aid in the identification of potential support or resistance to a proposed program. Second, it can indicate areas in which efforts at re-education, attitude change, etc., are likely to be necessary. Third, it can help in identifying specific sources of potential inter-agency conflict and lack of cooperation.

Citizen Involvement

Comprehensive planning efforts in juvenile justice should include participation by representatives of a variety of citizen groups.[16] The "power structure" of a community should be represented since this demonstrates a high probability that resulting programs will be able to continue after initial funds are gone. This, in turn, increases the likelihood of obtaining initial funding.[17]

Members of a cross-section of the adult public should be represented in the planning process. This is important, again, because of the necessity for support for new or changed programs and procedures. Delinquency prevention and rehabilitation programs need public acceptance and support for their success. Such support is likely to be based to some extent on beliefs regarding delinquency causation. Considerable evidence suggests that there are wide variations across various segments of the public in such beliefs. Beliefs concerning the causation of crime and delinquency differ across socio-economic strata, among age groups and according to sex.[18] Knowledge of such differences permits the identification of sources of support and resistance to a given program and specific groups where re-education may be necessary. Views among the public concerning the appropriate handling of delinquents by the juvenile justice system also seem to vary according to socio-economic status and often are quite different from those held by representatives of the juvenile justice system.[19]

Members of a cross-section of the youth population of the given area should be represented in planning efforts. This can function to obtain support from a very vital component of the general public; support which is likely to vary according to beliefs regarding delinquency causation. Cross-sectional representation is, again, desirable because such beliefs appear to vary according to age, sex, and socio-economic level.[20] Also, the views which youth hold regarding delinquency causation are often quite different from those held by their parents.[21] Again, this permits the identification of sources of support and resistance.

The final segment of the public which must be considered is the delinquent himself. Individuals who are actually caught up in the juvenile justice system should be very much involved in the planning process. Their experiences can make an invaluable contribution to any planning efforts. Also there is some suggestion that they may have quite different views of crime and delinquency causation than the general public.[22] This is important because these views may, in many respects, be more valid than any others and may have clear programmatic implications.

In brief, citizen participation is a vital component in comprehensive juvenile justice planning. Such participation should include representation of the power structure of the community, a cross-section of the general adult and youth populations as well as "clients" of the juvenile justice system. Involvement of these groups can lend broad-based support to the planning process as well as permit the identification of potential points of conflict (both among citizens and between citizens and agencies) and areas where efforts in attitude change and re-education may be desirable or necessary.

System Rates and Models

Almost since the beginning emphasis on comprehensive planning in the juvenile justice system there has been a recognition of the potential usefulness of system rates in the planning process.[23] The use of system rates enables some evaluation of the current functioning of the juvenile justice system, provides a way to determine the impact on the total system of a change introduced in some subsystem, and provides the basis for system simulation. The desirability of evaluating current functioning and determining the effects of changes are obvious. Perhaps not so obvious, however, is the place of system simulation or modeling in comprehensive planning. In brief, computer simulations or models permit the planner to conduct a variety of "experiments" on the effects of changes in the system. In real life, such experiments could not be conducted because of financial limitations or because of the accompanying disruption of the on-going functioning of the existing system. For example, the impact of the development of a Youth Services Bureau on the juvenile justice system of a given county could be assessed, within certain limits, through simulation rather than through the expensive process of actually establishing a Bureau. Similarly, the effects of detaining only those youths who commit offenses which are apparent felonies could be determined without disrupting current detention practices. In the latter case, possible outcomes which could be determined from an adequate model include changes in detention home personnel, changes in police personnel and procedures, changes in probation personnel and practices, and changes over time in rates for various types of offenses. Such information is obviously invaluable in comprehensive planning.

A number of models of the overall criminal justice system as well as models specifically relevant to the police, courts and corrections have been developed and are currently in limited use.[24] The use of models to date is rather limited largely due to resistance among agency personnel, a lack of inter-agency cooperation, and a lack of ready availabilty (or availability in any form) of the necessary baseline data. Suggestions for the successful implementation of models have been made by Chaiken and his associates.[25]

Optimism regarding the use of models in the criminal and juvenile justice fields is based largely on their success in other areas. It is far from an established fact that models can be successfully employed as a tool in comprehensive planning in juvenile justice, although the potential definitely exists. A clear problem which is endemic in current modeling efforts, and which must be overcome before models can realize their potential, is the limited number of variables which are included in the models. Considerable evidence exists which indicates that decisions at various points in the juvenile and criminal justice systems are based on a variety of factors. These factors include various characteristics of the offender such as sex, race, prior record, and current activities.[26] Also important are source of referral, degree of progression through the system, and current family situation.[27] In addition, various characteristics of the personnel of the system also affect decisions which are made regarding a given offender.[28] These and similar variables must be included in any model of the juvenile justice system before such a model is complete enough to fulfill its potential usefulness in comprehensive planning. Such variables can be readily accommodated within the limitations of current technology. What is lacking is sound empirical evidence regarding the effects of these variables, in essence baseline data.

Two additional procedures, closely related to modeling, have been proposed as useful in comprehensive planning. Cost/benefit analysis or the more sophisticated Planning/Performance Budgeting System (PPBS) currently in use in many Federal agencies has been suggested as a method to evaluate intra-organizational operations after decisions have been made and to compare the utility of various programs.[29] The rather sophisticated statistical technique of path anlaysis has been utilized in an effort to understand the effects of defense counsel, initial charge and charge alteration at various stages in court processing of cases.[30] Both of these procedures appear to have a definite potential in comprehensive juvenile justice planning, but require considerable additional development, experimentation, and experience in their application to this area.

Evaluation

The final procedure vital to comprehensive planning efforts is evaluation. After a given program or procedure has been implemented as a part of a comprehensive plan, this is not, by any means, the end of the planning process. Comprehensive planning ideally involves the on-going monitoring of the various components of the plan and at some point an intensive evaluation of each component. Procedures for conducting such evaluations and utilizing results have been discussed in detail.[31] In general the evaluation process should be included as an integral aspect of the comprehensive planning process. Both planning and evaluation should be viewed as having the same overall goal, that of reducing delinquency.

Conclusions

Comprehensive planning is an absolute necessity in any serious effort to reduce crimes committed by youthful offenders. This is recognized by virtually all individuals involved in the juvenile justice system and much time, effort, and funds have been devoted to planning in recent years. In spite of these efforts, delinquent activities seem to be increasing both in terms of frequency and seriousness. A contributor to this increase and to the prevailing confused state of affairs in the juvenile justice system in general may well be the lack of truly comprehensive planning.

Efforts in planning, in order to be truly comprehensive, must avoid both the error of exclusion and the error of inclusion. That is, all agencies which may potentially be affected by the outcomes of the planning process must be involved in that process. Also, "comprehensive" should not be equated with a given state as a planning entity. Comprehensive plans need not be all inclusive in a geographical sense. Planning can and should be conducted at the local and regional as well as state level.

Any serious effort in the area of comprehensive planning must include certain elements. These are resource assessment, need assessment, need projection, agency involvement, citizen involvement, consideration of system models, and evaluation. Some of these elements are integral to the planning process per se, others are necessary for successful implementation of outcomes of the planning process. The consideration of these elements in any effort at comprehensive planning should do much to alleviate the present unsatisfactory state of affairs which exists within the juvenile justice system.

Discussion Questions

1. Discuss the meaning of *comprehensive* planning as it relates to the juvenile justice system.

2. Discuss how comprehensive planning could result in the reduction of juvenile crime.

3. Discuss the elements of comprehensive planning in juvenile justice.

4. Speculate on the potential of system simulation or modeling in comprehensive juvenile justice planning.

Notes

1. *Uniform Crime Reports*—1975, Table 32, p. 184.

2. Walter B. Miller, *Violence by Youth Gangs and Youth Groups as a Crime Problem in Major American Cities* (Washington, D.C.: U.S. Government Printing Office, 1975), pp. 75–76.

3. U.S. Department of Justice, *Criminal Victimization Surveys in Eight American Cities: A Comparison of 1971/72 and 1974/75 Findings* (Washington, D.C.: U.S. Government Printing Office, 1976), pp. 5–8; and U.S. Department of Justice, *Criminal Victimization Surveys in Chicago, Detroit, Los Angeles, New York, Philadelphia: A Comparison of 1972 and 1974 Findings* (Washington, D.C.: U.S. Government Printing Office, 1976), pp. 5–7.

4. Office of Juvenile Justice and Delinquency Prevention, *First Comprehensive Plan for Federal Juvenile Delinquency Programs* (Washington, D.C.: U.S. Department of Justice, 1976), p. 1.

5. Lincoln J. Fry and Jon Miller, "Responding to Skid Row Alcoholism: Self-Defeating Arrangements in an Innovative Treatment Program," *Social Problems,* 22 (1975): 675–688; and Walter B. Miller, "Inter-Institutional Conflict as a Major Impediment to Delinquency Prevention," in Rose Giallombardo (ed.), *Juvenile Delinquency: A Book of Readings* (New York: Wiley, 1966), pp. 559–565.

6. The President's Commission on Law Enforcement and Administration of Justice, *The Challenge of Crime in a Free Society* (Washington, D.C.: U.S. Government Printing Office, 1967), pp. 79–88.

7. Ibid., pp. 279–280.

8. Alfred J. Kahn, *Planning Community Services for Children in Trouble* (New York: Columbia University Press, 1963), pp. 477–478.

9. Malcolm W. Klein, Solomon Kobrin, Alex W. McEachern, and Herbert R. Sigurdson, "System Rates: An Approach to Comprehensive Criminal Justice Planning," *Crime and Delinquency,* 17 (1971): 355–372.

10. Goodrich Walton (ed.), *Child and Youth Services Planning Project Report* (Ft. Logan, Colorado: State of Colorado, 1968); and Nicholas A. Reuterman, Rosalie A. Cates, Joyce J. Ashpole, and Robert B. Tabaka, *Total Youth Services Planning Study Report* (Edwardsville, Illinois: Delinquency Study and Youth Development Center, Southern Illinois University, Edwardsville, 1971).

11. Law Enforcement Assistance Administration, *Correctional Planning and Resource Guide* (Washington, D.C.: U.S. Department of Justice, 1969), pp. 9–29; and Paul F. Lazarsfeld, William H. Sewell, and Harold L. Wilensky (eds.), *The Uses of Sociology* (New York: Basic Books, 1967), pp. 437–642.

12. Herbert R. Sigurdson, Robert M. Carter, and Alex W. McEachern, "Methodological Impediments to Comprehensive Criminal Justice Planning," *Criminology,* 9 (1971): 248–267.

13. Desmond S. Cartwright, "Forecasting 1970 Delinquency from 1967 Data," *Criminology,* 11 (1973): 405–416.

14. William Dienstein, "Inter-Professional Differences in Beliefs about the Etiology of Juvenile Delinquency," *Journal of Criminal Law and Criminology,* 51 (1960): 79–80; and Nicholas A. Reuterman and Desmond S. Cartwright, "Practitioners' Views of Delinquency Causation: A Consideration in Comprehensive Juvenile Justice Planning," *Criminal Justice and Behavior,* 3 (1976): 67–84.

15. Doug Knight, *Delinquency Causes and Remedies: The Working Assumptions of the California Youth Authority Staff* (Sacramento, California: California Youth Authority, 1972), pp. 19–27.

16. William Clifford, *Planning Crime Prevention* (Lexington, Massachusetts: D.C. Heath, 1976) pp. 91–92; Carl W. Hamm, "Pluralistic Planning within the Criminal Justice System," *Crime and Delinquency,* 16 (1970): 393–402; and Herbert S. Miller, "The Citizen's Role in Changing the Criminal Justice System," *Crime and Delinquency,* 19 (1973): 343–353.

17. Miller, pp. 343–353.

18. C. Banks, E. Maloney, and H.D. Willcock, "Public Attitudes to Crime and the Penal System," *British Journal of Criminology,* 15 (1975): 228–240; David

Duffee and R. Richard Ritti, "Correctional Policy and Public Values," *Criminology,* 14 (1977): 449–460; Michael J. Hindelang, *Public Opinion Regarding Crime, Criminal Justice and Related Topics* (Washington, D.C.: U.S. Government Printing Office, 1975), pp. 19–20; and Nicholas A. Reuterman, "The Publics' Views of Deliquency Causation: A Consideration in Juvenile Justice Planning," *Juvenile & Family Court Journal,* 29 (1978): 39–45.

19. William P. Lentz, "Social Status and Attitudes Toward Delinquency Control," *Crime and Delinquency,* 3 (1966): 147–154; and William P. Lentz, "Research Note: Attitudinal Barriers to Delinquency Control," *Criminology,* 7 (1969) 68–75.

20. Nicholas A. Reuterman and Michael Durbin, "Youth Views of Delinquency Causation: A Consideration in Comprehensive Juvenile Justice Planning," *Juvenile and Family Court Journal,* 30 (1979): 41–46.

21. Nicholas A. Reuterman and Michael Durbin, *Inter-Generational Differences in Beliefs Regarding Delinquency Causation.* (Edwardsville, Ill.: Delinquency Study and Youth Development Center, Southern Illinois University, Edwardsville, Ill., 1977) pp. 12–13.

22. Frank O. Mathis and Martin D. Rayman, "The Ins and Outs of Crime and Corrections," *Criminology,* 10 (1972): 366–372.

23. Frederick W. Howlett and Hunter Hurst, "A Systems Approach to Comprehensive Criminal Justice Planning," *Crime and Delinquency,* 17 (1971): 345–354; and, Klein, Kobrin, McEachern and Sigurdson, pp. 355–372.

24. J. Chaiken, T. Crabill, L. Holliday, D. Jaquette, M. Lawless, and E. Quade, *Criminal Justice Models: An Overview* (Washington, D.C.: U.S. Government Printing Office, 1976), pp. 20–113; and Jacqueline Coben, Kenneth Fields, Michael Lettre, Richard Strafford, and Claire Walker, "Implementation of the Justice Planning Agency," *Journal of Research in Crime and Delinquency,* 10 (1973): 117–131.

25. *Ibid.* pp. 114–127.

26. Lawrence E. Cohen, *Delinquency Dispositions: An Empirical Analysis of Processing Decisions in Three Juvenile Courts* (Washington, D.C.: U.S. Government Printing Office, 1975), pp. 51–54; and Lawrence E. Cohen, *Pre-Adjudicatory Detention in Three Juvenile Courts: An Empirical Analysis of the Factors Related to Detention Decision Outcomes* (Washington, D.C.: U.S. Government Printing Office, 1975) pp. 38–43.

27. *Ibid.* pp. 51–54, 38–43.

28. Don M. Gottfredson and Gary D. Gottfredson, "Decision-Maker Attitudes and Juvenile Detention," *Journal of Research in Crime and Delinquency,* 6 (1969): 177–183; and, Nigel Lemon, "Training, Personality and Attitude as Determinants of Magistrates' Sentencing," *British Journal of Criminology,* 14 (1974): 34–48.

29. John E. Tropman and Karl H. Gohlke, "Cost/Benefit Analysis: Toward Comprehensive Planning in the Criminal Justice System," *Crime and Delinquency,* 19 (1973): 315–322.

30. John Hagan, "Parameters of Criminal Prosecution: An Application of Path Analysis to a Problem of Criminal Justice," *Journal of Criminal Law and Criminology,* 65 (1974): 536–544.

31. Law Enforcement Assistance Administration, "The National Conference on

Criminal Justice Evaluation: Abstracts of Presentations" (Papers read at the National Conference on Criminal Justice Evaluation, Washington, D.C., Feb. 1977); and, Donald R. Wridman, John D. Waller, Dona MacNeil, Francine L. Tolson, and Joseph S. Wholey, *Intensive Evaluation for Criminal Justice Planning Agencies* (Washington, D.C.: U.S. Government Printing Office, 1975), pp. 16–22.

The Female Delinquent: A Casualty of The Women's Liberation Movement?

Peggy C. Giordano

Stephen A. Cernkovich

Introduction

A WELL KNOWN REGULARITY in any given society is that succeeding generations of adults evidence considerable anxiety over the involvement of their youth in illegal activities. For the most part this concern traditionally has been generated by the continually increasing rates of male delinquency. As a result, most research on the delinquency problem, as well as treatment and prevention programs, has been focused on the male delinquent. More recently, however, as a result of the apparently large increases in illegal behavior on the part of women, female delinquency has become the focus of mass media and social scientific analyses of the crime problem. As if to make up for lost time, criminologists have begun a flurry of research efforts directed at studying the female offender. In particular, there is an increased awareness of the relative lack of reliable information on the female delinquent, as well as a realization that most explanatory models have been restricted to the male offender. Perhaps the most hotly debated issue, and one important reason for the increased focus on female crime and delinquency, centers around answering a number of related questions: Has there been a real increase in females' involvement in delinquent activity? If so, what is the nature of this increase—have females moved beyond involvement in relatively specific, less serious kinds of offenses, to participation in what traditionally have been considered to be "masculine crimes?" What effect, if any, has the "women's liberation movement" had on the apparently changing patterns of female delinquency? It is this last issue, in particular, which has fascinated the public consciousness.

There is no doubt that the women's movement has resulted in significant changes in sex role related attitudes and behavior. Furthermore, it is quite reasonable to assume that such changes are having an important impact on the behavior and attitudes of adolescent girls. While this is generally assumed to be the case, little is known about the way in which a broad social movement such as women's liberation actually filters down to the point where the everyday behavior and attitudes of adolescents are affected, particularly in ways which produce deviant outcomes. What seems to be at issue here, then, is the manner in which liberation affects delinquency, if it has any effect at all. Popular accounts[1] typically suggest a *direct* relationship between liberation and female crime—and imply that these "new female deviants" are themselves at least partly motivated by liberated or political concerns. A picture is presented of a kind of new competitive spirit, where females are no longer willing to accept the fact that males have traditionally gotten a bigger share of the illegal action.

It is our contention however, that this conception of the relationship between liberation and crime is oversimplified and leaves us with a distorted picture of the majority of girls who are actually involved in illegal activity. It is quite probable that these girls may not be at all "liberated" in the political sense, that they may not act out of a new found sense of elevated aspirations, or competition with their male counterparts. Rather, we would suggest that the various concerns of the liberation movement have caused much more mundane changes in the everyday lives of females, and these in turn have created the conditions under which delinquent activities become more probable.

This paper will be concerned with the effect of the liberation movement on increasing levels of female delinquency. Before examining this issue, however, it is necessary to understand something about recent changes in the extent and nature of female involvement in delinquent activities.

Changing Patterns of Female Delinquency

It has been suggested historically that males are much more likely than females to commit delinquent acts, and that when females are involved, their misconduct tends to be significantly less serious than that of their male counterparts. As for the kinds of crimes committed by females, the overriding belief is that girls' involvement is restricted to a limited number of specific offenses. At least one researcher[2] even goes so far as to argue that the crimes for which women are arrested and convicted have been much the same for hundreds of years. Generally, most research has indicated that the offenses females most often commit, and the ones for which they are most often arrested, referred to court, convicted and incarcerated are incorrigibility, various sexual offenses such as prostitution, running away from home, truancy, and shoplifting.[3] It appears that the general consensus in the professional and popular literature is that female delinquency is largely limited to these five basic categories of offenses. By comparison, female involvement in such deviant activities as armed robbery, assault, murder, and other serious offenses is thought to be relatively infrequent, or at least restricted to a very small population of female offenders with serious emotional or personality disorders. Further, much of this literature has tended to view the "typical" female delinquent as being characterized by a relatively poor self-image, feelings of loneliness, dependency, inferiority, and insecurity, emotional selfishness, a disturbed or unhappy family environment, abusive or neglectful parents, a general lack of love and affection, with a lack of sound discipline from the mother and a lack of affection from the father in particular.[4] In general, then, it has been maintained that female offenders typically suffer from a lack of sound, warm interpersonal relationships—and this is viewed as the root cause of their involvement in delinquency. Delinquent girls, when compared to their male counterparts, are found to more often evidence school failure, to be less well adjusted, less affected by status frustration, and more likely to come from broken or tension ridden homes.[5] Regarding group and friendship patterns, the traditional image has been that females are infrequently involved in gang structures, and that when they are they tend to play subordinate roles, are less active than the male members, are often used as decoys or to carry weapons for the boys, are usually sexually involved with male members, have relatively low status in the group, and are, in general, mere ornaments or accomplices.[6]

The relatively infrequent and assumed sexual or "moral" character of female misbehavior has resulted in the development of two entirely different sets of explanations for male and female delinquency involvement. Male delinquency is thought to be the result of such factors as a reaction to blocked educational and occupational opportunities, peer group pressure, and attempts to establish or prove one's masculinity, while female delinquency is most often explained within a psychological or personal problems framework; that is, the view that female delinquency is a function of such factors as loneliness, tension ridden homes, and poor self-concepts. An overriding theme in the literature is the "natural" or "inherent" difference between males and females (notably, females "lack of aggressive traits") which explain the lower crime rates for women. Where female delinquency or criminality does occur, then, it has largely been explained as representing some sort of "perversion or rebellion against their natural female roles."[7] The bulk of the literature, then, has perpetuated the notion that personal maladjustments characterize the female delinquent; she either must have a psychological problem, be unable to adequately perform her proper sex role, or suffer from the ill effects of a bad home life. More recently, however, the rather large increases in the female delinquency rates makes it more difficult to account for all female crime and delinquency in such purely psychological terms.

An indication of the increase in females' involvement in crime as well as in the versatility/seriousness of their activity, is provided by recent juvenile and adult arrest records. For example, between 1960 and 1975 the arrest rate for females under 18 years of age increased 254 percent for all offenses, 504 percent for violent crimes, and 420 percent for property crimes. This contrasts with increases of 125 percent, 278 percent, and 104 percent respectively for males in the same age bracket.[8] While females are not as yet anywhere near approaching the overall rate of males, such figures obviously indicate that the arrest rate for females is increasing at a much faster pace than that of males. It is also interesting to note that females are becoming much more *versatile* in their delinquency involvement than the various early formulations would indicate. Rather than restricting involvement to the traditional offenses of running away, truancy, prostitution, incorrigibility, and shoplifting, these statistics indicate significant female participation in such offenses as robbery (647 percent), aggravated assault (438 percent), and burglary (327 percent)[9] — offenses which were traditionally considered to be the province of the male offender. Recent studies[10] have found, as is usually the case, a greater *frequency* of delinquent acts on the part of males, but more importantly, that the *patterns* of delinquent conduct are becoming very similar for males and females — that it, males and females are beginning to commit the same kinds of offenses, although males tend to commit them more frequently. Other research[11] suggests that females are now committing more violent crimes than ever before in history. It also appears that when females are involved in crime they are now *active participants,* whereas previously their behavior was restricted to "traditional" areas of female misbehavior (such as prostitution or shoplifting), or as mere accomplices to males. Females are simply becoming more active members of male gangs, and are even beginning to form their own gangs, rather than being satisfied with their traditional role as ornamental appendages to male gangs.[12]

On the basis of this emerging picture of the "new female delinquent," criminologists and others interested in the delinquency problem, have come to recognize the inadequacy of the traditional "personal problems" explanatory framework in accounting for the increased frequency, seriousness, and versatility of female involvement in illegal behavior. As a result, there has been a determined search for a viable explanation which is capable of accounting for these changing patterns of female delinquency. Dominant among these explanations, and the one which has generated the greatest amount of professional and public discussion, is the notion that the women's liberation movement is somehow responsible for "producing" the "new female delinquent."

Liberation and Female Delinquency

Perhaps the appeal of "liberation" as a ready explanation of the changing patterns of female delinquency stems from the fact that delinquency rates for females began their dramatic increase at about the same time the current women's equal rights movement began to gain support and momentum. To many this juxtaposition is not just mere coincidence; rather, it is argued that the liberation movement is directly responsible for the increased frequency and versatility of female misconduct.

Adler,[13] the dominant proponent of this position, gives the impression that increases in criminality and delinquency are simply part of the price society must pay for greater involvement by females at all levels of the society. Just as women are becoming more integrated into the educational, occupational, and political structures of society, so too are they becoming more integrated into the worlds of crime and delinquency.

> In both hidden delinquency and overt deviancy, girls of all classes have departed from previously prescribed sex role behavior for the same reason that their sisters are choosing careers over domesticity or sexual experience over chastity.[14]

From such a perspective it is argued that teen-aged girls have become increasingly dissatisfied with traditional female roles, and have begun to explore new behavioral options. This is obvious in the occupational and educational worlds where many females are no longer satisfied with goals of housewife and mother alone. But this is also equally applicable in the worlds of crime and delinquency. It is this willingness, or perhaps, necessity, to explore new, not well understood roles, which Adler says often leads to delinquency.[15] While Adler does not consistently suggest that young girls who become involved in delinquency are necessarily aligned with the "movement" itself, the causal connection appears quite direct. For example, women who used to be satisfied with a petty theft are now beginning to ask themselves why they shouldn't get a bigger piece of the action—"If I can steal radios, why not T.V.'s?"[16] While the kind of motivation suggested by such a statement appears to be largely financial, Adler casts the argument from a strictly feminist, ideological perspective:

> Like her legitimate-based sister, the female criminal knows too much to pretend or return to her former role as a second rate criminal confined to 'feminine' crimes such as shoplifting and prostitution. She has had a taste of financial victory. In some cases, she has had a taste of blood. Her appetite however, appears to be only whetted.[17]

In general then, Adler's thesis suggests that just as "establishment women" are demanding and achieving integration within the heretofore male dominated educational, occupational, and power structures, so too are female delinquents reaching for and attaining a new level of integration within male delinquent subcultures, and are engaging in illegal activities which in the past were dominated by males.[18] In this regard, Adler clearly suggests that many female delinquents are beginning to adopt male attitudes and behavior patterns — that there is a spirit of competitiveness for many girls to be as tough and as "cool" as their male counterparts. The impression given is that as teen-aged girls become more "male-like" in behavior and attitude, they automatically become more delinquent.[19]

Adler argues[20] that this demonstrable convergence of sex-roles (that males and females are becoming more alike in terms of values, attitudes, and behavior) has not only freed the contemporary female from many traditional restraints, but also has *forced* her to compete more actively (with boys as well as with other girls) on academic, occupational, and criminal levels. The traditional, and somewhat stereotypic, female characteristics of passivity and virtue are no longer automatically rewarding or status-conferring. Rather, according to Adler, females are now being forced to compete on the same level with males according to the male rules of the game. The various pressures associated with the sex-role convergence simply make girls more vulnerable to delinquency — the traditional protective influence of the family has yielded to the necessity of the female to prove herself in the world. The role conflict and ambiguity associated with these recent role changes, Adler argues, creates complex identity problems for the female — problems that are much more intense for the female than for the male. The upshot of Adler's thesis is that the contemporary female's "departure from the safety of traditional female roles and the testing of uncertain alternative roles"[21] compounds the normal identity problems of adolescence and creates intense pressures to adopt traditional male-related behavior patterns — including delinquent ones — as a means of dealing with these problems. The implication is that delinquency provides an alternative means of achieving status, or a means of striking back at what is viewed as an unfair system.

Rather than representing a response to increased role conflicts, competitiveness with men, or any kind of overt politicization, we would argue that female crime emerges as a normal outcome of broadly based and small scale changes which themselves may have been brought about by the movement. We would emphasize that these effects, then, are much more indirect, complex than is depicted in these popular accounts, and importantly, that it is more correct to conceive of these girls as being *recipients* of such changing societal structures rather than themselves being the catalysts of these changes. Current models which suggest a direct relationship between liberation and crime fail to give us a complete understanding of the actual *process* through which these changes act in ways that influence girls in a delinquent direction.

The Process of Becoming Delinquent

One of the central tenets of most traditional theories of juvenile delinquency revolves around the fact that the *opportunity* to engage in illegal activities is not evenly distributed across the population: that is, while some individuals frequently find themselves in situations conducive to misbehavior of various kinds, others are most often in a social environment which is conducive to conformity. While such a notion has received considerable attention in the explanation of male delinquency,[22] scant consideration has been paid to the manner in which it contributes to increased levels of female delinquency. This is unfortunate in that such a factor seems quite useful in understanding females' traditionally low level of involvement in deviance, as well as the recent increases in their delinquency rates. Importantly, such a perspective also allows a specification of one of the ways in which the liberation movement is having a concrete effect on the everyday behavior of adolescent females. Simon[23] has utilized the notion of changing opportunity structures in an analysis of adult female criminality.

In an examination of current arrest statistics, she found the largest percentage increases for females in such crimes as larceny, fraud, embezzlement, and forgery. She attributed this, in large part, to the fact that women are now filling jobs which were formerly accessible primarily to males—that many women are now holding white-collar positions and thus have the opportunity to commit offenses typically associated with such positions. For example, to commit the crime of embezzlement one must first be in a position of having access to large amounts of money. To the extent that women are increasingly finding themselves in such occupations, we would expect their rate of involvement in the crime of embezzlement to increase. This indeed is what appears to be happening.

Such a model seems to be a reasonable explanation of *adult* female criminality. As women begin filling certain occupational roles we would expect their participation in crimes traditionally associated with these roles to increase. The dramatic increase in female crime at the *juvenile* level, however, is not as easily explained, since these girls have yet to enter the labor force. However, the argument can be fruitfully extended to an understanding of increasing levels of delinquency involvement by adolescents as well.

There has classically existed, even within the same family, more protection and restrictions on the behavior of young girls than is the case for boys. For example, while the young son was often allowed to use dad's car, to stay out until midnight, his sister was often simultaneously denied use of the car, had a curfew of ten o'clock, and in general, had many more restrictions on her movement. In such a situation, it should not be surprising that the son is more likely than the daughter to get into trouble with the law; he simply has more opportunity to do so—the fact that he has use of the car creates the possibility that he will violate certain driving regulations; similarly, the fact that he can stay out later than his sister gives him more time to get into trouble, either intentionally or accidentally. None of this, by any means, insures that he will violate the law. The point is that he has more opportunity than his sister to do so.

This classical protective pattern regarding the treatment of females has traditionally included more attention by all social institutions—the school, family, church—in guiding the moral and social life of the adolescent female, while the boy is expected, even encouraged, to sow a few wild oats. We would argue that recent social changes in sex role related attitudes and behavior has altered this traditional pattern. Sepcifically, it is our contention that such changes have caused a relaxing of the rather universal protection and sheltering of females, which, in turn, may have created new opportunities for them to engage in various kinds of delinquent activity. For example, parents, teachers and others may be attempting to equalize expectations and standards of judgment for males and females; that is, an orientation which dictates that if boys are allowed to do certain things, to go to certain places, girls should be given similar freedom of action. If this is indeed happening, and we think it clearly is, then many young females are now being exposed to new opportunities—many of which can lead to illegal behavior. For example, if the daughter now has an equal access to the family car, she too will find herself in more situations conducive to delinquency (as was her heretofore freer brother). These new opportunities are particularly likely to affect forms of delinquency which are highly situational in nature, such as drinking, drug use, or vandalism.

This sort of orientation even allows for a reinterpretation of previous research findings which suggest an important relationship between broken homes and female delinquency. The traditional argument has been that the broken home creates "deep emotional problems" for the young female, often resulting in delinquency as a response, adaptation, or reflection of such problems. While such a situation may indeed create all sorts of personal problems, we would suggest that the lack of a united two parent front (the broken home) to enforce rules, to watch over the daughter may result not *necessarily* in emotional problems, but simply in greater freedom and opportunity to commit delinquent acts. For example, there is some evidence[24] suggesting that those adolescents whose parents allowed them every evening out were likely to engage in delinquency than those who were not allowed many evenings out and who go home immediately after school.

In general then, we would suggest that the liberation movement may have created new opportunities for young females to be in situations in which delinquency is likely to occur. It is in this sense, we would suggest, that they are more correctly seen as the recipients of liberation-generated changes in the classical protective pattern, rather than ideological converts to the movement, committing illegal acts on the basis of political concerns. Additionally, we should reiterate here that we are not suggesting that increased freedom or new opportunities *cause* female delinquency. Rather, they simply free the individual from customary controls and allow her greater opportunities to be in situations where delinquent acts may be more likely to occur. It is once the individual has the opportunity to be in such situations that other factors begin operating to produce illegal behavior. Perhaps the most important of these other factors is group support and encouragement for delinquent conduct. Together with increased opportunity, these changes in the peer group are operating to produce the higher levels of female delinquency involvement.

As we have suggested previously, one must have the opportunity to engage in delinquency for such behavior to become a patterned regularity. In this sense, we view delinquency as being highly situational. Most adolescents engage in delinquency not so much because they are driven or forced into it, but rather because they often find themselves in situations which (1) weaken the customary controls on behavior, and (2) create group cultures which define delinquency as an appropriate, or even expected, behavioral expression.[25] The women's movement is important in this process to the extent that it has contributed to the weakening of traditional controls, as well as to changes in patterns of association and group support for various kinds of behavior.

Unfortunately, we know very little at present about the social world of adolescent females, and, more importantly, in what kind of social context the greatest levels of delinquency involvement are likely to occur. Nonetheless, it is important to isolate the processes through which "acceptable" kinds of social activity spill over into behavior which exceed legal boundaries. For example, what conditions have to be present for a relatively calm teen-age party to evolve into a liquor-drinking, marijuana-smoking event, characterized by vandalism and other illegal activities? It is clear that in order for many adolescent girls to engage in serious delinquent acts, they have had to move away from some aspects of the "traditional" female role. The classical definition of femininity simply would not permit these forms of behavior. However, the image of the "new," "liberated" female offender who is attempting to prove that she can do anything her male counterpart can do, or who is lashing out against her male oppressors simply is not an accurate reflection of the modern female delinquent. Rather, most contemporary female delinquents appear to be quite traditional in terms of sex role attitudes and values. Nonetheless, it is clear that they are receiving both support and encouragement from their peers, male and female, for engaging in delinquent activities.[26] Thus, while many of these girls appear to be liberated on a *behavioral* level (in that they are engaging in many forms of behavior traditionally regarded as patently "masculine") they are not liberated in any *ideological* sense.

The notion of group support for delinquency has received much attention in the delinquency literature. The generalized image, developed primarily on the basis of empirical studies of male delinquents, is that individuals derive some sort of moral support from the group which sanctions their delinquency. Regardless of personal values and attitudes, it is assumed that there is considerable conformity to peer expectations of appropriate, "cool" behavior. Most of the available evidence suggests that this is indeed the case for females as well as for males. Some of this research has indicated that while many female delinquents are not ideologically liberated as such, they do receive a great deal of peer support for engaging in non-traditional, typically masculine forms of delinquency. This is particularly evident for certain kinds of aggressive actions, such as fighting and the use of weapons. Many of these girls take great pride in discussing their membership in tough gangs, and their use of knives and other weapons.[27] Whether they may have been exaggerating their own involvement in such gangs, or their own use of various weapons is not as important as the fact that it was acceptable and considered "cool" by their various friends. Other evidence suggests that while definitions of the acceptability of certain kinds of illegal actions is likely to come from other girls, the delinquency of many girls is nevertheless tied to their friendships with males. Rather than competing with them, however, it is more likely that there is simply a greater probability of learning delinquent values/techniques from boys who have a longer history, tradition of delinquent involvement.

Changes in girls' perception of what is acceptable behavior for females are related, then, to both (1) increased opportunities and freedom to engage in other than traditional patterns of feminine behavior, and to (2) changing definitions made by the peer group about what constitutes "cool" behavior. Coleman[28] has presented the most popular and classic conception of this in his contention that the greatest "status enhancer" for young females is dating the "right boys." He suggests that while males have the "athletic hero," and to a somewhat lesser extent, the "good student" role as possible sources of status, girls have relatively little in the way of alternatives to the "popularity with-the-opposite-sex" role. Traditionally, this pattern had important consequences in severely restricting the limits of what was proper and acceptable behavior for girls, and was stressed within the peer group (e.g., pressures from friends to "be feminine," to date the "right" boys, etc.) as well as from without (e.g., parental admonitions, restrictions on inappropriate behavior, etc.). Thus, traditionally, there was neither the *opportunity* nor the *encouragement* and *support* to engage in what have been considered to be masculine forms of behavior. It is not surprising then, that in the past females' rates of participation in such behaviors as assault, burglary, robbery, and other "masculine offenses" were quite low. By the same token, participation in shoplifting, prostitution, and other typically "feminine offenses" was much more prevalent—mainly because there was both the opportunity to commit such offenses, and some, albeit limited, support for such behavior.

Summary

It is quite obvious that the traditional patterns of female delinquency have undergone major change. The limits of what constitutes acceptable feminine behavior are changing, permitting a wider range of behavioral alternatives for females—delinquent as well as non-delinquent. As we have attempted to show, this is not necessarily the result of young girls being liberated in an ideological, political sense. Rather, parents, teachers, and others are beginning to approve, or at least to acquiesce to a wider range of what constitutes acceptable behavior for females, to provide females with the same opportunities and freedom offered to males. This, of course, does not, as we have previously discussed, *cause* delinquency, but it certainly places many adolescent females in situations where they are subjected to the same pressures experienced by males. As such, we would expect the behavior of males and females to begin to converge, in both the delinquent and non-delinquent case. This indeed is what appears to be happening, although it would be a mistake to say that girls are engaging in as much delinquency as are males. Although the *patterns* of involvement are becoming more similar, the majority of all delinquent acts continues to be committed by males.

In addition to increased opportunities to engage in a wider range of behavior, the female peer subculture itself is beginning to tolerate, and even encourage and reward more aggressive, traditionally male kinds of behavior—again, both delinquent and non-delinquent. This has had the effect of broadening the range of acceptable behavior for females. While the liberation movement may have had a part in effecting these changes, the beneficiaries of the changes need not be liberated themselves. In other words, we would make an important distinction between liberation as a *social* phenomenon, and *personal* liberation. While liberation, as a social movement, may have importantly effected increased behavioral oppor- tunities and peer support/encouragement for heretofore unacceptable behavior, individuals who find themselves the recipients of these new opportunities and peer support need not themselves be personally liberated. In fact, they may be quite traditional in terms of their sex-role attitudes and values, as we have attempted to argue. The point is that there need not *necessarily* be any direct relationship between liberated attitudes and liberated behavior. While there may be some female delinquents who are engaging in illegal activities out of liberated, political motives, it is our contention that most are not—rather their enactment of traditionally masculine forms of behavior, delinquent and otherwise, is largely indepen- dent of their personal beliefs and attitudes regarding the liberation move- ment. It is in this sense that we feel the relationship between liberation and delinquency has been oversimplified in existing popular and professional accounts—in not recognizing the complexity of the relationship, in confus- ing personal liberation with liberation as a social movement, and in mistak- enly stressing a direct causal connection between personal liberation and increased female delinquency involvement.

There is a clear need to bring the study of female delinquency up to date with the theoretical and empirical work which has continued to focus on males. Recent increases in arrests for females suggest wider levels of involve- ment than can be explained within the traditional psychological or "personal problems" framework. We have argued that it is essential to concentrate on the *social context* in which delinquent acts occur. Even the most basic kinds of descriptive data are lacking—such as whether females' involvement typically is characterized by a dependence on male initiative, or whether they are engaging in delinquent acts largely with same-sex peers. Beyond this "how much" and "what kind" data, there is a need to study the *process* through which delinquent acts and situations arise. We have outlined some variables which we consider to have an important impact. It is obviously quite difficult to "get at" the *meaning* of these sorts of factors (e.g., group pressures, friendship patterns, etc.). However, this should not preclude dealing with these more qualitiative or subjective aspects of delinquents' social experiences.

While the effects of "womens' liberation" is currently a popular explana- tion for the increased frequency and versatility of female delinquency, there has been no real attempt to delineate the *specific* manner in which changes in female roles may have had an effect on patterns of delinquency involvement. It is doubtful that such changes have had the direct impact often suggested in the current literature. Rather, we have suggested that the effects have been much more indirect; that is, the changing opportunities, friendship patterns, and definitions of what is acceptable behavior for girls, which have resulted partly from the broader societal sex role changes, may themselves create the social context within which female participation in delinquent activities is more likely to occur. It is in these specific areas that research is needed to clarify the processes through which such changes affect the frequency of girls' participation in crime and the versatility of that involvement.

Discussion Questions

1. Compare and contrast males and females in terms of the nature and extent of their delinquency involvement. Is there any evidence to indicate that traditional sex differences in delinquent behavior are beginning to disappear?

2. Discuss the manner in which some theorists have suggested that changing sex roles ("women's liberation") has *directly* caused an increase in the extent of female delinquency as well as a change in the type of delinquent activities in which females engage.

3. In what ways has the presumed direct relationship between women's liberation and female delinquency been oversimplified in the popular and professional literature?

4. Discuss the manner in which the authors' suggest that changing sex roles may *indirectly*, by affecting opportunities and peer group expectations, contribute to female delinquency involvement.

Notes

Order of authorship is arbitrary and was randomly determined. The study from which this article is derived was supported by PHS Research Grant No. 29095-01, National Institute of Mental Health (Center for Studies of Crime and Delinquency).

1. See, for example, "Now, The Violent Woman," *Newsweek,* October 6 (1975): 6.

2. Ann D. Smith, *Women in Prison* (London: Stevens and Sons, Ltd., 1962).

3. Clyde B. Vedder, *The Juvenile Offender* (New York: Doubleday, 1954); Gordon H. Barker and William T. Adams, "Comparison of the Delinquencies of Boys and Girls," *Journal of Criminal Law, Criminology, and Police Science,* 53 (1962): 470–475; Charles O'Reilly, Frank Cizon, John Flanagan, and Steven Pflanczer, "Sentenced Women in a County Jail," *American Journal of Corrections,* 30 (1968): 23–25; Lois G. Forer, *No One Will Listen—How Our Legal System Brutalizes the Youthful Poor* (New York: The John Day Company, 1970); Clyde B. Vedder and Dora B. Somerville, *The Delinquent Girl* (Springfield: Charles C. Thomas, 1970); Meda Chesney-Lind, "Judicial Enforcement and the Female Sex Role," *Issues in Criminology,* 8 (1973): 51–69; Walter B. Miller, "The Molls," *Society,* 11 (1973): 32–35; Freda Adler, *Sisters in Crime,* (New York: McGraw-Hill, 1975); Susan K. Datesman, Frank R. Scarpitti, and Richard M. Stephenson, "Female Delinquency: An Application of Self and Opportunity Theories," *Journal of Research in Crime and Delinquency,* 12: 197–123.

4. Leontine R. Young, "Delinquency from the Child's Viewpoint," *The Juvenile Offender,* Clyde B. Vedder, ed. (New York: Doubleday, 1954): 62–68; Houston Brummit, "Observation on Drug Addicts in a House of Detention for Women," *Corrective Psychiatry and Journal of Social Therapy,* 9 (1963): 62–70; Bertha J. Payak, "Understanding the Female Offender," *Federal Probation,* 27 (1963): 7–12; Ruth Rittenhouse, "A Theory and Comparison of Male and Female Delinquency" (Unpublished Ph.D. Dissertation, University of Michigan, 1963); Ames Robey, Richard A. Rosewald, John Snell, and Rita Lee, "The Runaway Girl: A Reaction to Family Stress," *American Journal of Orthopsychiatry,* 34 (1964): 762–767; Harry Bluestone, Edward O'Malley, and Syndey Connell, "Homosexuals in Prison," *Corrective Psychiatry and Journal of Social Therapy,* 12 (1966): 13–24; Gisela Knopka, *The Adolescent Girl in Conflict* (Englewood Cliffs: Prentice-Hall, 1966); Wayne C. Richard, Catherine G. Mates, and Laura Whitten, "Personality Traits and Attitudes of Adolescent Girls with Behavior Disorders," *Corrective Psychiatry and Journal of Social Therapy,* 15 (1969): 34–44; Severin-Carlos Versele, "A Study of Female Shoplifters in Department Stores," *International Criminal Police Review,* 24 (1969); 66–70; Susan K. Datesman and Frank R. Scarpitti, "Female Delinquency and Broken Homes: A Re-Assessment," *Criminology,* 13 (1975): 33–55; Datesman, Scarpitti, and Stephenson; Margery L. Velimesis, "The Female Offender," *Crime and Delinquency Literature,* 7 (1975): 94–112.

5. William Wattenberg and Frank Saunders, "Sex Differences Among Juvenile Offenders," *Sociology and Social Research,* 39 (1965): 48–53; William Wattenberg, "Differences Between Girl and Boy Repeaters," *Journal of Educational Psychology,* 47 (1956): 48–53; William Wattenberg, "Girl Repeaters," National Probation and Parole Association, 3 (1957): 48–53; Barker and Adams; Ruth Shonle Cavan, "Delinquency Girls," *Juvenile Delinquency* (New York: J.B. Lippincott, 1962): 101–110; Rittenhouse; Cockbern E. Shaclay, "Sex Differentials in Juvenile Delinquency," *British Journal of Criminology,* 5 (1965): 289–308; Datesman and Scarpitti.

6. Vedder, James Galvin, "Some Dynamics of Delinquent Girls," *Journal of Nervous and Mental Disease,* 123 (1956): 292–295; Wattenberg; Cavan; Rittenhouse; Malcolm W. Klein and Gay Luce, "Delinquent Girl Gangs," *The Mental Health of the Child* (Washington, D.C.: U.S. Government Printing Office, 1971): 395–397.

7. Dorie Klein, "The Etiology of Female Crime: A Review of the Literature," *Issues in Criminology* 8 (1973): 3–30.

8. *Uniform Crime Reports for the United States—1975,* Clarence M. Kelley, Director, Federal Bureau of Investigation, U.S. Department of Justice (Washington, D.C.: U.S. Government Printing Office, 1975): 183.

9. *Ibid.,* p. 183.

10. See, for example, Michael J. Hindelang, "Age, Sex, and the Versatility of Delinquent Involvements," *Social Problems* 18 (1971): 522–535.

11. Lester David, "The Gentle Sex? I'd Rather Meet a Cougar," *Today's Health,* July (1972): 47–49.

12. *Ibid.*

13. Adler, 1975.

14. *Ibid.,* p. 90.

15. *Ibid.,* p. 93.

16. *Ibid.,* p. 11.

17. *Ibid.,* p. 15.

18. *Ibid.,* p. 99.

19. *Ibid.,* p. 106.

20. *Ibid.,* pp. 94–95.

21. *Ibid.,* p. 95.

22. Richard A. Cloward and Lloyd E. Ohlin, *Delinquency and Opportunity: A Theory of Delinquent Gangs* (New York: The Free Press, 1960).

23. Rita James Simon, *The Contemporary Woman and Crime* (Rockville, Maryland: National Institute of Mental Health: Crime and Delinquency Issues, 1975).

24. Walter L. Slocum and Carol L. Stone, "Family Culture Patterns and Delinquent-Type Behavior," *Marriage and Family Living* 25 (1963): 202–208.

25. David Matza, *Delinquency and Drift* (New York: John Wiley and Sons, 1964).

26. Peggy C. Giordano, "Changing Sex Roles and Females' Involvement in Delinquency" (Paper presented at the annual meeting of the Midwest Sociological Association, April 21–24, 1976, St. Louis, Missouri); Peggy C. Giordano and Stephen A. Cernkovich, *Social Change and Female Delinquency* (Research Proposal Submitted to the National Institute of Mental Health, February 25, 1976).

27. Giordano.

28. James S. Coleman, *The Adolescent Society* (New York: The Free Press, 1961).

5

Post-World War II Trends in Delinquency in the U.S.: Some Theoretical and Policy Implications

TONY G. POVEDA

AS THE STRUCTURE OF GROWING UP was transformed after World War II, with the emergence of a teen-culture in the 1950s and a counter-culture in the 1960s, the nature of delinquency in the postwar years was correspondingly changing. In this essay I shall provide an assessment of major trends in delinquency in the United States since 1940, consider the theoretical implications of my analysis, and finally examine the social policy implications for managing the delinquency problem in advanced-industrial society.

There are two major sources of national statistics on delinquency. The F.B.I.'s *Uniform Crime Reports* (U.C.R.) has provided information on juvenile arrests for a variety of offenses since 1930. Similarly, the Children's Bureau, through its publication *Juvenile Court Statistics*, has provided information on the number of delinquency cases disposed of by juvenile courts since 1927. Both of these series of national delinquency statistics have undergone changes. U.C.R. redefined some of its Part I offenses in 1958, and the Children's Bureau initiated a plan in 1957 for collecting juvenile court statistics from a representative national sample of 502 juvenile courts. Since the above changes may produce certain problems of comparability, the analysis of official delinquency trends will be divided between 1940-1956 and 1958-1975.

The use of police and judicial records on delinquency presents numerous, almost overwhelming, problems of interpretation. Before embarking upon an analysis of official delinquency trends, I shall consider some of these problems of interpretation.

Problems of Measurement and Interpretation

The problems of interpretation arise from difficulties in the measurement of delinquency. Official delinquency statistics do not represent a direct measure of delinquency. Instead "police arrest of juveniles" or "delinquency court cases" are used as indirect measures or indicators of delinquent behavior. They are not direct measures of delinquency because they measure not only the behavior of juveniles, but also police behavior in their discretion to make arrests and to refer cases to juvenile court. The interpretation involves sorting out the relative influence of juvenile behavior and police behavior on official delinquency statistics.

Since our concern is with illuminating long-term trends and changes in delinquency, one of the more obvious problems is the changing age composition of the U.S. population after World War II. An increase in arrests could be expected simply on the basis of a growing adolescent (10-17 years-old) population, which has been the case since the early 1950s. In 1950, 10-17 year-olds comprised 11.6% of the total U.S. population; 1957—12.9%; 1960—14.1%; 1965—15.1%; 1970—16.0% (U.S. Bureau of Census, 1957, 1962, and 1974). The analysis below is based not simply on trends in the number of arrests, but it is based on age-specific arrest rates which have been calculated from the number of arrests per 100,000 children 10-17 years-old. Since the base population in the U.C.R. data does not represent the total U.S. population, as all police departments do not report to U.C.R., the percentage of 10-17 year-olds in the U.C.R. base population was assumed to be the same as the percentage of 10-17 year-olds in the total U.S. population. So that increases in arrest rates in the following data have taken this growth of the adolescent population into consideration.

It is also possible that the increase in juvenile arrest rate is due to greater police efficiency since 1948. A common measure of police efficiency is the clearance rate (no. of arrests/no. of crimes reported to the police). Between 1958 and 1973 the police clearance rate for Part I offenses has consistently decreased from 26.4% to 21.0%—the opposite direction from which one would expect had the police become more efficient in the postwar years.

Similarly, the increase in the number of police officers between 1958 and 1973 might explain the increase in arrest rate. In 1958 there were 166,410 police officers (U.C.R.) or 1.6 per 1000 inhabitants; in 1973 there were 182,068 police officers (U.C.R.) or 2.1 per 1000 inhabitants. This represents an increase of 27% in the number of police officers per 1000 inhabitants, which is substantially less than the 104% increase in the juvenile arrest rate.

Still another problem involves changes in the definition of delinquency so that increases in arrest rates might simply reflect a broader definition of delinquency. This is most problematic when increases in the total delinquency rate are being assessed rather than comparisons in the same offense category over a period of time. Obviously, if more kinds of offenses are included as delinquency in recent years and fewer kinds in earlier years, an increase in arrests could be expected simply on the basis of a wider definition of delinquency. An examination of the offense categories in U.C.R. between

1952 and 1967 shows that the same offense categories have been used over this period with minor changes. Vandalism, runaways, and curfew and loitering violations are the only three offense categories added in fifteen years, which brings the total number of offense categories to twenty-five in 1967. There is also the possibility that diffusely defined offense categories may disproportionately contribute to the increase in delinquency rate. Teeters and Matza (1959) found little evidence that the bulk of the increase in delinquency rates could be attributed to vague and diffuse definitions. The percentage increase in the total delinquency rate (48%) between 1952 and 1956 exceeded all but one of the diffusely defined offense categories: suspicion (51%), all other offenses (41%), disorderly conduct (37%), and vagrancy (19%) (Teeters and Matza, 1959). We may therefore infer that the major increase in delinquency has occurred in relatively well-defined offense categories which have been consistently included in U.C.R.

A final problem with the use of arrest data as a measure of delinquency is that arrests are never made for the vast majority of delinquent acts. Murphy, Shirley, and Witmer (1946), in their study of a low-income area, found that of the 101 boys who committed delinquent acts (over a five-year period), only 40 became official delinquents, and of the 6416 infractions of the law which the researchers recorded, only 95 (1.5%) became official complaints. Gold's (1970) study of adolescents in Flint, Michigan in 1961 reported that 3.2% of all delinquents appeared in any police records. In any case, arrests are only the tip of the iceberg and probably not representative of all delinquent acts. An assumption that will be made in the analysis below is that the relationship between officially detected and undetected delinquent acts has been relatively constant during the historical period we are considering. This assumption would appear to be especially sound for violent offenses where one would not expect any dramatic changes in law enforcement policy. That the increase in the delinquency rate is a real increase is supported by the substantial increase in juvenile arrest rate for crimes against the person. This assumption, however, needs some qualification in the period after 1967. The proliferation of diversion as a strategy for avoiding official labelling in the juvenile justice system has meant a gradual change in the traditional relationship between official and unofficial delinquency, especially in the less serious delinquent offenses. This appears to be reflected in the tapering off of the increase in the delinquency rate after 1971 (for both police arrests of juveniles and delinquency court cases).

Trends in Official Delinquency

The official delinquency trends in the period immediately after World War II and into the mid-1950s have been carefully investigated and

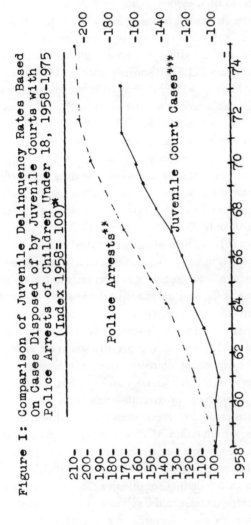

Figure I: Comparison of Juvenile Delinquency Rates Based
On Cases Disposed of by Juvenile Courts with
Police Arrests of Children Under 18, 1958-1975
(Index 1958= 100)*

*In both of these sources of delinquency rates, the rates
are based on adolescent population 10-17 years-old.

**Police arrest data are from Uniform Crime Reports (U.S.
Dept. of Justice, F.B.I., Washington, D.C.).

***Delinquency court cases (exclude traffic violations
but include juvenile status offenses) are from Juvenile Court
Statistics (U.S. Dept. of H.E.W., Children's Bureau,
Washington, D.C.).

analyzed by a number of students of delinquency. Both national series of delinquency statistics show remarkably similar trends between 1940 and 1951 (Robison, 1960: 20). This correspondence continued into the late 1950s.

> Police arrests of juveniles and juvenile court delinquency data, while differing in definitions, extent of coverage, geographic representation, and other factors, nevertheless show a remarkable similarity in their trends. Following a sharp increase during World War II, both arrests and court cases dropped abruptly until 1948. From then on until 1960 there was a steady increase in both series of data (Perlman, 1964: 27).

The picture revealed by official national statistics on delinquency (1940-1956) is one of continuous increase except for the immediate postwar years 1945-1948 when there was a gradual decrease. Between 1950 and 1956 delinquency court cases increased by 86% and the juvenile population (10-17) increased by 10% (Robison, 1960: 19). The increase in the police arrest rate for juveniles under 18 between 1952 and 1956 was 48% (Teeters and Matza, 1959). The similarity in trends between police arrests of juveniles and the number of juvenile delinquency court cases gives us some confidence in inferring the general direction of changes in the volume of delinquency in the United States. The actual volume of delinquency is impossible to infer from official statistics because of the problem of "hidden delinquency" and the selectivity of both police and judicial records.[1]

The more recent period 1958-1975 has not been so thoroughly analyzed with trends in official delinquency. An examination of Figure I, which plots changes in delinquency rates for both series of national delinquency statistics for this period, shows a continuing increase in the delinquency rate (which has been on the rise since 1948). Once again there is a remarkable similarity between changes in the delinquency rate as measured by the number of police arrests of juveniles and delinquency court cases. There is some variation in the two series between 1958 and 1961 with the number of delinquency court cases remaining relatively stable and decreasing somewhat in 1961, but showing an upturn after that which continued through 1971. The total percent increase in the delinquency rate between 1958 and 1975 as measured by police arrest of juveniles is 105.8%. The total percent increase in the delinquency rate between 1958 and 1973 as measured by delinquency court cases is 70%.

Let us now examine more closely the police arrest data on juveniles from *Uniform Crime Reports* for the period 1958-1975 as to what is revealed about the nature of the increase in delinquency in the U.S. If this increase is examined relative to crimes against property (burglary, larceny, and auto theft) and crimes against the person (robbery, aggravated assault), an

Table I. Changes in Juvenile Arrest Rates* for Property Crimes and Crimes Against the Person, 1958-1975.

	Property Crimes**	Crimes Against the Person***
1958	1529.3	82.1
1961	1743.5	123.8
% Change 58-61	+14.0%	+50.8%
1964	2052.8	136.8
% Change 61-64	+17.7%	+10.5%
1967	2315.9	205.2
% Change 64-67	+12.8%	+50.0%
1970	2618.6	256.8
% Change 67-70	+13.1%	+25.0%
1973	2542.8	294.6
% Change 70-73	-2.9%	+15.0%
1975	2968.9	336.1
% Change 73-75	+16.8%	+14.1%
% Change 58-75	+94.1%	+309.4%

*Arrest rates are based on number of arrests of youth under 18 per 100,000 children 10-17 years old (Cities over 2500).

**Larceny, burglary, and auto theft are used as an index of property crimes.

***Robbery and aggravated assault are used as an index of crimes against the person.

Table II. The Distribution of Arrests of Juveniles for Property Crimes* and Crimes Against the Person, 1958-1975 (Cities over 2500).

	Percent of Property Crime Arrests		Percent of Crime Against the Person Arrests	
	Under 18	Under 21	Under 18	Under 21
1958	51.2%	64.8%	13.7%	26.5%
1961	51.1%	65.0%	16.5%	30.0%
1964	56.1%	69.4%	19.4%	32.6%
1967	56.8%	71.2%	22.9%	38.4%
1970	52.4%	68.7%	24.1%	41.3%
1973	51.3%	67.7%	24.2%	40.9%
1975	48.9%	66.7%	25.2%	43.3%

*Larceny, auto theft, and burglary are used as an index of property crimes.

**Robbery, murder, and aggravated assault are used as an index of crimes against the person.

important difference appears. Between 1958 and 1975, while arrest rates for both property crimes and crimes against the person increased, the 309.4% increase in the juvenile arrest rate for crimes against the person was significantly greater than the 94.1% in the juvenile arrest rate for property crimes. Table I shows that this differential increase in arrest rate for property crimes and crimes against the person was consistently maintained during this period (at least until 1973).

Indeed, the total increase in arrest rates for crimes against the person between 1958 and 1972 is almost entirely accounted for by two age-groups: 18-24 year-olds and 15-17 year-olds (Exec. Office of Pres., 1973). Crimes against the person have traditionally been more characteristic of offenders in their early twenties rather than of juveniles. The 18-24 age group still has the highest arrest rate for crimes against the person relative to other age groups. The period 1958-1975, however, saw a downward redistribution of arrests for crimes against the person while the distribution of arrests by age for property crimes remained remarkably constant (Table II). In 1958, 26.5% of total arrests for crimes against the person were youth under 21 (13.7% were under 18). In 1975, 43.3% of total arrests for crimes against the person were youth under 21 (25.2% were under 18). Most of this increase in the arrest rate for youth under 21 for crimes against the person had occurred by 1970.

Total arrests for all U.C.R. offense categories also showed a downward redistribution by age between 1958 and 1975. In 1958, 19.7% of arrests for all U.C.R. offenses were youth under 21 (12.1% under 18); in 1975, 43.0% of arrests were youth under 21 (27.1% under 18).

One final aspect of the increase in official delinquency which we shall examine is whether this increase in juvenile arrest rates occurred differentially by social class. *Uniform Crime Reports* does not readily lend itself to this kind of analysis in that arrests are not reported in terms of traditional sociological indicators of social class—father's occupation, education, or income. If such an analysis is to be made, certain gross assumptions will have to be made. One approach would be to compare increases in arrest rates for offenses which are highly associated with a specific social class. Presumably differential increases in arrest rates for such class-linked offenses would reflect relative changes in delinquency rates for juveniles in those classes.

Auto theft is one such offense which has been identified as a predominantly middle-class delinquent act. Wattenberg and Balistrieri (1952) were the first to point out that auto theft was a "favored-group" delinquency in their study of Detroit police records in 1948. This finding was replicated in Chilton's (1967) specific offense analysis of lower- and middle-class delinquency in Indianapolis in 1958-60.[2]

Table III. A Comparison of Arrest Rates* for Auto Theft
and Larceny/Burglary, 1952-1975 (Cities over 2500).

	Auto Theft	Larceny/Burglary
%Change 52-56**	+60.0%	+52.0%
1958	276.5	1252.8
1961	295.3	1448.2
%Change 58-61	+6.8%	+15.6%
1964	367.5	1685.2
%Change 61-64	+24.4%	+16.4%
1967	377.3	1938.5
%Change 64-67	+2.7%	+15.0%
1970	346.7	2271.9
%Change 67-70	-8.2%	+17.2%
1973	310.7	2232.1
%Change 70-73	-10.4%	-1.8%
1975	257.8	2711.0
%Change 73-75	-17.0%	+21.5%
%Change 58-75	-6.8%	+116.4%

*Arrest rates are based on number of arrests of youth
under 18 per 100,000 children 10-17 years-old.

**The 1952-56 percent change calculation is based on
Teeters and Matza's (1959) analysis of U.C.R. data for
those years.

Table IV. A Comparison of Urban and Suburban Juvenile Arrest Rates* by Offense
1964-1975

	1964	1967	%Change 64-67	1970	%Change 67-70	1973	%Change 70-73	1975	%Change 73-75	%Change 64-75
Total Offenses										
Suburban:	4424	5323	+20.3%	6412	+20.4%	6541	+2.0%	7276	+11.2%	+64.5%
Urban:	5622	7684	+36.7%	7987	+3.9%	7915	-0.9%	8340	+5.4%	+48.3%
Crimes Against the Person*										
Suburban:	49.9	71.9	+44.0%	101.9	+42.0%	149.0	+46.0%	146.9	+10.7%	+230.5%
Urban:	136.8	205.2	+50.0%	256.8	+25.0%	294.6	+15.0%	336.1	+14.1%	+145.7%
Burglary										
Suburban:	402.1	491.1	+22.1%	521.1	+6.1%	616.8	+18.4%	785.0	+27.3%	+95.2%
Urban:	520.0	612.6	+17.8%	679.5	+10.9%	734.4	+8.1%	893.7	+21.7%	+71.9%
Auto Theft										
Suburban:	247.3	252.3	+2.0%	220.9	-12.4%	204.1	-7.6%	194.3	-4.8%	-21.4%
Urban:	367.5	377.3	+2.7%	346.7	-8.2%	310.7	-10.4%	257.8	-17.0%	-29.9%
Narcotic Law Violations										
Suburban:	9.1	93.3	+925.3%	281.7	+201.9%	560.0	+98.8%	465.9	-16.8%	+5020%
Urban:	20.4	111.8	+448.0%	365.5	+226.9%	559.5	+53.1%	479.1	-14.4%	+2249%
Juvenile Status Offenses*										
Suburban:	661	996	+46.2%	1197	+23.9%	1080	-9.8%			
Urban:	792	1140	+44.0%	1316	+15.4%	1335	+14.0%			

* Arrest rates are based on number of arrests of youth under 18 per 100,000 children 10-17 years old.

** Robbery and aggravated assault are used as an index of crimes against the person.

*** Curfew and loitering violations and running away from home are used as an index of juvenile status offenses.

Offenses involving property damage but no permanent material gain, such as vehicle taking, trespassing, and vandalism, are more frequently committed than would be expected by children from high income tracts. On the other hand, property offenses involving permanent material gain, such as larceny, robbery, and acts involving injury to people, such as assault, are committed more frequently than would be expected by children from low income tracts (Chilton, 1967: 96).

In Table III a comparison is made between changes in arrest rates for auto theft and for larceny and burglary, 1952-1975. Auto theft is used here to serve as an index of changes in middle-class delinquency (property offenses), and larceny/burglary as an index of changes in lower-class delinquency (property offenses). Between 1958 and 1975 the arrest rate for larceny/burglary increased by 116.4% and the arrest rate for auto theft decreased by 6.8%. While the arrest rates for both kinds of property offenses increased between 1952 and 1967, after 1967 the arrest rate for auto theft (associated with middle-class delinquency) continuously declined and the arrest rate for larceny/burglary (associated with lower-class delinquency) generally increased.

Another approach to the analysis of the relationship between social class and delinquency would be to compare delinquency rates in residential areas which are more or less associated with specific social classes. *Uniform Crime Reports* began reporting juvenile arrest rates according to rural-suburban-urban differences in the early 1960s. The suburban arrest rates are based on "suburban areas," which are communities located in S.M.S.A.s but which exclude the central cities of S.M.S.A.s. If we make another gross assumption that there is a positive relationship between suburban residential areas and the middle class,[3] a comparison between suburban juvenile arrest rates and urban juvenile arrest rates[4] may provide some insight into the increase in middle-class delinquency relative to the increase in all urban delinquency (Table IV). There does not appear to be any substantial difference in urban and suburban arrest rates with regard to all offenses reported by *Uniform Crime Reports* between 1964-1975 although the suburban arrest rate does increase at a faster rate after 1967. The suburban juvenile arrest rate for crimes against the person has increased at a faster rate than urban juvenile arrests, especially after 1967, although the urban arrest rate is still approximately double that of the suburbs. If we compare the burglary and auto theft arrest rates, two class-linked property offenses,[5] there are no significant differences in overall arrest rates between urban and suburban areas throughout the 1964-1975 period. There is a slight increasing trend in the urban burglary arrest rate, but nothing very substantial. Perhaps more unexpectedly is the lower arrest rate for auto theft in suburban areas and the striking similarity in changes in arrest rates between urban and suburban areas given the studies which show auto theft as a "favored-group" delinquency.

Table V.   Police Disposition of Juvenile Offenders Taken into Custody, 1961-1975.

	Handled within Dept. and Released			Referred to Juvenile Court		
	Total Cities	Cities over 250,000	Suburban Area	Total Cities	Cities over 250,000	Suburban Area
1961	45.3%*	36.2%		48.9%	59.8%	
1964	47.4%	38.0%	58.5%	46.8%	58.2%	36.0%
1967	46.9%	36.2%	55.0%	48.0%	60.5%	39.4%
1970	45.7%	37.7%	52.6%	49.8%	58.9%	42.0%
1973	45.8%	38.8%	52.5%	49.3%	59.0%	41.1%
1975	42.8%	29.5%	49.6%	51.7%	67.0%	45.1%

*The percent is of total number of police dispositions. The percentages do not add up to 100% in that several categories of police dispositions have been omitted (referred to welfare agency, referred to other police agency, and referred to criminal or adult court). These other categories account for only about 5% of the total dispositions and do not change the thrust of the above data.

A final consideration in interpreting urban and suburban arrest rates is the increasing tendency to handle the delinquent acts of middle-class boys in an official manner. The U.C.R. data (Table V) on police disposition of juvenile offenders show that "suburban areas" were the only category to show an increasing tendency to refer apprehended juveniles to juvenile court between 1964 and 1973.[6] This increase in official handling of middle-class delinquents has not been sufficient to explain the increase in the suburban juvenile arrest rate between 1964 and 1973 (25.3% increase in referral rate compared to 64.5% increase in arrest rate).

In conclusion, there does not appear to be any substantial difference in the increase in juvenile arrest rate for all offenses in urban and suburban areas, except after 1967 when the suburban arrest rate increases at a faster rate than the urban arrest rate. The pattern of increase, however, appears to be different. The increase in suburban areas has been most marked in the area of narcotics and crimes against the person. There is also some evidence for a change in the traditional pattern of property crimes with a decrease in the arrest rate for auto theft after 1967 and a slight increase in the burglary arrest rate relative to the urban rate after 1970. This suggests that the pattern of middle-class delinquency in the late 1960s and early 1970s may be changing in a way which more closely resembles the traditional lower-class pattern of delinquency characterized by assaults and property crimes involving economic material gain. The evidence on this is inconclusive. The possible convergence of lower-class and middle-class delinquency patterns is in need of further exploration.

Some Theoretical and Policy Implications

My analysis of official delinquency trends raises several problems for delinquency theory. The continuous increase in the delinquency rate after 1948 in both the lower and middle class needs to be explained as does the changing middle-class pattern of delinquency. In addition, the decreasing tolerance for middle-class delinquent behavior requires explanation.

The above anaysis also has social policy implications in that the continuous increase in the delinquency rate since World War II has occurred regardless of changes in social policy toward juvenile offenders at all levels of the juvenile justice system. Shifts in emphasis in social policy from treating the individual, to reorganizing poor neighborhoods, to radical non-intervention (Schur, 1973) appear to have had little impact on the long-term national trends and patterns of delinquency.

I shall propose in a preliminary way a theoretical perspective on delinquency which relates both to the above theoretical issues and to social policy issues for managing delinquency in advanced-industrial society.

The central theoretical problem is how the postwar increase in delinquency stems from problems of order and legitimacy produced by the
manpower requirements of American society. The transformation of the
U.S. political economy[7] after World War II has important implications for
the delinquency problem in terms of the demands of extended schooling and
extended dependency which it has placed upon young people growing up
since 1945. As Clark expressed it:

> Now, in a society where automation is taking over the tasks of routine
> labor, a large proportion of jobs increasingly falls into the upper ranges of
> skill and expertise, in the range from professional to technician. Large-
> scale enterprise—big business, big government, big labor, big education
> —demands managers, professionals, and technicians, and these posts
> demand training beyond the high school for the most part (Clark, 1962:
> 48).

In addition to technological manpower requirements, the U.S. cold war
foreign policy in the postwar period further contributed to the manpower
problems of American society. The fear of a monolithic Soviet communism
required an increase in military personnel as well as a growing number of
scientists and engineers.

In order to meet these various manpower requirements, young people had
to be channeled through military and educational institutions. The leverage
for channeling manpower was the selective service system where compulsory
military training was required by law or could be deferred until completion
of a college education (Spring, 1976: 52-92).

The manpower requirements of advanced-industrial society have thus
resulted in further changes in the structure of growing up—in particular,
the extension of schooling beyond the high school. In 1944, 12.7 percent of
the 18 to 21 year-olds in the population were enrolled in college; by 1972,
48.1 percent were enrolled (U.S. Bureau of Census, 1965, 1974). Inflated
education requirements for jobs have become an additional leverage to
ensure expanding enrollments in higher education. The result has been that
we have become a highly credentialled society where education requirements for jobs often bear little or no relationship to the skill requirements of
the job (Berg, 1970; Collins, 1971). As Berg (1970) has pointed out, the
growth in professional-technical jobs could only absorb part of the college
graduates in the postwar era. The surplus of college graduates had to be
absorbed in the middle-level jobs in the economy (lower white collar, sales,
clerical, teaching, service jobs, etc.) as the surplus of college graduates has
grown larger with each decade. In 1958, 13.8 percent of male college
graduates enterd non-managerial and nonprofessional jobs; in 1971, this
had increased to 30.5 percent (Freeman and Hollomon, 1975). The economy
has absorbed this surplus of college graduates by redefining education

requirements for employment at the middle-level jobs, not simply for the professional-technical ones. By the 1970s a large proportion of college graduates were faced with the prospect of underemployment, if not unemployment (O'Toole, 1975).

The manpower requirements of the postwar economy are at the core of the delinquency problem in post-World War II America. The prolonged schooling and dependency required of young people growing up in advanced-industrial society has reached a critical point. For middle-class youth the traditional "deferred gratification pattern" (Cohen, 1957) has been stretched beyond credibility, and for lower-class youth an over-credentialled society means fewer opportunities for early entrance into the work force and higher education requirements for entrance into middle-level and sometimes even lower-level jobs.

The emergence of a teen-culture in the 1950s, as England (1960) observed, represents an institutionalization of play and diversion from adult activities in an age-segregated setting as opposed to activities which are preparatory for adulthood. The counter-culture of the 1960s represents a further stage in the age-segregation of American youth although the major thrust of counter-cultural peer groups was to redefine the role of student in the school as well as to question the status of young people in the society generally. They sought an adolescence of increased participation and responsibility rather than one of extended dependency. By the early 1970s the political and cultural critique of American society that the counter-culture had been rooted in was at least partly dissipated. Although counter-cultural values had rapidly diffused, it had been in a selective and piecemeal fashion, which made the "new values" easily subject to cooptation (Yankelovich, 1974).

This crisis of prolonged adolescence in advanced-industrial society has been eased through the toleration of an adversary youth culture. The relaxation of traditional *in loco parentis* rules and regulations, which have regulated growing up since the turn of the century, is part of the management of this crisis. The easing, if not elimination, of dress codes in high schools; the proliferation of co-ed dorms in universities; the toleration of drug use and premarital sexual activity among students, especially college students; and the easing of academic standards ("grade inflation") are all symptomtic of this crisis. It is through this toleration of an adversary youth culture that social order and legitimacy are maintained even though the adversary youth culture may take expression in political radicalism, cultural bohemianism, and delinquency (Matza, 1961). This is the accommodation the postwar political and economic order has made to resolving the contradictions between its manpower requirements and the need to pacify an adversary youth culture which is discontent with the structure of extended schooling and prolonged dependency.

The above contradiction must be the central focus of a comprehensive social policy on delinquency in advanced-industrial society. Past efforts at preventing or controlling delinquency have been piecemeal; they treated the individual delinquent, attempted to reorganize urban poor neighbhorhoods, or attempted to increase the educational and occupational opportunities of lower-class youth. Their failure was in their inability or unwillingness to link the delinquency problem to the political and economic order. As I pointed out earlier, irrespective of which of the traditional approaches to delinquency were dominant in the postwar period, the delinquency rate continued to rise. This suggests that delinquency is rooted in structural contradictions of the society which traditional, piecemeal delinquency policies did not attempt to resolve.

It should be pointed out that the major thrust in delinquency policy since 1967 has been the diversion of young offenders from the juvenile and criminal justice system and the development of community-based corrections programs for juveniles. Both the President's Commission on Law Enforcement and Administration of Justice (1967) and the National Advisory Commission on Criminal Justice Standards and Goals (1973) endorsed this social policy in their various recommendations: establishing youth service bureaus so that delinquents could be handled nonjudicially in their own communities, narrowing the juvenile court's jurisdiction so that juvenile status offenses are eliminated from the court's jurisdiction, reducing the rate of delinquency cases disposed of by juvenile or family courts, etc. The rationale for this policy stems from labelling theory, which shows how agencies of social control unwittingly contribute to the development of delinquent careers and various forms of secondary deviance.

While there has been a levelling off in the overall delinquency rate since 1971, as measured by police arrest of juveniles and delinquency court cases, this does not necessarily mean that diversion policy has been effective in reducing delinquent behavior. Since diversion policy encourages less official handling of delinquents and more informal referrals of juvenile offenders, a decrease or levelling off in the rate of juvenile arrests and delinquency court cases is not unexpected. Since diversion normally involves the less serious delinquent offenses, diversion policy should not contaminate our measures of delinquency for the more serious offenses. Indeed, the juvenile arrest rate for crimes against the person continued to increase afer 1970 even though the juvenile arrest rate for all offenses tended to stabilize. If diversion policy has been effective in reducing the less serious delinquent offenses, it cannot be tested by using official measures for the reasons specified above. Diversion policy doesn't appear, however, to have substantially affected the rate of the more serious delinquent offenses although the rate of increase for violent delinquent offenses has not been so great since 1973.

A more appropriate test of diversion policy is in the hypothesis that the reduced labelling of juvenile offenders will have a subsequent impact by reducing the adult crime rate. Labelling theory predicts that an increase in unofficial handling of juvenile offenders will inhibit the development of delinquent and criminal careers. It is still too soon to test this particular proposition until the age cohort who were juveniles since the development of diversion policy are old enough to affect the adult crime rate in a substantial way.

Regardless of the merits of diversion policy for managing secondary aspects of the delinquency problem, it totally avoids resolving the structural contradictions, which I argued, are at the core of the delinquency problem in advanced-industrial society.

The implication of my formulation of the delinquency problem is that there are structural injustices which are at the root of the delinquency problem, and which are beyond the scope of the juvenile justice system and its operation. The loss of the adolescent's economic function and change of status to a minor at the turn of the century is one major source of injustice. The extended schooling and prolonged dependency, which the postwar economy has required of young people, is another. A national delinquency policy must go beyond simply reforming the juvenile justice system,[8] although this is no small task, and seek fundamental changes in manpower and education policies.[9] A national delinquency policy should be aimed at resolving the structural dilemma posed by the manpower requirements of the postwar political and economic order and the structure of extended schooling and prolonged dependency necessary to meet those requirements.

Summary

I have attempted to show that the increase in delinquency rate after World War II was a real increase, and that it occurred in spite of changes in social policy toward delinquency. I further argued that this continuous increase in the delinquency rate is related to structural contradictions in advanced-industrial society—in particular, the manpower needs of American society in the postwar era and the structure of extended schooling and prolonged dependency which this has required. A comprehensive delinquency policy must take as its central aim the resolution of this structural dilemma.

Discussion Questions

1. What are the problems of interpretation that arise from using official delinquency statistics as a measure of delinquency?

2. What general trends in official delinquency are revealed by the data?

3. Are there interpretations of the data in addition to those provided in the chapter?

4. What structural contradiction is at the core of the delinquency problem according to the chapter? Do you agree with this?

5. How do you interpret the continuous increase in the delinquency rate since World War II in spite of changes in social policy toward juvenile offenders during that period?

Notes

1. Some comparative data is available from studies of delinquency trends in western Europe which on the whole are similar to the above U.S. delinquency trends in the 1950s. Baur's (1964) analysis of delinquency in the U.S. and in the Netherlands between 1954 and 1961 shows a similar increase in both countries. Western European countries, however, experienced a postwar rise in delinquency with some decline in the early or mid-1950s, which was a departure from the U.S. pattern. There was a sharp upturn after 1954 in western Europe as well as in Norway, Denmark, Sweden, Canada, and Japan (Baur, 1964). The postwar rise in western Europe may be more due to the reorganization and reconstruction of police forces and child welfare agencies immediately after the war than to an actual increase in delinquency. Law enforcement in most of western Europe was so disrupted during the war years that any comparison during that period and the immediate postwar years with the U.S. is highly dubious. England, which was not occupied by Germany during the war, had a rapid increase in official delinquency after the war began, a decline following the war, and then a sharp increase after 1947—a pattern very similar to the U.S. one. The similarity ends, however, as the British rate began to fall after 1952 although there are indications that it began to increase again by the mid-1950s (Robison, 1960: 33-4). This comparative data on delinquency trends in the 1950s suggests that the increase in official delinquency in the U.S. during this period was not simply an artifact of distinctive features of U.S. crime reporting systems or of public alarm in the U.S. over the delinquency problem but rather reflects some real increase in delinquency in the Western industrialized nations. This was also the conclusion of Teeters and Matza (1959) in their analysis of delinquency rates for this period.

2. See also Gibbons (1970: 164-169) review of literature on juvenile automobile theft.

3. While the composition of U.S. suburbs as an aggregate is heterogeneous relative to social class and occupational groups, the suburban rings of S.M.S.A.s

nevertheless are disproportionately composed of white collar occupational groups than the general population and this was the case in both 1960 and 1970 (see table below). Clearly "suburban area" is a very crude index of middle class, but the weak positive relationship which does exist between suburban ring and social class (i.e., white collar) may be useful in discovering possible theoretical relationships between delinquency and the middle class.

The Percentage of White Collar/Blue Collar Occupational Groups Residing in 101 Suburban Rings and the Total Population: 1960 and 1970. (Kasarda, 1976; U.S. Bureau of Census, 1972).

Percent Residing in Sub. Ring and Total Pop.

Occupational Group:	1960		1970	
	Sub. Ring	Total Pop.	Sub. Ring	Total Pop.
Blue Collar (excl. farm):	50.6%	60.4%	45.3%	57.5%
White Collar:	49.4%	39.6%	54.7%	42.5%

4. The urban juvenile arrest rate includes arrests of juveniles in cities over 2500 (including suburban arrests).

5. Burglary has been more highly associated with lowerclass delinquents and auto theft with middle-class delinquents.

6. This is further substantiated by a study of middleclass delinquency in a wealthy suburb in California where Carter (1968) observed the community's declining willingness to "absorb" such behavior.

7. This transformation is characterized by the increasing domination of the economy by large-scale corporations, the growth of conglomerates and multinational corporations, an increase in productivity due to automation, the increasing use of the federal budget to stimulate the economy (Keynesian economics), and the growing reliance upon managers, professionals, and other experts in the operation of these large corporations (Clark, 1962; Galbraith, 1967; Bensman and Vidich, 1971; Mintz and Cohen, 1971; Mankoff, 1972; Anderson, 1974).

8. Present efforts consist in restoring constitutional safeguards, eliminating juvenile status offenses from the jurisdiction of the juvenile court, diverting juvenile offenders, and encouraging community-based corrections for juvenile offenders.

9. See Spring (1976) for an enlightening analysis of national manpower and education policies since 1945.

References Cited

Anderson, Charles H.
   1974   The Political Economy of Social Class. Englewood Cliffs, N.J.: Prentice-Hall.
Baur, E. Jackson
   1964   "The trend of juvenile offences in the Netherlands and the United States." J. of Crim. Law, Criminology, Police Sci. 55: 359–265.

Bensman, Joseph and Arthur Vidich
 1971 The New American Society. Chicago: Quadrangle.

Berg, Ivar
 1970 Education and Jobs. New York: Praeger.

Carter, Robert M.
 1968 Middle-Class Delinquency: An Experiment in Community Control. Univ. of Calif.: School of Criminology.

Chilton, Roland J.
 1967 "Middle-class delinquency and specific offense analysis." in Edmund Vaz, ed., Middle-Class Juvenile Delinquency. New York: Harper and Row.

Clark, Burton
 1962 Educating the Expert Society. San Francisco: Chandler Pub. Co.

Cohen, Albert K.
 1957 "Middle-class delinquency and the social structure." Paper read at annual meeting of A.S.A. Also in Edmund Vaz, ed., Middle-Class Juvenile Delinquency. New York: Harper and Row, 1967.

Collins, Randall
 1971 "Functional and conflict theories of educational stratification." Amer. Soc. Rev. 36 (December): 1002–1019.

England, Ralph
 1960 "A theory of middle class juvenile delinquency." J. of Crim. Law, Criminology, and Police Sci. 50 (March–April): 535–40.

Exec. Office of President
 1973 Social Indicators. Wash., D.C.: U.S. Government Printing Office.

Freeman, Richard and J. Herbert Hollomon
 1975 "The declining value of college going." Change (Sept.): 24–31, 62.

Galbraith, John Kenneth
 1967 The New Industrial State. Boston: Houghton Mifflin Co.

Gibbons, Don C.
 1970 Delinquent Behavior. Englewood Cliffs, N.J.: Prentice-Hall.

Gold, Martin
 1970 Delinquent Behavior in an American City. Belmont, Ca.: Brooks-Cole.

Kasarda, John
 1976 "The changing occupational structure of the American metropolis." in Barry Schwartz, ed., The Changing Face of the Suburbs. Chicago: Univ. of Chicago Press.

Mankoff, Milton
 1972 The Poverty of Progress: The Political Economy of American Social Problems. New York: Holt, Rinehart, and Winston.

Matza, David
 1961 "Subterranean traditions of youth." The Annals of the Amer. Acad. of Pol. and Soc. Sci. 338 (November): 103–118.

Mintz, Morton and Jerry Cohen
 1971 America, Inc. New York: Dell Pub. Co.

Murphy, Fred, M. Shirley, and H.L. Witmer
 1946 "The incidence of hidden delinquency." Amer. J. of Orthopsychiatry 16 (October): 686–96.

National Advisory Commission on Criminal Justice Standards and Goals
   1973   A National Strategy to Reduce Crime. Wash., D.C.: U.S. Government Printing Office.

O'Toole, James
   1975   "The reserve army of the underemployed: I and II." Change (May and June).

Perlman, Richard
   1964   "Anti-social behavior of the minor in the United States." Federal Probation 28 (December): 23–7.

President's Commission on Law Enforcement and Administration of Justice
   1967   The Challenge of Crime in a Free Society. Wash., D.C.: U.S. Government Printing Office.

Robison, Sophia
   1960   Juvenile Delinquency. New York: Holt, Rinehart and Winston.

Schur, Edwin M.
   1973   Radical Non-intervention. Englewood Cliffs, N.J.: Prentice-Hall.

Spring, Joel
   1976   The Sorting Machine. New York: McKay.

Teeters, Negley and David Matza
   1959   "The extent of delinquency in the United States." The J. of Negro Educ. 28 (Summer): 200–13.

U.S. Bureau of Census
   1957   Historical Statistics of the United States from Colonial Times to 1957.
   1962   Historical Statistics: Continuation to 1962.
   1965   Long-Term Economic Growth: 1860–1965.
   1972   General Population Characteristics: U.S. Summary.
   1974   Statistical Abstract of the U.S. Wash., D.C.: U.S. Government Printing Office.

U.S. Dept. of H.E.W.
   1958–73   Juvenile Court Statistics. Wash., D.C.: U.S. Government Printing Office.

U.S. Dept. of Justice
   1958–75   Uniform Crime Reports. Wash., D.C.: U.S. Government Printing Office.

Wattenberg, William and James Balistrieri
   1952   "Automobile theft: a 'favored-group' delinquency." Amer. J. of Soc. 57 (May): 575–9.

Yankelovich, Daniel
   1974   The New Morality: A Profile of American Youth in the '70s." New York: McGraw Hill.

Part VI
Why Not Capital Punishment?

1

Why Not Capital Punishment?

G. L. KUCHEL

IN DECISIONS OF JULY 2 AND JULY 6, 1976, the Supreme Court of the United States upheld the constitutionality of capital punishment under the laws of three states (Florida, Georgia, and Texas), and declared unconstitutional the laws of three states (Louisiana, North Carolina, and Oklahoma). [1] These decisions were simply the voice of the Supreme Court rejecting the constitutional arguments against capital punishment which had stopped all such activity since June 2, 1967. In effect, the way was now open for states to resume executions, provided the Court-established guidelines were followed.

The guidelines issued by the Supreme Court set forth a three step process that has been legislatively followed in all states where the death penalty has not been overturned. In summary form these steps are: (1) the usual trial to determined guilt or innocence; (2) if a finding of guilt is determined, a hearing is held to allow arguments of mitigation or aggravation. Following these arguments the penalty is determined and; (3) if the convicted person is sentenced to death, there should be an automatic appeal to the next higher-level court within that jurisdiction. This process disallows automatic death penalties for specific crimes and allows discretion by the court in those cases where mitigation exceeds aggravation. These were the circumstances that existed when Gary Gilmore was executed by a firing squad in Utah in January of 1977.

There is no need to recite the long history of opposition to capital punishment. The argument that no one, including the organized body of society, has a right to take a person's life is belied by centuries of example. The general argument is that no one has the right to murder (if you choose to call capital punishment "state murder"); hence, the state cannot commit a crime which it forbids. However, those who hold to that argument ignore the fact that executions are carried out in accordance with law and that killing under appropriate circumstances has always been legally excusable or justifiable.

There are a variety of other moral arguments that have been advanced in opposition to capital punishment. However, these were set aside at the same time the Supreme Court settled the constitutional arguments. The Court said that capital punishment does not constitute cruel or unusual punishment so long as the appropriate procedural safeguards are employed. In effect, the Court appears to be serving the purpose for which many say all courts were established: to carry out the will of the people. In 1966 a Gallup poll found 47 percent of the people polled were opposed to capital punishment and 42 percent favored it. However, by the Spring of 1976 Gallup found the tide of opinion had turned and 65 percent now favored executions while only 28 percent were in opposition.

Today our society is faced with a situation in which twenty-seven states have death penalty laws and legislative action is pending in six others.[2] In addition, we have seen a slight decline in the number of persons under sentence of death. At the start of 1976 there were 473 persons awaiting execution compared with 444 in January of 1977.[3] This decline resulted from court decisions voiding capital punishment statutes in some states.

The arguments generally supporting capital punishment are in some ways comparable to the arguments in opposition. They are mostly based on emotional discussions that cannot be empirically substantiated. The argument of deterrence is one that goes to the heart of this matter. Many argue that capital punishment does not deter while others are just as adamant in their claims of its deterrent value. Neither side can actually prove its argument. One can say, without fear of contradiction, that the death penalty does deter at least one person. The one executed will not commit another crime. This argument alone may be sufficient reason to establish a framework to again reinstitute this method of dealing with some offenders.

In recent years we have seen prison populations in this country grow until they reached an all time high. In addition to this, police departments across the country have recorded the first drop in violent crime since 1955. Perhaps the "get tough" policy for repetitive offenders or "career criminals" is having this effect. It is conceivable that a return to the use of executions may have a similar effect on this same area of crime. Today we believe that swift, certain and reasonably severe punishment can reduce crime rates. For that reason we hold that punishment can be both a deterrent and a rehabilitative tool.

The primary arguments that must be addressed when one discusses capital punishment are generally not brought forward and examined. In their simplest form they can be summarized under three general headings: (1) Capital punishment is necessary to protect persons inside as well as outside of prisons. (2) Society has the power and the legal right to impose any lawful punishment it desires. (3) Our system of law is based on individual responsibility and capital punishment, when administered according to law, is a logical extension of that philosophy. Let us examine the merit of each of these individually.

Capital Punishment is Necessary to Protect Persons Inside as Well as Those Outside of Prisons

One of the most difficult problems to handle in a penitentiary is the offender who has committed one or more murders and is serving one or more life sentences with little possibility of parole. In some cases parole possibility is totally removed by the fact of multiple life sentences ordered in a consecutive manner. These cases pose many questions that do not have ready answers.

What punishment is to be ordered if the multiple-lifer kills another inmate? Is it more humane to keep a person in close custody confinement for the rest of his life or is it more humane to put him to death? Opponents of capital pusnihment say killing is barbaric. What of the barbarian inside the walls who has no opportunity for release; what is to control his behavior? We have an obligation to maintain prisoners in a safe environment and this will require the execution of the dangerous multiple-lifer or the total isolation of those persons for the rest of their lives. If the argument in opposition to the death penalty is compassion, then we would do the taxpayer, the prison worker and other inmates a favor by executing some of those who must be forever confined. It is also true that compassion becomes an argument for the use of capital punishment if those executions will spare lives or injury of future victims.[4]

Society Has the Right to Impose Any Legal Punishment It Wants to Impose

Organized groups, including societies, gain and maintain their power and solidarity through their ability to carry out the will of the majority of their members. This is the essence of a democracy and is not to be taken lightly. The seriousness of this position is to be seen in the reaction of the courts to the general charge by the public that they were being too lenient with convicted offenders. As the media picked up the tenor of public hostility and reported it in newspapers, magazines and via radio and television, we saw courts of original jurisdiction begin to change tactics. Probation was offered to fewer individuals, hence more went to prison; longer sentences were being imposed and more consecutive as opposed to concurrent sentences became common. This has resulted in the largest prison population this country has ever seen and there is not a forseeable reduction in the current rate of commitments. This seems to be a strong indication that the public wants harsher penalties imposed upon certain classes of violators. Morality changes as the will of the people dictates it shall change (witness sexual permissiveness and the use of chemical stimulants and depressants). It is the same with the public attitude toward the execution of persons who commit certain crimes.

So long as the elected representatives of the people respond to the wishes of their constituents and enact legislation that meets the guidelines dictated by the Suprme Court for the imposition of capital punishment, that punishment cannot be legally or morally wrong. For certain kinds of offenses the majority of the people in many jurisdictions have made it clear that they want the death penalty imposed. Regardless of contrary arguments, the "voice of the people" must be considered the controlling factor in our society.

Our System of Law is Based on Individual Responsibility and Capital Punishment is an Extension of that Philosophy

One can summarize the philosophy of responsibility under criminal law in this country with the statement that all sane men are presumed to intend the natural and probable consequences of their voluntary acts. The law does not state that an individual is prohibited from committing any act. It spells out prohibited acts and establishes the penalty for each of these. In essence, the individual responsibility doctrine holds: one can do whatever one pleases to do, so long as he is willing to accept the penalty.

The individual who is found guilty to committing an offense that calls for the death penalty has been adjudged sane and to be an adult according to the laws in the jurisdiction where the offense occurred. That being the case it is only appropriate that the logical extension of that process is the imposition of the penalty called for by the law in that jurisdiction. If death is the prescribed penalty, then it should be imposed without regard to the deterrent effect or the moral implication of what is being done. One is not at liberty to consider the cause; the offender must be held accountable. To do less than that depreciates the value of law and certainly depreciates the value of the victim's life. It is ludicrous to oppose capital punishment when by its opposition we are in effect saying that we value the life of the killer more than we value the life of the viticm. If one of the high prices for living in a large, heterogeneous, complex society is a greater probability of becoming a victim of crime, then it seems logical that the probability of greater punishment should be the higher price for committing a crime. If this should also serve as a deterrent to some who would commit homicide then a dual benefit would accrue to society. The logical position of the deterrent effect of maximum punishment established in a legal framework is succinctly stated in an article that is more timely today than when it was published nearly two decades ago.

> Any case for the retention of the death penalty does not rest upon sentiment or hysteria. It is based quite simply on the fact that, human nature being what it is, potential criminals are most effectively deterred from crime by what they fear most. The penalty of death is obviously the most dreaded punishment, obviously it is more dreaded than life imprisonment, else why does every murderer sentenced to death thankfully accept a life sentence if and when he is reprieved? And even the strongest opponents of capital punishment admit it is necessary to provide the death penalty for murders committed by men under life sentences. This in itself is a complete admission that life imprisonment does not produce sufficient horror in the mind of the killer to deter him.

> There is no question that there are some murders committed upon sudden passion, so strong that the existence of no penalty would be sufficient to stay the hand of the murderer. But this is not an argument against capital punishment, as the abolitionists would have us believe. Indeed, it may be that men so dangerous that they kill when they lose their tempers should be executed for the safety of other people.[5]

Summary

Capital punishment is a punitive process that has a history as long as mankind. The arguments that have favored its retention or abolition have been carried on, mostly unchanged, for centuries and are of an emotional rather than an empirical nature. The primary argument of modern times has been upon the deterrent value of capital punishment and whether or not man is sufficiently logical to profit from an abstract example of punishment being applied to another.

The majority of our society is in favor of the use of capital punishment that is not arbitrarily nor capriciously used. The United States Supreme Court holds with this attitude and has established mandatory guidelines that the capital punishment statutes of the several states must meet.

The most primary arguments that establish a sound position for the continued use of capital punishment are generally not brought forward.

These are: (1) Capital punishment is necessary to protect persons inside as well as outside of prison. (2) Society has the power and legal right to impose any lawful punishment it desires. (3) Our system of law is based on individual responsibility and capital punishment is a logical extension of that philosophy.

The final analysis allows society to reduce the severity of punishment in situations where mitigation is sufficient. However, where there are no extenuating circumstances surrounding the offense, we must not allow the liberty to search for cause just to prevent us from facing the unpleasant reality that there are some people who are so dangerous and so clearly unable to control themselves that they must die so there will be harmonious conditions for those who control themselves sufficiently to live together.

Discussion Questions

1. Should the Supreme Court of the United States have the power to overrule the wishes of the several states and the majority of the citizens, and abolish capital punishment as a punishment in this country?

2. In deciding appropriate punishment for any offense, should moral considerations be utilized or should only legal considerations be the determinant?

3. Is it appropriate to use capital punishment if it can be proven that it has a deterrent effect? Is it appropriate if it has no deterrent effect?

4. Would capital punishment be a more effective deterrent if we were to return to the use of public executions?

5. Is it more humane to keep a person incarcerated without the possibility of release than it is to impose capital punishment?

Notes

1. *Gregg v. Georgia, Jurek v. Texas, Woodson and Waxson v. North Carolina, Profitt v. Florida, and Roberts v. Louisiana.*

2. New York Times, May 9, 1977

3. National Criminal Justice Reference Service, *Advance Report on Capital Punishment*, 1976 (Washington, D.C.).

4. Ernest van den Haag, *Punishing Criminals: Concerning a Very Old and Painful Question* (New York: Basic Books, Inc., 1975), p. 209.

5. Richard Gerstein, "A Prosecutor Looks at Capital Punishment", *Journal of Criminal Law, Criminology and Police Science*, Volume 51, Number 2, (1960).

2

Let's Ban Capital Punishment Permanently!

JOSEPH W. ROGERS

ON JUNE 29, 1972 THE UNITED STATES SUPREME COURT in the historic Furman Case rendered a landmark decision:

> In recognizing the humanity of our fellow beings, we pay ourselves the highest tribute. We . . . join the approximately 70 other jurisdictions in the world which celebrate their regard for civilization and humanity by shunning capital punishment.[1]

We now realize the premature nature of the above words in that the court's rejection of the death penalty was to be only temporary and on limited legal grounds. With the 1976 restoration and subsequent focus on such states as Florida, Georgia, and Texas the stage was set for a wide-scale revival of execution fever in America. At 8:07 A.M. on January 17, 1977 when Gary Mark Gilmore was declared dead of gunshot wounds fired from a Utah firing squad, a decade without executions came to a smoking halt.[2] The voices of celebration were now moving to the party of unrelenting supporters of capital punishment.

Not among the celebrants were Justices William Brennan and Thurgood Marshall who had been overridden six months earlier by their seven colleagues on the bench. At that time they reaffirmed the traditional liberal view that all executions are, as Justice Marshall put it, a "total denial of human dignity and worth."[3] Amid ensuing rounds of legal maneuvering, beyond comprehension of those awaiting decisions which would select them like winners or losers in a lottery, death-row tenants could find comfort in the biblical thought that many are called but few are chosen. Names such as those of Texans Jerry Lane Jurek, Calvin Woodkins, or Robert Excell White appeared in the press as possibilities to join the chosen few.[4]

The history of capital punishment is an interesting story; and when told with accompanying anecdotal or illustrative material, a provocative, if at times a gory one.[5] Our purposes here, however, are best served by omitting a historical account, and by moving directly to a stance on behalf of a permanent ban of the death penalty from modern society. This discussion will be cast within a frame of seven selected ideal characteristics with which a concept of punishment should be compared. We hold that the concept of capital punishment has not met all these criteria. They are: 1) Uniformity; 2) Celerity; 3) Certainty; 4) Correspondence; 5) Visibility; 6) Consistency; and 7) Impersonality.[6] Let's examine these one by one.

1. *Uniformity.* When we speak of uniformity in justice on the contemporary scene we speak to the notion of equal liability under law. Here we seek to strive for the parallel application of penalties and/or rewards regardless of such status characteristics as ethnicity, education, or income level. Uniformity is the antithesis of capriciousness as exemplified not only by the fluctuating differences among the laws of our fifty states, but by the empirical results in terms of death row residents.

Mindful that much of our law is derived through our English heritage, it is worth recalling that in 18th-century England, there were, reportedly, over 200 capital offenses such as coining, sheep stealing, and pick pocketing.[7] In the United States, as recently as 1952 (which is not exactly ancient history!) a U.S. Bureau of Prisons Criminologist identified 31 statutory capital offenses existing in one form or another. These ranged from the single offense of murder in New Hampshire to some 14 separate offenses on the law books of Georgia.[8] Consider then the implications of the statistic that during the period 1930-1960, only one person was executed in New Hampshire while 292 were meeting the same fate for various reasons in Georgia.[9] It does not follow, of course, that simply because laws exist in the book that they are utilized. But we can show this—that from 1930 through 1976 3,859 persons were executed for the following crimes:[10]

Murder	3334	Burglary	11
Rape	455	Aggravated Assault	6
Armed Robbery	25	Sabotage	6
Kidnapping	20	Espionage	2

Lack of uniformity is expressed not only in the lack of consensus among states as to what should be defined as capital crimes, but through the disproportionate number of Blacks among the executed. What does it imply when our own governmental figures show that while our U.S. population is approximately 11 percent Black, some 54 percent of the death penalties were inflicted upon this minority set? For the crime of rape, Blacks account for 89 percent of those executed![11]

Unfortunately, some persons see figures such as the foregoing and incorrectly attribute them to a bygone age. To demonstrate otherwise, we need only to take a look at the prisoners under sentence of death on December 31,

1975. On a data available basis, we find 53 percent were Black; less than 2 percent were female; 72 percent had not finished high school, 30 percent not even the eighth grade; only 35 percent were married; and the youngest was just 16 years of age, the oldest, 67. In summary, the typical portrait revealed a Death Row Convict as one likely to be Black, male, and single. He was about 26 years of age, a high school drop out, and had been sentenced to death for murder.[12] Is it possible then, the absence of uniformity is a function of such factors as ethnicity, sex, age, education, and regionalism, or others like poverty, competence of defense attorneys, and fickleness of law? Is so, men such as Ponce de Leon and Don Quixote have sought easier goals than the achievement of uniformity relative to capital punishment!

2. *Celerity.* This term refers to the "speed" with which sentence is followed by execution. The proximity of punishment to offensive behavior was considered an ideal characteristic within the classical school of criminology, and it is deemed to be an essential characteristic in child rearing discipline today. When we apply this concept to infliction of the death penalty, we discover troublesome variations.[13] For example, in 1959 (N = 49 deaths), the lapse time between sentence and execution ranged from a low of 65 days in a Nebraska homicide case to a high of over 9 years in a Pennsylvania case of murder. In 1960, (N = 56) the range was from a low of one month, 6 days for a Washington homicide to a high of 11 years, 10 months for the celebrated execution of a convicted kidnapper, Caryl Chessman.[14] The following year, 1961 (N = 42) the median elapsed time between sentence and its imposition was 16.2 months; in 1964, (N = 15) 20.5 months; in 1965 (N = 7),[15] 44.5 months; and in 1966 (N = 1) one lonely Oklahoman met his end after avoiding the electrocutioner for almost four full years. With a decade now of suspended infliction, a different statistic appears in more recent reports, namely "median length of death row incarceration." For 1973 this figure was 37 months; 1974, 10 months; 1975, 9 months; and for 1976, 14 months.[16]

Mindful that the above reflects lengthy, uneven, and probably unpredictable gaps in time between sentence and punishment, one could only speculate about the additional antecedent spreads between the alleged crime and sentence. In any case, one could take the view that such delays make for cruel and unusual punishment from, say, an eighth amendment constitutional perspective; or one could take the view that such delays make something of a farce of, at least, a portion of the deterrence argument. Even so there is no apparent way out, for as our system of justice demands, the defendant is entitled to every legal recourse, the matter of time not withstanding. In his brilliant work, wherein he eloquently argues for the abolition of capital punishment on grounds of its arbitrariness and irreparable error, Charles L. Black underscores a fourteenth amendment perspective. Listen to his words:

> If death, as the culture unambiguously assumes, is by far the worst punishment, then the requirements of 'due process' for death may reasonably be set higher that the requirements of 'due process' for other punishment.[17]

and later:

> . . . I have argued that there is not enough 'due process of *law*' in our system to make it an acceptable instrument for the 'deprivation of life?'[18]

This conclusion seems fair: celerity and due process are incompatible bed fellows in capital cases, leaving a singular choice in favor of due process.

3. *Certainty*. Some would argue that surety of sanction is the most important criterion of punishment. Yet our system of criminal justice is plagued by a near impossible task of approximating sanction certainty. Victim surveys and self-reports render support for such pessimism. For example, one recent study depicts the attrition or drop-outs in the legal process to be so large that only one percent of validated crimes (known to victims) result in convictions.[19] Moreover, our principal source of nation-wide crime statistics, *The Uniform Crime Reports,* reveals a 1974, 1975, & 1976 clearance rate for the key "index crimes" of only 21 percent. The 1976 clearance distribution is as follows: Murder (79%); Forcible Rape (52%); Aggravated Assault (63%); Robbery (27%); Burglary (17%); Larceny (19%); and Motor Vehicle Theft (14%).[20] Unfortunately, even here the percentages are misleading, for there still remains the long journey to conviction and beyond. For instance, Tappan was able to show in 1958 that only about 3 in 5 of the persons charged with murder were actually convicted.[21] Reports for recent years do not suggest any improvement.

Let's linger just a moment with the year 1958 long enough to observe that some 8,182 murders were estimated to have taken place (8,027 in 1957).[22] Now when we turn to the executions occuring in 1957, 1958, 1959, & 1960 we find the sequence to be 65, 49, 49, and 56. The point, of course, is that certainty of capital punishment becomes almost irrelevant to the issue. What does it imply when 65, or 49, or 56 individuals are selected out among thousands for extermination? Well, Professor Black asserts it represents mistake and caprice, and for many reasons these are beyond complete repair. It is his position,

> . . . that in one way or another, the official choices—by prosecutors, judges, juries, and governors—that divide those who are to die from

those who are to live are on the whole not made, and cannot be made, under standards that are consistently meaningful and clear, but that they are often made, and in the foreseeable future will continue often to be made, under no standards at all or under pseudo-standards without discoverable meaning.[23]

Following the 1972 Furman decision many states erroneously believed they could solve the Supreme Court's objections to capital punishment through statutes calling for *mandatory* execution upon conviction of first degree murder. Their goals included not only countering the cruel and unusual punishment flaw, but to bring about greater equalization and certainty of application. However it would have been instructive to have reviewed the classic McCafferty piece which was cited earlier. There he discusses an eleven year experience of the District of Columbia, a bastion in providing a mandatory death sentence for first-degree murder.[24] But before you read on, consider your own definition of the word *mandatory*. Now let's see if, indeed, the results agree with your definition. Examination of first degree homicides revealed that from July 1, 1947 through June 30, 1958, a total of 276 individuals were so indicted under the D.C. code. Of these, 44 percent were either aquitted or obtained a directed verdict from the court. The dispositions of the remaining 155 were as follows: 127 were convicted of a lesser offense and sentenced to incarceration while 28 were sentenced to death. Of those now awaiting execution, 7 had their sentences commuted, 7 were favored with reversals on appeal, 3 were transferred to a mental hospital, 1 was awaiting appeal outcome, and 10 were, in fact, executed.[25] McCafferty observed:

> This means that only 1 person was executed for about every 28 persons indicted for first degree murder!
> "Long dropped by most of the states as unworkable and self-defeating, the mandatory provision in the District of Columbia Code may give way to permitting the jury or court to set the penalty.[26]

Recalling that the foregoing researcher was making these remarks in 1961, adds emphasis to a similar conclusion reached some years later by Black who suspects the drawing of such laws is beyond "the wit of man." Why?—because it is impossible to foresee all the relevant circumstances, and even were that possible, the resultant statute would be "ridiculous." He asserts, "If strictly mandatory death-penalty statutes are enacted, the law will give somewhere; one of the places where it *can* give is at the stage of charging. . . ."[27]

It appears plausible to say that the only thing "certain" about the death penalty is its "*un*certainty."

4. *Correspondence.* By this term we infer a hypothetical relationship between seriousness of the crime and severity of sanction. Clearly, we commonly recognize this principle in our criminal codes through such concepts as simple and gross misdemeanor or felonies of varying degrees. Petty theivery and armed robbery, for instance rest at quite different levels of punishment risk. Framers of law, whether from a deterrence or some other perspective, have doubtlessly sought to build a fundamental sense of fairness in linking definitions of deviant behavior to corresponding penalties. Nevertheless the idea sounds so simple, yet it is so hard to achieve. And paradoxically, as we come to learn more about human behavior, the more difficult still it will be to achieve. Why would this be?

Perhaps at least partial insight can be gained through a brief return to the classical school of criminological theory as expounded by Cesare Beccaria almost two centuries ago. In attempting to match a scale of punishment with a scale of crimes, an objective basis was sought for what Sociologist George Vold calls "administrative and legal criminology."[28] Presumably it would be a procedural scheme easy to administer; judges would simply be instruments to apply the law; and the law itself would prescribe an exact penalty for every crime and degree thereof. Troublesome questions concerning reasons for or possible causes of behavior would be deemed irrelevant; matters of motive and intent would be ignored; and the unequal consequences of arbitrary rules or statutes would be disregarded for the sake of administrative purity. After all, said Baccaria, the act and not the intent is the real measure of injury done by crime, and you are mistaken if you imagine a crime to be less or greater according to the intention of the individual who commits it. Vold concludes:

> This was the classical conception of justice—an exact scale of punishments for equal acts without reference to the nature of the individual involved and with no attention to the question of special circumstances under which the act came about[29]

The early codes implementing such a policy could not long endure in the face of practical everyday situations; thus necessary modifications began to be introduced; curiously, in the name of administrative facilitation. Such "cookbook justice", simply could not go on neglecting individual differences, the significance of particular situations, and rapid developments in science and society. Questions emerged: Should first offenders and recidivists be treated exactly alike? Should minors and adults be penalized precisely the same? What is the relevance of intelligence or lack of it to the behavioral act? Should those we suspect are insane be treated as though they were competent? Does society play a role in the etiology of crime?—and so on.[30]

Paradoxically, parts of the above sound so strange yet so familiar. Strange in light of more than a century and a half of developments in the natural sciences, social sciences, and humanities; yet familiar in view of recent cries for law and order through more severe, determinate, or inflexible sentencing. But what makes us seriously believe that we can take capital crimes, put them in a "Cookbook of Favorite Capital Crime Recipes," disregarding contemporary knowledge of psychology, psychiatry, biology, chemistry, economics, anthropology, and sociology, among others, and be any more successful that the French of the 18th century? It would be about as useful as reviving Lombroso's "born criminal" and feeding him to the gas chamber. Why not? He has committed a capital crime, we don't understand why, and we don't know how to rehabilitate him. The point is this—that all murderers, all forcible rapists—the most common offenders for which the death penalty has been invoked—are sufficiently unique as individuals for society to retain sentencing and rehabilitation flexibility.[31] And this flexibility must incorporate the possibility of rectifying prior errors of fact and judgment.

5. *Visibility*. By this term is meant the saliency of penalties for the general public and for offenders both past and potential. Beccaria, for instance emphasized the publication of all laws so that the public would remain properly informed and thus would be led to support their intent and purpose.[32] As laudable as this is, there is evidence to suggest that visibility of criminal law is lacking on the contemporary scene. As a case in point, a California survey disclosed that its citizens were extremely uninformed about penalties for crimes. Out of 11 possible items, the mean score was only 2.6 responses correct. Most persons underestimated the severity of existing sanctions although about one-fourth of them felt crime would be reduced by stiffer penalties. After asking additional questions related to proposed legislation and other changes, the researchers observed: "In short, the general public simply *does not know* what the penalties are for various crimes. How then could increased penalties deter crime?"[33] Paradoxically, they found that persons who have already engaged in crime happened to be the most knowledgable about penalties. They concluded that penalties become of greater interest after persons violate the law, that penal institutions serve as good training grounds for learning about legal sanctions, and that such knowledge seems to possess little deterrence value.[34]

In an elaborate Arizona study, further doubt has been cast upon the relationship between perceived certainty of legal punishments and the deterrence doctrine. Significantly, these researches underscore the notion that although penal systems are social, deterrence denotes psychological phenomena in terms of fear, pain, and perceived risk. They point out that a truly narrow interpretation of the deterrence philosophy would maintain that the objective properties of legal penalties are irrelevant, thereby conceding that the doctrine is "purely *perceptual* theory."[35] Upon the basis of considerable data and intricate analysis, they assert:

> *Until defenders of the doctrine show that the relation between properties of legal punishments and the crime rate holds independently of the social condemnation of crime*, then all purported evidence of general deterrence is suspect.[36]

In another excellent study of the deterrent effects of formal sanctions, it was found that legal threat is a relatively weak source of compliance. Although legal factors generated some explanatory power, such influences tended to be indirect rather than direct. Contributing to greater inhibition were extralegal influences such as one's moral beliefs.[37]

Now suppose we were to attempt to reshape death penalty visibility through reinstituting a policy of public executions? Our imagination immediately permits us to wander from an old fashioned hanging in a town square to contemporary full scale multi-media prime time television coverage in the Astrodome with dramatic interviews and commentary similar to that to which we have now grown accustomed in connection with a World Series, Heavyweight Boxing Championship, or Kentucky Derby. One might assume we could not only inform but jointly deter. Yet it is not at all clear what the results would be. French Justice Marc Ancel has pointed out that many criminologists and penologists emphasize the criminogenic nature of the death penalty, which undermines public respect for human life. It may, in his view, even constitute a morbid stimulus to crime.[38] Reid reminds us of similar views expressed by Robespierre;[39] Bedau, of Thackeray's reaction: "I feel myself ashamed and degraded at the brutal curiosity which took me to that brutal sight."[40] He cites the observation by a British Chaplain that all but three of the 167 men sentenced to death whom he had interviewed had, at one time or another witnessed a hanging.[41] Warden Duffy also calls attention to similar experiences at San Quentin, where for instance, an inmate who helped install the gas chamber (while doing time for burglary) later returned to die in it![42] The warden, himself, never ceased to be amazed at requests to witness executions and at some who showed up. One sheriff, he recalls, persisted in attending six executions in order "to prove I can take it"; he fainted during the first five![43] Further, Sellin reports that a series of his studies on the relationship between publicity and homicides yielded only negative results.[44]

The notion of visibility requires more confidence, perhaps, in the concept of "rational man" than we should place in it. Not infrequently persons such as the sheriff above do strange things for odd reasons. One might speculate about crowd reactions as they turned thumbs down on fallen gladiators in the Roman Coliseum, or about apparent aggressive behavior of fellow drivers leaving a parking lot after a football game, auto race, or boxing match. Moreover, premature death may gain a person an especially permanent place in history; thus today such persons as Joan of Arc, Patrick Henry, John Kennedy, and Martin Luther King remain among our honored dead. For still others, execution may provide an unintended enduring heroic place they could not have achieved without becoming something of a "martyr" of the state. Candidates for such pseudoheroism would be Caryl Chessman or Sacco & Vanzetti, cases that Bedau believes cloud more objective discussion of capital punishment.[45] Nevertheless, the case of Sacco and Vanzetti has been revived through the pen of one of America's most gifted artists, Katherine Anne Porter who writes:

> Near the end of their ordeal Vanzetti said that if it had not been for 'these thing' he might have lived out his life talking at street corners to scorning men. He might have died unmarked, unknown, a failure.[46]

Interestingly, this type of event was one of the original bases for moving executions farther from public scrutiny as began to occur in the states of New York, Pennsylvania, and New Jersey during the 1830's.[47]—Shall we, go backward a century and a half, but with the full implementation of modern technology to public exposure of the final steps to a form of punishment that Mattick asserts is indefensible on any rational grounds? He feels the only purpose it can serve is one of irrational vengeance that is no better than "the original homicide to which it answers in kind."[48]

6. *Consistency*. When parents ordinarily think of disciplinary consistency relative to children they think of ways in which to *reduce confusion of expectations*. Family counselors often advise parents against the hazards of hit and miss, ambivalent, emotional-laden disciplinary measures. We are all too aware of victims of conflicting parents through a "scissors" sort of effect or a "yo-yo" type of response. Similarly, capital cases may be subject to "yo-yo" and "scissored" treatment. To the extent we can show *lack* of consensus about the death penalty there is the implication of inconsistency in American society. We shall try to demonstrate this through reference to several selected illustrations.

A. *Public Opinion*. From the outset we can show that the American public is far from indicating any overwhelming support for the death penalty. Table 1, which is based on data from the highly respected Gallup Polls, reveals that for six selected years representing the period 1936-1976, never has the supporting number exceeded two-thirds of their respondents. Moreover, the fluctuation has been as great as 20 percent, if not more.[49]

TABLE 1*

The Death Penalty and Public Opinion

	1936[a]	1953[a]	1960[a]	1965[b]	1972[b]	1976[c]
Yes	62%	68%	51%	45%	50%	65%
No	33	25	36	43	41	28
No Opinion	5	7	13	12	9	7

*The percentages shown are in response to the question: "Are you in favor of the death penalty for persons convicted of murder?"

The original source for all of these figures is The American Institute of Public Opinion, Princeton, New Jersey. These data, adapted to table form here, were drawn from the following:

a. The American Institute of Public Opinion, "Public Opinion and the Death Penalty" in Hugh Adam Bedau, (editor) *The Death Penalty in America* (Garden City, New York: Doubleday-Anchor, 1964), pp. 236-241.

b. Michael J. Hindelang, *Public Opinion Regarding Crime, Criminal Justice and Related Topics* (Washington, D.C.: U.S. Printing Office, 1975). This is a NCJIS/LEAA Report for the U.S Department of Justice.

c. *U.S. News and World Report,* Vol. 81, No. 2 (July 12, 1976) p. 50.

From additional data provided in connection with such surveys several generalizations can be made. Among them: 1) Blacks are considerably more opposed to the death penalty than are whites; 2) females are less in favor than are males; 3) a smaller percentage of persons under 30 are favorable than are those age 30 and over; and 4) lesser amounts of public sentiment favorable to capital punishment are found in the South and Midwest rather than in the East and West.[50] When demographic variables are employed, it is not uncommon to see the pro/con dichotomy to approximate 50/50 splits—or the differences to be statistically insignificant. Certainly these divisions lead *not* to a confident picture of consensus, but rather to one of dissensus.

B. *Governors.* In 1975 United Press International conducted a poll of the 50 U.S. Governors on this issue, with the results showing 28 favorable to the death penalty, 17 against, and 5 unwilling to express an opinion. Among those opposed were Gov. Ray Blanton of Tennessee, Gov. Richard Kneip of South Dakota, and Gov. Richard Lamm of Colorado. One of the strongest supporters was Gov. Otis Bowen of Indiana. Once an opponent, he stated he had changed his position because of a number of mass slayings such as those connected with the Charles Manson case.[51]

Some governors have been forced to display political courage in the face of pockets of pressure exerted upon them to favor the death penalty. For example, Gov. Jerry Apodaca of New Mexico left little doubt among his

TABLE 2*

The Death Penalty and Justice System Views

Position	Law Enf. off.	Inst. Cust.	Pol. Chiefs	Pros. Attys.	Sup. Ct. Judges	Par. Bd.	Inst. Other[1]	Inst. Treat.	Prob. & Par. Off.	Un-Weighted Totals[2]
(Ns)	113	92	19	19	44	14	25	19	56	401
For %	66	61	58	26	25	14	12	11	4	42
Against %	17	26	21	42	57	57	64	53	61	37
Neutral or No Opinion %	17	13	21	32	18	29	24	37	36	21
Mean Response[3]	5.18	4.89	4.89	3.21	2.84	2.21	2.24	2.89	2.38	3.89

*The percentages shown are based on 401 responses to a request to rate the item: "Greater use of the death penalty should be made throughout the United States," on a 1 to 7 scale reflecting a range from strong disagreement to strong agreement, with the number "4" reflecting a neutral position. *Here order of presentation is from high to low in terms of advocacy of greater use of capital punishment.* This particular item was part of a 12 item set within a 13 page questionnaire.

1. These were prison personnel (e.g. secretaries) who were not classifiable as either custody or treatment.

2. By unweighted totals I mean that the differences in organizational unit size were not taken into account.

3. These were based upon the seven point scale but were computed with non-respondents missing. In contrast to a simple dichotomy they are more sensitive to intensity of response, thus ordering changes would be expected.

SOURCE: Joseph W. Rogers, "The Parole Board: An Analysis of Role Within the Correctional Setting", unpublished Ph.D. dissertation, University of Washington, 1965. (Adapted from table 11, p. 86)

constituency of his stand: "I have always opposed capital punishment and I still do. . . . My position has been clear for the past 10 years."[52] Or consider the position of Gov. Edmund G. Brown Jr. who made good on his promise to veto legislation restoring capital punishment in California where both a majority of its citizens and its legislators would be known to condemn him for his veto.[53]

C. *Criminal Justice System*. If high degrees of consensus are lacking among the general public or governors we should not be surprised to discover dissensus within the justice system itself, as indicated in Table 2.[54] At one end, well over half of the police chiefs, law enforcement officers, and correctional custody staff favor greater use of capital punishment, yet no less than one third of even these groups remain neutral or opposed. While the modal responses among the remainder fall on the "con" side, it is clear that many probation officers, treatment personnel, and others want to remain uncommitted. In brief, either across organizational lines or within organizational units disagreement is present. Consider then the implication for persons proceeding from point of arrest to point of execution. To what extent is the image received by an individual likely to be one of consistency?—one of "scissors" (conflict)? one of "yo-yo" (changing)?

These results, incidentally, are not isolated: For example in a national survey, sampling prison line personnel, the results were very similar to our initial column of Table 1. In reply to the question: "Do you favor the death penalty?", 64 percent said "yes", 24 percent, 'no', and 12 percent were "not sure".[55] And, perhaps at times we may stereotype prison wardens as a group who would be overwhelmingly in favor of the death penalty. NOT so, for there is evidence of considerable opposition. Paul A. Thomas conducted a study two decades ago at which time he reported 89 percent of responding wardens did not consider capital punishment a deterrent; 92 percent did not believe murderers give actual forethought to consequences; 62 percent felt that execution of innocent persons provided a fallacy in the application of capital punishment; and for 31 percent of them this was sufficient basis for its abolition.[56] Data consistent with the results of Thomas were reported in 1960 by Balogh and Mueller.[57]

In reality, the above, sampling errors notwithstanding, should not be of genuine surprise, for some of the top and best known wardens or correctional administrators have made known their aversion—just to list a few—Clinton T. Duffy of San Quentin; Lewis E. Lawes of Sing Sing; James A. Johnston of Alcatraz; Hans W. Mattick of Chicago; Garrett W. Heyns of Michigan; John R. Cranor of Washington; and Austin H. MacCormick who has been called the "Dean of American Corrections". In particular it is worth noting the total abhorrence expressed by Wardens Duffy and Lawes who between them have witnessed probably more executions, 90 and 114 respectively, than any other pair.[58] Lawes says: "Strange to say, I have never received a request from a district attorney to witness the execution of the man whom he prosecuted, or from a judge to attend the execution of the man whom he sentenced."[59]

Adding further substance to the above is a resolution passed by one of our key professional organizations representing many correctional personnel including a number of U.S. Wardens. On September 1, 1966 the American Correctional Association (with over 5000 members) passed at their annual meeting in Baltimore, Maryland the following resolution:

> The 96th Annual Congress of Correction records its opposition to capital punishment; supports the Attorney General's recommendation that the death penalty be eliminated from the Federal Criminal Code; and commends the efforts of the abolition committees in the several states.[60]

Perhaps a final irony is revealed through the words of the British Chief Executioner who hanged at least 450 persons during a 26 year period.

> The fruit of my experience has this bitter aftertaste, that I do not now believe that any one of the hundreds of executions I carried out has in any way acted as a deterrent against future murder. Capital punishment, in my view, achieved nothing except revenge.[61]

Is it any wonder the recurring issue of capital punishment is one of dispair with consensus and consistency lacking among the general public, state governors, prison wardens, correctional system personnel, psychiatrists, and others?[62] Is it any wonder that in 1967 when the last execution prior to that of Gilmore took place there were 37 death penalty states and 13 abolition states? Is it any wonder that in the 1972 Furman decision lack of genuine agreement in either direction seemed to be present. Frankstone has pointed out that the precise holding in *Furman vs. Georgia* is difficult because the brief *per curiam* opinion reveals a majority opinion supplemented by five concurring opinions none of which were concurred in by another Justice! Additionally each of the four dissenters drafted separate opinions expressive of his minority position![63] On grounds such as those, lives hang in fragile balance—and one might add, with each new appointment to the Supreme Court bench, where a single "swing vote", in point of fact, is a matter of life or death.

7. *Impersonality*. This concept refers to an ideal form of discipline whereby we punish the act, not the actor; reject the deed rather than the doer; and sanction the offense while we treat the offender. This ideal is an abstraction, of course, but it is not without meaning to parents, counselors, and correctional officers alike. Nevertheless, the death penalty is perhaps

unsurpassed in its total destruction of ideal and aspiration. Through extermination there can be no retention of hope; only destruction of the complete human being—body, mind, self, and identity. Execution must be one of most personal acts of punishment devised by human beings in the name of being impersonal about the whole affair.

Additional Issues. Unfortunately, space limitations have prevented thorough discussion of the above criteria. Further, there are such other related matters as deterrence, error, cost, and the value of life. Each of these will receive only brief reference.

The matter of deterrence has been among the hottest correctional controversies since the 1975 publication of the impressive work of Economist, Isaac Ehrlich, who claims: ". . . an additional execution per year over the period in question may have resulted, on average in 7 or 8 fewer murders"[64] The accompanying footnote should provide interested parties with crucial leads to a debate of assured longevity.[65]

The matter of mistake is at least of parallel import to that of deterrence. Sutherland & Cressey call attention to a report that during a forty-year period, 12.3 percent of 406 individuals sentenced for execution at Sing Sing were found upon reexamination to have been sentenced in error.[66] They further cite Hartung's findings in Michigan, an abolition state where it was estimated that judges and juries erred in 10.9 percent of 759 life-imprisonment convictions in first-degree murder cases during the period 1942-1951.[67] Again, lest we think such findings are completely obsolete, one need only refer to the brief but sobering article by MacNamara providing glimpses of cases from the 50's and 60's.[68]

The death penalty at times is defended on the gound it is less costly than life imprisonment. According to Sutherland & Cressey the per capita cost of life imprisonment (at a time when it was about $2000 a year) was possibly less than the comparable cost of an execution. They assumed a term of twenty years at an expense of at least $40,000.[69] In another study Mattick found that thirty years of imprisonment cost the state about $45,000 at a time when the expenses of a capital trial and appeals, special detention handling in jail, plus an execution proper were in excess of $60,000.[70] Reid also believes capital punishment may actually cost more, citing the estimated expense of the Caryl Chessman case to have exceeded a half-million dollars! She was told by Warden Clinton Duffy that many capital cases cost the state over $50,000. The trials may be especially long with strung out appeals; the defendant may be less apt to plead guilty; jury selection is often long and expensive; prosecuting attorneys under publicity pressure may be less apt to accept a lesser plea; the cost of incarcerating a prisoner on death row is greater than the cost of other inmates; and the maintenance of the execution chamber and final processing represent additional expenditures.[71]

But just suppose society had never executed even a single one of those 3860 persons from 1930 to the present. And let's assess the cost of keeping all of them in prison at an average thirty years apiece at a hypothetical contemporary cost of $10,000 per capita. The total price would approximate slightly over a billion dollars—just a bit more than a *single* 1978 "Trident" submarine, projected at 949 million dollars! For each XM-1 tank with enormous killing capacity we spend $738,000; for each B-1 bomber, over $84,000,000![72] One would surmise there would not be an excessive compromise in national defense, were the cost of say, two or three of these military "mass executioners" to be diverted to a different "cause".[73]

Some might think had these 3860 been kept alive it would have created an overburdened prison population. But suppose that everyone of them had somehow survived until January 1, 1977. At that time there were 275,578 persons incarcerated in our state and federal institutions.[74] Seriously, how much difference would it be if the figure were 279,438?[75]

The final issue, the value of life argument, has been raised in a forceful, articulate position paper by Marlene W. Lehtinen who asserts that to "preserve the good life and to raise the quality of life" society should retain and impose the death penalty.[76] Her claim is this:

> The state's failure to use the death penalty when appropriate, stems from the unwarranted assumption that all life is equally valuable. All life is not equally worthy. Life in a living, breathing human body is not in and of itself of value. What is valuable and in need of preserving is a good life rather than a bad or dishonorable life.[77]

This particular argument strikes us as most debatable and especially dangerous, and opens a virtual "Pandora's box" of social-political hazards, far exceeding the matter at stake here. On grounds such as those invoked by Lehtinen, it does not take much imagination to procede to the facile infliction of death on those deemed less "worthy" by various powers that be. We remain genuinely concerned not only with the potential demagoguery, corruption and abuse of power, but with human fallibility of power which may be wrongly exercised for even well intentioned purposes.[78]

Summary and Conclusion. In the foregoing statement we have considered the dimensions of uniformity, celerity, certainty, correspondence, visibility, consistency, and impersonality, taking the position that the death penalty fails to meet these seven ideal punishment criteria. Moreover, but to a briefer extent we have expressed reservations about proponent arguments grounded on considerations of deterrence, cost, error, and unequal value of life. In sum, we are led not only to the overwhelming rejection of capital punishment, but to advocacy of its permanent abolition. Even so, we recognize the doubt, concern, anguish, and genuine controversy surrounding this issue, for they pervade many parts of our society. And clearly, these combined with fear and tensions tend to turn us towards impatient searches for an expedient way out. Nevertheless, we share with others, a sense of impending danger—that in response to agitation, turbulence, violence, and frustration we resort to a set of simplistic, illusory solutions to a complex problem when it deserves so much better.[79]

Discussion Questions

1. Among the seven criteria cited with which a concept of punishment should be considered, it was suggested that "certainty" is deemed by some to be the most important. Identify the criteria you believe to be the most crucial, giving the reasons for your choice.

2. Many persons are offended by vivid portrayals of the implications of the "visibility" dimension. Would you be willing to personally attend and witness a hanging or electrocution? Or, would you be willing to watch a television execution, thoroughly presented with "close-ups", etc.? Why or why not?

3. The "consistency" dimension introduced material drawn from various bodies of opinion. What would the current opinion of your class be? Your student body? Your home-town citizenry? Your college faculty? Consider doing a sample survey on the issue of capital punishment.

4. Carefully re-read the quotation of Marlene W. Lehtinen, taken from her article on the "value of life". Regardless of your personal position regarding the death penalty what implications do you see of her assertion that "All life is not equally worthy. Life in a living breathing human body is not in and of itself of value."? To be fair, you should read Professor Lehtinen's entire paper: "The Value of Life: An Argument for the Death Penalty", *Crime and Delinquency*, Vol. 23, No. 3 (July, 1977), pp. 237-252.

Notes

1. Furman v. Georgia, 408 U.S. 238 (1972), Justice Marshall concurring. Cited in Sue Titus Reid, *Crime and Criminology* (Hinsdale, IL: Dryden, 1976), p. 473. Among other major Western democracies only Mexico and France retain broad but seldom used, capital punishment laws. For relevant accounts of the

experiences of foreign countries see, James Avery Joyce, *Capital Punishment: A World View* (New York: Grove, 1961); Thorsten Sellin (editor) *Capital Punishment*, (New York: Harper and Row, 1967); and Walter C. Reckless, "The Use of the Death Penalty: A Factual Statement," *Crime and Delinquency*, vol. 15, no. 1 (January, 1969), pp. 43-56. These works contain extensive bibliographies.

2. Prior to Gilmore, the last execution took place in Colorado on June 2, 1967. Changing statistics dealing with such matters as executions and prisoners under sentence of death may be found in the *National Prison Statistics Bulletin, Capital Punishment, 1976* (Washington, DC: U.S. Department of Justice, November, 1977). This is a series, periodically brought up to date, and is available through the U.S. Government Printing Office.

3. Quoted in *Time*, Vol. 108, #2 (July 12, 1976), p. 35.

4. On December 31, 1976 the death row population numbered 444 in 23 states compared with 473 persons in 28 states a year earlier, as reported in *the NPS Bulletin, Capital Punishment, 1976* p. 6. However, according to Steve Gettinger this figure, in mid 1976 had risen to 588 distributed among 35 states. See "Death Row in America", *Corrections Magazine*, Vol. 2, No. 5 (September, 1976), pp. 37-48.

5. Historical coverage can be found in standard textbooks in criminology. One of the more classic treatments is that of Harry Elmer Barnes and Negley K. Teeters, *New Horizons in Criminology* (Englewood Cliffs, NJ: Prentice-Hall, 1959). For excellent word portraits of death row residents, see Clinton P. Duffy (with Al Hirshberg), *88 Men and 2 Women* (Garden City, NY: Doubleday, 1962), and David D. Cooper, *The Lesson of the Scaffold* (Athens, OH: Ohio University Press, 1974).

6. Punishment, it has been argued, serves a number of important societal functions. Among these are: 1) deterrence or crime prevention; 2) retribution or revenge; 3) reformation or rehabilitation; 4) expiation or guilt reduction; and 5) social solidarity. See, for example, Edwin H. Sutherland and Donald R. Cressey, *Criminology*, 10th edition (New York: Lippincott, 1978), pp. 334-341.

7. James A. McCafferty, "Major Trends in the Use of Capital Punishment", *Federal Probation*, Vol 25, No. 3 (September, 1961), p. 16. Although it has been estimated that Henry VIII executed 72,000 of his subjects for theft and robbery, prior to his own death in 1547, this figure has been seriously questioned. See, Graeme Newman, *The Punishment Response* (Philadelphia: Lippincott, 1978), p. 111.

8. Ibid. p. 16. For pieces on selected individual states, see *The Annals of the American Acadamy of Political and Social Science*, Vol. 284 (November, 1952); *Crime and Delinquencey*, Vol. 15, No. 1 (January, 1969); and Hugh Adam Bedau (editor), *The Death Penalty in America* (Garden City, NY: Doubleday-Anchor, 1964).

9. Ibid., p. 16.

10. *NPS Bulletin, Capital Punishment, 1976*, pp. 13-15. The 1977 execution of Gary Gilmore makes the grand total 3,860; the subtotal for murders, 3335.

11. Ibid., pp. 13; 16-17. As would be expected, a disproportionate share occurred in the southern region of the U.S.

12. *NPS Bulletin, Capital Punishment, 1975* (Washington, DC: U.S. Department of Justice, July 1976) pp. 2-3. These summaries are supported by a number

of tables supplying more specific catagorical details (e.g. by region). A year later, whites made up the majority (55%), although the Black proportion of the total far exceeded their representation in the national population. Additionally, there has been little uniformity even in method of execution. For example, in 1961 a year in which 42 persons were put to death, there were 43 jurisdictions with designated methods; 24 by electrocution; 11 by gas; 6 by hanging; and one (Utah) permitting a choice between shooting or hanging. Executions ordered by the Federal Courts are carried out in accordance with the method used by the state in which the death sentence is imposed; or if an "abolition" state, a substitute state is designated.

13. The data cited were selected from various NPS Bulletins on capital punishment. These are available for closer scrutiny by any reader with access to a good governmental documents section in a public or university library.

14. Chessman's execution is among the most controversial and publicized of all time. For example, a chapter in the book by former San Quentin Warden Clinton T. Duffy, *88 Men and 2 Women* is devoted to this case. Although Duffy did not have the slightest doubt of Chessman's guilt, and believed the man dangerous if ever released, he was firm in his conviction that Chessman should not have died (p. 149). For one of his own polemics against capital punishment see, Caryl Chessman, *Trial by Ordeal*, (Englewood Cliffs, NJ: Prentice-Hall, 1955).

15. Four of the seven executions in 1965 took place in Kansas—among them were the notorious slayers of the Herbert Clutter family known to the public through the dramatization by Truman Capote, *In Cold Blood* (New York: Random House, 1965).

16. About 60 percent of the inmates under the death sentence on December 31, 1975 had been sentenced during 1975; the others at an earlier date. A total of 15 prisoners had spent more than 8 years on death row, the longest period of time being 18½ years. (*NPS Bulletin, Capital Punishment, 1975*) p. 3. A year later for reasons related to the Supreme Court decisions, it could be stated that no prisoner had spent more than 4 years on death row. *NPS Bulletin, Capital Punishment, 1976*, p. 2 (fn. 4).

17. Charles L. Black, Jr., *Capital Punishment: The Inevitability of Caprice and Mistake* (New York: W.W. Norton, 1974) p. 33. The author is professor of jurisprudence at Yale Law School and has been called one of the nation's leading constitutional scholars.

18. Ibid., p. 94.

19. Philip H. Ennis, "Crime, Victims, and the Police," *Transaction* Vol. 4 (June 1967), pp. 36-44.

20. U.S. Department of Justice, *Uniform Crime Reports for the United States, 1976* (Washington, DC: U.S. Printing Office, September 28, 1977), pp. 160-161.

21. Paul W. Tappan, *Crime, Justice, and Correction.* (New York: McGraw-Hill, 1960). pp. 361-364.

22. Ibid., p. 37.

23. Black, *Capital Punishment*, p. 21.

24. McCafferty, "Major Trends in the Use of Capital Punishment", pp. 17-18.

25. Ibid., pp. 17-18.

26. Ibid., p. 18. McCafferty noted that the press reported many lawyers believed the elimination of the mandatory death penalty for the District would relieve a burden on the prosecutors. This "Burden" was perceived as arising from the reluctance of juries to sentence persons to death (p. 17).

27. Black, *Capital Punishment,* p. 40.

28. George B. Vold, *Theoretical Criminology* (New York: Oxford University, 1958), pp. 14-26. Also see the anthology edited by Stanley E. Grupp, *Theories of Punishment*, (Bloomington, IN: Indiana University Press, 1971).

29. Ibid., p. 23. Also see, Norval Morris, *The Future of Imprisonment*, (Chicago: University of Chicago, 1974), esp. pp. 60-62 for reference to the principle of parsimony which means that the least restrictive or punitive sanction necessary to accomplish defined social purposes should be imposed.

30. Ibid., pp. 22-26. How very complex these issues are! For example, Morris also discusses companion principles of "dangerousness" and "desert". In turn, the "Just Deserts" principle remained to plague "The Committee for the Study of Incarceration". See, Andrew von Hirsch, *Doing Justice: The Choice of Punishments* (New York: Hill and Wang, 1976).

31. During 1977 the U.S. Supreme Court considered a Georgia rape case, that of Ehrlich Coker. The court was being asked to permit capital punishment for crimes in which no life has been actually taken. Although Florida and Mississippi have laws providing execution for rape of a child; Georgia was the only state calling for the death penalty for rape of an adult woman. (*Time*, Vol. 109, No. 15—April 11, 1977—p. 80.) The court concluded a sentence of death to be grossly disproportionate and excessive punishment for the crime of rape, and therefore forbidden by the Eight Amendment as cruel and unusual punishment. See, Coker v. Georgia, 97 S. Ct. 2861 at 2865-66 (1977).

32. Vold, *Theoretical Criminology,* p. 22.

33. Dorothy Miller, Ann Rosenthal, Don Miller, and Sheryl Ruzek, "Public Knowledge of Criminal Penalities" in Grupp, *Theories of Punishment*, p. 224.

34. Ibid., p. 219.

35. Maynard L. Erickson, Jack P. Gibbs, and Gary F. Jensen, "The Deterrence Doctrine and the Perceived Certainty of Legal Punishments", *American Sociological Review*, Vol. 42, No. 2 (April 1977) P. 305. Also see, Richard L. Henshel and Robert A. Silverman (editors), *Perception in Criminology* (New York: Columbia University Press, 1975).

36. Ibid., p. 316.

37. Robert F. Meier and Weldon T. Johnson, "Deterrence as Social Control: The Legal and Extralegal Production of Conformity." *American Sociological Review*, Vol. 42, No. 2 (April, 1977), pp. 292-304. Also see, Joseph W. Rogers, *Why Are You Not a Criminal?* (Englewood Cliffs, NJ: Prentice-Hall, Inc., 1977).

38. Marc Ancel, "The Problem of the Death Penalty" in Thorsten Sellin, *Capital Punishment,* p. 18.

39. Reid, *Crime and Criminology,* p. 484.

40. Bedau, *The Death Penalty in America*, p. 20. This is an excellent collection of articles by one who acknowledges his opposition to capital punishment. Also, see,

Hugh Adam Bedau and Charles M. Pierce (editors) *Capital Punishment in the United States* (New York: AMS Press, 1976)

41. Ibid., p. 20.

42. Duffy, *88 Men and 2 Women*, pp. 155-164.

43. Ibid., p. 243.

44. Sellin, *Capital Punishment*, pp. 246-247. In reversing a district judge's order, the 5th U.S. Circuit Court of Appeals decided that television cameramen can be barred from filming Texas executions. The court held that the protection which the First Amendment provides to the news gathering process does not extend to matters not accessible to the public generally, such as the filming of executions in Texas state prisons. *Las Cruces* (New Mexico) *Sun-News* (August 4, 1978), p. 14B. United Press International release.

45. Bedau, *The Death Penalty in America*, pp. v-vi; Duffy, *88 Men and 2 Women*, pp. 142-154.

46. Katherine Anne Porter, "The Never-Ending Wrong", *Atlantic Monthly*, Vol. 239, No. 6 (June, 1977), pp. 63-64.

47. Bedau, *The Death Penalty in America*, pp. 20-23. The last state to stage a public execution was Kentucky in August of 1936 with an estimated crowd of 20,000 present.

48. Hans W. Mattick, *The Unexamined Death: An Analysis of Capital Punishment,* (Chicago: World Correctional Service Center, 1972), pp. 41-42.

49. In 1966, one Gallup poll reported only 42 percent in favor of capital punishment. The 1976 figure of 65 percent was the highest in nearly a quarter century. (*U.S. News and World Report*, Vol. 81, No. 2 (July 12, 1976), p. 50. Other surveys have reported similar spreads. According to a 1958 Roper Poll, only 42 percent favored capital punishment over life imprisonment for those convicted of "the worst crimes like murder". Fifty percent preferred life imprisonment; 8 percent were of no opinion. (Bedau, *The Death Penalty in America*, p. 234) The Marvin Field poll reported that 49 percent of Californians favored capital punishment in 1956, compared to 74 percent in 1975. (*New York Times*, March 26, 1975—cited by Ernest van den Haag, *Punishing Criminals: Concerning a Very Old and Painful Question* (New York: Basic Books, 1975), p. 226.

50. For instance, see Michael Hindelang. *Public Opinion Regarding Crime, Criminal Justice and Related Topics,* (Washington, DC: U.S. Printing Office, 1975), pp. 13-14.

51. *Las Cruces Sun-News* (June 2, 1975), p. 1. By United Press International. Of the 17 governors against capital punishment, 7 said it was not a deterrent; 5 expressed personal aversion to it; others said the state has no right to take a life, that the penalty is cruel and unusual; or that there is no post-execution appeal. cf. Bedau, *The Death Penalty in America*, pp. 234-235.

52. *Las Cruces Sun-News* (July 4, 1976), p. 1, U.P.I. release. Gov. Apodaca's threatened veto of pending legislation did not require implementation.

53. *Las Cruces Sun-News* (May 29, 1977), p. 8A, U.P.I. release, Gov. Brown is the son of the former Gov. Edmund G. Brown who was in office at the time of the Caryl Chessman execution. For an eloquent plea, read Caryl Chessman, "A Letter

to the Governor" in David M. Petersen and Marcello Truzzi (editors) *Criminal Life: Views from the Inside* (Englewood Cliffs, NJ: Prentice-Hall, Inc., 1972), pp. 204-212. The California Legislature subsequently voted 54-26—the exact number needed—to override Brown's veto, thereby restoring capital punishment in California. *Las Cruce Sun-News* (August 12, 1977), p. 2. U.P.I. release.

54. Cf. Table 1, especially the poll results of 1960 and 1965. Also see, Joseph W. Rogers, "Optimism and Accuracy in the Perception of Selected Parole Prediction Items", *Social Forces*, Vol 46, No. 3 (March, 1968), pp. 388-400.

55. South Carolina Department of Corrections, *Collective Violence in Correctional Institutions: A Search for Causes*, (Columbia, SC: South Carolina Department of Corrections, 1973), p. 107; p. 22.

56. Paul A. Thomas, "Attitudes of Wardens toward the Death Penalty" in Bedau, *The Death Penalty in America*, pp. 242-252.

57. Cited by Bedau, Ibid., pp. 235-236. Also see, Joseph Balogh and Mary Mueller, "A Scaling Technique for Measuring Social Attitudes toward Capital Punishment", *Sociology and Social Research*, Vol. 45, No. 1 (October, 1960).

58. Duffy, *88 Men and 2 Women,* p. 252; the number for Lawes is quoted by Frank E. Hartung, "Trends in the Use of Capital Punishment", *The Annals of the American Academy of Political and Social Science*, Vol. 284 (November, 1952), p. 19.

59. Ibid., p. 18. Hartung, upon quoting Lawes, suggests it might be appropriate for legislators who enact the laws to be required to attend the executions resulting from their "legislative activities".

60. *Time*, Vol 89, No. 11 (March 17, 1967), p. 16. Serving under President Lyndon B. Johnson, principal figures would have been former Attorneys General Nicholas Katzenback and Ramsey Clark.

61. *El Paso Times,* (October 22, 1974).

62. Many psychiatrists such as Dr. Karl Menninger and Dr. Joseph Satten have voiced their aversion to capital punishment. For example, see Philip Roche, "A Psychiatrist Looks at the Death Penalty" *The Prison Journal* (October, 1958) p. 47, and Grant S. McClellen (editor) *Capital Punishment* (New York: H.W. Wilson, 1961). Further, numerous national church conferences have adopted abolition stances. Between 1956 and 1966 some dozen resolutions were passed by bodies representing, among others, the Baptist, Episcopal, Hebrew, Lutheran, Methodist, and Presbyterian faiths. (Sellin, *Capital Punishment,* pp. 121-122). Also see, John Howard Yoder, *The Christian and Capital Punishment* (Newton, KS: Institute on Mennonite Studies, Faith and Life Press, 1961).

63. The *majority* included Justices Brennan, Douglas, Marshall, Stewart, and White; the *minority*, Chief Justice Burger, plus Justices Blackmun, Powell, and Rehnquist. See, David R. Frankstone, "Criminal Procedure—Judicial Legislation of Capital Punishment: State v. Waddell", *North Carolina Law Review*, Vol. 52 (1974), esp. pp. 875-878; Leonard Orland, *Justice Punishment and Treatment: The Correctional Process* (New York: Free Press/Macmillan, 1973), pp. 279-290; and Reid, *Crime and Criminology*, pp. 490-492; 509-510. Reid states, "The four justices who voted in the minority in *Furman* indicated that although they were personally opposed to the death penalty, the issue was whether or not capital punishment constitutes cruel and unusual punishment." (p. 491).

64. Isaac Ehrlich, "The Deterrent Effect of Capital Punishment: A Question of Life and Death", *The American Economic Review*, Vol. 65, No. 3 (June, 1975), p. 414.

65. The following list is restricted to selections within the last few years. They contain ample references to prior bibliographical sources.

David C. Baldus and James W.L. Cole, "A Comparision of the Work of Thorsten Sellin and Isaac Ehrlich on the Deterrence of Capital Punishment", *The Yale Law Journal*, Vol. 85, No. 2 (December, 1975), pp. 170-186; William J. Bowers and Glenn L. Pierce, "The Illusion of Deterrence in Isaac Ehrlich's Research on Capital Punishment", Ibid., pp. 187-208; Isaac Ehrlich, "Deterrence Evidence and Inference", Ibid., pp. 209-227; Jon K. Peck, "The Deterrent Effect of Capital Punishment; Ehrlich and His Critics", *The Yale Law Journal*, Vol. 85, No. 3 (January, 1976), pp. 359-367; Isaac Ehrlich, "Rejoinder", Ibid., pp. 368-369; Jan Palmer, "Economic Analysis of the Deterrent Effect of Punishment", *Journal of Research in Crime and Delinquency*, Vol. 14, No. 1 (January 1977), pp. 4-21. For another exchange, see Daniel Glaser and Max S. Ziegler, "Use of the Death Penalty v. Outrage at Murder" *Crime and Delinquency*, Vol. 20, No. (October, 1974), pp. 333-338; William C. Bailey, "Use of the Death Penalty v. Outrage at Murder; Some Additional Evidence and Considerations", *Crime and Delinquency*, Vol. 22, No. 1 (January, 1976), pp. 31-39; Daniel Glaser, "A Response to Bailey: More Evidence on Capital Punishment as Correlate to Tolerance for Murder", pp. 40-43.

Significantly, two entire issues of *The Journal of Behavioral Economics*, Vol. 6, Nos. 1 & 2 (Summer/Winter 1977) were assigned to a symposium on capital punishment. Covering over 400 pages, it contains fifteen articles whose primary focus is on deterrence. Also see, Henry Pontell, Jack Gibbs, Charles Tittle, and Richard Henshel, "Deterrence: A Statement and Three Commentaries", *Criminology An Interdisciplinary Journal*, Vol. 16, No. 1 (May 1978), pp. 3-46.

66. Cited by Sutherland and Cressey, 1978, p. 347, from Lewis E. Lawes, *Twenty Thousand Years in Sing Sing*, (New York: R. Long and R.R. Smith, 1932), pp. 146-148, 156. The general period of time covered was 1889-1927.

67. Ibid., p. 347. Also see, Otto Pollock, "The Errors of Justice", *Annals of the American Academy of Political and Social Science*, Vol. 284 (November, 1952), pp. 115-123. Cf. Black, *Capital Punishment,* esp. pp. 29-36.

68. Donal E.J. MacNamara, "Convicting the Innocent", *Crime and Delinquency*, Vol. 15, No. 1 (January, 1969), pp. 57-61. This entire issue of this journal is devoted to the subject of the death penalty. Also see, William J. Bowers, *Executions in America* (Lexington, MA: D.C. Heath, 1974), and Porter, "The Never Ending Wrong", p. 39. Further, ponder the tragic case of Ralph Lobaugh, age 60, who was recently released from the Indiana State Prison more than 25 years after state investigators determined he was innocent of the crimes for which he was incarcerated. An earlier death sentence was commuted to a life term, but no further rectification of the error was made for over two decades. *Las Cruces Sun-News* (August 24, 1977) p. 8A, U.P.I. release.

69. Edwin H. Sutherland and Donald R. Cressey, *Criminology,* Ninth edition (New York: Lippencott, 1974)., pp. 335-336.

596

70. Mattick, *The Unexamined Death,* p. 30.

71. Reid, *Crime and Criminology*, pp. 480-481.

72. *Time*, Vol. 109, No. 2 (May 23, 1977), p. 18.

73. I am not really suggesting a weakened military, of course. The point is simply one of recognizing some "excuses" for why we do or do not spend money. Something called an "Airframe" is said to cost $37.6 million; the wings alone $18.6 million per pair! (Ibid., p. 18). Assuming, again an annual cost of $10,000 per prisoner, about 125 persons could be retained on "life-sentences" for three decades at the sacrifice of just one airframe. Actually, our calculations tend to be "conservative" compared to those suggested in the tenth edition of Sutherland and Cressey (1978). By assuming an average "life-term" of twenty years, the total cost would be $200,000 per inmate—two thirds of our estimate. (pp. 346-347).

74. Rob Wilson, "U.S. Prison Population Sets Another Record", *Corrections Magazine*, Vol. 3, No. 1 (March 1977), p. 4.

75. Actually, our U.S. prisons *are* overcrowded with an increase of 13 percent in our prison population from January 1, 1976. In addition to the figure cited for January 1, 1977, there were 7690 sentenced inmates waiting in local facilities pending availability of prison space.

76. Marlene W. Lehtinen, "The Value of Life: An Argument for the Death Penalty" *Crime and Delinquency*, Vol. 23, No. 3 (July 1977) pp. 237-252. Immediately following this piece is a comparably brief but pointed rejoinder by Gerald W. Smith, "The Value of Life: Arguments against the Death Penalty: A Reply to Professor Lehtinen", Ibid., pp. 253-259. Incidentally, at the time of writing, both authors were members of the sociology department, University of Utah.

77. Ibid., p. 252.

78. Consider the compassionate, insightful response of President Truman to a Columbia University student asking for his opinion of capital punishment.

"President Truman: Why, I've never really believed in capital punishment. I commuted the sentence of the fellow who was trying to shoot me to life imprisonment. That's the best example I can give you. But I know what you're trying to get at. You'll understand that when enough people know the actual facts behind one of these periods of hysteria they help to cure it." Harry S. Truman, *Truman Speaks* (New York: Columbia University Press, 1960), p. 119.

79. Cf. John V. Lindsey, "Assessment and Perspective" in Warren H. Schmidt, ed., *Organizational Frontiers and Human Values* (Belmont, CA: Wasdworth, 1970), pp. 65-69.

In spite of polemics on one side or the other, the thoughts of Governor Edmund G. Brown Jr. seem especially fitting for the age which we are entering.

"Statistics can be marshalled and arguments propounded. But at some point each of us must decide for himself what sort of future he would want. For me, this would be a society where we do not attempt to use death as a punishment" Quoted in *The Las Cruces Sun-News* (May 29, 1977), p. 8A.

3

The Death Penalty—A National Dilemma

ARTHUR J. CROWNS, Jr.

Introduction

THE PREPONDERANCE OF ARTICLES WRITTEN ABOUT the death penalty argue for its abolition. An analysis of these articles leads one to the assumption that the death penalty serves no useful purpose. The abolitionists argue on the basis of morality, decency and human dignity. On the other hand the supporters of the death penalty assert its use as a deterrent to crime especially for those criminals who have nothing more to lose than their lives.

The trend in the United States has been toward a less frequent use of the death penalty as a final solution for serious crime. Only one American soldier, since the Civil War, was executed for desertion in the face of the enemy, (Private Eddie D. Slovik).[1] Since 1930 there have been 3,860 executions in the United States. This number represents a very small segment of the total crime population during that period.[2]

Between the execution of Luis Jose Monge, in the Colorado State Penitentiary's gas chamber on June 2, 1967;[3] and Gary Gilmore's execution by a firing squad at Point of the Mountain, Utah, on January 17, 1977 nine and one-half years elapsed. When the infrequent use of the death penalty is considered one could ask the question; Why, then, is so much emotion encountered when the subject of the death penalty is approached?

Of all the serious unsolved problems faced by our society the execution of a few serious criminals seems of minor importance. What justifiable reason can be advanced for mass murderers' right to life? Are their lives more precious than those of their many victims and future victims?

If the death penalty is evil are not the alternatives such as life imprisonment without possibility of release or the subsequent parole of a convicted murderer to perhaps kill again, equally as evil?

It is difficult to reconstruct the early history of the death penalty, however, we can find its roots in the reaction of the kin group. The group whose member was killed or injured wanted revenge. However, when revenge was sought there were frequent conflicts with the established religious beliefs. These conflicts required justification for dealing with the offender. Concern arose about what should be done with the offender. The

597

various suggestions for dealing with the offender have been supported by rationalizations. These rationalizations have become accepted beliefs and theories in support of punishment.

The Theoretical Basis for the Death Penalty

According to John L. Gillin there are five theories which emerged in the course of history. These five theories identify the purpose of punishment and they are: (1) retaliation or retribution (2) expiation, (3) deterrence, (4) reformation or treatment and (5) protection of society.[4]

Retaliation or retribution is the simplest justification for the death penalty. When retaliation is considred from the viewpoint of the victim it is difficult to find a more adequate justification. The victim usually wants to hurt the person causing the injury. His primary reaction to injury is impulsive; an injury for an injury. This is the eye for an eye argument first documented by Hammurabi.

The United States Supreme Court supports retribution and the possibility of deterrence of capital crimes by prospective offenders as permissible justification for a legislative body to weigh in the determination of whether the death penalty should be imposed. In the words of the high court "The death penalty is said to serve two principal social purposes: retribution and deterrence of capital crimes by prospective offenders."[5]

In part, capital punishment is an expression of society's moral outrage at particularly offensive conduct. This approach may be unappealing to many, but it is essential in an ordered society that asks its citizens to rely on legal processes rather than selfhelp to vindicate their wrongs. "The instinct of retribution is part of the nature of man, and channeling that instinct in the administration of criminal justice serves an important purpose in promoting the stability of a society governed by law. When people begin to believe that organized society is unwilling or unable to impose upon criminal offenders the punishment they deserve, then there are sown the seeds of anarchy—of self-help, vigilante justice and lynch law."[6] "Retribution is no longer the dominant objective of the criminal law, but neither is it a forbidden objective nor one inconsistent with our respect for the dignity of men."[7]

The theory of deterrence has stimulated serious debate as to its validity in the control of human behavior. Originally the act and who was responsible for it were all that was considered in the determination of guilt. Under classical criminology the individual was responsible for all the acts he committed. A criminal homicide is not difficult to prove and after responsibility is fixed on a particular individual, no further justification is necessary to prescribe penalty. The act, not the individual who committed the act, was the object of consideration. The question of intent was not raised because it was irrelevant. When attention is focused on the individual who committed the act, modification of the classical position was required. This modification is identified as neo-classical criminology.

Under neo-classical criminology the criminal intent of the accused becomes important. In order to hold the criminal responsible for his action, it is necessary to assume intent. In a trial court, however, a wide range of evidence offered by expert witnesses can negate intent. The individual who committed the act of murder is then the object of consideration. The act of killing another human being is irrelevant except as a symptom which indicates an outside force which controlled the killer.

Since the M'Naghten rule was promulgated the "so-called experts" on human behavior, such as the psychologists, psychiatrists and the sociologists, have questioned the doctrine of self-responsibility.[8] In place of self-responsibility the experts on human behavior have substituted the doctrine of determinism. Simply stated, the doctrine of determinism assumes the behavior in question was caused by forces outside the control of the individual, thereby negating the concept of self-responsibility. It is then argued that deterrence has no effect on the potential criminal's behavior because he cannot control his behavior.

The position of the experts on human behavior also rests upon assumptions which must be accepted on faith. The logic of this argument leads us to the absurd position that the more serious and uncontrolled the behavior, the less justification society has for action against the criminal.

The theory of "protection of society" rests on the concept of self-defense. The right to take life in self-defense has long been recognized as justified in all law traditions. The police officer has the authority to kill in the line of duty if he is placed in danger of losing his life. In most jurisdictions he may also kill to prevent a felony from being committed or to prevent a known felon from escaping. A soldier in time of war can kill the enemy within the rules of humanity. The recognized legal authority of civil government has the same right to protect itself from a serious threat. If a specific crime is defined as a serious threat, the death penalty can be used to permanently remove the individual who committed the crime.

The execution of a criminal, without question, protects the group from further harm by that criminal. The wrongdoer is gone forever and, therefore can do nothing in the future.

The theory based on expiation is archaic in a complex urban society, a society in which there are either confliciting or no religious beliefs. Expiation is defined as the act or means by which atonement or reparation is made. In a culture where the religious beliefs are based upon superstition and fear, the group can view an impious act by one of its members as possibly invoking the wrath of the ancestral spirits or of the vengeful gods upon the whole group. This was especially true if the rules which governed the group were thought to have come from the offended ancestral spirits or god. To prevent this reaction the group developed an appeasement ritual. The ritual usually took the form of a sacrifice to the ancestral spirit or god offended by the act committed. Frequently the wrongdoer's life was sacrificed to protect the group. The statements "may God have mercy on your soul" and "you must pay for the wrong done" made by some judges when imposing the death sentence reflect a survival of the expiation theory.

The imposition of the death penalty is incompatible with the theories based on reformation or treatment. Theories based on treatment and reformation have not been affective in reducing the crime rate. This is most obvious in the recidivist rate. These theories also overlook the danger and potential victims. All resources are focused on the offender to the exclusion of their victims. It would be logical to conserve our limited resources by use of the death penalty for those criminals who do not respond to rehabilitative attempts.

The State Legislatures and the Death Penalty

Throughout United States history relatively few offenses have been subject to death penalty. First degree murder was punishable by death in every state prior to the Furman decision[9] in which the death penalty was authorized. The list of other capital crimes included kidnapping, rape, robbery, burglary, arson, train wrecking and treason. Kidnapping was a recent addition, starting with the federal "Lindburgh law" passed in 1932. More recently the sale of narcotic drugs was made a capital crime in several jurisdictions.[a]

In the six states in which train wrecking was punishable by death no records can be found which show that anyone had been executed for this offense. Another capital crime was assault of a law enforcement officer. In California assaulting a prison guard was also included. The federal penal code authorized the death penalty for a number of federal offenses but few persons were actually executed under it.[10]

An analysis of the United States Code indicates the death penalty can be imposed for the following federal crimes for military personnel:

1. Desertion
2. Assaulting or disobeying superior officer

[a]United States, Louisiana, Maine (sale to minors), New Mexico, Missouri (sale to minors).

3. Mutiny or sedition

4. Misbehavior before the enemy

5. Subordinate compelling surrender

6. Improper use of countersign

7. Forcing a safeguard

8. Aiding the enemy

9. Spies

10. Improper hazarding of vessel

11. Misbehavior of sentinel

12. Murder

13. Rape and carnal knowledge

For civilians found guilty of crimes involving aircraft or motor vehicles if death results, the death penalty can be imposed:

1. For gathering or delivering defense information to aid foreign government

2. Kidnapping

3. Wrecking Trains

4. Rape

5. Bank robbery and incidental crimes

6. Treason[11]

The most marked indication of the United States endorsement of the death penalty was the various state legislatures' response to the Furman vs. State of Georgia case.[b] The legislatures of at least 35 states have enacted new statutes that provide for the death penalty for at least some crimes that result in the death of another person.[12]

Most authorities who support the states' right to employ capital punishment identify the crimes of murder which justify the death penalty as:

1. Murder of a policeman while in performance of duty.

2. Murder done for hire such as a murder under contract.

3. Murder perpetrated during a kidnapping.

4. Murder by an assassin who lays in wait or stalks his victim.

5. Murder committed by a parolee or inmate previously convicted of first degree murder.

[b]The Furman v. State of Georgia case was one of three cases which involved the constitutionality of the death penalty to reach the Supreme Court during the 1971-72 term. The companion cases were Lucious Jackson, Jr. v. State of Georgia and Elmer Branch v. State of Texas. All defendants were black. Furman was convicted of murder in the first degree; Jackson and Branch were convicted of rape. All defendants were sentenced to death for their crimes. The court held in a 5/4 decision that the death penalty as applied in these particular cases was unconstitutional. The decision in these cases is discussed at a later point in this chapter.

6. Murder committed during any arson, rape, robbery or burglary when the defendant had previously been convicted of one of those crimes.
7. Murder which results when an airplane, train, bus ship or other commerical vehicles are high jacked.
8. Murder committed by political terrorists especially when bombs are used and helpless hostages are killed. [13]

The United States Supreme Court on the Death Penalty

The Fifth Amendment of the Federal Constitution recognizes the possibility of the death penalty in its wording: "Nor shall any person be subject for the same offense to be twice put in jeopardy of life or limb." The Fourteenth Amendment permits the state the option of the death penalty by the following words: "nor shall any state deprive any person of life, liberty or property without due process of law." These constitutional references assure that all laws dealing with the death penalty are presumed constitutional until tested by the courts.

The statutes provide various methods for the execution of the death penalty. About half the states are electrocution; eleven states use lethal gas; eight use hanging; and Utah gives the convicted individual a choice of hanging or shooting. All of the different methods used by the states have been upheld by the courts. [14] The major consitutional problem is whether the death penalty violates the prohibition against cruel and unusual punishment as set forth in the Eighth Amendment.

Robert W. Ferguson identifies three major themes which run through the Eighth Amendment cases considered by the United States Supreme Court. These three themes become three questions which the court recurringly asks in one way or another in testing the constitutionality of a punishment: (1) Is the punishment grossly disproportionate to the offense? (2) Is the punishment barbaric in some absolute sense? (3) Were the intentions of the authorities in the infliction of the punishment humane or inhumane? [15]

The Eighth Amendment's prohibition against inflicting "cruel and unusual punishments" has not until recent years been the subject of extensive interpretation by the Supreme Court of the United States. As is the case with other specific provisions of the Bill of Rights and the due process and equal protection clauses of the Fourteenth Amendment, the prohibition has been applied to the substance of legislation, that is, the words themselves, as well as its application to specific factual situations.

The high court has ruled on a number of issues involving the death sentence. During the 1947 term of the court it was asked to rule on the constitutionality of a second attempt at execution of a condemned man after the first attempt at execution failed.[16] The petitioner, Willie Francis, was a black citizen of Louisiana. He was duly convicted of murder and in September, 1945, was sentenced to be electrocuted for the crime. Upon a proper death warrant, Francis was prepared for execution and on May 3, 1946, pursuant to the warrant, was placed in the official electric chair of the State of Louisiana in the presence of the authorized witnesses. The executioner threw the switch but, presumably because of some mechanical difficulty, death did not result he was then removed from the chair and returned to prison. A new death warrant which fixed the execution for May 9, 1946, was issued by the governor of the State of Louisiana.

Applications to the Supreme Court of the state were filed for writs of certiorari,[c] mandamus,[d] prohibition[e] and habeas corpus,[f] and were directed to the appropriate officials in the state. Execution of sentence was stayed. In the applications the petitioner claimed the protection of the due process

---

[c]*Certiorari* is a Latin word meaning to be informed of, to be made certain in regard to. A Writ of Certiorari is a request to a superior court to direct an inferior court to send up to the higher court the record of a specific case for review. If the superior court grants the request the inferior court is ordered to send up the record and the case is reviewed on the record by the higher court. The decision of the inferior court can be affirmed, modified or reversed by the higher court. If the writ is denied by the superior court the lower court's decision stands.

[d]*Mandamus* is a Latin word meaning "We Command." This is the name of a writ issued from a court of superior jurisdiction, and is directed to a private or municipal corporation, or any of its officers, or to an executive, administrative or judicial officer, or to an inferior court, commanding the performance of a particular act specified in the writ, and belonging to his/her or their public, official, or ministerial duty, or directing the restoration of the complainant to rights or privileges of which he has been illegally deprived.

[e]*Prohibition* is the name of a writ issued by a superior court, directed to the judge and parties of a suit in an inferior court, commanding them to cease from prosecution of the case involving the applicant. The writ of prohibition is a request directed to the superior court to prevent the inferior court from exceeding its jurisdiction either by prohibiting it from assuming jurisdiction in a matter over which it has no control, or from going beyond its legitimate powers in a matter of which it has jurisdiction.

[f]*Habeas Corpus* is a Latin phrase meaning "You have the body." This is the name given to a writ directed to the person detaining another and commanding him to produce the body of the person detained in the court issuing the writ to show cause why the person is so detained or to obey an order of the court to release the prisoner.

clause of the Fourteenth Amendment on the ground that an execution under the circumstances would deny due process to him because of the double jeopardy provision of the Fifth Amendment and the cruel and unusual punishment provision of the Eighth Amendment. These federal constitutional protections, it was claimed, would be denied because he had once gone through the difficult preparation for execution and had once received through his body a current of electricity intended to cause death. The Supreme Court of the State of Louisiana denied the applications due to lack of any basis for judicial relief. The Supreme Court of the United States granted certiorari on a petition. The Supreme Court Judges found no cruel and unusual punishment in the constitutional sense in the proceedings.

In United States v. Jackson, 390 U.S. 570 (1967) the threat of the death penalty to force a plea of guilty was attacked. Under the federal kidnapping act, only the defendants who exercised their constitutional right of a jury trial could be subjected to the death penalty if found guilty. In this case the majority of the courts held that the death penalty clause in the "Lindburgh Act" permitted imposition of capital punishment only on defendants who assert their right to be tried by jury. This would, of course, needlessly discourage the defendant from exercising his right to plead innocent and demand jury trials. The court concluded that the Fifth and Sixth Amendments were violated by this intimidation of the federal kidnapping defendant.

In Witherspoon v. Illinois 391 U.S. 510, 10L. Ed. 2d 776, 88 S. Ct. 1770 (1968) the court heard arguments in regard to the state's right to exclude from the jury in a capital case those persons who say that they could never vote to impose the death penalty or that they would refuse even to consider its imposition in the case before them.

The court held that a prospective juror cannot be expected to say in advance of trial whethe he could, in fact, vote for the extreme penalty in the case before him. The most that can be demanded of a veniereman[g] in this regard is that he be willing to consider all the penalties provided by state law, and that he not be irrevocably committed, before trial has begun, to vote against the penalty of death regardless of the facts and circumstances that might emerge in the course of the proceedings. If the *voir dire*[h]

---

[g]*Venireman*—A member of a panel of jurors.

[h]*Voir Dire* is a Latin and French phrase meaning "To speak the truth." This phrase denotes the preliminary examination which the court may make of one present as a witness or juror, when his or her competency, interest, veracity, etc., is objected to.

testimony in the given case indicates that veniremen were excluded on any broader basis than this, the death sentence cannot be carried out even if applicable statutory or case law in the relevant jurisdiction would appear to support only a narrow ground of exclusion.

The court then emphasized that this ruling did not bear upon the power of a state to execute a defendant sentenced to death by a jury from which the only veniremen who were excluded for cause were those who made unmistakably clear (1) that they would automatically vote against the imposition of capital punishment without regard to any evidence that might be developed at the trial of the case before them, or (2) that their attitude toward the death penalty would prevent them from making an impartial decision as to the defendant's guilt. Nor does the decision in this case affect the validity of any senence other than one of death. Nor, finally, does the court ruling render invalid the conviction, as opposed to the sentence, in this or any other case.

Maxwell v. Bishop, 389 U.S. 262, 26L. Ed (2d) 221, 90 S. Ct. 1578 (1970), dealt with an Arkansas jury selection procedure which excluded prospective jurors who oppose capital punishment in violation of Witherspoon v. Illinois, 391 U.S. 510. The court reached the conclusion that excluding jurors with a bias toward the imposition of capital punishment was not proper; that all the state could require was that the jury member would consider the death penalty and remanded this case to the district court for consideration of possible violations of the rule of Witherspoon v. Illinois, 321 U.S. 510.

Late in the 1970-71 term the court considered McGautha v. California, and Crampton v. Ohio, 402 U.S. 183, 28 L. Ed. 2d 711, 91 S. Ct. 1454 (1971). The constitutional issue of a jury's fixing the death penalty without any guidelines as to when the death penalty should be imposed was presented in these two cases: McGautha was convicted of first degree murder in the Superior Court of Los Angeles County, California, and was sentenced to death after a separate penalty trial (a bifurcated procedure)[i] and an automatic appeal, of this conviction was affirmed by the California Supreme

---

[i]*Bifurcated Procedure* is when there is a separation of the criminal trial for determination of guilt of the defendant from the sentencing of the guilty defendant. A bifurcated proceeding can be two separate stages with the same jury or by two separate juries; one responsible for the trial and the other for sentencing. During the trial stage only evidence supporting the guilt or innocence of the accused may be revealed. In the sentencing stage evidence of the defendant's personality and past behavior as well as mitigating circumstances may be received by the jury, which at the trial stage would not have been relevant.

Court (70 Cal 2d 770, 76 Cal. Rptr. 434, 452 P2d 650); and Crampton was convicted of first degree murder, with no recommendation for mercy and sentenced to death, after a trial in Lucas County, Ohio. His conviction was affirmed by the Lucas County Court of Appeals, which was affirmed by the Supreme Court of Ohio (18 Ohio St. 2d 182, 47 Ohio Aps. 394, 248 NE2d 614).

On certiorari, the United States Supreme Court affirmed both convictions. The court held that in both cases the absence of standards to guide the jury's discretion in determining whether to impose or withhold the death penalty did not violate due process. In Crampton's case Ohio's single verdict procedure for determining guilt and punishment in capital cases was not unconstitutional.

Throughout the 1960s, the Supreme Court rejected repeated opportunities to consider the constitutionality of the death penalty judged by the Eighth Amendment standard. This policy was reversed during the 1971-72 term when the high court decided to grant certiorari and hear arguments in the cases of Furman v. Georgia; Jackson v. Georgia and Branch v. Texas, 408 U.S. 238, 33 L. Ed. 2d 346, 92 S. Ct. 2726. Each of the three petitioners was black and had been convicted in a state court. They each had been sentenced to death following a trial by jury which, under applicable state statutes, had discretion to determine whether or not to impose the death penalty. William Henry Furman was convicted of murder and his death sentence was upheld by the Georgia Supreme Court (225 Ga 253, 167 SE 2d 628). Lucious Jackson, Jr. was convicted of rape and his death sentence was upheld by the Georgia Supreme Court (225 Ga 790, 171 SE2d 501). Elmer Branch was convicted of rape and his death sentence was upheld by the Texas Court of Criminal Appeals (447 SW2d 932).

On certiorari, the United States Supreme Court reversed the judgment of the state courts in each case insofar as it left undistrubed the death sentence imposed, and the cases were remanded for further proceedings. In a per curiam opinionʲ expressing the view of five members of the court, it was held that the imposition and discharge of the death sentence in these three cases constituted cruel and unusual punishment which violated the Eighth and Fourteenth Amendments.

The separate opinions of the nine justices reflected the diversity of thought in regard to the death penalty issue. Justice William J. Brennan,

---

ʲ*Per Curiam* is a Latin phrase meaning "by the court" and is used to identify an opinion of the whole court from an opinion written by any one judge. In the Furman, Jackson and Branch cases each justice, including the chief justice wrote a separate opinion.

Jr. considered the death penalty as cruel and unusual because it was a denial of human dignity for a state to arbitrarily subject a person to an unusually severe punishment. He believed the death penalty was a punishment which society did not regard as acceptable. Also, it could not be shown to serve any penal purpose more effectively than a less drastic punishment. Justice William O. Douglas emphasized that it was cruel and unusual to apply the death penalty selectively to minorities whose members were few, who were considered outcasts of society and who were unpopular but whom society was willing to see suffer. Justice Potter Stewart felt the Eighth and Fourteenth Amendments could not tolerate the infliction of the death penalty under legal systems which permitted this unique penalty to be so wantonly and freakishly imposed. Justice Byron R. White stated that as the state statutes involved in these cases were administered, the death penalty was so infrequently imposed that the threat of execution was too attenuated to be of substantial service to criminal justice. Justice Thurgood Marshall was the only justice to rule that the death penalty violated the Eighth Amendment because it was an excessive and unneccessary punishment and it was morally unacceptable to the people of the United States.

It was clear from these opinions that the common factor supporting the coalition of five justices was "race prejudice." If the court could find prejudice in how the death penalty was imposed and administered, then it could rule state statutes as unconstitutional.

The minority of four justices, Chief Justice Warren E. Burger, Justices Harry A. Blackmun, Lewis F. Powell, Jr., and Willam H. Rehnquist, who were all appointed to the high court by President Nixon, argued for judicial restraints. It was their opinion that the death penalty was not unconsitutional and that the various state legislatures had the authority to decide this issue for a specific state.

The issue of the manditory death penalty for a specific crime which eliminated any decision on the part of judge or jury in imposing the death sentence, was not considered by the court. Several justices speculated in their decisions that a new alliance of justices would develop if that issue reached the high court.

These three cases touched off a national debate on the issue of the death penalty. By its ruling in the Furman case, the court virtually overturned every state statute which provided for jury discretion in the imposition of the death penalty.

Between 1972 and 1976, 35 states and the United States Congress re-enacted the death penalty in some form. These new enactments, in general, either provided a mandatory penalty in certain cases or established special sentencing procedures and defined which aggravating and mitigating circumstances should be considered in capital punishment cases.

The single most significant event during this period was the November, 1975 retirement of Justice Douglas. He was the last of President Franklin Roosevelt's appointments who was considered a judicial activist. The activists were liberal justices who indicated a willingness to use the Supreme Court decision making powers to influence public policy and current affairs. They were frequently criticized for assuming the role usually reserved for the legislatures in deciding public policy. On the other hand, President Nixon's appointments were considered strict constructionists; a group willing to let the various state legislatures establish public policy if it was not in conflict with a conservative interpretation of the Constitution.

With the retirement of Justice Douglas the high court only had two liberal justices remaining, Justice Marshall and Justice Brennen. Justice Douglas' influence was gone in the all important private conferences which the nine justices hold. In these conferences the issues are argued, and the cases are discussed. Through the interaction of the justices, decisions are achieved. The cases are then assigned for written opinions to the justices best reflecting the majority position consistent with their work responsibility.

President Ford appointed John Stevens to fill the vacancy created by the retirement of Justice Douglas. Justice Stevens was considered a "middle of the roader," neither a conservative nor a liberal. However, with his appointment the high court became more conservative. Greater responsibility is now given the states on the issue of the death penalty.

On July 2, 1976, the United States Supreme Court again ruled on the capital punishment issue in deciding five capital punishment cases. These case were: (1) Gregg v. Georgia, 428 U.S. 153 96 S. Ct. 2909 (1976) 49 L. Ed. 2d 859; (20 Jurek v. Texas, 428 U.S. 262 96 S. Ct. 2950 (1976) 49 L. Ed. 2d 929; (3) Proffitt v. Florida 428 U.S. 242 96 S. Ct. 2960 (1976) 49 L. Ed. 2d 913; (4) Woodson v. North Carolina, 428 U.S. 280 96 S. Ct. 2978 (1976) 49 L. Ed. 2d 944; (5) Roberts v. Louisiana, 428 U.S. 325 96 S. Ct. 3001 (1976), 49 L. Ed. 2d 974.

Troy Leon Gregg was charged with committing armed robbery and murder on the basis of evidence that he had killed and robbed two men. At the trial stage of Georgia's bifurcated procedure, the jury found the petitioner guilty of two counts of armed robbery and two counts of murder. At the penalty stage, the judge instructed the jury that it could recommend either a death sentence or a life prison sentence on each count; that the jury was free to consider mitigating or aggravating circumstances, if any, as presented by the parties; and that the jury would not be authorized to consider imposing the death sentence unless it first found beyond a reasonable doubt (1) that the murder was committed while the offender was engaged in the commission of other capital felonies, such as armed robberies of the victims; (2) that he committed the murder for the purpose of receiving the victims' money and automobile; or (3) that the murder was "outrageously and wantonly vile, horrible and inhuman" in that it "involved the depravity of the mind of the defendant." The jury found the first and second of these aggravating circumstances and returned a sentence of death. The Georgia Supreme Court affirmed the convictions and concluded that the death sentence imposed conformed to similar cases and was not the result of prejudice, but vacated the armed robbery sentences on the ground that the death penalty had rarely been imposed in Georgia for that offense. Gregg, on appeal to the United States Supreme Court, challenged imposition of the death sentence under the Georgia statute as "cruel and unusual" punishment under the Eighth and Fourteenth Amendments. Georgia had reinstated the death penalty for murder and for other crimes to conform to suggestions of Furman v. Georgia.[17] Guilt or innocence was determined in the first stage of a bifurcated trial, and if the trial is by jury, the judge must charge lesser included offenses when supported by any view of the evidence. Upon a guilty verdict or plea a presentence hearing is held where the judge or jury hears additional extenuating or mitigating evidence and evidence in aggravation of punishment if made known to the defendant before trial. At least one of ten specified aggravating circumstances must be found to exist beyond a reasonable doubt and designated in writing before a death sentence can be imposed.[k] In jury cases, the trial judge is bound by the recommended

[k]The Georgia statute provides in part (Section 27-2534.1 (Supp. 1975)). "(a) The death penalty may be imposed for the offenses of aircraft hijacking or treason, in any case.

(b) In all cases of other offenses for which the death penalty may be authorized, the judge shall consider, or he shall include in his instructions to the jury for it to consider, any mitigating circumstances or aggravating circumstances otherwise authorized by law and any of the following statutory aggravating circumstances which may be supported by the evidence:

(1) The offense of murder, rape, armed robbery, or kidnapping was committed by a person with a prior record of conviction for a capital felony, or the offense of murder was committed by a person who has a substantial history of serious assaultive criminal convictions.

(2) The offense of murder, rape, armed robbery or kidnapping was committed while the offender was engaged in the commission of another capital felony, or aggravated battery, or the offense of murder was committed while the offender was engaged in the commission of burglary or arson in the first degree.

(3) The offender by his act of murder, armed robbery, or kidnapping knowingly created a great risk of death to more than one person in a public place by means of a weapon or device which would normally be hazardous to the lives of more than one person.

sentence. In its automatic review of a death sentence the state supreme court must consider whether the sentence was influenced by passion, prejudice, or any other arbitrary factor; also whether the evidence supports the finding of a statutory aggravating circumstance; and whether the death sentence "is excessive or disproportionate to the penalty imposed in similar cases, considering both the crime and the defendant." If the court affirms the death penalty, it must include in its decision reference to similar cases that it has considered.

The majority of the court held that the punishment of death for the crime of murder does not, under all circumstances, violate the Eighth and Fourteenth Amendments. The United States Supreme Court felt that the concerns expressed in the Furman case that the death penalty not be imposed arbitrarily or capriciously was met by a carefully drafted statute which ensured that the sentencing authority was given adequate information and guidance. These concerns, in the opinion of the court, were best met by a system that provided for a bifurcated proceeding at which the sentencing authority would be appraised of the information relevant to the imposition of sentence and provided with standards to guide its use of that information.

---

(4) The offender committed the offense of murder for himself or another, for the purpose of receiving money or any other thing of monetary value.

(5) The murder of a judicial officer, former judicial officer, district attorney or solicitor or former district attorney or solicitor during or because of the exercise of his official duty.

(6) The offender caused or directed another to commit murder or committed murder as an agent or employee of another person.

(7) The offense of murder, rape, armed robbery, or kidnapping was outrageously or wantonly vile, horrible or inhuman in that it involved torture, depravity of mind, or an aggravated battery to the victim.

(8) The offense of murder was committed against any peace officer, corrections employee or fireman while engaged in the performance of his official duties.

(9) The offense of murder was committed by a person in, or who has escaped from, the lawful custody of a peace officer or place of lawful confinement.

(10) The murder was committed for the purpose of avoiding, interfering with, or preventing a lawful arrest or custody in place of lawful confinement, of himself or another.

(c) The statutory instructions as determined by the trial judge to be warranted by the evidence shall be given in charge and in writing to the jury for its deliberation. The jury, if its verdict by a recommendation of death, shall designate in writing, signed by the foreman of the jury, the aggravating circumstance or circumstances which it found beyond a reasonable doubt. In non-jury cases the judge shall make such designation. Except in cases of treason or aircraft hijacking, unless at least one of the statutory aggravating circumstances enumerated in section 27-2534.1 (b) is so found the death penalty shall not be imposed."

The Supreme Court held that the Georgia statutory system under which Gregg was sentenced to death was constitutional.

Jerry Lane Jurek was convicted of murder in a Texas trial. His death sentence was upheld on appeal to the Texas Court of Criminal Appeals. The Texas code enacted after Furman v. Georgia,[18] limits capital homicides to intentional and knowing murders committed in five situations. Texas also adopted a new capital sentencing procedure, which requires the jury to answer the following three questions in a proceeding that takes place after verdict finding a person guilty of one of the specified murder categories; (1) whether the conduct of the defendant causing the death was committed deliberately and with the reasonable expectation that the death would result; (2) whether it is probable that the defendant would commit criminal acts of violence constituting a continuing threat to society and (3) if raised by the evidence, whether the defendant's conduct was an unreasonable response to the provocation, if any, by the deceased.[19] If the jury found that the state had proved beyond a reasonable doubt that the answer to each of the three questions was affirmative, the death sentence was imposed; if it found that the answer to any question was negative, a sentence of life imprisonment resulted. The Texas Court of Criminal Appeals in this case indicated that it interpreted the "continuing threat to society" question to mean that the jury could consider various mitigating factors.

The United States Supreme Court held in this case the Texas capital sentencing procedures do not violate the Eighth and Fourteenth Amendments. Texas' action in narrowing capital offenses to five categories[1] in

---

[1]Texas law prescribed the punishment for murder as follows: "(a) except as provided in subsection (b) of this Article, the punishment for murder shall be confinement in the penitentiary for life or for any term of years not less than two.

(b) The punishment for murder with malice aforethought shall be death or imprisonment for life if:

(1) the person murdered a peace officer or fireman who was acting in the lawful discharge of an official duty and who the defendant knew was a peace officer or fireman;

(2) the person intentionally committed the murder in the course of committing or attempting to commit kidnapping, burglary, robbery, forcible rape, or arson;

(3) the person committed the murder for remuneration or the promise of remuneration or employed another to commit the murder for remuneration or the promise of remuneration;

(4) the person committed the murder while escaping or attempting to escape from a penal institution;

(5) the person, while incarcerated in a penal institution murdered another who was employed in the operation of the penal institution."

Texas Penal Code, Art. 1257 (1973).

essence required the jury to find the existence of a statutory aggravating circumstance before the death penalty was imposed, thus requiring the sentencing authority to focus on the particularized nature of the crime. Though the Texas statute did not explicity speak of mitigating circumstances, it was construed to embrace the jury's consideration of such circumstances.

Charles William Proffitt was convicted of first-degree murder in the State of Florida. He attacked the constitutionality of the Florida capital sentencing procedure, that was enacted in response to Furman v. Georgia.[20] Under the new Florida statute, the trial judge (who is the sentencing authority) must weigh eight statutory aggravating factors against seven statutory mitigating factors[m] to determine whether the death penalty should be imposed. This

[m]The aggravating circumstances are:

"(a) The capital felony was committed by a person under sentence of imprisonment.

(b) the defendant was previously convicted of another capital felony or of a felony involving the use or threat of violence to the person.

(c) The defendant knowingly created a great risk of death to many people.

(d) The capital felony was committed while the defendant was engaged, or was an accomplice, in the commission of, or an attempt to commit, or flight after committing or attempting to commit, any robbery, rape, arson, burglary, kidnapping, or aircraft piracy or the unlawful throwing, placing, or discharging of a destructive device or bomb.

(3) The capital felony was committed for the purpose of avoiding or preventing a lawful arrest or effecting an escape from custody.

(f) The capital felony was committed for pecuniary gain.

(g) The capital felony was committed to disrupt or hinder the lawful exercise of any governmental function or the enforcement of laws.

(h) The capital felony was especially heinous, atrocious, or cruel."

The mitigating circumstances are:

"(a) The defendant has no significant history of prior criminal activity.

(b) The capital felony was committed while the defendant was under the influence of extreme mental or emotional disturbance.

(c) The victim was a participant in the defendant's condition or consented to the act.

(d) The defendant was an accomplice in the capital felony committed by another person and his participation was relatively minor.

(e) The defendant acted under extreme duress or under the substantial domination of another person.

(f) The capacity of the defendant to appreciate the criminality of his conduct or to conform his conduct to the requirements of law was substantially impaired.

(g) The age of the defendant at the time of the crime." § 921,14 (6) (supp. 1976-1977).

procedure requires him to focus on the circumstances of the crime and the character of the individual defendant. The basic difference in the Florida case was that the sentence was determined by the trial judge rather than by the jury. The jury has an advisory role with respect to the sentencing phase of the trial.

The Supreme Court held that on its face, the Florida procedures for imposition of the death penalty satisfied the constitutional deficiencies identifed in Furman.[21] Florida trial judges are given specific and detailed guidance to assist them in deciding whether to impose a death penalty or imprisonment for life, and their decisions are reviewed to ensure that they comport with other sentences imposed under similar circumstances.

The argument advanced by Proffitt that the Florida system was constitutionally invalid because it allowed discretion to be exercised at each stage of the criminal proceedings was, in the court's opinion, a fundamental misinterpretation of Furman.

The Woodson and the Roberts cases dealt with the issue of a mandatory death sentence. The State of North Carolina and Louisiana enacted a mandatory sentence for first degree murder following the Furman v. Georgia case.[22] In these two cases the Supreme Court held that the mandatory death sentence for first degree murder violated the Eighth and Fourteenth Amendments. The court stated that the imposition of mandatory death sentence failed to curb arbitrary and wanton jury discretion with the objective standards to guide, regularize and make rationally reviewable the process for imposing a sentence of death. The courts further affirmed that imposition of the mandatory death sentence without consideration of the character and record of the individual offender or the circumstances of the particular offense was inconsistent with the fundamental respect for humanity which underlies the Eighth Amendment.

In the 1977 term the Supreme Court declared the mandatory death sentence unconstitutional for first degree murder of a police officer in performance of his lawful duties.[23] The court held that the Eighth Amendment barred both punishments which are "barbaric" and "excessive" in relation to the crime committed. This ruling stated that death for rape was excessive if the victim was not killed.[24]

In 1978 the high court ruled that a death penalty statute must permit individualized consideration of mitigating factors in order to satisfy the requirements of the Eighth and Fourteenth Amendments. An Ohio statute, which was held unconstitutional, specified only three factors which could be considered in mitigation of a defendant's sentence. These factors were: (1) the victim induced or facilitated the offense; (2) it is unlikely that the offense would have been committed but for the fact that the offender was under duress, coercion, or strong provocation; or (3) the offense was primarily the product of the offender's psychosis or mental deficiency.[25]

In summary, these cases tend to indicate that the position of the majority of the justices composing the United States Supreme Court is that, while capital punishment is not cruel and unusual punishment under the Eighth Amendment, it must be subject to strict legislative limitations. These recent opinions also indicate that the mandatory death penalty for certain crimes is not Constitutionally permissible.

Frequently Overlooked Issues in the National Debate

The major issue involved in the debate over capital punishment centers on its appropriateness for the crime of murder. These debates usually overlook several basic facts. First, murder destroys the victim as a human being. Murder usually brings forth exteme brutality. The victim lives his last moments in utter terror. There is no "Bill of Rights" to protect the victim nor are there constitutional protections which extend to the victim.

After the act of murder there is only evidence that a crime has been committed. The murdered victim is examined for cause of death by the state police authority. Evidence is gathered by the taking of measurements and pictures also by interviewing witnesses. The police authority seldom, if ever, has seen the victim as a living person. However, they are the ones who view the horror the victim has experienced. Words which the authorities often use to describe the crimes are: most heinous; most brutal or most savage acts they have witnessed. These descriptions often fall short of describing the actual scene.

In the course of the investigation the police authority is closely scrutinized by both the defense attorney and the court. If the court maintains the pictures obtained as evidence show too much brutality they are rejected because they might tend to prejudice the jury. A change of venue may be granted the accused if the crime has been to well publicized. Witnesses in an attempt to prove the existence of a crime are subjected to cross examination to test their reliability, dependability and credibility.

The accused has no responsibility to assist the police authority in any manner during the investigation. He may remain silent and no inference of guilt may be drawn from his silence. The best informed person is the murderer; only he knows what really took place. The police authority can only "theorize." If the authorities become to aggressive in trying to obtain a confession from the accused it is disregarded as evidence and any leads obtained due to the confession are also barred.

The trial of a criminal case is a depersonalized matter. The state is alleged to have suffered a harm and becomes the prosecutor. The accused becomes the defendant and the victim becomes only evidence. The police authority must present its case by means of verbal testimony and all testimony must conform to established rules of evidence. If it does not it is stricken from the record. The presumption of innocence protects the accused during the trial. This presumption can only be overcome by evidence which can convince the jury "beyond a reasonable doubt" of the defendant's guilt. In a murder case a jury usually consists of twelve members who have the responsibility to determine the facts on all matters in issue. The judge makes the decisions on all points of law which the state and defence disagree on. The defendant is not compelled to offer evidence on his own behalf. He can remain silent or he can testify, however, if he does testify he usually will deny any involvement in the crime. The defendant may exercise a number of affirmative defenses as the reason for explaining the murder such as a plea of innocence by reason of insanity or self-defense.

The focal point of the trial is whether or not the defendant is guilty and if so, did he commit the crime after forming the intent to kill. The jury's decision on these questions will determine the probability of a finding of guilty.

After the trial the defendant is turned over to the executive branch of the government for execution of his sentence. At this stage a new group of functionaries (the correctional authority) represents the state and assumes control of the defendant. The correctional authority has never seen the victim and usually knows nothing of the circumstances of the crime, except for trial records or what the defendant tells them. The police authority files are closed and they cease to be involved with the case. The correctional authority sees the defendant as a person and it is understandable that they frequently over identify with the defendant and seek to minimize the "harshness" of the sentence imposed.

Another point frequently overlooked in arguments dealing with capital punishment is the role of the attorney. The legal profession is a business based on the "ability to pay." If a defendant accused of a crime can afford the best he can have the best. If he is poor he must take what the state provides in the way of assigned counsel or a public defender. The important consideration here is who pays the bill. The rich defendant has the advantage because he can afford better pretrial preparation and better pre-trial investigation. He also has the advantage because his attorney must satisfy him. On the other hand the poor defendant has no money for pre-trial preparation or investigation. He has little control over who his attorney is because the state pays the bill and if satisfaction is necessary it is the state which must be satisfied.

This distressing issue is overlooked in the debate because opponents of the death penalty assume that racial prejudice is the determining factor, not economics and the legal profession based on the ability to pay.

The Abolitionists Arguments Analyzed

Opponents to the death penalty argue two basic positions. The first argument is that the government cannot ethically or morally execute an offender for a specific crime. There is no argument that the government can and does execute offenders for certain crimes. The opponents argue that government "ought not" execute criminals based on a self serving assumption that the "state shall not commit murder." By using the same logic "God" should be the only one who can take a life other than the murderer. Are we to believe then, that the murderer is the "instrument of God" and the state is not?

The second argument advanced is based on economics. It is alleged to cost more to execute a criminal than to keep him alive. This argument is a good example of the academic cliche that statistics don't lie but liers use statistics. An analysis by Vernon Fox indicated the cost factor for keeping a criminal alive in a correctional institution ranges from a high of $23.69 per day in Montana to a low of $1.90 in Mississippi. The average cost when all states were averaged together was $9.99 per day.[26] If a criminal is twenty-five years of age when committed life expectancy for a white male inmate is 46.5 years and for a nonwhite male inmate 41.5 years.[27] For one person to be institutionalized for one year the average cost is $3,648.85. The formula for the calculation of this cost is: $9.99 multiplied by 365.25.[n] The average yearly cost times the life expectancy gives us total expense of a "true" life sentence, which is $159,671.41 for white male inmates and $151,427.28 for nonwhite male inmates. If interest on the above amounts is calculated the loss to the tax payers is even greater. The total average cost of a first degree murder trial and appeal is approximately $20,000.[o]

Some opponents seem to think that the small number of executions carried to completion is justification for elimination of the death penalty. The point overlooked in this position is the difficulty of obtaining a first degree murder conviction due to the accused's constitutional protections.

Summary

There is no doubt that the legislatures of the various states and the United States Congress have the authority to make specific crimes punishable by the death penalty. If safeguards are taken to prevent prejudice in the imposition of the death penalty, it has the backing of the United States Supreme Court.

[n]Leap year adjustment.

[o]The author of this article has made inquiries of a number trial attorneys throughout the United States to arrive at this figure.

There are no reasons why execution should not be legal. Until the United States Supreme Court or the various legislative bodies decide otherwise, the debate over the death penalty is only academic.

Discussion Questions

1. What are the arguments pro and con in the national debate on capital punishment?

2. Why does the national debate on capital punishment evoke so much emotion?

3. Are there any crimes which justify capital punishment?

4. What reasons account for the frequent disregard of the victim or future victims in the national debate on capital punishment?

5. What is the present theme that the majority of the United States Supreme Court follow in deciding capital punishment issues?

6. If there is no agreement on a major premise, in the debate on capital punishment, is any method short of force possible for a solution?

Notes

1. William Bradford Huie. *The Execution of Private Slovik*, (New York: The New American Library of World Literature, Inc., 1954).

2. Vernon Fox. *Introduction to Corrections*, (Englewood Cliffs, New Jersey: Prentice-Hall, Inc., 1972), p. 43.

3. *Ibid*. pp. 41-43.

4. John L. Gillin. *Criminology and Penology*, 3rd ed., (New York: D. Appleton Century Co., 1945), p. 247.

5. Gregg v. State of Georgia, 428 U.S. 153 96 S. Ct., at 2930, 49 L. Ed. 2d, 859.

6. Furman v. State of Georgia, 408 U.S., at 308, 92 S. Ct., at 2761 (Justice stewart concurring).

7. Williams v. State of New York, 337 U.S. 241, 248, 69 S. Ct. 1079, 1084, 93 L. Ed. 1337 (1949).

8. Queen v. M'Naghten (1843), 10 Clark and Finnelly, 200, 8 English Reprint 718.

9. Furman.

10. U.S. Senate, The Report of the Committee on the Judiciary, Report #1478 (April 28, 1958).

11. *Ibid*.

12. Gregg.

13. U.S. Senate.

14. Shooting—Wilkerson v. State of Utah, 99 U.S. 130, 25 L. Ed. 345 (1878); 30 A. L. R. 1457, 35 L. R. A. 575; Hanging Ex parte Medley, 134 U.S. 160, 10 S. Ct. 384, 33 L. Ed. 835 (1889); Dutton v. State, 123 Md. 373, 91 A. 417 (1914); Lethal Gas—State v. Gee Jon 46 Nev. 418, 211 P. 676, 30 A. L. R. 1443, 217 P. 587, 30 A. L. R. 1443 (1923); Electricity—McElvaine v. Brush, 142 U.S. 155, 12 S. Ct. 156, 35 L. Ed. 971 (1891); in re Kemmler, 136 U.S. 436, 10 S. Ct. 930, 34 L. Ed. 519 (1890); Storti v. Com of Mass., 183 U.S. 138, 22 S. Ct 72, 46 L. Ed. 120 (1901).

15. Robert W. Ferguson. *Concept of Criminal Law: Selected Readings*, (St. Paul, Minnesota: West Pubishing Company, 1975), p. 351.

16. Louisiana ex rel. Francis v. Resweber 329 U.S. 459, 67 S. Ct. 374, 91 L. Ed. 122 (1947).

17. Furman.

18. *Ibid.*

19. Jurik v. State of Texas 148 U.S. 262 96 S. Ct 2950, 49 L. Ed. 2d 929, (1976).

20. Furman.

21. *Ibid.*

22. *Ibid.*

23. Roberts (Stanislaus) v. Louisiana 428 U.S. 325, (1976).

24. Coker v. Georgia 433 U.S. 584, (1977).

25. Lockett v. Ohio cited 38 Commercial Clearing House Supreme Court Bulletin p. B4388 (argued January 17, 1978—decided July 3, 1978).

Bell v. Ohio cited 38 Commercial Clearing House Supreme Court Bulletin p. B4442 (argued January 17, 1978—decided July 3, 1978).

26. Fox. *Introduction to Corrections*, p. 167.

27. Martin A. Bacheller, Editor in Chief. *The CBS News Alamanc, 1977*, (Maplewood, N.J.: Hammond Almanac, Inc.) p. 247.